About the Author

Sander van Vugt is an independent Linux trainer, author, and consultant living in the Netherlands. Sander is the author of the best-selling *Red Hat Certified System Administrator (RHCSA) Complete Video Course* and also of the *Red Hat Certified Engineer (RHCE) Complete Video Course*. He has also written numerous books about different Linux-related topics, and many articles for Linux publications around the world. Sander has been teaching Red Hat, SUSE, and LPI Linux classes since 1994. As a consultant, he specializes in Linux high-availability solutions and performance optimization. You can find more information about Sander on his website at http://www.sandervanvugt.com.

For more information about RHAT certification and additional resources, visit the author's Red Hat Certification page at http://www.rhatcert.com/.

About the Technical Reviewers

Frederik Vos is a senior technical trainer in Linux training and also in several virtualization solutions, such as VMware vSphere, XenServer, and KVM. For the past 8 years Frederik has working for XTG in Gouda, a training center specializing in virtualization solutions and Linux, as a teacher and Linux evangelist, responsible for the Linux portfolio at XTG.

He has specialized in data center infrastructures (several Linux distributions), hypervisors, networking, and storage solutions and cloud computing (Cloudstack, Cloudplatform, and OpenStack). He has a lot of knowledge as a teacher and also real-world experience as a system engineer and as a long-time (1997) Linux user.

Ross Brunson has more than 20 years of experience as a Linux and open source trainer, training manager, and technologist and is author of the popular LPIC-1 Exam Cram (Que Publishing), as well as the Pearson LPIC-1 Certification Guide.

Ross recently spent almost 5 years as the director of member services for the Linux Professional Institute, building the member program, conducting dozens of Train-the-Trainer sessions, and providing support for the worldwide Master Affiliate network spanning 100+ countries.

Ross holds a number of key IT certifications and is also author of several successful technical books, dozens of technical courses for major organizations (including the first LPI Certification Bootcamp). He is also skilled at both contributing to and building community around IT products.

He lives in Paradise Valley, Montana, with his family and enjoys traveling far and wide, winter sports, and photography.

William "Bo" Rothwell, at the impressionable age of 14, crossed paths with a TRS-80 Micro Computer System (affectionately known as a Trash 80). Soon after, the adults responsible for Bo made the mistake of leaving him alone with the TSR-80. He immediately dismantled it and held his first computer class, showing his friends what made this "computer thing" work.

Since this experience, Bo's passion for understanding how computers work and sharing this knowledge with others has resulted in a rewarding career in IT training. His experience includes Linux, UNIX, and programming languages such as Perl, Python, Tcl, and Bash. Bo owns several IT certifications, including earning his original RHCE in 2003. He is a former RHCI (Red Hat Certified Instructor) and the founder and president of One Course Source, an IT training organization.

Dedication

This book is dedicated to my family: Florence, Franck, and Alex. Together we've made great accomplishments over the past year.

Acknowledgments

This book could not have been written without the help of all the people who contributed to it. To start, I want to thank the people at Pearson, Denise Lincoln and Ellie Bru in particular. We've worked a lot together over the past year, and this book is another milestone on our road to success!

Next I want to thank my technical proofreaders. What has made this book special is that the first round of technical proofreading was completely done by volunteers. We started with 10 volunteers, but just 1 made it all the way to the end. Many thanks to Giles, the man behind the great and very useful website certdepot.net, the only one who reviewed all the chapters.

I also want to thank Jaques Weewer, Rob Mokkink, and all the other volunteer technical reviewers. You made many suggestions without which the book would not have the high quality that it has right now.

We Want to Hear from You!

As the reader of this book, you are our most important critic and commentator. We value your opinion and want to know what we're doing right, what we could do better, what areas you'd like to see us publish in, and any other words of wisdom you're willing to pass our way.

We welcome your comments. You can email or write to let us know what you did or didn't like about this book[md]as well as what we can do to make our books better.

Please note that we cannot help you with technical problems related to the topic of this book.

When you write, please be sure to include this book's title and author as well as your name and email address. We will carefully review your comments and share them with the author and editors who worked on the book.

Email: feedback@pearsonitcertification.com

Mail: Pearson IT Certification
ATTN: Reader Feedback
800 East 96th Street
Indianapolis, IN 46240 USA

Reader Services

Visit our website and register this book at www.pearsonitcertification.com/register for convenient access to any updates, downloads, or errata that might be available for this book.

Contents at a Glance

Contents

DVD and Companion Website Elements

Command Syntax Conventions

The conventions used to present command syntax in this book are the same conventions used in the IOS Command Reference. The Command Reference describes these conventions as follows:

- **Boldface** indicates commands and keywords that are entered literally as shown. In actual configuration examples and output (not general command syntax), boldface indicates commands that are manually input by the user (such as a **show** command).

Introduction

Welcome to the Red Hat RHCSA/RHCE 7 Cert Guide. The Red Hat exams are some of the toughest in the business, and this guide will be an essential tool in helping you prepare to take both the Red Hat Certified System Administrator (RHCSA) and the Red Hat Systems Engineer (RHCE) exams.

As a Red Hat instructor with more than 20 years of experience, I have taken both the RHCSA and RHCE exams numerous times so that I can keep current on the progression of the exam, what is new, and what is different. I share my knowledge with you in this comprehensive Cert Guide so that you get the guidance you need to pass both exams.

The RHCSA and RHCE exams were recently updated for Red Hat Enterprise Linux 7. This book contains all you need to know to pass these exams. As you will see, this Cert Guide covers every objective in both exams: 42 chapters, more than 100 exercises, 4 practice exams (2 RHCSA and 2 RHCE), interactive quizzes and exercises, 4 advanced command-line interface (CLI) simulations, 3 virtual machines, and hours of video training. This Red Hat RHCSA/RHCE 7 Cert Guide is the best resource you can get to prepare for and pass the exams.

Goals and Methods

To learn the topics described in this book, it is recommended that you create your own testing environment. You cannot become an RHCSA or RHCE without practicing a lot. Within the exercises included in every chapter of the book, you will find all the examples you need to understand what is on the exam and thoroughly learn the material needed to pass it. The exercises in the chapters provide step-by-step procedure descriptions that you can work through to find working solutions so that you can get real experience before taking the tests.

Each chapter also includes an end-of-chapter lab. These labs ask questions that are very similar to the questions that you might encounter on the exam. There are no solutions for these labs provided, and that is on purpose, because you need to train yourself to verify your work before you take the exams. On the exam, you also have to be able to verify for yourself whether the solution is working as expected.

Before you begin, you can test your knowledge by taking the theoretical pre-assessment exams in Chapter 42. These exams help you determine what you know and what you do not know so that you can better prepare your study plan. When you feel ready to take the exams, take a look at the practice exams that come with this book, two RHCSA and two RHCE. These will help you test your skills and get comfortable with the exam content and how questions might be presented in the testing facility.

This book contains everything you need to pass the exams, but if you want more guidance and practice, I have a number of video training titles available to help you study, including the following:

- Red Hat Certified System Administrator (RHCSA) Complete Video Course
- Red Hat Certified Engineer (RHCE) Complete Video Course
- Red Hat Certified System Administrator (RHCSA) Exam Prep Video Workshop
- Red Hat Certified Engineer (RHCE) Exam Prep Video Workshop

Apart from these products, you might also appreciate my website rhatcert.com. Through this website, I provide updates on anything that is useful to exam candidates. I recommend that you register on the website so that I can send you messages about important updates that I've made available. Also, you'll find occasional video updates on my YouTube channel rhatcertification.com. I hope that all these resources provide you with everything you need to pass the Red Hat exams in an affordable way! Good luck!

Who Should Read This Book?

This book is written as an RHCSA/RHCE exam preparation guide. That means that you should read it if you want to increase your chances of passing either the RHCSA or RHCE exam. A secondary use of this book is as a reference guide for Red Hat system administrators. As an administrator, you'll like the explanations and procedures that describe how to get things done on Red Hat Enterprise Linux.

So, why should you consider passing the RHCSA/RHCE exams? That question is simple to answer. Linux has become a very important operating system, and qualified professionals are sought after all over the world. If you want to work as a Linux professional, and prove your skills, the RHCSA or RHCE certificate really helps. Having these certificates dramatically increases your chances of becoming hired as a Linux professional.

How This Book Is Organized

This book is organized as a reference guide to help you prepare for the exams. If you're new to the topics, you can just read it cover to cover. It is a smart idea, though, to distinguish between the RHCSA part and the RHCE part of this book. Finish RHCSA before starting with RHCE, because it will be too much to learn all of it at once.

You can also read the individual chapters that you need to fine-tune your skills in this book. Every chapter starts with a "Do I Know This Already?" quiz. This quiz asks questions about 10 topics that are covered in each chapter and provides a simple tool to check whether you're already familiar with the topics covered in a chapter. Remember, though, the RHCSA and RHCE practice exams; these are an essential part of readying yourself for the real testing experience. You may be able to provide the right answer to the multiple-choice chapter questions, but that doesn't mean that you can create the configurations when you take the tests. The companion files, included on the DVD and through the book's companion web page, also includes more than 40 interactive exercises to help you learn and retain the knowledge needed to pass the exam and 4 simulations that take you through complex CLI exercises so that you can feel sure you're ready not only for the exams but also to actually use Red Hat Linux.

The core chapters are organized in two parts. The first part, which includes Chapters 1 through 24, covers RHCSA topics; the second part, which consists of Chapters 25 through 40, covers RHCE objectives. All the objectives in both exams are covered in these chapters.

The following topics are covered in the chapters:

Part 1: RHCSA

Part 1-1: Performing Basic System Management Tasks

- Chapter 1: Installing Red Hat Enterprise Linux Server

  In this chapter, you learn how to install Red Hat Enterprise Linux Server (RHEL). It also shows how to set up an environment that can be used for working on the labs and exercises in this book.

- Chapter 2: Using Essential Tools

  This chapter covers some of the Linux basics, including working with the shell and Linux commands. This chapter is particularly important if you're new to working with Linux.

- Chapter 3: Essential File Management Tools.

  In this chapter, you learn how to work with tools to manage the Linux file system. This is an important skill because everything on Linux is very file system oriented.

- Chapter 4: Working with Text Files

  In this chapter, you learn how to work with text files. The chapter teaches how to create text files, but also how to look for specific contents in the different text files.

- Chapter 5: Connecting to a Red Hat Enterprise Linux 7

  This chapter teaches about the different methods that can be used to connect to RHEL 7. It explains local login as well as remote log in, and the different terminal types used for this purpose as well.

- Chapter 6: User and Group Management

  On Linux, users are used as an entity that can be used by people or processes that need access to specific resources. This chapter explains how to create users and make user management easier by working with groups.

- Chapter 7: Configuring Permissions

  In this chapter, you learn how to manage Linux permissions through the basic read, write, and execute permissions, but also through the special permissions and access control lists.

- Chapter 8: Configuring Networking

  A server is useless if it isn't connected to a network. In this chapter, you learn the essential skills required for managing network connections.

Part 1-2: Operating Running Systems

- Chapter 9: Managing Processes

  As an administrator, you need to know how to work with the different tasks that can be running on Linux. This chapter shows how to do this, by sending signals to processes and by changing process priority.

- Chapter 10: Working with Virtual Machines

  Red Hat Enterprise Linux includes KVM, a complete solution that allows you to run virtual machines on top of RHEL. This chapter explains how to manage virtual machines.

- Chapter 11: Managing Software

  Red Hat offers an advanced system for managing software packages. This chapter teaches you how it works.

- Chapter 12: Scheduling Tasks

  In this chapter, you learn how to schedule a task for execution on a moment that fits you best.

- Chapter 13: Configuring Logging

  As an administrator, you need to know what's happening on your server. The rsyslogd and journald services are used for this purpose. This chapter explains how to work with them.

- Chapter 14: Managing partitions

  Storage management is an important skill of a Linux administrator. This chapter explains how hard disks can be organized in partitions, and how these partitions can be mounted in the file system.

- Chapter 15: Managing LVM Logical Volumes

  Dividing disks in partitions isn't very flexible. If you need optimal flexibility, you need LVM logical volumes, which are used by default while installing Red Hat Enterprise Linux. This chapter shows how to create and manage those logical volumes.

Part 1-3: Performing Advanced System Administration Tasks

- Chapter 16: Basic Kernel Management

  The kernel is the part of the operating system that takes care of handling hardware. This chapter explains how that works, and what an administrator can do to analyze the current configuration and manage hardware devices in case the automated procedure doesn't work well.

- Chapter 17: Configuring a Basic Apache Server

  Apache is the most commonly used service on Linux. This chapter shows how to set up Apache web services, including the configuration of Apache virtual hosts.

- Chapter 18: Managing and Understanding the Boot Procedure

  Many things are happening when a Linux server boots. This chapter describes the boot procedure in detail and zooms in on vital aspects of the boot procedure, including the GRUB 2 boot loader and the systemd service manager.

- Chapter 19: Troubleshooting the Boot Procedure

  Sometimes a misconfiguration might cause your server no longer to boot properly. This chapter teaches you some of the techniques that can be applied when normal server startup is no longer possible.

Part 1-4: Managing Network Services

- Chapter 20: Using Kickstart

  If you want to install one server, you can go through a manual installation procedure. If you need to install many servers, you're better off using an installation server. This chapter teaches you how to set up such a server.

- Chapter 21: Managing SELinux

  Many Linux administrators only know how to switch it off, because SELinux is hard to manage and is often the reason why services cannot be accessed. In this chapter, you learn how SELinux works and what to do to configure it so that your services are still working and will be much better protected against possible abuse.

- Chapter 22: Configuring a Firewall

  Apart from SELinux, RHEL 7 comes with a firewall, which is implemented by the firewalld service. In this chapter, you learn how this service is organized and what you can do to block or enable access to specific services.

- Chapter 23: Configuring Remote Mounts and FTP

  While working in a server environment, managing remote mounts is an important skill. A remote mount allows a client computer to access a file system offered through a remote server. These remote mounts can be made through a persistent mount in /etc/fstab, or by using the automount service. This chapter teaches how to set up either of them, and also shows how to configure an FTP server.

- Chapter 24: Configuring Time Services

  For many services, such as databases and Kerberos, it is essential to have the right time. That's why as an administrator you need to be able to manage time on Linux. This chapter teaches you how.

Part 2: RHCE

Part 2-1: System Configuration and Management

- Chapter 25: Configuring External Authentication and Authorization

  If you have multiple servers to manage, it makes sense to use an external authentication and authorization server, such as a Lightweight Directory Access Protocol (LDAP) server that uses Kerberos for authorization. This chapter teaches you how to set up a server for usage of an existing LDAP server that uses Kerberized authorization. It also explains Kerberos protocol fundamentals.

- Chapter 26: Configuring an iSCSI SAN

  RHEL 7 includes everything that is needed to set up a storage-area network (SAN). This chapter explains how to set up the SAN itself, using the iSCSI target software, and how to connect to a SAN, using the iSCSI initiator software on the client server.

- Chapter 27: System Performance Reporting

  Your server might sometimes have problems replying to a user request adequately. If that happens, you need to be able to find out what is wrong with it. This chapter explains performance reporting and all the different tools available to do this in an efficient way.

- Chapter 28: System Optimization Basics

  If you've found that something is wrong with your server's performance, you need to optimize it. In this chapter, you learn how to optimize your server for specific workloads.

- Chapter 29: Configuring Advanced Log Features

  The rsyslog service used for logging on RHEL 7 contains some advanced features, such as working with modules and setting up a remote log server. This chapter explains how to use these features.

- Chapter 30: Configuring Routing and Advanced Networking

  To integrate a server in a datacenter, advanced network configurations are often needed. This chapter explains how to do so and includes configuring aggregated network interfaces using bonding or teaming, as well as routing and IPv6 configurations.

- Chapter 31: An Introduction to Bash Shell Scripting

  Some tasks are complex and need to be performed repeatedly. Such tasks are ideal candidates for optimization through shell scripts. In this chapter, you learn how to use conditional structures in shell scripts to automate tasks efficiently.

Part 2-2: System Security

- Chapter 32: Advanced Firewall Configuration

  In Chapter 22, you learned how to set up a firewalld based firewall, using the default components of this firewall. This chapter zooms in on some more advanced configurations, including port forwarding and rich rules.

- Chapter 33: Managing Advanced Apache Services

  The Apache web server offers many solutions to access web content. That includes using virtual servers, but also includes authentication and the use of Transport Layer Security (TLS) certificates. This chapter teaches you how to manage these advanced features.

- Chapter 34: Configuring DNS

  In this chapter, you learn how to set up a caching-only DNS name server, which is useful to handle DNS requests more efficiently.

- Chapter 35: Configuring a MariaDB Database

  As a Linux administrator, you'll have to deal with database management as well. That is, you do not have to become a skilled DBA, but at least you need to know how to manage database backups, set up a simple database and perform database queries. This chapter teaches how to do all this.

- Chapter 36: Configuring NFS

  The Network File System (NFS) protocol is used to share files between Linux servers or between Linux servers and clients. This chapter teaches you how to set up Domain Name System (DNS), including advanced setups such as Kerberized NFS servers.

- Chapter 37: Configuring Samba File Services

  The Samba file server offers a solution to share directories on Linux to make them accessible for Windows clients. This chapter shows you how to set up a Samba server, and also discusses some of the advanced methods that Samba shares can be integrated in the client file system.

- Chapter 38: Setting Up an SMTP Server

  A Linux server occasionally needs to send email messages to other servers. This chapter shows how to set up a simple configuration for sending email using other mail servers as a relay host.

- Chapter 39: Configuring SSH

  The Secure Shell (SSH) service is used for remote access, but it can do so much more. In this chapter, you learn how to optimize the SSH service through its many parameters in the configuration files. You also learn how to set up SSH port forwarding.

- Chapter 40: Managing Time Synchronization

  As discussed earlier, time is a critical factor for many services to work successfully. This chapter explains how to manage time synchronization by using the Network Time Protocol (NTP).

Part 3: Final Preparation

- Chapter 41: Final Preparation

  In this chapter, you get some final exam preparation tasks. It contains some test exams and many tips that help you maximize your chances of passing the exam.

- Chapter 42: Theoretical Pre-Assessment Exams

  In this chapter, you'll get an RHCSA Theoretical Pre-Assessment Exam and an RHCE Theoretical Pre-Assessment Exam, so you can pre-assess your skills and determine the best route forward for studying for the exams.

- Practice Exams: This section supplies two RHCSA Practice Exams and two RHCE Practice Exams, so you can test your knowledge and skills before taking the exams. These exams are also available on the book's companion website and DVD as PDF files.

Chapter Features

To help you customize your study time using these books, the core chapters have several features that help you make the best use of your time:

- **"Do I Know This Already?" Quizzes:** Each chapter begins with a quiz that helps you determine the amount of time you need to spend studying that chapter.
- **Foundation Topics:** These are the core sections of each chapter. They explain the protocols, concepts, and configuration for the topics in that chapter.
- **Exam Preparation Tasks:** At the end of the "Foundation Topics" section of each chapter, the "Exam Preparation Tasks" section lists a series of study activities that should be done at the end of the chapter. Each chapter includes the activities that make the most sense for studying the topics in that chapter. The activities include the following:

- **Review Key Topics:** The Key Topic icon is shown next to the most important items in the "Foundation Topics" section of the chapter. The Key Topics Review activity lists the key topics from the chapter and their corresponding page numbers. Although the contents of the entire chapter could be on the exam, you should definitely know the information listed in each key topic.
- **Complete Tables and Lists from Memory:** To help you exercise your memory and memorize some lists of facts, many of the more important lists and tables from the chapter are included in a document on the DVD and companion website. This document lists only partial information, allowing you to complete the table or list.
- **Define Key Terms:** This section lists the most important terms from the chapter, asking you to write a short definition and compare your answer to the glossary at the end of this book.
- **Review Questions:** Questions at the end of each chapter that measure insight in the topics that were discussed in the chapter.
- **End-of-Chapter Labs:** Real labs that give you the right impression on what an exam assignment looks like. The end of chapter labs are your first step in finding out what the exam tasks really look like.

Other Features

In addition to the features in each of the core chapters, this book, as a whole, has additional study resources on the DVD and companion website, including the following:

- **Four practice exams:** The companion website and DVD contains the four practice exams, two RHCSA and two RHCE, provided in the book as PDFs so that you can readily test your skills before taking the exams in the testing facility.
- **Interactive exercises and quizzes:** The companion website and DVD contains more than 40 interactive hands-on exercises and 40 interactive quizzes so that you can test your knowledge on the spot.
- **Four advanced CLI simulations:** The companion website and DVD contains four advanced CLI simulations—two RHCSA and two RHCE—that allow you to walk through multistep CLI scenarios in a simulated environment.
- **Glossary quizzes:** The companion website and DVD contains interactive quizzes that allow you to test yourself on every glossary term in the book.

- **More than 2.5 hours of video training:** The companion website and DVD contains 30 minutes of unique test-prep videos plus more than 2 hours of instruction from the best-selling RHCSA and RHCE Complete Video Course series.
- **Virtual Machines:** The companion website and DVD contains three virtual machines so that you can easily get access to an environment where you can work on the labs and exercises in this book.

Book Organization, Chapters, and Appendixes

I have also included two tables that detail where every objective in the the RHCSA and RHCE exams is covered in this book so that you can more easily create a successful plan for passing the tests.

Table 1 RHCSA Objectives

<table>
<tr><th>Objective</th><th>Chapter Title</th><th>Chapter</th><th>Page</th></tr>
<tr><td colspan="4">Understand and use essential tools</td></tr>
<tr><td>Access a shell prompt and issue commands with correct syntax</td><td>Using Essential Tools</td><td>2</td><td>33</td></tr>
<tr><td>Use input-output redirection (>, >>, |, 2>, etc.)</td><td>Using Essential Tools</td><td>2</td><td>33</td></tr>
<tr><td>Use grep and regular expressions to analyze text</td><td>Working with Text Files</td><td>4</td><td>85</td></tr>
<tr><td>Access remote systems using ssh</td><td>Connecting to an RHEL Server</td><td>5</td><td>103</td></tr>
<tr><td>Log in and switch users in multiuser targets</td><td>Connecting to an RHEL Server</td><td>5</td><td>103</td></tr>
<tr><td>Archive, compress, unpack, and uncompress files using tar, star, gzip, and bzip2</td><td>Essential File Management Tools</td><td>3</td><td>57</td></tr>
<tr><td>Create and edit text files</td><td>Working with Text Files</td><td>4</td><td>85</td></tr>
<tr><td>Create, delete, copy, and move files and directories</td><td>Essential File Management Tools</td><td>3</td><td>57</td></tr>
<tr><td>Create hard and soft links</td><td>Essential File Management Tools</td><td>3</td><td>57</td></tr>
<tr><td>List, set, and change standard ugo/rwx permissions</td><td>Permissions Management</td><td>7</td><td>151</td></tr>
</table>

Objective	Chapter Title	Chapter	Page
Locate, read, and use system documentation including man, info, and files in /usr/share/doc Note: Red Hat may use applications during the exam that are not included in Red Hat Enterprise Linux for the purpose of evaluating candidate's abilities to meet this objective.	Using Essential Tools	2	33
Operate running systems			
Boot, reboot, and shut down a system normally	Connecting to an RHEL Server	5	103
Boot systems into different targets manually	Essential Book Procedure Troubleshooting	19	429
Interrupt the boot process in order to gain access to a system	Essential Book Procedure Troubleshooting	19	429
Identify CPU/memory intensive processes, adjust process priority with renice, and kill processes	Process Management	9	205
Locate and interpret system log files and journals	Configuring Logging	13	295
Access a virtual machine's console	Working with Virtual Machines	10	225
Start and stop virtual machines	Working with Virtual Machines	10	225
Start, stop, and check the status of network services	Configuring Networking	8	177
Securely transfer files between systems	Connecting to an RHEL Server	5	103
Configure local storage			
List, create, and delete partitions on MBR and GPT disks	Managing Partitions	14	319
Create and remove physical volumes, assign physical volumes to volume groups, and create and delete logical volumes	Managing LVM Logical Volumes	15	349
Configure systems to mount file systems at boot by Universally Unique ID (UUID) or label	Managing Partitions	14	319

Objective	Chapter Title	Chapter	Page
Add new partitions and logical volumes, and swap to a system non-destructively	Managing Partitions	14	319
Create and configure file systems			
Create, mount, unmount, and use vfat, ext4, and xfs file systems	Managing Partitions	14	319
Mount and unmount CIFS and NFS network file systems	Configuring Remote Mounts and FTP	23	515
Extend existing logical volumes	Managing LVM Logical Volumes	15	349
Create and configure set-GID directories for collaboration	Permissions Management	7	151
Create and manage access control lists (ACLs)	Permissions Management	7	151
Diagnose and correct file permission problems	Permissions Management	7	151
Deploy, configure, and maintain systems			
Configure networking and hostname resolution statically or dynamically	Configuring Networking	8	177
Schedule tasks using at and cron	Scheduling Tasks	12	281
Start and stop services and configure services to start automatically at boot	Managing and Understanding the Boot Procedure	18	405
Configure systems to boot into a specific target automatically	Managing and Understanding the Boot Procedure	18	405
Install Red Hat Enterprise Linux automatically using Kickstart	Using Kickstart	20	451
Configure a physical machine to host virtual guests	Working with Virtual Machines	10	225
Install Red Hat Enterprise Linux systems as virtual guests	Working with Virtual Machines	10	225
Configure systems to launch virtual machines at boot	Working with Virtual Machines	10	225
Configure network services to start automatically at boot	Configuring Networking	8	177
Configure a system to use time services	Configuring Time Services	24	539

Objective	Chapter Title	Chapter	Page
Install and update software packages from Red Hat Network, a remote repository, or from the local file system	Installing Software Packages	11	249
Update the kernel package appropriately to ensure a bootable system	Basic Kernel Management	16	369
Modify the system bootloader	Managing and Understanding the Boot Procedure	18	405
Manage users and groups			
Create, delete, and modify local user accounts	User and Group Management	6	123
Change passwords and adjust password aging for local user accounts	User and Group Management	6	123
Create, delete, and modify local groups and group memberships	User and Group Management	6	123
Configure a system to use an existing authentication service for user and group information	User and Group Management	6	123
Manage security			
Configure firewall settings using firewall-config, firewall-cmd, or iptables	Configuring a Firewall	22	499
Configure key-based authentication for SSH	Connecting to an RHEL Server	5	103
Set enforcing and permissive modes for SELinux	Managing SELinux	21	473
List and identify SELinux file and process context	Managing SELinux	21	473
Restore default file contexts	Managing SELinux	21	473
Use boolean settings to modify system SELinux settings	Managing SELinux	21	473
Diagnose and address routine SELinux policy violations	Managing SELinux	21	473

Table 2 RHCE Objectives

Objective	Chapter Title	Chapter	Page
System configuration and management			
Use network teaming or bonding to configure aggregated network links between two Red Hat Enterprise Linux systems	Configuring Routing and Advanced Networking	30	655
Configure IPv6 addresses and perform basic IPv6 troubleshooting	Configuring Routing and Advanced Networking	30	655
Route IP traffic and create static routes	Configuring Routing and Advanced Networking	30	655
Use firewalld and associated mechanisms such as rich rules, zones and custom rules, to implement packet filtering and configure Network Address Translation (NAT)	Managing Linux-Based Firewalls	32	701
Use /proc/sys and sysctl to modify and set kernel runtime parameters	System Optimization Basics	28	627
Configure a system to authenticate using Kerberos	Configuring External Authentication and Authorization	25	557
Configure a system as either an iSCSI target or initiator that persistently mounts an iSCSI target	Configuring an iSCSI SAN	26	577
Produce and deliver reports on system utilization (processor, memory, disk, and network)	System Performance Reporting	27	607
Use shell scripting to automate system maintenance tasks	An Introduction to Bash Shell Scripting	31	683
Network services			
Install the packages needed to provide the service	Installing Software Packages	11, 25, 26, 31, 33, 34, 35, 36, 37, 38	249, 557, 577, 683, 719, 781, 801, 825
Configure SELinux to support the service	Managing SELinux	21, 33, 35, 36, 37, 39	473, 719, 759, 781, 801, 845
Use SELinux port labeling to allow services to use non-standard ports	Managing SELinux	2, 33, 391	33, 719, 845

Objective	Chapter Title	Chapter	Page
Configure the service to start when the system is booted	Managing and Understanding the Boot Procedure	18, 25, 26, 33, 34, 35, 36, 37, 38	405, 557, 577, 719, 741, 759, 781, 801, 825
Configure the service for basic operation	Sander please insert chapter names and numbers	25, 26, 29, 30, 31, 32, 33, 34, 35, 36, 37, 38, 39, 40	557, 577, 641, 655, 683, 701, 719, 741, 759, 781, 801, 825, 845, 859
Configure host-based and user-based security for the service	Sander please insert chapter names and numbers	25, 26, 29, 30, 31, 32, 33, 34, 35, 36, 37, 38, 39, 40	557, 577, 641, 655, 683, 701, 719, 741, 759, 781, 801, 825, 845, 859
HTTP/HTTPS			
Configure a virtual host	Managing Advanced Apache Services	33	719
Configure private directories	Managing Advanced Apache Services	33	719
Deploy a basic CGI application	Managing Advanced Apache Services	33	719
Configure group-managed content	Managing Advanced Apache Services	33	719
Configure TLS security	Managing Advanced Apache Services	33	719
DNS			
Configure a caching-only name server	Configuring DNS	34	741
Troubleshoot DNS client issues	Configuring DNS	34	741
NFS			
Provide network shares to specific clients	Configuring NFS	36	781
Provide network shares suitable for group collaboration	Configuring NFS	36	781
Use Kerberos to control access to NFS network shares	Configuring NFS	36	781
SMB			
Provide network shares to specific clients	Configuring Samba File Services	37	801

Objective	Chapter Title	Chapter	Page
Provide network shares suitable for group collaboration	Configuring Samba File Services	37	801
SMTP			
Configure a system to forward all email to a central mail server	Setting up an SMTP Server	38	825
SSH			
Configure key-based authentication	Configuring SSH	39	845
Configure additional options described in documentation	Configuring SSH	39	845
NTP			
Synchronize time using other NTP peers	Managing Time Synchronization	40	859
Database services			
Install and configure MariaDB	Configuring a MariaDB Database	35	759
Backup and restore a database	Configuring a MariaDB Database	35	759
Create a simple database schema	Configuring a MariaDB Database	35	759
Perform simple SQL queries against a database	Configuring a MariaDB Database	35	759

About the Virtual Machines

On the companion website and DVD that comes with this book, you can find a set of virtual machines that you can use to work through the labs in this book. Alternatively, you can set up an IPA server as instructed in Appendix D of this book and install your own environment according to the instructions in Chapter 1.

To use the virtual machines, you need VMware Workstation/Player or Fusion. Using the VMs if one of these virtualization platforms is installed on your computer is easy—just doubleclick the files that you'll find in the archive after uncompressing it. Notice that you'll need the following to use these virtual machines:

- A total of 30 GB of disk space
- A total of 3 GB of available RAM

Where are the Companion Content Files?

Register this print version of Red Hat RHCSA/RHCE 7 Cert Guide to access the Bonus content online.

This print version of this title comes with a disc of companion content. You have online access to these files by following the steps below:

1. Go to www.pearsonITcertification.com/register and log in or create a new account.
2. Enter the ISBN: 9780789754059
3. Answer the challenge question as proof of purchase.
4. Click on the “Access Bonus Content” link in the Registered Products section of your account page, to be taken to the page where your downloadable content is available.

Please note that many of our companion content files can be very large, especially image and video files.

If you are unable to locate the files for this title by following the steps at left, please visit www.pearsonITcertification.com/ contact and select the “Site Problems/ Comments” option. Our customer service representatives will assist you.

This book also includes an exclusive offer for 70% off the Premium Edition eBook and Practice Tests edition of this title. Please see the coupon code included with the DVD for information on how to purchase the Premium Edition.

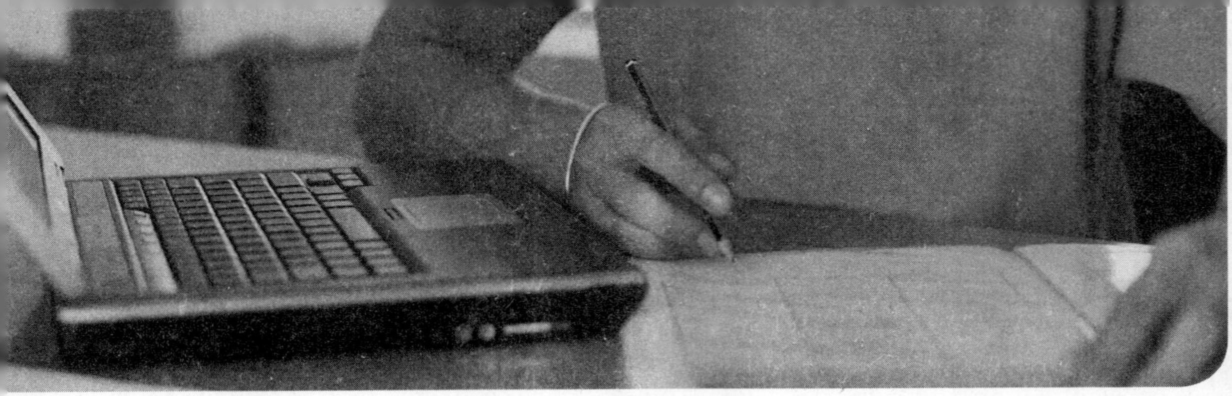

PART 1

RHCSA

The following topics are covered in this chapter:

- Preparing to Install Red Hat Enterprise Linux
- Performing a Manual Installation

This chapter covers no exam objectives.

CHAPTER 1

Installing Red Hat Enterprise Linux Server

To learn how to work with Red Hat Enterprise Linux Server as an administrator, you first need to install it. This chapter teaches you how to set up an environment in which you can perform all exercises in this book.

On the RHCSA exam, you do not need to install Red Hat Enterprise Linux Server. However, because you need to install an environment that allows you to test all items discussed in this book, you start by installing Red Hat Enterprise Linux in this chapter. This chapter describes all steps that you will encounter while performing an installation of RHEL 7. It also discusses how to set up an environment in which you can perform all exercises in this book.

"Do I Know This Already?" Quiz

The "Do I Know This Already?" quiz allows you to assess whether you should read this entire chapter thoroughly or jump to the "Exam Preparation Tasks" section. If you are in doubt about your answers to these questions or your own assessment of your knowledge of the topics, read the entire chapter. Table 1-1 lists the major headings in this chapter and their corresponding "Do I Know This Already?" quiz questions. You can find the answers in Appendix A, "Answers to the 'Do I Know This Already?' Quizzes and 'Review Questions.'"

Table 1-1 "Do I Know This Already?" Section-to-Question Mapping

Foundation Topics Section	Questions
Preparing to Install Red Hat Enterprise Linux	1, 2, 6
Performing a Manual Installation	3–5, 7–10

1. You want to install a test environment to practice for the RHCSA/RHCE exams. Which of the following distributions should you avoid?
   a. The most recent Fedora version
   b. CentOS 7
   c. Scientific Linux 7
   d. RHEL 7

2. Which of the following features is not just available in RHEL but also in CentOS?
   a. Hardware certification
   b. Software certification
   c. The right to make support calls
   d. Software updates

3. Why should you install the server with a GUI installation pattern?
   a. To prepare for RHCSA/RHCE, you need some tools that run in a GUI only.
   b. The minimal installation is incomplete.
   c. If you do not install a GUI immediately, it is very hard to add it later.
   d. The Server with GUI is the default installation that is recommended by Red Hat.

4. Which is the default file system that is used in RHEL 7?
   a. Ext3
   b. Ext4
   c. XFS
   d. Btrfs

5. Which feature is supported in Ext4 but not in XFS?
   a. Shrinking the file system
   b. Snapshots
   c. File system quota
   d. A maximum size that goes beyond 2TB

6. Which of the following is not a reason why Fedora should be avoided?
    a. Fedora contains features that may or may not be available in future RHEL releases.
    b. Fedora distributions show a much later state of development than RHEL.
    c. Fedora software is not stable.
    d. Software in Fedora may differ from the same software in RHEL.
7. Which of the following options is not available from the Installation Summary screen?
    a. Date & Time
    b. Keyboard
    c. Language Support
    d. Troubleshoot an Existing Installation
8. After setting the root password you want to use, you cannot proceed in the installation. What is the most likely cause that you cannot move on?
    a. The password is unsecure, and unsecure passwords are not accepted.
    b. The password does not meet requirements in the password policy.
    c. You also need to create a user.
    d. If an unsecure password is used, you need to click **Done** twice.
9. Which statement about the system language is *not* true?
    a. You can change the system language from the Installation Summary screen.
    b. You can change the system language directly after booting from the installation media.
    c. When setting the installation language, you can also select a keyboard layout.
    d. After installation, you cannot change the language settings.

10. When installing a server that uses LVM logical volumes, you'll get at least three storage volumes (partitions or LVM). Which of the following is not part of them?

a. /boot

b. /home

c. /

d. swap

Foundation Topics

Preparing to Install Red Hat Enterprise Linux

Before you start installing Red Hat Enterprise Linux, you want to take care of a few things. These things are discussed in this section. You'll first learn what exactly Red Hat Enterprise Linux is. Then you'll learn how you can get access to the software. We then discuss the Red Hat Enterprise Linux add-ons, as well as the setup requirements. After you know all about these, you move on to the next section, where you learn how to install Red Hat Enterprise Linux.

What Is Red Hat Enterprise Linux 7 Server?

RHEL 7 is a Linux distribution. As you probably know, Linux is a free operating system. That means that the source code of all programs is available for free, which is also the case for Red Hat Enterprise Linux 7. However, you cannot download RHEL 7 for free (with the exception of a 30-day evaluation version).

To use RHEL 7, you need a subscription. This subscription entitles you to a few additional items, such as support and patches. When you pay for Red Hat Enterprise Linux, Red Hat offers you a supported Enterprise Linux operating system. It is not just an operating system, but it is an operating system that is offered with some key benefits that are a normal requirement in corporate environments:

- Monitored updates and patches, which is not just updates and patches, but updates and patches that have gone through a thorough testing procedure
- Different levels of support and help, according to the kind of subscription that you have purchased
- A certified operating system that is guaranteed to run and to be supported on specific hardware models
- A certified platform for running enterprise applications such as SAP, Oracle Database, and many more
- Access to the Red Hat customer portal at access.redhat.com, where you can find much detailed documentation that is available to customers only

Red Hat understands that not all potential customers are interested in these enterprise features. That is why Red Hat is involved in two free alternatives also:

- CentOS 7
- Fedora

You'll learn more about these in the upcoming sections of this chapter.

Getting the Software

There are different ways to get the software required to perform all exercises in this book. In this section, you learn what your options are.

Using Red Hat Enterprise Linux Server

If you want to learn how to work with the different programs, tools, and services that are provided in Red Hat Enterprise Linux 7, the easiest way is to use Red Hat Enterprise Linux 7 on a paid version, not a free derivative such as CentOS or Scientific Linux. Red Hat Enterprise Linux 7 is not a freely available operating system, though. If you want to use it, you need to buy it. The only thing that you can get for free is a 30-day evaluation version, which you can get from https://access.redhat.com/products/red-hat-enterprise-linux/evaluation.

The most important thing that you get in the RHEL 7 Server evaluation version and which is not available in the freely available derivatives is access to the Red Hat customer portal. Through this portal, you have access to different kinds of information, in addition to updates provided through Red Hat Network.

After installing Red Hat Enterprise Linux and first registering it at the Red Hat Network, you'll get access to patches and updates for a period of 30 days. Once this period expires, you can still use Red Hat Enterprise Linux, but you can no longer install software through the Red Hat Network, nor update or patch the software, which makes RHEL a less-ideal candidate for use in this course if you do not want to pay for it.

Using CentOS

CentOS 7 is the Community Enterprise Operating System. CentOS 7 started as a recompiled version of RHEL, where all items that were not available for free were removed from the software. Basically, that meant that just the name was changed and that the Red Hat logo (which is proprietary) was removed from all the CentOS software packages. The result was an operating system that offered exactly the same functionality as RHEL 7 but was available for free (and without the enterprise support services).

Recently, Red Hat has incorporated CentOS. According to Red Hat CTO Brian Stevens in 2014, "That is to offer something to those customers that aren't ready for Enterprise support yet." The idea behind that is that eventually many customers will need enterprise support, because their Linux distribution is becoming increasingly important. And by giving away CentOS 7 for free, and under the Red Hat brand, it is just natural that the customer will upgrade to Red Hat Enterprise Linux 7.

CentOS 7 is also an excellent choice to work with in this book; it offers all that RHEL has to offer but you do not have to pay for it. That is why I'm using it myself, and I recommend you to use it as well. You can download CentOS 7 from http://www.centos.org.

TIP Another benefit of CentOS is that it has a bigger hardware compatibility list than RHEL 7, because more drivers are compiled in the CentOS 7 kernel.

Other Distributions

CentOS is not the only distribution that offers Red Hat packages without having to pay for them. Another commonly used Linux distribution that is doing the same is Scientific Linux, a Linux distribution that was developed at Fermi National Accelerator Laboratory. Even if Scientific Linux is known to be offering an excellent Linux distribution, while writing this book I have not used it, and so I do not guarantee the perfect working of all exercises in this book on Scientific Linux. In theory, it should work as well, though. In addition, it differs from CentOS because it provides additional repositories and its own updates and patches. So, you do run the risk of working with software in Scientific Linux that you will not find in the exact same way when taking the RHCSA or RHCE exams, which are based on Red Hat Enterprise Linux.

Another Linux distribution closely related to Red Hat Enterprise Linux is Fedora. Fedora is a completely open source Linux distribution available for free. Red Hat is dedicating a lot of staff to contribute to the Fedora project, because Red Hat uses Fedora as the development platform for RHEL. The result is that Fedora offers access to the latest and greatest software, which in most cases is much more recent than the thoroughly tested software components of Red Hat Enterprise Linux (which is why you should not use Fedora to prepare for the RCHSA or RHCE exam). Fedora is also used by Red Hat as a testing ground for new features that might or might not be included in future RHEL releases. In Fedora, you will work with items that are not available in RHEL, which means that you will have to do things differently on the exam. So, don't use it!

Understanding Access to Repositories

An important difference between RHEL and the other distributions is the access to repositories. A repository is the installation source used for installing software. If you are using free software such as CentOS, correct repositories are automatically set up, and no further action is required. If you are using Red Hat Enterprise Linux with a subscription, you'll get access to the Red Hat repositories on the Red Hat Network (RHN).

> **TIP** If you are installing Red Hat from the RHEL 7 installation disc, but you do not register it, you will not have access to any repository at all, which is why you need to know how to set up repository access manually. In Chapter 11, "Managing Software," you learn how to do this.

Understanding Red Hat Enterprise Linux 7 Server Variants and Add-Ons

This book focuses on the default version of RHEL 7. However, it is good to know that there are some server variants and add-ons available. A server variant is developed to be used for specific purposes or platforms. Server variants are modified versions of the RHEL 7 platform. A server add-on is an additional installation that offers functionality to RHEL 7 that is not available by default. Add-ons also require additional payment.

The following server variants are offered:

- **Red Hat Enterprise Linux Server for High-Performance Computing (HPC):** A tuned version of RHEL that is created to be used in an HPC cluster, so that challenging workloads can be handled in the most efficient way possible.
- **Red Hat Enterprise Linux Server for IBM Power:** IBM Power is a specific platform that is used in high-demand environments. To run RHEL on this hardware platform, Red Hat is offering the RHEL for IBM Power server variant.
- **Red Hat Enterprise Linux Server for IBM System z:** This platform-specific version of RHEL allows you to run RHEL on IBM mainframes.
- **Red Hat Enterprise Linux for SAP Business Applications:** This is a version of RHEL that was specifically developed for SAP application deployments. It contains the infrastructure software stack that is needed for the best operation of SAP apps, and the service and support that is required for running SAP on RHEL.
- **Red Hat Enterprise Linux for SAP HANA:** A version of RHEL that has been optimized to run SAP HANA, an enterprise relational database management system that was designed to run completely from server memory without needing any disk access.

Apart from the server variants, Red Hat also offers server add-ons to enrich the features offered through RHEL:

- **High Availability:** An add-on that helps you to make applications highly available through failover to another node after failure.
- **Resilient Storage:** A solution that allows you to access the same storage device over a network, through shared storage or a clustered file system.
- **Smart management:** An add-on that makes managing and updating RHEL systems easier, and integrates well with Red Hat Satellite.
- **Extended support:** This add-on offers 24 months of additional support after the ending of the default RHEL support life cycle.

Setup Requirements

RHEL 7 can be installed on physical as well as virtual hardware. For the availability of specific features, it does not really matter which type of hardware is used, as long as the following conditions are met:

- 512MB of RAM
- A 4GB hard disk
- A network card

The preceding requirements allow you to run a minimal installation of RHEL, but if you want to create an environment that enables you to perform all exercises described in this book, make sure to meet the following minimal requirements

- 64-bit platform support
- 1GB of RAM
- A 10GB hard disk
- A DVD drive
- A network card

NOTE Some resources on the Internet will mention different minimal requirements. This is not a big deal for the RHCSA or RHCE exams.

Course Environment Description

To perform all exercises in this book, I recommend installing three different servers, named as follows:

- Server1
- Server2
- FreeIPA

TIP Although I recommend setting up all parts that are required for this course manually, if you are having a problem you might like the environment that I provide at http://www.rhatcert.com. Go to the download area of this website to get access to all software required to work on the exercises in this book.

Server1 is a base RHEL 7 installation used in the RHCSA part of this book. Server2 is used when client/server functionality needs to be tested. The FreeIPA server is required in some of the labs related to authentication and Network File System (NFS). To install server1 and server2, you can follow the generic guidelines in this chapter; all specific parts of the setup are explained in the specific exercises. To install the FreeIPA server, you can follow the directions in Appendix D, "Setting Up Identity Management," after you have installed a base installation of RHEL 7.

NOTE Even if in this book I'm using CentOS 7, because this is a book about RHEL and no functional difference exists between CentOS 7 and RHEL 7, I just refer to RHEL 7. If items are discussed that apply to RHEL7 only, and not to CentOS, I mention that specifically.

To set up the course environment, I recommend that you use a solution for desktop virtualization, such as VMware Workstation (or Fusion if you are on Mac) or Oracle VirtualBox. Using one of these has the benefit that you can use snapshots which enable you to easily revert to a previous state of the configuration. Other virtualization solutions, such as KVM, are supported as well. You can also install on real hardware, but you will be less flexible.

> **TIP** In all chapters, you'll find step-by-step exercises that tell you exactly what to do to configure specific services. At the end of all chapters, you'll find end-of-chapter labs which provide assignments that are very similar to the types of assignments that you will get on the exam. To get the most out of the end-of-chapter labs, it is a good idea to start from a clean environment. The most efficient way to do this is by creating snapshots of the state of your virtual machines when you are starting the chapter. This allows you to revert to the state your virtual machines were in when you started working on the chapter, while still keeping all the work that you have done in previous chapters.

Performing a Manual Installation

Even if RHEL 7 can be installed from other media such as an installation server or a USB key, the most common installation starts from the installation DVD. So, take your installation DVD and boot the computer on which you want to install RHEL 7. The following steps describe how to proceed from the moment that you see the installation DVD boot screen:

Key Topic

1. After booting from DVD, you'll see the CentOS 7 boot menu. From this menu, you can choose from different options:

   - **Install CentOS 7:** Choose this for a normal installation.
   - **Test This Media & Install CentOS 7:** Select this if before installing you want to test the installation media. Notice that this will take a significant amount of time.
   - **Troubleshooting:** Select this option for some troubleshooting options. This option is useful if you cannot normally boot from your computer's hard drive anymore.

   When the installation program starts, you can pass boot options to the kernel, so enable or disable specific features. To get access to the prompt where you can add these options, press **Tab** from the installation menu. This will show you the kernel boot line that will be used and offers an option to change boot parameters.

   To start a normal installation, just select the **Install CentOS** 7 boot option.

2. Once the base system from which you will perform the installation has loaded, you see the Welcome to CentOS 7 screen. From this screen, you can select the language and the keyboard setting. For the RHCSA and RHCE exams, it makes no sense to choose anything but English. If you are working on a non-US keyboard, from this screen you can select the keyboard setting. Make sure

to select the appropriate keyboard setting, after which you click **Continue** to proceed (see Figure 1.1).

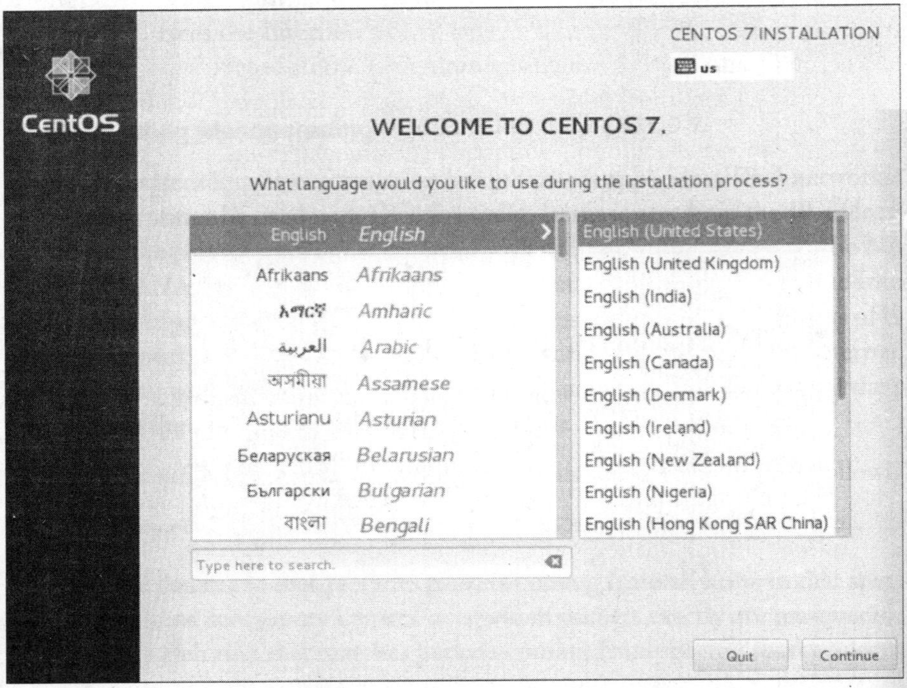

Figure 1.1 Select the appropriate keyboard setting before continuing.

3. After selecting the keyboard and language settings, you'll see the Installation Summary screen (see Figure 1.2). From this screen, you specify all settings you want to use. On this screen, you have seven different options:

   - Date & Time
   - Keyboard
   - Language Support
   - Installation Source
   - Software Selection
   - Installation Destination
   - Network & Hostname

From this overview screen, you can see whether items still need to be configured. So long as this is the case, you cannot click the Begin Installation button. You will not have to change settings at each option in all cases, but for completeness, you'll learn what is behind the different settings in the subsections that follow.

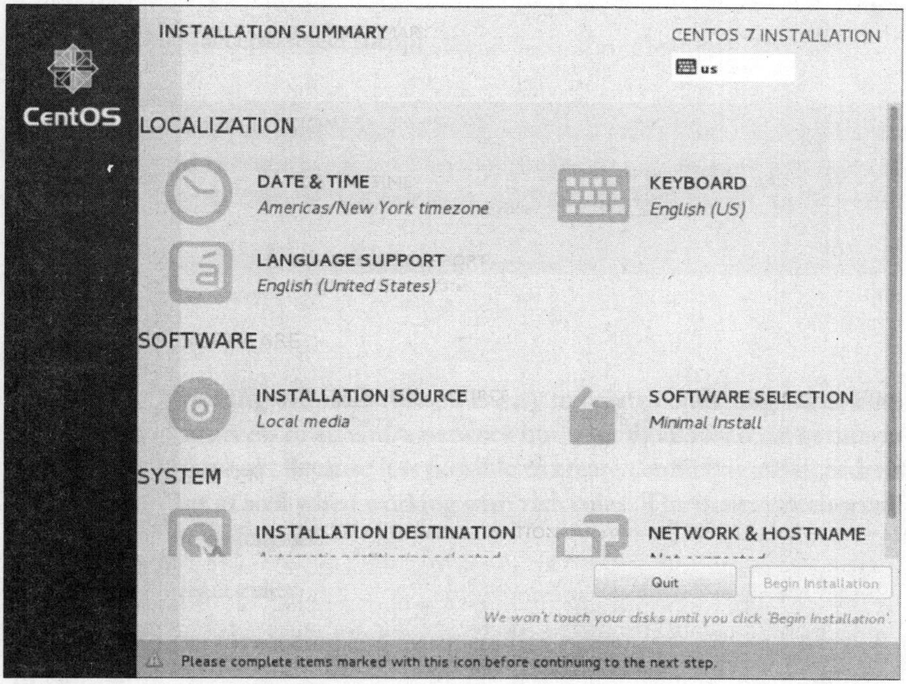

Figure 1.2 You specify the complete configuration of your server from the Installation Summary screen.

4. After selecting Date & Time, you'll see a map of the world on which you can easily click the time zone that you are in (see Figure 1.3). Alternatively, you can select the region and city you are in. You can also set the current date and time, and after setting the network, you can specify the Network Time Protocol (NTP) to be used. This option is not accessible if you have not configured the network yet. When using network time, you can add network time servers to be used by clicking the configuration icon in the upper-right part of the screen. After specifying the settings you want to use, click **Done** in the upper-left corner of the screen to write the settings.

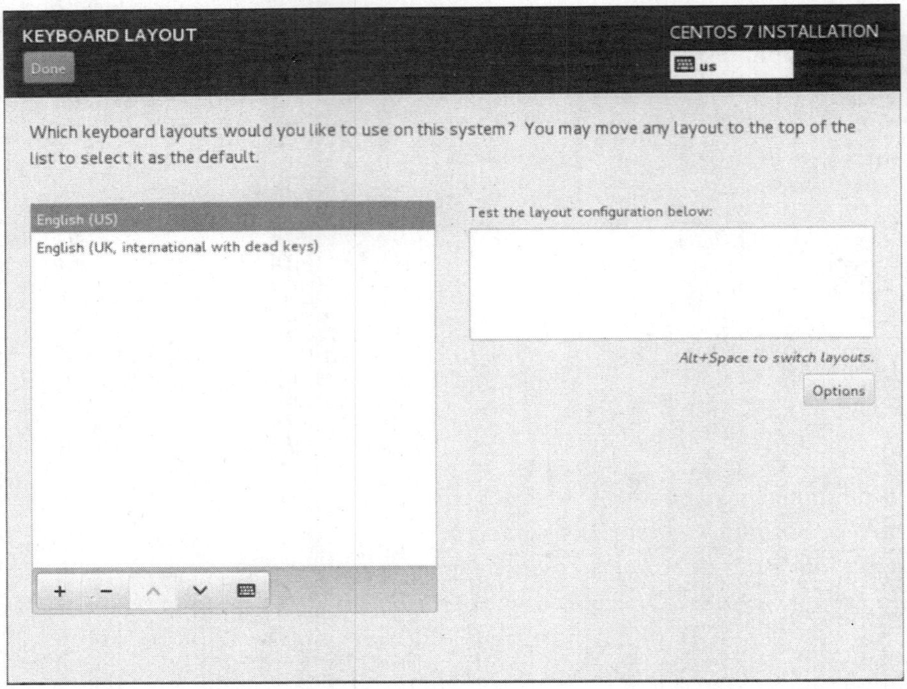

Figure 1.3 Selecting date and time settings.

5. Under the Keyboard Layout option, you'll find what you need to configure the keyboard layout. From this screen, shown in Figure 1.4, you can also select a secondary keyboard layout, which is useful if your server is used by administrators using different keyboard layouts. Not only different language settings are supported, but also different hardware layouts. If many administrators are using an Apple Macintosh computer, for instance, you can select the standard keyboard layout for Mac in the appropriate region.

   After adding another keyboard layout, you can also configure layout switching options. This is a key sequence that is used to switch between different kinds of layout. Select **Options** to specify the key combination you want to use for this purpose. After specifying the configuration you want to use, click **Done** to complete.

6. The Language Support option is the same as the Language Support option that you used in Step 2 of this procedure. If you've already configured the language settings to be used, you do not need to change anything here.

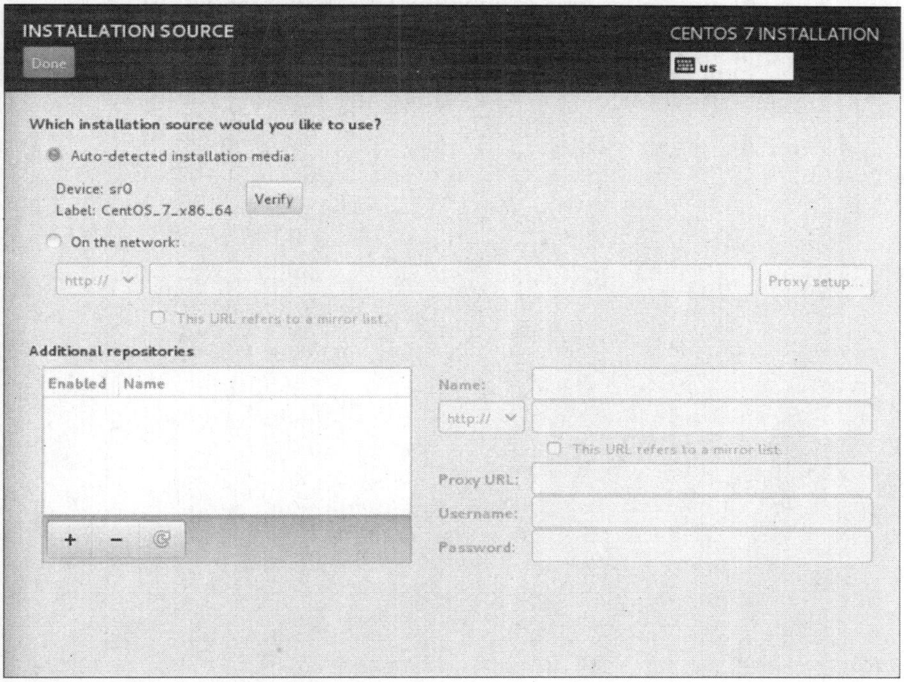

Figure 1.4 Selecting additional keyboard layout.

7. In the Software section, the first option available is Installation Source (see Figure 1.5). If you have booted from a regular installation disc, there is nothing to be specified from this option. If you have booted from a minimal boot environment, you can specify the network URL where additional packages are available, as well as additional repositories that need to be used. You do not have to do this for the RHCSA or RHCE exam, but if ever you are setting up an installation server, it is useful to know that this option exists.

8. An important part of the installation procedure is the Software Selection screen. From here, you select the base environment (see Figure 1.6) and add-ons that are available for the selected environment. By default, a Minimal Installation is selected. This base environment allows you to install RHEL on a minimal-size hard disk. For this course, I assume that you install the **Server with GUI** option. To perform the tasks that need to be performed on the RHCSA and RHCE exams, some easy-to-use graphical tools are available, so it does make sense to install a server with a graphical user interface (GUI) (even if you would never do this in a production environment). All additional packages can be added later. At this point, you do not have to select any additional packages.

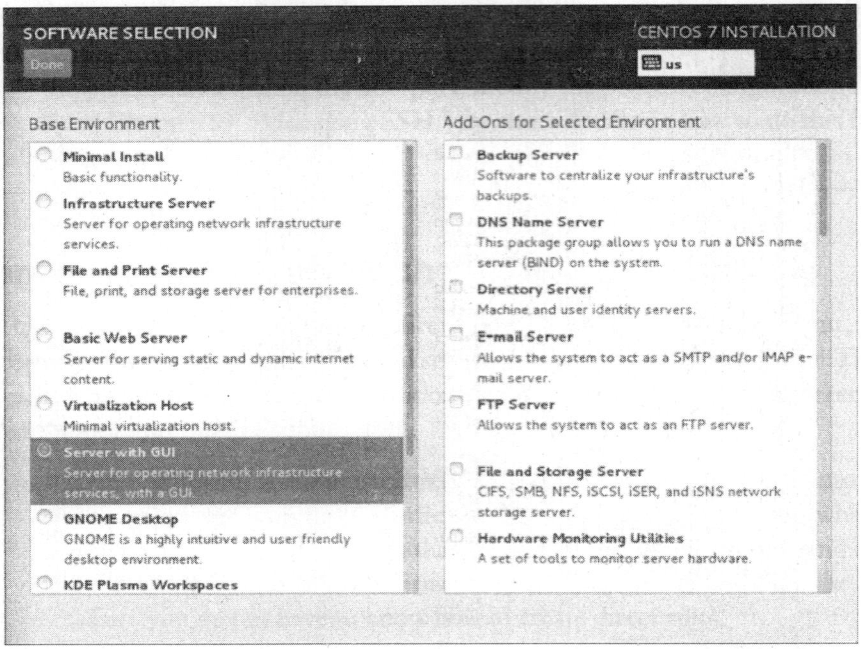

Figure 1.5 Selecting the installation source.

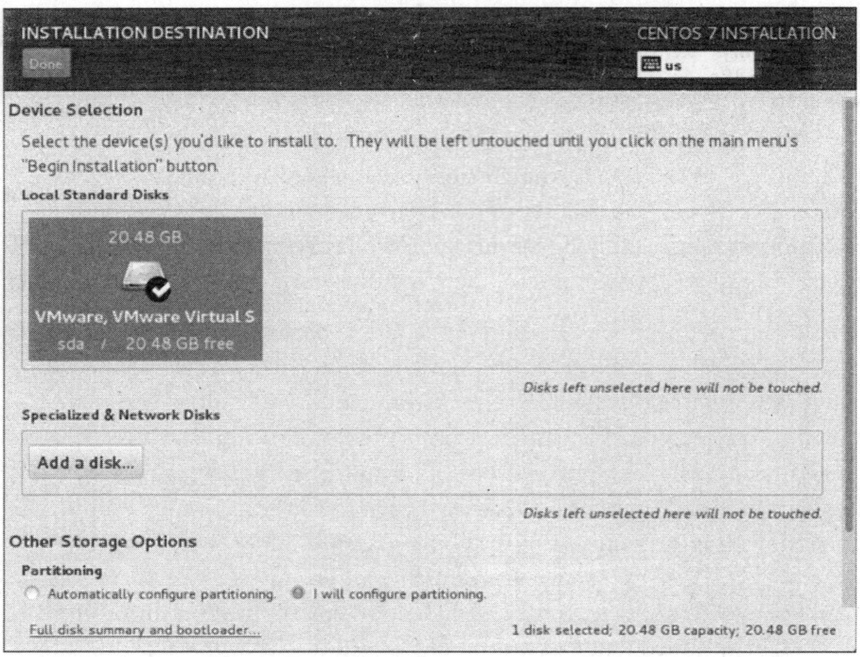

Figure 1.6 Make sure you select **Server with GUI** for every server you are going to use for the exercises in this book.

NOTE Some people say that *real* administrators do not use the Server with GUI installation pattern. Preparing for the RHCSA and RHCE exams is not about being a real administrator. The big advantage of using the Server with GUI installation pattern is that it provides an easy to use interface. Some tools discussed in this book only run on a GUI. Also, you'll notice that an increasing number of Linux servers run with a GUI.

9. Next, you need to specify where you want to install to. By default, automatic partitioning is selected and you only need to approve the disk device you want to use for automatic partitioning (see Figure 1.7). Many advanced options are available, as well. To prepare your installation for all the exercises that are in later chapters in this book, you cannot just use the default partitioning. Instead, you need a setup that uses LVM and also keeps some disk space available. To do this, from the screen you see in Figure 1.7, select **I Will Configure Partitioning**. Then, make sure that the disk you want to use is selected and click **Done** to proceed. Notice that sometimes not all options are shown, and you'll see a scrollbar to the right of the screen. If this is the case, scroll down to show additional installation options. You'll see the Encryption option, which allows you to set up an encrypted disk.

TIP If you want to use this server to perform the exercises in the upcoming chapters, make sure you keep some disk space that is not allocated to any partition. You need unpartitioned disk space to work through the partitioning and LVM exercises, which is an essential part of the RHCSA exam objectives.

After specifying that you want to set up disk layout manually, you'll see the screen that is in Figure 1.8. From this screen, click **+** to add new disk devices. For setting up the environment that is required in this course, I recommend using the following disk layout (based on a 20GB hard disk).

- /boot mounted on an XFS formatted traditional partition, size 500MB
- An XFS formatted logical volume with a size of 10GB that is mounted on /
- A 1GB logical volume that is used as swap space

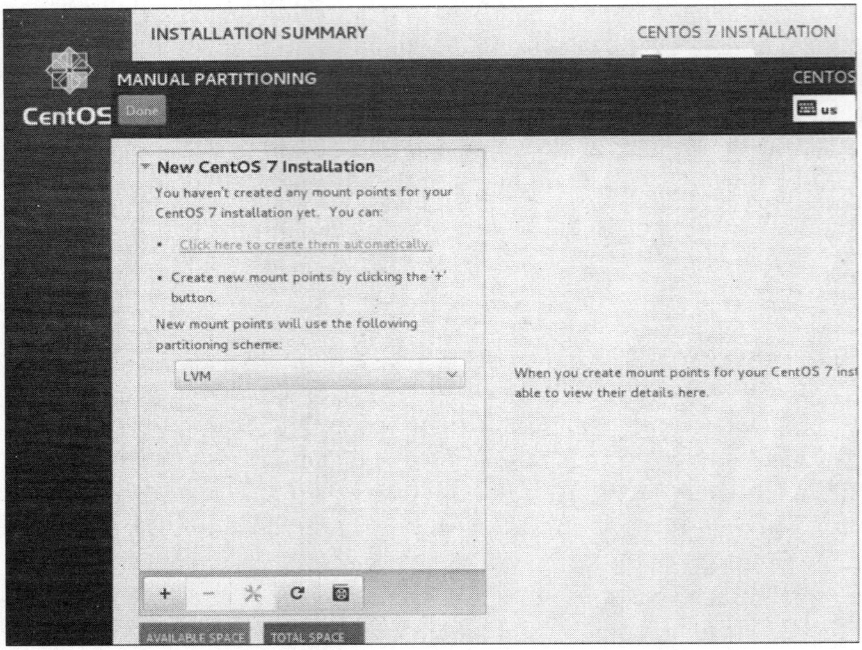

Figure 1.7 Select **I Will Configure Partitioning**, and click **Done** to proceed.

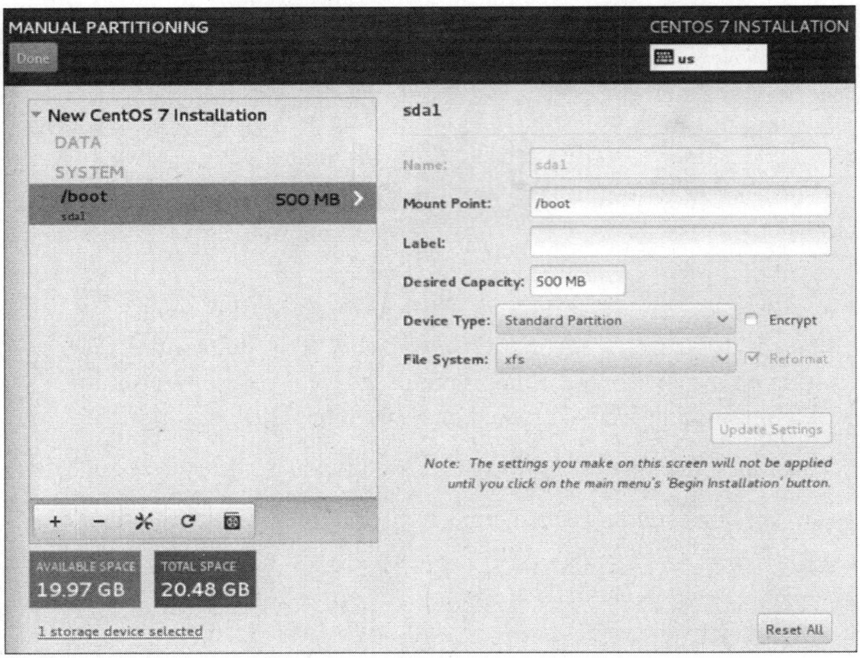

Figure 1.8 Configuring advanced disk layout.

NOTE RHEL 7 by default uses the XFS file system. This file system cannot be shrunk; it can only be expanded. Therefore, it is sometimes a better choice to use ext4.

To create this configuration, from the screen in Figure 1.8, click the **+** sign. You'll now see a pop-up in which you can specify a mount point and the desired capacity. From the Mount Point drop-down list, select **/boot** and add the desired capacity **500M**. Then, click **Add Mount Point**. You'll now get to the screen that you see in Figure 1.9, in which you can specify specific details about the mount point you just created.

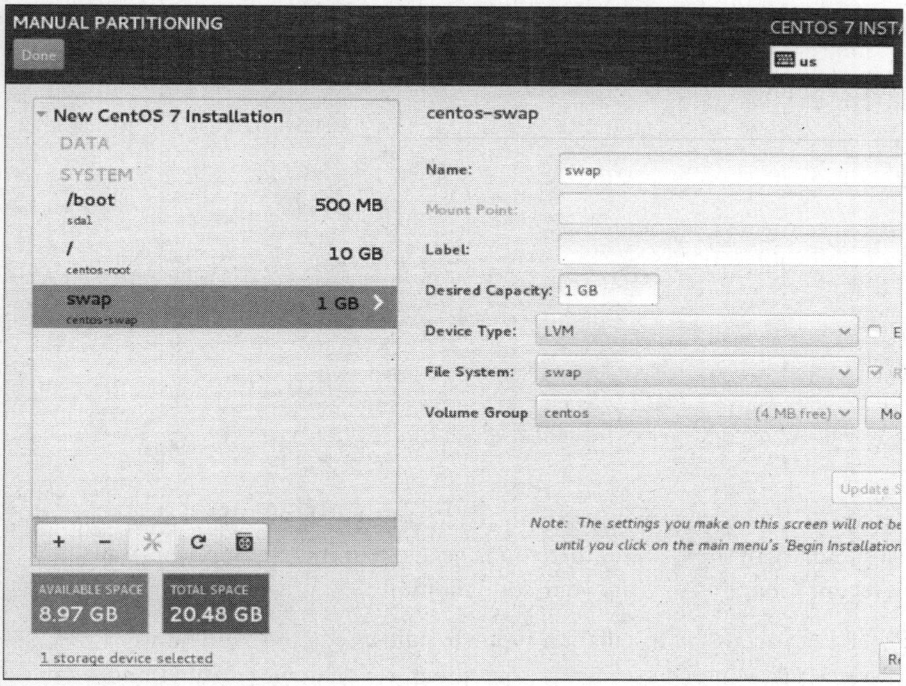

Figure 1.9 Specifying details for the mount point you just created.

At this point, from the interface that you see in Figure 1.9, click the **+** sign again and specify the mount point **/** and a capacity of **10G**. On the Mount Point Details screen that you see now, make sure that the device type LVM is set and that the file system XFS is selected. You do not have to modify anything else.

Now click the **+** sign once more to add a swap device. From the Mount Point drop-down list, select **swap**, and specify the desired capacity of **1G**. Then, click **Add Mount Point**. The layout at this point should look like Figure 1.10. If this is the case, click **Done** to write the configuration.

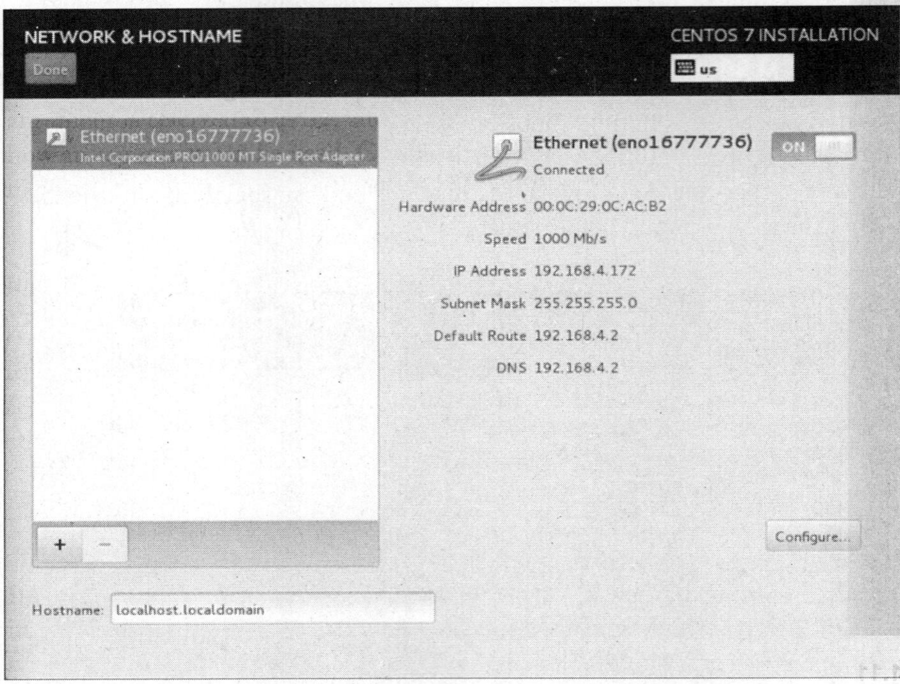

Figure 1.10 If the configuration looks like this, you can write it to disk.

Before the configuration is committed to disk, you'll see a screen showing a summary of the changes that you have applied. If it all looks good, click **Accept Changes** to write your configuration.

10. The last part of the installation summary allows you to set up networking. Notice that you must configure something. If you do not do anything, your server will not be able to connect to any network. From the Installation Summary screen, click **Network & Hostname** to set up networking. This shows the screen that you see in Figure 1.11.

    The network connection by default is set to off. Make sure to switch it on. After switching on the network connection, you could click **Configure** to add the further configuration. Networking is discussed in detail in Chapter 8, "Configuring Networking," and so you do not have to do that now and can just leave the default settings that get an IP address from the Dynamic Host Configuration Protocol (DHCP) server. You can also leave the hostname at its default setting; you learn how to change it in Chapter 8 as well.

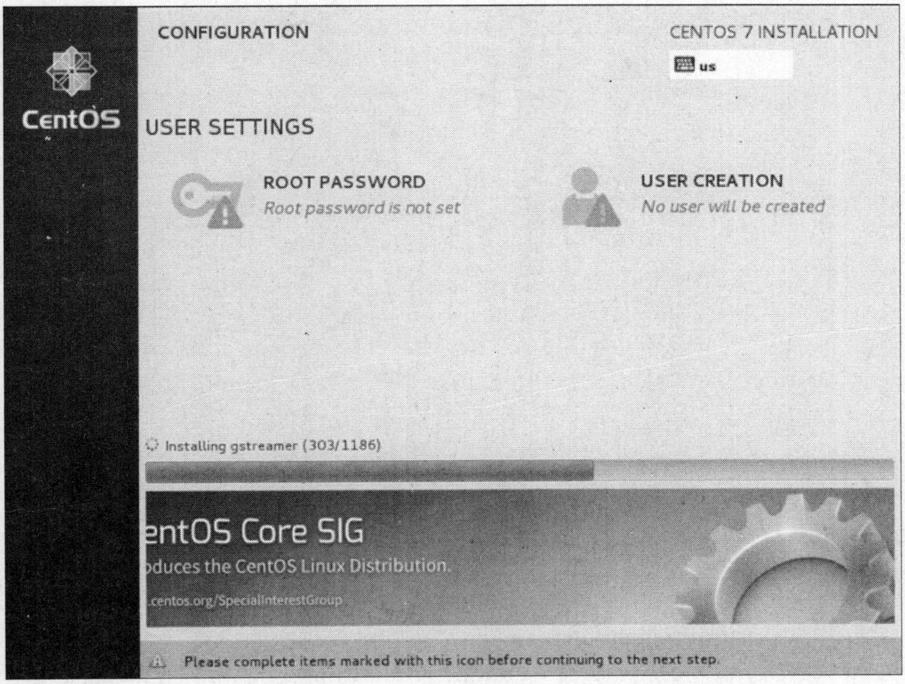

Figure 1.11 In the Network & Hostname screen, you must set the network card to on.

11. After specifying all settings in the installation summary, you can click **Begin Installation** to start the installation. This immediately starts the installation procedure but also prompts for user settings (see Figure 1.12).

    From this screen, click **Root Password** first, and set the password to **password**. That is not very secure, but by using a simple password like this, you'll avoid the issues later on that might result from not remembering the password. You have to specify the password twice, and you also need to click **Done** twice. This is because you have to confirm that you really want to use a weak password.

    Next, click **User Settings** to create a user. Enter the full name and username you want to use, and for this user, set the password to **password** also. Again, you have to click **Done** twice to confirm that you really want to use a weak password.

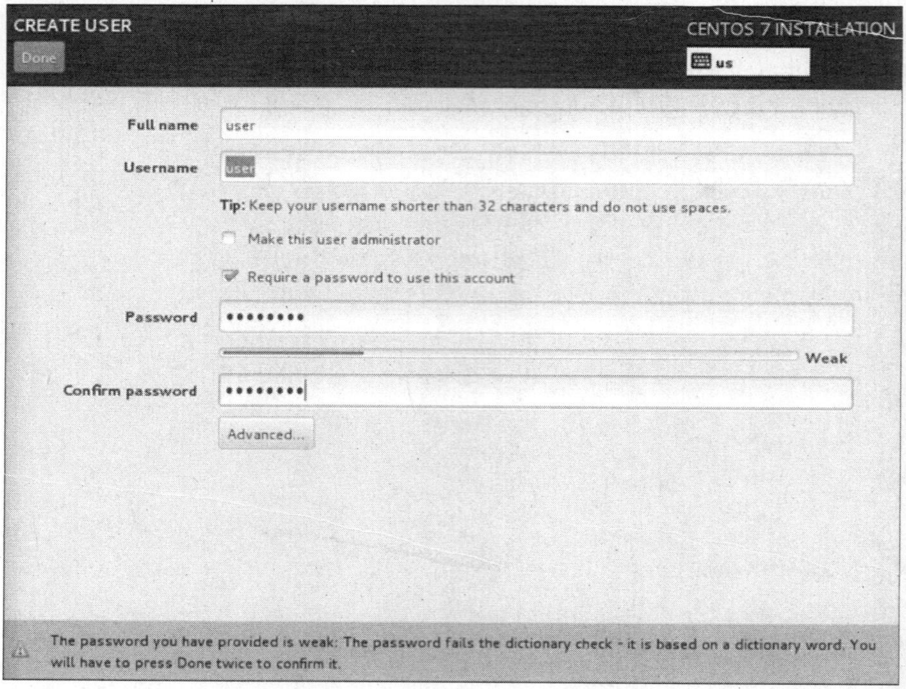

Figure 1.12 Specifying additional user settings.

12. When the installation has completed, you'll see the screen shown in Figure 1.13. You'll now need to click **Reboot** to restart the computer and finalize the installation.

13. After rebooting, you have to go through a couple of additional setup steps. Fist, you need to accept the license agreement. To do this, click the red text **License Not Accepted**, select **I Accept the License Agreement**, and then click **Done** to complete. You can now click **Finish the Configuration** to finalize the configuration, which brings you to the graphical login prompt.

NOTE The procedure described above is based on the installation of version 7.0. In 7.1, once the step has been added, you can now configure Kdump from the installer. Kdump is used to set up a process that is started with your server to allow you to create a memory core dump in case the kernel crashes. As Linux kernel crashes don't occur very frequently, and as setting up Kdump is not a part of the RHCSA or RHCE objectives, you can just click Next on this step to accept the default settings. If your server does have enough RAM available, that will result in Kdump being active automatically. If your server is low on memory, you won't have it running by default.

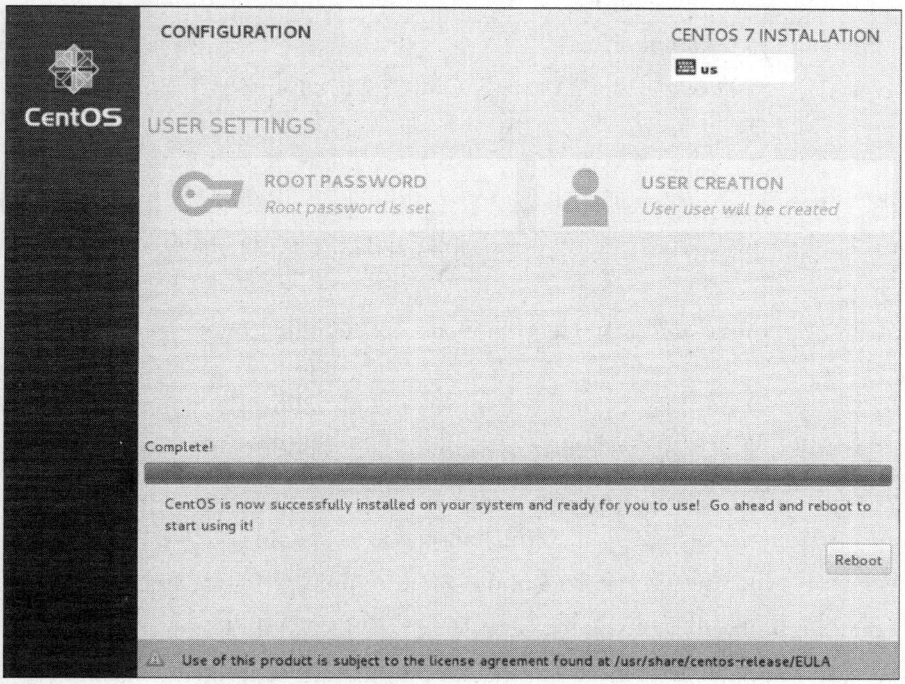

Figure 1.13 Reboot to finalize the installation.

Summary

In this chapter, you learned what Red Hat Enterprise Linux is and how it relates to some other Linux distributions. You also learned how to install Red Hat Enterprise Linux 7. You are now ready to set up a basic environment that you can use to work on all the exercises in this course.

Exam Preparation Tasks

Review All Key Topics

Review the most important topics in the chapter, noted with the Key Topic icon in the outer margin of the page. Table 1.2 lists a reference of these key topics and the page numbers on which each is found.

Table 1.2 Key Topics for Chapter 1

Key Topic Element	Description	Page Number
Step List	How to perform a manual CentOS 7 installation	17

Define Key Terms

Define the following key terms from this chapter and check your answers in the glossary:

distribution, Linux, Red Hat, CentOS, Fedora, Scientific Linux

Review Questions

1. You do not want to buy a RHEL license, but you want to create an environment to practice for the exam. Which distribution should you use?
2. Why can't you use a 32-bit version of RHEL to prepare for the exam?
3. You want to install a minimal system. How much RAM do you need?
4. Why is it a good idea to have Internet access on all servers you are installing?
5. You want to install a virtual machine on a computer that does not have an optical disk drive. What is the easiest alternative to perform the installation?
6. Why is it a good idea to install a GUI?
7. What is the default file system on RHEL 7?
8. Can you install RHEL if you do not have Internet access?
9. What is the most important feature offered through RHN?
10. Which installation pattern should you use if you have a very limited amount of disk space available?

End-of-Chapter Labs

In this chapter, you learned how to set up Red Hat Enterprise Linux. At this point, you should have one server up and running. For exercises in later chapters in this book, two additional servers are needed.

Lab 1.1

Repeat the procedure "Performing a Manual Installation" to install two more servers. Details about the additional configuration on these servers follow in exercises in later chapters. For now, it is sufficient to ensure that the following conditions are met:

- Use the server names server1 and server2.
- Set the obtain an IP address automatically.
- Make sure to keep at least 1GB of disk space as unallocated disk space (which is not assigned to any partition) so that you have free space to work on the partitioning exercises in later chapters.
- Install one server using the Minimal installation pattern, and another server using the Server with GUI installation pattern.

The following topics are covered in this chapter:

- Basic Shell Skills
- Understanding the Shell Environment
- Editing Files with vim
- Finding Help

The following RHCSA exam objectives are covered in this chapter:

- Use input-output redirection
- Create and edit text files
- Locate, read, and use system documentation including man, info, and files in /usr/share/doc

CHAPTER 2

Using Essential Tools

Even though this book is written for people who have at least some experience working with Linux, you need to know about some of the basic topics as well. This chapter is dedicated to the basic Linux skills that everyone should have before attempting to take the RHCSA exam.

"Do I Know This Already?" Quiz

The "Do I Know This Already?" quiz allows you to assess whether you should read this entire chapter thoroughly or jump to the "Exam Preparation Tasks" section. If you are in doubt about your answers to these questions or your own assessment of your knowledge of the topics, read the entire chapter. Table 2.1 lists the major headings in this chapter and their corresponding "Do I Know This Already?" quiz questions. You can find the answers in Appendix A, "Answers to the 'Do I Know This Already?' Quizzes and 'Review Questions.'"

Table 2.1 "Do I Know This Already?" Section-to-Question Mapping

Foundation Topics Section	Questions
Basic Shell Skills	1, 3, 4–7
Editing Files with vim	8
Understanding the Shell Environment	2, 9
Finding Help	10

1. Which of the following enables you to redirect standard output as well as errors to a file?
   - **a.** **1&2> file**
   - **b.** **2>&1 file**
   - **c.** **>1&2 file**
   - **d.** **1>2& file**

2. You are looking for a variable that is set in a bash login shell for all users. Which of the following files is the most likely location where this variable is set? (Choose two.)
   a. /etc/profile
   b. /etc/bashrc
   c. ~/.bash_profile
   d. ~/.bashrc

3. A user has created a script with the name myscript. He tries to run it using the command **myscript**, but it is not started. The user has verified that the script permissions are set as executable. Which of the following is the most likely explanation?
   a. An internal command is preventing the startup of the script.
   b. Users are not allowed to run scripts.
   c. The directory that contains the script is not in the PATH.
   d. The script does not have appropriate permissions.

4. You need the output of the command **ls** to be used as input for the **less** command. Which of the following examples will do that for you?
   a. **ls > less**
   b. **ls >> less**
   c. **ls >| less**
   d. **ls | less**

5. A user wants to remove his complete history. Which of the following approaches would do that?
   a. Remove the ~/.bash_history file and type **history -c**.
   b. Type **history -c**.
   c. Remove the ~/.bash_history file.
   d. Type **history -c** and close the current shell.

6. Which of the following is *not* a valid method to repeat a command from history?
   a. Use **Ctrl+R** and start typing a part of the command.
   b. Use **!** followed by the first letters in the command.
   c. Use **!** followed by the number of the command as listed in history.
   d. Use **Ctrl+X** followed by the number in history.

7. For which of the following items can bash completion be used?
   - a. Commands
   - b. Files
   - c. Variables
   - d. All of the above

8. Which of the following commands enables you to replace every occurrence of *old* with *new* in a text file that is opened with vi?
   - a. **:%s/old/new/g**
   - b. **:%r/old/new/**
   - c. **:s/old/new/g**
   - d. **r:/old/new**

9. Which approach works best if during the login process you want to show a message to all users who have just logged in to a shell session on your server?
   - a. Put the message in /etc/issue.
   - b. Put the message in /etc/motd.
   - c. Put the message in /etc/profile.
   - d. Put the message in /etc/bashrc.

10. You are using **man -k user**, but you get the message "nothing appropriate." Which of the following solutions is most likely to fix this for you?
    - a. Type **updatedb** to update the man database.
    - b. Type **makewhatis** to update the man database.
    - c. Type **mandb** to update the man database.
    - d. Use **man -K**, not **man -k**.

Foundation Topics

Basic Shell Skills

The shell is the default working environment for a Linux administrator. It is the environment where users and administrators enter commands that are executed by the operating system. Different shells for Linux are available, but bash is the common shell. So when we are talking about "the shell" in this book, we are actually talking about the *bash* shell. This chapter provides an overview of some of the items that you will encounter when working with the shell.

Executing Commands

The purpose of the Linux shell is that it provides an environment in which commands can be executed. The shell takes care of interpreting the command that a user has entered correctly. To do this, the shell makes a difference between three kinds of commands:

- Aliases
- Internal commands
- External commands

An alias is a command that a user can define as needed. Some aliases are provided by default; type **alias** on the command line to get an overview. To define an alias, use **alias newcommand='oldcommand'**, as in the default alias **ll='ls -l --color=auto'**. Aliases are executed before anything else.

An internal command is a command that is a part of the shell itself. It is available when the shell is loaded and can be executed from memory without any lookup from disk. An external command is a command that exists as an executable file on disk of the computer. Because it has to be read from disk, it is a bit slower. When a user executes a command, the shell first looks to determine whether it is an internal command; if it is not, it looks for an executable file with a name that matches the command on disk. To find out whether a command is a bash internal, or an executable file on disk, you can use the **type** command.

To look up external commands, the **$PATH** variable is used. This variable defines a list of directories that is searched for a matching filename when a user enters a command. To find out which exact command the shell will be using, you can use the **which** command. For instance, type **which ls** to find out where the shell will get the **ls** command from.

You should notice that for security reasons that the current directory is not in the **$PATH** variable and that Linux does not look in the current directory to see whether a specific command is available from that directory. That is why you need to start a command that is in the current directory but nowhere in the **$PATH** by including **./** in front of it. The dot stands for the current directory, and by running it as **./**, you'll tell bash to look for the command in the current directory.

The **$PATH** variable can be set for specific users, but in general, most users will be using the same PATH variable. The only exception to this is the user root, who needs access to specific administration commands. In Exercise 2.1, you learn some of the basics about working with commands.

Exercise 2.1 Using Internal and External Commands from the Shell

1. Authenticate as the user user who you created in Chapter 1, "Installing Red Hat Enterprise Linux Server," when installing your server.
2. Type **time ls**. This executes the **ls** command where the bash internal **time** shows information about the time it took to complete this command.
3. Now type **which time**. This shows the filename /bin/time that was found in the $PATH variable.
4. Type **echo $PATH** to show the contents of the $PATH variable. You can see that /bin is included in the list, but because there also is an internal command **time**, the time command from the path will not be executed unless you tell the shell specifically to do so.
5. Type **/bin/time ls** to run the **/bin/time** command when executing **ls**. You'll notice that the output differs completely.

I/O Redirection

By default when a command is executed it shows its results on the screen of the computer you are working on. The computer monitor is the so-called standard output, which is also referred to as the STDOUT. The shell also has default destinations to send error messages to and to accept input. Table 2.2 gives an overview of all three.

Table 2.2 Standard Input, Output, and Error Overview

Name	Default destination	Use in Redirection	File Descriptor Number
STDIN	Computer keyboard	< (same as 0<)	0
STDOUT	Computer monitor	> (same as 1>)	1
STDERR	Computer monitor	2>	2

So if you run a command, that command would expect input from the keyboard, and it would normally send its output to the monitor of your computer without making a difference between normal output and errors. Some commands, however, are started at the background and not from a current terminal session, so these commands do not have a monitor or console session to send their output to, and they do not listen to keyboard input to accept their standard input. That is where redirection comes in handy.

Programs started from the command line have no idea what they are reading from or writing to. They just read from channel (file descriptor) 0 if they want to read from standard input, and they write to file descriptor number 1 to display output and to file descriptor 2 if they have error messages to be output. By default, these are connected to the keyboard and the screen. If you use redirection symbols such as <, >, and |, the shell connects the file descriptors to files or other commands. We first look at < and >. Later we discuss pipes (using the | symbol). Table 2.3 shows the most common redirectors that are used from the bash shell.

Table 2.3 Common Bash Redirectors

Redirector	Explanation
> (same as 1>)	Redirects STDOUT. If redirection is to a file, the current contents of that file are overwritten.
>> (same as 1>>)	Redirects STDOUT. If output is written to a file, the output is appended to that file.
2>	Redirects STDERR.
2>&1	Redirects STDERR to the same destination as STDOUT.
< (same as 0<)	Redirects STDIN.

In I/O redirection, files can be used to replace the default STDIN, STDOUT, and STDERR. You can also redirect to *device files*. A device file on Linux is a file that is used to access specific hardware. Your hard disk for instance can be referred to as /dev/sda, the console of your server is known as /dev/console or /dev/tty1, and if you want to discard a commands output, you can redirect to /dev/null. Notice that to access most device files you need to be root.

Using Pipes

Where an I/O redirector is used to use alternatives for keyboard and computer monitor, a pipe can be used to catch the output of one command and use that as input for a second command. If a user runs the command **ls**, for instance, the output of the command is shown onscreen. If the user uses **ls | less**, the commands **ls** and **less** are started in parallel. The standard output of the **ls** command is connected to the standard input of **less**. Everything that **ls** writes to the standard output will become available for read from standard input in **less**. The result is that the output of **ls** is shown in a pager, where the user can browse up and down through the results easily.

As a Linux administrator, you'll use pipes a lot. Using pipes makes Linux a flexible operating system; by combining multiple commands using pipes, you can create kind of super commands that make almost anything possible. In Exercise 2.2, you use I/O redirectors and pipes.

Exercise 2.2 Using I/O Redirection and Pipes

1. Open a shell as user user and type **cd** without any arguments. This ensures that the home directory of this user is the current directory while working on this exercise. Type **pwd** to verify this.
2. Type **ls.** You'll see the results onscreen
3. Type **ls > /dev/null**. This redirects the STDOUT to the null device, with the result that you will not see it.
4. Type **ls ilwehgi > /dev/null**. This command shows a "no such file or directory" message onscreen. You see the message because it is not STDOUT, but an error message that is written to STDERR.
5. Type **ls ilwehgi 2> /dev/null**. Now you will not see the error message anymore.
6. Type **ls ilwehgi Documents 2> /dev/null**. This shows the name of the Documents folder in your home directory while hiding the error message.
7. Type **ls ilwehgi Documents 2> /dev/null > output**. In this command, you still write the error message to /dev/null while sending STDOUT to a file with the name output that will be created in your home directory.
8. Type **cat output** to show the contents of this file.

9. Type **echo hello > output**. This overwrites the contents of the output file.
10. Type **ls >> output**. This appends the result of the **ls** command to the output file.
11. Type **ls -R /**. This shows a long list of files and folders scrolling over your computer monitor. (You may want to type **Ctrl+C** to stop [or wait a long time]).
12. Type **ls -R | less**. This shows the same result, but in the pager **less**, where you can scroll up and down using the arrow keys on your keyboard.
13. Type **q** to close **less**. This will also end the **ls** program.
14. Type **ls > /dev/tty1**. This gives an error message because you are executing the command as an ordinary user (unless you were logged in to tty1). Only the user root has permission to write to device files directly.

History

A convenient feature of the bash shell is the bash history. Bash is configured to keep the last 1,000 commands you have used (and if shell session is never closed, the exact number can grow even much beyond that). When a shell session is closed, the history of that session is updated to the history file. The name of this file is .bash_history, and it is created in the home directory of the user who started a specific shell session. Notice that the history file is closed only when the shell session is closed; until that moment, all commands in the history are kept in memory.

The history feature makes it easy to repeat complex commands. There are several ways of working with history:

- Type **history** to show a list of all commands in the bash history.
- Use **Ctrl+R** to open the prompt from which you can do backward searches in commands that you have previously used. Just type a part of the command you are looking for, and it will be displayed automatically. Use **Ctrl+R** to search further backward based on the same search criteria.
- Type **!number** to execute a command with a specific number from history.
- Type **!sometext** to execute the last command that starts with sometext. Notice that this is a potentially dangerous command because the command that was found is executed immediately!

Exercise 2.3 guides you through some history features.

Exercise 2.3 Working with History

1. Make sure that you have opened a shell as user user.
2. Type **history** to get an overview of commands that you have previously used.
3. Type some commands, such as the following:
```
ls
pwd
cat /etc/hosts
ls -l.
```
   The goal is to fill the history a bit.
4. Open a second terminal on your server by right-clicking the graphical desktop and selecting the **Open in Terminal** menu option.
5. Type **history** from this second terminal window. Notice that you do not see the commands that you just typed in the other terminal. That is because the history file has not been updated yet.
6. From the first terminal session, type **Ctrl+R**. From the prompt that opens now, type **ls**. You'll see the last **ls** command you used. Press **Ctrl+R** again. You'll now see that you are looking backward and that the previous **ssh** command is highlighted. Press **Enter** to execute it.
7. Type **history | grep cat**. The **grep** command searches the history output for any commands that contained the text *cat*. Remember the command number of one of the **cat** commands you have previously used.
8. Type **!nn**, where *nn* is replaced by the number you remembered in Step 7. You'll see that the last **cat** command is repeated.
9. Close this terminal by typing **exit**.
10. From the remaining terminal window, type **history -c**. This wipes all history that is currently in memory. Close this terminal session as well.
11. Open a new terminal session and type **history**. It may be a bit unexpected, but you'll see a list of commands anyway. That is because **history -c** clears the in-memory history, but it does not remove the .bash_history file in your home directory.
12. As an alternative to deleting the history file, you can also use **history -w** after using **history -c**.

Bash Completion

Another useful feature of the bash shell is automatic completion. This feature helps you in finding the command you need, and it also works on variables and filenames, and on some occasions even within command shells that are opened.

Bash completion is used most on commands. Just type the beginning of a command and press the **Tab** key on your computer's keyboard. If there is only one option for completion, bash will complete the command automatically for you. If there are several options, you need to press the **Tab** key once more to get an overview of all the available options. In Exercise 2.4, you learn how to work with these great features.

Exercise 2.4 Using Bash Completion

1. Still from a user shell, type **gd** and press **Tab**. You'll see that nothing happens.
2. Press **Tab** again. Bash now shows a short list of all commands that start with the letters *gd*.
3. To make it clear to bash what you want, type **i** (so that your prompt at this point shows a command **gdi**. Press **Tab** again. Bash now knows what you want and opens gdisk for you. Press **Enter** to close the prompt that was just opened.
4. Use **cd /etc** to go to the /etc directory.
5. Type **cat pas[Tab]**. Because there is one file only that starts with *pas*, bash knows what to do and automatically completes the filename. Press **Enter** to execute the command.

Editing Files with vim

Managing Linux often means working with files. Most of the things that are configured on Linux are configured through files. To get things done, you often need to change the contents of a configuration file with a text editor.

Over the years, many text editors have been created for Linux. One editor really matters, though, and that is vi. Even if some other text editors are easier to use, vi is the only text editor that is always available. That is why as a Linux administrator you need to know how to work with vi. Only one alternative is permitted, and that is vim. Vim is "vi improved;" it is a complete rewrite of vi with a lot of enhancements that make working with vi easier, such as syntax highlighting for many configuration files which makes it easy to recognize typing errors that you have made. All that you learn in this section about vim works on vi as well.

An important concept when working with vim is that it uses different modes. Two of them are particularly important: command mode and input mode. These modes often cause confusion because in command mode you can just enter a command and you cannot change the contents of a text file. To change the contents of a text file, you need to get to input mode.

The challenge when working with vim is the vast number of commands that are available. Some people have even produced vi cheat sheets, listing all available commands. Do not use them. Instead, focus on the minimal number of commands that are really important. Table 2.4 summarizes the most essential vim commands. Use these (and only these) and you'll get around on the exam.

TIP Do *not* try to work with as many commands as possible when working with vim. Just use a minimal set of commands and use them often. You'll see, you'll get used to these commands and remember them on the exam. Also, you may like the **vimtutor** command. (Use **yum install vim-enhanced** to install it.) This command opens a vim tutorial that has you work through some nice additional exercises.

Table 2.4 Vim Essential Commands

Key Topic

vim command	explanation
Esc	Switches from input mode to command mode. Use this before typing any command.
i, a	Switches from command mode to input mode at (i) or after (a) the current cursor position.
o	Opens a new line below the current cursor position and goes to input mode.
:wq	Writes the current file and quits.
:q!	Quits the file without applying any changes. The **!** forces the command to do its work. Only add the **!** if you really know what you are doing.
:w filename	Writes the current file with a new filename.
dd	Deletes the current line.
yy	Copies the current line.
p	Pastes the current selection.
v	Enters visual mode, which allows you to select a block of text using the arrow keys. Use **d** to cut, or **y** to copy the selection.
u	Undoes the last command. Repeat as often as necessary.
Ctrl+r	Redoes the last undo.
gg	Goes to the first line in the document.
G	Goes to the last line in the document.

vim command	explanation
/text	Searches for *text* from the current cursor position forward.
?text	Searches for *text* from the current cursor position backward.
^	Goes to the first position in the current line.
$	Goes to the last position in the current line.
!ls	Adds the output of **ls** (or any other command) in the current file.
:%s/old/new/g	Replaces all occurrences of *old* with *new*.

You know have acquired sufficient skills about working with bash. In Exercise 2.5, you practice these skills.

Exercise 2.5 Vim Practice

1. Type **vim ~/testfile**. This starts vim and opens a file with the name testfile in ~, which represents your current home directory.
2. Press **i** to enter input mode and type the following text

```
cow
sheep
ox
chicken
snake
fish
oxygen
```

3. Press **Esc** to get back to command mode and type **:w** to write the file using the same filename.
4. Type **:3** to go to line number 3.
5. Type **dd** to delete this line.
6. Type **dd** again to delete another line.
7. Type **u** to undo the last deletion.
8. Type **o** to open a new line.
9. Enter some more text at the current cursor position:

```
tree
farm
```

10. Press **Esc** to get back into command mode.
11. Type **:%s/ox/OX/g.**
12. Type **:wq** to write the file and quit. If for some reason that does not work, use **:wq!**.

Understanding the Shell Environment

When you are working from a shell, an environment is created to ensure that all that is happening is happening the right way. This environment consists of variables that define the user environment, such as the $PATH variable discussed earlier. In this section, you get a brief overview of the shell environment and how it is created.

Understanding Variables

The Linux shell environment consists of many variables. Variables are fixed names that can be assigned dynamic values. An example of a variable is LANG, which in my shell is set to en_US.UTF-8. This value (which may differ on your system) ensures that I can work in the English language using settings that are common in the English language (think of the way document contents are sorted and how date and time are displayed).

The advantage for scripts and programs of working with variables is that the program only has to use the name of the variable without taking interest in the specific value that is assigned to the variable. Because the needs for different users are different, the variables that are set in a user environment will differ. To get an overview of the current variables defined in your shell environment, type the **env** command. Listing 2.1 shows the last lines of the output of this command.

Listing 2.1 Displaying the Current Environment

```
[user@server1 ~]$ env
MAIL=/var/spool/mail/user
PATH=/usr/local/bin:/bin:/usr/bin:/usr/local/sbin:/usr/sbin:/home/
  user/.local/bin:/home/user/bin
PWD=/home/user
LANG=en_US.UTF-8
HISTCONTROL=ignoredups
SHLVL=1
HOME=/home/user
LOGNAME=user
```

```
LESSOPEN=||/usr/bin/lesspipe.sh %s
_=/bin/env
OLDPWD=/etc
```

As you can see from Listing 2.1, to define a variable, the name of the variable is mentioned followed by an equals sign (=) and the value that is assigned to the specific variable. To read the value of a variable, a user can use the **echo** command, followed by the name of the variable, as in **echo $PATH**, which reads the current value of the PATH variable and prints that on the STDOUT. For now, you do not have to know much more about variables; knowing that they are there and how you can get an overview of current variables is enough for the RHCSA exam. You can read about more advanced use of variables in Chapter 31, "An Introduction to Bash Shell Scripting."

Environment Configuration Files

When a user logs in, an environment is created for that user automatically. This happens based on four different files where some script code can be specified and where variables can be defined for use by one specific user:

- **/etc/profile:** This is the generic file that is processed by all users upon login.
- **/etc/bashrc:** This file is processed when subshells are started.
- **~/.bash_profile:** In this file, user-specific login shell variables can be defined.
- **~/.bashrc:** In this user-specific file, subshell variables can be defined.

As you have seen, in these files a difference is made between a login shell and a subshell. A login shell is the first shell that is opened for a user after the user has logged in. From the login shell, a user may run scripts, which will start a subshell of that login shell. Bash allows for the creation of a different environment in the login shell and in the subshell but to synchronize settings; by default the subshell settings are included when entering a login shell.

Using /etc/motd and /etc/issue

Bash offers an option to include messages in the /etc/motd and the /etc/issue files. Messages in /etc/motd display after a user has successfully logged in to a shell. (Notice that users in a graphical environment do not see its contents after a graphical login.) Using /etc/motd can be a convenient way for system administrators to inform users.

Another way to send information to users is by using /etc/issue. The contents of this file display before the user logs in. This provides an excellent means of specifying specific login instructions to users who are not logged in yet.

In Exercise 2.6, you can review the topics that have been discussed in this section.

Exercise 2.6 Managing the Shell Environment

1. Open a shell in which you are user.
2. Type **echo $LANG** to show the contents of the variable that sets your system keyboard and language settings.
3. Type **ls --help**. You'll see that help about the **ls** command is displayed in the current language settings of your computer.
4. Type **LANG=fr_FR.UTF-8**. This temporarily sets the language variable to French.
5. Type **ls --help** again. You'll see that now the ls help text is displayed in French.
6. Type **exit** to close your terminal window. Because you have not changed the contents of any of the previously mentioned files, while opening a new shell the original value of the LANG variable will be used.
7. Open a shell as user again.
8. Verify the current value of the LANG variable by typing echo **$LANG**.
9. Use **vim .bashrc** to open the .bashrc configuration file.
10. In this file, add the line **COLOR=red** to set a variable with the name COLOR and assign it the value red.
11. Close the user shell and open a new user shell.
12. Verify that the variable COLOR has been set, by using **echo $COLOR**. Because the .bashrc file is included in the login procedure, the variable is set after logging in.

Finding Help

On an average Linux system, hundreds of commands are available (way too many to ever be able to remember all of them, which is why using the help resources on your computer is so very important). This section provides a brief overview about using man, and (more important) what you can do with man if you do not know the exact command you are looking for.

Using --help

The quickest way to get an overview of how to use a command is by running the command with the **--help** option. Nearly all commands will display a usage summary when using this option. The list of options that is shown in this way is of use mainly when you already have a generic understanding of how to use the command and need a quick overview of options available with the command.

TIP Nearly all commands provide a short overview of help when the option **--help** is used. Some commands do not honor that option and consider it erroneous. Fortunately, these commands will be so friendly to show an error message, displaying valid options with the command, which effectively means that you'll get what you needed anyway.

Using man

When using the Linux command line, you will at some point consult man pages. Man is what makes working from the command line doable. If you do not know how a command is used, the man page of that command will provide valuable insight. This section covers a few man essentials.

To start with, the most important parts of the man page in general are at the bottom of the man page. Here you'll find two important sections: In many cases there are examples; if there are no examples, there is always a "see also" section. This brings you to related man pages, which is useful if you have just not hit the right man page. To get to the bottom of the man page as fast as possible, use the **G** command. You can also type **/example** to search the man page for any examples. Figure 2.1 shows what the end of a man page may look like.

Finding the Right man Page

To find information in man pages, you can search the mandb database by using **apropos** or **man -k**. If the database is current, getting access to the information you need is easy. Just type **man -k**, followed by the keyword you want to search for. This command looks in the summary of all man pages that are stored in the mandb database. Listing 2.2 shows a partial result of this command.

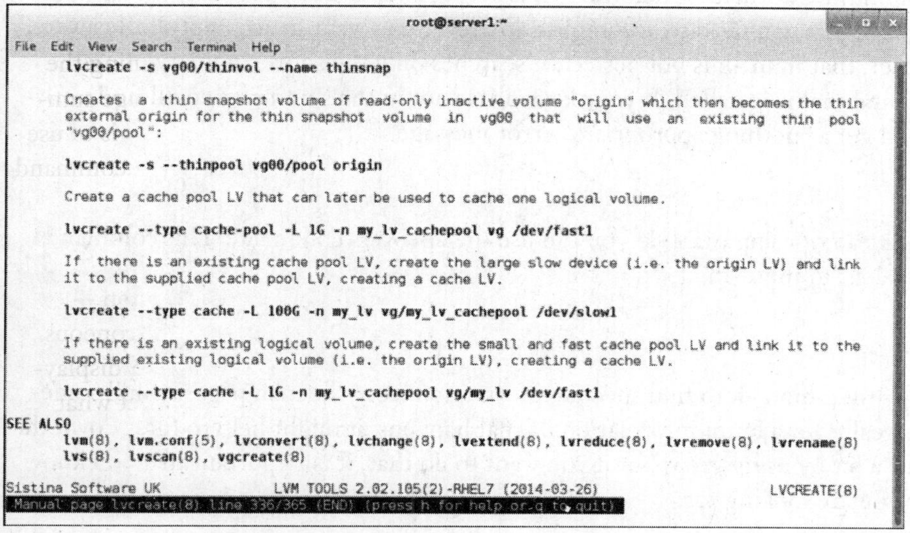

Figure 2.1 Sample man page contents.

Listing 2.2 Searching man Pages with **man -k**

```
[root@server1 ~]# man -k partition
addpart (8)          - simple wrapper around the "add partition" ioctl
cfdisk (8)           - display or manipulate disk partition table
cgdisk (8)           - Curses-based GUID partition table (GPT) manipulator
delpart (8)          - simple wrapper around the "del partition" ioctl
fdisk (8)            - manipulate disk partition table
fixparts (8)         - MBR partition table repair utility
gdisk (8)            - Interactive GUID partition table (GPT) manipulator
iostat (1)           - Report Central Processing Unit (CPU) statistics and in...
kpartx (8)           - Create device maps from partition tables
mpartition (1)       - partition an MSDOS hard disk
os-prober (1)        - Discover bootable partitions on the local system.
partprobe (8)        - inform the OS of partition table changes
partx (8)            - tell the Linux kernel about the presence and numbering...
pvcreate (8)         - initialize a disk or partition for use by LVM
pvresize (8)         - resize a disk or partition in use by LVM2
resizepart (8)       - simple wrapper around the "resize partition" ioctl
sfdisk (8)           - partition table manipulator for Linux
sgdisk              (- Command-line GUID partition table (GPT) manipulator fo...
systemd-efi-boot-generator (8) - Generator for automatically mounting the EFI...
systemd-gpt-auto-generator (8) - Generator for automatically discovering and ..
```

Based on the information that **man -k** is giving you, you can probably identify the man page that you need to accomplish whatever you want to accomplish. Be aware, however, that **man -k** is not perfect; it searches only the short summary of each command that is installed. If your keyword is not in the summary, you'll find nothing and get a "nothing appropriate" error message.

> **TIP** Instead of using **man -k**, you can use the **apropos** command. This command is equivalent to **man -k**.

While using **man -k** to find specific information from the man pages, you'll sometimes really get a lot of information. If that happens, it might help to filter down the results a bit by using grep. But if you want to do that, it is important that you know what you are looking for.

Man pages are categorized in different sections. The most relevant sections for system administrators are as follows

Key Topic

- **1:** Executable programs or shell commands
- **5:** File formats and conventions
- **8:** System administration commands

There are also sections that provide in-depth detail, such as the sections about system calls and library calls. When using **man -k**, you'll get results from all of these sections. To limit the results that display, it makes sense to use grep to show only those sections that are relevant for what you need. So, if you are looking for the configuration file that has something to do with passwords, use **man -k password | grep 5**, or if you are looking for the command that an administrator would use to create partitions, use **man -k partition | grep 8**.

Another useful man option is **-f**. The command **man -f <somecommand>** displays a short description of the item as found in the man database. This may help you when deciding whether this man page contains the information you are looking for.

Updating mandb

When using the **man -k** command, the mandb database is consulted. It can sometimes happen that you are looking for something that should obviously be documented but you cannot find anything anyway and all you get is "nothing appropriate." If that happens, you might need to update the man database. Doing that is easy: Just run the **mandb** command as root without any arguments. It will see whether new man pages have been installed and update the man database accordingly.

> **TIP** Do not try to memorize all the commands that you need to accomplish specific tasks. Instead, memorize how to find these commands and which man page to read to get more information about the command. In Exercise 2.7, you'll see how that works.

Let's assume that you are looking for a command, using **man -k**, but all you get is a message "nothing appropriate" and you do not remember how to fix it. Exercise 2.7 shows what you can do in such cases.

Exercise 2.7 Using man -k

1. Because **man -k** does not give the expected result, it makes sense to look in the man page for the **man** command. Type **man man** to open the man page of man. Once in the man page, type **/-k** to look for a description of the **-k** option. Type **n** a few times until you get to the line that describes the option. You'll see that **man -k** is equivalent to **apropos** and that you can read the man page of apropos for more details.
2. Type **man apropos** and read the first paragraphs of the description. You'll see that the database searched by apropos is updated by the mandb program.
3. Type **man mandb**. This man page explains how to run mandb to update the man database. As you'll read, all you need to do is type **mandb**, which does the work for you.
4. Type **mandb** to update the man database.

Using info

Apart from the information that you'll find in man, another system provides help about command usage. This is the info system. Most commands are documented in man, but some commands are documented only in the info system. If that is the case, the "see also" section of the man page of that command will tell you that "The full documentation for ... is maintained as a Texinfo manual." If that happens, you can read the Info page using the command **pinfo** or **info**. Both commands work, but in **pinfo**, special items such as menu items are clearly indicated, which is why using **pinfo** is recommended.

When working with info, take a look at the top line of the viewer. This shows the current position in the info document. Particularly interesting are the Up, Next, and Previous indicators which tell you how to navigate. Info pages are organized like web pages, which means that they are organized in a hierarchical way. To browse through that hierarchy, type **n** to go to the next page, **p** to go to the previous page, or **u** to move up in the hierarchy.

In an info page, you'll also find menus. Each item that is marked with an asterisk (*) is a menu item. Use the arrow keys to select a specific menu item. This brings you down one level. To get back up again, press **u**. This brings you back to the original starting point in the pinfo hierarchy. Figure 2.2 shows what an info page looks like.

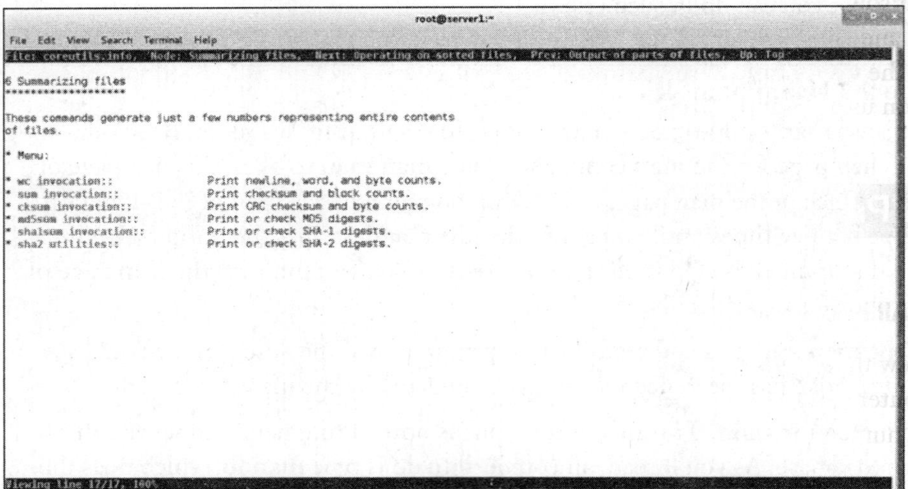

Figure 2.2 Getting more command usage information using **pinfo**.

Exercise 2.8 shows an example of such a command, and in this exercise you learn how to get the information out of the info page.

Exercise 2.8 Using info

1. Type **man ls**. Type **G** to go to the end of the man page and look at the "see also" section. It tells you that the full documentation for ls is maintained as a Texinfo manual. Quit the man page by pressing **Q**.
2. Type **pinfo coreutils 'ls invocation'**. This shows the information about ls usage in the pinfo pager. Read through it and press **Q** when done.

Using /usr/share/doc Documentation Files

A third source of information consists of files that are sometimes copied to the /usr/share/doc directory. This happens in particular for services and larger systems that are a bit more complicated. You will not typically find much information about a command like **ls**, but some services do provide useful information in /usr/share/doc.

Some services store very useful information in this directory, like rsyslog, bind, Kerberos, and OpenSSL. For setting up advanced services, you need access to this information. For setting up services on the RHCSA and RHCE exams, you can probably do without.

Summary

In this chapter, you read about essential Linux administration tasks. You learned about some of the important shell basics, such as I/O redirection, working with history, and management of the environment. You also learned how to edit text files with the vim editor. In the last part of this chapter, you learned how to find information using **man** and related commands.

Exam Prep Tasks

Review All Key Topics

Review the most important topics in the chapter, noted with the Key Topic icon in the outer margin of the page. Table 2.5 lists a reference of these key topics and the page numbers on which each is found.

Table 2.5 Key Topics for Chapter 2

Key Topic Element	Description	Page
Table 2.4	vim essential commands	43
List	Significant sections in man	50

Complete Tables and Lists from Memory

Print a copy of Appendix B, “Memory Tables” (found on the disc), or at least the section for this chapter, and complete the tables and lists from memory. Appendix C, “Memory Tables Answer Key,” also on the disc, includes completed tables and lists to check your work.

Define Key Terms

Define the following key terms from this chapter and check your answers in the glossary:

shell, bash, internal command, external command, $PATH, variable, STDIN, STDOUT, STDERR, file descriptor, pipe, redirect, device files, environment, login shell, subshell

Review Questions

1. What is a variable?
2. Which command enables you to find the correct man page based on keyword usage?
3. What file do you need to change if you want a variable to be set for every shell that is started?
4. When analyzing how to use a command, you read that the documentation is maintained with the Techinfo system. How can you read the information?
5. What is the name of the file where bash stores its history?
6. Which command enables you to update the database that contains man keywords?
7. How can you undo the last modification you have applied in vim?
8. What can you add to a command to make sure that it does not show any error message, assuming that you do not care about the information that is in the error messages either?
9. How do you read the current contents of the PATH variable?
10. How do you repeat the last command you used that contains the string *dog* somewhere in the command?

End-of-Chapter Labs

You have now learned about some of the most important basic skills that a Linux administrator should have. In this section, you apply these skills by doing some end-of-chapter labs.

Lab 2.1

1. Modify your shell environment so that on every subshell that is started a variable is set. The name of the variable should be COLOR, and the value should be set to red. Verify that it is working.
2. Use the appropriate tools to find the command that you can use to set the system time 1 minute ahead.

This chapter covers the following subjects:

- Working with the File System Hierarchy
- Managing Files
- Using Links
- Working with Archives and Compressed Files

The following RHCSA exam objectives are covered in this chapter:

- Archive, compress, unpack, and uncompress files
- Create, delete, copy, and move files directories
- Create hard and soft links

CHAPTER 3

Essential File Management Tools

Linux is a file-oriented operating system. That means that many things an administrator has to do on Linux can be traced down to managing files on the Linux operating system. This chapter introduces you to essential file management skills. You learn how the Linux file system is organized and how you can work with files and directories. You also learn how to manage links and compressed or uncompressed archives.

Do I Know This Already Quiz

The "Do I Know This Already?" quiz allows you to assess whether you should read this entire chapter thoroughly or jump to the "Exam Preparation Tasks" section. If you are in doubt about your answers to these questions or your own assessment of your knowledge of the topics, read the entire chapter. Table 3.1 lists the major headings in this chapter and their corresponding "Do I Know This Already?" quiz questions. You can find the answers in Appendix A, "Answers to the 'Do I Know This Already?' Quizzes and 'Review Questions.'"

Table 3.1 "Do I Know This Already?" Section-to-Question Mapping

Foundation Topics Section	Questions
Working with the File System Hierarchy	1–4
Managing Files	5, 7
Using Links	8
Working with Archives and Compressed Files	10

1. Under which directory would you expect to find nonessential program files?

    a. /boot

    b. /bin

    c. /sbin

    d. /usr

2. Under which directory would you expect to find log files?
   a. /proc
   b. /run
   c. /var
   d. /usr

3. Which of the following directories would typically not be mounted on its own dedicated device?
   a. /etc
   b. /boot
   c. /home
   d. /usr

4. Which of the following commands would give the most accurate overview of mounted disk devices (without showing much information about mounted system devices as well)?
   a. **mount**
   b. **mount -a**
   c. **df -T**
   d. **du -h**

5. Which command enables you to show all files in the current directory so that the newest files are listed last?
   a. **ls -lRt**
   b. **ls -lrt**
   c. **ls -alrt**
   d. **ls -alr**

6. Which command enables you to copy hidden files as well as regular files from /home/$USER to the current directory?
   a. **cp -a /home/$USER .**
   b. **cp -a /home/$USER/* .**
   c. **cp -a /home/$USER/. .**
   d. **cp -a home/$USER. .**

7. Which command enables you to rename the file myfile to mynewfile?

   a. **mv myfile mynewfile**

   b. **rm myfile mynewfile**

   c. **rn myfile mynewfile**

   d. **ren myfile mynewfile**

8. Which statement about hard links is *not* true?

   a. Hard links cannot be created to directories.

   b. Hard links cannot refer to files on other devices.

   c. The inode keeps a hard link counter.

   d. If the original hard link is removed, all other hard links become invalid.

9. Which command creates a symbolic link to the directory /home in the directory /tmp?

   a. **ln /tmp /home**

   b. **ln /home /tmp**

   c. **ln -s /home /tmp**

   d. **ln -s /tmp /home**

10. Which option enables you to add one single file to a tar archive?

   a. **-a**

   b. **-A**

   c. **-r**

   d. **-u**

Foundation Topics

Working with the File System Hierarchy

To manage a Linux system, you should be familiar with the default directories that exist on almost all Linux systems. This section describes these directories and explains how mounts are used to compose the file system hierarchy.

Defining the File System Hierarchy

The file system on most Linux systems is organized in a similar way. The layout of the Linux file system is defined in the Filesystem Hierarchy Standard (FHS), and this file system hierarchy is described in **man 7 hier**. Table 3.2 shows an overview of the most significant directories that you'll encounter on a Red Hat Enterprise Linux (RHEL) system, as specified by the FSH.

Key Topic

Table 3.2 FSH Overview

Directory	Use
/	The root directory. This is where the file system tree starts.
/bin	In here, you find executable programs that are needed to repair a system in a minimal troubleshooting mode. This directory is essential during boot.
/boot	Contains all files and directories that are needed to boot the Linux kernel.
/dev	Device files that are used for accessing physical devices. This directory is essential during boot.
/etc	Contains configuration files that are used by programs and services that are used on your server. This directory is essential during boot.
/home	Used for local user home directories.
/lib, /lib64	Shared libraries that are used by programs in /boot, /bin and /sbin.
/media, /mnt	Directories that are used for mounting devices in the file system tree.
/opt	This directory is used for optional packages that may be installed on your server.
/proc	This directory is used by the proc file system. This is a file system structure that gives access to kernel information.
/root	The home directory of the root user.
/run	Contains process and user specific information that has been created since the last boot.
/sbin	Like /bin, but for system administration commands that are not necessarily needed by regular users.

Directory	Use
/srv	Directory that may be used for data that is used by services like NFS, FTP and HTTP.
/sys	Used as an interface to different hardware devices that is managed by the Linux kernel and associated processes.
/tmp	Contains temporary files that may be deleted without any warning during boot.
/usr	Directory that contains subdirectories with program files, libraries for these program files and documentation about them. Typically, many subdirectories exist in this directory that mimic the contents of the / directory. The contents of /usr are not required during boot.
/var	Directory that contains files which may change in size dynamically, such as log files, mail boxes, and spool files.

Understanding Mounts

To understand the organization of the Linux file system, the concept of mounting is important. A Linux file system is presented as one hierarchy, with the root directory (/) as its starting point. This hierarchy may be distributed over different devices and even computer systems that are mounted into the root directory.

Mounting devices makes it possible to organize the Linux file system in a flexible way. There are several disadvantages to storing all files in just one file system:

- High activity in one area may fill up the entire file system, which will negatively impact services running on the server.
- If all files are on the same device, it is difficult to secure access and distinguish between different areas of the file system with different security needs. By mounting a separate file system, mount options can be added to meet specific security needs.
- If a one-device file system is completely filled, it may be difficult to make additional storage space available.

To avoid these pitfalls, it is common to organize Linux file systems in different devices (and even shares on other computer systems), such as disk partitions and logical volumes, and mount these devices into the file system hierarchy. By configuring a device as a dedicated mount, it is also possible to use specific mount options that can restrict access to the device. Some directories are commonly mounted on dedicated devices:

- **/boot:** This directory is often mounted on a separate device because it required essential information your computer needs to boot. As the root directory (/) is often on a Logical Volume Manager (LVM) logical volume, from which Linux cannot boot, the kernel and associated files need to be stored separately on a dedicated /boot device.
- **/var:** This directory is often on a dedicated device because it grows in a dynamic and uncontrolled way. By putting it on a dedicated device, you can ensure that it will not fill up all storage on your server.
- **/home:** This directory often is on a dedicated device for security reasons. By putting it on a dedicated device, it can be mounted with specific options to enhance the security of the server. When reinstalling the operating system, it is an advantage to have home directories in a separate file system. The home directories can then survive the system reinstall.
- **/usr:** This directory contains operating system files only, to which normal users normally do not need any write access. Putting it on a dedicated device allows administrators to configure it as a read-only mount.

Apart from these directories, you may find servers that have other directories that are mounted on dedicated partitions or volumes also. After all, it is up to the discretion of the administrator to decide which directories get their own dedicated devices.

To get an overview of all devices and their mount points, you can use different commands:

- The **mount** command gives an overview of all mounted devices. To get this information, the /proc/mounts file is read, where the kernel keeps information about all current mounts. It shows kernel interfaces also, which may lead to a long list of mounted devices being displayed. Listing 3.1 shows sample output of this command.

Listing 3.1 Sample **mount** Command Output

```
[root@server1 ~]# mount
proc on /proc type proc (rw,nosuid,nodev,noexec,relatime)
sysfs on /sys type sysfs (rw,nosuid,nodev,noexec,relatime,seclabel)
devtmpfs on /dev type devtmpfs (rw,nosuid,seclabel,size=929784k,nr_
  inodes=232446,mode=755)
securityfs on /sys/kernel/security type securityfs (rw,nosuid,nodev,
  noexec,relatime)
tmpfs on /dev/shm type tmpfs (rw,nosuid,nodev,seclabel)
```

```
devpts on /dev/pts type devpts (rw,nosuid,noexec,relatime,seclabel,
  gid=5,mode=620,ptmxmode=000)
tmpfs on /run type tmpfs (rw,nosuid,nodev,seclabel,mode=755)
tmpfs on /sys/fs/cgroup type tmpfs (rw,nosuid,nodev,noexec,seclabel,
  mode=755)
cgroup on /sys/fs/cgroup/systemd type cgroup
(rw,nosuid,nodev,noexec,relatime,xattr,release_agent=/usr/lib/systemd/
  systemd-cgroups-agent,name=systemd)
pstore on /sys/fs/pstore type pstore (rw,nosuid,nodev,noexec,relatime)
cgroup on /sys/fs/cgroup/cpuset type cgroup (rw,nosuid,nodev,noexec,
  relatime,cpuset)
cgroup on /sys/fs/cgroup/cpu,cpuacct type cgroup (rw,nosuid,nodev,
  noexec,relatime,cpuacct,cpu)
cgroup on /sys/fs/cgroup/memory type cgroup (rw,nosuid,nodev,noexec,
  relatime,memory)
cgroup on /sys/fs/cgroup/devices type cgroup (rw,nosuid,nodev,noexec,
  relatime,devices)
cgroup on /sys/fs/cgroup/freezer type cgroup (rw,nosuid,nodev,noexec,
  relatime,freezer)
cgroup on /sys/fs/cgroup/net_cls type cgroup (rw,nosuid,nodev,noexec,
  relatime,net_cls)
cgroup on /sys/fs/cgroup/blkio type cgroup (rw,nosuid,nodev,noexec,
  relatime,blkio)
cgroup on /sys/fs/cgroup/perf_event type cgroup (rw,nosuid,nodev,
  noexec,relatime,perf_event)
cgroup on /sys/fs/cgroup/hugetlb type cgroup (rw,nosuid,nodev,noexec,
  relatime,hugetlb)
configfs on /sys/kernel/config type configfs (rw,relatime)
/dev/mapper/centos-root on / type xfs (rw,relatime,seclabel,attr2,
  inode64,noquota)
selinuxfs on /sys/fs/selinux type selinuxfs (rw,relatime)
systemd-1 on /proc/sys/fs/binfmt_misc type autofs (rw,relatime,fd=32,
  pgrp=1,timeout=300,minproto=5,maxproto=5,direct)
debugfs on /sys/kernel/debug type debugfs (rw,relatime)
hugetlbfs on /dev/hugepages type hugetlbfs (rw,relatime,seclabel)
mqueue on /dev/mqueue type mqueue (rw,relatime,seclabel)
sunrpc on /var/lib/nfs/rpc_pipefs type rpc_pipefs (rw,relatime)
sunrpc on /proc/fs/nfsd type nfsd (rw,relatime)
/dev/sda1 on /boot type xfs (rw,relatime,seclabel,attr2,inode64,
  noquota)
fusectl on /sys/fs/fuse/connections type fusectl (rw,relatime)
gvfsd-fuse on /run/user/1000/gvfs type fuse.gvfsd-fuse
  (rw,nosuid,nodev,relatime,user_id=1000,group_id=1000)
```

- The **df -Th** command was designed to show available disk space on mounted devices; it includes most of the system mounts. Because it will look on all mounted file systems, it is a convenient command to get an overview of current system mounts. The **-h** option summarizes the output of the command in a human-readable way, and the **-T** option shows which file system type is used on the different mounts.
- The **findmnt** command shows mounts and the relation that exists between the different mounts. Because the output of the **mount** command is a bit overwhelming, you may like the output of **findmnt**. Listing 3.2 shows sample output of this command.

Listing 3.2 Sample **findmnt** Command Output

```
[root@server1 ~]# findmnt
TARGET                                  SOURCE      FSTYPE     OPTIONS
/                                       /dev/mapper/centos-root
                           xfs           rw,relatime,seclabel,attr2,
           inode64,noquota
├─/proc                        proc       rw,nosuid,nodev,noexec,relatime
│ ├─/proc/sys/fs/binfmt_misc            systemd-1  autofs     rw,relatime,
           fd=32,pgrp=1,timeout=300,minpr
│ └─/proc/fs/nfsd                      sunrpc     nfsd        rw,relatime
├─/sys                                sysfs      sysfs        rw,nosuid,
           nodev,noexec,relatime,seclabel
│ ├─/sys/kernel/security               securityfs
           securityf rw,nosuid,nodev,noexec,relatime
│ ├─/sys/fs/cgroup                    tmpfs      tmpfs        rw,nosuid,
           nodev,noexec,seclabel,mode=755
│ │ ├─/sys/fs/cgroup/systemd          cgroup     cgroup       rw,nosuid,
           nodev,noexec,relatime,xattr,rele
│ │ ├─/sys/fs/cgroup/cpuset           cgroup     cgroup       rw,nosuid,
           nodev,noexec,relatime,cpuset
│ │ ├─/sys/fs/cgroup/cpu,cpuacct cgroup     cgroup       rw,nosuid,
           nodev,noexec,relatime,cpuacct,cp
│ │ ├─/sys/fs/cgroup/memory           cgroup     cgroup       rw,nosuid,
           nodev,noexec,relatime,memory
│ │ ├─/sys/fs/cgroup/devices          cgroup     cgroup       rw,nosuid,
           nodev,noexec,relatime,devices
│ │ ├─/sys/fs/cgroup/freezer          cgroup     cgroup       rw,nosuid,
           nodev,noexec,relatime,freezer
│ │ ├─/sys/fs/cgroup/net_cls          cgroup     cgroup       rw,nosuid,
           nodev,noexec,relatime,net_cls
```

```
| | ├─/sys/fs/cgroup/blkio         cgroup      cgroup      rw,nosuid,
        nodev,noexec,relatime,blkio
| | ├─/sys/fs/cgroup/perf_event    cgroup      cgroup      rw,nosuid,
        nodev,noexec,relatime,perf_event
| | └─/sys/fs/cgroup/hugetlb       cgroup      cgroup      rw,nosuid,
        nodev,noexec,relatime,hugetlb
| ├─/sys/fs/pstore                 pstore      pstore      rw,nosuid,
        nodev,noexec,relatime
| ├─/sys/kernel/config             configfs    configfs    rw,relatime
| ├─/sys/fs/selinux                selinuxfs   selinuxfs   rw,relatime
| ├─/sys/kernel/debug              debugfs     debugfs     rw,relatime
| └─/sys/fs/fuse/connections       fusectl     fusectl     rw,relatime
├─/dev                           devtmpfs    devtmpfs      rw,nosuid,
        seclabel,size=929784k,nr_inodes=
| ├─/dev/shm                       tmpfs       tmpfs       rw,nosuid,
        nodev,seclabel
| ├─/dev/pts                       devpts      devpts      rw,nosuid,
        noexec,relatime,seclabel,gid=5,m
| ├─/dev/hugepages                 hugetlbfs   hugetlbfs rw,relatime,
        seclabel
| └─/dev/mqueue                    mqueue      mqueue    rw,relatime,
        seclabel
├─/run                             tmpfs       tmpfs     rw,nosuid,nodev,
        seclabel,mode=755
| └─/run/user/1000/gvfs            gvfsd-fuse fuse.gvfs rw,nosuid,nodev,
        relatime,user_id=1000,grou
├─/var/lib/nfs/rpc_pipefs          sunrpc      rpc_pipef rw,relatime
└─/boot                            /dev/sda1   xfs       rw,relatime,
        seclabel,attr2,inode64,noquota
```

In Exercise 3.1, you learn how to work with these commands.

Exercise 3.1 Getting an Overview of Current Mounts

In this exercise, you use different commands to get an overview of currently mounted devices.

1. Log in as an ordinary user and type **mount**. Notice that the output of the command is quite overwhelming. If you read carefully, though, you'll see a few directories from the Linux directory structure and their corresponding mounts.
2. Now type **df -hT**. Notice that a lot fewer devices are shown. An example of the output of this command is in Listing 3.3.

Listing 3.3 df -hT Sample Output

```
[root@server1 ~]# df -hT
   Filesystem              Type      Size  Used Avail Use% Mounted on
   /dev/mapper/centos-root xfs       5.9G  3.9G  2.1G  66% /
   devtmpfs                devtmpfs  908M     0  908M   0% /dev
   tmpfs                   tmpfs     918M  144K  917M   1% /dev/shm
   tmpfs                   tmpfs     918M   21M  897M   3% /run
   tmpfs                   tmpfs     918M     0  918M   0% /sys/fs/cgroup
   /dev/sda1               xfs       197M  131M   67M  67% /boot
```

Now that you have entered the **mount** and **df** commands, let's have a closer look at the output of the **df -h** command in Listing 3.1.

The output of **df** is shown in seven columns:

- **Filesystem:** The name of the device file that interacts with the disk device that is used. The real devices in the output start with /dev (which refers to the directory that is used to store device files). You can also see a couple of tmpfs devices. These are kernel devices that are used to create a temporary file system in RAM.
- **Type:** The type of file system that was used.
- **Size:** The size of the mounted device.
- **Used:** The amount of disk space the device has in use.
- **Avail:** The amount of unused disk space.
- **Use%:** The percentage of the device that currently is in use.
- **Mounted on:** The directory the device currently is mounted on.

Note that when using the **df** command, the sizes are reported in kibibytes. The option **-m** will display these in mebibytes, and using **-h** will use a human-readable format in KiB, MiB, GiB, TiB, or PiB.

Managing Files

As an administrator, you need to be able to perform common file management tasks. These tasks include the following:

- Working with wildcards
- Managing and working with directories
- Working with absolute and relative pathnames

- Listing files and directories
- Copying files and directories
- Moving files and directories
- Deleting files and directories

The following subsections explain how to perform these tasks.

Working with Wildcards

When working with files, using wildcards can make your work a lot easier. A wildcard is a shell feature that helps you referring to multiple files in an easy way. Table 3.3 gives an overview.

Table 3.3 Wildcard Overview

Key Topic

Wildcard	Use
*	Refers to an unlimited number of all characters. **ls ***, for instance, shows all files in the current directory (except those that have a name starting with a dot).
?	Used to refer to one specific character that can be any character. **ls c?t** would match cat as well as cut.
[auo]	Refers to one character that may be selected from the range that is specified between square brackets. **ls c[auo]t** would match cat, cut, and cot.

Managing and Working with Directories

To organize files, Linux works with directories (also referred to as folders). You have already read about some default directories as defined by the FHS. When users start creating files and storing them on a server, it makes sense to provide a directory structure as well. As an administrator, you have to be able to walk through the directory structure. Let's do Exercise 3.2, in which you can discover how working with directories works.

Exercise 3.2 Working with Directories

In this exercise, you learn how to work with directories.

1. Open a shell as a normal user. Type **cd**. Next, type **pwd**, which stands for print working directory. You'll see that you are currently in your home directory, a directory with the name /home/<username>.

2. Type **touch file1**. This command creates an empty file with the name file1 on your server. Because you currently are in your home directory, you can create any file you want to.
3. Type **cd /**. This changes the current directory to the root (/) directory. Type **touch file2**. You'll see a "permission denied" message. Ordinary users can create files only in directories where they have the permissions needed for this.
4. Type **cd /tmp**. This brings you to the /tmp directory, where all users have write permissions. Again, type **touch file2**. You'll see that you can create items in the /tmp directory (unless there is already a file2 that is owned by somebody else).
5. Type **cd** without any arguments. This command brings you back to your home directory.
6. Type **mkdir files**. This creates a directory with the name files in the current directory. The **mkdir** command uses the name of the directory that needs to be created as a relative pathname; it is relative to the position you are currently in.
7. Type **mkdir /home/$USER/files**. In this command, you are using the variable **$USER**, which is substituted with your current username. The complete argument of **mkdir** is an absolute filename to the directory files you are trying to create. Because this directory already exist, you'll get a "file exists" error message.
8. Type **rmdir files** to remove the directory files you have just created. The **rmdir** command enables you to remove directories, but it works only if the directory is empty and does not contain any files.

Working with Absolute and Relative Pathnames

In the previous section, you have worked with the commands **cd** and **mkdir**. You have used these commands to browse through the directory structure. You have also worked with a relative filename and an absolute filename.

Key Topic

An absolute filename, or absolute pathname, is a complete path reference to the file or directory you want to work with. This pathname starts with the root directory, followed by all subdirectories up to the actual filename. No matter what your current directory is, absolute filenames will always work. An example of an absolute filename is /home/lisa/file1.

Key Topic

A relative filename is relative to the current directory as shown with the **pwd** command. It contains only the elements that are required to get from the current directory up to the item you need. Suppose that your current directory is /home (as shown by the **pwd** command). When you refer to the relative filename lisa/file1, you are referring to the absolute filename /home/lisa/file1.

When working with relative filenames, it is sometimes useful to move up one level in the hierarchy. Imagine you are logged in as root and you want to copy the file /home/lisa/file1 to the directory /home/lara. A few solutions would work:

- Use **cp /home/lisa/file1 /home/lara**. Because in this command you are using absolute pathnames, this command will work at all times.
- Make sure your current directory is /home and use **cp lisa/file1 lara**. Notice that both the source file and the destination file are referred to as relative filenames and for that reason do *not* start with a /.
- If the current directory is set to /home/lisa, you could also use **cp file1 ../lara**. In this command, the name of the target file uses .., which means go up one level. The .. is followed by /lara, so the total name of the target file would be interpreted as "go up one level" (so you would be in /home), and from there, look for the /lara subdirectory.

TIP If you are new to working with Linux, understanding relative filename is not always easy. There is an easy workaround though. Just make sure that you always work with absolute pathnames. It is more typing, but it is easier and so you'll make fewer mistakes.

In Chapter 2, "Using Essential Tools," you learned how you can use tab completion to complete commands. Using tab completion makes it a lot easier to work with long commands. Tab completion works on filenames, too. If you have a long filename, like my-long-file-name, try typing **my-** and press the **Tab** key. If in the current directory, just one file has a name starting with my-, the filename will automatically be completed. If there are more files that have a name starting with my-, you have to press the Tab key twice to see a list of all available filenames.

Listing Files and Directories

While working with files and directories, it is useful if you can show the contents of the current directory. For this purpose, you can use the **ls** command. If used without arguments, **ls** shows the contents of the current directory. Some common arguments make working with **ls** easier. Table 3.4 gives an overview.

Key Topic

Table 3.4 ls Common Command-Line Options

Command	Use
ls -l	Shows a long listing, which includes information about file properties, such as creation date and permissions.
ls -a	Shows all files, including hidden files.
ls -lrt	This is a very useful command. It shows commands sorted on modification date. You'll see the most recently modified files last in the list.
ls -d	Shows the names of directories, not the contents of all directories that match the wildcards that have been used with the **ls** command.
ls -R	Shows the contents of the current directory, in addition to all of its subdirectories; that is, it **R**ecursively descends all subdirectories.

TIP A hidden file on Linux is a file that has a name that starts with a dot. Try the following: **touch .hidden**. Next, type **ls**. You will not see it. Then type **ls -a**. You'll see it.

When using **ls** and **ls -l**, you'll see that files are color-coded. The different colors that are used for different file types make it easier to distinguish between different kinds of files. Do not focus too much on them, though, because the colors that are used are the result of a variable setting that might be different in other Linux shells or on other Linux servers.

Copying Files

To organize files on your server, you'll often be copying files. The **cp** command helps you do so. Copying a single file is not difficult: Just use **cp /path/to/file /path/to/destination**. To copy the file /etc/hosts to the directory /tmp for instance, use **cp /etc/hosts /tmp**. This results in the file hosts being written to /tmp.

With the **cp** command, you can also copy an entire subdirectory, with its contents and everything beneath it. To do so, use the option **-R**, which stands for recursive. (You'll see the option **-R** with many other Linux commands also.) To copy the directory /etc and everything in it to the directory /tmp, you would, for instance, use the command **cp -R /etc /tmp**.

While using the **cp** command, permissions and other properties of the files are to be considered. Without extra options, you risk permissions not being copied. If you want to make sure that you keep the current permissions, use the **-a** option, which has **cp** work in archive mode. This option ensures that permissions and all other file properties will be kept while copying. So, to copy an exact state of your home directory and everything within it to the /tmp directory, use **cp -a ~ /tmp**.

A special case when working with **cp** are hidden files. By default, hidden files are not copied over. There are three solutions to work hidden files as well:

- **cp /somedir/.* /tmp** This copies all files that have a name starting with a dot (the hidden files, that is) to /tmp. It gives an error message for directories whose name starts with a dot in /somedir, because the **-R** option was not used.
- **cp -a /somedir/ .** This copies the entire directory /somedir, including its contents, to the current directory. So, as a result, a subdirectory somedir will be created in the current directory.
- **cp -a /somedir/. .** This copies all files, regular and hidden, to the current directory.

Moving Files

To move files, you use the **mv** command. This command removes the file from its current location and puts it in the new location. You can also use it to rename a file (which, in fact, is nothing else than copying and deleting the original file anyway). Let's take a look at some examples:

- **mv myfile /tmp** Moves the file myfile from the current directory to /tmp.
- **mkdir somefiles; mv somefiles /tmp** This first creates a directory with the name somefiles and then moves this directory to /tmp. Notice that this also works if the directory contains files.
- **mv myfile mynewfile** Renames the file myfile to a new file with the name mynewfile.

Deleting Files

The last common file administration task is file deletion. To delete files and directories, you use the **rm** command. When used on a single file, the single file is removed. You can also use it on directories that contain files. To do so, include the **-r** option, which again stands for recursive.

NOTE Many commands have an option that creates recursive behavior. On some commands you use the option **-R**, on other commands you use the option **-r**. That is confusing, but it is just the way it is.

On RHEL 7, the **rm** command prompts for confirmation. If you do not like that, you can use the **-f** option. Make sure that you know what you are doing when using this option, because after using it, there is no way back but the backup tape!

Exercise 3.2 Working with Files

In this exercise, you work with the common file management utilities. Figure 3.1 provides an overview of the directory structure you are working with in this exercise.

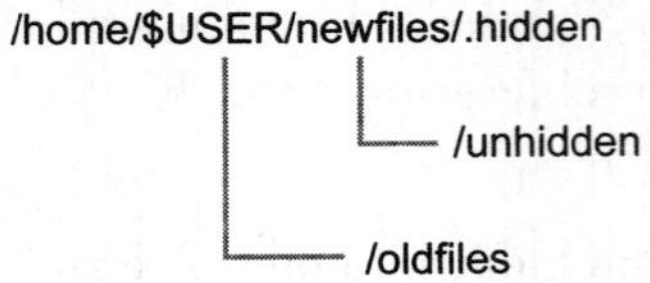

Figure 3.1 Sample directory structure overview.

1. Open a shell as an ordinary user.
2. Type **pwd**. You should be in the directory /home/$USER.
3. Type **mkdir newfiles** and **mkdir oldfiles**. Type **ls**. You'll see the directories you have just created.
4. Type **touch newfiles/.hidden** and **touch newfiles/unhidden**. This creates two files in the directory newfiles.
5. Type **cd oldfiles**.
6. Type **ls -al**. This shows two items only: ., which refers to the current directory; and .., which refers to the item above this (the parent directory).
7. Type **ls -al ../newfiles**. In this command, you are using a relative pathname to refer to the contents of the /home/$USER/newfiles directory.
8. Use the command **cp -a newfiles/..**.
9. Type **ls -a**. You see that you have created the subdirectory newfiles into the directory oldfiles.
10. Make sure that you are still in /home/$USER/oldfiles, and type **rm -rf newfiles**.
11. Now use the command **cp -a newfiles/*..**. Type **ls -l** to see what has been copied now. You'll see that the hidden file has not been copied.

12. To make sure that you'll copy hidden files as well as regular files, use **cp -a newfiles/.**.
13. Verify the command worked this time, using **ls -al**. You'll notice that the hidden as well as the regular files have been successfully copied this time.

Using Links

Links on Linux are like aliases that are assigned to a file. There are symbolic links, and there are hard links. To understand a link, you need to know a bit about the organization of the Linux file system.

Understanding Hard Links

Key Topic

Linux stores administrative data about files in inodes. Every file on Linux has an inode, and in the inode, important information about the file is stored:

- The data block where the file contents are stored
- The creation, access, and modification date
- Permissions
- File owners

Just one important piece of information is not stored in the inode: the name. Names are stored in the directory, and each filename knows which inode it has to address to access further file information. It is interesting to know that an inode does not know which name it has; it just knows how many names are associated with the inode. These names are referred to as hard links.

When you create a file, you give it a name. Basically, this name is a hard link. On a Linux file system, multiple hard links can be created to a file. This can be useful, because it enables you to access the file from multiple different locations. Some restrictions apply to hard links though:

- Hard links must exist all on the same device.
- You cannot create hard links to directories.
- The number of aliases the original file has. When the last name is removed, the contents are also removed.

The nice thing about hard links is that no difference exists between the first hard link and the second hard link. They are both just hard links, and if the first hard link that ever existed for a file is removed, that does not impact the other hard links that still exist. The Linux operating system uses links on many locations to make files more accessible.

Understanding Symbolic Links

A symbolic link (also referred to as soft link) does not link directly to the inode but to the name of the file. This makes symbolic links much more flexible, but it also has some disadvantages. The advantage of symbolic links is that they can link to files on other devices, as well as on directories. The major disadvantage is that when the original file is removed, the symbolic link becomes invalid and does not work any longer.

Figure 3.2 gives a schematic overview of how inodes, hard links, and symbolic links relate to one another.

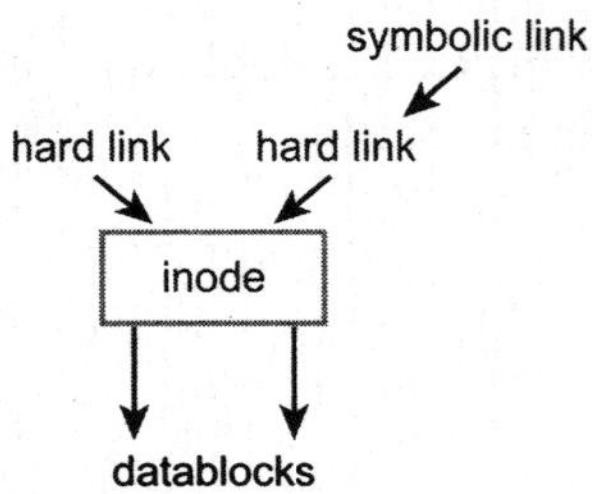

Figure 3.2 Links and inodes overview.

Creating Links

Use the **ln** command to create links. It uses the same order of parameters as **cp** and **mv**; first you mention the source name, followed by the destination name. If you want to create a symbolic link, you use the option **-s**, and then you specify the source and target file or directory. One important restriction applies, however; to be able to create hard links, you must be the owner of the item that you want to link to. This is a new security restriction that has been introduced in RHEL 7.

Table 3.5 shows some examples.

Key Topic

Table 3.5 ln Usage Examples

Command	Explanation
ln /etc/hosts .	Creates a link to the file /etc/hosts in the current directory
ln -s /etc/hosts .	Creates a symbolic link to the file /etc/hosts in the current directory
ln -s /home /tmp	Creates a symbolic link to the directory /home in the directory /tmp

The **ls** command will reveal whether a file is a link:

- In the output of the **ls -l** command, the first character is an l if the file is a symbolic link.
- If a file is a symbolic link, the output of **ls -l** shows the name of the item it links to after the filename.
- If a file is a hard link, **ls -l** shows the hard link counter. In the output in Listing 3.4, this is the number 3 that is right before root root for the hosts file.

Listing 3.4 Showing Link Properties with **ls -l**

```
[root@localhost tmp]# \ls -l
total 3
lrwxrwxrwx. 1 root root   5 Jan 19 04:38 home -> /home
-rw-r--r--. 3 root root 158 Jun  7  2013 hosts
```

NOTE In Listing 3.4, the command that was used is **\ls -l**, not **ls -l**. The **ls** command by default is an alias, which takes care of using the different colors when showing **ls** output; the \ in front of the command causes the alias not to be used.

Removing Links

Removing links can be dangerous. To show you why, let's consider the following procedure.

1. Make a directory test in your home directory: **mkdir ~/test**.
2. Copy all files that have a name starting with a, b, c, d, or e from /etc to this directory: **cp /etc/[a-e]* ~/test**.
3. Make sure that you are in your home directory, by using **cd** without arguments.
4. Type **ln -s test link**.
5. Use **rm link**. This removes the link. (Do *not* use **-r** or **-f** to remove links, even if they are subdirectories.)
6. Type **ls -l**. You'll see that the symbolic link has been removed.
7. Let's do it again. Type **ln -s test link** to create the link again.
8. Type **rm -rf link/** (which is what you would get by using bash command line completion)

9. Type **ls**. You'll see that the directory link still exists.
10. Type **ls test/** You'll see the directory test is now empty.

In Exercise 3.4, you learn how to work with symbolic links and hard links.

Exercise 3.4 Working with Symbolic Links and Hard Links

In this exercise, you work with symbolic links and hard links.

1. Open a shell as a regular (nonroot) user.
2. From your home directory, type **ln /etc/passwd .**. (Make sure that the command ends with a dot!) This command gives you an "operation not permitted" error because you are not the owner of /etc/passwd.
3. Type **ln -s /etc/passwd .**. (Again, make sure that the command ends with a dot!) This works; you do not have to be the owner to create a symbolic link.
4. Type **ln -s /etc/hosts**. (This time with no dot at the end of the command.) You'll notice this command also works. If the target is not specified, the link is created in the current directory.
5. Type **touch newfile** and create a hard link to this file by using **ln newfile linkedfile**.
6. Type **ls -l** and notice the link counter for newfile and linkedfile, which is currently set to 2.
7. Type **ln -s newfile symlinkfile** to create a symbolic link to newfile.
8. Type **rm newfile**.
9. Type **cat symlinkfile**. You will get a "no such file or directory" error message because the original file could not be found.
10. Type **cat linkedfile**. This gives no problem.
11. Type **ls -l** and look at the way the symlinkfile is displayed. Also look at linkedfile, which now has the link counter set to 1.
12. Type **ln linkedfile newfile**.
13. Type **ls -l** again. You'll see that the original situation has been restored.

Working with Archives and Compressed Files

Another important file-related task is managing archives and compressed files. To create an archive of files on a Linux computer, the **tar** command is often used. This command was originally designed to stream files to a tape without any compression of the files. If you want to compress files as well, a specific compression tool has to be used, or you need to specify an option that compresses the archive while it is created. In this section, you learn how to work with archives and compressed files.

Managing Archives with tar

The Tape ARchiver (tar) utility is used to archive files. Although originally designed to stream files to a backup tape, in its current use tar is used mostly to write files to an archive file. You have to be able to perform three important tasks with tar on the RHCSA exam:

- Create an archive
- List the contents of an archive
- Extract an archive

Creating Archives with tar

To create an archive, you use the **tar -cf archivename.tar /files-you-want-to-archive** command. If you want to see what is happening, use **the -v** option as well. To put files in an archive, you need at least read permissions to the file. Use **tar -cvf /root/homes.tar /home** as user root to write the contents of the /home directory and everything below it to the file homes.tar in the directory /root. Notice the options that are used; the order in these options is important.

Originally, tar did not use the dash (-) in front of its options. Modern tar implementations use that dash, as do all other Linux programs, but they still allow the old usage without a dash for backward compatibility. For a complete overview of relevant options used, see Table 3.4.

While managing archives with tar, it is also possible to add a file to an existing archive, or to update an archive. To add a file to an archive, you use the **-r** options. Use for instance **tar -rvf /root/homes.tar /etc/hosts** to add the /etc/hosts file to the archive.

To update a currently existing archive file, you can use the **-u** option. So, use **tar -uvf /root/homes.tar /home** to write newer versions of all files in /home to the archive.

Monitoring and Extracting Tar Files

Before extracting a file, it is good to know what might be expected. The option **-t** can be used to find out. Type for instance **tar -tvf /root/homes.tar** to see the contents of the tar archive.

TIP It is good practice to create archive files with an extension such as .tar or .tgz so that they can be easily recognized, but not everyone is doing that. If you think that a file is a tar archive, but you are not sure, use the **file** command. If you type **file somefile**, for instance, the **file** command analyzes its contents and shows on the command line what type of file it is.

To extract the contents of an archive, use **tar -cvf /archivename**. This extracts the archive in the *current* directory. That means that if you are in /root when typing **tar -xvf /root/homes.tar**, and the file contains a directory /home, after extracting you'll have a new directory /root/home that contains the entire contents of the file. This might not be what you wanted to accomplish. There are two solutions to put the extracted contents right where you want to have them:

- Before extracting the archive file, **cd** to the directory where you want to extract the file.
- Use the option **-C /targetdir** to specify the target directory where you want to extract the file in. If you want to put the contents of the file /root/homes.tar in the directory /tmp, for instance, you can use **tar -xvf homes.tar -C /tmp**.

NOTE The RHCSA objectives mention that you need to know how to work with **star** as well. The **star** utility was designed to offer support for archiving nondefault file attributes, such as access control lists (see Chapter 7, "Permissions Management") or SELinux file context (see Chapter 21, "Managing SELinux"). In its current release, tar offers this functionality also, so there is no real need for using **star** anymore.

Apart from extracting an entire archive file, it is also possible to extract one file out of the archive. To do so, use **tar -xvf /archivename.tar /file-you-want-to-extract.** If your archive etc.tar contains the file /etc/hosts that you want to extract, for instance, use **tar -xvf /root/etc.tar /etc/hosts**.

Using Compression

Many files contain a lot of redundancy. Compression programs allow you to make files take less disk space by taking out that redundancy. In all examples of the **tar** command that you have seen so far, not a single byte has been compressed. Originally, after creating the archive, it had to be compressed with a separate compression utility, such as **gzip** or **bzip2**. After having created home.tar, you can compress it with **gzip home.tar**. **gzip** replaces home.tar with its compressed version, home.tar.gz, which takes significantly less space.

As an alternative to using **gzip**, you can use the **bzip2** utility. Originally, bzip2 used a more efficient encryption algorithm, which resulted in smaller file sizes, but currently it hardly makes a difference anymore with the result of the **gzip** utility.

To decompress files that have been compressed with **gzip** or **bzip2**, you can use the **gunzip** and **bunzip2** utilities; you work with some examples of this command in Exercise 3.5.

As an alternative to using these utilities from the command line, you can include the **-z** (gzip) or **-j** (bzip2) options while creating the archive with tar. This will immediately compress the file size. There is no need to use these options while extracting. The tar utility will recognize the compressed contents and automatically decompress it for you. In Exercise 3.5, you apply the newly acquired tar skills. Table 3.6 gives an overview of the most significant tar options.

Table 3.6 Overview of tar Options

Key Topic

Option	Use
c	Creates an archive.
v	Shows verbose output while tar is working.
f	Used to specify the name of the tar archive that is to be used. Without using this option, the default destination is STDIN for **-x** and STDOUT for **-c**.
t	Shows the contents of an archive.
z	Compresses/decompresses the archive while creating it, by using gzip.
j	Compresses/decompresses the archive by using bzip2.
x	Extracts an archive.
u	Updates an archive; only newer files will be written to the archive.
C	Changes the working directory before performing the command.
r	Appends files to an archive.

Exercise 3.5 Using `tar`

In this exercise, you work with the tar command to manage archives.

1. Open a root shell on your server. By logging in, the home directory of user root will become the current directory, so all relative filenames used in this exercise refer to /root/.
2. Type **tar -cvf etc.tar /etc** to archive the contents of the /etc directory.

3. Type **file etc.tar** and read the information that is provided by the command. This should look like the following:

```
[root@server1 ~]# file etc.tar
etc.tar: POSIX tar archive (GNU)
```

4. Type **gzip etc.tar**.
5. Type **tar tvf etc.tar.gz**. Notice that the **tar** command has no issues reading from a gzip compressed file. Also notice that the archive content consists of all relative filenames.
6. Type **tar xvf etc.tar.gz etc/hosts**.
7. Type **ls -R**. Notice that a subdirectory etc has been created in the current directory. In this subdirectory, the file hosts has been restored.
8. Type **gunzip etc.tar.gz**. This decompresses the compressed file but does not change anything else with regard to the **tar** command.
9. Type **tar xvf etc.tar -C /tmp etc/passwd**. This extracts the password file to the /tmp directory.
10. Type **tar xjvf homes.tar /home**. This creates a compressed archive of the home directory to the home directory of user root.
11. Type **rm -f *gz *tar** to remove all files resulting from exercises in this chapter from the home directory of /root.

Summary

In this chapter, you learned how to work with essential file management tools. You learned how the Linux directory structure is organized by default, and you learned what file types to expect in which directories. You also learned how to find your way in the directory structure and to work with files.

Exam Preparation Tasks

Review All Key Topics

Review the most important topics in the chapter, noted with the Key Topic icon in the outer margin of the page. Table 3.7 lists a reference of these key topics and the page numbers on which each is found.

Table 3.7 Key Topics for Chapter 3

Key Topic Element	Description	Page Number
Table 3.2	FHS overview	60
Table 3.3	Wildcard overview	67
Paragraph	Definition of an absolute filename	68
Paragraph	Definition of a relative filename	68
Table 3.4	**ls** common command; line options	70
Paragraph	Definition of an inode	73
Table 3.5	**ln** usage examples	74
Table 3.6	Overview of tar options	79

Complete Tables and Lists from Memory

Print a copy of Appendix B, "Memory Tables" (found on the disc), or at least the section for this chapter, and complete the tables and lists from memory. Appendix C, "Memory Tables Answer Key," also on the disc, includes completed tables and lists to check your work.

Define Key Terms

Define the following key terms from this chapter and check your answers in the glossary:

FSH, directory, mount, device, folder, root directory, path, hard link, symbolic link, absolute filename, relative filename, inode, tar, gzip, compression, archiving

Review Questions

1. Which directory would you go to if you were looking for configuration files?
2. What command enables you to display a list of current directory contents, where the newest files are listed first?
3. Which command enables you to rename the file myfile to your file?
4. Which command enables you to wipe an entire directory structure, including all of its contents?
5. How do you create a link to the directory /tmp in your home directory?

6. How would you copy all files that have a name that starts with a, b, or c from the directory /etc to your current directory?
7. Which command enables you to create a link to the directory /etc in your home directory?
8. What is the safe option to remove a symbolic link to a directory?
9. How do you create a compressed archive of the directories /etc and /home and write that to /tmp/etchome.tgz?
10. How would you extract the file /etc/passwd from /tmp/etchome.tgz that you have created in the previous step?

End-of-Chapter Labs

In this chapter, you learned how to perform basic file management tasks. Managing files is an essential task for a Linux administrator. In the end-of-chapter labs with this chapter, you can practice these skills and make sure that you master them before taking the RHCSA exam.

Lab 3.1

1. Log in as user root. In the home directory of root, create one archive file that contains the contents of the /home and the /etc directory. Use the name **/root/essentials.tar** for the archive file.
2. Copy this archive to the /tmp directory. Also create a hard link to this file in the / directory.
3. Rename the file /essentials.tar to /archive.tar.
4. Create a symbolic link in the home directory of the user root that refers to /archive.tar. Use the name **link.tar** for the symbolic link.
5. Remove the file /archive.tar and see what happened to the symbolic link. Remove the symbolic link also.
6. Compress the /root/essentials.tar file.

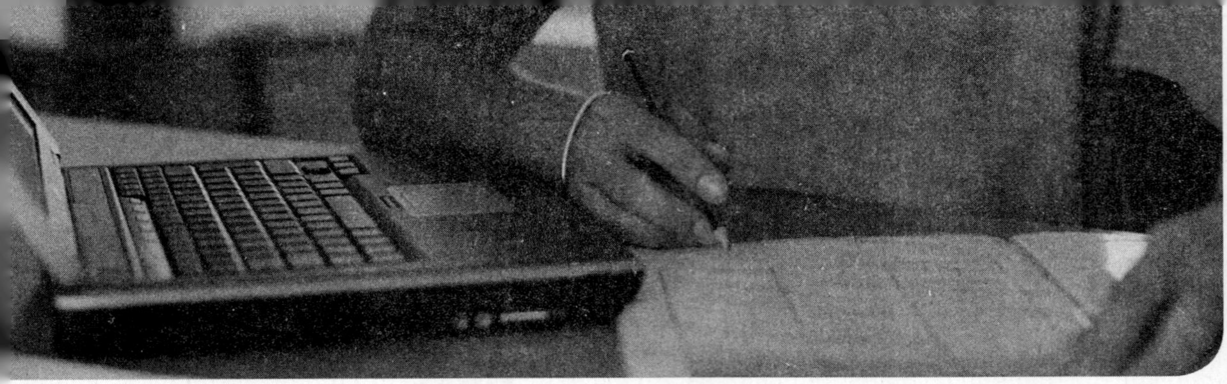

The following topics are covered in this chapter:

- Using Common Text File-Related Tools
- A Primer to Using Regular Expressions
- Using grep to Analyze Text
- Working with Other Useful Text Processing Utilities

The following RHCSA exam objectives are covered in this chapter:

- Using grep and regular expressions to analyze text
- Create and edit text files

CHAPTER 4

Working with Text Files

Since the early days of UNIX, working with text files has been an important administrator skill. Even on modern Linux versions such as Red Hat Enterprise Linux 7, working with text files is still an important skill. By applying the correct tools, you'll easily find the information you need. This chapter is about these tools. Make sure that you master them well, because good knowledge of these tools really will make your work as a Linux administrator a lot easier. And at the same time, it will increase your chances of passing the RHCSA test.

"Do I Know This Already?" Quiz

The "Do I Know This Already?" quiz allows you to assess whether you should read this entire chapter thoroughly or jump to the "Exam Preparation Tasks" section. If you are in doubt about your answers to these questions or your own assessment of your knowledge of the topics, read the entire chapter. Table 4.1 lists the major headings in this chapter and their corresponding "Do I Know This Already?" quiz questions. You can find the answers in Appendix A, "Answers to the 'Do I Know This Already?' Quizzes and 'Review Questions.'"

Table 4.1 "Do I Know This Already?" Section-to-Question Mapping

Foundation Topics Section	Questions
Using Common Text File-Related Tools	1–5
A Primer to Using Regular Expressions	6–8
Using grep to Analyze Text	10
Working with Other Useful Text Processing Utilities	9

1. Which command was developed to show only the first 10 lines in a text file?
   a. **head**
   b. **top**
   c. **first**
   d. **cat**
2. Which command enables you to count the number of words in a text file?
   a. **count**
   b. **list**
   c. **ls -l**
   d. **wc**
3. Which key on your keyboard do you use in less to go to the last line of the current text file?
   a. End
   b. PageDown
   c. q
   d. G
4. Which option is missing from the following command, assuming that you want to filter the first field out of the /etc/passwd file and assuming that the character that is used as the field delimiter is a:? **cut .... : -f 1 /etc/passwd**
   a. **-d**
   b. **-c**
   c. **-t**
   d. **-x**
5. Which option is missing if you want to sort the third column of the output of the command **ps aux**?

   ```
   ps aux | sort ...
   ```

   a. **-k3**
   b. **-s3**
   c. **-k f 3**
   d. **-f 3**

6. Which of the following lines would only show lines in the file /etc/passwd that start with the text anna?
   a. **grep anna /etc/passwd**
   b. **grep -v anna /etc/passwd**
   c. **grep $anna /etc/passwd**
   d. **grep ^anna /etc/passwd**
7. Which regular expression do you use to make the previous character optional?
   a. ?
   b. .
   c. *
   d. &
8. Which regular expression is used as a wildcard to refer to any single character?
   a. ?
   b. .
   c. *
   d. &
9. Which command prints the fourth field of a line in the /etc/passwd file if the text *user* occurs in that line?
   a. **awk '/user/ { print $4 }' /etc/passwd**
   b. **awk -d : '/user/ { print $4 }' /etc/passwd**
   c. **awk -F : '/user/ $4 ' /etc/passwd**
   d. **awk -F : '/user/ { print $4 }' /etc/passwd**
10. Which option would you use with grep to show only lines that do *not* contain the regular expression that was used?
    a. **-x**
    b. **-v**
    c. **-u**
    d. **-q**

Foundation Topics

Using Common Text File-Related Tools

Before we start talking about the best possible way to find text files containing specific text, let's take a look at how you can display text files in an efficient way. Table 4.2 provides an overview of some common commands often used for this purpose.

Key Topic

Table 4.2 Essential Tools for Managing Text File Contents

Command	Explanation
less	Opens the text file in a pager, which allows for easy reading of the text file
cat	Dumps the contents of the text file on the screen
head	Shows the first 10 lines of the text file
tail	Shows the last 10 lines of the text file
cut	Used to filter specific columns or characters from a text file
sort	Sorts contents of a text file
wc	Counts the number of lines, words, and characters in a file

Apart from using these commands on a text file, they may also prove very useful when used in pipes. You can use the command **less /etc/passwd**, for example, to open the contents of the /etc/passwd file in the **less** pager, but you can also use the command **ps aux | less**, which sends the output of the command **ps aux** to the pager less to allow for easy reading.

Doing More with Less

In many cases, as a Linux administrator you'll need to read the contents of text files. The less utility offers a convenient way to do so. To open the contents of a text file in less, just type **less** followed by the name of the file you want to see, as in **less /etc/passwd**.

From less, you can use the PageUp and PageDown keys on your keyboard to browse through the file contents. Seen enough? Then you can press **q** to quit less. Also very useful is that you can easily search for specific contents in less using **/sometext** for a forward search and **?sometext** for a backward search. Repeat the last search by using **n**.

If you think this sounds familiar, it should. You have seen similar behavior in **vim** and **man**. That is because all of these commands are based on the same code.

NOTE Once upon a time, less was developed because it offered more features than the classical UNIX tool that was developed to page through file contents page by page, more. So, the idea was to do more with less. Developers did not like that, so they enhanced more features as well. The result is that both more and less offer many features that are similar and it doesn't really matter that much anymore which of these tools you are using. There is one significant difference, though, and that is that the more utility ends if the end of the file is reached. To prevent this behavior, you can start more with the **-p** option. In Exercise 4.1, you'll apply some basic less skills.

Exercise 4.1 Applying Basic Less Skills

In this exercise, you apply some basic less skills working with file contents and command output.

1. From a terminal, type **less /etc/passwd**. This opens the /etc/passwd file in the less pager.
2. Type **G** to go to the last line in the file.
3. Type **/root** to look for the text *root*. You'll see that all occurrences of the text *root* are highlighted.
4. Type **q** to quit less.
5. Type **ps aux | less**. This sends the output of the **ps aux** command (which shows a listing of all processes) to less. Browse through the list.
6. Press **q** to quit less.

Showing File Contents with cat

The less utility is useful to read long text files. If a text file is not that long, you are probably better off using cat. This tool just dumps the contents of the text file on the terminal it was started from. This is convenient is the text file is short. If the text file is long, however, you'll see all contents scrolling by on the screen, and only the lines that fit on the terminal screen are displayed. Using cat is simple. Just type **cat** followed by the name of the file you want to see. For instance, use **cat /etc/passwd** to show the contents of this file on your computer screen.

TIP The cat utility dumps the contents of a file to the screen from the beginning to the end, which means that for a long file you'll see the last lines of the file only. If you are interested in the first lines, you can use the tac utility, which gives the inversed result of cat.

Displaying the First or Last Lines of a File with head and tail

If a text file contains much information, it can be useful to filter the output a bit. You can use the head and tail utilities to do that. Using head on a text file will show by default the first 10 lines of that file. Using tail on a text file shows the last 10 lines by default. You can adjust the number of lines that are shown by adding **-n** followed by the number you want to see. So, **tail -n 5 /etc/passwd** shows the last five lines of the /etc/passwd file.

TIP On older versions of head and tail, you had to use the **-n** option to specify the number of lines you wanted to see. On current versions of both utilities, you may also omit the **-n** option. So, **tail -5 /etc/passwd** or **tail -n 5 /etc/passwd** gives you the exact same results.

Another useful option that you can use with tail is **-f**. This option starts by showing you the last 10 lines of the file you've specified, but it refreshes the display as new lines are added to the file. This is convenient for monitoring log files. The command **tail -f /var/log/messages** is a common command to show in real-time messages that are written to the main log file /var/log/messages.

When combining tail and head, you can do smart things as well. Suppose, for instance, that you want to see line number 11 of the /etc/passwd file. To do that, use **head -n 11 /etc/passwd | tail -n 1**. The command before the pipe shows the first 11 lines from the file. The result is sent to the pipe, and on that result **tail -n 1** is used, which leads to only line number 11 being displayed. In Exercise 4.2, you apply some basic head and tail operations.

Exercise 4.2 Using Basic head and tail Operations

In this exercise, you learn how to use head and tail to get exactly what you want.

1. Type **tail -f /var/log/messages**. You'll see the last lines of /var/log/messages being displayed. The file doesn't close automatically.

2. Type **Ctrl+C** to quit the previous command.
3. Type **head -n 5 /etc/passwd** to show the first five lines in /etc/passwd.
4. Type **tail -n 2 /etc/passwd** to show the last two lines of /etc/passwd.
5. Type **head -n 5 /etc/passwd | tail -n 1** to show only line number 5 of the /etc/passwd file.

Filtering Specific Columns with cut

When working with text files, it can be useful to filter out specific fields. Imagine that you need to see a list of all users in the /etc/passwd file. In this file, several fields are defined, of which the first contains the name of the users who are defined. To filter out a specific field, the **cut** command is useful. To do this, use the **-d** option to specify the field delimiter followed by **-f** with the number of the specific field you want to filter out. So, the complete command is **cut -d : -f 1 /etc/passwd** if you want to filter out the first field of the /etc/passwd file. You can see the result in Listing 4.1.

Listing 4.1 Filtering Specific Fields with **cut**

```
[root@localhost ~]# cut -f 1 -d : /etc/passwd
root
bin
daemon
adm
lp
sync
shutdown
halt
...
```

Sorting File Contents and Output with sort

Another very useful command to use on text file is **sort**. As you can probably guess, this command sorts text. If you type **sort /etc/passwd**, for instance, the content of the /etc/passwd file is sorted in alphabetic order. You can use the **sort** command on the output of a command also, as in **cut -f 1 -d : /etc/passwd | sort**, which sorts the contents of the first column in the /etc/passwd file.

By default, the **sort** command sorts in alphabetic order. In some cases, that is not convenient because the content that needs sorting may be numeric or in another format. The **sort** command offers different options to help sorting these specific types of data. Type, for instance, **cut -f 2 -d : /etc/passwd | sort -n** to sort the second field of the /etc/passwd file in numeric order. It can be useful also to sort in reverse order; if you use the command **du -h | sort -rn**, you get a list of files sorted with the biggest file in that directory listed first.

You can also use the **sort** command and specify which column you want to sort. To do this, use **sort -k3 -t : /etc/passwd**, for instance, which uses the field separator : to sort the third column of the /etc/passwd file.

You might also like the option to sort on a specific column of a file or the output of a command. An example is the command **ps aux**, which gives an overview of the busiest processes on a Linux server. (Listing 4.2 shows partial output of this command.)

Listing 4.2 The Command **ps aux** Gives an Overview of the Busiest Processes on a Linux Server

```
[root@localhost ~]# ps aux | tail -n 10
postfix    1350  0.0  0.7  91872  3848 ?       S    Jan24   0:00 qmgr -l
    -t unix -u
root       2162  0.0  0.3 115348  1928 tty1    Ss+  Jan24   0:00 -bash
postfix    5131  0.0  0.7  91804  3832 ?       S    12:10   0:00 pickup
    -l -t unix -u
root       5132  0.0  0.0      0     0 ?       S    12:10   0:00
    [kworker/0:1]
root       5146  0.0  0.9 133596  4868 ?       Ss   12:12   0:00 sshd:
    root@pts/0
root       5150  0.0  0.3 115352  1940 pts/0   Ss   12:12   0:00 -bash
root       5204  0.0  0.0      0     0 ?       S    12:20   0:00
    [kworker/0:2]
root       5211  0.0  0.0      0     0 ?       S    12:26   0:00
    [kworker/0:0]
root       5212  0.0  0.2 123356  1320 pts/0   R+   12:26   0:00 ps aux
root       5213  0.0  0.1 107928   672 pts/0   R+   12:26   0:00 tail
    -n 10
```

To sort the output of this command directly on the third column, use the command **ps aux | sort -k3**.

Counting Lines, Words, and Characters with wc

When working with text files, you sometimes get a large amount of output. Before deciding which approach works best in a specific case, you might want to have an idea about the amount of text you are dealing with. In that case, the **wc** command is useful. In its output, this command gives three different results: the number of lines, the number of words, and the number of characters.

Consider, for example, the **ps aux** command. When executed as root, this command gives a list of all processes running on a server. One solution to count how many processes there are exactly is to pipe the output of **ps aux** through **wc**, as in **ps aux | wc**. You can see the result of the command in Listing 4.3. In the result in Listing 4.3, you can see that the total number of lines is 90 and that there are 1,045 words and 7,583 characters in the command output.

Listing 4.3 Counting the Number of Lines, Words, and Characters with **wc**

```
[root@localhost ~]# ps aux | wc
     90    1045    7583
```

A Primer to Using Regular Expressions

Working with text files is an important skill for a Linux administrator. You not only have to know how to create and modify existing text files, but it is also very useful if you can find the text file that contains specific text.

If will be clear sometimes which specific text you are looking for. Other times, it might not. For example, are you looking for color or colour? Both spellings might give a match. This is just one example of why using flexible patterns while looking for text can prove useful. These flexible patterns are known as *regular expressions* in Linux.

To understand regular expressions a bit better, let's take a look at a text file example (Listing 4.4). This file contains the last six lines from the /etc/passwd file. (This file is used for storing Linux accounts; see Chapter 6, "User and Group Management," for more details about it.)

Listing 4.4 Example Lines from **/etc/passwd**

```
[root@localhost ~]# tail -n 6 /etc/passwd
anna:x:1000:1000::/home/anna:/bin/bash
rihanna:x:1001:1001::/home/rihanna:/bin/bash
```

```
annabel:x:1002:1002::/home/annabel:/bin/bash
anand:x:1003:1003::/home/anand:/bin/bash
joanna:x:1004:1004::/home/joanna:/bin/bash
joana:x:1005:1005::/home/joana:/bin/bash
```

Now suppose that you are looking for the user anna. In that case, you could use the general regular expression parser grep to look for that specific string in the file /etc/passwd by using the command **grep anna /etc/passwd**. Listing 4.5 shows the results of that command, and as you can see, way too many results are shown.

Listing 4.5 This is Why You Need to Know About Regular Expressions

```
[root@localhost ~]# grep anna /etc/passwd
anna:x:1000:1000::/home/anna:/bin/bash
rihanna:x:1001:1001::/home/rihanna:/bin/bash
annabel:x:1002:1002::/home/annabel:/bin/bash
joanna:x:1004:1004::/home/joanna:/bin/bash
```

Key Topic

A regular expression is a search pattern that allows you to look for specific text in an advanced and flexible way.

Using Line Anchors

In Listing 4.5, you might want to specify that you are looking for lines that are starting with the text *anna*. The type of regular expression that specifies where in a line of output the result is expected is known as a *line anchor*.

To show only lines that start with the text you are looking for, you can use the regular expression ^ (in this case, to indicate that you are looking only for lines where *anna* is at the beginning of the line; see Listing 4.6).

Listing 4.6 Looking for Lines Starting with a Specific Pattern

```
[root@localhost ~]# grep ^anna /etc/passwd
anna:x:1000:1000::/home/anna:/bin/bash
annabel:x:1002:1002::/home/annabel:/bin/bash
```

Another regular expression that relates to the position of specific text in a specific line is $, which states that the line ends with some text. For instance, the command **grep ash$ /etc/passwd** shows all lines in the /etc/passwd file that end with the text *ash*.

Using Escaping in Regular Expressions

Although not mandatory, when using regular expressions it is a good idea to use escaping to prevent the regular expression from being interpreted by the shell. In many cases, it is not really necessary to use escaping; in some cases, the regular expression fails without escaping. To prevent this from ever happening, it is a good idea to put the regular expression between quotes. So, instead of typing **grep ^anna /etc/passwd**, it is better use **grep '^anna' /etc/passwd,** even if in this case both examples work.

Using Wildcards and Multipliers

In some cases, you might know which text you are looking for, but you might not know how the specific text is written. Or you just want to use one regular expression to match different patterns. In those cases, wildcards and multipliers come in handy.

To start with, there is the . regular expression. This is used as a wildcard character to look for one specific character. So, the regular expression **r.t** would match the strings rat, rot, and rut.

In some cases, you might want to be more specific about the characters you are looking for. If that is the case, you can specify a range of characters that you are looking for. For instance, the regular expression r[aou]t matches the strings rat, rut, as well as rot.

Another useful regular expression is the multiplier *. This matches zero or more of the previous character. That does not seem to be very useful, but indeed it is, as you will see in the examples at the end of this section.

If you know exactly how many of the previous character you are looking for, you can specify a number also, as in re\{2\}d, which would match red as well as reed. The last regular expression that is useful to know about is ?, which matches zero or one of the previous character. Table 4.3 provides an overview of the most important regular expressions.

Key Topic

Table 4.3 Most Significant Regular Expressions

Regular Expression	Use
^text	Line starts with text.
text$	Line ends with text.
.	Wildcard. (Matches any single character.)
[abc]	Matches a, b, or c.
*	Match 0 to an infinite number of the previous character.
\{2\}	Match exactly 2 of the previous character.
\{1,3\}	Match a minimum of 1 and a maximum of 3 of the previous character.
colou?r	Match 0 or 1 of the previous character. This makes the previous character optional, which in this example would match both *color* and *colour*.

Let's take a look at an example of a regular expression that comes from the man page semanage-fcontext and relates to managing SELinux (see Chapter 21, "Managing SELinux"). The example line contains the following regular expression:

```
"/web(/.*)?"
```

In this regular expression, the text */web* is referred to. This text string can be followed by the regular expression (/.*)?, which means zero or one (/.*), which in fact means that it can be followed by nothing or (/.*). The (/.*) refers to a slash which may be followed by an unlimited number of characters. To state it differently, the regular expression refers to the text */web* which may or may not be followed by any characters.

Using grep to Analyze Text

The ultimate utility to work with regular expressions is grep, which stands for "general regular expression parser." Quite a few examples that you have seen already were based on the **grep** command. The **grep** command has a couple of useful options to make it even more efficient. Table 4.4 describes some of the most useful options.

Table 4.4 Most Useful **grep** Options

Key Topic

Option	Use
-i	Not case sensitive. Matches uppercase as well as lowercase.
-v	Only show lines that do *not* contain the regular expression.
-r	Search files in the current directory and all subdirectories.
-e	Use this to search for lines matching more than one regular expression.
-A <number>	Show <number> of lines after the matching regular expression.
-B <number>	Show <number> of lines before the matching regular expression.

In Exercise 4.3, you work through some examples using these grep options.

Exercise 4.3 Using Common grep Options

In this exercise, you work through some common grep options.

1. Type **grep '^#' /etc/sysconfig/sshd**. This shows that the file /etc/sysconfig/sshd contains a number of lines that start with the comment sign #.
2. To view the configuration lines that really matter, type **grep -v '^#' /etc/sysconfig/sshd**. This shows only lines that do not start with a #.
3. Now type **grep -v '^#' /etc/sysconfig/sshd -B 5**. This shows lines that are not starting with a # sign but also the five lines that are directly before that line, which is useful because in these lines you'll typically find comments on how to use the specific parameters. However, you'll also see that many blank lines are displayed.
4. Type **grep -v -e '^#' -e '^$' /etc/sysconfig/sshd**. This excludes all blank lines and lines that start with #.

Working with Other Useful Text Processing Utilities

The grep utility is a powerful utility that allows you to work with regular expressions. It is not the only utility, though. Some even more powerful utilities exist, like awk and sed. Both utilities are extremely rich and merit a book by themselves. As a Linux administrator in the twenty-first century, you do not have to be a specialist in using these utilities anymore. It does make sense, however, to know how to perform some common tasks using these utilities. The most useful use cases are summarized in the following examples:

```
awk -F : '{ print $4 }' /etc/passwd
```

This command shows the fourth line from /etc/passwd. This is something that can be done by using the cut utility as well, but the awk utility is more successful in distinguishing the fields that are used in command output of files. The bottom line is that if cut does not work, you should try the awk utility.

You can also use the awk utility to do tasks that you might be used to using grep for. Consider the following example:

```
awk -F : '/user/ { print $4 }' /etc/passwd
```

This command searches the /etc/passwd file for the text user and will print the fourth field of any matching line:

```
sed -n 5p /etc/passwd
```

In this example, the "stream editor" sed is used to print the fifth line from the /etc/passwd file. The sed utility is a very powerful utility for filtering text from text files (like grep), but it has the benefit that it also allows you to apply modifications to text files, as shown in the following example:

```
sed -i s/old-text/new-text/g ~/myfile
```

In this example the sed utility is used to search the text *old-text* in ~/myfile and on all occurrences replace it with the text *new-text*. Notice that the default sed behavior is to write the output to STDOUT, but the option **-i** will write the result directly to the file. Make sure that you know what you are doing before using this command, because it might be difficult to revert file modifications that are applied in this way:

```
sed -i -e '2d' ~/myfile
```

You will like the preceding example if you've ever had a utility containing a specific line in a file that was erroneous. With this command, you can delete a line based on a specific line number. You can also make more complicated references to line numbers. Use, for instance, **sed -i -e '2d;20,25d' ~/myfile** to delete lines 2 and 20 through 25 in the file ~/myfile.

> **TIP** Do not focus on awk and sed too much. These are amazing utilities, but many of the things that can be accomplished using awk and sed can be done using other tools as well. The awk and sed tools are very rich, and you can easily get lost in them if you are trying to dig too deep.

Summary

In this chapter, you learned how to work with text files. You acquired some important skills like searching text files with grep and displaying text files or part of them with different utilities. You have also learned how regular expressions can be used to make the search results more specific and learned about the very sophisticated utilities awk and sed, which allow you to perform more advanced operations on text files.

Exam Preparation Tasks

Review All Key Topics

Review the most important topics in the chapter, noted with the Key Topic icon in the outer margin of the page. Table 4.5 lists a reference of these key topics and the page numbers on which each is found.

Table 4.5 Key Topics for Chapter 4

Key Topic Element	Description	Page
Table 4.2	Essential tools for managing text file contents	88
Paragraph	Definition of regular expressions	94
Table 4.3	Most useful regular expressions	96
Table 4.4	Most useful grep options	97

Complete Tables and Lists from Memory

Print a copy of Appendix B, "Memory Tables" (found on the disc), or at least the section for this chapter, and complete the tables and lists from memory. Appendix C, "Memory Tables Answer Key," also on the disc, includes completed tables and lists to check your work.

Define Key Terms

Define the following key terms from this chapter and check your answers in the glossary:

regular expression, pager, escaping, wildcards, multipliers, line anchors

Review Questions

1. Which command enables you to see the results of the **ps aux** command in a way that you can easily browse up and down in the results?
2. Which command enables you to show the last five lines from ~/samplefile?
3. Which command do you use if you want to know how many words are in ~/samplefile?
4. After opening command output using **tail -f ~/mylogfile,** how do you stop showing output?
5. Which grep option do you use to exclude all lines that are starting with either a # or a ;?
6. Which regular expression do you use to match one or more of the preceding characters?
7. Which **grep** command enables you to see *text* as well as *TEXT* in a file?
8. Which **grep** command enables you to show all lines starting with *PATH*, as well as the five lines just before that line?
9. Which **sed** command do you use to show line 9 from ~/samplefile?
10. Which command enables you to replace the word *user* with the word *users* in ~/samplefile?

End-of-Chapter Labs

In these end-of-chapter labs, you work with some of the most significant text processing utilities.

Lab 4.1

1. Describe two ways to show line 5 from the /etc/passwd file?
2. How would you locate all text files on your server that contain the current IP address? Do you need a regular expression to do this?

3. You have just used the **sed** command that replaces all occurrences of the text *Administrator* with *root*. Your Windows administrators do not like that very much. How do you revert?
4. Assuming that in the **ps aux** command the fifth line contains information about memory utilization, how would you process the output of that command to show the process that has the most heavy memory utilization first in the results list?
5. Which command enables you to filter the sixth column of **ps aux** output?
6. How do you delete the sixth line from the file ~/myfile?

The following topics are covered in this chapter:

- Working on Local Consoles
- Using SSH and Related Utilities

The following RHCSA exam objectives are covered in this chapter:

- Access remote systems using SSH
- Switch users in multiple targets
- Boot, reboot, and shut down a system normally
- Securely transfer files between systems
- Configure key-based authentication for SSH

CHAPTER 5

Connecting to Red Hat Enterprise Linux 7

You have already learned how to log in on Linux from a graphical environment. In this chapter, you learn about some other methods to access a Linux shell and start working. You learn how to work from local consoles, as well as Secure Shell (SSH) to connect to Linux. You also learn how to perform some basic tasks from these environments.

"Do I Know This Already?" Quiz

The "Do I Know This Already?" quiz allows you to assess whether you should read this entire chapter thoroughly or jump to the "Exam Preparation Tasks" section. If you are in doubt about your answers to these questions or your own assessment of your knowledge of the topics, read the entire chapter. Table 5.1 lists the major headings in this chapter and their corresponding "Do I Know This Already?" quiz questions. You can find the answers in Appendix A, "Answers to the 'Do I Know This Already?' and 'Review Questions.'"

Table 5.1 "Do I Know This Already?" Section-to-Question Mapping

Foundation Topics Section	Questions
Working on Local Consoles	1–6
Using SSH and Related Utilities	7–10

1. Which is the correct word for the description here?

   "Used to refer to the physical screen you are currently looking at as a user?"

   a. Terminal

   b. Console

   c. Shell

   d. Interface

2. Which is the correct word for the description here?

   "The environment from which a shell is used where users can enter their commands"

   a. Terminal
   b. Console
   c. Shell
   d. Interface

3. Which is the correct word for the description here?

   "The environment that offers a command line on which users type the commands they want to be using"

   a. Terminal
   b. Console
   c. Shell
   d. Interface

4. Which device file is associated with the virtual console that is opened after using the Alt+F6 key sequence?

   a. /dev/console6
   b. /dev/tty6
   c. /dev/vty6
   d. /dev/pts/6

5. Which of the following methods will open a pseudo terminal device?

   a. Log in using an SSH session
   b. Use Alt+F2 to open a new nongraphical login
   c. Right-click the graphical desktop and select Open in Terminal
   d. Enter your username and password on a nongraphical console

6. Sometimes a server reboot may be necessary. Which of the following is *not* typically one of them?

   a. To recover from serious problems such as server hangs and kernel panics
   b. To apply kernel updates
   c. To apply changes to kernel modules that are used and because of that cannot be reloaded easily
   d. To apply changes to the network configuration

7. Which of the following is true about remote access to Linux servers from a Windows environment?
   a. Open a shell terminal on Windows and type **ssh**. The **ssh** command is available as a default part of the Windows operating system.
   b. Configure Remote Access on Windows if you want to access Linux servers running the sshd process.
   c. Install the PuTTY program on Windows to access sshd services on Linux from Windows.
   d. You cannot remotely access Linux machines from Windows.

8. What is the name of the file in which the public key fingerprint of the SSH servers you have connected to in the past are stored?
   a. /etc/ssh/remote_hosts
   b. /etc/ssh/known_hosts
   c. ~/.ssh/remote_hosts
   d. ~/.ssh/known_hosts

9. To allow graphical applications to be used through an SSH session, you can set a parameter in the /etc/ssh/ssh_config file. Using this parameter makes it unnecessary to use the **-X** command-line option each time an SSH session is initiated. Which of the following parameters should be used?
   a. **Host ***
   b. **TunnelX11 yes**
   c. **ForwardX11 yes**
   d. **Xclient yes**

10. Which of the following statements about key-based SSH authentication is true?
    a. After creating the key pair, you need to copy the private key to the remote server.
    b. Use **scp** to copy the public key to the remote server.
    c. Use **ssh-copy-id** to copy the public key to the remote server.
    d. Use **ssh-keygen** on the server to generate a key pair that matches the client keys.

Foundation Topics

Working on Local Consoles

You have already learned how to log in on Linux by using a graphical console. In this section, you learn some more about the possibilities you have while working from either a graphical Linux console or a text-based Linux console.

Key Topic

Before we get into details, it makes sense to highlight the difference between the words console and terminal. In this book, I follow the common notion of a console as the environment the user is looking at. That means that the console is basically what you see when you are looking at your computer screen.

A terminal is an environment that is opened on the console, and which provides access to a text shell, which is the command-line environment that can be used to type commands. A terminal can be offered through a window while using a graphical console, but it can also be opened as the only thing that you see in a textual console. This means that on a textual environment, the words *console* and *terminal* are more or less equivalent. In a graphical environment, they are not. Think of it like this: You can have multiple terminals open on a console, but you cannot have multiple consoles open in one terminal.

Logging In to a Local Console

Roughly, there are two ways to make yourself known to a Linux server. Sometimes you just sit behind the Linux console and interactively log in from the login prompt that is presented. In other cases, a remote connection is established. The second part of this chapter is about logging in from a remote session; in this part, you learn how to work from a local console.

If a Linux server boots with a graphical environment (the so-called graphical target), you see a login prompt on which a user name and password can be entered. Many Linux servers do not use a graphical environment at all, though, and are just presenting a text-based console, as shown in Figure 5.1.

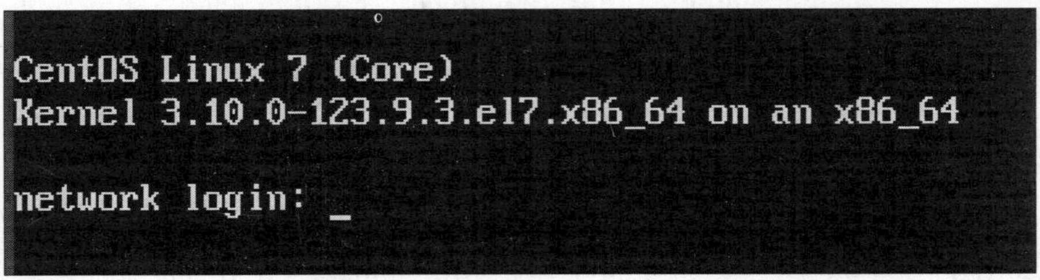

Figure 5.1 Logging in from a text console.

To log in from a text console, you need to know which user account you should use. A user root is always available, but using this account to do your work is often not a good idea; the user root has no limitations to access the system and can therefore do a lot of damage. A small mistake can have huge impact. Typically, it is a better idea to log in as one of the locally defined users, and there are many reasons to do so, including the following:

- It will make it more difficult to make critical errors.
- On many occasions, you will not need root permissions anyway.
- If you only allow access to normal users and not to root, it will force an attacker to guess three different things: the name of that specific user, the password of that user, and the root password as well.
- If you do need root access anyway, you can use the **su -** command from the local user environment to open a root shell. This opens one root shell only, while you will still be an ordinary user in all other parts of your current session.
- Use sudo to configure specific administration tasks for specific users only. See Chapter 6, "User and Group Management," for more information.

Switching Between Terminals in a Graphical Environment

When working in a graphical environment, it is relatively easy to open several different working environments. Just right-click the graphical desktop and select Open in Terminal. This opens several terminal windows as a subshell of the current environment. Because all of these terminals are opened as a subshell, you do not have to log in to each terminal again, and will get access as the same user account that was originally used to log in to the graphical environment (see Figure 5.2).

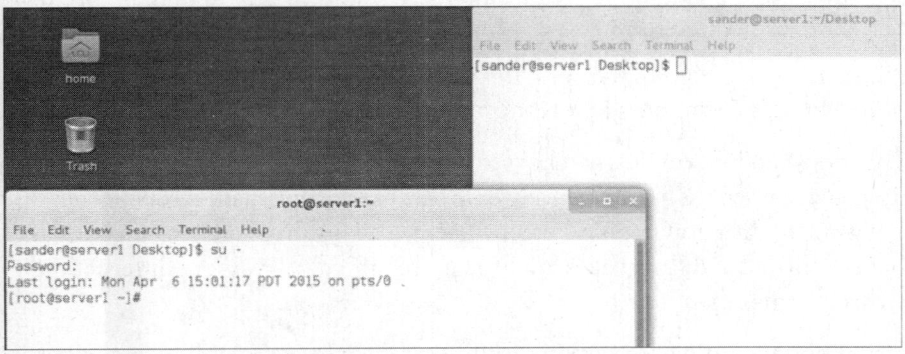

Figure 5.2 Using different terminal windows from the graphical environment.

Working from a graphical environment is convenient. As an administrator, you can open several terminal windows, and in each terminal window you can use the **su -** command to open a shell in which you can work with a different user identity. This allows you to easily test features and see the results of these tests immediately. Exercise 5.1 guides you through a common scenario where you can do this and see how it can be convenient to test things from one terminal window, while monitoring from another terminal window.

Exercise 5.1 Working from Several Terminal Windows Simultaneously

In this exercise, you learn how an administrator can benefit from working in several terminal windows simultaneously.

1. Start your computer and make sure to log in as non-root user account from the graphical log in window that is presented. You should have a local user with the name user and the password password that you can use for this purpose.
2. Right-click an empty spot on the graphical desktop, and from the drop-down menu select Open in Terminal.
3. Repeat step 2 so that you have two terminal windows that are open simultaneously.
4. From one of the terminal windows, type the command **su -** and enter the password of the root user. Then, type **tail -f /var/log/secure**. This opens a trace on the file /var/log/secure, where you can monitor security events in real time.
5. From the other terminal windows, type **su -**. When asked for a password, you normally enter the password for the user root. Enter a wrong password.
6. Now look at the terminal where the trace on /var/log/secure is still open. You will see that an error message has been written to this file.
7. Use the **Ctrl+C** key sequence to close the **tail -f** session on the /var/log/secure file.

Working with Multiple Terminals in a Nongraphical Environment

In the previous section, you learned how to work with multiple terminals in a graphical environment. This is relatively easy because you just have to open a new terminal window. In a nongraphical environment, you just have one terminal interface that is available and that makes it a little more difficult to work in different user shell environments.

To offer an option that makes working from several consoles from the same server possible, Linux uses the concept of a virtual terminal. This feature allows you to open six different terminal windows from the same console at the same time. To open these terminal windows, you can use the key sequences **Alt+F1** through **Alt+F6**.

TIP A convenient alternative to using the Alt+Function key sequences is offered by the **chvt** command. This command enables you to switch to a different virtual environment directly from the current environment. If you are in a graphical console right now, open a terminal and type **chvt 3**. This brings you to a login prompt on virtual terminal 3. Switch back to the graphical environment using the **chvt 1** command.

Of these virtual consoles, the first one is used as the default console. It is commonly known as the *virtual console tty1*, and it has a corresponding device file in the /dev directory that has the name /dev/tty1. The other virtual consoles also have corresponding device files, which are numbered /dev/tty1 through /dev/tty6.

When working from a graphical environment, it is also possible to open different virtual consoles. Because the combinations between the Alt key and the Function keys typically already have a meaning in the graphical environment, you need to use **Ctrl+Alt+Function key** instead. So do not use **Alt+F2** to open /dev/tty2 from a graphical environment, but use **Ctrl+Alt+F2**. To get back to the graphical console, you can use the **Alt+F1** key sequence. The **Alt+F6** and the **Ctrl+Alt+F6** key sequences are essentially the same. It just is important to use the Ctrl key as well when going from a GUI to a text environment. To go back from the text environment to the GUI environment, using the Ctrl key is optional.

NOTE A long time ago, big central computers were used to which dumb terminal devices were connected. These dumb terminal devices consisted of nothing more than a monitor and keyboard attached to it. From each of these dumb terminal devices, a console session to the operating system could be started. On a modern Linux server, no dumb terminals are attached anymore. The dumb terminals have been replaced with the virtual terminals, as described in the previous section.

Understanding Pseudo Terminal Devices

Every terminal used in a Linux environment has a device file associated with it. You've just learned that terminals that are started in a nongraphical environment are typically referred to through the devices /dev/tty1 through /dev/tty6.

For terminal windows that are started from a graphical environment, pseudo terminals are started. These pseudo terminals are referred to using numbers in the /dev/pts directory. So, the first terminal window that is started from a graphical environment shows as /dev/pts/1, the second terminal windows is /dev/pts/2, and so on. In Exercise 5.2, you learn how to work with these pseudo terminal devices and see which user is active on which pseudo terminal.

NOTE On earlier versions of Linux, pseudo terminals were seen as pty devices. These types of terminals are now deprecated and replaced with the pts terminal types, as described before.

Exercise 5.2 Working with Pseudo Terminals

In this exercise, you learn how to work with pseudo terminals. You also learn how to get more information on user activity on specific pseudo interfaces.

1. Log in to the graphical console, using a non-root user account.
2. Right-click on the desktop and select Open in terminal.
3. From the terminal window, type **w**. This will give an overview of all users that are currently logged in. Notice the column that mentions the tty the users are on, in which you see :0 that refers to the console, and pts/0 which refers to the terminal window.
4. Right-click on the desktop and select Open in terminal again. Type **su -** to become root.
5. Type **w** to display once more an overview of all users that are currently logged in. Notice that the root terminal shows as owned by the nonroot user as well.

At this point, you know how to work with the console, terminals, virtual terminals, and pseudo terminals. In the section "Using SSH and Related Utilities" later in this chapter, you use SSH to open terminal sessions to your server. These sessions show as pseudo terminals as well.

Booting, Rebooting, and Shutting Down Systems

As an administrator of a Linux server, you occasionally have to reboot the Linux server. Rebooting a server is not often a requirement, but it can make your work a lot easier because it will make sure that all processes and tasks that were running on your server have re-read their configurations and initialized properly.

TIP Rebooting a Linux server is an important task on the RHCSA as well as on the RHCE exam. Everything you have configured should still be working after the server has rebooted. So, make sure that you reboot at least once during the exam, but also after making critical modifications to the server configuration. If your server cannot reboot anymore after applying critical modifications to your server's configuration, at least you know where to look to fix the issues.

For an administrator who really knows Linux very thoroughly, rebooting a server is seldom necessary. Experienced administrators can often trigger the right parameter to force a process to reread its configurations. There are some cases, though, that even experienced Linux administrators have to reboot:

Key Topic

- To recover from serious problems such as server hangs and kernel panics
- To apply kernel updates
- To apply changes to kernel modules that are used and because of that cannot be reloaded easily

When a server is rebooted, all processes that are running need to shut down properly. If the server is just stopped by pulling the power plug, much data will typically be lost. That is because processes that have written data do not typically write that data directly to disk, but instead store it in memory buffers from where it is committed to disk when it is convenient for the operating system.

To issue a proper reboot, the systemd process has to be alerted. The systemd process is the first process that was started when the server was started, and it is responsible for managing all other processes, directly or indirectly. As a result, on system reboots or halts, the systemd process needs to make sure that all these processes are stopped. To tell the systemd process this has to happen, a few commands can be used:

- **systemctl reboot** or **reboot**
- **systemctl halt** or **halt**
- **systemctl poweroff** or **poweroff**

When stopping a machine, you can use the **systemctl halt** or the **systemctl poweroff** commands. The difference between these two commands is that the **systemctl poweroff** command talks to power management on the machine to shut off power on the machine. This often does not happen when using **systemctl halt**.

NOTE Using the methods that have just been described will normally reboot or stop your machine. In some cases, these commands might not work. If that is the case, there is an emergency reset option as well. Using this option may prove useful if the machine is not physically accessible. To force a machine to reset, you can type **echo b > /proc/sysrq-trigger**. This command immediately resets the machine without saving anything. Notice that this command should be used only if there are no other options!

Using SSH and Related Utilities

In the previous sections in this chapter, you learned how to access a terminal if you have direct access to the server console. Many administrators work with servers that are not physically accessible. To manage these servers, Secure Shell (SSH) is normally used. In this section, you learn how to work with SSH.

On modern Linux distributions, Secure Shell is the common method to gain access to other machines over the network. In SSH, cryptography is used to ensure that you can be sure that you are connecting to the intended server. Also, traffic is encrypted while transmitted.

Accessing Remote Systems Using SSH

To access a server using SSH, two components are needed. On the remote server that you want to access, the **sshd** service must be running and offering services at port 22, and it should not be blocked by the firewall. If the SSH port is open, you can access it using the **ssh** command from the command line. The **ssh** command by default tries to reach the ssh process on the server port 22. If you have configured the sshd process to offer its services on a different port, use **ssh -p** followed by the port number you want to connect to.

The **ssh** command is available on all Linux distributions, and on Apple Macintosh computers as well, where it can be launched from an Apple Macintosh terminal.

The **ssh** command is not a native part of the Windows operating system. If you want to access Linux servers through SSH from a Windows computer, you need to install an SSH client like PuTTY on Windows. From PuTTY, different types of remote sessions can be established with Linux machines. Alternative SSH clients for Windows are available as well, such as MobaXterm, Kitty, mRemoteNG, Bitvise, and also Xshell.

Accessing another Linux machine from a Linux terminal is relatively easy. Just type **ssh** followed by the name of the other Linux machine. After connecting, you will be prompted for a password if a default configuration is used.

When remotely connecting to a Linux server, the SSH client tries to do that as the user account you are currently logged in with on the local machine. If you want to connect using a different user account, you can specify the name of this user on the command line, in the user@server format. If, for instance, you want to establish an SSH session as user root to a remote server, type **ssh root@remoteserver**. An alternative way of specifying the user account is by using the option **-l username**. So, **ssh remoteserver -l root** will also try to establish a root session to the remote server. In Exercise 5.3, you learn how to log in using SSH.

Exercise 5.3 Using SSH to Log In to a Remote Server

In this exercise, you log in to a remote server using SSH. This exercise assumes that a remote server is available and reachable. In this exercise, server1 is used as the local server, and server2 is the remote server on which the SSH process should be up and running. If you cannot access a remote server to perform the steps in the exercise, you might alternatively replace server2 with localhost. It is obvious that by doing so you will not log in to a remote server, but you still use the **ssh** command to connect to an sshd process.

1. Open a root shell on server2. Type **systemctl status sshd**. This should show you that the sshd process is currently up and running.
2. To avoid any firewall-related problems, type **systemctl stop firewalld**. (In Chapter 22, "Configuring a Firewall," you learn how to configure the firewall to allow for SSH traffic).
3. Type **ip a | grep 'inet '**. (Notice the space between **inet** and the closing quote.) Notice the IPv4 address your server is currently using. In the rest of this exercise, it is assumed that server2 is using IP address 192.168.122.220. Replace that address with the address that you have found here.
4. Open a shell as a nonprivileged user on server1.
5. On server1, type **ssh 192.168.122.220 -l root**. This connects to the sshd process on server2 and opens a root shell.
6. Before being prompted for a password, you see a message indicating that the authenticity of host 192.168.122.220 cannot be established (see Listing 5.1). This message is shown because the host you are connecting to is not yet known on your current host, which might involve a security risk. Type **yes** to continue.
7. When prompted, enter the root password. After entering it, you now are logged in to server2.
8. Type **w**. Notice that the SSH session you have just opened shows as just another pseudo terminal session.
9. Type **exit** to close the SSH session.

Listing 5.1 When Logging In to a Remote Server for the First Time, You See a Security Message

```
[root@server1 ~]# ssh 192.168.4.220 -l root
The authenticity of host '192.168.4.220 (<no hostip for proxy
command>)' can't be established.
ECDSA key fingerprint is 35:64:36:f8:ac:4f:8a:94:aa:6e:4b:85:ed:76:0a:
eb.
Are you sure you want to continue connecting (yes/no)?
```

NOTE On some occasions, using **ssh** to get access to a server will be slow. If you want to know why, use the **-v** option with the **ssh** command. This will start SSH in verbose mode and show all the individual components that are contacted. By doing so, you might get an indication why your server is being slow.

You have noticed that while using SSH to connect to the remote server a security message was displayed. This is because the remote server has never been contacted before and therefore there is no way to verify the identity of the remote server. After connecting to the remote server, a public key fingerprint is stored in the file ~/.ssh/known_hosts.

The next time you connect to the same server, this fingerprint is checked with the encryption key that was sent over by the remote server to initialize contact. If the fingerprint matches, you will not see this message anymore.

In some cases, the remote host key fingerprint does not match the key fingerprint that is stored locally. That is a potentially dangerous situation. Instead of being connected to the intended server, you might be connected to the server of an evildoer. It does, however, also happen if you are connecting to an IP address that you have been connected to before, but this IP address is now in use by a different server. In that case, you just have to remove the key fingerprint from the ~/.ssh/known_hosts file on the client computer.

Using Graphical Applications in an SSH Environment

From an SSH session, by default you cannot start graphical applications. That is because of security; a remote host cannot draw screens on your computer without specific permission to do that. There are two requirements for starting graphical applications through an SSH connection:

- An X server must be running on the client computer. The X server is the software component that creates the graphical screens.
- The remote host must be allowed to display screens on the local computer.

The easiest way to allow the remote host to draw graphical screens on your computer is by adding the **-X** option to the **ssh** command. So, use **ssh -X linda@server2** if you want to connect as linda to server2, and also be able to start graphical applications.

As you have noticed, the **ssh** command gives you a few options. Table 5.2 shows some of the most common options available.

Key Topic

Table 5.2 Common **ssh** Options

Option	Use
-v	Verbose, shows in detail what is happening while establishing the connection
-X	Enables support for graphical applications
-p <PORT>	Used to connect to an SSH service that is not listening on the default port 22

As an administrator, you can also create a systemwide configuration that allows you to use "X forwarding," which is starting graphical applications through an SSH session. As root, open the configuration file **/etc/ssh/ssh_config** and make sure it includes the following line:

```
ForwardX11 yes
```

The next time you use the **ssh** command, X forwarding will be available by default.

NOTE In this lesson, you learned about SSH basics. In Chapter 39, "Configuring SSH," you learn in more detail about the advanced options that can be used when working with SSH.

Securely Transferring Files Between Systems

If a host is running the sshd service, that service can also be used to securely transfer files between systems. To do that, you can use the **scp** command. This command is very similar to the **cp** command, which is used to copy local files, but it does include an option that allows it to work with remote hosts. You can use **scp** to copy files and subdirectories to remote hosts, and subdirectories as well. To copy, for instance, the /etc/hosts file to the /tmp directory on server2 using your current user account, use the following command:

```
scp /etc/hosts server2:/tmp
```

If you want to connect to server2 as user root to copy the /etc/passwd file to your home directory, you use the following command:

```
scp root@server2:/etc/passwd ~
```

You can also use **scp** to copy an entire subdirectory structure. To do so, use the **-r** command, as in the following command:

```
scp -r server2:/etc/ /tmp
```

Notice that the **scp** command can be configured to connect to a non-default SSH port also. It is a bit confusing, but to do this with the **scp** command, you need the **-P** option followed by the port number you want to connect to. Notice that **ssh** uses **-p** (lowercase) to specify the port it needs to connect to; the **scp** command uses an uppercase **-P**.

> **TIP** As an alternative to using **scp** for copying files between servers, you might be interested in the **rsync** command. The basic use of rsync is similar to the use of **scp**, and it also uses the sshd service to securely copy files. Rsync, however, does offer advanced options that enable you to synchronize files and directories based on a delta sync. That means that only differences are synchronized, which makes this a very efficient solution for keeping files and directories the same between hosts.

Configuring Key-Based Authentication for SSH

If SSH is used on the Internet, it might not be a good idea to allow password logins. To make SSH a bit more secure, it will always first try whether login using public/private keys is possible. Only if that is not possible is a password login used. The only thing you need to do to enable key-based login is to create a key pair.

When using public/private key-based authentication, the user who wants to connect to a server generates a public/private key pair. The private key needs to be kept private and will never be distributed. The public key is stored in the home directory of the target user on the SSH server.

When authenticating using key pairs, the user generates a hash derived from the private key. This hash is sent to the server, and if on the server it proves to match the public key that is stored on the server, the user is authenticated.

Using Passphrases or Not?

When creating a public/private key pair, you are prompted for a passphrase. If you want maximal security, you should enter a passphrase. You are prompted for that passphrase each time that you are using the private key to authenticate to a remote host. That is very secure, but it is not very convenient. To create a configuration that allows for maximal convenience, you can just press the **Enter** key twice to confirm that you do not want to set a passphrase. This is a typical configuration that is used for authentication between servers in a trusted environment where no outside access is possible anyway. In Chapter 39, you learn how to create SSH keys using passphrases.

To create a key pair, use the **ssh-keygen** command. The **ssh-copy-id** command is next used to copy the public key over to the target server. In Exercise 5.4, you learn how to do this.

Exercise 5.4 Connecting to a Remote Server with Public/Private Keys

In this exercise, you create a public/private key pair to log in to the server2 host. If no remote host is available, you can use localhost as an alternative to verify the procedure.

1. On server1, open a root shell.
2. Type **ssh-keygen**. When asked whether you want to use a passphrase, press **Enter** to use the passphrase-less setup.
3. When asked for the filename in which to store the (private) key, accept the default filename ~/.ssh/id_rsa.
4. When asked to enter a passphrase, press **Enter** twice.
5. The private key will now be written to the ~/.ssh/id_rsa file and the public key is written to the ~/.ssh/id_rsa.pub file.
6. Use **ssh-copy-id server2** to copy the public key you have just created over to server2. You are then asked for the password on the remote server one last time.
7. After copying the public key, verify that it can actually be used for authentication. To do this, type **ssh server2**. You should now authenticate without having to enter the password for the remote user account.

After copying over the public key to the remote host, it will be written to the ~/.ssh/authorized_keys file on that host. Notice that if multiple users are using keys to log in with that specific account, the authorized_keys file may contain a lot of public keys. Make sure never to overwrite it because that will wipe all keys that are used by other users as well!

Using the screen Command

You do not have to know about it for either RHCSA or RHCE, but the screen command is a useful command that allows you to open multiple terminal sessions, even if you are not in a graphical session. It does not just allow you to run multiple terminals but also allows you to share a session with other users, or to attach and detach to remote terminal sessions. Before you can use screen, you need to install it. To do this, use the **yum install -y screen** command. Then, type **screen** to open a screen session. From the screen session, you can start any command you like.

The **screen** command is particularly useful when used from an SSH session. You can start a task that takes a long time from a screen session, detach from it, and attach to it later. The command continues running, even if you are going home and shut down your computer. The next day, you can easily attach to the screen session again to complete the task. To do this, just follow a simple procedure:

1. Open an SSH session.
2. From the SSH session, type screen to open a screen session.
3. Start whichever task you want to start and keep it running.
4. Use the **Ctrl+a, d** key sequence to detach from the screen session and log out from the SSH session.
5. When you are ready to reconnect, start the SSH session again. It is essential that you are using the same user account that you used before.
6. Attach to the screen session again using **screen -r**. You can now conveniently finish the work that you have started from the screen session before.

While working with screen, you are working in a specific application. From within this application you can issue specific commands. To use these specific screen commands, start by typing **Ctrl+a, ?**. This shows a list of all commands that are available. Every screen command is started with the **Ctrl+a** key sequence. An important command to remember is **Ctrl+a, /**, which will close the screen session. Make sure to remove screen sessions that you do not need anymore, otherwise they will stay active until the next time you reboot your server!

If while trying to attach to a screen session you get a message that multiple screen sessions are currently running, you need to be more specific. To find out which screen sessions currently are running, use the **screen -ls** command. This command shows you all screen sessions that are currently running. In Listing 5.2, you can see how multiple screen sessions are detached from, and how the **screen -r** command gives a list of all currently available screen sessions, from which you can select the screen session you want to connect to by adding the number of the screen session to the **screen -r** command.

Listing 5.2 Selecting the Right screen Session

```
[sander@lab ~]$ screen
[detached from 30500.pts-0.lab]
[sander@lab ~]$ screen
[detached from 30532.pts-0.lab]
[sander@lab ~]$ screen -r
There are several suitable screens on:
        30532.pts-0.lab     (Detached)
        30500.pts-0.lab     (Detached)
Type "screen [-d] -r [pid.]tty.host" to resume one of them.
[sander@lab ~]$ screen -r 30500
```

You can also use screen to work together with other users in the same session. To do this, follow these steps:

1. Make sure that both users are using SSH to connect to the system where you want to work on together. Both users must use the same user account when using SSH to connect.
2. One user needs to start a screen session, using the **screen** command.
3. The second user can just connect to the screen session, using **screen -x**.

Summary

In this chapter, you learned how to connect to Red Hat Enterprise Linux 7. You learned the difference between consoles, terminals, and shells, and you learned how to set up terminal sessions locally as well as remotely. You also learned how to use SSH to connect to a remote server, and how to securely copy files between servers. At the end of this chapter you learned how you can use the screen utility to start jobs in a session you can detach from and then reattach to it later.

Exam Preparation Tasks

Review All Key Topics

Review the most important topics in the chapter, noted with the Key Topic icon in the outer margin of the page. Table 5.3 lists a reference of these key topics and the page numbers on which each is found.

Table 5.3 Key Topics for Chapter 5

Key Topic Element	Description	Page
Paragraph	Definition of the words console and terminal	106
List	Situations that typically require a server reboot	111
Table 5.2	Common SSH options	115

Define Key Terms

Define the following key terms from this chapter and check your answers in the glossary:

console, terminal, tty, login shell, subshell, reboot, systemd, key-based login, public key, private key

Review Questions

1. What is the console?
2. On a server that currently has an operational graphical interface, you are on a text-based login prompt. Which key sequence do you use to switch back to the graphical interface?
3. What command(s) shows all users that currently have a terminal session open to a Linux server?
4. On a server where no GUI is operational, what would you expect to be the device name that is used by the first SSH session that is opened to that server?
5. Which command would you use to get detailed information on what SSH is doing while logging in?
6. How do you initiate an SSH session with support for graphical applications?
7. What is the name of the configuration file that needs to be edited to modify SSH client settings?

8. How do you copy over the /etc/hosts file to the directory /tmp on server2 using the username lisa?
9. What is the name of the file in which public keys are stored for remote users that want to log in to this machine using key-based authentication?
10. Which command enables you to generate an ssh public/private key pair?

End-of-Chapter Labs

The end-of-chapter labs help you practice what you learned throughout the chapter. The first lab is about connecting to RHEL 7 locally, and the second lab is about using SSH to log in to a remote server.

Lab 5.1

1. Log in to the local console on server1. Make sure that server1 does *not* show a graphical interface anymore, but just a text-based login prompt. Log in from that environment and activate tty6. From tty6, switch back on the graphical interface and use the correct key sequence to go to the graphical interface.
2. Set up SSH based authentication. From server2, use SSH to connect to server1. Make sure that graphical applications are supported through the SSH session. Also set up key-based authentication so that no password has to be entered while connecting to the remote server.

The following topics are covered in this chapter:

- Creating and Managing User Accounts
- Creating and Managing Group Accounts
- Logging in Through an External Authentication Server

The following RHCSA exam objectives are covered in this chapter:

- Create, delete, and modify local user accounts
- Change passwords and adjust password aging for local user accounts
- Create, delete, and modify local groups and group memberships
- Configure a system to use an existing authentication service for user and group information

CHAPTER 6

User and Group Management

On a Linux system, a wide variety of processes are normally being used. These processes need access to specific resources on the Linux system. To determine how these resources can be accessed, a difference is made between processes that run in kernel mode and processes that run without full permissions to the operating system. In the latter case user accounts are needed. This chapter explains how to set up user and group accounts.

Apart from setting up user and group accounts, you also learn how to connect to an external authentication service, such as LDAP. Make sure not to miss this part, it might be new to you!

"Do I Know This Already?" Quiz

The "Do I Know This Already?" quiz allows you to assess whether you should read this entire chapter thoroughly or jump to the "Exam Preparation Tasks" section. If you are in doubt about your answers to these questions or your own assessment of your knowledge of the topics, read the entire chapter. Table 6-1 lists the major headings in this chapter and their corresponding "Do I Know This Already?" quiz questions. You can find the answers in Appendix A, "Answers to the 'Do I Know This Already?' Quizzes and 'Review Questions.'"

Table 6-1 "Do I Know This Already?" Section-to-Question Mapping

Foundation Topics Section	Questions
Creating and Managing User Accounts	1–6
Creating and Managing Group Accounts	7
Logging In Through an External Authentication Server	8–10

1. Which statement about privileged users (root) is true?
   a. A privileged user is a user who has access to a Linux system.
   b. A privileged user with no access permissions can do nothing at all.
   c. Privileged users are not restricted in any way.
   d. On every server, at least one privileged user must be manually created while installing the server.

2. On a default installation of a RHEL 7 server, which group does the user typically need to be a member of to be able to use sudo to run all administration commands?
   a. admin
   b. root
   c. sys
   d. wheel

3. There are different ways that users can run tasks with root permissions. Which of the following is not one of them?
   a. sudo
   b. runas
   c. su
   d. PolicyKit

4. Which of the following is used to store the hash of the user's encrypted password?
   a. /etc/passwd
   b. /etc/shadow
   c. /etc/users
   d. /etc/secure

5. Which configuration file should you change to set the default location for all new user home directories?
   a. /etc/login.defaults
   b. /etc/login.defs
   c. /etc/default/useradd
   d. /etc/default/login.defs

6. Which command enables you to get information about password properties such as password expiry?

   a. **chage -l**

   b. **usermod --show**

   c. **passwd -l**

   d. **chage --show**

7. Which of the following files is not processed when a user starts a login shell?

   a. /etc/profile

   b. /etc/.profile

   c. ~/.bashrc

   d. ~/.bash_profile

8. Which of the following is not a property of a typical LDAP server?

   a. It is hierarchical.

   b. It is replicated.

   c. It is secure by default.

   d. It is distributed.

9. Which of the following is not a valid tool in RHEL7 to configure LDAP authentication?

   a. system-config-authentication

   b. authconfig

   c. authconfig-tui

   d. authconfig-gtk

10. When setting up authentication against an LDAP server, you need to specify different items. Which of the following is *not* part of them?

   a. Base DN

   b. LDAP URI

   c. TLS certificate

   d. Administrator name

Foundation Topics

Different User Types

In this chapter, you learn how to create and manage user accounts. Before diving into the details of user management, you learn how users are used in a Linux environment.

Users on Linux

Key Topic

On Linux, there are two ways to look at system security. There are privileged users, and there are unprivileged users. The default privileged user is root. This user account has full access to everything on a Linux server and is allowed to work in system space without restrictions. The root user account is meant to perform system administration tasks and should be used for that only. For all other tasks, an unprivileged user account should be used.

To get information about a user account, you can use the **id** command. When using this command from the command line, you can see details about the current user. You can also use it on other user accounts to get details about those accounts. Listing 6.1 shows an example of the output of the command.

Listing 6.1 Getting More Information About Users with **id**

```
[root@localhost ~]# id linda
uid=1001(linda) gid=1001(linda) groups=1001(linda)
```

Working as Root

On all Linux systems, by default there is the user root, also known as the superuser. This account is used for managing Linux. Root, for instance, can create other user accounts on the system. For some tasks, root privileges are required. Some examples are installing software, managing users, and creating partitions on disk devices. Generically speaking, all tasks that involve direct access to devices need root permissions.

Because the root account is so useful for managing a Linux environment, some people make a habit of logging in as root directly. That is not recommended, especially not when you are logging in to a graphical environment. When you log in as root in a graphical environment, all tasks that are executed are running as root as well, and that involves an unnecessary security risk. Therefore, you should instead use one of the following alternative methods. Table 6.1 provides an overview of these methods.

Table 6.2 Methods to Run Tasks with Elevated Permissions

Key Topic

su	Opens a subshell as a different user, with the advantage that only in the subshell commands are executed as root
sudo	Allows you to set up an environment where specific tasks are executed with administrative privileges
PolicyKit	Allows you to set up graphical utilities to run with administrative privileges

Using su

The **su** command allows users to open a terminal window, and from that terminal start a sub shell in which the user has another identity. To perform administrative tasks, for instance, you can log in with a normal user account and type **su** to open a root shell. This brings the benefit that only in the root shell root privileges are used.

If just the command **su** is typed, the username root is implied. But su can be used to run tasks as another user as well. Type **su linda** to open a subshell as the user linda, for example. When using **su** as an ordinary user, you are prompted for a password and after entering that you have acquired the credentials of the target user:

```
[linda@localhost ~]$ su
Password:
[root@localhost linda]#
```

When using **su**, a sub shell is started. This is an environment where you are able to work as the target user account, but environment settings for that user account have not been set. If you need complete access to the entire environment of the target user account, you can use **su -** to start a login shell. If you start a login shell, all scripts that make up the user environment are processed, which makes you work in an environment that is exactly the same as when logging in as that user.

TIP Using **su -** is better than using **su**. When the **-** is used, a login shell is started, without the **-**, some variables may not be set correctly. So, you are better off using **su -** immediately.

sudo

Instead of using the root user account, unprivileged users can be configured for using administrator permissions on specific tasks by using sudo. When sudo is configured, ordinary users have sudo privileges and to use these privileges, they will start the command using **sudo**. So, instead of using commands like **useradd** as the root user, you use an ordinary user account and type **sudo useradd**. This is definitely more secure because you will only be able to act as if you have administrator permissions while running this specific command.

When creating Linux users during the installation process, you can select to grant administrator permissions to that specific user. If you select to do so, the user will be able to use all administrator commands using sudo. It is also possible to set up sudo privileges after installation. To do that in a very easy way, you have to accomplish a simple two-step procedure:

1. Make the administrative user account member of the group wheel by using **usermod -aG wheel user**.
2. Type **visudo** and make sure the line %wheel ALL=(ALL) ALL is included.

PolicyKit

Most administration programs with a graphical user interface use PolicyKit to authenticate as the root user. If a normal user who is not a member of the group wheel accesses such an application, he will be prompted for authentication. If a user who is a member of the group wheel opens a PolicyKit application, he will have to enter his own password. For the RHCSA exam, you do not have to know PolicyKit. If you are interested, you can take a look at the man pages of the **pkexec** and **polkit** commands for more details.

Exercise 6.1 Switching User Accounts

1. Log in to your system as a non-privileged user and open a terminal.
2. Type **whoami** to see which user account you are currently using. Type **id** as well, and notice that you get more detail about your current credentials when using **id**.
3. Type **su**. When prompted for a password, enter the root password. Type **id** again. You see that you are currently root.
4. Type **visudo** and make sure that the line %wheel ALL=(ALL) ALL is included.

5. Type **useradd -G wheel lisa** to create a user lisa who is a member of the group wheel.
6. Type **id lisa** to verify that she has been added to the group wheel.
7. Set the password for lisa by typing **passwd lisa**. Enter the password **password** twice.
8. Log out and log in as lisa.
9. Type **sudo useradd lori**. Enter the password when asked. You notice that user lori will be created.

Managing User Accounts

Now that you know how to perform tasks as administrative or nonadministrative user, it is time to learn how to manage user accounts on Linux. In this section, you learn what is involved.

System and Normal Accounts

On a typical Linux environment, two kinds of user accounts exist. There are user accounts for the people who need to work on a server and who need limited access to the resources on that server. These user accounts typically have a password that is used for authenticating the user to the system. There are also system accounts that are used by the services the server is offering. Both user accounts share common properties, which are kept in the files /etc/passwd and /etc/shadow. Listing 6.2 shows the contents of the /etc/passwd file.

Listing 6.2 Partial Contents of the /etc/passwd user Configuration File

```
ntp:x:38:38::/etc/ntp:/sbin/nologin
chrony:x:994:993::/var/lib/chrony:/sbin/nologin
abrt:x:173:173::/etc/abrt:/sbin/nologin
pulse:x:171:171:PulseAudio System Daemon:/var/run/pulse:/sbin/nologin
gdm:x:42:42::/var/lib/gdm:/sbin/nologin
gnome-initial-setup:x:993:991::/run/gnome-initial-setup/:/sbin/nologin
postfix:x:89:89::/var/spool/postfix:/sbin/nologin
sshd:x:74:74:Privilege-separated SSH:/var/empty/sshd:/sbin/nologin
tcpdump:x:72:72::/:/sbin/nologin
user:x:1000:1000:user:/home/user:/bin/bash
```

> **NOTE** On many Linux servers, there are no user accounts that are used by people. Many Linux servers are installed to run a specific service, and if people interact with that service, they will authenticate within the service.

As you can see, to define a user account different fields are used in /etc/passwd. The fields are separated from each other by a colon. Below is a summary of these fields, followed by a short description of their purpose.

Key Topic

- **Username:** This is a unique name for the user. User names are important to match a user to his password, which is stored separately in /etc/shadow (see next). On Linux, there can be no spaces in the user name.
- **Password:** In the old days, the second field of /etc/passwd was used to store the hashes password of the user. Because the /etc/passwd file is readable by all users, this poses a security threat, and for that reason on current Linux systems the hashes passwords are stored in /etc/shadow (discussed in the next section).
- **UID:** Each user has a unique user ID (UID). This is a numeric ID. It is the UID that really determines what a user can do. When permissions are set for a user, the UID is stored in the file metadata (and not the user name). UID 0 is reserved for root, the unrestricted user account. The lower UIDs (typically up to 999) are used for system accounts, and the higher UIDs (from 1000 on by default), are reserved for people that need to connect directory to the server. The range of UIDs that are used to create regular user accounts is set in /etc/login.defs.
- **GID:** On Linux, each user is a member of at least one group. This group is referred to as the *primary group*, and this group plays a central role in permissions management, as discussed later in this chapter.
- **Comment field:** The Comment field, as you can guess, is used to add comments for user accounts. This field is optional, but it can be used to describe what a user account is created for. Some utilities, such as the obsolete finger utility, can be used to get information from this field. The field is also referred to as the GECOS field, which stands for General Electric Comprehensive Operating System and had a specific purpose for identifying jobs in the early 1970s when General Electric was still an important manufacturer of servers.
- **Directory:** This is the initial directory where the user is placed after logging in, also referred to as the *home directory*. If the user account is used by a person, this is where the person would store his personal files and programs. For a system user account, this is the environment where the service can store files it needs while operating.

- **Shell:** This is the program that is started after the user has successfully connected to a server. For most users this will be /bin/bash, the default Linux shell. For system user accounts, it will typically be a shell like /sbin/nologin. The **/sbin/nologin** command is a specific command that silently denies access to users (to ensure that if by accident an intruder logs in to the server he cannot get any shell access). You can create a file with the name /etc/nologin.txt that contains a message that will be displayed when a user who has /sbin/nologin as its shell tries to log in.

A part of the user properties is stored in /etc/passwd, which was just discussed. Another part of the configuration of user properties is in /etc/shadow. The settings in this file are used to define the validity of the password. Typical for /etc/shadow is that no one except the superuser root and processes running with root permissions, such as the authentication mechanisms on the server, have permissions to access it, which makes sense as it contains all the information that is required for connecting to a system. Listing 6.3 shows an example of /etc/shadow contents.

Listing 6.3 Sample Content from /etc/shadow

```
[root@localhost ~]# tail -n 10 /etc/shadow
ntp:!!:16420::::::
chrony:!!:16420::::::
abrt:!!:16420::::::
pulse:!!:16420::::::
gdm:!!:16420::::::
gnome-initial-setup:!!:16420::::::
postfix:!!:16420::::::
sshd:!!:16420::::::
tcpdump:!!:16420::::::
user:$6$3VZbGx1djo6FfyZo$/Trg7Q.3foIsIFYxBm6UnHuxxBrxQxHDnDuZxgS.We/
MAuHn8HboBZzpaMD8gfm.fmlB/ML9LnuaT7CbwVXx31:16420:0:99999:7:::
```

The following fields are defined in /etc/shadow:

- **Login name:** Notice that /etc/shadow does not contain any UIDs, but usernames only. This opens a possibility for multiple users using the same UID but different passwords (which, by the way, is not really recommended).

Key Topic

- **Encrypted password:** This field contains all that is needed to store the password in a secure way.

- **Days since Jan 1, 1970, that the password was last changed:** Many things on Linux refer to this date, which on Linux is considered the beginning of days. It is also referred to as *epoch*.
- **Days before password may be changed:** This allows system administrators to use a more strict password policy, where it is not possible to change back to the original password immediately that a password has been changed. Typically this field is set to the value 0.
- **Days after which password must be changed:** This field contains the maximal validity period of passwords. Notice that by default it is set to 99,999 (about 273 years).
- **Days before password is to expire that user is warned:** This field is used to warn a user when a forced password change is upcoming. Notice that the default is set to 7 (even if the password validity is set to 99,999 days!).
- **Days after password expires that account is disabled:** Use this field to enforce a password change. After password expiry, users can log in no longer.
- **Days since Jan 1, 1970, that account is disabled:** An administrator can set this field to disable an account. This is typically a better approach than removing an account, as all associated properties and files of the account will be kept, but it can be used no longer to authenticate on your server.
- **A reserved field, which was once added "for future use":** That was a long time ago; it will probably never be used.

Most of the password properties can be managed with the **passwd** or **chage** command, which are discussed later in this chapter.

Creating Users

There are many solutions for creating users on a Linux server. To start, you can edit the contents of the /etc/passwd and /etc/shadow files directly (with the risk of making an error that could make logging in impossible to anyone; so better just do not). There is also useradd. useradd is the utility that you should use for creating users. To remove users, you can use the **userdel** command. Use **userdel -r** to remove a user, including the complete user environment.

Modifying the Configuration Files

To add user accounts, it suffices that one line is added to /etc/passwd and another line is added to /etc/shadow, in which the user account and all of its properties are defined. It is not recommended, though. By making an error, you might mess up the consistency of the file and make logging in completely impossible to anyone. Also, you might encounter locking problems if one administrator is trying to modify the file contents directly while another administrator wants to write a modification with some tool.

If you insist on modifying the configuration files directly, you should use **vipw**. This command opens an editor interface on your configuration files, and more important, it sets the appropriate locks on the configuration files to prevent corruption. It does *not* check syntax, however, so make sure that you know what you are doing because even by making a typo you might still severely mess up your server. If you want to use this tool to modify the /etc/shadow file, use **vipw -s**. To edit the contents of the /etc/group file where groups are defined, a similar command with the name **vigr** exists.

NOTE It is nice to know that vipw and vigr exist, but it is better not to use these utilities or anything else that opens the user and group configuration files directly. Instead, use tools like useradd and groupmod.

Using useradd

The useradd utility is probably the most common tool on Linux for managing users. It allows you to add a user account from the command line by using many of its parameters. Use, for instance, the command **useradd -m -u 1201 -G sales,ops linda** to create a user linda who is a member of the groups sales and ops with UID 1201 and add a home directory to the user account as well.

Home Directories

All normal users will have a home directory. For people, the home directory is the directory where personal files can be stored. For system accounts, the home directory often contains the working environment for the service account.

As an administrator, you normally will not change home directory-related settings for system accounts because they are created automatically from the RPM postinstallation scripts when installing the related software packages. If you have people who need a user account, you probably do want to manage home directory contents a bit.

If when creating user accounts you tell your server to add a home directory as well (for instance, by using **useradd -m**), the content of the "skeleton" directory is copied to the user home directory. The skeleton directory is /etc/skel, and it contains files that are copied to the user home directory at the moment this directory is created. These files will also get the appropriate permissions to ensure that the new user can use and access them.

By default, the skeleton directory contains mostly configuration files that determine how the user environment is set up. If in your environment specific files need to be present in the home directories of all users, you take care of that by adding the files to the skeleton directory.

Managing User Properties

For changing user properties, the same rules apply as for creating user accounts. You can either work directly in the configuration files using **vipw** or you can use command-line tools.

The ultimate command-line utility for modifying user properties is usermod. It can be used to set all properties of users as stored in /etc/passwd and /etc/shadow, plus some additional tasks, such as managing group membership. There is just one task it does not do well: setting passwords. Although usermod has an option **-p** that tells you to "use encrypted password for the new password," it expects you to do the password encryption before adding the user account. That does not make it particularly useful. If as root you want to change the user password, you'd better use the **passwd** command.

Configuration Files for User Management Defaults

When working with tools as useradd, some default values are assumed. These default values are set in two configuration files: /etc/login.defs and /etc/default/useradd. Listing 6.4 shows the contents of /etc/default/useradd.

Listing 6.4 Useradd Defaults in /etc/default/useradd

```
[root@localhost skel]# cat /etc/default/useradd
# useradd defaults file
GROUP=100
HOME=/home
INACTIVE=-1
EXPIRE=
SHELL=/bin/bash
SKEL=/etc/skel
CREATE_MAIL_SPOOL=yes
```

As shown in Listing 6.4, the /etc/default/useradd file contains some default values that are applied when using useradd.

In the file /etc/login.defs, different login-related variables are set. This file is used by different commands, and it relates to setting up the appropriate environment for new users. Here is a list of some of the most significant properties that can be set from /etc/login.defs:

Key Topic

- **MOTD_FILE:** Defines the file that is used as "message of the day" file. In this file, you can include messages to be displayed after the user has successfully logged in to the server.
- **ENV_PATH:** Defines the $PATH variable, a list of directories that should be searched for executable files after logging in.
- **PASS_MAX_DAYS, PASS_MIN_DAYS**, and **PASS_WARN_AGE:** Define the default password expiration properties when creating new users.
- **UID_MIN:** The first UID to use when creating new users.
- **CREATE_HOME:** Indicates whether or not to create a home directory for new users.
- **USERGROUPS_ENAB:** Set to yes to create a private group for all new users. That means that a new user has a group with the same name as the user as its default group. If set to no, all users are made a member of the group users.

Managing Password Properties

You learned about the password properties that can be set in /etc/shadow. You can use two commands to change these properties for users: **chage** and **passwd**. The commands are rather straightforward. For instance, the command **passwd -n 30 -w 3 -x 90 linda** sets the password for user linda to a minimal usage period of 30 days and an expiry after 90 days, where a warning is generated 3 days before expiry.

Many of the tasks that can be accomplished with **passwd** can be done with **chage** also. For instance, use **chage -E 2015-12-31 bob** to have the account for user bob expire on December 31, 2015. To see current password management settings, use **chage –l** (see Listing 6.5).

Listing 6.5 Showing Password Expiry Information with **chage -l**

```
linux:~ # chage -l linda
Last password change                                    : Apr 11, 2015
Password expires                                        : Jul 10, 2015
Password inactive                                       : never
Account expires                                         : never
Minimum number of days between password change          : 30
Maximum number of days between password change          : 90
Number of days of warning before password expir         : 3
```

Creating a User Environment

When a user logs in, an environment is created. The environment consists of some variables that determine how the user environment is used. One such variable, for instance, is $PATH, which defines a list of directories that should be searched when a user types a command.

To construct the user environment, a few files play a role:

Key Topic

- **/etc/profile:** Used for default settings for all users when starting a login shell
- **/etc/bashrc:** Used to define defaults for all users when starting a subshell
- **~/.profile:** Specific settings for one user applied when starting a login shell
- **~/.bashrc:** Specific settings for one user applied when starting a subshell

When logging in, the files are read in this order, and variables and other settings that are defined in these files are applied. If a variable or setting occurs in more than one file, the last one wins.

Exercise 6.2 Creating User Accounts

In this exercise, you apply common solutions to create user accounts.

1. Type **vim /etc/login.defs** to open the configuration file /etc/login.defs and change a few parameters before you start creating logging. Look for the parameter **CREATE_HOME** and make sure it is set to "yes." Also set the parameter **USERGROUPS_ENAB** to "no," which makes that a new user is added to a group with the same name as the user and nothing else.
2. Use **cd /etc/skel** to go to the /etc/skell directory. Type **mkdir Pictures** and **mkdir Documents** to add two default directories to all user home directories.

Also change the contents of the file .bashrc to include the line **export EDITOR=/usr/bin/vim**, which sets the default editor for tools that need to modify text files.

3. Type **useradd linda** to create an account for user linda. Then, type **id linda** to verify that linda is a member of a group with the name linda and nothing else. Also verify that the directories Pictures and Documents have been created in linda's home directory.
4. Use **passwd linda** to set a password for the user you have just created. Use the password **password.**
5. Type **passwd -n 30 -w 3 -x 90 linda** to change the password properties. This has the password expire after 90 days (**-x 90**). Three days before expiry, the user will get a warning (**-w 3**), and the password has to be used for at least 30 days before (**-n 30**) it can be changed.
6. Create a few more users: lisa, lori, and bob, using **for i in lisa lori bob; do useradd $i; done.**
7. Use **grep lori /etc/passwd /etc/shadow /etc/group**. This shows the user lori created in all three critical files and confirms they have been set up correctly.

Creating and Managing Group Accounts

Every Linux user has to be a member of at least one group. In this section, you learn how to manage settings for Linux group accounts.

Understanding Linux Groups

Linux users can be a member of two different kinds of groups. First, there is the primary group. Every user must be a member of a primary group and there is only one primary group. When creating files, the primary group becomes group owner of these files. (File ownership is discussed in detail in Chapter 7, "Permissions Management.") Users can also access all files their primary group has access to. The users primary group membership is defined in /etc/passwd; the group itself is stored in the /etc/group configuration file.

Besides the mandatory primary group, users can be a member of one or more secondary groups as well. Secondary groups are important to get access to files. If the group a user is a member of has access to specific files, the user will get access to these files also. Working with secondary groups is important, in particular in environments where Linux is used as a file server to allow people working for different departments to share files with one another.

Creating Groups

As is the case for creating users, there are also different options for creating groups. The group configuration files can be modified directly using **vigr** or the command-line utility groupadd.

Creating Groups with vigr

With the **vigr** command, you open an editor interface directly on the /etc/group configuration file. In this file, groups are defined in four fields per group (see Listing 6.6).

Listing 6.6 Sample /etc/group Content

```
kvm:x:36:qemu
qemu:x:107:
libstoragemgmt:x:994:
rpc:x:32:
rpcuser:x:29:
"/etc/group.edit" 65L, 870C
```

The following fields are used in /etc/group:

- **Group name:** As is suggested by the name of the field, this contains the name of the group.
- **Group password:** A feature that is hardly used anymore. A group password can be used by users that want to join the group on a temporary basis, so that access to files the group has access to is allowed.
- **Group ID:** A unique numeric group identification number.
- **Members:** Here you find the names of users that are a member of this group as a secondary group. Note that it does not show users that are a member of this group as their primary group.

Using groupadd to Create Groups

Another method to create new groups is by using the **groupadd** command. This command is easy to use. Just use **groupadd** followed by the name of the group you want to add. There are some advanced options, the only significant of them is **-g**, which allows you to specify a group ID when creating the group.

Managing Group Properties

To manage group properties, **groupmod** is available. You can use this command to change the name or group ID of the group, but it does not allow you to add group members. To do this, you use **usermod**. As discussed before, **usermod -aG** will add users to new groups that will be used as their secondary group. Because a group does not have many properties, it is quite common that group properties are managed directly in the /etc/group file by using the **vigr** command.

TIP Because users group membership is defined in two different locations, it can be difficult to find out which groups exactly a user is a member of. A convenient command to check this is **groupmems**. Use, for example, the command **groupmems -g sales -l** to see which users are a member of the group sales. This shows users who are a member of this group as a secondary group assignment, but also users who are a member of this group as the primary group assignment.

Exercise 6.3 Working with Groups

In this exercise, you create two groups and add some users as members to these groups.

1. Type **groupadd sales** followed by **groupadd account** to add groups with the names sales and account.
2. Use **usermod** to add users linda and lisa to the group sales, and lori and bob to the group account:

```
usermod -aG sales linda
usermod -aG sales lisa
usermod -aG account lori
usermod -aG account bob
```

3. Type **id linda** to verify that user linda has correctly been added to the group sales. In the results of this command, you see that linda is assigned to the group with gid=100(users). This is her primary group. With the **groups** parameter, all groups she is a member of as secondary group are mentioned:

```
linux:~ # id linda
uid=1000(linda) gid=100(users) groups=1000(sales),100(users)
```

Logging In Through an External Authentication Service

When a user enters his login name and password, these are normally checked on the local server. If in your environment many servers are used, this approach is not the most convenient, and you might benefit from a centralized service that helps you managing users and groups. To provide such centralized authentication services, LDAP is a common solution.

Understanding LDAP

The Lightweight Directory Access Protocol (LDAP) was developed as a protocol to get information from an X.500 directory service. This service was originally developed as an address book. Currently, LDAP has developed further into a service that can be used as a centralized authentication service.

LDAP is an open standard, and many directory services are available that are using LDAP as their access protocol. Some common LDAP solutions are OpenLDAP, or the LDAP server that is integrated in the Red Hat Identity Management solution, which is also known as FreeIPA. For the RHCSA exam, you do not need to know how to set up an LDAP server yourself, but you do need to be able to set up a client for authentication on LDAP.

LDAP directory servers are organized in a hierarchical, distributed and replicated way:

- LDAP is hierarchical; it is organized like DNS, using domains (which in LDAP are called containers) to organize the leaf objects (such as users) in a way that makes sense.
- LDAP is distributed because the entire database does not have to be available on one single server. The different containers in the LDAP hierarchy can be spread over multiple servers to make the information available where it needs to be available. To distribute the information in the LDAP directory, the directory tree is partitioned into different parts.
- LDAP is replicated; multiple copies of one partition can be created.

In Figure 6.1, you can see a schematic overview of an LDAP directory. This is the imaginary LDAP environment that matches the DNS domain rhatcert.com. This LDAP environment spreads two geographic regions: SFO and AMS. Because it will not happen often that users in SFO are logging in or accessing resources in AMS, the directory tree is split in two parts, one for the SFO geographic and one for the AMS geographic. Every server in each geographic will know how to access information in the other partition; it will just be a bit slower because a remote server needs to be accessed.

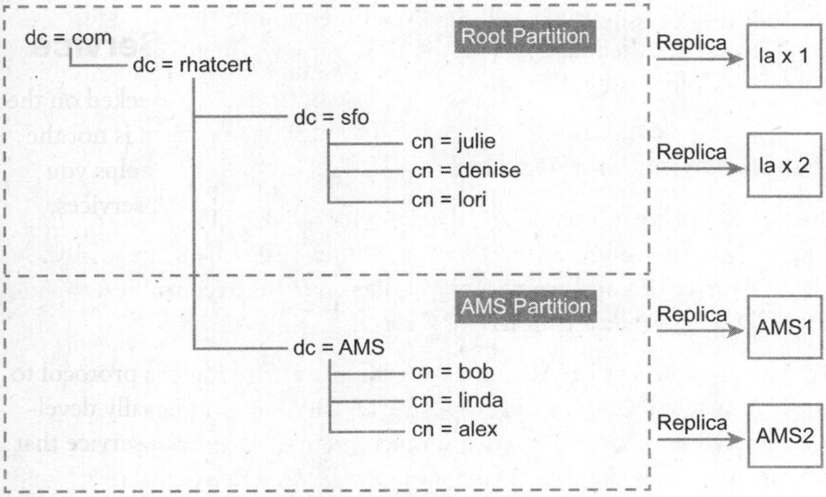

Figure 6.1 LDAP schematic overview.

To increase the accessibility, as well as fault tolerance, each geographic has two different servers. On each server, a replica of the partition is stored. This allows the workload to be load balanced across the servers, and it also allows for fault tolerance. When users are connecting to LDAP, they need to specify which specific server to access.

Key Topic

Figure 6.1 also shows that the users are in two specific containers in LDAP. When enabling LDAP access, users need to specify which container they are using as their base environment. This is referred to as the *base context*. The name of the base context is always written out as a name that includes the complete path (a fully distinguished name). This name includes type indicators and commas to separate the different parts. The two containers that contain users are therefore dc=sfo,dc=rhatcert,dc=com and dc=ams,dc=rhatcert,dc=com.

To access an LDAP server, security is important. To ensure a base level of security, Transport Layer Security (TLS) certificates are used. These certificates ensure that the server that LDAP users are authenticating against is verified, and that user credentials are secured while transported over the network.

To authenticate on an LDAP server, there are two options:

- Password authentication
- Kerberos authentication

To pass the RHCSA exam, you need to be able to set up password based LDAP authentication. Kerberos authentication is in the RHCE requirements and is covered in Chapter 24, "Configuring Time Services."

Making the Authentication Platform Available

You do not have to know how to set up an LDAP server for the RHCSA test. You only need to know how to configure your server to authenticate on an already existing external LDAP server. If you want to test whether you can successfully authenticate on an external server, you need an LDAP server.

The easiest way to configure an LDAP authentication platform is by installing a Red Hat Identity Management server. In Appendix D, "Setting Up Identity Management," you can read how to do that. Also, a preconfigured server is available for download at http://www.rhatcert.com. Make sure to register. After registering, you have access to a completely configured environment that includes a FreeIPA server. You find a readme file in the archive file that contains the virtual machine files that explain how to set up this environment.

Configuring RHEL 7 for LDAP Authentication

To set up RHEL7 for LDAP authentication, you need to create a configuration file that explains which LDAP server to use, which TLS certificate to use, and which container in LDAP should be used as the base LDAP URL. To specify all this, three different tools can be used:

Key Topic

- **authconfig:** A command-line utility in which you have to specify all you want to do by using command-line options
- **authconfig-tui:** A menu-driven text user interface that allows you to select options to be used from a list. Use of this utility is recommended
- **authconfig-gtk:** A utility with a GUI, which for that reason can be used from a GUI environment only

Depending on which tool you use, a different authentication backend is configured. The nslcd service is configured and started when using autconfig-tui. When authconfig-gtk is used, the sssd service is used as the backend.

TIP If you install the sshd package before you configure anything, you should be able to deal with authentication through the sssd service and not using the nslcd service. It is easy to find yourself in a situation where nslcd is used instead of sssd, which is why you learn about both of them in the following sections.

Managing nslcd

When you use authconfig-tui, the nslcd service is configured on your server to connect to the LDAP service. This service ensures that your local system will look beyond the local user information and get to LDAP. The nscld service is using a configuration file with the name /etc/nslcd.conf. In this file, you find all relevant settings that are required to connect to LDAP. In Listing 6.7, you can see the contents of this configuration file.

Listing 6.7 LDAP Connection Parameters in nslcd.conf

```
[root@localhost ~]# cat /etc/nslcd.conf | grep -v ^# | grep ^[a-Z]
uid nslcd
gid ldap
uri ldap://ipa.example.com
base dc=example,dc=com
tls_reqcert never
ssl start_tls
tls_cacertdir /etc/openldap/cacerts
```

The important parameters that were added by authconfig-tui are as follows:

- **uri** This specifies the name of the LDAP server.
- **base** This is the base container where LDAP users should be looked for.
- **tls_reqcert** This option was added to allow TLS connections without a trusted certificate authority (CA).
- **ssl** This option specifies that TLS should be used for establishing trusted connections.

After configuring your server for LDAP authentication, use **systemctl status nslcd** to verify it is running. If it is not, check whether the sssd service is used instead, as described in the following subsection.

If the nslcd service is not running, and neither is sssd, you can start it using the **systemctl start nslcd** command. Once it is running, you can use the **systemctl status nslcd** command for troubleshooting also. This command tells you exactly what is wrong if you receive an error when connecting to the LDAP server.

Managing sssd

If you have initialized the connection to the LDAP server using authconfig-gtk after making sure that the sssd service is installed, the configuration is written to sssd. The sssd service integrates with the local authentication procedure and redirects all authentication requests to LDAP in that case.

When sssd is used, you should check whether the service is running by using **systemctl status sssd**. If it is, you can check the configuration in /etc/sss/sssd.conf. Normally, there should not be a need to modify the configuration in /etc/sssd/sssd.conf directly because it is written by authconfig-gtk, but for verification purposes you might want to take a look anyway. You find all LDAP-related configuration lines in this file.

TIP On the exam, be prepared to work with both nslcd and sssd. Being prepared for both ensures that you will not get into trouble because you do not know what is happening. The best tool to focus on during the exam is authconfig-tui, because it does not require many resources and additional programs to work.

NOTE When you use authconfig-tui, the variable FORCELEGACY=yes is set in /etc/sysconfig/authconfig. This makes that nslcd is used instead of sssd.

TIP Also read Chapter 25, "Configuring External Authentication and Authorization," for more information about setting up external authentication.

Exercise 6.4 Connecting to an External LDAP Server

This exercise assumes that you have installed an LDAP server as offered by FreeIPA. Setup of this server is described in Appendix D. Alternatively, a complete lab environment is available for download at http://rhatcert.com. Make sure to register. The lab environment is available as a free download for registered users only. All tasks described here are performed on your test server:

1. Set up hostname resolution on your server so that the LDAP server can be used by its name. In this exercise, the IP address 192.168.122.200 is used for the

LDAP server. Change this according to the setup you are using and enter the following line in the /etc/hosts file:

```
192.168.122.200            ipa.example.com
```

2. Type **yum groupinstall -y "Directory Client"**.
3. Type **scp ipa.example.com:/root/cacert.p12/etc/openldap/cacerts**.
4. As root, type **authconfig-tui**. In the text user interface that opens now, under User Information select Use LDAP, and under Authentication, select Use LDAP Authentication. Do not unselect any option that is selected by default (see Figure 6.2).

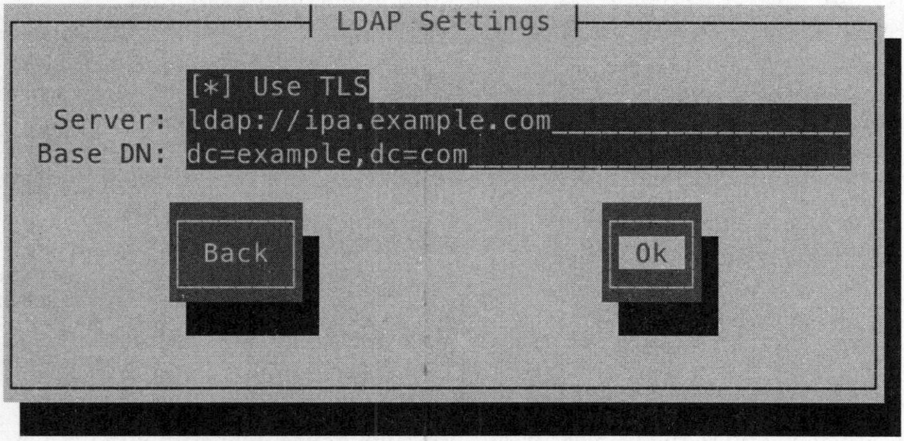

Figure 6.2 Configuring authentication from authconfig-tui.

5. In the next screen, you are prompted as to whether TLS should be used, see Figure 6.3. Select Use TLS, and then enter the server URL **ldap://ipa.example.com**. Make sure the base DN is set to dc=example,dc=com. Then click OK to continue.
6. You now see a message indicating that you need to copy the certificate of the CA that has signed the public key certificate of the LDAP server to /etc/openldap/cacerts. You have already done this in step 3 of this exercise, so no action is required here.
7. Open the file /etc/nslcd.conf and make sure that it contains the line tls_reqcert never. Use **systemctl restart nslcd** to restart the nslcd service.

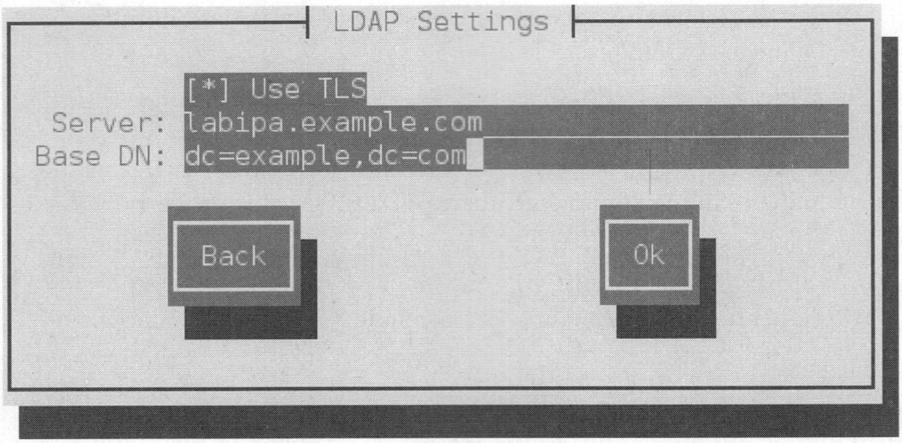

Figure 6.3 Configuring TLS settings.

8. Use **su - lara** to verify that you now have access to users on the IPA server. On the IPA server, a user with the name lara has been created. You notice that you are logged in as this user, but you also get a warning that the home directory could not be set. For the moment, you can ignore that warning.

Summary

In this chapter, you learned how to create users and groups. You learned which configuration files are used to store users and groups, and you learned which properties are used in these files. You also learned which utilities are available to manage user and group accounts.

Exam Preparation Tasks

Review All Key Topics

Review the most important topics in the chapter, noted with the Key Topic icon in the outer margin of the page. Table 6.3 lists a reference of these key topics and the page numbers on which each is found.

Table 6.3 Key Topics for Chapter 6

Key Topic Element	Description	Page Number
Section	Users on Linux	126
Table 6.2	Methods to run tasks with elevated permissions	127
List	Definitions of user account fields	130
List	Fields defined in /etc/shadow	131
List	Significant properties that can be set from /etc/login.defs	135
List	Files that play a role in constructing the user environment	136
Paragraph	Definition of "base context"	141
List	Tools that can be used for managing external authentication.	142

Complete Tables and Lists from Memory

Print a copy of Appendix B, "Memory Tables" (found on the disc), or at least the section for this chapter, and complete the tables and lists from memory. Appendix C, "Memory Tables Answer Key," also on the disc, includes completed tables and lists to check your work.

Define Key Terms

Define the following key terms from this chapter and check your answers in the glossary:

User, password, GECOS, group, primary group, secondary group, privileged user, unprivileged user, root, LDAP

Review Questions

1. What is the UID of user root?
2. What is the configuration file in which sudo is defined?
3. Which command should you use to modify a sudo configuration?
4. Which two files can be used to define settings that will be used when creating users?
5. How many groups can you create in /etc/passwd?

6. If you want to grant a user access to all admin commands through sudo, which group should you make that user a member of?
7. Which command should you use to modify the /etc/group file manually?
8. Which two commands can you use to change user password information?
9. What is the name of the file where user passwords are stored?
10. What is the name of the file where group accounts are stored?

End-of-Chapter Labs

You have now learned how to set up an environment where user accounts can log in to your server and access resources on your server. In the two end-of-chapter labs, you learn how to configure an environment for users and groups, as well as LDAP authentication.

Lab 6.1

1. Set up a shared group environment that meets the following requirements:
   - Create two groups: sales and account.
   - Create users bob, betty, bill, and beatrix. Make sure they have their primary group set to a private group that has the name of the user.
   - Make bob and betty a member of the group sales, and bill and beatrix a member of the group account.
   - Set a password policy that requires users to change their password every 90 days.

Lab 6.2

1. Configure your server for authentication on an LDAP server. You can use the LDAP server that is available from the test environment at http://www.rhatcert.com, or set up an LDAP server as described in Appendix D of this book. After configuring LDAP login, try logging in as an LDAP user. The LDAP server on rhatcert.com has users linda, lisa, and lara preconfigured, which you can use for testing.

The following topics are covered in this chapter:

- Managing File Ownership
- Managing Basic Permissions
- Managing Advanced Permissions
- Managing ACLs
- Setting Default Permissions with umask
- Working with User Extended Attributes

The following RHCSA exam objectives are covered in this chapter:

- List, set, and change standard UGO/rwx permissions
- Create and configure set-GID directories for collaboration
- Create and manage access control lists
- Diagnose and correct file permissions problems

CHAPTER 7

Configuring Permissions

To get access to files on Linux, permissions are used. These permissions are assigned to three entities: the file owner, the group owner, and the others entity (which is everybody else). In this chapter, you learn how to apply permissions. The chapter starts with an overview of the basic partitions, after which the special permissions and access control lists (ACLs) are discussed. At the end of this chapter, setting default permissions through the umask is covered, as is managing user extended attributes.

"Do I Know This Already?" Quiz

The "Do I Know This Already?" quiz allows you to assess whether you should read this entire chapter thoroughly or jump to the "Exam Preparation Tasks" section. If you are in doubt about your answers to these questions or your own assessment of your knowledge of the topics, read the entire chapter. Table 7.1 lists the major headings in this chapter and their corresponding "Do I Know This Already?" quiz questions. You can find the answers in Appendix A, "Answers to the 'Do I Know This Already?' Quizzes and 'Review Questions.'"

Table 7.1 "Do I Know This Already?" Section-to-Question Mapping

Foundation Topics Section	Questions
Managing File Ownership	1–3
Managing Basic Permissions	4
Managing Advanced Permissions	5
Managing ACLs	6–8
Setting Default Permissions with umask	9
Working with User Extended Attributes	10

1. A user who is a member of several groups wants to change default group ownership for all newly created files and set it to the group sales. Which command would do that?
   a. **chgrp sales**
   b. **setgid sales**
   c. **newgrp sales**
   d. **setgroup sales**

2. Which command enables you to find all files on a system that are owned by user linda?
   a. **find / -user linda**
   b. **find / -uid linda**
   c. **ls -l | grep linda**
   d. **ls -R | find linda**

3. Which of the following commands does not set group ownership to the group sales for the file myfile?
   a. **chgrp sales myfile**
   b. **chown .sales myfile**
   c. **chgrp myfile sales**
   d. **chown :sales myfile**

4. Which of the following would be used to allow read and write permissions to the user and group owners and no permissions at all to anyone else?
   a. **chown 007 filename**
   b. **chmod 077 filename**
   c. **chmod 660 filename**
   d. **chmod 770 filename**

5. Which command enables you to set the SGID permission on a directory?
   a. **chmod u+s /dir**
   b. **chmod g-s /dir**
   c. **chmod g+s /dir**
   d. **chmod 1770 /dir**

6. You are trying to use the **setfacl** command to set ACLs on the directory /data, but you are getting an "operation not supported" message. Which of the following is the most likely explanation?
   a. The **setfacl** command is not installed on your computer.
   b. You are making an error typing the command.
   c. The user or group to which you want to grant ACLs does not exist.
   d. The file system lacks ACL support.

7. Which of the following commands grants rw permissions for the group sales to all new files that will be created in the /data directory and all of its subdirectories?
   a. **setfacl -m d:g:sales:rw /data**
   b. **setfacl -m d:g:sales:rwx /data**
   c. **setfacl -R -m g:sales:rwx /data**
   d. **setfacl -R -m g:sales:rw /data**

8. Which command enables you to make sure that others have no access to any new files that will be created in the /data directory, assuming that you want others to have read permissions on all other files?
   a. **setfacl -m d:o::- /data**
   b. **setfacl -m o::- /data**
   c. **umask 027 /data**
   d. **umask 027**

9. Which of the following umask settings meets the following requirements:
   - Grants all permissions to the owner of the file.
   - Grants read permissions to the group owner of the file.
   - Grants no permissions to others.

   a. 740
   b. 750
   c. 027
   d. 047

10. Which command enables you to check all attributes that are currently set on myfile.

   a. **ls --attr myfile**

   b. **getattr myfile**

   c. **lsattr myfile**

   d. **listattr myfile**

Foundation Topics

Managing File Ownership

Before discussing permissions, you must know about the role of file and directory ownership. File and directory ownership is vital for working with permissions. In this section, you first learn how you can see ownership. Then you learn how to change user and group ownership for files and directories.

Displaying Ownership

On Linux, every file and every directory has two owners: a user and a group owner. These owners are set when a file or directory is created. On creation, the user who creates the file becomes the user owner, and the primary group of that user becomes the group owner. To determine whether you as a user have permissions to a file or a directory, the shell checks ownership. This happens in the following order:

1. The shell checks whether you are the user owner of the file you want to access, which is also referred to as the user of the file. If you are the user, you get the permissions that are set for the user, and the shell looks no further.
2. If you are not the user owner, the shell will check whether you are a member of the group owner, which is also referred to as the group of the file. If you are a member of the group, you get access to the file with the permissions of the group, and the shell looks no further.
3. If you are neither the user, nor the group owner, you get the permissions of others.

To see current ownership assignments, you can use the **ls -l** command. This command shows the user and the group owner. In Listing 7.1, you can see the ownership settings for directories in the directory /home.

Listing 7.1 Displaying Current File Ownership

```
[root@server1 home]# ls -l
total 8
drwx------.  3 bob      bob        74 Feb  6 10:13 bob
drwx------.  3 caroline caroline   74 Feb  6 10:13 caroline
drwx------.  3 fozia    fozia      74 Feb  6 10:13 fozia
drwx------.  3 lara     lara       74 Feb  6 10:13 lara
drwx------.  5 lisa     lisa     4096 Feb  6 10:12 lisa
drwx------. 14 user     user     4096 Feb  5 10:35 user
```

Using the **ls** command, you can display ownership for files in a given directory. It may on occasion be useful to get a list of all files on the system that have a given user or group as owner. To do this, you may use **find**. The **find** argument **-user** can be used for this purpose. For instance, the following command shows all files that have user linda as their owner:

```
find / -user linda
```

You can also use **find** to search for files that have a specific group as their owner. For instance, the following command searches all files that are owned by the group users:

```
find / -group users
```

Changing User Ownership

To apply appropriate permissions, the first thing to consider is ownership. To do this, there is the **chown** command. The syntax of this command is not hard to understand:

```
chown who what
```

For instance, the following command changees ownership for the file account to user linda:

```
chown linda account
```

The **chown** command has a few options, of which one is particularly useful: **-R**. You might guess what it does, because this option is available for many other commands as well. It allows you to set ownership recursively, which allows you to set ownership of the current directory and everything below. The following command changes ownership for the directory /home and everything beneath it to user linda:

```
chown -R linda /home/linda
```

Changing Group Ownership

There are actually two ways to change group ownership. You can do it using **chown**, but there is also a specific command with the name **chgrp** that does the job. If you want to use the **chown** command, use a **.** or **:** in front of the group name. The following changes the group owner of directory /home/account to the group account:

```
chown .account /home/account
```

You can use **chown** to change user and/or group ownership in a number of ways, an overview of which follows:

- **chown lisa myfile** Sets user lisa as the owner of myfile
- **chown lisa.sales myfile** Sets user lisa as user owner and group sales as group owner of myfile
- **chown lisa:sales myfile** Sets user lisa as user owner and group sales as group owner of myfile
- **chown .sales myfile** Sets group sales as group owner of myfile without changing the user owner
- **chown :sales myfile** Sets group sales as group owner of myfile without changing the user owner

You can also use the **chgrp** command to change group ownership. Consider the following example, where you can use **chgrp** to set group ownership for the directory /home/account to the group account:

```
chgrp account /home/account
```

As is the case for **chown**, you can use the option **-R** with **chgrp** as well to change group ownership recursively.

Understanding Default Ownership

You might have noticed that when a user creates a file, default ownership is applied. The user who creates the file automatically becomes user owner, and the primary group of that user automatically becomes group owner. Normally, this is the group that is set in the **/etc/passwd** file as the user's primary group. If the user is a member of more groups, however, he can change the effective primary group.

To show the current effective primary group, a user can use the **groups** command:

```
[root@server1 ~]# groups lisa
lisa : lisa account sales
```

If the current user linda wants to change the effective primary group, she can use the **newgrp** command, followed by the name of the group she wants to set as the new effective primary group. This group will be continued to be used as effective primary group until the user uses the **exit** command or logs out. Listing 7.2 shows how user linda uses this command to make sales her effective primary group.

Listing 7.2 Using **newgrp** to Change the Effective Primary Group

```
[lisa@server1 ~]$ groups
lisa account sales
[lisa@server1 ~]$ newgrp sales
[lisa@server1 ~]$ groups
sales lisa account
[lisa@server1 ~]$ touch file1
[lisa@server1 ~]$ ls -l
total 0
-rw-r--r--. 1 lisa sales 0 Feb  6 10:06 file1
```

After you change the effective primary group, all new files that the user creates will get this group as their group owner. To return to the original primary group setting, use **exit**.

To be able to use the **newgrp** command, a user has to be a member of that group. Alternatively, a group password can be set for the group using the **gpasswd** command. If a user uses the **newgrp** command but is not a member of the target group, the shell prompts for the group password. After you enter the correct group password, the new effective primary group is set.

Managing Basic Permissions

The Linux permissions system was invented in the 1970s. Because computing needs were limited in those years, the basic permission system that was created was rather limited. This basic permission system uses three permissions that can be applied to files and directories. In this section, you learn how the system works and how to modify these permissions.

Understanding Read, Write, and Execute Permissions

The three basic permissions allow you to read, write, and execute files. The effect of these permissions differs when applied to files or directories. If applied to a file, the read permission gives you the right to open the file for reading. Therefore, you can read its contents, but it also means that your computer can open the file to do something with it. A program file that needs access to a library needs, for example, read access to that library. From that follows that the read permission is the most basic permission you need to work with files.

If applied to a directory, read allows you to list the contents of that directory. You should be aware that this permission does not allow you to read files in the directory as well. The Linux permission system does not know inheritance, and the only way to read a file is by using the read permissions on that file. To open a file for reading, however, you do need read permissions to the directory because you would not see the file otherwise.

As you can probably guess, the write permission, if applied to a file, allows you to write in the file. Stated otherwise, write allows you to modify the contents of existing files. It does not, however, allow you to create or delete new files or modify permissions of a file. To do that, you need write on the directory where you want to create the file. On directories, this permission also allows you to create and remove new subdirectories.

The execute permission is what you need to execute a file. It will never be set by default, which makes Linux almost completely immune to viruses. Only someone with administrative rights to a directory can apply the execute permission. Typically, this is the user root, but a user who is owner of a directory also has the right to change permissions in that directory.

Whereas the execute permission on files means that you are allowed to run a program file, if applied to a directory it means that the user is allowed to use the **cd** command to go to that directory. This means that execute is an important permission for directories and you will see that it is normally applied as the default permission to directories. Without it, there is no way to change to that directory! Table 7.2 summarizes the use of the basic permissions.

Table 7.2 Use of Read, Write, and Execute Permissions

Key Topic

Permission	Applied to Files	Applied to Directories
Read	Open a file	List contents of directory
Write	Change contents of a file	Create and delete files and modify permissions on files
Execute	Run a program file	Change to the directory

Applying Read, Write, and Execute Permissions

To apply permissions, you use the **chmod** command. When using **chmod**, you can set permissions for user, group, and others. You can use this command in two modes: the relative mode and the absolute mode. In absolute mode, three digits are used to set the basic permissions. Table 7.3 provides an overview of the permissions and their numeric representation.

Table 7.3 Numeric Representation of Permissions

Key Topic

Permission	Numeric Representation
Read	4
Write	2
Execute	1

When setting permissions, calculate the value that you need. If you want to set read, write, and execute for the user, read and execute for the group, and read and execute for others on the file /somefile, for example, you use the following **chmod** command:

```
chmod 755 /somefile
```

When you use **chmod** in this way, all current permissions are replaced by the permissions you set. If you want to modify permissions relative to the current permissions, you can use **chmod** in relative mode. When using **chmod** in relative mode, you work with three indicators to specify what you want to do:

- First, you specify for whom you want to change permissions. To do this, you can choose between user (**u**), group (**g**), and others (**o**).
- Then, you use an operator to add or remove permissions from the current mode, or set them in an absolute way.
- At the end, you use **r**, **w**, and **x** to specify what permissions you want to set.

When changing permissions in relative mode, you may omit the "to whom" part to add or remove a permission for all entities. For instance, the following adds the execute permission for all users:

```
chmod +x somefile
```

When working in relative mode, you may use more complex commands as well. For instance, the following adds the write permission to the group and remove read for others:

```
chmod g+w,o-r somefile
```

TIP When using **chmod -R o+rx /data**, you set the execute permission on all directories as well as files in the /data directory. To set the execute permission to directories only, and not to files, use **chmod -R o+rX /data**. The uppercase X ensures that files will not get the execute permission unless the file has already set the execute permission for some of the entities. That makes X the more intelligent way of dealing with execute permissions; it will avoid setting that permission on files where it is not needed.

Exercise 7.1 Managing Basic Permissions

In this exercise, you create a directory structure for the groups that you have created earlier. You also assign the correct permissions to these directories.

1. From a root shell, type **mkdir -p /data/sales /data/account**.
2. Before setting the permissions, change the owners of these directories using **chown linda.sales /data/sales and chown linda.account /data/account**.
3. Set the permissions to enable the user and group owners to write files to these directories, and deny all access for all others: **chmod 770 /data/sales, and next chmod 770 /data/account**.
4. Use **su - lisa** to become lisa and change into the directory /data/account. Use **touch emptyfile** to create a file in this directory. Does this work?
5. Still as lisa, use **cd /data/sales** and use **touch emptyfile** to create a file in this directory. Does this work?

Managing Advanced Permissions

Apart from the basic permissions that you have just read about, Linux has a set of advanced permissions as well. These are not permissions that you would set by default, but they sometimes provide a useful addition. In this section, you learn what they are and how to set them.

Understanding Advanced Permissions

There are three advanced permissions. The first of them is the set user ID (SUID) permission. On some very specific occasions, you may want to apply this permission to executable files. By default, a user who runs an executable file runs this file with his own permissions. For normal users, that normally means that the use of the program is restricted. In some cases, however, the user needs special permissions, just for the execution of a certain task.

Consider, for example, the situation where a user needs to change his password. To do this, the user needs to write his new password to the /etc/shadow file. This file, however, is not writeable for users who do not have root permissions:

```
[root@hnl ~]# ls -l /etc/shadow
----------. 1 root root 1184 Apr 30 16:54 /etc/shadow
```

The SUID permission offers a solution for this problem. On the /usr/bin/passwd utility, this permission is applied by default. That makes that when changing his password, the user temporarily has root permissions, which allows him to write to the /etc/shadow file. You can see the SUID permission with **ls -l** as an **s** at the position where normally you would expect to see the **x** for the user permissions:

```
[root@hnl ~]# ls -l /usr/bin/passwd
-rwsr-xr-x. 1 root root 32680 Jan 28  2010 /usr/bin/passwd
```

The SUID permission may look useful (and it is in some cases), but at the same time, it is potentially dangerous. If applied wrongly, you may give away root permissions by accident. I therefore recommend using it with greatest care only. Most administrators will never have to use it; you'll only see it on some files where the operating system needs to set it as a default.

The second special permission is set group ID (SGID). This permission has two effects. If applied on an executable file, it gives the user who executes the file the permissions of the group owner of that file. So, SGID can accomplish more or less the same thing that does SUID. For this purpose, however, SGID is hardly used. As is the case for the SUID permission, SGID is applied to some system files as a default setting.

When applied to a directory, SGID may be useful, because you can use it to set default group ownership on files and subdirectories created in that directory. By default, when a user creates a file, his effective primary group is set as the group owner for that file. That is not always very useful, especially because on Red Hat users have their primary group set to a group with the same name as the user, and of which the user is the only member. So by default, files that a user creates will be group shared with nobody else.

Imagine a situation where users linda and lori work for the accounting department and are both members of the group account. By default, these users are members of the private group of which they are the only member. Both users, however, are members of the accounting group as well but as a secondary group setting.

The default situation is that when either of these users creates a file, the primary group becomes owner. So by default, linda cannot access the files that lori has created and vice versa. However, if you create a shared group directory (say, /groups/account) and make sure that the SGID permission is applied to that directory, and that the group accounting is set as the group owner for that directory, all files created in this directory and all its subdirectories also get the group accounting as the default group owner. For that reason, the SGID permission is a very useful permission to set on shared group directories.

The SGID permission shows in the output of **ls -l** as an **s** at the position where you normally find the group execute permission:

```
[root@hnl data]# ls -ld account
drwxr-sr-x. 2 root account 4096 Apr 30 21:28 account
```

The third of the special permissions is sticky bit. This permission is useful to protect files against accidental deletion in an environment where multiple users have write permissions in the same directory. If sticky bit is applied, a user may delete a file only if he is the user owner of the file or of the directory that contains the file. It is for that reason applied as a default permission to the /tmp directory, and it can be useful on shared group directories as well.

Without sticky bit, if a user can create files in a directory, he can also delete files from that directory. In a shared group environment, this may be annoying. Imagine users linda and lori again, who both have write permissions to the directory /data/account and get these permissions because of their membership of the group accounting. Therefore, linda can delete files that lori has created and vice versa.

When you apply the sticky bit, a user can delete files only if either of the following is true:

- The user is owner of the file.
- The user is owner of the directory where the file exists.

When using **ls -l**, you can see sticky bit as a **t** at the position where you normally see the execute permission for others:

```
[root@hnl data]# ls -ld account/
drwxr-sr-t. 2 root account 4096 Apr 30 21:28 account/
```

TIP Make sure that you know how to manage these advanced permissions. The RHCSA objectives specifically mention that you need to be able to use set GID to create a shared group directory.

Applying Advanced Permissions

To apply SUID, SGID, and sticky bit, you can use **chmod** as well. SUID has numeric value 4, SGID has numeric value 2, and sticky bit has numerical value 1. If you want to apply these permissions, you need to add a four-digit argument to **chmod**, of which the first digit refers to the special permissions. The following line would, for example, add the SGID permission to a directory, and set rwx for user and rx for group and others:

```
chmod 2755 /somedir
```

It is rather impractical if you have to look up the current permissions that are set before working with **chmod** in absolute mode. (You risk overwriting permissions if you do not.) Therefore, I recommend working in relative mode if you need to apply any of the special permissions:

- For SUID, use **chmod u+s**.
- For SGID, use **chmod g+s**.
- For sticky bit, use **chmod +t**, followed by the name of the file or the directory that you want to set the permissions on.

Table 7.4 summarizes all that is important to know about managing special permissions.

Key Topic

Table 7.4 Working with SUID, SGID, and Sticky Bit

Permission	Numeric Value	Relative Value	On Files	On Directories
SUID	4	u+s	User executes file with permissions of file owner.	No meaning.
SGID	2	g+s	User executes file with permissions of group owner.	Files created in directory get the same group owner.
Sticky bit	1	+t	No meaning.	Prevents users from deleting files from other users.

Exercise 7.2 Working with Special Permissions

In this exercise, you use special permissions to make it easier for members of a group to share files in a shared group directory. You assign the set group ID bit, as well as sticky bit, and see that after setting these, features are added that make it easier for group members to work together.

1. Open a terminal in which you are user linda.
2. Use **cd /data/sales** to go to the sales directory. Use **touch linda1** and **touch linda2** to create two files of which linda is the owner.
3. Use **su - lisa** to switch the current user identity to user lisa, who also is a member of the sales group.
4. Use **cd /data/sales** and from that directory, use **ls -l**. You'll see the two files that were created by user linda that are group-owned by the group linda. Use **rm -f linda***. This will remove both files.
5. Use the commands **touch lisa1** and **touch lisa2** to create two files that are owned by user lisa.
6. Use **su -** to escalate your current permissions to root level.
7. Use **chmod g+s,o+t /data/sales** to set the group ID bit as well as sticky bit on the shared group directory.
8. Use **su - linda**. First, use **touch linda3** and **touch linda4**. You should now see that the two files you have created are owned by the group sales who is group owner of the directory /data/sales.
9. Use **rm -rf lisa***. Sticky bit prevents you from removing these files as user linda because you are not the owner of the files. Note that if user linda is directory owner of /data/sales, she can remove the files in question anyway!

Managing ACLs

Even if the advanced permissions that were discussed in the previous section add useful functionality to the way Linux works with permissions, it does not allow you to give permissions to more than one user or one group on the same file. Access control lists do offer this feature. Apart from that, they allow administrators to set default permissions in a sophisticated way where the permissions that are set can differ on different directories.

Understanding ACLs

Although the ACL subsystem adds great functionality to your server, there is one drawback: Not all utilities support it. Therefore, you might lose ACL settings when copying or moving files, and your backup software might not be able to back up ACL settings.

The tar utility does not support ACLs. To make sure that your ACL settings are not lost when you make a backup, use **star** instead of tar. **star** works with exactly the same options as tar; it just adds support for ACL settings as well.

> **TIP** You can also create a backup of ACLs using **getfacl**, which can be restored using the **setfacl** command. To create the backup, use **getfacl -R /directory > file.acls**. To restore the settings from the backup file, use **setfacl --restore=file.acl**.

The lack of support by some tools does not have to be a problem though. ACLs are often applied to directories as a structural measure and not on individual files. Therefore, you will not have lots of them, but just a few applied in smart places in the file system. Hence, it is relatively easy to restore the original ACLs you were working with, even if your backup software does not support them.

Preparing Your File System for ACLs

Before starting to work with ACLs, you might have to prepare your file system for ACL support. Because the file system metadata needs to be extended, there is not always default support for ACLs in the file system. If while setting ACLs to a file system you are getting an "operation not supported" message, your file system probably lacks support for ACLs. To fix this, you need to add the **acl mount** option in the /etc/fstab file so that the file system will be mounted with ACL support by default. Read Chapter 14, "Managing Partitions," for more information about the /etc/fstab file and options that you can use in that file.

Changing and Viewing ACL Settings with setfacl and getfacl

To set ACLs, you need the **setfacl** command. To see current ACL settings, you need **getfacl**. The **ls -l** command does not show any existing ACLs; it just shows a + after the listing of the permissions, which indicates that ACLs apply to the file as well. Before setting ACLs, it is always a good idea to show current ACL settings using **getfacl**. In Listing 7.3, you can see the current permissions as shown with

ls -l and also as shown with **getfacl**. If you look closely enough, you can see that the information shown is exactly the same.

Listing 7.3 Checking Permissions with **ls -l** and **getfacl**

```
[root@server1 /]# ls -ld /dir
drwxr-xr-x. 2 root root 6 Feb  6 11:28 /dir
[root@server1 /]# getfacl /dir
getfacl: Removing leading '/' from absolute path names
# file: dir
# owner: root
# group: root
user::rwx
group::r-x
other::r-x
```

In the result of the **getfacl** command in Listing 7.4, you can see that the permissions are shown for three different entities: the user, the group, and others. Now let's add an ACL to give read and execute permissions to the group sales as well. The command to use for this is **setfacl -m g:sales:rx /dir**. In this command, **-m** indicates that the current ACL settings need to be modified. After that, **g:sales:rx** tells the command to set the ACL to read and execute (**rx**) for the group (**g**) sales. In Listing 7.4, you can see what the command looks like, as well as the output of the **getfacl** command after changing the current ACL settings.

Listing 7.4 Changing Group ACLs Using **setfacl**

```
[root@server1 /]# setfacl -m g:sales:rx /dir
[root@server1 /]# getfacl /dir
getfacl: Removing leading '/' from absolute path names
# file: dir
# owner: root
# group: root
user::rwx
group::r-x
group:sales:r-x
mask::r-x
other::r-x
```

Now that you understand how to set a group ACL, it is easy to understand ACLs for users and others as well. For instance, the command **setfacl -m u:linda:rwx /data** gives permissions to user linda on the /data directory without making her the owner and without changing the current owner assignment.

The **setfacl** command has many possibilities and options. One option is particularly important, the option **-R**. If used, the option makes the ACL setting for all files and subdirectories currently existing in the directory where you set the ACL. It is a good idea to always use this option while changing ACLs for existing directories.

Working with Default ACLs

One benefit of using ACLs is that you can give permissions to more than one user or group at a directory. Another benefit is that you can enable inheritance by working with default ACLs. By setting a default ACL, you'll determine the permissions that will be set for all new items that are created in the directory. Be aware, though, that a default ACL does not change the permissions for existing files and subdirectories. To change those as well you need to add a normal ACL, too!

TIP This is important to know. If you want to use ACLs to configure access for multiple users or groups to the same directory, you have to set ACLs twice. First, use **setfacl -R -m** to modify the ACLs for current files. Then, use **setfacl -m d:** to take care of all new items that will be created also.

To set a default ACL, you just have to add the option d after the option **-m** (order does matter!). So, use **setfacl -m d:g:sales:rx /data** if you want group sales to have read and execute on everything that will ever be created in the /data directory.

When using default ACLs, it can also be useful to set an ACL for others. Normally, this does not make much sense because you can also change the permissions for others by using **chmod**. What you cannot do using **chmod**, though, is specify the permissions that should be given to others on every new file that will ever be created. If you want others not to get any permissions on anything that is created in /data, for example, use **setfacl -m d:o::- /data**.

TIP ACLs and regular permissions are not always very well integrated. Problems may arise if you have applied default ACLs to a directory, after which items have been added to that directory and next try to change the regular permissions. The changes that are applied to the regular permissions will not be reflected well in the ACL overview. To avoid problems, set regular permissions first, after which you set default ACLs (and after doing that, try to not change them again).

Exercise 7.3 Managing Advanced Permissions Using ACLs

In this exercise, you work further on the /data/account and /data/sales directories that you created before. In earlier exercises, you ensured that the group sales has permissions on /data/sales, and the group account has permissions on /data/account. Up to now, you have not been able to upgrade the design, which you do in this exercise. You first make sure that the group account gets read permissions on the /data/sales directory and that group sales gets read permissions on the /data/account directory. Then, you set default ACLs to make sure that on all new files the permissions are properly set for all new items.

1. Open a root terminal.
2. Use **setfacl -m g:account:rx /data/sales** and **setfacl -m g:sales:rx /data/account**.
3. Use **getfacl** to verify that the permissions have been set the way you intended to.
4. Use **setfacl -m d:g:account:rwx,g:sales:rx /data/sales** to set the default ACL for the directory sales.
5. Add the default ACL for the directory /data/account by using **setfacl -m d:g:sales:rwx,g:account:rx /data/account**.
6. Verify that the ACL settings are effective by adding a new file in /data/sales. Use **touch /data/sales/newfile** and use **getfacl /data/sales/newfile** to check the current permission assignments.

Setting Default Permissions with umask

In the section about ACLs, you learned how to work with default ACLs. If you do not use ACLs, there is a shell setting that determines the default permissions that you will get: the umask. In this section, you learn how to modify default permissions using umask.

You have probably noticed that when creating a new file, some default permissions are set. These permissions are determined by the umask setting. This shell setting is applied to all users when logging in to the system. In the umask setting, a numeric value is used that is subtracted from the maximum permissions that can be set automatically to a file; the maximum setting for files is 666, and for directories is 777. Some exceptions apply to this rule, however. You can find a complete overview of umask settings in Table 7.5.

Of the digits used in the umask, like with the numeric arguments for the **chmod** command, the first digit refers to user permissions, the second digit refers to the group permissions, and the last refers to default permissions set for others. The default umask setting of 022 gives 644 for all new files and 755 for all new directories that are created on your server. A complete overview of all umask numeric values and their result is shown in Table 7.5.

Table 7.5 umask Values and Their Result

Key Topic

Value	Applied to Files	Applied to Directories
0	Read and write	Everything
1	Read and write	Read and write
2	Read	Read and execute
3	Read	Read
4	Write	Write and execute
5	Write	Write
6	Nothing	Execute
7	Nothing	Nothing

An easy way to see how the umask setting works is as follows: Start with the default permissions for a file set to 666 and subtract the umask to get the effective permissions. Do the same for a directory and its default permissions 777.

There are two ways to change the umask setting: for all users and for individual users. If you want to set the umask for all users, you must make sure the umask setting is considered when starting the shell environment files as directed by /etc/profile. The right approach is to create a shell script with the name umask.sh in the /etc/profile.d directory and specify the umask you want to use in that shell script. If the umask is changed in this file, it applies to all users after logging in to your server.

An alternative to setting the umask through /etc/profile and related files where it is applied to all users logging in to the system is to change the umask settings in a file with the name .profile, which is created in the home directory of an individual user. Settings applied in this file are applied for the individual user only; therefore, this is a nice method if you need more granularity. I personally like this feature to change the default umask for user root to 027, whereas normal users work with the default umask 022.

Working with User Extended Attributes

When you work with permissions, a relation always exists between a user or group object and the permissions these user or group objects have on a file or directory. An alternative method of securing files on a Linux server is by working with attributes. Attributes do their work regardless of the user that accesses the file.

As is the case for ACLs, for file attributes a **mount** option may have to be enabled. This is the **user_xattr** option. If you are getting an operation not supported message while working with user extended attributes, make sure to set this **mount** option in the /etc/fstab file.

Many attributes are documented. Some attributes are available but not yet implemented. Do not use them; they bring you nothing. Following are the most useful attributes that you can apply:

- **A** This attribute ensures that the file access time of the file is not modified. Normally, every time a file is opened, the file access time must be written to the file's metadata. This affects performance in a negative way; therefore, on files that are accessed on a regular basis, the **A** attribute can be used to disable this feature.
- **a** This attribute allows a file to be added to but not to be removed.
- **c** If you are using a file system where volume level compression is supported, this file attribute makes sure that the file is compressed the first time the compression engine gets active.
- **D** This attribute makes sure that changes to files are written to disk immediately, and not to cache first. This is a useful attribute on important database files to make sure that they do not get lost between file cache and hard disk.
- **d** This attribute makes sure the file is not backed up in backups where the dump utility is used.
- **I** This attribute enables indexing for the directory where it is enabled. This allows faster file access for primitive file systems like Ext3 that do not use a B-tree database for fast access to files.
- **i** This attribute makes the file immutable. Therefore, no changes can be made to the file at all, which is useful for files that need a bit of extra protection.
- **j** This attribute ensures that on an ext3 file system the file is first written to the journal and only after that to the data blocks on hard disk.
- **s** Overwrite the blocks where the file was stored with 0s after the file has been deleted. This makes sure that recovery of the file is not possible after it has been deleted.
- **u** This attribute saves undelete information. This allows a utility to be developed that works with that information to salvage deleted files.

NOTE Although there are quite a few attributes that can be used, be aware that most attributes are rather experimental and are only of any use if an application is used that can work with the given attribute. For example, it does not make sense to apply the u attribute if no application has been developed that can use this attribute to recover deleted files.

If you want to apply attributes, you can use the **chattr** command. For example, use **chattr +s somefile** to apply the attributes to somefile. Need to remove the attribute again? Then use **chattr -s somefile** and it will be removed. To get an overview of all attributes that are currently applied, use the **lsattr** command.

Summary

In this chapter, you learned how to work with permissions. You read about the three basic permissions, the advanced permissions, and how to apply ACLs on the file system. You also learned how to use the umask setting to apply default permissions. Toward the end of this chapter, you learned how to use user-extended attributes to apply an additional level of file system security.

Exam Preparation Tasks

Review All Key Topics

Review the most important topics in the chapter, noted with the Key Topic icon in the outer margin of the page. Table 7.6 lists a reference of these key topics and the page numbers on which each is found.

Table 7.6 Key Topics for Chapter 7

Key Topic Element	Description	Page
Table 7.2	Use of the basic permissions	159
Table 7.3	Numeric representation of permissions	160
Table 7.4	Special permissions overview	164
Table 7.5	umask overview	170

Define Key Terms

Define the following key terms from this chapter and check your answers in the glossary:

ownership, permissions, access control list, inheritance, attribute

Review Questions

1. How do you use chown to set the group owner to a file?
2. Which command finds all files that are owned by a specific user?
3. How would you apply read, write, and execute permissions to all files in /data for the user and group owners while setting no permissions to others?
4. Which command enables you in relative permission mode to add the execute permission to a file that you want to make executable?
5. Which command enables you to ensure that group ownership on all new files that will be created in a directory are set to the group owner of that directory?
6. You want to ensure that users can only delete files of which they are the owner, or which are in a directory of which they are the owner. Which command will do that for you?
7. Which command adds an ACL that grants members of the group sales read permissions to all existing files in the current directory?
8. What do you need to do to ensure that members of the group sales get read permissions to all files in the current directory and all of its subdirectories, as well as all files that will be created in this directory in the future?
9. Which umask do you need to set if you never want "others" to get any permissions on new files?
10. Which command ensures that nobody can delete myfile by accident?

End-of-Chapter Labs

In Chapter 6, "User and Group Management," you created some users and groups. These users and groups are needed to perform the exercises in this lab.

Lab 7.1

1. Set up a shared group environment. Create two directories: /data/account and /data/sales. Make the group sales owner of the directory sales, and make the group account owner of the directory account.

2. Configure the permissions so that the user owner (which must be root) and group owner have full access to the directory. There should be no permissions assigned to the others entity. Also make sure that "others" will get no permissions on newly created files and directories within the entire /data structure.
3. Create a configuration that allows members of the group sales read files in the directory /data/account. Also make sure that members of the group account have read permissions in the directory /data/sales.
4. Ensure that all new files in both directories inherit the group owner of the /data/sales and /data/account directory. This means that all files that will be created in /data/sales will be owned by the group sales, and all files in /data/account will be owned by the group account.
5. Ensure that users are only allowed to remove files of which they are the owner.

This chapter covers the following subjects:

- Networking Fundamentals
- Managing Network Addresses and Interfaces
- Validating Network Configuration
- Configuring Network Configuration with nmtui and nmcli
- Working on Network Configuration Files
- Setting Up Hostname and Name Resolution

The following RHCSA exam objectives are covered:

- Configure networking and hostname resolution statically or dynamically

CHAPTER 8

Configuring Networking

Networking is one of the most essential items on a modern server. On RHEL 7, networking is managed by the NetworkManager service, and with the release of RHEL 7, some completely new tools have been introduced to help manage networks. If you have already worked with networking on previous RHEL versions, you will notice that networking has changed a lot in RHEL 7 and that some approaches that were default in earlier versions will no longer work.

"Do I Know This Already?" Quiz

The "Do I Know This Already?" quiz allows you to assess whether you should read this entire chapter thoroughly or jump to the "Exam Preparation Tasks" section. If you are in doubt about your answers to these questions or your own assessment of your knowledge of the topics, read the entire chapter. Table 8.1 lists the major headings in this chapter and their corresponding "Do I Know This Already?" quiz questions. You can find the answers in Appendix A, "Answers to the 'Do I Know This Already?' Quizzes and 'Review Questions.'"

Table 8.1 "Do I Know This Already?" Section-to-Question Mapping

Foundation Topics Section	Questions
Networking Fundamentals	1–2
Managing Network Addresses and Interfaces	3
Validating Network Configuration	4
Configuring Network Configuration with nmtui and nmcli	5–8
Setting Up Hostname and Name Resolution	9–10

1. Which of the following IP addresses belong to the same network?

I. 192.168.4.17/26

II. 192.168.4.94/26

III. 192.168.4.97/26

IV. 192.168.4.120/26

a. I and II

b. II and III

c. III and IV

d. II, III, and IV

2. Which of the following is *not* a private IP address?

a. 10.10.10.10

b. 169.254.11.23

c. 172.19.18.17

d. 192.168.192.192

3. Which of the following would be the default network interface name on a RHEL 7 system?

a. p6p1

b. eth0

c. eno1677783

d. e0

4. Which command shows the recommended way to display information about the network interface as well as its IP configuration?

a. **ifconfig -all**

b. **ipconfig**

c. **ip link show**

d. **ip addr show**

5. Which statement about NetworkManager is *not* true?

a. It is safe to disable NetworkManager and work with the network service instead.

b. NetworkManager manages network connections that are applied to network interfaces.

c. NetworkManager has a text based user interface with the name nmtui.

d. NetworkManager is the default service to manage networking in RHEL 7.

6. Which man page contains excellent examples on nmcli usage?
   a. nmcli
   b. nmcli-examples
   c. nm-config
   d. nm-tools

7. Which of the following is the name of the text user interface to specify network connection properties?
   a. system-config-network
   b. system-config-networkmanager
   c. nmtui
   d. nmcli

8. Which of the following commands shows correct syntax to set a fixed IP address to a connection using nmcli?
   a. **nmcli con add con-name "static" ifname eth0 autoconnect no type ethernet ipv4 10.0.0.10/24 gw4 10.0.0.1**
   b. **nmcli con add con-name "static" ifname eth0 autoconnect no type ethernet ipv4 10.0.0.10/24 gwv4 10.0.0.1**
   c. **nmcli con add con-name "static" ifname eth0 type ethernet ipv4 10.0.0.10/24 gw4 10.0.0.1**
   d. **nmcli con add con-name "static" ifname eth0 autoconnect no type ethernet ip4 10.0.0.10/24 gw4 10.0.0.1**

9. Which of the following is *not* a recommended way to specify which DNS servers to use?
   a. Edit /etc/resolv.conf
   b. Set the DNS options in /etc/sysconfig/network-scripts/ifcfg-<ID>
   c. Set the DNS server names using nmcli
   d. Use nmtui to set the DNS server names

10. In which configuration file would you set the hostname?
   a. /etc/sysconfig/network
   b. /etc/sysconfig/hostname
   c. /etc/hostname
   d. /etc/defaults/hostname

Foundation Topics

Networking Fundamentals

To set up networking on a server, your server needs a unique address on the network. For this purpose, IP (Internet Protocol) addresses are used. Currently, two versions of IP addresses are relevant:

Key Topic

- **IPv4 addresses:** These are based on 32-bit addresses and look like 192.168.10.100.
- **IPv6 addresses:** These are based on 128-bit addresses and are written in eight hexadecimal written parts that are based on 16 bits each. An IPv6 address may look like fe80:badb:abe01:45bc:34ad:6723:8798.

In this chapter, you learn how to work with IPv4 addresses on RHEL 7.

IP Addresses

Originally, IP addresses were assigned to computers and routers. Nowadays, many other devices also need IP addresses to communicate, such as smartphones, industrial equipment, and almost all other devices that are connected to the Internet. This chapter refers to all of those devices by using the word *node*. You'll also occasionally encounter the word *host*. A host is typically a server providing services on the network.

To make it easier for computers to communicate to one another, every IP address belongs to a specific network, and to communicate to computers on another network, the router is used. The router is a machine (often dedicated hardware that has been created for that purpose) that connects networks to one another.

To communicate on the Internet, every computer needs a worldwide unique IP address. These addresses are scarce, however; a theoretical maximum of four billion IP addresses is available, and that is not enough to provide every device with an IP address. IPv6 is the ultimate solution for that problem, because a very large number of IP addresses can be created in IPv6. Because many networks still work with IPv4, though, another solution exists: the private network addresses.

Private network addresses are addresses that are for use in internal networks only. Some specific IP network addresses have been created for this purpose:

Key Topic

- 10.0.0.0/8 (a single Class A network)
- 172.16.0.0/12 (16 Class B networks)
- 192.168.0.0/16 (256 Class C networks)

When private addresses are used, the nodes that are using them cannot access the Internet, and nodes from the Internet cannot easily access them. Because that is not very convenient, Network Address Translation (NAT) is often used. In NAT, the nodes use a private IP address, but when accessing the Internet, this private IP address is replaced with the IP address of the NAT router. Hence, nodes on the Internet think that they are communicating with the NAT router, and not with the individual hosts.

The NAT router on its turn uses tables to keep track of all connections that are currently existing for the hosts in the network. Based on this table, the NAT router helps make it possible for computers with a private IP address to connect to hosts on the Internet anyway. The use of NAT is very common; it is embedded in most routers that are used in home and small business networks to connect computers and other devices in those networks to the Internet.

IPv6 Addresses

An IPv6 address may look like fe80::225:90ff:fe23:8998. In an IPv6 address, there may be components that have leading 0s. Multiple sequences of 0000 can be written as ::, as you can see in this IPv6 address example. By using IPv6 addresses, billions of nodes can be addressed, which is why IPv6 addresses are slowly being introduced in current network configurations.

Network Masks

To know to which network a computer belongs, a subnet mask is used. The subnet mask defines which part of the network address indicates the network and which part indicates the node. Network masks may be written in the classless interdomain routing (CIDR) notation, or in the classical notation, and they always need to be specified with the network address. Examples include 192.168.10.100/24, which indicates that a 24-bit network address is used, and 192.168.10.100/255.255.255.0, which indicates exactly the same.

Often, network masks use multiple bytes. In the example using 192.168.10.100/24, the first three bytes (which is the 192.168.10 part) form the network part, and the last part (the number 100) is the host part on that network.

When talking about network addresses, you use a 4-byte number, as well, in which the node address is set to 0. So in the example of 192.168.10.100/24, the network address is 192.168.10.0. In IPv4 networks, there is also always a broadcast address. This is the address that can be used to address all nodes in the network. In the broadcast address, all node bits are set to 1, which makes for the decimal number 255 if an entire byte is referred to. So in the example of the address 192.168.10.100/24, the broadcast address is 192.168.10.255.

Binary Notation

Because the number of IPv4 addresses is limited, in modern IPv4 networks variable network masks are used. These are network masks such as 212.209.113.33/27. In a variable subnet mask, only a part of the byte is used for addressing nodes, and another part is used for addressing the network. In the subnet mask /27, the first 3 bits of the last byte are used to address the network, and the last 5 bits are used for addressing nodes. This becomes a bit clearer if you write down the address in a binary notation:

IP address:

```
212.209.113.33 = 11010100.11010001.00001010.00100001
```

Subnet mask:

```
/27            = 11111111.11111111.11111111.11100000
```

When applying the subnet mask to the IP address, you can see that the first 3 bits of the IP address belong to the network, so the network is 00100000. And if you use a binary calculator, you can see that that corresponds with the decimal IP address 32. Using the /27 subnet mask allows for the creation of multiple networks. Table 8.2 gives an overview.

Key Topic

Table 8.2 Binary-Decimal Conversion Overview

Binary Value	Decimal Value
00000000	0
00100000	32
01000000	64
01100000	96
10000000	128
10100000	160
11000000	192
11100000	224

So, if based on this information, you consider the IP address 212.209.113.33/27 again, you can see that it belongs to the network 212.209.113.32/27, and that in this network the broadcast address (which has the node part of the IP address set to all 1s) is 212.209.113.63, and therefore with a /27 subnet mask 30 nodes can be addressed per network. You'll get 32 IP addresses, but 2 of them are the network address and the broadcast address, which cannot be used as a host IP address.

EXAM TIP You do not need to make this kind of calculation on the RHCSA exam, but it helps understanding how IP network addressing works.

MAC Addresses

IP addresses are the addresses that allow nodes to communicate to any other node on the Internet. They are not the only addresses in use though. Each network card also has an address, which is known as the MAC address. MAC addresses are for use on the local network (that is, the local cable or local WLAN, just up to the first router that is encountered); they cannot be used for communications between nodes that are on different networks. They are important, though, because MAC addresses help computers find the specific network card that an IP address belongs to.

Protocol and Ports

IP addresses are used to address nodes, and that is useful, but addressing nodes is not what it is all about. Nodes are useful because they offer specific services on the network, such as a web server or a mail server. To identify these services, port addresses are used. Every service has a specific port address, such as port 80 for Hypertext Transfer Protocol (HTTP) or port 22 for a Secure Shell (SSH) server, and in network communication, the sender and the receiver are using port addresses. So, there is a destination port address as well as a source port address involved in network communications.

Because not all services are addressed in a similar way, a specific protocol is used between the IP address and the port address, such as Transfer Control Protocol (TCP), User Datagram Protocol (UDP), or Internet Control Message Protocol (ICMP). Every protocol has specific properties: TCP is typically used when the network communication must be reliable and delivery must be guaranteed; UDP is used when it must be fast and guaranteed delivery does not count.

Managing Network Addresses and Interfaces

As a Linux server administrator, you need to manage network addresses and network interfaces. The network addresses can be assigned in two ways:

Key Topic

- **Fixed IP addresses:** Useful for servers that always need to be available at the same IP address.
- **Dynamically assigned IP addresses:** Useful for end-users devices, and for instances in a cloud environment. To dynamically assign IP addresses, a Dynamic Host Configuration Protocol (DHCP) server is usually used.

For a long time, network cards in Linux have had default names, such as eth0, eth1, and eth2. This naming was assigned based on the order of detection of the network card. So, eth0 was the first network card that got detected, eth1 the second, and so on. This worked well in an environment where a node has one or two network cards only. If a node has multiple network cards that need to be dynamically added and removed, however, this approach does not work so well anymore.

In RHEL 7, the default names for network cards are based on firmware, device topology, and device types. This leads to network card names that always consist of the following parts:

- Ethernet interfaces begin with en, WLAN interfaces begin with wl, and WWAN interfaces begin with ww.
- The next part of the name represents the type of adapter. An o is used for onboard, s is for a hotplug slot, and p is for a PCI location. Administrators can also use the x to create a device name that is based on the MAC address of the network card.
- Then follows a number, which is used to represent an index, ID, or port.
- If the fixed name cannot be determined, traditional names such as eth0 are used.

Based on this information, device names such as eno16777734 can be used, which stands for an onboard Ethernet device, with its unique index number.

Apart from this default device naming, network cards can be named based on the BIOS device name as well. In this naming, names such as em1 (embedded network card 1) or p4p1 (which is PCI slot 4, port 1) can be used. To use this kind of naming, the biosdevname package must be installed.

Validating Network Configuration

Before you can learn how to set network information, you must know how to verify current network information. In this section, you learn how to do that, and you learn how to check the following networking items:

- IP address and subnet mask
- Routing
- Availability of ports and services

Validating Network Address Configuration

To verify the configuration of the network address, you need to use the **ip** utility. The **ip** utility is a modern utility that can consider advanced networking features that have been introduced recently. With the **ip** utility, many aspects of networking can be monitored:

- Use **ip addr** to configure and monitor network addresses
- Use **ip route** to configure and monitor routing information
- Use **ip link** to configure and monitor network link state

Apart from these items, the **ip** utility can manage many other aspects of networking, but you do not need to know about them for the RHCSA exam.

WARNING In earlier Linux versions, and some other UNIX-like operating systems, the **ifconfig** utility was and is used for validating network configuration. Do not use this utility on modern Linux distributions. Because Linux has become an important player in cloud computing, networking has evolved a lot to match cloud computing requirements, and many new features have been added to Linux networking. With the **ifconfig** utility, you cannot manage or validate these concepts.

To show current network settings, you can use the **ip addr show** command (which can be abbreviated as **ip a s** or even as **ip a**). The **ip** command is relatively smart and does not always require you to type the complete option.

The result of the **ip addr show** command looks as in Listing 8.1

Listing 8.1 Monitoring Current Network Configuration with **ip addr show**

```
[root@server2 ~]# ip a
1: lo: <LOOPBACK,UP,LOWER_UP> mtu 65536 qdisc noqueue state UNKNOWN
    link/loopback 00:00:00:00:00:00 brd 00:00:00:00:00:00
    inet 127.0.0.1/8 scope host lo
       valid_lft forever preferred_lft forever
    inet6 ::1/128 scope host
       valid_lft forever preferred_lft forever
2: eno16777736: <BROADCAST,MULTICAST,UP,LOWER_UP> mtu 1500 qdisc
  pfifo_fast state UP qlen 1000
    link/ether 00:0c:29:b8:8c:eb brd ff:ff:ff:ff:ff:ff
```

```
    inet 192.168.4.220/24 brd 192.168.4.255 scope global eno16777736
       valid_lft forever preferred_lft forever
    inet6 fe80::20c:29ff:feb8:8ceb/64 scope link
       valid_lft forever preferred_lft forever
```

In the result of this command, you see a listing of all network interfaces in your computer. You'll normally see at least two interfaces, but on specific configurations, there can be many more interfaces. In Listing 8.1, two interfaces are shown: the loopback interface lo, and the onboard Ethernet card eno16777736. The important part of the output of the command is for the onboard Ethernet card. The command shows the following items about its current status:

- **Current state:** The most important part of this line is the text state UP, which shows that this network card is currently up and available.
- **MAC address configuration:** This is the unique MAC address that is set for every network card. You can see the MAC address itself (00:0c:29:b8:8c:eb), as well as the corresponding broadcast address.
- **IPv4 configuration:** This line shows the IP address that is currently set, as well as the subnet mask that is used. You can also see the broadcast address that is used for this network configuration.
- **IPv6 configuration:** This line shows the current IPv6 address and its configuration.

If you are just interested in the link state of the network interfaces, you can use the **ip link show** command. This command (of which you can see the output in Listing 8.2) repeats the link state information of the **ip addr show** command.

Listing 8.2 ip link show Output

```
[root@server2 ~]# ip link show
1: lo: <LOOPBACK,UP,LOWER_UP> mtu 65536 qdisc noqueue state UNKNOWN
mode DEFAULT
    link/loopback 00:00:00:00:00:00 brd 00:00:00:00:00:00
2: eno16777736: <BROADCAST,MULTICAST,UP,LOWER_UP> mtu 1500 qdisc pfifo_
fast state UP mode DEFAULT qlen 1000
    link/ether 00:0c:29:b8:8c:eb brd ff:ff:ff:ff:ff:ff
```

In case the **ip link show** command shows the current link state as down, you can temporarily bring it up again by using **ip link set**, which is followed by **dev devicename** and **up** (for example, **ip link set dev eno16777736 up**).

In Exercise 8.1, you learn how to manage and monitor networking with the **ip** utility and other utilities.

Exercise 8.1 Validating Network Configuration

1. Open a root shell.
2. Type **ip -s link**. This shows all existing network connections, in addition to statistics about the number of packets that have been sent and associated error messages.
3. Type **ip addr show**. You'll see the current address assignments for network interfaces on your server.

Validating Routing

One important aspect of networking is routing. On every network that needs to communicate to nodes on other networks, routing is a requirement. Every network has, at least, a default router (also called the default gateway) that is set, and you can see which router is used as the default router by using the command **ip route show** (see Listing 8.3). You should always perform one quick check to verify that your router is set correctly: the default router at all times must be on the same network as the local IP address that your network card is using.

Listing 8.3 ip route show Output

```
[root@server2 ~]# ip route show
default via 192.168.4.2 dev eno16777736  proto static  metric 1024
192.168.4.0/24 dev eno16777736  proto kernel  scope link  src
192.168.4.220
```

Validating the Availability of Ports and Services

Network problems can be related to the local IP and router settings but can also be related to network ports that are not available on your server or on a remote server. To verify availability of ports on your server, you can use the **netstat** command, or the newer **ss** command, which provides the same functionality. Example 8.2 shows how to verify network settings. By typing **ss -lt**, you'll see all listening TCP ports on the local system (see Listing 8.4).

Listing 8.4 Use **ss -lt** to Display All Listening Ports on the Local System

```
[root@server2 ~]# ss -lt
State       Recv-Q Send-Q    Local Address:Port         Peer Address:Port
LISTEN      0      100       127.0.0.1:smtp             *:*
LISTEN      0      128       *:56601                    *:*
LISTEN      0      128       .0.0.1:x11-ssh-offse       *:*
LISTEN      0      128       *:sunrpc                   *:*
LISTEN      0      128       *:ssh                      *:*
LISTEN      0      128       127.0.0.1:ipp              *:*
LISTEN      0      100       ::1:smtp                   :::=*
LISTEN      0      128       :1:x11-ssh-offset          :::  *
LISTEN      0      128       :::sunrpc                  :::*
LISTEN      0      128       :::34449                   :::*
LISTEN      0      128       :::ssh                     :::*
LISTEN      0      128       ::1:ipp                    :::*
```

Notice where the port is listening on. Some ports are only listening on the IPv4 loopback address 127.0.0.1 or the IPv6 loopback address ::1, which means that they are locally accessible only. Other ports are listening on *, which stands for all IPv4 addresses, or on :::*, which represents all ports on all IPv6 addresses.

Exercise 8.2 Verifying Network Settings

1. Open a root shell to your server and type **ip addr show**. This shows the current network configuration. Note the IPv4 address that is used. Notice the network device names that are used; you need these later in this exercise.
2. Type **ip route show** to verify routing configuration.
3. If your computer is connected to the Internet, you can now use the **ping** command to verify the connection to the Internet is working properly. Type **ping -c 4 8.8.8.8**, for instance, to send four packets to IP address 8.8.8.8. If your Internet connection is up and running, you should get "echo reply" answers.
4. Type **ip addr add 10.0.0.10/24 dev <yourdevicename>**.
5. Type **ip addr show**. You'll see the newly set IP address, in addition to the IP address that was already in use.

6. Type **ifconfig**. Notice that you do not see the newly set IP address (and there are no options with the **ifconfig** command that allow you to see it). This is one example why you should not use the **ifconfig** command anymore.
7. Type **ss -tul**. You'll now see a list of all UDP and TCP ports that are listening on your server.

Configuring Network Configuration with nmtui and nmcli

As mentioned earlier in this chapter, networking on RHEL 7 is managed by the NetworkManager service. You can use the **systemctl status NetworkManager** command to verify its current status. When NetworkManager comes up, it reads the network card configuration scripts, which are in /etc/sysconfig/network-scripts and have a name that starts with ifcfg and is followed by the name of the network card.

When working with network configuration in RHEL 7, you should know the difference between a device and a connection:

- A device is a network interface card.
- A connection is the configuration that is used on a device.

In RHEL 7, you can create multiple connections for a device. This can make sense on mobile computers, to make a difference between settings that are used while connected to the home network and settings that are needed to the corporate network. Switching between connections on devices is something that is common on end-user computers, and not so common on servers. To manage the network connections that you want to assign to devices, you use the **nmtui** or the **nmcli** command.

EXAM TIP Red Hat wants you to know how to work with **nmcli**. This command is not so very easy to use, however, and in the end, on the exam you will need to configure a network device with the appropriate settings. For that reason, on the RHCSA exam, it is perfectly fine to use the **nmtui** text user interface command; you will get things done a lot easier with this command.

Configuring the Network with nmcli

Earlier in this chapter, you learned how to use **ip** to verify network configuration. You have also applied the **ip addr add** command to temporarily set an IP address on a network interface. Everything you do with the **ip** command, though, is nonpersistent. If you want to make your configuration persistent, use **nmtui** or **nmcli**.

A good start is to use **nmcli** to show all connections. This shows active *and* inactive connections. You can easily see the difference because inactive connections are not currently assigned to a device (see Listing 8.5)

Listing 8.5 Showing Current Connection Status

```
[root@server2 ~]# nmcli con show
NAME  UUID                                  TYPE            DEVICE
eth0  3b2a6a84-ea82-45d1-a173-6674e770c096  802-3-ethernet  eno16777736
```

After finding the name of the connection, you can use **nmcli con show** followed by the name of the connection to see all properties of the connection. Notice that this command shows many properties. Listing 8.6 shows the output of this command.

Listing 8.6 Displaying Connection Properties

```
[root@server2 ~]# nmcli con show eno16777736
connection.id:                          eno16777736
connection.uuid:                        3b2a6a84-ea82-45d1-a173-
6674e770c096
connection.interface-name:              --
connection.type:                        802-3-ethernet
connection.autoconnect:                 yes
connection.timestamp:                   1418466791
connection.read-only:                   no
connection.permissions:
connection.zone:                        --
connection.master:                      --
connection.slave-type:                  --
connection.secondaries:
connection.gateway-ping-timeout:        0
802-3-ethernet.port:                    --
802-3-ethernet.speed:                   0
802-3-ethernet.duplex:                  --
802-3-ethernet.auto-negotiate:          yes
802-3-ethernet.mac-address:             00:0C:29:B8:8C:EB
802-3-ethernet.cloned-mac-address:      --
802-3-ethernet.mac-address-blacklist:
```

```
802-3-ethernet.mtu:             auto
802-3-ethernet.s390-subchannels:
802-3-ethernet.s390-nettype:  --
802-3-ethernet.s390-options:
ipv4.method:                   manual
ipv4.dns:                      192.168.4.200, 8.8.8.8
ipv4.dns-search:
ipv4.addresses:                { ip = 192.168.4.220/24, gw = 192.168.4.2 }
ipv4.routes:
ipv4.ignore-auto-routes:        no
ipv4.ignore-auto-dns:           no
ipv4.dhcp-client-id:            --
ipv4.dhcp-send-hostname:        yes
ipv4.dhcp-hostname:            --
ipv4.never-default:            no
ipv4.may-fail:                 yes
ipv6.method:                   auto
ipv6.dns:
ipv6.dns-search:
ipv6.addresses:
ipv6.routes:
ipv6.ignore-auto-routes:        no
ipv6.ignore-auto-dns:           no
ipv6.never-default:             no
ipv6.may-fail:                 yes
ipv6.ip6-privacy:              -1 (unknown)
ipv6.dhcp-hostname:            --
GENERAL.NAME:                  eth0
GENERAL.UUID:                  3b2a6a84-ea82-45d1-a173-6674e770c096
GENERAL.DEVICES:               eno16777736
GENERAL.STATE:                 activated
GENERAL.DEFAULT:               yes
GENERAL.DEFAULT6:              no
GENERAL.VPN:                 no
GENERAL.ZONE:                  --
GENERAL.DBUS-PATH:             /org/freedesktop/NetworkManager/
                               ActiveConnection/0
GENERAL.CON-PATH:               /org/freedesktop/NetworkManager/Settings/0
GENERAL.SPEC-OBJECT:            --
GENERAL.MASTER-PATH:            --
```

```
IP4.ADDRESS[1]:               ip = 192.168.4.220/24, gw = 192.168.4.2
IP4.DNS[1]:                   192.168.4.200
IP4.DNS[2]:                   8.8.8.8
IP6.ADDRESS[1]:               ip = fe80::20c:29ff:feb8:8ceb/64, gw = ::
```

To find out what exactly these settings are doing, read man 5 nm-settings. You can also use **nmcli** to show an overview of currently configured devices and the status of these devices. Type, for instance, the **nmcli dev status** command to show a list of all devices, and **nmcli dev show <devicename>** to show settings for a specific device.

In Exercise 8.3, you learn how to create connections and switch between connections using the **nmcli** command:

Exercise 8.3 Managing Network Connections with nmcli

1. Create a new network connection using **nmcli con add con-name "dhcp" type ethernet ifname eth0**.
2. Create a connection with the name static to define a static IP address and gateway: **nmcli con add con-name "static" ifname eth0 autoconnect no type ethernet ip4 10.0.0.10/24 gw4 10.0.0.1**. The gateway might not exist in your configuration, but that does not matter. (Make sure to change the ifname eth0 into the interface name that matches your hardware!)
3. Type **nmcli con show** to show the connections, and use **nmcli con up "static"** to activate the static connection. Switch back to the DHCP connection using **nmcli con up "dhcp"**.

In this exercise, you created network connections using **nmcli con add**. You can also change current connection properties by using **nmcli con mod**. In Exercise 8.4, you use **nmcli** to change some connection parameters.

Exercise 8.4 Changing Connection Parameters with nmcli

1. Make sure that the static connection does not connect automatically by using **nmcli con mod "static" connection autoconnect no**.
2. Add a DHCP server to the static connection by using **nmcli con mod "static" ipv4.dns 10.0.0.10**. Notice that while adding a network connection you used

ip4, but while modifying parameters for an existing connection, you'll often use **ipv4** instead. This is not a typo; it is just an inconsistency in the command.

3. To add a second item for the same parameters, use a + sign. Test this by adding a second DNS server, using **nmcli con mod "static" + ipv4.dns 8.8.8.8**.
4. Using **nmcli con mod**, you can also change parameters such as the existing IP address. Try this by using **nmcli con mod "static" ipv4.addresses "10.0.0.20/24" 10.0.0.100**.
5. And to add a second IP address you use the + sign again: **nmcli con mod "static" +ipv4.addresses 10.20.30.40/16**.
6. After changing connection properties, you need to activate them. To do that, you can use **nmcli con up "static"**.

This is all you need to know about nmcli for RHCSA. Did you like it? Probably not. The exact syntax of this command may be hard to remember. Fortunately, though, there is an excellent man page with examples. Type **man nmcli-examples** to show this man page; you'll notice that if you can find this man page, you can do almost anything with nmcli.

Configuring the Network with nmtui

If you do not like the complicated syntax of the nmcli command line, you might like **nmtui**. This is a text user interface that allows you to create network connections easily. Figure 8.1 shows what the nmtui interface looks like.

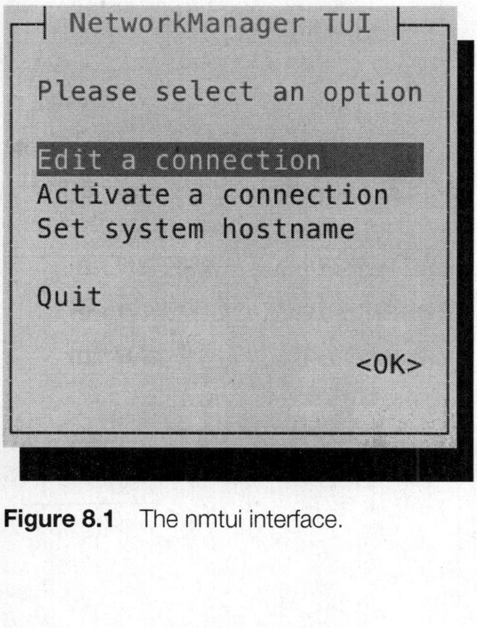

Figure 8.1 The nmtui interface.

The nmtui interface consists of three menu options:

- **Edit a Connection:** Use this option to create new connections or edit existing connections.
- **Activate a Connection:** Use this to (re)activate a connection.
- **Set System Hostname:** Use this to set the hostname of your computer.

The option to edit a connection offers almost all features that you might ever need to do while working on network connections. It sure allows you to do anything you need to be doing on the RHCSA exam. You can use it to add any type of connection. Not just Ethernet connections, but also advanced connection types such as network bridges and teamed network drivers are supported.

When you select the option Edit Connection, you get access to a rich interface that allows you to edit most properties of network connections. After editing the connection, you need to deactivate it and activate it again. This should work automatically, but the fact is it does not.

TIP If you like graphical user interface (GUI) tools, you are lucky. Use nm-connection-editor instead of nmtui, but be prepared that this interface offers a relatively restricted option set. It does not contain advanced options such as the options to create network team interfaces and manage network bridge interfaces. It does, however, offer all you need to manage address configuration on a network connection. Start it by using the **nm-connection-editor** command, or by using the applet in the GNOME graphical interface. Figure 8.2 shows what the default interface of this tool looks like.

Working on Network Configuration Files

Every connection that you create is stored as a configuration file in the directory /etc/sysconfig/network-scripts. The name of the configuration files starts with ifcfg- and is followed by the name of the network interface. In Listing 8.7, you can see what such a configuration file looks like.

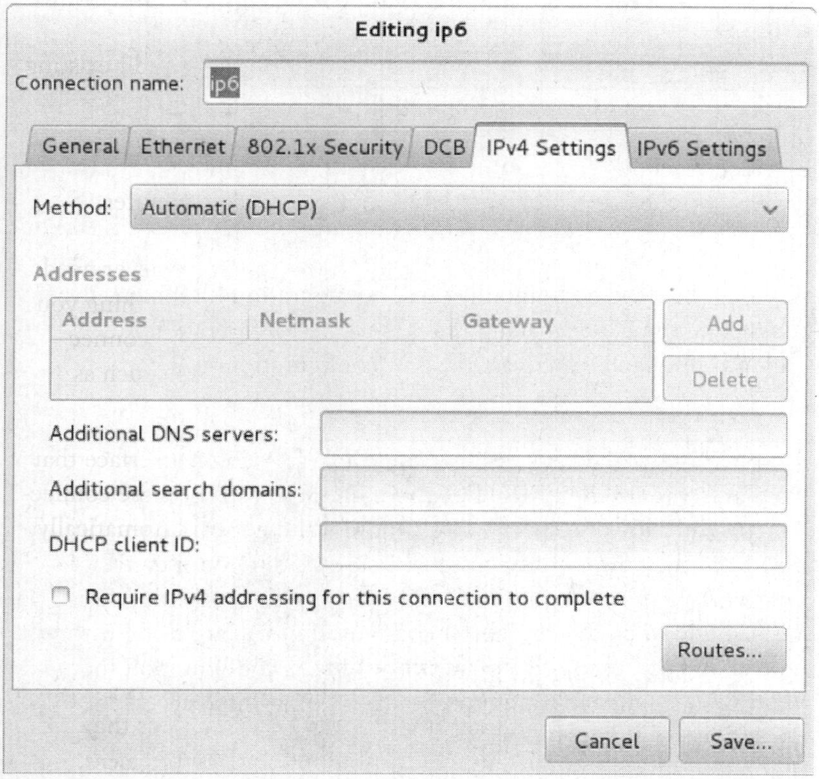

Figure 8.2 The nm-connection-editor interface.

Listing 8.7 Example of an ifcfg Configuration File

```
[root@server2 network-scripts]# cat ifcfg-eno16777736
TYPE="Ethernet"
BOOTPROTO=none
DEFROUTE="yes"
IPV4_FAILURE_FATAL="no"
IPV6INIT="yes"
IPV6_AUTOCONF="yes"
IPV6_DEFROUTE="yes"
IPV6_FAILURE_FATAL="no"
NAME=eno16777736
UUID="3b2a6a84-ea82-45d1-a173-6674e770c096"
ONBOOT="yes"
IPADDR0=192.168.4.220
PREFIX0=24
```

```
GATEWAY0=192.168.4.2
DNS1=192.168.4.200
HWADDR=00:0C:29:B8:8C:EB
DNS2=8.8.8.8
IPV6_PEERDNS=yes
IPV6_PEERROUTES=yes
```

Normally, there should be no need to modify these configuration files manually. If you want to, though, you can. After making changes to the configuration file, use the **nmcli con reload** command to activate the new configuration.

> **TIP** You can set both a fixed IP address as a dynamic IP address in one network connection. To do that, set the BOOTPROTO option in the connection configuration file to dhcp, while you also specify an IP address and network prefix. You can do this also from the nmtui utility; just make sure that in nmtui the IPv4 configuration is set to automatic (and not to manual), and specify an IP address as well. I recommend that you to do this in the test configuration you are using with this book, because it allows you to use a static network address configuration for internal use, in addition to a dynamic configuration that allows you to access the Internet and install software from repositories.

Setting Up Hostname and Name Resolution

To communicate with other hosts, hostnames are used. As an administrator, it is important that you know how to set the hostname. You also need to make sure that hosts can contact one another based on hostnames by setting up hostname resolution. In this section, you learn how to do that.

Hostnames

Because hostnames are used to access servers and the services they're offering, it is important to know how to set the system hostname. A hostname typically consists of different parts. These are the name of the host and the DNS domain in which the host resides. These two parts together make up for the fully qualified domain name (FQDN), which looks like server1.example.com. It is good practice to always specify an FQDN, and not just the hostname. There are different ways to change the hostname:

- Use nmtui and select the option **Change Hostname**.
- Use **hostnamectl set-hostname**.
- Edit the contents of the configuration file /etc/hostname.

To configure the hostname with **hostnamectl**, you can use a command like **hostnamectl set-hostname myhost.example.com**. After setting the hostname, you can use **hostnamectl status** to show the current hostname. Listing 8.8 shows the output of this command.

Listing 8.8 Showing Current Hostname Configuration

```
[root@server2 ~]# hostnamectl status
   Static hostname: server2.example.com
         Icon name: computer
           Chassis: n/a
        Machine ID: 708ab34cdfca454d908224e0b37a8bf6
           Boot ID: 9fa3baf6fe46420aaa44c324a76f40b2
    Virtualization: vmware
  Operating System: CentOS Linux 7 (Core)
       CPE OS Name: cpe:/o:centos:centos:7
            Kernel: Linux 3.10.0-123.el7.x86_64
      Architecture: x86_64
```

The **hostnamectl** command is new in RHEL 7. When using **hostnamectl status**, you see not only information about the hostname but also information about the Linux kernel, virtualization type, and much more.

Alternatively, you can set the hostname using the nmtui interface. Figure 8.3 shows the screen from which this can be done.

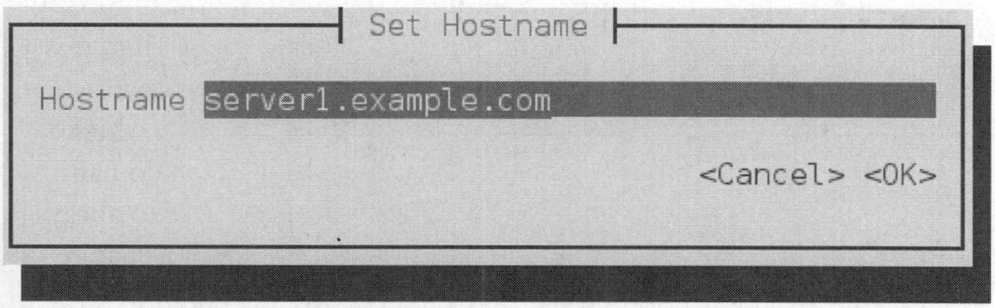

Figure 8.3 Changing the hostname using nmtui.

To set host name resolution, DNS is typically used. Configuring DNS is not an RHCSA objective. Apart from DNS, you can configure host name resolution in the /etc/hosts file. Listing 8.9 shows the contents of an /etc/hosts file.

Listing 8.9 /etc/hosts Sample Contents

```
[root@server1 ~]# cat /etc/hosts
127.0.0.1    localhost localhost.localdomain localhost4 localhost4.localdomain4
::1          localhost localhost.localdomain localhost6 localhost6.localdomain6
```

All hostname - IP address definitions as set in /etc/hosts will be applied before the hostname in DNS is used. This is configured as a default in the hosts line in /etc/nsswitch.conf, which by default looks like this:

```
hosts:    files dns
```

Setting up an /etc/hosts file is easy; just make sure that it contains at least two columns. The first column has the IP address of the specific host, and the second column specifies the hostname. The hostname can be provided as a short name (like server1), or an FQDN. In an FQDN, the hostname as well as the complete DNS name are included, as in server1.example.com.

If a host has more than one name, like a short name and a fully qualified DNS name, you can specify both of them in /etc/hosts. In that case, the second column must contain the FQDN, and the third column can contain the alias. Listing 8.10 shows a hostname configuration example.

Listing 8.10 /etc/hosts Configuration Example

```
[root@server2 ~]# cat /etc/hosts
127.0.0.1    localhost localhost.localdomain localhost4 localhost4.localdomain4
::1          localhost localhost.localdomain localhost6 localhost6.localdomain6
10.0.0.10      server1.example.com     server1
10.0.0.20      server2.example.com     server2
```

DNS Resolving

Just using an /etc/hosts file is not enough for name resolution if you want to be able to communicate with other hosts on the Internet. You should use DNS, too. To specify which DNS server should be used, set the DNS server via Network-Manager. The NetworkManager configuration stores the DNS information in the configuration file for the network connection, which is in /etc/sysconfig/network-scripts, and from there pushes the configuration to the /etc/resolv.conf file, which is used for DNS name server resolving.

It is recommended to always set up at least two DNS name servers to be contacted. If the first name server does not answer, the second name server is contacted. So, this is why you want to use a second name server. If the first name server times out or cannot be reached, the second server is used. To specify which DNS name servers you want to use, you have a few different options:

- Use **nmtui** to set the DNS name servers. Figure 8.4 shows the interface from which you can do this.
- Set the DNS1 and DNS2 in the ifcfg network connection configuration file in /etc/sysconfig/network-scripts.
- Use a DHCP server that is configured to hand out the address of the DNS name server.
- Use **nmcli con mod <connection-id> [+]ipv4.dns <ip-of-dns>**.

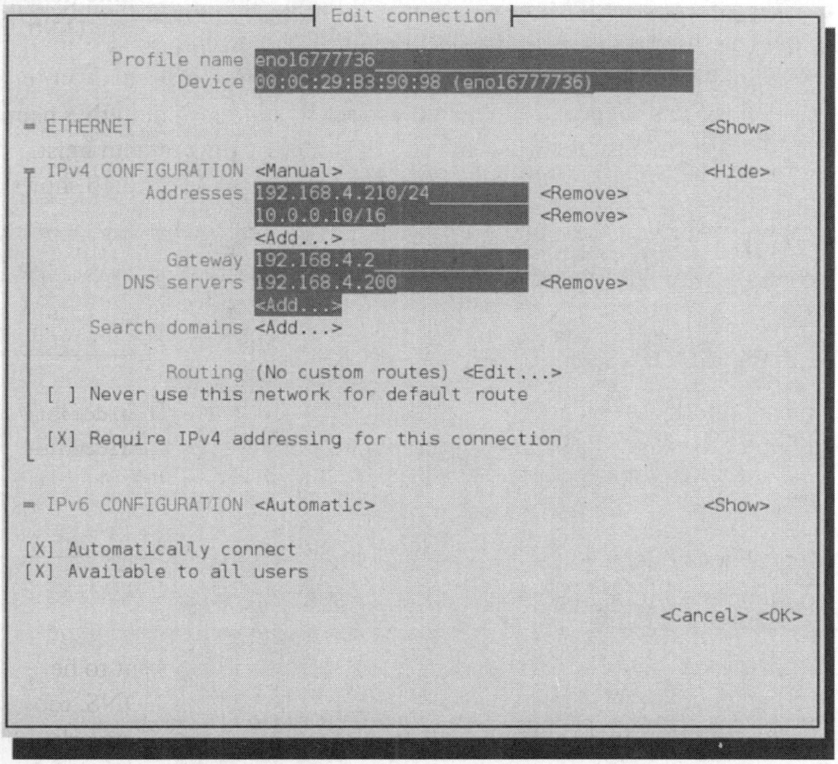

Figure 8.4 Setting DNS servers from the nmtui interface

Notice that if your computer is configured to get the network configuration from a DHCP server, the DNS server is also set via the DHCP server. If you do not want this to happen, you have two options:

- Edit the ifcfg configuration file to include the option **PEERDNS=no**.
- Use **nmcli con mod <con-name> ipv4.ignore-auto-dns yes**.

To verify host name resolution, you can use the **getent hosts <servername>** command. This command searches in both /etc/hosts and DNS to resolve the hostname that has been specified.

EXAM TIP Do *not* specify the DNS servers directly in /etc/resolv.conf. They will be overwritten by NetworkManager.

Summary

In this chapter, you learned how to configure networking in RHEL 7. First you read how the IP protocol is used to connect computers together, and then you read which techniques are used to make services between hosts accessible. Next you read how to verify the network configuration using the **ip** utility and some related utilities. In the last part of this chapter, you read how to set IP addresses and other host configuration in a permanent way by using either the nmcli or the nmtui utility.

Exam Prep Tasks

Review All Key Topics

Review the most important topics in the chapter, noted with the Key Topic icon in the outer margin of the page. Table 8.3 lists a reference of these key topics and the page numbers on which each is found.

Table 8.3 Key Topics for Chapter 8

Key Topic Element	Description	Page
List	IPv4 / IPv6 short description	180
List	Private network addresses	180
Table 8.2	Binary-decimal conversion overview	182
List	IP address types	183

Complete Tables and Lists from Memory

Print a copy of Appendix B, "Memory Tables" (found on the disc), or at least the section for this chapter, and complete the tables and lists from memory. Appendix C, "Memory Tables Answer Key," also on the disc, includes completed tables and lists to check your work.

Define Key Terms

Define the following key terms from this chapter and check your answers in the glossary:

ip, ipv4, ipv6, protocol, port, subnet mask, DNS, DHCP, connection, interface, FQDN

Review Questions

1. What is the network address in the address 213.214.215.99/29?
2. Which command only shows link status and not the IP address?
3. Which service manages networking in RHEL 7?
4. Which file contains the hostname in RHEL 7?
5. Which command enables you to set the hostname in an easy way?
6. Which command do you need to run after manually changing the contents of the /etc/sysconfig/ifcfg files?
7. Which configuration file can you change to enable hostname resolving for a specific IP address?
8. Which command shows current routing configuration?
9. How do you verify the current status of the NetworkManager service?
10. Which command enables you to change the current IP address and default gateway on your network connection?

End-of-Chapter Labs

For exercises in later chapters in this book, it is recommended to have a test environment in which at least two servers are present. To do the exercises in this lab, make sure that you have a second server installed. For your convenience, a complete test environment is available as a free download at http://www.rhatcert.com. Notice that you need to register on this site (for free), after which you have access to the test environment. You can do the end-of-chapter labs in this chapter based on the servers you have installed yourself or based on this free test environment.

Lab 8.1

1. Set up the first server to use the FQDN server1.example.com. The second server should use server2.example.com.
2. On server1.example.com, use nmtui and configure your primary network card to automatically get an IP address through DHCP. Also set a fixed IP address to 192.168.122.100. On server2, set the fixed IP address to 192.168.122.110.
3. Make sure that from server1 you can ping server2, and vice versa.
4. To allow you to access servers on the Internet, make sure that your local DHCP server provides the default router and DNS servers.

The following topics are covered in this chapter:

- Introduction to Process Management
- Managing Shell Jobs
- Using Common Command-Line Tools for Process Management
- Using top to Manage Processes

The following RHCSA exam objectives are covered in this chapter:

- Identify CPU/memory-intensive processes, adjust process priority with renice, and kill processes

CHAPTER 9

Managing Processes

Process management is an important task for a Linux administrator, which is why in this book you find three chapters dedicated to this topic. In this chapter, you learn what you need to know to manage processes from a perspective of daily operation of a server. In Chapter 27, "System Performance Reporting," the topic is explored more in depth, and process management is covered from the performance analysis perspective. In Chapter 28, "System Optimization Basics," you learn how you can use the data that is gathered this way to optimize system performance.

TIP If you are interested in more information about some of the utilities discussed in this chapter, see Chapter 27.

"Do I Know This Already?" Quiz

The "Do I Know This Already?" quiz allows you to assess whether you should read this entire chapter thoroughly or jump to the "Exam Preparation Tasks" section. If you are in doubt about your answers to these questions or your own assessment of your knowledge of the topics, read the entire chapter. Table 9.1 lists the major headings in this chapter and their corresponding "Do I Know This Already?" quiz questions. You can find the answers in Appendix A, "Answers to the 'Do I Know This Already?' Quizzes and 'Review Questions.'"

Table 9.1 "Do I Know This Already?" Section-to-Question Mapping

Foundation Topics Section	Questions
Introduction to Process Management	1
Managing Shell Jobs	2–3
Using Common Command-Line Tools for Process Management	4–9
Using top to Manage Processes	10

1. Which of the following is not generally considered a type of process?
   a. A shell job
   b. A cron job
   c. A daemon
   d. A thread

2. Which of the following can be used to move a job to the background?
   a. Type &
   b. Type **Ctrl+Z**, followed by **bg**
   c. Type **Ctrl+D**, followed by **bg**
   d. Type **Ctrl+Z**, followed by &

3. Which keystroke enables you to cancel a current interactive shell job?
   a. **Ctrl+C**
   b. **Ctrl+D**
   c. **Ctrl+Z**
   d. **Ctrl+Break**

4. Which of the following statements are true about threads?
   a. Threads cannot be managed individually by an administrator.
   b. Multithreaded processes can make the working of processes more efficient.
   c. Threads can be used only on supported platforms.
   d. Using multiple processes is more efficient, in general, than using multiple threads.

5. Which of the following commands is most appropriate if you're looking for detailed information about the command and how it was started?
   a. **ps ef**
   b. **ps aux**
   c. **ps**
   d. **ps fax**

6. Of the following nice values, which will increase the priority of the selected process?
   a. 100
   b. 20
   c. -19
   d. -100

7. Which of the following shows correct syntax to change the priority for the current process with PID 1234?
   a. **nice -n 5 1234**
   b. **renice 5 1234**
   c. **renice 5 -p 1234**
   d. **nice 5 -p 1234**

8. Which of the following commands cannot be used to send signals to processes?
   a. **kill**
   b. **mkill**
   c. **pkill**
   d. **killall**

9. Which signal would you send to a process if you want to force it to stop, even if that means potential loss of data that the process is currently working with?
   a. SIGKILL
   b. SIGSTOP
   c. SIGTERM
   d. SIGHUP

10. Which of the following commands would you use from top to change the priority of a process?
    a. **r**
    b. **n**
    c. **c**
    d. **k**

Foundation Topics

Introduction to Process Management

For everything that happens on a Linux server, a process is started. For that reason, process management is among the key skills that an administrator has to master. To do this efficiently, it is important to know which type of process you are dealing with. A major distinction can be made between two process types:

- Shell jobs are commands started from the command line. They are associated with the shell that was current when the process was started. Shell jobs are also referred to as interactive processes.
- Daemons are processes that provide services. They normally are started when a computer is booted and often (but certainly not in all cases) they are running with root privileges.

When a process is started, it can use multiple threads. A thread is a task started by a process and that a dedicated CPU can service. The Linux shell offers tools to manage individual threads. Thread management should be taken care of from within the command.

To manage a process efficiently, it is paramount that you know what type of process you are dealing with. Shell jobs require another approach than the processes that are automatically started when a computer boots.

Managing Shell Jobs

When a user types a command, a shell job is started. If no particular measures have been taken, the job is started as a foreground process, occupying the terminal it was started from until it has finished its work. As a Linux administrator, you need to know how to start shell jobs in the foreground or background and what can be done to manage shell jobs.

Running Jobs in the Foreground and Background

By default, any executed command is started as a foreground job. For many commands, that does not really matter because the command often takes a little while to complete, after which it returns access to the shell from which it was started. Sometimes it might prove useful to start commands in the background. This makes sense for processes that do not require user interaction. A process that does require user interaction will not be able to get that when running in the background, and for that reason will typically stall when moved to the background. You can take two different approaches to run a process in the background.

If you know that a job will take a long time to complete, you can start it with an **&** behind it. This immediately starts the job in the background to make room for other tasks to be started from the command line. To move the last job that was started in the background back as a foreground job, use the **fg** command. This command immediately, and with no further questions, brings the last job back to the foreground.

A job might sometimes have been started that takes (much) longer than predicted. If that happens, you can use **Ctrl+Z** to temporarily stop the job. This does not remove the job from memory; it just pauses the job so that it can be managed. Once paused, it can be continued as a background job using the **bg** command. An alternative key sequence that you can use to manage shell jobs is **Ctrl+C**. This stops the current job and removes it from memory.

A related keystroke combination is **Ctrl+D**, which sends the End Of File (EOF) character to the current job. The result is that the job stops waiting for further input so that it can complete what it was currently doing. The result of sending **Ctrl+D** is sometimes very similar to the result of sending **Ctrl+C**, but there is a difference. When **Ctrl+C** is used, the job is just canceled, and nothing is closed properly. When **Ctrl+D** is used, the job stops waiting for further input, which often is just what is needed to complete in a proper way.

Managing Shell Jobs

When moving jobs between the foreground and background, it may be useful to have an overview of all current jobs. To get such an overview, use the **jobs** command. As you can see in Table 9.2, this command gives an overview of all jobs currently running as a background job, including the job number assigned to the job when starting it in the background. These job numbers can be used as an argument to the **fg** and **bg** commands to perform job management tasks. In Exercise 9.1, you learn how to perform common job management tasks from the shell.

Table 9.2 Job Management Overview

Key Topic

Command	Use
& (used at the end of a command line)	Starts the command immediately in the background.
Ctrl+Z	Stops the job temporarily so that it can be managed. For instance, it can be moved to the background.
Ctrl+D	Send the End Of File (EOF) character to the current job to indicate that it should stop waiting for further input.

Command	Use
Ctrl+C	Can be used to cancel the current interactive job
bg	Continues the job that has just been frozen using **Ctrl+Z** in the background.
fg	Brings the last job that was moved to background execution back to the foreground.
jobs	Shows which jobs are currently running from this shell. Displays job numbers that can be used as an argument to the commands **bg** and **fg**.

Exercise 9.1 Managing jobs

In this exercise, you apply the commands that you just learned about to manage jobs that have been started from the current shell.

1. Open a root shell and type the following commands:

```
sleep 3600 &
dd if=/dev/zero of=/dev/null &
sleep 7200
```

2. Because you started the last command with no & after the command, you have to wait 2 hours before you get control to the shell back. Type **Ctrl+Z** to stop it.
3. Type **jobs**. You will see the three jobs that you just started. The first two of them have the Running state, and the last job currently is in the Stopped state.
4. Type **bg 3** to continue running job 3 in the background. Notice that because it was started as the last job, you did not really have to add the number 3.
5. Type **fg 1** to move job 1 to the foreground.
6. Type **Ctrl+C** to cancel job number 1 and use **jobs** to confirm that it is now gone.
7. Use the same approach to cancel jobs 2 and 3 also.
8. Open a second terminal on your server.
9. From that second terminal, type **dd if=/dev/zero of=/dev/null &**.
10. Type **exit** to close the second terminal.
11. From the other terminal, start **top**. You will see that the **dd** job is still running. From top, use **k** to kill the dd job.

NOTE You read how to manage interactive shell jobs in this section. Notice that all of these jobs are processes as well. As the user that started the job, you can also manage it. In the next section, you learn how to use process management to manage jobs started by other users.

Managing Parent Child Relations

When a process is started from a shell, it becomes a child process of that shell. In process management, the parent-child relationship between processes is very important. The parent is needed to manage the child. For that reason, all processes started from a shell are terminated when that shell is stopped. This also offers an easy way to terminate processes no longer needed.

Processes started in the background will not be killed when the parent shell from which they were started is killed. To terminate these processes, you need to use the **kill** command, as described later in this chapter.

NOTE In earlier versions of the bash shell, background processes were also killed when the shell they were started from was terminated. To prevent that, the process could be started with the **nohup** command in front of it. Using **nohup** for this purpose is no longer needed in RHEL 7.

Using Common Command-Line Tools for Process Management

On a Linux server, many processes are usually running. On an average server or desktop computer, there are often more than a hundred active processes. With so many processes being active, things may go wrong. If that happens, it is good to know how noninteractive processes can be stopped, or how the priority of these processes can be adjusted to make more system resources available for other processes.

Understanding Processes and Threads

Tasks on Linux are typically started as processes. One process can start several worker threads. Working with threads makes sense, because if the process is very busy, the threads can be handled by different CPUs or CPU cores available in the machine. As a Linux administrator, you cannot manage individual threads; you can manage processes, though. It is the programmer of the multithreaded application that has to define how threads relate to one another.

Before talking about different ways to manage processes, it is good to know that there are two different types of background processes. To start, there are kernel threads. These are a part of the Linux kernel, and each of them is started with its own process identification number (PID). When managing processes, it is easy to recognize the kernel processes because they have a name that is between square brackets. Listing 9.1 shows a list of a few processes as output of the command **ps aux | head** (discussed later in this chapter), in which you can see a couple of kernel threads.

As an administrator, it is important to know that kernel threads cannot be managed. You cannot adjust their priority; neither is it possible to kill them, except by taking the entire machine down.

Listing 9.1 Showing Kernel Threads with **ps aux**

```
[root@server1 /]# ps aux | head
USER       PID %CPU %MEM    VSZ   RSS TTY   STAT START   TIME COMMAND
root         1  0.0  0.4  52984  4272 ?     Ss   Feb05   0:03 /usr/lib/
    systemd/systemd --switched-root --system --deserialize 23
root         2  0.0  0.0      0     0 ?     S    Feb05   0:00 [kthreadd]
root         3  0.0  0.0      0     0 ?     S    Feb05   0:00 [ksoftirqd/0]
root         5  0.0  0.0      0     0 ?     S<   Feb05   0:00 [kworker/0:0H]
root         7  0.0  0.0      0     0 ?     S    Feb05   0:00 [migration/0]
root         8  0.0  0.0      0     0 ?     S    Feb05   0:00 [rcu_bh]
root         9  0.0  0.0      0     0 ?     S    Feb05   0:00 [rcuob/0]
root        10  0.0  0.0      0     0 ?     S    Feb05   0:00 [rcuob/1]
root        11  0.0  0.0      0     0 ?     S    Feb05   0:00 [rcuob/2]
```

Using ps to Get Process Information

The most common command to get an overview of currently running processes is **ps**. If used without any arguments, the **ps** command shows only those processes that have been started by the current user. You can use many different options to display different process properties. If you are looking for a short summary of the active processes, use **ps aux** (as you saw in Listing 9.1). If you are not only looking for the name of the process but also for the exact command that was used to start the process, use **ps -ef**. Alternative ways to use **ps** exist as well, such as the command **ps fax**, which shows hierarchical relationships between parent and child processes (see Listings 9.2 and 9.3).

Listing 9.2 Use **ps -ef** to See the Exact Command Used to Start Processes

```
[root@server2 ~]# ps -ef
UID         PID   PPID  C STIME TTY          TIME CMD
root        874      1  0 May14 ?        00:00:00 /sbin/auditd -n
root        885    874  0 May14 ?        00:00:00 /sbin/audispd
root        889    885  0 May14 ?        00:00:00 /usr/sbin/sedispatch
root        898      1  0 May14 ?        00:00:00 /usr/sbin/alsactl -s -n
19 -c -E ALSA_CONFIG_PATH=/etc/alsa/alsactl.conf --initfile=/lib/alsa/
root        899      1  0 May14 ?        00:00:00 /usr/sbin/bluetoothd -n
root        900      1  0 May14 ?        00:00:00 /usr/bin/python -Es /
usr/sbin/firewalld --nofork --nopid
avahi       902      1  0 May14 ?        00:00:00 avahi-daemon: running
[server2.local]
libstor+    903      1  0 May14 ?        00:00:00 /usr/bin/lsmd -d
root        905      1  0 May14 ?        00:02:14 /usr/bin/vmtoolsd
root        908      1  0 May14 ?        00:00:00 /usr/sbin/rsyslogd -n
root        910      1  0 May14 ?        00:00:00 /usr/sbin/abrtd -d -s
root        911      1  0 May14 ?        00:00:00 /usr/bin/abrt-watch-log
-F BUG: WARNING: at WARNING: CPU: INFO: possible recursive locking det
avahi       912    902  0 May14 ?        00:00:00 avahi-daemon: chroot
helper
```

NOTE For some commands, using a hyphen before options is optional. Some commands do not. The **ps** command is one of those latter commands. There is a historical reason why this is the case: The commands derive from the old BSD UNIX flavor, where it was common to specify command-line options without a - in front of them.

Listing 9.3 Use **ps fax** to Show Parent-Child Relationships Between Processes

```
[root@server2 ~]# ps fax
  PID TTY      STAT   TIME COMMAND
1603 ?         Ss     0:00 /usr/sbin/sshd -D
35395 ?        Ss     0:00  \_ sshd: root@pts/1
```

```
35417 pts/1    Ss     0:00   \_ -bash
35568 pts/1    R+     0:00   \_ ps fax
 1612 ?        Ss     0:00 /usr/sbin/vsftpd /etc/vsftpd/vsftpd.conf
 1613 ?        Ssl    0:07 /usr/sbin/nslcd
 1652 ?        Ss     0:01 /usr/sbin/nmbd
 1689 ?        Ss     0:02 /usr/sbin/smbd
 1717 ?        S      0:00   \_ /usr/sbin/smbd
 1721 ?        Ss     0:00 /usr/sbin/cupsd -f
 1778 ?        Ss     0:00 /usr/libexec/postfix/master -w
 1780 ?        S      0:00   \_ qmgr -l -t unix -u
33145 ?        S      0:00   \_ pickup -l -t unix -u
 1824 ?        Ss     0:02 /usr/sbin/crond -n
 1825 ?        Ss     0:00 /usr/sbin/atd -f
 1827 ?        Ssl    0:00 /usr/sbin/gdm
 1839 ?        Sl     0:00   \_ /usr/libexec/gdm-simple-slave --display-id
/org/gnome/DisplayManager/Displays/_0
 1860 tty1     Ss+    0:04   \_ /usr/bin/Xorg :0 -background none -verbose
-auth /run/gdm/auth-for-gdm-Fm1P1C/database -seat seat0 -noliste
34159 ?        Sl     0:00   \_ gdm-session-worker [pam/gdm-password]
34192 ?        Ssl    0:00   \_ gnome-session --session gnome-classic
34344 ?        Ss     0:00   \_ /usr/bin/ssh-agent /bin/sh -c exec -l /bin/
bash -c "env GNOME_SHELL_SESSION_MODE=classic gnome-sess
34382 ?        Sl     0:00   \_ /usr/libexec/gnome-settings-daemon
34478 ?        Sl     0:08   \_ /usr/bin/gnome-shell
34563 ?        Sl     0:00   \_ nautilus --no-default-window --force-
desktop
34583 ?        S      0:00   \_ /usr/bin/seapplet
34600 ?        SNl    0:00   \_ /usr/libexec/tracker-miner-fs
34605 ?        Sl     0:00   \_ /usr/libexec/tracker-store
34611 ?        Sl     0:00   \_ abrt-applet
```

An important piece of information to get out of the **ps** command is the PID. Many tasks require the PID to operate, and that is why a command like **ps aux | grep dd**, which will show process details about dd, including its PID, is quite common. An alternative way to get the same result is to use the **pgrep** command. Use **pgrep dd** to get a list of all PIDs that have a name containing the string dd.

Adjusting Process Priority with nice

When Linux processes are started, they are started with a specific priority. By default, all regular processes are equal and are started with the same priority, which is the priority number 20. In some cases, it is useful to change the default priority that was assigned to the process when it was started. You can do that using the **nice** and **renice** commands. Use **nice** if you want to start a process with an adjusted priority. Use **renice** to change the priority for a currently active process. Alternatively, you can use the **r** command from the **top** utility to change the priority of a currently running process.

Changing process priority may make sense in two different scenarios. Suppose, for example, that you are about to start a backup job that does not necessarily have to finish fast. Typically, backup jobs are rather resource intensive, so you might want to start it in a way that it is not annoying other users too much, by lowering its priority.

Another example is where you are about to start a very important calculation job. To ensure that it is handled as fast as possible, you might want to give it an increased priority, taking away CPU time from other processes.

On earlier Linux versions, it could be dangerous to increase the priority of one job too much, because other processes (including vital kernel processes) might risk being blocked out completely. On current Linux kernels, the situation is not that urgent anymore:

- Modern Linux kernels differentiate between essential kernel threads that are started as real-time processes and normal user processes. Increasing the priority of a user process will never be able to block out kernel threads or other processes that were started as real-time processes.
- Modern computers often have multiple CPU cores. A single threaded process that is running with the highest priority will never be able to get beyond the boundaries of the CPU it is running on.

When using **nice** or **renice** to adjust process priority, you can select from values ranging from -20 to 19. The default niceness of a process is set to 0 (which results in the priority value of 20). By applying a negative niceness, you increase the priority. Use a positive niceness to decrease the priority. It is a good idea not to use the ultimate values immediately. Instead, use increments of 5 and see how it affects the application.

TIP Do not set process priority to -20; it risks blocking other processes from getting served.

Let's take a look at examples of how to use **nice** and **renice**. The command **nice -n 5 dd if=/dev/zero of=/dev/null &** starts an infinite I/O-intensive job, but with an adjusted niceness so that some place remains for other processes as well. To adjust the niceness of a currently running process, you need the PID of that process. The following two commands show how **ps aux** is used to find the PID of the dd job from the previous example. Next, you see how the **renice** command is used to change the niceness of that command:

1. Use **ps aux | grep dd** to find the PID of the dd command that you just started. The PID is in the second column of the command output.
2. Use **renice -n 10 -p 1234** (assuming that 1234 is the PID you just found).

Note that regular users can only decrease the priority of a running process. You must be root to give processes increased priority.

Sending Signals to Processes with kill, killall, and pkill

Before starting to think about using the **kill** command or sending other signals to processes, it is good to know that Linux processes have a hierarchical relationship. Every process has a parent process, and as long as it lives, the parent process is responsible for the child processes it has created. This is particularly important when processes are terminated, because it is the parent that has to clean up the resources that were used by the children. When using kill on a parent process that still has active children, you will for that reason not just kill the parent process in question but also all of its currently active child processes.

> **NOTE** Over time, many different utilities have been developed for process monitoring and managing. I apologize if your favorite tool is not mentioned here. However, it does not really make sense to try to know all the available tools, because many tools offer comparable functionality.

The Linux kernel allows many signals to be sent to processes. Use **man 7 signals** for a complete overview of all the available signals. Three of these signals work for all processes:

Key Topic

- The signal SIGTERM (15) is used to ask a process to stop.
- The signal SIGKILL (9) is used to force a process to stop.
- The SIGHUP (1) signal is used to hang up a process. The effect is that the process will reread its configuration files, which makes this a useful signal to use after making modifications to a process configuration file.

To send a signal to a process, the **kill** command is used. The most common use is the need to stop a process, which you can do by using the **kill** command followed by the PID of the process. This sends the SIGTERM signal to the process, which normally causes the process to cease its activity.

Sometimes the **kill** command does not work because the process you want to kill is busy. In that case, you can use **kill -9** to send the SIGKILL signal to the process. Because the SIGKILL signal cannot be ignored, it forces the process to stop, but you also risk losing data while using this command. In general, it is a bad idea to use **kill -9**:

- You risk losing data.
- Your system may become unstable if other processes depend on the process you have just killed.

TIP Use **kill -l** to show a list of available signals that can be used with **kill**.

There are some commands that are related to kill: **killall** and **pkill**. The **pkill** command is a bit easier to use because it takes the name rather than the PID of the process as an argument. You can use the **killall** command if multiple processes using the same name need to be killed simultaneously.

Using **killall** was particularly common when Linux environments were multiprocessing instead of multithreading. In a multiprocessing environment where a server starts several commands, all with the same name, it is not easy to stop these commands one by one based on their individual PID. Using **killall** enables you to terminate all these processes simultaneously.

NOTE Back in the 1990s when using the Netscape browser on Linux, many (many!) netscape processes were started. To terminate all of them all at once using **killall netscape** was very efficient.

In a multithreaded environment, the urge to use **killall** is smaller. Because there is often just one process that is generating several threads, all these threads are terminated anyway by stopping the process that started them. You still can use **killall**, though, to terminate lots of processes with the same name that have been started on your server. In Exercise 9.2, you practice using the commands that you just learned about.

Exercise 9.2 Managing Processes from the Command Line

In this exercise, you learn how to work with ps, nice, kill, and related utilities to manage processes.

1. Open a root shell. From this shell, type **dd if=/dev/zero of=/dev/null &**. Repeat this command three times.
2. Type **ps aux | grep dd**. This shows all lines of output that have the letters dd in them; you will see more than just the dd processes, but that should not really matter. The processes you just started are listed last.
3. Use the PID of one of the dd processes to adjust the niceness, using **renice -n 5 <PID>**. Notice that in top you cannot easily get an overview of processes and their current priority.
4. Type **ps fax | grep -B5 dd**. The **-B5** option shows the matching lines, including the five lines before that. Because **ps fax** shows hierarchical relationships between processes, you should also find the shell and its PID from which all the dd processes were started.
5. Find the PID of the shell from which the dd processes were started and type **kill -9 <PID>**, replacing **<PID>** with the PID of the shell you just found. You will see that your root shell is closed, and with it, all of the dd processes. Killing a parent process is an easy and convenient way to kill all of its child processes also.

Using top to Manage Processes

A convenient tool to manage processes is top. This tool is described in detail in Chapter 27. For common process management tasks, top is so great because it gives an overview of the most active processes currently running (hence the name top). This enables you to easily find processes that might need attention. From top, you can also perform common process management tasks, such as adjusting the current process priority and killing processes.
Figure 9.1 shows the interface that appears when you start top.

Among the information that you can conveniently obtain from the top utility is the process state. Table 9.3 provides an overview of the different process states that you may be observing.

Table 9.3 Linux Process States Overview

Key Topic

State	Meaning
Running (R)	The process is currently active and using CPU time, or in the queue of runnable processes waiting to get services.
Sleeping (S)	The process is waiting for an event to complete.
Uninterruptable sleep (D)	The process is in a sleep state that cannot be stopped. This usually happens while a process is waiting for I/O.
Stopped (S)	The process has been stopped, which typically has happened to an interactive shell process, using the **Ctrl+Z** key sequence.
Zombie (Z)	The process has been stopped but could not be removed by its parent, which has put it in an unmanageable state.

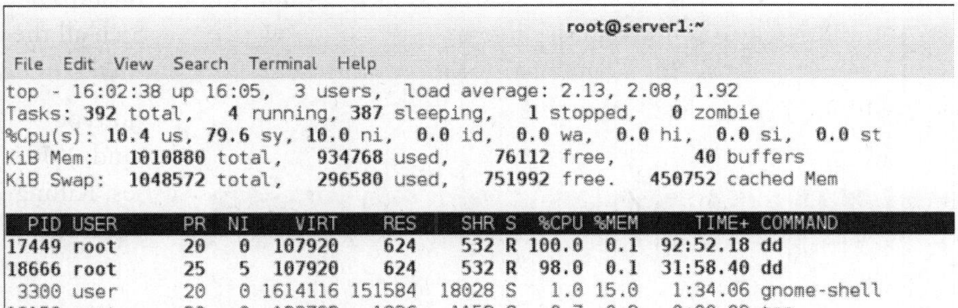

Figure 9.1 Using top makes process management easy.

Now that you know how to use the **kill** and **nice** commands from the command line, using the same functionality from top is even easier. From top, type **k**. top will then prompt for the PID of the process you want to send a signal to. By default, the most active process is selected. After you enter the PID, top asks which signal you want to send. By default, signal 15 for SIGTERM is used. However, if you want to insist a bit more, you can type **9** for SIGKILL. Now press **Enter** to terminate the process.

To renice a running process from top, type **r**. You are first prompted for the PID of the process you want to renice. After entering the PID, you are prompted for the nice value you want to use. Enter a positive value to increase process priority or a negative value to decrease process priority.

Summary

Managing processes is a common task for a Linux system administrator. In this chapter, you learned how to look up specific processes and how to change their priority using nice and kill. See Chapter 27 for more advanced information about process monitoring.

Exam Preparation Tasks

Review All Key Topics

Review the most important topics in the chapter, noted with the Key Topic icon in the outer margin of the page. Table 9.4 lists a reference of these key topics and the page numbers on which each is found.

Table 9.4 Key Topics for Chapter 9

Key Topic Element	Description	Page
Table 9.2	Job management overview	209
List	Essential signal overview	216
Table 9.3	Process state overview	219

Complete Tables and Lists from Memory

Print a copy of Appendix B, "Memory Tables," (found on the disc), or at least the section for this chapter, and complete the tables and lists from memory. Appendix C, "Memory Tables Answer Key," also on the disc, includes completed tables and lists to check your work.

Define Key Terms

Define the following key terms from this chapter and check your answers in the glossary:

job, process, background, foreground, nice, kill, signal, PID, thread

Review Questions

1. Which command gives an overview of all current shell jobs?
2. How do you stop the current shell job to continue running it in the background?
3. Which keystroke combination can you use to cancel the current shell job?
4. A user is asking you to cancel one of the jobs he has started. You cannot access the shell that user currently is working from. What can you do to cancel his job anyway?
5. Which command would you use to show parent-child relationships between processes?
6. Which command enables you to change the priority of PID 1234 to a higher priority?
7. On your system, 20 dd processes are currently running. What is the easiest way to stop all of them?
8. Which command enables you to stop the command with the name mycommand?
9. Which command do you use from top to kill a process?
10. How would you start a command with a reasonably high priority without risking that no more resources are available for other processes?

End-of-Chapter Labs

In the end-of-chapter labs, you apply some of the most important process management tasks. Use the tools that you find the most convenient to perform these labs.

Lab 9.1

1. Launch the command **dd if=/dev/zero of=/dev/null** three times as a background job.
2. Increase the priority of one of these commands using the nice value -5. Change the priority of the same process again, but use this time the value -15. Observe the difference.
3. Kill all the dd processes you just started.

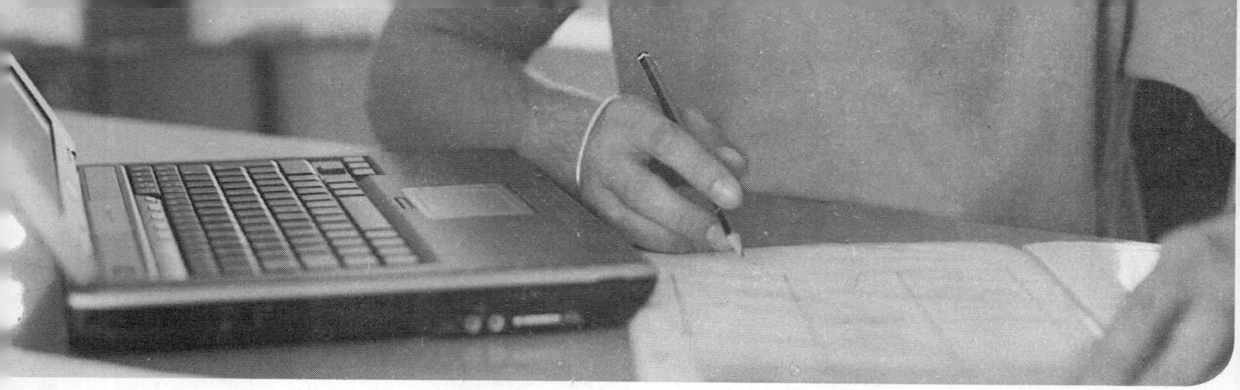

The following topics are covered in this chapter:

- Understanding RHEL 7 Virtualization
- Making Your Server a KVM Host
- Managing Virtual Machines

The following RHCSA exam objectives are covered in this chapter:

- Access a virtual machine's console
- Start and stop virtual machines
- Configure a physical machine to host virtual guests
- Install Red Hat Enterprise Linux systems as virtual guests
- Configure systems to launch virtual machines at boot

CHAPTER 10

Working with Virtual Machines

To become an RHCSA, you need to be able to work with virtual machines (VMs). In this chapter, you learn which virtualization options are available in RHEL 7. You also learn how to set up your server as a KVM host and how to manage VMs.

"Do I Know This Already?" Quiz

The "Do I Know This Already?" quiz allows you to assess whether you should read this entire chapter thoroughly or jump to the "Exam Preparation Tasks" section. If you are in doubt about your answers to these questions or your own assessment of your knowledge of the topics, read the entire chapter. Table 10.1 lists the major headings in this chapter and their corresponding "Do I Know This Already?" quiz questions. You can find the answers in Appendix A, "Answers to the 'Do I Know This Already?' Quizzes and 'Review Questions.'"

Table 10.1 "Do I Know This Already?" Section-to-Question Mapping

Foundation Topics Section	Questions
Understanding RHEL 7 Virtualization	1–2
Making Your Server a KVM Host	3, 4, 6
Managing Virtual Machines	5, 7–10

1. Which statement about KVM virtualization is *not* true?
    a. KVM is implemented through the Linux kernel.
    b. If you shut down the virt-manager utility, all virtual machines that are running within it will shut down as well.
    c. KVM virtualization is not installed by default.
    d. To configure a server as a KVM virtualization platform, you need a 64-bit operating system platform.

2. Which process must be running to manage KVM virtual machines?
   a. kvmd
   b. libvirtd
   c. qemu
   d. virt-manager

3. How do you enable hardware virtualization support?
   a. Enable it in your servers BIOS
   b. Load the kvm module
   c. Start the libvirtd service
   d. Add virt=kvm at the kernel boot line in GRUB 2

4. How can you check whether hardware virtualization support is enabled on your servers CPU?
   a. **cat /proc/kvm**
   b. **cat /proc/cpu**
   c. **cat /proc/cpuinfo**
   d. **lscpu**

5. What command enables you to load kernel KVM support?
   a. **modprobe kvm**
   b. **insmod kmv**
   c. **lsmod kvm**
   d. **modload kvm**

6. In which directory are virtual machine disk files stored by default?
   a. /etc/libvirt/images
   b. /var/lib/libvirt/fileystems
   c. /var/lib/libvirt/images
   d. /var/lib/qemu/images

7. What will be the (default) name of the configuration file that is used by the virtual machine vm1?

   a. /etc/kvm/vm1.xml

   b. /etc/libvirt/vm1.xml

   c. /etc/libvirt/kvm/vm1.xml

   d. /etc/libvirt/qemu/vm1.xml

8. Which approach would you use to enable a virtual machine for automatic starting while booting?

   a. On the virtual machine properties, select the automatic boot option in Virtual Machine Manager.

   b. Use systemctl enable followed by the name of the virtual machine.

   c. From the Virtual Machine Manager Boot Options interface, under Autostart, select the Start Virtual Machine on Host Boot Up option.

   d. Add the virtual machine name as a boot option to GRUB on the hypervisor host.

9. From a command-line interface, which command enables you to list all virtual machines that are available, including VMs that haven't been started?

   a. **virsh list**

   b. **virsh --list**

   c. **virsh list --all**

   d. **virsh list all**

10. You want to stop a virtual machine in the fastest way possible. Which command enables you to do this?

   a. **virsh shutdown vmname**

   b. **virsh shutdown --now vmname**

   c. **virsh poweroff vmname**

   d. **virsh destroy vmname**

Foundation Topics

Understanding RHEL 7 Virtualization

Red Hat Enterprise Linux is an important platform for virtualization. Since RHEL 6, Red Hat has been using KVM as the default virtualization solution. This section provides an overview of different Red Hat virtualization solutions as well as components that are used in a KVM virtualization environment.

Understanding KVM Virtualization

Different virtualization solutions are available on RHEL 7. The default virtualization solution, though, is KVM (Kernel Virtual Machine). KVM is included in the Linux kernel, and the solution offers hypervisor-based virtualization. That means that you do not have to run a specific program to host VMs; instead, virtualization support is inside the operating system kernel.

KVM virtualization is not supported by default on every RHEL 7 server; you'll have to install it separately on a server that meets the minimal requirements, as described later in this chapter. KVM virtualization can be used only on 64-bit computer architecture.

If you are used to using a desktop virtualization solution, such as VMware Workstation or Oracle Virtual Box, you need to be aware of one important difference between desktop-based virtualization and hypervisor-based virtualization. In desktop-based virtualization, the VMs are provided by the virtualization application. As a result, if you shut down the virtualization application, the VMs running within it shut down as well.

In KVM hypervisor virtualization, the VMs are running directly on top of the Linux kernel. As a result, you will not have an application that is running to support VMs by default, and you might not even notice that the VMs are running on your server.

Understanding QEMU

While installing a Red Hat Enterprise Linux 7 server as a KVM hypervisor host, you also automatically install some QEMU components. QEMU (Quick Emulator) is open source software that was originally created to offer hardware virtualization through binary emulation. QEMU can be used by itself, but it is also used together with KVM to run VMs on near-native speed. Some important parts on KVM hypervisor hosts are not provided by KVM itself but are instead integrated from the QEMU project. An example of this is the disk format of image files in VMs, but many other parts come from QEMU as well.

Red Hat Beyond KVM

The Red Hat product offering goes way beyond just KVM on individual hypervisors. Red Hat also has the Red Hat Enterprise Virtualization (RHEV) product in its portfolio. This solution was developed to compete with VMware vSphere environments. It offers an infrastructural server that consists of multiple hypervisor nodes that are managed from a central RHEV Manager node, on which a web user interface makes managing a complex environment easy.

Red Hat also puts a lot of effort in showing itself as a major cloud provider. Red Hat is an important contributor to the OpenStack cloud project and offers its own cloud solution that is based on OpenStack. In that solution, KVM virtualization is also offered.

Understanding the Role of Libvirtd

To access VMs that are offered through KVM, you use libvirtd. Libvirtd is a process that sits between the virtualization layer and the application that an administrator is using to access the VMs. Without libvirtd, you cannot manage VMs. Virtual machine management options also are configured through the libvirtd configuration file /etc/libvirt/libvirtd.conf. In this file, you can set some advanced parameters. For instance, you can open a TCP port that allows you to connect to a libvirt process that is running on another host. This is convenient, because in a multihost environment it allows you to manage VMs that are not just running on your server but also VMs that are running on other hosts as well.

Although the method to connect remotely directly to libvirtd works well and is convenient for hypervisors that have a minimal number of software packages installed, alternatively you can use Secure Shell (SSH) from virt-manager to connect to remote libvirtd processes.

If you are experiencing problems accessing VMs, libvirtd is the primary suspect, and you should at least ensure that it is running, by using the **systemctl status -l libvirtd** command. In Listing 10.1, you can see how this command shows that libvirtd is running; the command also shows information about recent activity on the process.

Listing 10.1 Using **systemctl status -l libvirtd** to Get Details About the libvirtd Process Status

```
[root@lab ~]# systemctl status -l libvirtd
libvirtd.service - Virtualization daemon
   Loaded: loaded (/usr/lib/systemd/system/libvirtd.service; enabled)
   Active: active (running) since Mon 2015-03-09 16:39:45 EDT;
  2 weeks 4 days ago
 Main PID: 1538 (libvirtd)
   CGroup: /system.slice/libvirtd.service
           ├─1538 /usr/sbin/libvirtd
           └─2914 /sbin/dnsmasq --conf-file=/var/lib/libvirt/dnsmasq/
  default.conf


Mar 28 10:23:12 lab.sandervanvugt.nl dnsmasq-dhcp[2914]:
  DHCPACK(virbr0) 192.168.122.13
52:54:00:41:45:35 ubuntu
Mar 28 10:37:30 lab.sandervanvugt.nl libvirtd[1538]: stream aborted at
  client request
Mar 28 10:38:49 lab.sandervanvugt.nl dnsmasq-dhcp[2914]:
DHCPREQUEST(virbr0) 192.168.122.30
52:54:00:f5:19:bf
Mar 28 10:38:49 lab.sandervanvugt.nl dnsmasq-dhcp[2914]:
DHCPACK(virbr0) 192.168.122.30
52:54:00:f5:19:bf labipa
Mar 28 10:43:31 lab.sandervanvugt.nl dnsmasq-dhcp[2914]:
DHCPREQUEST(virbr0) 192.168.122.221
52:54:00:59:b4:7c
Mar 28 10:43:31 lab.sandervanvugt.nl dnsmasq-dhcp[2914]:
DHCPACK(virbr0) 192.168.122.221
52:54:00:59:b4:7c server2
Mar 28 10:50:18 lab.sandervanvugt.nl dnsmasq-dhcp[2914]:
DHCPREQUEST(virbr0) 192.168.122.13
52:54:00:41:45:35
Mar 28 10:50:18 lab.sandervanvugt.nl dnsmasq-dhcp[2914]:
DHCPACK(virbr0) 192.168.122.13
52:54:00:41:45:35 ubuntu
Mar 28 11:01:58 lab.sandervanvugt.nl dnsmasq-dhcp[2914]:
DHCPREQUEST(virbr0) 192.168.122.30
52:54:00:f5:19:bf
Mar 28 11:01:58 lab.sandervanvugt.nl dnsmasq-dhcp[2914]:
DHCPACK(virbr0) 192.168.122.30
52:54:00:f5:19:bf labipa
```

Several management utilities can be used on top of libvirtd. The Virtual Machine Manager (offered through the virt-manager binary) is a commonly used graphical user interface (GUI) to manage KVM. Alternatively, the **virsh** command is available as a shell interface to manage KVM VMs. In following sections in this chapter, you learn how to use both.

Making Your Server a KVM Host

In this section, you learn what is needed to make your server a KVM host. You first learn about the requirements for doing so. You then learn how to install the required KVM software packages. In the last part of this section, you learn how networking is enhanced to support for VM networking.

Checking Host Requirements

Before starting to configure a RHEL server as a hypervisor host, verify support. There really are just two requirements to start KVM hypervisor backend services:

Key Topic

- You must be using a 64-bit CPU architecture.
- Your CPU must support hardware virtualization.

To verify whether you are running 64-bit architecture is not difficult; just type **arch** to show the architecture that is currently used. If you are good, you'll see the architecture x86_64 being displayed. Alternatively, you can use the **uname -i** command, which also shows which type of kernel is used.

Checking the availability of virtualization support on your CPU can be a bit more complicated. To start, you need to make sure that virtualization support is switched on in the BIOS of your computer. After you have done that, you can use the command **cat /proc/cpuinfo**. In the output of this command (see Listing 10.2), you should see **vmx** on an intel CPU, and **svm** on an AMD CPU.

Listing 10.2 Partial Contents of /proc/cpuinfo

```
processor          : 1
vendor_id          : GenuineIntel
cpu family         : 6
model              : 58
model name         : Intel(R) Core(TM) i7-3740QM CPU @ 2.70GHz
stepping           : 9
microcode          : 0x15
cpu MHz            : 2693.276
```

```
cache size          : 6144 KB
physical id         : 2
siblings            : 1
core id             : 0
cpu cores           : 1
apicid              : 2
initial apicid      : 2
fpu                 : yes
fpu_exception       : yes
cpuid level         : 13
wp                  : yes
flags               : fpu vme de pse tsc msr pae mce cx8 apic sep
  mtrr pge mca cmov pat pse36 clflush
dts mmx fxsr sse sse2 ss syscall nx rdtscp lm constant_tsc
  arch_perfmon pebs bts nopl xtopology
tsc_reliable nonstop_tsc aperfmperf eagerfpu pni pclmulqdq vmx ssse3
  cx16 pcid sse4_1 sse4_2
x2apic popcnt aes xsave avx f16c rdrand hypervisor lahf_lm ida arat
  epb xsaveopt pln pts dtherm
tpr_shadow vnmi ept vpid fsgsbase smep
bogomips            : 5386.55
clflush size        : 64
cache_alignment     : 64
address sizes       : 40 bits physical, 48 bits virtual
power management:
```

Installing the KVM Software

After verifying that you meet all hardware requirements, you can install the virtualization software. The most convenient way of doing so is by using **yum groupinstall "Virtualization Host"**. This command installs everything you need to set up a virtualization host environment.

Another important consideration is the availability of storage. When you are installing a VM, it needs to create a virtual disk. This virtual disk by default is stored in an image file in the directory /var/lib/libvirt/images. Make sure that you have enough available disk space in the partition where you want to install the VMs before starting the installation.

NOTE As an alternative to working with disk image files, you may prefer working with LVM logical volumes as the storage backend. This offers some advantages, such as the possibility to easily create backups by using the LVM snapshot feature. For this reason, LVM is often used as a storage backend in production KVM servers. For the RHCSA and RHCE exams, you do not need to know how to set this up.

In Exercise 10.1, you learn how to set up your server as a KVM installation host.

Exercise 10.1 Setting Up Your Server as a KVM Hypervisor Host

In this exercise, you set up your server as a KVM hypervisor host. For optimal performance, it works best if you perform this exercise on a physical server. For study purposes, you can also set up a KVM or VMware VM as a hypervisor host. That has you using virtualization within virtualization, which is bad for performance, but at least allows you to see how it works. To do this, in your virtualization program check the CPU features and make sure that hypervisor options are enabled. Currently, KVM and VMware VMs support nested virtualization (a hypervisor host in a VM). VirtualBox does not support this kind of setup.

1. On the server that you want to use as hypervisor host, type **arch** to verify that you are using a 64-bit CPU architecture.
2. Next type **cat /proc/cpuinfo | egrep 'svm|vmx'** and read the CPU flags section to see whether either vmx or svm is listed as one of the flags.
3. Type **yum groupinstall "Virtualization Host"** to install everything that is needed to make your server a virtualization host.

Understanding KVM Host Networking

After installing the virtualization software on a host computer, networking also changes significantly. On the host, a virtual bridge is created. This virtual bridge works like an embedded switch, and it is used to connect one or more of the physical network interfaces in the host to the different VMs.

While communicating on the network, a VM sends out packets through its internal (virtual) network interface, which typically has the name eth0. At the hypervisor level, this network is represented by a vnet interface. The first VM that starts gets the interface vnet0, the second machine that starts gets vnet1, and so on.

This vnet interfaces on their turn connect to the virtual bridge. The virtual bridge itself is connected to the physical network interface on your host. To get an overview of the virtual networking configuration, you can use the command **brctl show**. This command for which you can see the output in Listing 10.3 shows the name of the bridge, the unique ID that has been assigned to the bridge, an indicator that shows if the bridging protocol STP (Spanning Tree Protocol) has been enabled, and all the interfaces that are connected to the bridge.

Listing 10.3 Displaying Bridging Configuration with **brctl show**

```
[root@lab ~]# brctl show
    bridge name     bridge id              STP enabled     interfaces
    virbr0          8000.fe5400414535      yes             vnet0
                                                           vnet1
                                                           vnet2
                                                           vnet3
```

Notice that on Red Hat Enterprise Linux 7 that there are two different methods to manage network bridges. When installing RHEL as a KVM host, a bridge interface with the name virbr0 is created automatically. Alternatively, you can configure a bridge manually, using the bridging utilities that are available in the NetworkManager-related utilities nmtui and nmcli. For an easy way to set up virtual networking configuration, it is recommended to have the bridge installed while configuring your server as a KVM host.

Managing Virtual Machines

After installing the required software packages, you can move on and start creating and managing VMs. In this section, you learn how.

Installing Virtual Machines

In Exercise 10.2, you learn how to install a VM using the Virtual Machine Manager. After the exercise, a small section explains where you can find the VM configuration that has been written to disk.

Exercise 10.2 Installing a Virtual Machine

In this exercise, you learn how to install a VM. Before starting this exercise, make sure that an installation disk containing RHEL or CentOS 7 is available. The easiest way to do so is by inserting a physical CD-ROM into the CD drive of the KVM host.

If that is not an option, the second best option is to copy the ISO of the installation disk to the hypervisor host and use that.

1. Open a root shell. From the root shell, type **lsmod | grep kvm**. You are looking for the **kvm** and **kvm_intel** module (**kvm_amd** in case you are using an AMD platform). If these modules are not currently loaded, type **modprobe -r kvm** to load them.
2. Type **systemctl status libvirtd**. This command checks to see whether the libvirtd service is currently loaded. If it is, you are good. If not, type **systemctl start libvirtd** to start the service.
3. Type **df -h** to verify the amount of available disk space.
4. Type **virt-manager &** to start the Virtual Machine Manager.
5. In Virtual Machine Manager, click **Create a New Virtual Machine**. This opens the step 1 of 5 window of the New VM Wizard (see Figure 10.1)

Key Topic

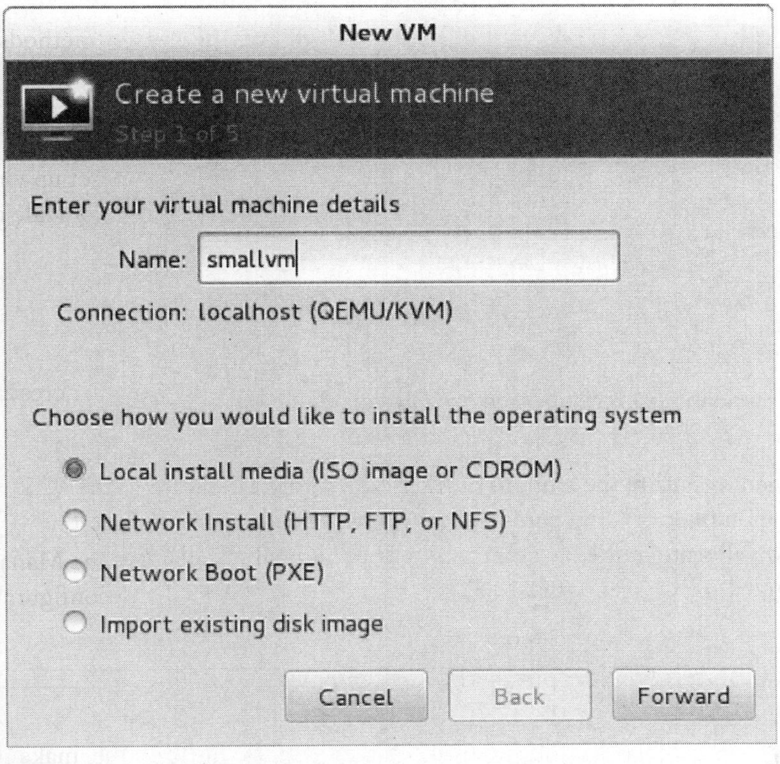

Figure 10.1 Step 1 of 5 of the Create a New Virtual Machine Wizard.

6. In step 2 of 5 of the wizard, you need to specify the source where the installation disk can be found, as well as the operating system and operating system version you want to install. Make sure to use the same settings as in Figure 10.2.

Figure 10.2 Specifying the installation source and OS settings.

7. Next you need to specify the amount of RAM you want to dedicate to the VM, as well as the number of CPU cores. Of course, you need to have at least the resources you allocate in the host machine. For a minimal installation, use 512 MB RAM and 1 CPU (see Figure 10.3).

Figure 10.3 Entering VM properties.

8. Now enter the properties of the virtual disk you want to create. For a basic installation, a minimum of 2GB is recommended (see Figure 10.4).

TIP If you have a limited amount of disk space available, just create the VM with the disk space you have got available. You do not have to complete the entire installation procedure (so you do not need all the disk space that is normally needed to complete an installation). All that counts is that you know how to go through the steps in Virtual Machine Manager. (You already know how to install RHEL 7.)

9. At this point, you have entered all properties that are to be used for the VM. You can now click **Finish** to write the VM settings to disk and start the installation procedure. Notice that you do not have to complete the installation procedure. You do not have to use the VM that you are installing here for anything else anymore in later chapters in this book.

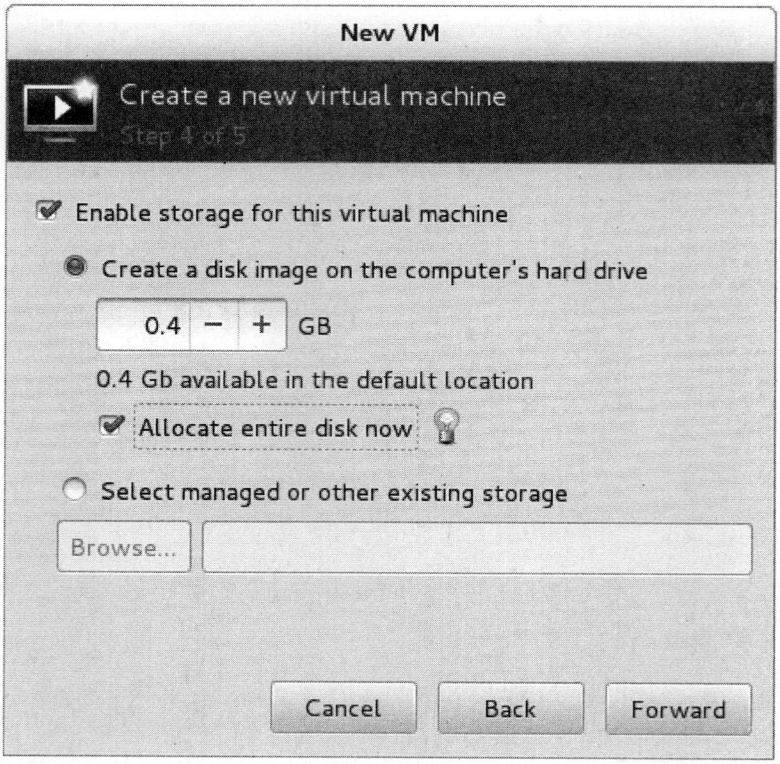

Figure 10.4 Entering the virtual disk size.

In this procedure, you have defined the virtual hardware settings that your VM is going to use. The installation can now be started. The VM settings themselves have been written to an XML configuration file that is stored in the /etc/libvirtd/qemu directory. Listing 10.4 shows the partial contents of the configuration file that was just created.

Listing 10.4 Verifying the Virtual Machine Configuration File XML Code

```
[root@server1 qemu]# cat vmthin1.xml
<!--
WARNING: THIS IS AN AUTO-GENERATED FILE. CHANGES TO IT ARE LIKELY TO
  BE
OVERWRITTEN AND LOST. Changes to this xml configuration should be made
  using:
  virsh edit vmthin1
```

```
or other application using the libvirt API.
-->

<domain type='qemu'>
  <name>vmthin1</name>
  <uuid>61d74270-548b-4176-b34a-73faf7b421d8</uuid>
  <memory unit='KiB'>524288</memory>
  <currentMemory unit='KiB'>524288</currentMemory>
  <vcpu placement='static'>1</vcpu>
  <os>
    <type arch='x86_64' machine='pc-i440fx-rhel7.0.0'>hvm</type>
    <boot dev='hd'/>
  </os>
  <features>
    <acpi/>
    <apic/>
    <pae/>
  </features>
  <clock offset='utc'/>
  <on_poweroff>destroy</on_poweroff>
  <on_reboot>restart</on_reboot>
  <on_crash>restart</on_crash>
  <devices>
    <emulator>/usr/libexec/qemu-kvm</emulator>
    <disk type='block' device='disk'>
      <driver name='qemu' type='raw' cache='none' io='native'/>
      <source dev='/dev/vgthin/lvthin1'/>
      <target dev='hda' bus='ide'/>
      <address type='drive' controller='0' bus='0' target='0'
 unit='0'/>
    </disk>
    <disk type='block' device='cdrom'>
      <driver name='qemu' type='raw'/>
      <target dev='hdc' bus='ide'/>
      <readonly/>
      <address type='drive' controller='0' bus='1' target='0'
 unit='0'/>
    </disk>
```

As the virtual hardware settings are easily accessible in the configuration file, you might be tempted to modify them from the file as well. That is not what you should be doing. To change virtual hardware settings, you can use the VM properties in Virtual Machine Manager, or use the **virsh edit <vmname>** command. This is because access to the VM settings is streamlined through libvirtd, accessing the configuration directly will mess up your VM.

Using KVM Virtual Machines

After installing a KVM VM, there are multiple ways to access it, including the following:

Key Topic

- SSH into the VM
- Through Virtual Machine Manager
- Through GNOME Boxes
- Using virt-viewer
- Optionally, through third-party utilities.

Of these listed methods, accessing VMs through Virtual Machine Manager is the easiest way to use them. Virtual Machine Manager shows an overview of all the available VMs (see Figure 10.5), and you just have to access the VM window to use them.

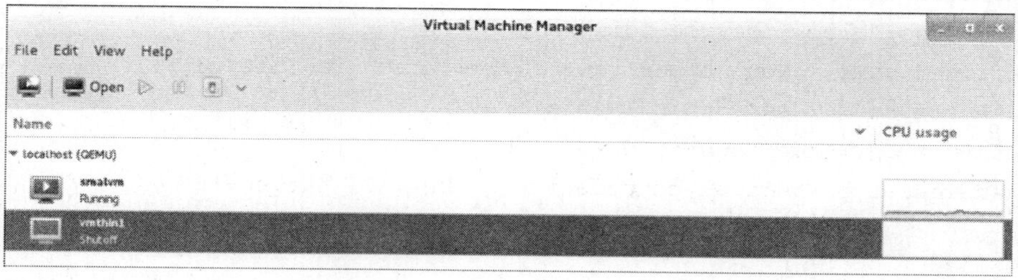

Figure 10.5 Accessing VMs through Virtual Machine Manager.

Key Topic

When accessing a VM in a mode that gives access to the full console environment, the mouse cursor is captured in the VM. To release the mouse cursor, press the left **Ctrl+Alt** keys on your keyboard simultaneously.

From Virtual Machine Manager, you also have access to different icons that enable you to perform specific tasks on the VM easily. For instance, you can use a play button to start a VM, and you can a use a pause button to pause it.

Another common way to access VMs is by SSH-ing into them. In production environments, this is how VMs are usually accessed. Virtual machines are often hosted on servers that do not even have a monitor attached to them, and often they are put away in a data center that cannot be easily accessed. Therefore, using SSH or VNC to connect to them is the most practical method in production environments.

The virt-viewer utility is similar to Virtual Machine Manager. It was developed to provide access to VM to users without also granting the option to change VM settings.

The GNOME Boxes utility is an addition to the GNOME 3 interface that is used on RHEL 7 servers that have a graphical interface installed. It was developed as an end-user utility that makes it easy for users to use and access VMs.

Accessing Virtual Machines from a Text-Only Console

You do not have to know how to do this on the exam, but in real life it can really help if you know how to access the console of a VM if you are in a text-only environment, which is the case, for instance, if you are working directly from the console of the KVM host. This procedure describes how to do it on server1:

1. Log in to the server1 VM and make sure that you have root privileges.
2. Type **grubby --update-kernel=ALL --args="console=ttyS0"**. Using the **grubby** command allows you to change the configuration of the GRUB2 boot loader without having to go through the GRUB2 configuration files. Alternatively, you can edit the /etc/default/grub file and add the argument **console=ttyS0** to the line that specifies the kernel arguments to be used. If you are modifying the grub.conf file, use **grub2-mkconfig -o /boot/grub2/grub.cfg** to write the changes to the boot loader main configuration file.
3. Restart your VM, using the **reboot** command.
4. From the KVM host, use the **virsh console server1.example.com** command to connect to the VM. You'll now get access to the VM console, as shown in Listing 10.5. Press **Ctrl+]** to get out of the virsh console session. Notice that the name of the VM you are connecting to has to match the VM name, as you can see it using the **virsh list** command.

Listing 10.5 Using **virsh console** to Connect to a VM

```
[root@lab ~]# virsh console sander-vm1
Connected to domain sander-vm1
Escape character is ^]

CentOS Linux 7 (Core)
Kernel 3.10.0-123.el7.x86_64 on an x86_64

server2 login:
```

Managing Virtual Machine Properties

As an administrator, you'll occasionally have to change VM properties. The easiest way to do this is through Virtual Machine Manager. To access the properties in Virtual Machine Manager, you first must open the VM. It does not have to be started; it just needs to be open. After opening it, click the icon that looks like a lamp to open the interface shown in Figure 10.6.

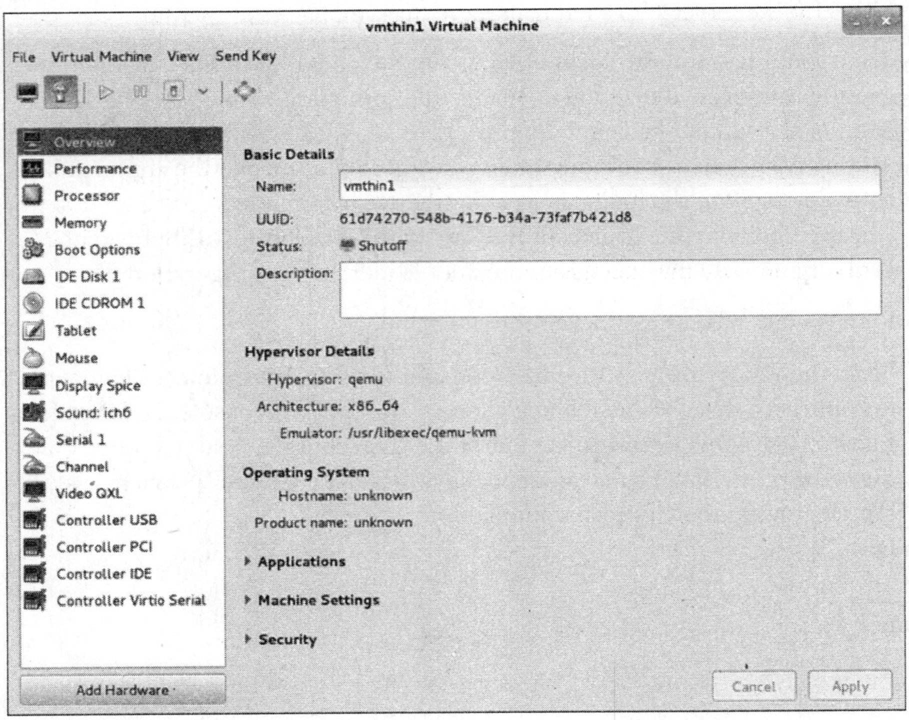

Figure 10.6 Accessing VM properties through Virtual Machine Manager.

As you can see, you have many options available from the Virtual Machine Manager properties interface. Many of them are self-explanatory. Some of the most common configuration tasks that you can access through this interface are as follows:

Key Topic

- To add new hardware, click the **Add Hardware** button in the lower-left part of the window. This opens an interface from which you can select the hardware device to be added, as well as its additional properties.
- Click the **Performance** option to show performance graphs about VM usage.
- Click the **Memory** option to grow or reduce the size of memory that is allocated to the VM.
- Click **Boot Options** to enable Autostart. This will start the VM upon host boot.
- Also from the Boot Options interface, you'll find the **Boot Device Order**. Select this to specify the order in which devices in your VM will be used for booting.

Managing Virtual Machines from the Command Line

RHEL offers a versatile command-line interface to manage VMs directly from the command line. You can start the **virsh** command with many different arguments to perform specific tasks. You can also just type **virsh** to open a command-line interface from which you can type the specific commands immediately. Table 10.2 shows some of the most common **virsh** commands.

Table 10.2 virsh Command Interface

Key Topic

Command	Use
list	Shows all VMs that are currently active
list --all	Shows all VMs, including machines that are not currently active
help	Gives a list of all parameters that can be used with the virsh command
shutdown <vmname>	Shuts down the VM properly
destroy <vmname>	Halts a VM, similar to pulling the power plug on a real computer
edit <vmname>	Opens a vi interface that allows you to edit the XML configuration file belonging to a specific VM

Command	Use
console <vmname>	Connects to a VM directly from the console of a KVM host server
start <vmname>	Starts a VM
reboot <vmname>	Reboots a VM

When using **virsh** commands, you often have to specify the VM name. An alternative is to use the VM ID. To get an overview of VM IDs, use **virsh list**. You'll see IDs listed for all VMs that are currently active (see Listing 10.6).

Listing 10.6 Generating a List of Active Virtual Machines

```
[root@lab ~]# virsh list
 Id     Name                                     State
----------------------------------------------------
 3      dan-vm1                                  running
 4      dan-vm2                                  running
 6      sander-vm1                               running
 7      sander-vm2                               running
 8      sander-ipa                               running
 10     vm1-rhel6-svv                            running
 12     vm2-rhel6-svv                            running
 16     sander-server1                           running
 18     dan-labipa                               running
```

Monitoring Virtual Machine Activity from Top

On Linux, you can use the **top** utility to monitor the activity of processes. As mentioned earlier in this chapter, a VM is just like any other process from the perspective of the host it is running on. That means that VMs are using resources like any other processes. In the **top** utility, an interesting parameter is used to display such activity; the **st** parameter in the CPU utilization line indicates the percentage of CPU time that was "stolen" from the hypervisor by VMs. The VM itself on the hypervisor host shows as one single process in top.

So, using **top** on the host allows you to see how busy a VM is related to other processes running on that machine. You cannot see what is happening within the VM by using **top** from the host, but you will have to do that by using the appropriate tools from within the VM. Figure 10.7 shows **top** on a KVM host that is running different VMs. Each of the VMs shows as a qemu-kvm process.

```
root@lab:~                                   root@server1:/usr/lib/systemd/system
top - 10:37:47 up 18 days, 17:58,  2 users,  load average: 0.00, 0.01, 0.05
Tasks: 171 total,   1 running, 170 sleeping,   0 stopped,   0 zombie
%Cpu(s):  0.2 us,  0.2 sy,  0.0 ni, 99.7 id,  0.0 wa,  0.0 hi,  0.0 si,  0.0 st
KiB Mem:  16196548 total,  4158596 used, 12037952 free,     1336 buffers
KiB Swap: 20479996 total,        0 used, 20479996 free.   247696 cached Mem

  PID USER      PR  NI    VIRT    RES    SHR S  %CPU %MEM     TIME+ COMMAND
10821 qemu      20   0 3658648 1.156g   7312 S   2.3  7.5 523:09.19 qemu-kvm
 3028 qemu      20   0 1793264 1.160g   7460 S   2.0  7.5 525:42.93 qemu-kvm
10840 qemu      20   0 3127136 416508   7356 S   1.7  2.6 336:15.41 qemu-kvm
    1 root      20   0   52980   6896   3756 S   0.0  0.0   0:27.02 systemd
    2 root      20   0       0      0      0 S   0.0  0.0   0:00.31 kthreadd
    3 root      20   0       0      0      0 S   0.0  0.0   0:01.89 ksoftirqd/0
    5 root       0 -20       0      0      0 S   0.0  0.0   0:00.00 kworker/0:0H
    7 root      rt   0       0      0      0 S   0.0  0.0   0:00.67 migration/0
    8 root      20   0       0      0      0 S   0.0  0.0   0:00.00 rcu_bh
    9 root      20   0       0      0      0 S   0.0  0.0   0:00.00 rcuob/0
   10 root      20   0       0      0      0 S   0.0  0.0   0:00.00 rcuob/1
   11 root      20   0       0      0      0 S   0.0  0.0   0:00.00 rcuob/2
   12 root      20   0       0      0      0 S   0.0  0.0   0:00.00 rcuob/3
   13 root      20   0       0      0      0 S   0.0  0.0   1:02.29 rcu_sched
   14 root      20   0       0      0      0 S   0.0  0.0   0:22.01 rcuos/0
   15 root      20   0       0      0      0 S   0.0  0.0   0:23.95 rcuos/1
   16 root      20   0       0      0      0 S   0.0  0.0   0:25.96 rcuos/2
   17 root      20   0       0      0      0 S   0.0  0.0   0:23.15 rcuos/3
   18 root      rt   0       0      0      0 S   0.0  0.0   0:07.93 watchdog/0
   19 root      rt   0       0      0      0 S   0.0  0.0   0:07.92 watchdog/1
   20 root      rt   0       0      0      0 S   0.0  0.0   0:00.13 migration/1
   21 root      20   0       0      0      0 S   0.0  0.0   0:00.89 ksoftirqd/1
   23 root       0 -20       0      0      0 S   0.0  0.0   0:00.00 kworker/1:0H
   24 root      rt   0       0      0      0 S   0.0  0.0   0:06.73 watchdog/2
   25 root      rt   0       0      0      0 S   0.0  0.0   0:00.30 migration/2
```

Figure 10.7 Monitoring VM activity with **top**.

Summary

In this chapter, you learned how to work with VMs in Red Hat Enterprise Linux 7. You learned about virtualization in RHEL7 and how to set up a KVM host server. You also learned how to install a VM and how to manage it, using a graphical utility like Virtual Machine Manager or the **virsh** command-line interface.

Exam Prep Tasks

Review All Key Topics

Review the most important topics in the chapter, noted with the Key Topic icon in the outer margin of the page. Table 10.3 lists a reference of these key topics and the page numbers on which each is found.

Table 10.3 Key Topics for Chapter 10

Key Topic Element	Description	Page Number
List	KVM hardware requirements	231
Figure 10.1	Step 1 of 5: Create a new virtual machine wizard	235
List	Ways to access VMs	240
Paragraph	Releasing the mouse cursor from a VM	240
List	Virtual Machine Manager interface configuration tasks	243
Table 10.2	**virsh** command Interface	243

Define Key Terms

Define the following key terms from this chapter and check your answers in the glossary:

hypervisor, KVM, libvirt, cloud, openstack, virsh, virbr, virtual bridge qemu

Review Questions

1. Which kernel modules must be loaded on all KVM hypervisor hosts?
2. Which CPU flag would you expect to see on a server that has hardware virtualization support on an Intel CPU?
3. How can you release the mouse cursor if it is captured in a virtual machine?
4. Which command enables you to check whether you are using a 64-bit hardware platform?
5. Which command enables you to show CPU properties, which allows you to verify that your platform is appropriate for running KVM virtual machines?
6. How do you start the Virtual Machine Manager from the command line?
7. Which service needs to be running to perform KVM management tasks?
8. In which directory are disk image files stored by default?
9. How do you show a list of all virtual machines, including machines that are not currently operational?
10. What is the fastest way to immediately shut down a VM named vm1?

End-of-Chapter Labs

You have now learned how to work with KVM virtualization on Red Hat Enterprise Linux 7. In the end-of-chapter labs with this chapter you practice these skills and use the Virtual Machine Manager to install virtual machines.

Lab 10.1

1. Set up one server as a KVM hypervisor host. Notice that if you're doing these labs on a virtual machine, you'll need to enable the hypervisor extensions in the virtual machine software. Consult the documentation of your virtualization software to find out how to do this.
2. On this host, install a KVM virtual machine. You do not have to complete the entire installation procedure. Just make sure that the virtual machine configuration is created and written to disk.

The following topics are covered in this chapter:

- Managing Software with yum
- Using yum
- Managing Software Packages with RPM

The following RHCSA exam objectives are covered in this chapter:

- Install and update software packages from Red Hat Network, a remote repository, or from the local file system

CHAPTER 11

Managing Software

Managing software packages is an important task for an administrator of Red Hat Enterprise Linux. In this chapter, you learn how to manage software packages from the command line by using the yum utility. You also learn which role repositories play in software management with yum. In the second part of this chapter, you learn how to manage software with the **rpm** command, which is particularly important to query new and installed software packages.

"Do I Know This Already?" Quiz

The "Do I Know This Already?" quiz allows you to assess whether you should read this entire chapter thoroughly or jump to the "Exam Preparation Tasks" section. If you are in doubt about your answers to these questions or your own assessment of your knowledge of the topics, read the entire chapter. Table 11.1 lists the major headings in this chapter and their corresponding "Do I Know This Already?" quiz questions. You can find the answers in Appendix A, "Answers to the 'Do I Know This Already?' Quizzes and 'Review Questions.'"

Table 11.1 "Do I Know This Already?" Section-to-Question Mapping

Foundation Topics Section	Questions
Managing Software with yum	1–4
Using yum	5–7
Managing Software Packages with RPM	8–10

1. Which of the following is *not* a mandatory component in a .repo file that is used to indicate which repositories should be used?
   - **a.** [label]
   - **b.** name=
   - **c.** baseurl=
   - **d.** gpgcheck=

2. Which installation source is used on RHEL if a server is not registered with RHN?
   a. The installation medium
   b. Nothing
   c. The base RHN repository, without updates
   d. You have full access to RHN repositories, but the software you are using is just not supported.
3. Which of the following should be used in the repo file to refer to a repository that is in the directory /repo on the local file system?
   a. file=/repo
   b. baseurl=file://repo
   c. baseurl=file:///repo
   d. file=http:///repo
4. Which of the following is true about GPG-based repository security?
   a. If packages in the repository have been signed, you need to copy the GPG key to the correct location.
   b. GPG package signing is mandatory.
   c. GPG package signatures prevent packages in a repository from being changed.
   d. GPG package signing is recommended on Internet repositories, but not required on local repositories that are for internal use only.
5. Which command enables you to search the package that contains the file semanage?
   a. **yum search semanage**
   b. **yum search all semanage**
   c. **yum provides semanage**
   d. **yum whatprovides */semanage**
6. Which command enables you to show all installed packages using the **yum** command?
   a. **yum show**
   b. **yum show all**
   c. **yum list**
   d. **yum list all**

7. Which command enables you to find out the yum ID number that is needed to roll back a command that was issued with yum?

   a. **yum show all**

   b. **yum show recent**

   c. **yum show history**

   d. **yum history**

8. Which command should you use to install an RPM file that has been downloaded to your computer?

   a. **yum install**

   b. **yum localinstall**

   c. **rpm -ivh**

   d. **rpm -Uvh**

9. Which command enables you to find the RPM a specific file belongs to?

   a. **rpm -ql /bin/file**

   b. **rpm -qlf /bin/file**

   c. **rpm -qf /bin/file**

   d. **rom -qa /bin/file**

10. Which command enables you to analyze whether there are scripts in an RPM package file that you have just downloaded?

    a. **rpm -qs packagename.rpm**

    b. **rpm -qps packagename.rpm**

    c. **rpm -qp --scripts packagename.rpm**

    d. **rpm -q --scripts packagename.rpm**

Foundation Topics

Managing Software Packages with yum

The default utility used to manage software packages on Red Hat Enterprise Linux is yum, which stands for Yellowdog update manager. Yum is designed to work with repositories, which are online depots of available software packages. In this section, you learn how to create and manage repositories and how to manage software packages based on the contents of the repositories.

Understanding the Role of Repositories

Software on Red Hat Enterprise Linux is provided in the RPM (Red Hat Package Manager) format. This is a specific format used to archive the package and provide package metadata as well.

When you are working with software in Red Hat Enterprise Linux, repositories play a key role. Working with repositories makes it easy to keep your server current: The maintainer of the repository publishes updated packages in the repository, and the result is that whenever you use yum (discussed later in this chapter) to install software, the most recent version of the software is automatically used.

Another major benefit of working with yum is the way that package dependencies are dealt with. On Linux (as on most other modern operating systems) software packages have dependencies. This means that to install one package, other packages have to be present as well. Without using repositories, that would mean that these packages have to be installed manually.

The yum repository system takes care of resolving these dependencies automatically. If a package is going to be installed, it contains information about the required dependencies. The **yum** command then looks in the repositories configured on this system to fetch the dependencies automatically. If all goes well, the installer just sees a short list of the dependencies that will be installed as a dependency to install the package. If you are using Red Hat Enterprise Linux with the repositories that are provided through Red Hat Network, there is no reason why this procedure should not work, and the attempts to install software will usually succeed.

While installing Red Hat Enterprise Linux, it asks you to register with Red Hat Network (RHN). From RHN, different repositories are provided. After registering with RHN, you can install software packages that are verified by Red Hat automatically. If you are using CentOS, you get access to the CentOS repositories. If you choose to install Red Hat Enterprise Linux without a registration key, however, it cannot get in touch with the RHN repositories, and you end up with no repositories at all. In that case, you have to be able to specify yourself which repository you want to use.

Note that repositories are specific to an operating system. Therefore, if you are using RHEL, you should use RHEL repositories only. Do not try, for instance, to add CentOS repositories to an RHEL server. If you want to provide additional software from the Fedora project to an RHEL server (which for support reasons is not recommended), you can consider adding the EPEL (Extra Packages for Enterprise Linux) repositories. See https://fedoraproject.org/wiki/EPEL for more information.

WARNING Do not install EPEL repositories on RHEL; you break your support if you do.

Specifying Which Repository to Use

On most occasions, after the installation of your server has finished, it is configured with a list of repositories that should be used. You sometimes have to tell your server which repositories should be used:

- You want to distribute nondefault software packages through repositories.
- You are installing Red Hat Enterprise Linux without registering it on RHN.

Telling your server which repository to use is not difficult, but it is important that you know how to do it (for the RHCSA and RHCE exams, too).

To tell your server which repository to use, you need to create a file with a name that ends in .repo. In that file you need the following contents: Key Topic

- **[label]** The .repo file can contain different repositories, each section starting with a label that identifies the specific repository.
- **name=** Use this to specify the name of the repository you want to use.
- **baseurl=** Contains the URL that points to the specific repository location.
- In the repository files that are provided by default, you may find several repositories in one file, as is the case in Listing 11.1. This is useful to group repositories that belong together in one file, and is often done in repository files that are provided as a default. If you are creating repository files yourself, you are free to create separate files for each repository.

TIP RHEL 7 does not have an easy-to-use graphical user interface (GUI) tool that makes it easy to create your own repository file. So, you have to make sure you know how to do this, in case a related exam question comes up. To help with that, type **man yum.conf** and search for "example." This shows an example containing just these minimal ingredients that should be present in the repository file.

Listing 11.1 shows a repository file that is based on the default repositories that are installed on CentOS 7.

Listing 11.1 Repository File Example

```
[root@server1 yum.repos.d]# cat CentOS-Base.repo
# CentOS-Base.repo
#
# The mirror system uses the connecting IP address of the client and
the
# update status of each mirror to pick mirrors that are updated to and
# geographically close to the client.  You should use this for CentOS
updates
# unless you are manually picking other mirrors.
#
# If the mirrorlist= does not work for you, as a fall back you can try
the
# remarked out baseurl= line instead.
#
#

[base]
name=CentOS-$releasever - Base
mirrorlist=http://mirrorlist.centos.org/?release=$releasever&arch=$bas
earch&repo=os
#baseurl=http://mirror.centos.org/centos/$releasever/os/$basearch/
gpgcheck=1
gpgkey=file:///etc/pki/rpm-gpg/RPM-GPG-KEY-CentOS-7

#released updates
[updates]
name=CentOS-$releasever - Updates
mirrorlist=http://mirrorlist.centos.org/?release=$releasever&arch=$base
arch&repo=updates
```

```
#baseurl=http://mirror.centos.org/centos/$releasever/updates/$basearch/
gpgcheck=1
gpgkey=file:///etc/pki/rpm-gpg/RPM-GPG-KEY-CentOS-7

#additional packages that may be useful
[extras]
name=CentOS-$releasever - Extras
mirrorlist=http://mirrorlist.centos.org/?release=$releasever&arch=$base
arch&repo=extras
#baseurl=http://mirror.centos.org/centos/$releasever/extras/$basearch/
gpgcheck=1
gpgkey=file:///etc/pki/rpm-gpg/RPM-GPG-KEY-CentOS-7

#additional packages that extend functionality of existing packages
[centosplus]
name=CentOS-$releasever - Plus
mirrorlist=http://mirrorlist.centos.org/?release=$releasever&arch=$base
arch&repo=centosplus
#baseurl=http://mirror.centos.org/centos/$releasever/
centosplus/$basearch/
gpgcheck=1
enabled=0
gpgkey=file:///etc/pki/rpm-gpg/RPM-GPG-KEY-CentOS-7
```

In the repository configuration file from Listing 11.1, you can see that some options are used. Table 11.2 summarizes these options.

Table 11.2 Key Options in .repo Files

Option	Explanation
[label]	The label used as an identifier in the repository file.
name=	The name of the repository.
mirrorlist=	Refers to a URL where information about mirror servers for this server can be obtained. Typically used for big online repositories only.
baseurl=	The base URL where to go to find the RPM packages
gpgcheck=	Set to 1 if a GPG integrity check needs to be performed on the packages. If set to 1, a gpgkey is required.
gpgkey=	Specifies the location of the GPG key that is used to check package integrity.

When creating a repository file, the baseurl parameter is the most important because it tells your server where to find the files that are to be installed. The baseurl takes as its argument the URL where files need to be installed from. This will often be an HTTP or FTP URL, but it can be a file-based URL as well.

When using a URL, two components are used. First, the URI identifies the protocol to be used and is in the format protocol://, such as http://, ftp:// or file://. Following the URI is the exact location on that URL. That can be the name of a web server or an FTP server, including the subdirectory where the files are found. If the URL is file based, the location on the file system starts with a / as well. Therefore, for a file system-based URL, there will be three slashes in the baseurl, such as baseurl:///repo, which refers to the directory /repo on the local file system.

To help you determine the status of packages provided, Red Hat (as well as CentOS) groups packages in different repositories. Each of these has a different support status, so it is important to know where you are installing software from if you are interested in keeping the support status of your server. Table 11.3 lists the different default repository types.

Table 11.3 Repository Types and Their Support Status

Type	Description
base	This is the base repository that contains all essential Red Hat software. Its packages are fully supported.
updates	A specific repository that contains updates only.
optional	This repository contains packages that are provided for the convenience of Red Hat customers. The packages in this repository are open source and not supported by Red Hat.
supplementary	This repository contains packages that are provided for the convenience of Red Hat customers. The packages in this repository are proprietary and not supported by Red Hat.
extras	This repository contains packages that are provided for the convenience of Red Hat customers. Software in this repository comes from different sources and is not supported by Red Hat.

Understanding Repository Security

Using repositories allows you to transparently install software packages from the Internet. This is convenient, but it also involves a security risk. When installing RPM packages, you do that with root permissions, and if in the RPM package script code is executed, that is executed as root as well. For that reason, you want to make sure that you can trust the software packages you are trying to install. This is why repositories in general use keys for package signing. This is also why on Red Hat Enterprise Linux it is a good idea to use repositories provided though RHN only.

To secure packages in a repository, these packages are often signed with a GPG key. This makes it possible to check whether packages have been changed since the owner of the repository provided them. The GPG key used to sign the software packages is typically made available through the repository as well. The users of the repository can download that key and store it locally so that the package signature check can be performed automatically each time a package is downloaded from the repository.

If repository security is compromised and an intruder manages to hack the repository server and put some fake packages on it, the GPG key signature will not match, and the **yum** command will complain while installing new packages. This is why it is highly recommended to use GPG keys when using Internet repositories.

If you are using a repository where GPG package signing has been used, on first contact with that repository the RPM command will propose to download the key that was used for package signing (see Listing 11.2). This is a transparent procedure that requires no further action. The GPG keys that were used for package signing are installed to the /etc/pki/rpm-gpg directory by default.

> **TIP** For using internal repositories, the security risks are not that high. For that reason, you do not have to know how to work with GPG-signed packages on the exam.

Listing 11.2 On First Contact with a Repository, the GPG Key Is Downloaded

```
[root@server1 ~]# yum install kernel
Loaded plugins: fastestmirror
Loading mirror speeds from cached hostfile
 * base: centos.mirror1.spango.com
 * extras: mirror.netrouting.net
 * updates: mirrors.supportex.net
Resolving Dependencies
--> Running transaction check
---> Package kernel.x86_64 0:3.10.0-229.1.2.el7 will be installed
--> Processing Dependency: linux-firmware >= 20140911 for package:
kernel-3.10.0-229.1.2.el7.x86_64
--> Running transaction check
---> Package linux-firmware.noarch 0:20140213-0.3.git4164c23.el7 will
be updated
```

```
---> Package linux-firmware.noarch 0:20140911-0.1.git365e80c.el7 will
be an update
--> Finished Dependency Resolution

Dependencies Resolved

=======================================================================
=======================================================================
 Package                              Arch                       Version
Repository                 Size
=======================================================================
==============
Installing:
 kernel                               x86_64                     3.10.0-
229.1.2.el7                                updates                      31
M
Updating for dependencies:
 linux-firmware                       noarch
20140911-0.1.git365e80c.el7                     base
17 M

Transaction Summary
=======================================================================
Install  1 Package
Upgrade              ( 1 Dependent package)


Total size: 48 M
Is this ok [y/d/N]: y
Downloading packages:
warning: /var/cache/yum/x86_64/7/base/packages/linux-firmware-20140911-
0.1.git365e80c.el7.noarch.rpm: Header V3 RSA/SHA256 Signature, key ID
f4a80eb5: NOKEY
Retrieving key from file:///etc/pki/rpm-gpg/RPM-GPG-KEY-CentOS-7
Importing GPG key 0xF4A80EB5:
 Userid     : "CentOS-7 Key (CentOS 7 Official Signing Key) <security@
centos.org>"
 Fingerprint: 6341 ab27 53d7 8a78 a7c2 7bb1 24c6 a8a7 f4a8 0eb5
 Package    : centos-release-7-0.1406.el7.centos.2.3.x86_64 (@anaconda)
 From       : /etc/pki/rpm-gpg/RPM-GPG-KEY-CentOS-7
Is this ok [y/N]:
```

Creating Your Own Repository

It is not a requirement for the RHCSA or RHCE exam, but it can be useful to know how to create your own repository if you want to test setting up and working with repositories. This allows you to put your own RPMs in a directory and publish that directory as a repository. It is also useful to know how to do this if you have installed RHEL and not connected it to RHN, which means that you would not have any repositories at all.

The procedure itself is not hard to summarize. You need to copy all RPM packages to a directory that you want to use as a repository, and after doing that, you need to use the **createrepo** command to generate the metadata that enables you to use that directory as a repository. Exercise 11.1 describes how to do this.

Exercise 11.1 Creating Your Own Repository

In this exercise, you learn how to create your own repository. To perform this exercise, you need to have access to the CentOS installation disk or ISO file.

1. Insert the installation disk in your virtual machine. This mounts it on the directory /run/media/user/CentOS 7 x86_64. Alternatively, you can manually mount the ISO on the /mnt directory, using **mount -o loop /path/to/centos.iso /mnt**.
2. Type **mkdir /repo** to create a directory /repo that can be used as repository.
3. If you want to create a complete repository, containing all the required files, type **cp $MOUNTPATH/Packages/* repo**. (Replace $MOUNTPATH with the name of the directory on which the installation disk is mounted.) If you do not need a complete repository, you can copy just a few files from the installation disk to the /repo directory.
4. Type **yum install -y createrepo** to ensure that the createrepo RPM package is installed.
5. Type **createrepo /repo**. This generates the repository metadata, which allows you to use your own repository.
6. Now that you have created your own repository, you might as well start using it. In the /etc/yum.repos.d directory, create a file with the name my.repo. Make sure this file has the following contents:

```
[myrepo]
name=myrepo
baseurl=file:///repo
```

7. Type **yum repolist** to verify the availability of the newly created repository. It should show the name of the myrepo repository, including the number of packages that is offered through this repository (see Listing 11.3).

TIP In Exercise 11.1, you have mounted the ISO file of the installation disk to copy files from it. Another convenient way to get repository files is by using the yumdownloader utility. This utility enables you to download single packages directly from the repository to the current directory. For instance, type **yumdownloader nmap** to download the nmap RPM package to the current directory.

Listing 11.3 Verifying Repository Availability with **yum repolist**

```
[root@server1 Packages]# yum repolist
Loaded plugins: fastestmirror, langpacks
myrepo                                               | 2.9 kB     00:00
myrepo/primary_db                                    |  77 kB   00:00
Loading mirror speeds from cached hostfile
 * base: mirror.nl.leaseweb.net
 * extras: mirror.nl.leaseweb.net
 * updates: mirror.nl.leaseweb.net
repo id                    repo name                              status
base/7/x86_64              CentOS-7 - Base                  8,465
extras/7/x86_64            CentOS-7 - Extras                  104
myrepo                     myrepo                             130
updates/7/x86_64           CentOS-7 - Updates               1,668
repolist: 10,367
```

Using yum

At this point, you should have operational repositories, so it is time to start using them. To use repositories, you need the **yum** command. This command enables you to perform several tasks on the repositories. Table 11.4 provides an overview of common yum tasks.

Key Topic

Table 11.4 Common yum Tasks

Task	Explanation
search	Search for the exact name of a package
[what]**provides */name**	Perform a deep search in the package to look for specific files within the package
info	Provide more information about the package

Task	Explanation
install	Install the package
remove	Remove the package
list [all | installed]	List all or installed packages
group list	List pacakge groups
group install	Install all packages from a group
update	Update packages specified
clean all	Remove all stored metadata

Using yum to Find Software Packages

To install packages with yum, you first need to know the exact name of the package. The **yum search** command can help you with that. When you use **yum search**, it first gets in touch with the online repositories (which might take a minute), after which it downloads the most recent repository metadata to the local machine. Then, **yum search** looks in the package name and description for the string you have been looking for. In Listing 11.4, you can see what the result looks like after using **yum search user**.

Listing 11.4 yum search Sample Output

```
[root@server1 Packages]# yum search user
Loaded plugins: fastestmirror, langpacks
Loading mirror speeds from cached hostfile
 * base: mirror.sitbv.nl
 * extras: mirror.sitbv.nl
 * updates: mirror.sitbv.nl
============================== N/S matched: user
==============================
gnome-user-docs.noarch : GNOME User Documentation
libuser.i686 : A user and group account administration library
libuser.x86_64 : A user and group account administration library
libuser-devel.i686 : Files needed for developing applications which use
libuser
libuser-devel.x86_64 : Files needed for developing applications which
use
                     : libuser
```

Because the **yum search** command looks in the package name and summary only, it often does not show what you need. You often need to look for packages containing a specific file. To do this, the **yum whatprovides** or **yum provides** command will help you. (There is no functional difference between these two commands.) To make it clear that you are looking for packages containing a specific file, you need to specify the filename as */filename, or use the full path name to the file you want to use. So if you need to look for the package containing the file semanage, for example, use **yum whatprovides */semanage**. It will show the name of the package as a result.

Getting More Information About Packages

Before installing a package, it is a good idea to get some more information about the package. Because the **yum** command was developed to be intuitive, it is almost possible to guess how that works. Just use **yum info**, followed by the name of the package. In Listing 11.5, you see what this looks like for the nmap package (which, by the way, is a very useful tool). It is a network sniffer that allows you to find ports that are open on other hosts. Just use **nmap 192.168.122.100** to give it a try, but be aware that some network administrators really do not like nmap and might consider this a hostile attack.

Listing 11.5 Example Output of **yum info nmap**

```
[root@localhost ~]# yum info nmap
Loaded plugins: fastestmirror
Loading mirror speeds from cached hostfile
 * base: centos.mirror.triple-it.nl
 * extras: centos.mirror.triple-it.nl
 * updates: centos.mirror.triple-it.nl
Available Packages
Name         : nmap
Arch         : x86_64
Epoch        : 2
Version      : 6.40
Release      : 4.el7
Size         : 3.9 M
Repo         : base/7/x86_64
Summary      : Network exploration tool and security scanner
URL          : http://nmap.org/
License      : GPLv2 and LGPLv2+ and GPLv2+ and BSD
```

```
Description : Nmap is a utility for network exploration or security
auditing.  It supports
            : ping scanning (determine which hosts are up), many port
scanning techniques
            : (determine what services the hosts are offering), and
TCP/IP fingerprinting
            : (remote host operating system identification). Nmap also
offers flexible target
            : and port specification, decoy scanning, determination of
TCP sequence
            : predictability characteristics, reverse-identd scanning,
and more. In addition
            : to the classic command-line nmap executable, the Nmap
suite includes a flexible
            : data transfer, redirection, and debugging tool (netcat
utility ncat), a utility
            : for comparing scan results (ndiff), and a packet
generation and response analysis
            : tool (nping).
```

Installing and Removing Software Packages

If after looking at the **yum info** output you are happy with the package, the next step is to install it. As anything else you are doing with yum, it is not hard to guess how to do that: Just use **yum install nmap**. When used in this way, the **yum** command asks for confirmation. If when you type the **yum install** command you are sure about what you are doing, you might as well use the **-y** option, which passes a "yes" to the confirmation prompt that yum normally issues. Listing 11.6 shows what the result looks like.

Listing 11.6 Installing Software with yum

```
[root@localhost ~]# yum install nmap
Loaded plugins: fastestmirror
base
3.6 kB  00:00:00
extras
| 3.4 kB  00:00:00
updates
| 3.4 kB  00:00:00
Loading mirror speeds from cached hostfile
```

```
 * base: centos.mirror.triple-it.nl
 * extras: centos.mirror.triple-it.nl
 * updates: centos.mirror.triple-it.nl
Resolving Dependencies
--> Running transaction check
---> Package nmap.x86_64 2:6.40-4.el7 will be installed
--> Processing Dependency: nmap-ncat = 2:6.40-4.el7 for package:
2:nmap-6.40-4.el7.x86_64
--> Running transaction check
---> Package nmap-ncat.x86_64 2:6.40-4.el7 will be installed
--> Finished Dependency Resolution

Dependencies Resolved

========================================================================
 Package            Arch            Version            Repository  Size
========================================================================
Installing:
 nmap                x86_64      2:6.40-4.el7   base      3.9 M
Installing for dependencies:
 nmap-ncat          x86_64     2:6.40-4.el7    base      200 k

Transaction Summary
========================================================================
Install  1 Package (+1 Dependent package)

Total download size: 4.1 M
Installed size: 17 M
Is this ok [y/d/N]: y
Downloading packages:
(1/2): nmap-ncat-6.40-4.el7.x86_64.rpm
| 200 kB  00:00:00
(2/2): nmap-6.40-4.el7.x86_64.rpm
| 3.9 MB  00:00:01
------------------------------------------------------------------------
Total
3.2 MB/s | 4.1 MB  00:00:01
Running transaction check
Running transaction test
Transaction test succeeded
Running transaction
  Installing : 2:nmap-ncat-6.40-4.el7.x86_64
1/2
```

```
  Installing  : 2:nmap-6.40-4.el7.x86_64
2/2
  Verifying   : 2:nmap-6.40-4.el7.x86_64
1/2
  Verifying   : 2:nmap-ncat-6.40-4.el7.x86_64
2/2

Installed:
  nmap.x86_64 2:6.40-4.el7

Dependency Installed:
  nmap-ncat.x86_64 2:6.40-4.el7

Complete!
[root@localhost ~]#
```

In Listing 11.6, you can see that yum starts by analyzing what is going to be installed. Once that is clear, it gives an overview of the package that is going to be installed, including its dependencies. Then, the package itself is installed to the system.

To remove software packages from a machine, use the **yum remove** command. This command also will do a dependency analysis, which means that it will not only remove the selected package but also all packages that depend on it. This may sometimes lead to a long list of software packages that are going to be removed. To avoid unpleasant surprises, you should never use **yum remove** with the **-y** option.

NOTE Some packages are protected. Therefore, you cannot easily remove them. If **yum remove** encounters protected packages, it refuses to remove them.

Showing Lists of Packages

When working with yum, you may also use the **yum list** command to show lists of packages. Used without arguments, **yum list** shows a list of all software packages that are available, including the repository they were installed from. You see the repository names as listed in Table 11.2 and the @anaconda repository as well. If a repository name is shown, the package is available in that specific repository. If @ anaconda is listed, the package has already been installed on this system. Listing 11.7 shows the partial output of the **yum list** command.

Listing 11.7 Partial Output of the **yum list** Command

```
Installed Packages
...
zenity.x86_64                    3.8.0-4.el7              @anaconda
zip.x86_64                       3.0-10.el7               @anaconda
zlib.x86_64                      1.2.7-13.el7             @anaconda
Available Packages
389-ds-base.x86_64               1.3.3.1-16.el7_1         updates
389-ds-base-devel.x86_64         1.3.3.1-16.el7_1         updates
389-ds-base-libs.x86_64          1.3.3.1-16.el7_1         updates
Cython.x86_64                    0.19-3.el7               base
ElectricFence.i686               2.2.2-39.el7             base
ElectricFence.x86_64             2.2.2-39.el7             base
GConf2.i686                      3.2.6-8.el7              base
```

If you want to see which packages are installed on your server, you can use the **yum list installed** command. The **yum list** command can also prove useful when used with the name of a specific package as its argument. For instance, type **yum list kernel** to show which version of the kernel is actually installed and which version is available as the most recent version in the repositories. Listing 11.8 shows the result of this command.

Listing 11.8 Use **yum list packagename** for Information About Installed and Available Versions

```
[root@localhost ~]# yum list kernel
Loaded plugins: fastestmirror
Loading mirror speeds from cached hostfile
 * base: centos.mirror.triple-it.nl
 * extras: centos.mirror.triple-it.nl
 * updates: centos.mirror.triple-it.nl
Installed Packages
kernel.x86_64                   3.10.0-123.el7
@anaconda
Available Packages
kernel.x86_64
```

Updating Packages

One of the major benefits of working with yum repositories is that repositories make it easy to update packages. The maintainer of the repositories copies updated packages to the repositories. The index in the repository always contains the current version of a package in the repository. On the local machine also, a database is available with the current versions of the packages that are used. When using the **yum update** command, current versions of packages that are installed are compared to the version of these packages in the repositories. As shown in Listing 11.9, yum next shows an overview of updatable packages. From this overview, type **y** to install the updates.

Notice that while updating packages the old version of the package is replaced with a newer version of the package. There is one exception, which is for the kernel package. Even if you are using the **yum update kernel** command, the kernel package is not updated, but the newer kernel is installed beside the old kernel, so that while booting you can select the kernel that you want to use. This is useful because you may find that because of hardware compatibility issues the new kernel will not work. In that case, you can interfere on the GRUB 2 boot prompt (see Chapter 18, "Managing and Understanding the Boot Procedure," for more details) to start the older kernel.

Listing 11.9 Using **yum update**

```
systemd-sys           x86_64      208-11.el7_0.6        updates          36 k
tuned                 noarch      2.3.0-11.el7_0.3      updates         145 k
 tzdata               noarch      2015a-1.el7_0         updates         432 k
 wpa_supplicant       x86_64      1:2.0-13.el7_0        updates         801 k
 yum-plugin-fastestmirror         noarch      1.1.31-25.el7_0
updates       28 k

Transaction Summary
================================================================================
Install    1 Package
Upgrade   79 Packages

Total download size: 95 M
Is this ok [y/d/N]:
```

Working with yum Package Groups

While managing specific services on a Linux machine, you often need several different packages. If, for instance, you want to make your machine a virtualization host, you need the KVM packages, but also all supporting packages such as qemu, libvirt, and the client packages. Or while configuring your server as a web server, you need to install additional packages like PHP as well in many cases.

To make it easier to manage specific functionality, instead of specific packages, you can work with package groups as well. A package group is defined in the repository, and yum offers the group management commands to work with these groups. For an overview of all current groups, use **yum groups list**. This shows output as in Listing 11.10.

> **TIP** The name of the command is **yum groups**, but there are aliases that ensure that **yum group** and even commands like **yum groupinstall** are also working. So, you can use either of these commands.

Listing 11.10 Showing Available yum Groups

```
[root@localhost ~]# yum groups list
Loaded plugins: fastestmirror
Loading mirror speeds from cached hostfile
 * base: centos.mirror.triple-it.nl
 * extras: centos.mirror.triple-it.nl
 * updates: centos.mirror.triple-it.nl
Available environment groups:
   Minimal Install
   Infrastructure Server
   File and Print Server
   Basic Web Server
   Virtualization Host
   Server with GUI
   GNOME Desktop
   KDE Plasma Workspaces
   Development and Creative Workstation
Installed groups:
   Console Internet Tools
   System Administration Tools
Available Groups:
   Compatibility Libraries
```

```
   Development Tools
   Graphical Administration Tools
   Legacy UNIX Compatibility
   Scientific Support
   Security Tools
   Smart Card Support
   System Management
```

Notice that some yum groups are not listed by default. To show those as well, type **yum groups list hidden**. You see the list of groups that is displayed is considerably longer. The difference is that **yum groups list** shows environment groups, which contain basic functionality. Within an environment group, different subgroups can be used; these are displayed only when using **yum groups list hidden**.

To get information about packages available in a group, you use **yum groups info**. Because group names normally contain spaces, do not forget to put the entire group name between quotes. So, type **yum groups info "Basic Web Server"** to see what is in the Basic Web Server group. As shown in Listing 11.11, this command shows mandatory items and optional items in the group. The items can be groups and individual packages.

Listing 11.11 Showing Group Contents with **yum groups info**

```
[root@localhost ~]# yum groups info "Basic Web Server"
Loaded plugins: fastestmirror
Loading mirror speeds from cached hostfile
 * base: centos.mirror.triple-it.nl
 * extras: centos.mirror.triple-it.nl
 * updates: centos.mirror.triple-it.nl

Environment Group: Basic Web Server
 Environment-Id: web-server-environment
 Description: Server for serving static and dynamic internet content.
 Mandatory Groups:
   +base
    core
    web-server
 Optional Groups:
   +backup-client
```

```
 directory-client
+guest-agents
+hardware-monitoring
+java-platform
+large-systems
+load-balancer
+mariadb-client
+network-file-system-client
+performance
+perl-web
+php
+postgresql-client
+python-web
+remote-system-management
+web-servlet
```

Using yum History

While working with yum, all actions are logged to the /var/log/yum.log file. You can use the **yum history** command to get an overview of all actions that have been issued. From the history file, it is possible to undo specific actions; use **yum history undo** followed by the number of the specific action you want to undo.

In Listing 11.12, you see the result of the **yum history** command where every action has its own ID.

Listing 11.12 Showing Past yum Actions Using **yum history**

```
[root@localhost ~]# yum history
Loaded plugins: fastestmirror
ID     | Login user               | Date and time    | Action(s)      | Altered
-------------------------------------------------------------------------------
    14 | root <root>              | 2015-02-10 04:07 | I, U           |   80
    13 | root <root>              | 2015-02-10 03:48 | Install        |    2
    12 | root <root>              | 2015-01-23 12:29 | Install        |    1
    11 | root <root>              | 2015-01-23 12:17 | I, U           |    4
    10 | root <root>              | 2015-01-19 05:35 | Install        |    2
     9 | root <root>              | 2015-01-19 02:53 | Install        |    1
     8 | root <root>              | 2015-01-18 05:14 | Install        |    3
     7 | root <root>              | 2015-01-17 13:47 | Install        |   30
     6 | root <root>              | 2015-01-17 11:40 | Install        |    5
```

```
    5 | root <root>          | 2015-01-11 10:19 | Install        |    1
    4 | root <root>          | 2015-01-09 17:36 | I, U           |    8
    3 | root <root>          | 2015-01-09 17:30 | Install        |    1
    2 | root <root>          | 2015-01-09 17:27 | Install        |    1
    1 | System <unset>       | 2014-10-03 02:17 | Install        |  297
history list
```

As you can see, action number 14 altered 80 packages and was used to install and update packages. To undo this action completely, type **yum history undo 14**. In Exercise 11.2, you apply some of the most useful **yum** commands as discussed previously.

Exercise 11.2 Using yum for Package Management

In this exercise, you use yum for common package management tasks.

1. Type **yum repolist** to show a list of the current repositories that your system is using.
2. Type **yum search xeyes**. This will give no matching result.
3. Type **yum provides */xeyes**. The command shows that the xorg-x11-apps-<version> package contains this file.
4. Install this package using **yum install -y xorg-x11-apps**. Depending on your current configuration, you might notice that quite a few dependencies have to be installed also.
5. Type **yum list xorg-x11-apps**. You see that the package is listed as installed.
6. Type **yum history** and notice the number of the last **yum** command you used.
7. Type **yum history undo <nn>** (where **<nn>** is replaced with the number that you found in step 6). This undoes the last action, so it removes the package you just installed.
8. Repeat the **yum list xorg-x11-apps** command. The package is now listed as available but not as installed.

Managing Software Packages with rpm

Once upon a time, repositories did not exist, and the **rpm** command was used to install package files after they had been downloaded. That worked, but there was one major issue: the dependency hell. Because RPM packages have always focused on specific functionality, to install specific software, a collection of RPM packages was normally required. Therefore, a "missing dependency" message was often issued while users were trying to install RPM packages, which means that to install the selected package, other packages needed to be installed first.

It sometimes even happened that a whole chain of dependencies needed to be installed to finally get the desired functionality. That did not really make working with RPM packages a joyful experience.

On modern RHEL systems, repositories are used, and packages are installed using yum. The **yum** command considers all package dependencies and tries to look them up in the currently available repositories. On an RHEL system configured to get updates from the RHN network, or on a CentOS system where consistent repositories are used, the result is that package installation nowadays is without problems and the RPM command is needed no longer for software installation.

Even after downloading an RPM package file, you do not need to use the **rpm -Uvh packagename** command anymore to install it (even if it still works). A much better alternative is **yum install packagename**, which installs the package and also considers the repositories to resolve dependencies automatically. (In earlier versions of RHEL, the **yum localinstall** command was used to do this; in RHEL 7, **yum localinstall** was deprecated.) That does not mean the **rpm** command has become totally useless. You can still use it to query RPM packages.

TIP On your system, two package databases are maintained: the yum database and the rpm database. When you are installing packages through yum, the yum database is updated first, after which the updated information is synchronized to the RPM database. If you install packages using the **rpm** command, the update is written to the rpm database only and will not be updated to the yum database, which is an important reason not to use the **rpm** command anymore to install software packages.

Understanding RPM Filenames

When working with RPM packages directly, it makes sense understanding how the RPM filename is composed. A typical RPM filename looks like autofs-5.0.7-40.el7.x86_64.rpm. This name consists of several parts:

Key Topic

- **autofs:** The name of the actual package.
- **5.0.7:** The version of the package. This normally corresponds to the name of the package as it was released by the package creator.
- **-40:** The subversion of the package.
- **el7:** The Red Hat version this package was created for.
- **x86_64:** The platform (32 bits or 64 bits) this package was created for.

Querying the RPM Database

The **rpm** command enables you to get much information about packages. Using RPM queries can be a really useful way to find out how software can be configured and used. To start, you can use the **rpm -qa** command. Like **yum list installed**, this shows a list of all software that is installed on the machine. Use **grep** on this command to find out specific package names. To perform queries on RPM packages, you just need the name and not the version information.

After finding the package about which you want to have more information, you can start with some generic queries to find out what is in the package. In the following examples, I assume that you are using RPM queries on the nmap RPM package. To start, type **rpm -qi nmap** to get a description of the package.

The next step is to use **rpm -ql nmap**, which shows a list of all files that are in the package. On some packages, the result can be a really long list of filenames that is not particularly useful. To get more specific information, use **rpm -qd nmap**, which shows all documentation available for the package, or **rpm -qc nmap**, which shows all configuration files in the package.

Using RPM queries can really help in finding out more useful information about packages. The only thing that you need to know is the RPM package name a specific file belongs to. To find this, use **rpm -qf**, followed by the specific filename you are looking for. Use, for instance, **rpm -qf /bin/ls** to find the name of the RPM the **ls** command comes from. In Exercise 11.3, you see how useful it can be to use RPM queries in this way.

Querying RPM Package Files

RPM queries by default are used on the RPM database, and what you are querying are installed RPMs. It sometimes makes sense to install an RPM before it is actually installed. To do this, you need to add the **-p** option to the query, because without the **-p** option, you will be querying the database not the package file. Also, when querying a package file, you need to refer to the complete filename, including the version number and all other information that you do not have to use when querying the RPM database. As an example, the **rpm -qp --scripts httpd-2.4.6-19.el7.centos.x86_64.rpm** command queries the specific RPM file to see whether there are scripts contained with the RPM.

A query option that needs special attention is **--scripts**. This option queries an RPM package to see which scripts it contains (if any). This option is especially important when combined with the **-p** option, to find out whether a package that you are going to install includes any scripts.

When you are installing RPM packages, you will be doing that as root. Before installing an RPM package from an unknown source, you really need to make sure that it does not include any rogue scripts. If you do not, you do risk installing malware on your computer without even knowing it.

Table 11.5 describes the most important RPM querying options.

Table 11.5 Common RPM Query Commands

Key Topic

Command	Use
rpm -qf	Uses a filename as its argument to find the specific RPM package a file belongs to.
rpm -ql	Uses the RPM database to provide a list of files in the RPM package.
rpm -qi	Uses the RPM database to provide package information (equivalent to yum info).
rpm -qd	Uses the RPM database to show all documentation that is available in the package.
rpm -qc	Uses the RPM database to show all configuration files that are available in the package.
rpm -q --scripts	Uses the RPM database to show scripts that are used in the package. Particularly useful if combined with the **-p** option.
rpm -qp ...	The **-p** option is used with all the previously listed options to query individual RPM package files instead of the RPM package database. Using this option before installation helps you find out what is actually in the package before it is installed.
rpm -qR	Shows dependencies for a specific package.
rpm -V	Use on an individual package to see which parts of the package have been changed since installation.
rpm -Va	Verifies all installed packages and shows which parts of the package have been changed since installation. This is an easy and convenient way to do a package integrity check.
rpm -qa	Lists all packages that are installed on this server

Using repoquery

While **rpm -qp** provides useful tools to query packages before installation, there is a slight problem with this command: It works only on RPM package files, and it cannot query files directly from the repositories. If you want to query packages from the repositories before they have been installed, you need **repoquery**. This binary is not installed by default, so make sure to install the **yum-utils** RPM package to use it.

The **repoquery** command is pretty similar to the **rpm -q** command and uses many similar options. There is just one significant option missing: the **--script** option. A simple solution is to make sure that you are using trusted repositories only, to prevent installing software that contains dangerous script code.

If you need to thoroughly analyze what an RPM package is doing when it is installed, you can download it to your machine, which allows you to use the **rpm -qp --scripts** command on the package. To download a package from the repository to the local directory, you can use the **yumdownloader** command, which comes from the **yum-utils** package.

Now that you learned all about RPM querying options, you can practice these newly acquired skills in Exercise 11.3.

Exercise 11.3 Using RPM Queries

In this exercise, you learn how to use RPM queries to get more information about software that is installed on your RHEL system.

1. Type **which dnsmasq**. This command gives the complete path name of the **dnsmasq** command.
2. Type **rpm -qf $(which dnsmasq)**. This will do an RPM file query on the result of the **which dnsmasq** command; you learn more about this technique in Chapter 31, "An Introduction to Bash Shell Scripting."
3. Now that you know that the dnsmasq binary comes from the dnsmasq package, use **rpm -qi dnsmasq** to show more information about the package.
4. The information that is shown with **rpm -qi** is useful, but it does not give the details that are needed to start working with the software in the package. Use **rpm -ql dnsmasq** to show a list of all files in the package.
5. Use **rpm -qd dnsmasq** to show the available documentation. Notice that this command reveals that there is a man page, but there is also a doc.html and a setup.html file in the /usr/share/doc/dnsmasq-version directory. Open these files with your browser to get more information about the use of dnsmasq.

6. Type **rpm -qc dnsmasq** to see which configuration files are used by dnsmasq.
7. After installation, it does not make much sense, but it is always good to know which scripts are executed when a package is installed. Use **rpm -q --scripts dnsmasq** to show the script code that can be executed from this RPM.

TIP Working with RPM queries is an extremely valuable skill on the RHCSA and the RHCE exams. If you know how to handle queries, you can find all relevant configuration files and the documentation.

Summary

In this chapter, you learned how to work with software on Red Hat Enterprise Linux. You learned how to use yum to manage software packages coming from repositories. You also learned how to use the **rpm** command to perform queries on the packages on your system. Make sure that you master these essential skills well; they are key to getting things done on Red Hat Enterprise Linux.

Exam Preparation Tasks

Review All Key Topics

Review the most important topics in the chapter, noted with the Key Topic icon in the outer margin of the page. Table 11.5 lists a reference of these key topics and the page numbers on which each is found.

Table 11.5 Key Topics for Chapter 11

Key Topic Element	Description	Page
Paragraph	Description of how to create a repository	253
Table 11.4	Common yum tasks	260
List	RPM package name components	273
Table 11.5	Common RPM query commands	274

Complete Tables and Lists from Memory

Print a copy of Appendix B, "Memory Tables," (found on the disc), or at least the section for this chapter, and complete the tables and lists from memory. Appendix C, "Memory Tables Answer Key," also on the disc, includes completed tables and lists to check your work.

Define Key Terms

Define the following key terms from this chapter and check your answers in the glossary:

yum, repository, dependency, package, Red Hat Network, RHN, package groups, dependency hell, RPM

Review Questions

1. You have a directory containing a collection of RPM packages and want to make that directory a repository. Which command enables you to do that?
2. What needs to be in the repository file to point to a repository on http://server.example.com/repo?
3. You have just configured a new repository to be used on your RHEL computer. Which command enables you to verify that the repository is indeed available?
4. Which command enables you to search the RPM package containing the file useradd?
5. Which two commands do you need to use to show the name of the yum group that contains security tools and shows what is in that group?
6. Which command enables you to install an RPM that you have downloaded from the Internet and which is not in the repositories?
7. You want to make sure that an RPM package that you have downloaded does not contain any dangerous script code. Which command enables you to do so?
8. Which command reveals all documentation in an RPM?
9. Which command shows the RPM a file comes from?
10. Which command enables you to query software from the repository?

End-of-Chapter Labs

In the end-of-chapter labs, you use some of the essential RHEL package management skills. All assignments can be done on one server.

Lab 11.1

1. Copy some RPM files from the installation disk to the /myrepo directory. Make this directory a repository and make sure that your server is using this repository.
2. List the repositories currently in use on your server.
3. Search for the package that contains the cache only DNS name server. Do not install it yet.
4. Perform an extensive query of the package so that you know before you install it which files it contains, which dependencies it has, and where to find the documentation and configuration.
5. Check whether the RPM contains any scripts. You may download it, but you may not install it yet; you want to know which scripts are in a package before actually installing it, right?
6. Install the package you have found in step 3.
7. Undo the installation.

The following topics are covered in this chapter:

- Scheduling once-only future tasks with at
- Scheduling regular future tasks with cron

The following RHCSA exam objectives are covered in this chapter:

- Scheduling tasks using at and cron

CHAPTER 12

Scheduling Tasks

On a Linux server it is important that certain tasks run at certain times. This can be done by using the atd and crond services, which can be configured to run tasks in the future. The atd service is for executing future tasks once only, the crond service is for recurring regular tasks. In this chapter you learn how to configure both.

"Do I Know This Already?" Quiz

The "Do I Know This Already?" quiz allows you to assess whether you should read this entire chapter thoroughly or jump to the "Exam Preparation Tasks" section. If you are in doubt about your answers to these questions or your own assessment of your knowledge of the topics, read the entire chapter. Table 12.1 lists the major headings in this chapter and their corresponding "Do I Know This Already?" quiz questions. You can find the answers in Appendix A, "Answers to the 'Do I Know This Already?' Quizzes and 'Review Questions.'"

Table 12.1 "Do I Know This Already?" Section-to-Question Mapping

Foundation Topics Section	Questions
Scheduling Once-Only Future Tasks with at	9–10
Scheduling Regular Future Tasks with cron	1–8

1. Which of the following commands enables you to check the current status of the crond service?
   a. **service crond status**
   b. **systemctl status crond**
   c. **/usr/sbin/crond --status**
   d. **chkconfig crond --show**

2. Which of the following would run a cron task Sunday at 11 a.m.?
    a. *** 11 7 * ***
    b. **0 11 * 7 ***
    c. **0 11 * * 7**
    d. **11 0 * 7 ***

3. Which of the following launches a job every five minutes from Monday through Friday?
    a. ***/5 * * * 1-5**
    b. ***/5 * 1-5 * ***
    c. **0/5 * * * 1-5**
    d. **0/5 * 1-5 * ***

4. How do you create a cron job for a specific user?
    a. Log in as that user and type **crontab -e** to open the cron editor.
    b. Open the crontab file in the user home directory and add what you want to add.
    c. As root, type **crontab -e username**.
    d. As root, type **crontab -u username –e**.

5. Which directory is mainly used by cron files that are installed automatically through RPM?
    a. /etc/crond.d
    b. /etc/cron.d
    c. /var/cron
    d. /var/spool/cron

6. Which of the following is not a recommended way to specify jobs that should be executed with cron?
    a. Modify /etc/crontab.
    b. Put the jobs in separate scripts in /etc/cron.d.
    c. Use crontab -e to create user specific cron jobs.
    d. Put scripts in /etc/cron.{hourly|daily|weekly|monthly} for automatic execution.

7. Which service takes care of executing cron jobs in /etc/cron.hourly, cron.daily, cron.weekly, and cron.monthly?
   a. cron
   b. crontab
   c. atd
   d. anacron
8. Which of the statements about cron security is true?
   a. By default, all users are allowed to schedule tasks through cron because the /etc/cron.allow file has the keyword **all** in it.
   b. If the cron.deny file exists, a cron.allow file must be created also and list users who are allowed to schedule tasks through cron.
   c. For every user, a matching entry must exist in either the cron.allow file, or in the cron.deny file.
   d. If the cron.allow file exists, a user must be listed in it to be able to schedule jobs through cron.
9. After entering commands in the at shell, which command enables you to close the at shell?
   a. **Ctrl+V**
   b. **Ctrl+D**
   c. **exit**
   d. **:wq**
10. Which command enables you to see current at jobs scheduled for execution?
   a. **atrm**
   b. **atls**
   c. **atq**
   d. **at**

Foundation Topics

Configuring cron to Automate Recurring Tasks

On a Linux system, some tasks have to be automated on a regular basis. It would be one option to configure each process with a process-specific solution to handle recurring tasks, but that would not be efficient to deal with. That is why on Linux the cron service is used as a generic service to run processes automatically at specific times.

The cron service consists of two major components. First, there is the cron daemon crond. This daemon looks every minute to see whether there is work to do. This work to do is defined in the cron configuration, which consists of multiple files working together to provide the right information to the right service at the right time. In this section, you learn how to configure cron.

Managing the cron Service

The cron service is started by default on every RHEL system. The service is needed because some system tasks are running through cron as well. An example of these is logrotate, a service that cleans up log files and runs on a regular basis, but other important maintenance processes are started automatically through cron also.

Managing the cron service itself is easy: It does not need much management. Where other services need to be reloaded or restarted to activate changes to their configuration, this is not needed by cron. The cron daemon wakes up every minute and checks its configuration to see whether anything needs to be started.

To monitor the current status of the cron service, you can use the **systemctl status crond -l** command. Listing 12.1 shows the output of this command.

Listing 12.1 Monitoring the Current State of the crond Service

```
[root@server2 ~]# systemctl status crond -l
crond.service - Command Scheduler
   Loaded: loaded (/usr/lib/systemd/system/crond.service; enabled)
   Active: active (running) since Wed 2015-02-11 03:50:14 EST; 5 days
ago
 Main PID: 550 (crond)
   CGroup: /system.slice/crond.service
           └─550 /usr/sbin/crond -n
```

```
Feb 11 03:50:14 localhost.localdomain systemd[1]: Started Command
Scheduler.
Feb 11 03:50:15 localhost.localdomain crond[550]: (CRON) INFO (RANDOM_
DELAY will be scaled with factor 46% if used.)
Feb 11 03:50:15 localhost.localdomain crond[550]: (CRON) INFO (running
with inotify support)
```

The most significant part of the output of the **systemctl status crond** command is in the beginning: It mentions that the cron service is loaded and that it is enabled as well. The fact that the service is enabled means that it will automatically be started whenever this service is restarting. The last part of the command shows current status information. Through the journald service, the **systemctl** command can find out what is actually happening to the crond service.

Understanding cron Timing

When scheduling services through cron, you need to specify when exactly the services need to be started. In the crontab configuration (which is explained more in depth in the next section), you use a time string to indicate when tasks should be started. Table 12.2 shows the time and date fields used (in the order specified)

Table 12.2 cron Time and Date Fields

Key Topic

Field	Values
minute	0–59
hour	0–23
day of month	1–31
month	1–12 (or names which are better avoided)
day of week	0–7 (Sunday is 0 or 7, or names [which are better avoided])

In any of these fields, you can use an * to refer to any value. Ranges of numbers are allowed, as are lists and patterns. Some examples are listed next:

Key Topic

- *** 11 * * *** Any minute between 11:00 and 11:59 (probably not what you want)
- **0 11 * * 1-5** Every day at 11 a.m. on weekdays only
- **0 7-18 * * 1-5** Every hour on weekdays on the hour

- **0 */2 2 12 5** Every 2 hours on the hour on December second and every Friday in December

> **TIP** No need trying to remember all this, **man 5 crontab** shows all possible constructions.

Managing cron Configuration Files

The main configuration file for cron is /etc/crontab, but you will not change this file directly. It does give you a convenient overview, though, of the different time specifications that can be used in cron. It also sets environment variables that are used by the commands that are executed through cron (see Listing 12.2). To make modifications to the cron jobs, there are other locations where cron jobs should be specified.

Listing 12.2 /etc/crontab Sample Content

```
[root@server2 ~]# cat /etc/crontab
SHELL=/bin/bash
PATH=/sbin:/bin:/usr/sbin:/usr/bin
MAILTO=root

# For details see man 4 crontabs

# Example of job definition:
# .---------------- minute (0 - 59)
# |  .------------- hour (0 - 23)
# |  |  .---------- day of month (1 - 31)
# |  |  |  .------- month (1 - 12) OR jan,feb,mar,apr ...
# |  |  |  |  .---- day of week (0 - 6) (Sunday=0 or 7) OR
sun,mon,tue,wed,thu,fri,sat
# |  |  |  |  |
# *  *  *  *  * user-name  command to be executed
```

Key Topic

Instead of modifying /etc/crontab, different cron configuration files are used:

- Cron files in /etc/cron.d
- Scripts in /etc/cron.hourly, cron.daily, cron.weekly, and cron.monthly
- User-specific files that are created with **crontab -e**

In this section, you get an overview of these locations.

NOTE If you want to experiment how cron works, you should allow for a sufficient amount of time for the job to be executed. The crond service reads its configuration every minute, after which new jobs can be scheduled for execution on the next minute. So, if you want to make sure your job is executed as fast as possible, allow for a safe margin of 3 minutes between the moment you save the cron configuration and execution time.

To start, cron jobs can be started for specific users. To create a user specific cron job, type **crontab -e** after logging in as that user, or as root type **crontab -e -u username**.

When you are using **crontab -e**, the vi editor opens and creates a temporary file. After you edit the cron configuration, the temporary file is moved to its final location in the directory /var/spool/cron. In this directory, a file is created for each user. These files should never be edited directly! When the file is saved by **crontab -e**, it is activated automatically.

Whereas in the early days the /etc/crontab file was modified directly, on RHEL 7 you do not do that anymore. If you want to add cron jobs that are not bound to a specific user account (and which for that reason by default will be executed as root if not specified otherwise), you add these to the /etc/cron.d directory. Just put a file in that directory (the exact name does not really matter) and make sure that it meets the syntax of a typical cron job. In Listing 12.3, you can see an example of the /etc/cron.d/unbound-anchor cron configuration file (which was inserted to the /etc/cron.d directory upon installation of the unbound Domain Name System [DNS] server).

Listing 12.3 Example cron Job in /etc/cron.d

```
[root@server1 cron.d]# cat unbound-anchor
# Look to see whether the DNSSEC Root key got rolled, if so check trust
and update

10 3 1 * * unbound /usr/sbin/unbound-anchor -a /var/lib/unbound/root.
anchor -c /etc/unbound/icannbundle.pem
```

This example file contains three elements. First there is the time indication, which has the command start at 3:10 a.m. on the first of every month. Then, the configuration indicates that the command has to be started as the unbound user. The last part has the actual command that needs to be started with some arguments specific to the command and show how this command should be used.

The last way to schedule cron jobs is through the following directories:

- /etc/cron.hourly
- /etc/cron.daily
- /etc/cron.weekly
- /etc/cron.monthly

In these directories, you typically find scripts that are put in there from RPM package files. When opening these scripts, notice that no information is included about the time when the command should be executed. That is because the exact time of execution does not really matter. The only thing that does matter is that the job is launched once an hour, day, week, or month.

Understanding the Purpose of anacron

To ensure regular execution of the job, cron uses the anacron service. This service takes care of starting the hourly, daily, weekly, and monthly cron jobs, no matter at which exact time. To determine how this should be done, anacron uses the /etc/anacrontab file. Listing 12.4 shows the contents of the /etc/anacrontab file, which is used to specify how anacrontab jobs should be executed.

Listing 12.4 anacrontab Configuration

```
[root@server1 spool]# cat /etc/anacrontab
# /etc/anacrontab: configuration file for anacron

# See anacron(8) and anacrontab(5) for details.

SHELL=/bin/sh
PATH=/sbin:/bin:/usr/sbin:/usr/bin
MAILTO=root
# the maximal random delay added to the base delay of the jobs
RANDOM_DELAY=45
# the jobs will be started during the following hours only
START_HOURS_RANGE=3-22
```

```
#period in days   delay in minutes   job-identifier   command
1         5        cron.daily          nice run-parts /etc/cron.daily
7         25       cron.weekly         nice run-parts /etc/cron.weekly
@monthly 45        cron.monthly        nice run-parts /etc/cron.monthly
```

In /etc/anacrontab, the jobs to be executed are specified in lines that contain three fields, as shown in Listing 12.4. The first field specifies the frequency of job execution, expressed in days. The second column specifies how long anacron waits before executing the job, and in the last part is the command that should be executed.

TIP Although useful to know how anacron works, it typically is not a service that is configured directly. The need to configure services through anacron is taken away by the /etc/cron.hourly, cron.daily, cron.weekly, and cron.monthly files.

NOTE It is not easy to get an overview of the cron jobs actually scheduled for execution. There is no single command that would show all currently scheduled cron jobs. The **crontab-l** command does list cron jobs, but only for the current user account.

Managing cron Security

By default, all users can enter cron jobs. It is possible to limit which user is allowed to schedule cron jobs by using the /etc/cron.allow and /etc/cron.deny configuration files. If the cron.allow file exists, a user must be listed in it to be allowed to use cron. If the /etc/cron.deny file exists, a user must not be listed in it to be allowed to set up cron jobs.

In Exercise 12.1, you learn how to run jobs through cron.

Exercise 12.1 Running Scheduled Tasks Through cron

In this exercise, you apply some of the cron basics. You schedule cron jobs using different mechanisms.

1. Open a root shell. Type **cat /etc/crontab** to get an impression of the contents of the /etc/crontab configuration file.

2. Type **crontab -e**. This opens an editor interface that by default uses vi as its editor. Add the following line:

```
0 2 * * 1-5 logger message from root
```

3. Use the vi command **:wq!** to close the editing session and write changes.
4. Use **cd /etc/cron.hourly**. In this directory, create a script file with the name **eachhour** that contains the following line:

```
logger This message is written at $(date)
```

5. Use **chmod +x eachhour** to make the script executable; if you fail to make it executable, it will not work.
6. Now enter the directory /etc/crond.d and in this directory create a file with the name **eachhour**. Put the following contents in the file:

```
11 * * * *  root  logger This message is written from /etc/cron.d
```

7. Save the modifications to the configuration file and go work on the next section. (For optimal effect, perform the last part of this exercise after a couple of hours.)
8. After a couple of hours, type **grep written /var/log/messages** and read the messages that have been written which verifies correct cron operations.

Configuring at to Schedule Future Tasks

Whereas cron is used to schedule jobs that need to be executed on a regular basis, the atd service is available for services that need to be executed only once. On RHEL 7, the atd service is available by default, so all that needs to be done is scheduling jobs.

To run a job through the atd service, you would use the **at** command, followed by the time the job needs to be executed. This can be a specific time, as in **at 14:00**, but it can also be a time indication like **at teatime** or **at noon**. After you type this, the at shell opens. From this shell, you can type several commands that will be executed at the specific time that is mentioned. After entering the commands, use **Ctrl+D** to quit the at shell.

After scheduling jobs with at, you can use the **atq** command (*q* for *queue*) to get an overview of all jobs currently scheduled. It is also possible to remove current at jobs. To do this, use the **atrm** command, optionally followed by the number of the at job that you want to remove. In Exercise 12.2, you learn how to work with at to schedule jobs for execution at a specific time.

> **TIP** The **batch** command works like **at**, but it's a bit more sophisticated. When using **batch**, you can specify that a job is only started when system performance parameters allow. Typically, that is when system load is lower than 0.8. This value is a bit low on modern multi-CPU systems, which is why the load value can be specified manually when starting atd, using the **-l** command-line option. Use for instance **atd -l 3.0** to make sure that no batch job is started when system load is higher than 3.0.

Exercise 12.2 Scheduling Jobs with at

In this exercise, you learn how to schedule jobs using the atd service.

1. Type **systemctl status atd**. In the line that starts with Loaded:, this command should show you that the service is currently loaded and enabled, which means that it is ready to start receiving jobs.
2. Type **at 15:00** (or replace with any time near to the time at which you are working on this exercise).
3. Type **logger message from at**. Use **Ctrl+D** to close the at shell.
4. Type **atq** to verify that the job has indeed been scheduled.

Summary

In this chapter, you learned how to schedule jobs for future execution. You also learned how to configure cron to execute jobs repeatedly at a specific time. You learned that different methods exist to tell cron when a job should be executed. In addition, you learned about the anacron service, which is used to make sure that the jobs in the directories /etc/cron.{hourly|daily|weekly|monthly} are indeed executed, even if the system temporarily is not available. At the end of this chapter, you learned how to use the **atd** service to schedule tasks to be executed once.

Exam Preparation Tasks

Review All Key Topics

Review the most important topics in the chapter, noted with the Key Topic icon in the outer margin of the page. Table 12.3 lists a reference of these key topics and the page numbers on which each is found.

Table 12.3 Key Topics for Chapter 12

Key Topic Element	Description	Page
Table 12.2	crontab time indicators	285
Bullet list	crontab time indicators examples	285
Bullet list	Methods to enter crontab information	286

Define Key Terms

Define the following key terms from this chapter and check your answers in the glossary:

cron, anacron, at

Review Questions

1. Where do you configure a cron job that needs to be executed once every 2 weeks?
2. How do you specify the execution time in a cron job that needs to be executed twice every month, on the 1st and the 15th of the month at 2 p.m.?
3. How do you specify cron execution time for a job that needs to run every 2 minutes on every day?
4. How do you specify a job that needs to be executed on September 19 and every Thursday in September?
5. Which three valid day indicators can you use to specify that a cron job needs to be executed on Sunday?
6. Which command enables you to schedule a cron job for user lisa?
7. How do you specify that user boris is never allowed to schedule jobs through cron?
8. You need to make sure that a job is executed every day, even if the server at execution time is temporarily unavailable. How do you do this?
9. Which service must be running to schedule at jobs?
10. Which command enables you to find out whether any current at jobs are scheduled for execution?

End-of-Chapter Labs

In this end-of-chapter lab, you work on at jobs and on cron jobs.

Lab 12.1

1. Create a cron job that performs an update of all software on your computer every evening at 11 p.m.
2. Schedule your machine to be rebooted at 3 a.m. tonight.

The following topics are covered in this chapter:

- Understand System Logging
- Configuring rsyslogd
- Rotating Log Files
- Working with journald

The following RHCSA exam objectives are covered in this chapter:

- Locate and interpret system log files and journals

CHAPTER 13

Configuring Logging

Analyzing log files is an important system administrator task. If anything goes wrong on a Linux system, the answer is often in the log files. On RHEL 7, two different log systems are used side by side, and it is important to know which information can be found where. This chapter teaches you all about it. You learn how to read log files, configure rsyslogd and journald, and also how to set up your system for log rotation so that you can prevent your disks from being completely filled up by services that are logging too enthusiastically.

"Do I Know This Already?" Quiz

The "Do I Know This Already?" quiz allows you to assess whether you should read this entire chapter thoroughly or jump to the "Exam Preparation Tasks" section. If you are in doubt about your answers to these questions or your own assessment of your knowledge of the topics, read the entire chapter. Table 13.1 lists the major headings in this chapter and their corresponding "Do I Know This Already?" quiz questions. You can find the answers in Appendix A, "Answers to the 'Do I Know This Already?' Quizzes and 'Review Questions.'"

Table 13.1 "Do I Know This Already?" Section-to-Question Mapping

Foundation Topics Section	Questions
Understand System Logging	1–3
Configuring rsyslogd	4–7
Rotating Log Files	8
Working with journald	9–10

1. Which of the following statements about journald is *not* true?
   a. journald logs kernel messages.
   b. journald writes to the journal, which by default does not persist between boots.
   c. journald is a replacement of rsyslogd.
   d. To read files from the journal, the **journalctl** command is used.

2. Which log would you read to find messages related to authentication errors?
   a. /var/log/messages
   b. /var/log/lastlog
   c. /var/log/audit/audit.log
   d. /var/log/secure

3. Which log would you read to find information that relates to SELinux events?
   a. /var/log/messages
   b. /var/log/lastlog
   c. /var/log/audit/audit.log
   d. /var/log/secure

4. What is the name of the rsyslogd configuration file?
   a. /etc/rsyslog.conf
   b. /etc/sysconfig/rsyslogd.conf
   c. /etc/sysconfig/rsyslog.conf
   d. /etc/rsyslog.d/rsyslogd.conf

5. You need to change the startup behavior of the rsyslogd service. Which of the following describes the recommended approach to do so?
   a. Include the startup parameter in the main rsyslog configuration file.
   b. Create a snap-in file in the directory /etc/rsyslog.d and specify the required parameters in there.
   c. Change the systemd unit file in /usr/lib/systemd/system to include the required startup parameter.
   d. Use the SYSLOGD_OPTIONS line in the file /etc/sysconfig/rsyslog and include the startup parameter here.

6. In the rsyslog.conf file, which of the following destinations refers to a specific rsyslogd module?
   a. -/var/log/maillog
   b. /var/log/messages
   c. :omusrmsg:*
   d. *

7. Which facility is the best solution if you want to configure Apache to log messages through rsyslog?
   a. daemon
   b. apache
   c. syslog
   d. local0-7
8. You want to maximize the file size of a log file to 10MB. Where do you configure this?
   a. Create a file in /etc/logrotate.d and specify the maximal size in that file.
   b. Put the maximal size in the logrotate cron job.
   c. Configure the destination with the maximal size option.
   d. This cannot be done.
9. Which directory is used to store the journald journal?
   a. /var/log/journal
   b. /var/run/journal
   c. /run/log
   d. /run/log/journal
10. What do you need to do to make the journald journal persistent?
    a. Create the directory /var/log/journal, set appropriate permissions and reboot your machine.
    b. Open /etc/sysconfig/journal and set the PERSISTENT option to yes.
    c. Open the /etc/systemd/journald.conf file and set the PERSISTENT option to yes.
    d. Create the /var/log/journal file and set appropriate permissions.

Foundation Topics

Understanding System Logging

Most services used on a Linux server write information to log files. This information can be written to different destinations, and there are multiple solutions to find the relevant information in system logs. No less than three different approaches can be used by services to write log information:

- **Direct write:** Some services write logging information directly to the log files, even some important services such as the Apache web server and the Samba file server.
- **rsyslogd:** rsyslogd is the enhancement of syslogd, a service that takes care of managing centralized log files. Syslogd has been around for a long time.
- **journald:** With the introduction of systemd, the journald log service systemd-journald has been introduced also. This service is tightly integrated with systemd, which allows administrators to read detailed information from the journal while monitoring service status using the **systemctl status** command.

Understanding the Role of rsyslogd and journald

Key Topic

On RHEL 7, journald (which is implemented by the systemd-journald daemon) provides an advanced log management system. journald collects messages from the kernel, the entire boot procedure, and services and writes these messages to an event journal. This event journal is stored in a binary format, and it can be queried using the **journalctl** command.

Key Topic

Because the journal that is written by journald is not persistent between reboots, messages are also forwarded to the rsyslogd service. Rsyslogd writes the messages to different files in the /var/log directory. rsyslogd also offers features that do not exist in journald, such as centralized logging and filtering messages by using modules. In the current state of Red Hat Enterprise Linux 7, journald is not a replacement for rsyslog; it is just another way of logging information. journald is tightly integrated with systemd and therefore logs everything that your server is doing. rsyslogd adds some services to it. In particular, it takes care of writing log information to specific files (that will be persistent between reboots), and it allows you to configure remote logging and log servers.

To get more information about what has been happening on a machine running RHEL, administrators of Red Hat Enterprise Linux have to take three approaches:

- The files in /var/log that are written by rsyslogd must be monitored.
- The **journalctl** command can be used to get more detailed information from the journal.
- For a short overview of the last significant events that have been logged by systemd units through journald, administrators can use the **systemctl status <unit>** command. This command shows the status of services, as well as the last couple of lines that have been logged. Listing 13.1 shows an example where this command clearly indicates what went wrong while starting a service.

Listing 13.1 Using **systemctl** Status to Show Relevant Log Information

```
[root@server1 ~]# systemctl status httpd
httpd.service - The Apache HTTP Server
   Loaded: loaded (/usr/lib/systemd/system/httpd.service; disabled)
   Active: failed (Result: exit-code) since Wed 2015-03-25 05:25:18
PDT; 2s ago
  Process: 2893 ExecStop=/bin/kill -WINCH ${MAINPID} (code=exited,
  status=0/SUCCESS)
  Process: 2890 ExecStart=/usr/sbin/httpd $OPTIONS -DFOREGROUND
  (code=exited, status=1/FAILURE)
 Main PID: 2890 (code=exited, status=1/FAILURE)

Mar 25 05:25:18 server1.example.com httpd[2890]: (13)Permission
  denied: AH00072: make_sock: could not bind to address [::]:443
Mar 25 05:25:18 server1.example.com httpd[2890]: (13)Permission
  denied: AH00072: make_sock: could not bind to address 0.0.0.0:443
Mar 25 05:25:18 server1.example.com httpd[2890]: no listening sockets
  available, shutting down
Mar 25 05:25:18 server1.example.com httpd[2890]: AH00015: Unable to
  open logs
Mar 25 05:25:18 server1.example.com systemd[1]: httpd.service: main
  process exited, code=exited, status=1/FAILURE
Mar 25 05:25:18 server1.example.com systemd[1]: Failed to start The
  Apache HTTP Server.
Mar 25 05:25:18 server1.example.com systemd[1]: Unit httpd.service
  entered failed state.
```

Reading Log Files

Apart from the messages that are written by journald to the journal, and which can be read using the **journalctl** command, on a Linux system you'll also find different log files in the directory /var/log. These files can be read using a pager utility like **less**.

The exact number of files in the /var/log directory will change, depending on the configuration of a server and the services that are running on that server. Some files, however, do exist on most occasions, and as an administrator, you should know which files they are and what kind of contents can be expected in these files. Table 13.2 provides an overview of some of the standard files that are created in this directory.

Key Topic

Table 13.2 System Log Files Overview

Log File	Explanation
/var/log/messages	The most commonly used log file, it is the generic log file where most messages are written to.
/var/log/dmesg	Contains kernel log messages.
/var/log/secure	Contains authentication related messages. Look here to see which authentication errors have occurred on a server.
/var/log/boot.log	Look here for messages that are related to system startup.
/var/log/audit/audit.log	Contains audit messages. SELinux writes to this file.
/var/log/maillog	Look here for mail-related messages.
/var/log/samba	Provides log files for the Samba service. Notice that Samba by default is not managed through rsyslog, but writes directly to the /var/log directory.
/var/log/sssd	Contains messages that have been written by the sssd service, which plays an important role in the authentication process.
/var/log/cups	Contains log messages that were generated by the print service CUPS.
/var/log/httpd/	Directory that contains log files that are written by the Apache web server. Notice that Apache writes messages to these files directly and not through rsyslog.

Understanding Log File Contents

As an administrator, you need to be able to interpret the contents of log files. For example, Listing 13.2 shows partial content from the /var/log/messages file.

Listing 13.2 /var/log/messages Sample Content

```
[root@server1 log]# tail -n 20 /var/log/messages
Mar 25 05:25:50 server1 systemd: Starting Network File System Server.
Mar 25 05:25:50 server1 systemd: Reached target Network File System
  Server.
Mar 25 05:25:50 server1 systemd: Starting Multi-User System.
Mar 25 05:25:50 server1 systemd: Reached target Multi-User System.
Mar 25 05:25:50 server1 systemd: Starting Graphical Interface.
Mar 25 05:25:50 server1 systemd: Reached target Graphical Interface.
Mar 25 05:25:50 server1 systemd: Starting Update UTMP about System
  Runlevel Changes...
Mar 25 05:25:50 server1 systemd: Started Stop Read-Ahead Data
  Collection 10s After Completed Startup.
Mar 25 05:25:50 server1 systemd: Started Update UTMP about System
  Runlevel Changes.
Mar 25 05:25:50 server1 systemd: Startup finished in 983ms (kernel)
  + 1.797s (initrd) + 1min 2.306s (userspace) = 1min 5.087s.
Mar 25 05:27:21 server1 chronyd[851]: Selected source 65.19.178.219
Mar 25 05:27:52 server1 systemd: Time has been changed
Mar 25 05:28:54 server1 systemd: Time has been changed
Mar 25 05:29:56 server1 systemd: Time has been changed
Mar 25 05:30:03 server1 systemd: Starting Session 2 of user root.
Mar 25 05:30:03 server1 systemd: Started Session 2 of user root.
Mar 25 05:30:10 server1 NetworkManager[1058]: <info> NetworkManager
  state is now CONNECTED_GLOBAL
Mar 25 05:30:11 server1 goa[3009]: goa-daemon version 3.8.5 starting
  [main.c:113, main()]
Mar 25 05:30:11 server1 goa[3009]: GoaKerberosIdentityManager: Using
  polling for change notification for credential cache type 'KEYRING'
  [goakerberosidentitymanager.c:1393, monitor_credentials_cache()]
Mar 25 05:30:57 server1 systemd: Time has been changed
```

As you can see in Listing 13.2, each line that is logged has specific elements:

- **Date and time:** Every log message starts with a timestamp. For filtering purposes, the timestamp is written as military time.
- **Host:** The host the message originated from. This is relevant because rsyslogd can be configured to handle remote logging as well.
- **Service or process name:** The name of the service or process that generated the message.

- **Message content:** The content of the message, which contains the exact message that has been logged.

To read the content of a log file, you can use a pager utility, like **less**, or you can live monitor what is happening in the log file, as described in the next section.

Live Log File Monitoring

When you are configuring services on Linux, it might be useful to see in real time what is happening. You could, for example, open two terminal sessions at the same time. In one terminal session, you configure and test the service. In the other terminal session, you see in real time what is happening. The **tail -f <logfile>** command shows in real time which lines are added to the log file. Exercise 13.1 shows a small example in which **tail -f** is used. When monitoring a log file with **tail -f**, the trace remains open until you use **Ctrl+C** to close it.

Using logger

Most services write information to the log files all by themselves. The **logger** command enables users to write messages to rsyslog from the command line. Using this command is simple. Just type **logger**, followed by the message you want to write to the logs. The logger utility, in this way, offers a convenient solution to write messages from scripts. This allows you to have a script write to syslog if something goes wrong.

When using logger, you can also specify the priority and facility to log to. The command **logger -p kern.err message** writes **message** to the kernel facility, for example, using the error priority. This option enables you to test the working of specific rsyslog facilities. In Exercise 13.1, you use logger to write log messages.

Exercise 13.1 Using Live Log Monitoring and logger

In this exercise, you use **tail -f** to monitor a log file in real time. You also use **logger** to write messages to a log file.

1. Open a root shell.
2. From the root shell, type **tail -f /var/log/messages**.
3. Open a second terminal window. In this terminal window, type **su - user** to open a subshell as user.
4. Type **su -** to open a root shell, but enter the wrong password.
5. Notice that nothing appears in /var/log/messages. That is because login-related errors are not written here.

6. From the user shell, type **logger hello**. You'll see the message appearing in the /var/log/messages file in real time.
7. In the **tail -f** terminal, use **Ctrl+C** to stop tracing the messages file.
8. Type **tail -n 20 /var/log/secure**. This shows the last 20 lines in /var/log/secure, which also shows the messages that the **su -** password errors have generated previously.

Configuring rsyslogd

To make sure that the information that needs to be logged is written to the location where you want to find it, you can configure the rsyslogd service through the /etc/rsyslog.conf file. In this file, you find different sections that allow you to specify where and how information should be written.

Understanding rsyslogd Configuration Files

Like many other services on RHEL 7, the configuration for rsyslogd is not defined in just one configuration file. The /etc/rsyslogd.conf file is the central location where rsyslogd is configured. From this file, the content of the directory /etc/rsyslog.d is included. This directory can be populated by installing RPM packages on a server. When looking for specific log configuration, make sure to always consider the contents of this directory also.

If specific options need to be passed to the rsyslogd service on startup, you can do this by using the /etc/sysconfig/rsyslog file. This file by default contains one line, which reads SYSLOGD_OTIONS="". On this line, you can specify rsyslogd startup parameters. The SYSLOGD_OPTIONS variable is included in the systemd configuration file that starts rsyslogd. Theoretically, you could change startup parameters in this file, as well, but that is not recommended. (See Chapter 18, "Managing and Understanding the Boot Procedure," for more details about systemd configuration.)

TIP It is important to remember that RHEL 7 often has configuration files in two locations. Do not ever change configuration files that are in the /usr/lib directory; only apply modifications to configuration files in the /etc directory.

Understanding rsyslog.conf Sections

The rsyslog.conf file is used to specify what should be logged and where it should be logged. To do this, you'll find different sections in the configuration file:

- **#### MODULES ####:** rsyslogd is modular. Modules are included to enhance the supported features in rsyslogd. See Chapter 29, "Configuring Advanced Log Features," for more information about rsyslogd modules.
- **#### GLOBAL DIRECTIVES ####:** This section is used to specify global parameters, such as the location where auxiliary files are written or the default timestamp format.
- **#### RULES ####:** This is the most important part of the rsyslog.conf file. It contains the rules that specify what information should be logged to which destination.

Understanding Facilities, Priorities, and Log Destinations

To specify what information should be logged to which destination, rsyslogd uses facilities, priorities, and destinations:

- A *facility* specifies a category of information that is logged. Rsyslogd uses a fixed list of facilities, which cannot be extended. This is because of backward compatibility with the legacy syslog service.
- A *priority* is used to define the severity of the message that needs to be logged. When specifying a priority, by default all messages with that priority and all higher priorities are logged.
- A *destination* defines where the message should be written to. Typical destinations are files, but rsyslog modules can be used as a destination as well, to allow further processing through an rsyslogd module.

Listing 13.3 shows an example of the RULES section in rsyslog.

Listing 13.3 An example of the RULES Section in rsyslog

```
#### RULES ####


# Log all kernel messages to the console.
# Logging much else clutters up the screen.
#kern.*                                          /dev/console


# Log anything (except mail) of level info or higher.
```

```
# Do not log private authentication messages!
*.info;mail.none;authpriv.none;cron.none    /var/log/messages

# The authpriv file has restricted access.
authpriv.*                                  /var/log/secure

# Log all the mail messages in one place.
mail.*                                     -/var/log/maillog


# Log cron stuff
cron.*                                     /var/log/cron

# Everybody gets emergency messages
*.emerg                                    :omusrmsg:*

# Save news errors of level crit and higher in a special file.
uucp,news.crit                              /var/log/spooler
```

In Listing 13.3, you can see how different facilities and priorities are used to define locations where information can be logged to. The available facilities and priorities are fixed and cannot be added to. Table 13.3 shows which facilities are available, and Table 13.4 shows a list of all priorities.

When specifying a destination, a file is often used. If the filename starts with a hyphen (as in -/var/log/maillog), the log messages will not be immediately committed to the file but will be buffered to make writes more efficient. Device files can also be used, as in /dev/console. If this device is used, messages are written in real time to the console. On modern servers, this often does not make sense, because administrators often log in remotely and do not see what is happening on the server console.

To enhance rsyslogd functionality, modules can be used for further processing of messages. If this is required, the module name can be specified as :modulename:. In Chapter 29, you learn more about the configuration of rsyslog modules.

Table 13.3 rsyslogd Facilities

Key Topic

Facility	Used by
auth / authpriv	Messages related to authentication.
cron	Messages generated by the crond service.

Facility	Used by
daemon	Generic facility that can be used for nonspecified daemons.
kern	Kernel messages.
lpr	Messages generated through the legacy lpd print system.
mail	Email-related messages.
mark	Special facility that can be used to write a marker periodically.
news	Messages generated by the NNTP news system.
security	Same as auth / authpriv. Should not be used anymore.
syslog	Messages generated by the syslog system.
user	Messages generated in user space.
uucp	Messages generated by the legacy UUCP system.
local0-7	Messages generated by services that are configured by any of the local0 through local7 facilities.

The syslog facilities were defined in the 1980s, and to guarantee backward compatibility, no new facilities can be added. The result is that some facilities still exist that basically serve no purpose anymore, and some services that have become relevant at a later stage do not have their own facility. As a solution, two specific facility types can be used. The daemon facility is a generic facility that can be used by any daemon. In addition, the local0 through local7 facilities can be used.

If there are services that do not have their own rsyslogd facility that need to write log messages to a specific log file anyway, these services can be configured to use any of the local0 through local7 facilities. You next have to configure the services to use these facilities as well. The procedure you follow to do that is specific to the service you are using. Then you need to add a rule to the rsyslog.conf file to send messages that come in through that facility to a specific log file. Exercise 13.2 shows how you can do this.

To determine which types of messages should be logged, different severities can be used in rsyslog.conf lines. These severities are the syslog priorities. Table 13.4 provides an overview of the available priorities in ascending order.

Table 13.4 rsyslogd Priorities

Key Topic

Priority	Used for
debug	Debug messages that will give as much information as possible about service operation.
info	Informational messages about normal service operation.
notice	Used for informational messages about items that might become an issue later.
warning / warn	Something is suboptimal, but there is no real error yet.
err /error	A noncritical error has occurred.
crit	A critical error has occurred.
alert	Used when the availability of the service is about to be discontinued.
emerg / panic	Message generated when the availability of the service is discontinued.

When a specific priority is used, all messages with that priority and higher are logged according to the specifications used in that specific rule. If you need to configure logging in a detailed way, where messages with different priorities are sent to different files, you can specify the priority with an equals sign (=) in front of it, as in the following configuration file, which will send all cron debug messages to a specific file with the name /var/log/cron.debug. Notice the use of the hyphen (-) in front of the destination filename, which ensures that messages are buffered and not written immediately to disk (which is good for disk performance).

Consider the following line, where all cron messages with only the debug priority are written to a specific file. Notice the - in front of the line, which buffers writes so that information is logged in a more efficient way:

```
cron.=debug        -/var/log/cron.debug
```

TIP There is no need to learn the names of rsyslogd facilities and priorities by heart. They are all listed in man 5 rsyslog.conf. On the exam, you have access to the man pages, so this information will be easily accessible.

Exercise 13.2 Changing rsyslog.conf Rules

In this exercise, you learn how to change rsyslog.conf. You configure the Apache service to log messages through syslog, and you create a rule that logs debug messages to a specific file.

1. By default, the Apache service does not log through rsyslog, but keeps its own logging. You are going to change that. To start, type **yum install -y httpd** to install the Apache service.
2. After installing the Apache service, open its configuration file /etc/http/conf/httpd.conf and add the following line to it:

```
ErrorLog   syslog:local1
```

3. Type **systemctl restart httpd**.
4. Now create a line in the rsyslog.conf file that will send all messages that it receives for facility local1 (which is now used by the httpd service) to the file /var/log/httpd-error.log. To do this, include the following line:

```
local1:error                    -/var/log/httpd-error.log
```

5. Tell rsyslogd to reload its configuration, by using **systemctl restart httpd**.
6. All Apache error messages will now be written to the httpd-error.log file.
7. From the Firefox browser, go to http://localhost/nowhere. Because the page you are trying to access does not exist, this will be logged to the Apache error log.
8. Now let's create a snap-in file that logs debug messages to a specific file as well. To do this, type **echo "*.debug /var/log/messages/messages-debug" > /etc/rsyslogd/debug.conf**.
9. Again, restart rsyslogd using **systemctl restart rsyslogd**.
10. Use the command **tail -f /var/log/messages-debug** to open a trace on the newly created file.
11. Type **logger -p daemon.debug "Daemon Debug Message"**. You'll see the debug message passing by.
12. Use **Ctrl+C** to close the debug log file.

Rotating Log Files

To prevent syslog messages from filling up your system completely, the log messages can be rotated. That means that when a certain threshold has been reached, the old log file is closed and a new log file is opened. The logrotate utility is started periodically through the crond service to take care of rotating log files.

When a log file is rotated, the old log file is typically copied to a file that has the rotation date in it. So, if /var/log/messages is rotated on January 17, 2015, the rotated filename will be /var/log/messages-20150115. As a default, four old log files are kept on the system. Files older than that period are removed from the system automatically.

> **WARNING** Log files that have been rotated are not stored anywhere; they are just gone. If your company policy requires you to be able to access information about events that have happened more than 5 weeks ago, you should take measures. You could decide either to back up log files or to configure a centralized log server where logrotate keeps rotated messages for a significantly longer period. In Chapter 29, you can read about how to do this.

The default settings for log rotation are kept in the file /etc/logrotate.conf (see Listing 13.4).

Listing 13.4 /etc/logrotate.conf Sample Content

```
# see "man logrotate" for details
# rotate log files weekly
weekly

# keep 4 weeks worth of backlogs
rotate 4

# create new (empty) log files after rotating old ones
create

# use date as a suffix of the rotated file
dateext

# uncomment this if you want your log files compressed
#compress

# RPM packages drop log rotation information into this directory
include /etc/logrotate.d

# no packages own wtmp and btmp -- we'll rotate them here
/var/log/wtmp {
    monthly
```

```
    create 0664 root utmp
        minsize 1M
    rotate 1
}

/var/log/btmp {
    missingok
    monthly
    create 0600 root utmp
    rotate 1
}
```

The most significant settings used in this configuration file tell logrotate to rotate files on a weekly basis and keep four old versions of the file. You can obtain more information about other parameters in this file through the **man logrotate** command.

If specific files need specific settings, you can create a configuration file for that file in /etc/logrotate.d. The settings for that specific file overwrite the default settings in /etc/logrotate.conf.

Working with journald

The systemd-journald service stores log messages in the journal, a binary file that is stored in the file /run/log/journal. This file can be examined using the **journalctl** command.

Using journalctl to Find Events

The easiest way to use journalctl is by just typing the command. It shows you recent events that have been written to the journal since your server last started. Notice that the result of this command is shown in the less pager, and by default you'll see the beginning of the journal. Because the journal is written from the moment your server boots, this is showing boot-related log messages. If you want to see the last messages that have been logged, you can use **journalctl -f**, which shows the last lines of the messages where new log lines are automatically added. You can also type **journalctl** and use (uppercase) **G** to go to the end of the journal. Also note that the search options / and ? work in the journalctl output. Listing 13.5 shows a partial result of this command.

Listing 13.5 Watching Log Information Generated by journald

```
-- Logs begin at Wed 2015-03-25 05:24:43 PDT, end at Wed 2015-03-25
05:46:46 PDT. --
Mar 25 05:24:43 localhost.localdomain systemd-journal[207]: Runtime
journal is using 6.1M (max 49.3M, leaving 74.0M of free 487.3M, cu
Mar 25 05:24:43 localhost.localdomain systemd-journal[207]: Runtime
journal is using 6.1M (max 49.3M, leaving 74.0M of free 487.3M, cu
Mar 25 05:24:43 localhost.localdomain kernel: Initializing cgroup
subsys cpuset
Mar 25 05:24:43 localhost.localdomain kernel: Initializing cgroup
subsys cpu
Mar 25 05:24:43 localhost.localdomain kernel: Initializing cgroup
subsys cpuacct
Mar 25 05:24:43 localhost.localdomain kernel: Linux version 3.10.0-123.
el7.x86_64 (builder@kbuilder.dev.centos.org) (gcc version 4.8.2
Mar 25 05:24:43 localhost.localdomain kernel: Command line: BOOT_
IMAGE=/vmlinuz-3.10.0-123.el7.x86_64 root=UUID=432d640e-3339-45fa-a66
Mar 25 05:24:43 localhost.localdomain kernel: Disabled fast string
operations
Mar 25 05:24:43 localhost.localdomain kernel: e820: BIOS-provided
physical RAM map:
Mar 25 05:24:43 localhost.localdomain kernel: BIOS-e820: [mem
0x0000000000000000-0x000000000009efff] usable
Mar 25 05:24:43 localhost.localdomain kernel: BIOS-e820: [mem
0x000000000009f000-0x000000000009ffff] reserved
Mar 25 05:24:43 localhost.localdomain kernel: BIOS-e820: [mem
0x00000000000dc000-0x00000000000fffff] reserved
Mar 25 05:24:43 localhost.localdomain kernel: BIOS-e820: [mem
0x0000000000100000-0x000000003fedffff] usable
Mar 25 05:24:43 localhost.localdomain kernel: BIOS-e820: [mem
0x000000003fee0000-0x000000003fefefff] ACPI data
Mar 25 05:24:43 localhost.localdomain kernel: BIOS-e820: [mem
0x000000003feff000-0x000000003fefffff] ACPI NVS
Mar 25 05:24:43 localhost.localdomain kernel: BIOS-e820: [mem
0x000000003ff00000-0x000000003fffffff] usable
Mar 25 05:24:43 localhost.localdomain kernel: BIOS-e820: [mem
0x00000000f0000000-0x00000000f7ffffff] reserved
Mar 25 05:24:43 localhost.localdomain kernel: BIOS-e820: [mem
0x00000000fec00000-0x00000000fec0ffff] reserved
Mar 25 05:24:43 localhost.localdomain kernel: BIOS-e820: [mem
0x00000000fee00000-0x00000000fee00fff] reserved
Mar 25 05:24:43 localhost.localdomain kernel: BIOS-e820: [mem
0x00000000fffe0000-0x00000000ffffffff] reserved
Mar 25 05:24:43 localhost.localdomain kernel: NX (Execute Disable)
protection: active
Mar 25 05:24:43 localhost.localdomain kernel: SMBIOS 2.4 present.
```

```
Mar 25 05:24:43 localhost.localdomain kernel: DMI: VMware, Inc. VMware
Virtual Platform/440BX Desktop Reference Platform, BIOS 6.00 07
Mar 25 05:24:43 localhost.localdomain kernel: Hypervisor detected:
VMware
Mar 25 05:24:43 localhost.localdomain kernel: e820: update [mem
0x00000000-0x00000fff] usable ==> reserved
Mar 25 05:24:43 localhost.localdomain kernel: e820: remove [mem
0x000a0000-0x000fffff] usable
Mar 25 05:24:43 localhost.localdomain kernel: No AGP bridge found
Mar 25 05:24:43 localhost.localdomain kernel: e820: last_pfn = 0x40000
max_arch_pfn = 0x400000000
Mar 25 05:24:43 localhost.localdomain kernel: MTRR default type:
uncachable
Mar 25 05:24:43 localhost.localdomain kernel: MTRR fixed ranges
enabled:
Mar 25 05:24:43 localhost.localdomain kernel:   00000-9FFFF write-back
Mar 25 05:24:43 localhost.localdomain kernel:   A0000-BFFFF uncachable
Mar 25 05:24:43 localhost.localdomain kernel:   C0000-CBFFF write-
protect
Mar 25 05:24:43 localhost.localdomain kernel:   CC000-EFFFF uncachable
Mar 25 05:24:43 localhost.localdomain kernel:   F0000-FFFFF write-
protect
Mar 25 05:24:43 localhost.localdomain kernel: MTRR variable ranges
enabled:
Mar 25 05:24:43 localhost.localdomain kernel:   0 base 0000000000 mask
FFC0000000 write-back
```

What makes journalctl a flexible command is that its many filtering options allow you to show exactly what you need. Exercise 13.3 shows some of the most interesting options.

Exercise 13.3 Discovering journalctl

In this exercise, you learn how to work with different journalctl options.

1. Type **journalctl**. You'll see the content of the journal since your server last started, starting at the beginning of the journal. The content is shown in **less**, so you can use common **less** commands to walk through the file.
2. Type **q** to quit the pager. Now type **journalctl --no-pager**. This shows the contents of the journal without using a pager.
3. Type **journalctl -f**. This opens the live view mode of journalctl, which allows you to see new messages scrolling by in real time. Use **Ctrl+C** to interrupt.

4. Type **journalctl** and press the **Tab** key twice. This shows specific options that can be used for filtering. Type, for instance, **journalctl _UID=0**.
5. Type **journalctl -n 20**. The **-n 20** option displays the last 20 lines of the journal (just like **tail -n 20**).
6. Now type **journalctl -p err**. This command shows errors only.
7. If you want to view journal messages that have been written in a specific time period, you can use the **--since** and **--until** commands. Both options take the time parameter in the format YYYY-MM-DD hh:mm:ss. Also, you can use **yesterday**, **today**, and **tomorrow** as parameters. So, type **journalctl --since yesterday** to show all messages that have been written since yesterday.
8. **journalctl** allows you to combine different options, as well. So, if you want to show all messages with a priority err that have been written since yesterday, use **journalctl --since yesterday -p err**.
9. If you need as much detail as possible, use **journalctl -o verbose**. This shows different options that are used when writing to the journal (see Listing 13.3). All these options can be used to tell the **journalctl** command which specific information you are looking for. Type, for instance, **journalctl _SYSTEMD_UNIT=sshd.service** to show more information about the sshd systemd unit.

In the preceding exercise, you typed **journalctl -o verbose** to show verbose output. Listing 13.6 shows an example of the **verbose** output. You can see that this is providing detailed information for all items that have been logged, including the PID, the ID of the associated user and group account, the command that is associated, and more.

Listing 13.6 Showing Detailed Log Information with **journalctl -o verbose**

```
-- Logs begin at Thu 2015-01-08 08:28:16 EST, end at Sun 2015-01-18
03:13:41 EST. --
Thu 2015-01-08 08:28:16.531278 EST [s=8759b876dde1477a801fa58ffb4bf0ce;
i=1;b=0eebc0595e384c56b9b4079dfc26918a;
    PRIORITY=6
    _TRANSPORT=driver
    MESSAGE=Runtime journal is using 4.0M (max 24.5M, leaving 36.7M of
free 241.0M, current limit 24.5M).
    MESSAGE_ID=ec387f577b844b8fa948f33cad9a75e6
    _PID=80
    _UID=0
```

```
    _GID=0
    _COMM=systemd-journal
    _EXE=/usr/lib/systemd/systemd-journald
    _CMDLINE=/usr/lib/systemd/systemd-journald
    _CAP_EFFECTIVE=4402800cf
    _SYSTEMD_CGROUP=/system.slice/systemd-journald.service
    _SYSTEMD_UNIT=systemd-journald.service
    _SYSTEMD_SLICE=system.slice
    _SELINUX_CONTEXT=kernel
    _BOOT_ID=0eebc0595e384c56b9b4079dfc26918a
    _MACHINE_ID=223a4aa0398843c497ecff431a4f0567
    _HOSTNAME=localhost.localdomain
Thu 2015-01-08 08:28:16.531445 EST
[s=8759b876dde1477a801fa58ffb4bf0ce;i=2;
b=0eebc0595e384c56b9b4079dfc26918a;
    PRIORITY=6
    _TRANSPORT=driver
    MESSAGE=Runtime journal is using 4.0M (max 24.5M, leaving 36.7M of
free 241.0M, current limit 24.5M).
    MESSAGE_ID=ec387f577b844b8fa948f33cad9a75e6
```

Preserving the systemd Journal

By default, the journal is stored in the file /run/log/journal. The entire /run directory is used for current process status information only, which means that the journal is cleared when the system reboots. To make the journal persistent between system restarts, you should make sure that a directory /var/log/journal exists.

Even when the journal is written to the permanent file in/var/log/journal, that does not mean that the journal is kept forever. The journal has built-in log rotation that will be used monthly. Also, the journal is limited to a maximum size of 10% of the file system size that it is on, and it will also stop growing if less than 15% of the file system is still free. If that happens, the oldest messages from the journal are dropped automatically to make place for newer messages. To change these settings, you can modify the file /etc/systemd/journald.conf. You'll see that in this file some other parameters can be set also (see Listing 13.5).

Listing 13.5 Setting journald Parameters Through /etc/systemd/journald.conf

```
[Journal]
#Storage=auto
#Compress=yes
#Seal=yes
#SplitMode=login
#SyncIntervalSec=5m
#RateLimitInterval=30s
#RateLimitBurst=1000
#SystemMaxUse=
#SystemKeepFree=
#SystemMaxFileSize=
#RuntimeMaxUse=
#RuntimeKeepFree=
#RuntimeMaxFileSize=
#MaxRetentionSec=
#MaxFileSec=1month
#ForwardToSyslog=yes
#ForwardToKMsg=no
#ForwardToConsole=no
#TTYPath=/dev/console
#MaxLevelStore=debug
#MaxLevelSyslog=debug
#MaxLevelKMsg=notice
#MaxLevelConsole=info
```

Making the journal permanent is not hard to do. Exercise 13.4 shows how to proceed.

Exercise 13.4 Making the journald Journal Permanent

Key Topic

In this exercise, you learn how to make the journald journal permanent.

1. Open a root shell and type **mkdir /var/log/journal**.
2. Before journald can write the journal to this directory, you have to set ownership. Type **chown root:systemd-journal /var/log/journal**, followed by **chmod 2755 /var/log/journal**.
3. Next, you can either reboot your system (restarting the systemd-journald service is not enough) or use the **killall -USR1 systemd-journald** command.
4. The systemd journal is now persistent across reboots. If you want to see the log messages since last reboot, use **journalctl -b**.

TIP It is nowhere in the RHCSA objectives, but this procedure just feels like a nice exam assignment. Make sure that you know how to apply it!

Summary

In this chapter, you learned how to configure logging. You read how the rsyslogd and journald services are used on RHEL 7 to keep log information, and you learned how to manage logs that are written by these services. You also learned how to configure log rotation and make the journal persistent.

Exam Prep Tasks

Review All Key Topics

Review the most important topics in the chapter, noted with the Key Topic icon in the outer margin of the page. Table 13.5 lists a reference of these key topics and the page numbers on which each is found.

Table 13.5 Key Topics for Chapter 13

Key Topic Element	Description	Page
Paragraph	journald explanation	298
Paragraph	rsyslogd explanation	298
Table 13.2	System log files overview	300
Table 13.3	rsyslogd facilities	305
Table 13.4	rsyslogd priorities	307
Exercise 13.4	Making the journald journal permanent	315

Define Key Terms

Define the following key terms from this chapter and check your answers in the glossary:

journald, journalctl, rsyslogd, facility, priority, destination, log rotation

Review Questions

1. Which file is used to configure rsyslogd?
2. Which configuration file contains messages related to authentication?
3. If you do not configure anything, how long will it take for log files to be rotated away?
4. Which command enables you to log a message from the command line to the user facility, using the notice priority?
5. Which line would you add to write all messages with a priority of info to the file /var/log/messages.info?
6. Which configuration file enables you to allow the journal to grow beyond its default size restrictions?
7. Which command enables you to see new messages in the journal scrolling by in real time?
8. Which command enables you to see all journald messages that have been written for PID 1 between 9:00 a.m. and 3:00 p.m.?
9. Which command enables you to see journald messages since last reboot on a system where a persistent journal has been configured?
10. Which procedure enables you to make the journald journal persistent?

End-of-Chapter Labs

You have now learned how to work with logging on Red Hat Enterprise Linux 7 and know how to configure rsyslogd and journald. You can now complete the end-of-chapter labs to enforce these newly acquired skills.

Lab 13.1

1. Configure the journal to be persistent across system reboots.
2. Make a configuration file that writes all messages with an info priority to the file /var/log/messages.info.
3. Configure logrotate to keep 10 old versions of log files.

The following topics are covered in this chapter:

- Understanding MBR and GPT Partitions
- Managing Partitions and File Systems
- Mounting File Systems

The following RHCSA exam objectives are covered in this chapter:

- List, create, delete partitions on MBR and GPT disks
- Configure systems to mount file systems at boot by universal unique ID (UUID) or label
- Add new partitions and logical volumes, and swap to a system non-destructively
- Create, mount, unmount, and use vfat, Ext4, and xfs file systems

CHAPTER 14

Managing Partitions

Working with storage is an important task for a Linux administrator. In this chapter, you acquire the first set of essential storage skills. You learn how to create and manage partitions, format them with the file system you need to use, and mount these file systems.

"Do I Know This Already?" Quiz

The "Do I Know This Already?" quiz allows you to assess whether you should read this entire chapter thoroughly or jump to the "Exam Preparation Tasks" section. If you are in doubt about your answers to these questions or your own assessment of your knowledge of the topics, read the entire chapter. Table 14.1 lists the major headings in this chapter and their corresponding "Do I Know This Already?" quiz questions. You can find the answers in Appendix A, "Answers to the 'Do I Know This Already?' Quizzes and 'Review Questions.'"

Table 14.1 "Do I Know This Already?" Section-to-Question Mapping

Foundation Topics Section	Questions
Understanding MBR and GPT Partitions	1–2
Managing Partitions and File Systems	3–6
Mounting File Systems	7–10

1. Which of the following is *not* an advantage of using a GUID partition table over using an MBR partition table?
   a. Access time to a directory is quicker.
   b. A total amount of 8 ZiB can be addressed by a partition.
   c. With GUID partitions, a backup copy of the partition table is created automatically.
   d. There can be up to 128 partitions in total.

2. You want to create a partition with a size of 1024^5 bytes. What size should it be?
   a. 1 PB
   b. 1 PiB
   c. 1 EB
   d. 1 EiB
3. Which partition type is commonly used to create a Linux partition?
   a. 81
   b. 82
   c. 83
   d. 8e
4. What is the default disk device name you would expect to see in KVM virtual machines?
   a. /dev/sda
   b. /dev/hda
   c. /dev/vda
   d. /dev/xvda
5. Which of the following statements is *not* true?
   a. Do not ever use gdisk on an MBR disk.
   b. fdisk offers support to manage GPT partitions as well, but it is not stable as of yet.
   c. Depending on your needs, you can create MBR and GPT partitions on the same disk.
   d. If your server boots from EFI, you must use GPT partitions.
6. Which of the following file systems is used as the default in RHEL7?
   a. Ext4
   b. XFS
   c. btrfs
   d. Ext3

7. Which command enables you to find current UUIDs set to the file systems on your server?

- **a. mount**
- **b. df -h**
- **c. lsblk**
- **d. blkid**

8. What would you put in the device column of /etc/fstab to mount a file system based on its unique ID 42f419c4-633f-4ed7-b161-519a4dadd3da?

- **a.** 42f419c4-633f-4ed7-b161-519a4dadd3da
- **b.** /dev/42f419c4-633f-4ed7-b161-519a4dadd3da
- **c.** ID=42f419c4-633f-4ed7-b161-519a4dadd3da
- **d.** UUID=42f419c4-633f-4ed7-b161-519a4dadd3da

9. Which of the following /etc/fstab lines would perform a file system check on the file system, but only after the root file system has been checked successfully?

```
/dev/sda1        /data          xfs    defaults       1 1
/dev/sda1        /dat           xfs    defaults       1 2
/dev/sda1        /data          xfs    defaults       1 1
/dev/sda1        /data          xfs    defaults       0 2
```

10. Which mount option would you use in /etc/fstab to specify that the file system can only be mounted once the network is available?

- **a. network**
- **b. _netdev**
- **c. _network**
- **d. netdev**

Foundation Topics

Understanding MBR and GPT Partitions

To use a hard drive, there need to be partitions on the hard drive. Some operating systems are installing everything to one partition, while other operating systems such as Linux normally have several partitions on one hard disk. Using more than one partition on a system makes sense because it makes it easier to distinguish between the different types of data.

> **NOTE** Instead of using multiple different partitions, you can also use different LVM logical volumes. Managing logical volumes is covered in Chapter 15, "Managing LVM Logical Volumes."

On RHEL 7, two different partitioning schemes are available. Before creating your first partition, you should know which schemes these are and which scheme would work best in a specific environment.

Understanding the MBR Partitioning Scheme

When the personal computer was invented in early 1982, a system was needed to define hard disk layout. This system became known as the Master Boot Record partitioning scheme. While booting a computer the Basic Input Output System (BIOS) was loaded to access hardware devices. From the BIOS, the bootable device was read, and on this bootable device, the Master Boot Record (MBR) was allocated. The MBR contains all that is needed to start a computer, including a boot loader and a partition table.

When hard disks first came out for PCs in the early 1980s, you could have different operating systems on them. Some of these included MS-DOS/PC-DOS, PC/IX (IBM's UNIX for 8086 PCs), CPM86, and MPM86. The disk would be partitioned so each operating system you installed got a part of the disk. One of the partitions would be made active, meaning the code in the boot sector in the MBR would read the first sector of that active partition and run the code. That code would then load the rest of the OS. This explains why four partitions were deemed "enough." Some operating systems (such as SCO Xenix and SCO Unix) would have another layer of partitions in the dedicated UNIX partition (in SCO's case, called *divisions*), with its own partition program (SCO: *divvy*)

The MBR was defined as the first 512 bytes on a computer hard drive, and in the MBR an operating system boot loader (such as GRUB 2; see Chapter 18, "Managing and Understanding the Boot Procedure") was present, as well as a partition table. The size that was used for the partition table was relatively small, just 64 bytes, with the result that in the MBR no more than four partitions could be created. Since partition size data was stored in 32-bit values, and a default sector size of 512 bytes is used, the maximum size that could be used by a partition was limited to 2 TiB (hardly a problem in the early 1980s).

In the MBR, just four partitions could be created. Because many PC operating systems needed more than four partitions, a solution was found to go beyond the number of four. In the MBR, one partition could be created as an extended partition, as opposed to the other partitions that were created as primary partitions. Within the extended partition, a number of logical partitions could be created to reach a total number of 15 partitions that can be addressed by the Linux kernel.

Understanding the Need for GPT Partitioning

Current computer hard drives have become too big to be addressed by MBR partitions. That is why a new partitioning scheme was needed. This partitioning scheme is the GUID Partition Table (GPT) partitioning scheme. On computers that are using the new Unified Extensible Firmware Interface (UEFI) as a replacement for the old BIOS system, GPT partitions are the only way to address disks. Also older computer systems that are using BIOS instead of GPT can be configured with GUID partitions.

Using GUID offers many benefits:

- The maximum partition size is 8 zebibyte (ZiB), which is 1024 * 1024 * 1024 * 1024 gibibytes.
- In GPT, up to a maximum number of 128 partitions can be created.
- The 2 TiB limit no longer exists.
- Because space that is available to store partitions is much bigger than 64 bytes, which was used in MBR, there is no longer a need to distinguish between primary, extended, and logical partitions.
- GPT uses a 128-bit global unique ID (GUID) to identify partitions.
- A backup copy of the GUID partition table is created by default at the end of the disk, which eliminates the single point of failure that exists on MBR partition tables.

Understanding Storage Measurement Units

When talking about storage, different measurement units are used. In some cases, units like megabyte (MB) are used. In other cases, units like mebibyte (MiB) are used. The difference between these two is that a megabyte is a multiple of 1,000, and a Mebibyte is a multiple of 1,024. In computers, it makes sense to talk about multiples of 1,024 because that is how computers address items. The misunderstanding was created though when hardware vendors a long time ago started talking about megabytes instead.

In the early days of computing, the difference was not that important. Between a kilobyte (KB) and a kibibyte (KiB), it is just 24 bytes. The bigger the numbers grow, the bigger the difference becomes. A gigabyte, for instance, is 1,000 * 1,000 * 1,000 bytes, so 1,000,000,000 bytes, whereas a gibibyte is 1,024 x 1,024 x 1,024 bytes, which makes a total of 1,073,741,824 bytes, which is over 70MB larger than 1GB.

On current Linux distributions, the binary numbers (MiB, not MB) have become the standard. In Table 14.2, you can see an overview of the values that are used.

In the past, KB, MB, and so on, were used both in decimal and binary situations; sometimes they were even mixed. For example, 1Mbps line speed is one million bits per second. The once famous "1.44MB" floppy disk was really 1,440,000 bytes in size (80 tracks * 2 heads * 9 sectors * 512 byte sectors), creating a mixed meaning of MB: 1.44 * (decimal K) * (binary K).

Table 14.2 Disk Size Specifications

Key Topic

Symbol	Name	Value	Symbol	Name	Value
KB	Kilobyte	1000^1	KiB	Kibibyte	1024^1
MB	Megabyte	1000^2	MiB	Mebibyte	1024^2
GB	Gigabyte	1000^3	GiB	Gibibyte	1024^3
TB	Terabyte	1000^4	TiB	Tebibyte	1024^4
PB	Petabyte	1000^5	PiB	Pebibyte	1024^5
EB	Exabyte	1000^6	EiB	Exbibyte	1024^6
ZB	Zettabyte	1000^7	ZiB	Zebibyte	1024^7
YB	Yottabyte	1000^8	YiB	Yobibyte	1024^8

Managing Partitions and File Systems

As discussed in the previous section, there are two different types of partitions that can be used on RHEL 7. To match the different partition types, there are also two different partitioning utilities. The fdisk utility has been around for a long time and is used to create MBR partitions. The gdisk utility is used to create GPT partitions. In the next subsections, you learn how to use both.

For both MBR and GPT partitions, you need to specify the name of the disk device as an argument. Table 14.3 shows the most common disk device names that you work with on RHEL7:

Table 14.3 Common Disk Device Types

Key Topic

Device Name	Description
/dev/sda	A hard disk that uses the SCSI driver. Used for SCSI and SATA disk devices. Common on physical servers but also in VMware virtual machines.
/dev/hda	The (legacy) IDE disk device type. You will seldom see this device type on modern computers.
/dev/vda	A disk in a KVM virtual machine that uses the virtio disk driver. This is the common disk device type for KVM virtual machines.
/dev/xvda	A disk in a Xen virtual machine that uses the Xen virtual disk driver. You see this when installing RHEL as a virtual machine in Xen. RHEL 7 cannot be used as a Xen hypervisor, but you might see RHEL 7 virtual machines on top of the Xen hypervisor using these disk types.

As you can see in Table 14.3, all disk device names end with the letter a. That is because it is the first disk that was found in your server. The second SCSI disk, for instance, would have the name /dev/sdb. If many disks are installed in a server, you can have up to /dev/sdz and even beyond. After /dev/sdz, the kernel continues creating devices with names like /dev/sdaa and /dev/sdab.

Creating MBR Partitions with fdisk

To create an MBR disk partition, you have to apply a multiple step procedure. In Exercise 14.1, you learn how to apply this procedure.

Exercise 14.1 Creating MBR Partitions with fdisk

This exercise has been written to use an installation of RHEL/CentOS that contains nonpartitioned disk space. If you do not have such an installation, you can use a second disk device on your demo environment. This can be a virtual disk that is added through your virtualization program, or a USB flash drive if working on a physical installation. In that case, make sure the device names in this exercise are replaced with the device names that match your hardware.

TIP In the end-of-chapter labs, you have to create partitions again. It will be a lot easier if at that point you can start from a clean installation. The following two steps help you to revert easily to a system on which you have not created any partitions yet.

1. Type **dd if=/dev/vda of=/root/diskfile bs=1M count=1**. (If your disk is /dev/sda and not /dev/vda, change the disk name accordingly.) Using this command allows you to create a backup of the first megabyte of raw blocks and write that to the file /root/diskfile. This file allows you to easily revert to the situation that existed at the start of this exercise.
2. Type **cp /etc/fstab /root/fstab** to make a backup of the /etc/fstab file as well.

At this point you are ready to start working on the exercise.

1. Open a root shell and run the **fdisk** command. This command needs the name of the disk device where you want to create the partition as its argument. In this exercise I'll use /dev/vda. Change if needed according to your hardware.

```
[root@localhost ~]# fdisk /dev/vda
Welcome to fdisk (util-linux 2.23.2).
```

   Changes will remain in memory only until you decide to write them. Be careful before using the **write** command.

2. Before doing anything, it is a good idea to check how much disk space you have available. Press **p** to see an overview of current disk allocation.

```
Command (m for help): p

Disk /dev/vda: 6442 MB, 6442450944 bytes, 12582912 sectors
Units = sectors of 1 * 512 = 512 bytes
Sector size (logical/physical): 512 bytes / 512 bytes
I/O size (minimum/optimal): 512 bytes / 512 bytes
Disk label type: dos
Disk identifier: 0x000a056b

   Device Boot      Start         End      Blocks   Id  System
/dev/vda1   *        2048      514047      256000   83  Linux
/dev/vda2          514048     8984575     4235264   8e  Linux LVM
```

In the output of this command, in particular look for the total number of sectors and the last sector that is currently used (marked in bold in the above command output). If the last partition does not end on the last sector, you have available space to create a new partition.

3. Type **n** to add a new partition.

```
Command (m for help): n
Partition type:
   p   primary (2 primary, 0 extended, 2 free)
   e   extended
Select (default p):
```

4. Assuming you have a /dev/vda1 and a /dev/vda2 partition and nothing else, select **p** to create a primary partition. Accept the partition number that is now suggested.
5. Specify the first sector on disk that the new partition will start on. The first available sector is suggested by default, press Enter to accept.
6. Specify the last sector that the partition will end on. By default, the last sector available on disk is suggested. If you use that, after this exercise you will not have any disk space left to create additional partitions or logical volumes, so you should use another last sector. To use another last sector, you can do the following:
   - Enter the number of the last sector you want to use.
   - Enter **+number** to create a partition that sizes a specific number of sectors.
   - Enter **+number(K,M,G)** to specify the size you want to assign to the partition in KiB, MiB, or GiB.
   - Type **+100M** to make this a 100 MiB partition.

   ```
   Partition number (3,4, default 3):
   First sector (8984576-12582911, default 8984576):
   Using default value 8984576
   Last sector, +sectors or +size{K,M,G} (8984576-12582911,
   default 12582911): +100M
   Partition 3 of type Linux and of size 100 MiB is set
   ```

   After you enter the partition's ending boundary, fdisk will show a confirmation.
7. At this point, you can define the partition type. By default, a Linux partition type is used. If you want the partition to be of any other partition type, use **t** to change it. Common partition types include the following:

- 82: Linux swap
- 83: Linux
- 8e: Linux LVM

Press **Enter** to accept the default Linux partition type **83**.

8. If you are happy with the modifications, press **w** to write them to disk and exit fdisk. If you have created a partition on a disk that is already in use, you now see the following message:

```
Command (m for help): w
The partition table has been altered!

Calling ioctl() to re-read partition table.

WARNING: Re-reading the partition table failed with error 16:
Device or resource busy.
The kernel still uses the old table. The new table will be used
at
the next reboot or after you run partprobe(8) or kpartx(8)
Syncing disks.
[root@localhost ~]#
```

9. This message indicates that the partition has successfully been added to the partition table, but the in-memory kernel partition table could not be updated. You can see that by comparing the output of **fdisk -l /dev/vda** with the output of the command **cat /proc/partitions**, which shows the kernel partition table.

10. Type **partprobe /dev/vda** to write the changes to the kernel partition table. The partition has now been added and you can create a file system on it as described in the section "Creating File Systems."

NOTE You see the "re-reading the partition table failed with error 16" message only if you are adding partitions to a disk that already has some mounted partitions. If you are working on a new disk that does not have any mounted partitions, you will not see this error and you will not have to use the **partprobe** command.

Using Extended and Logical Partitions on MBR

In the previous procedure, you learned how to add a primary partition. If three partitions have been created already, there is room for one more primary partition, after which the partition table is completely filled up. If you want to go beyond four partitions on an MBR disk, you have to create an extended partition. Following that, you can create logical partitions within the extended partition.

Using logical partitions does allow you to go beyond the limitation of four partitions in the MBR; there is a disadvantage as well, though. All logical partitions exist within the extended partition. If something goes wrong with the extended partition, you have a problem with all logical partitions existing within it as well. If you need more than four separate storage allocation units, you might be better off using LVM instead of logical partitions.

NOTE An extended partition is only used for the purpose of creating logical partitions. You cannot create file systems directly on an extended partition!

Exercise 14.2 Creating Logical Partitions

1. To create a logical partition, when fdisk prompts which partition type you want to create, enter **e**.

```
Command (m for help): n
Partition type:
   p   primary (3 primary, 0 extended, 1 free)
   e   extended
Select (default e):
```

2. If the extended partition is the fourth partition that you are writing to the MBR, it will also be the last partition that can be added to the MBR. For that reason, it should fill the rest of your computer's hard disk. Press **Enter** to accept the default first sector and press **Enter** again when **fdisk** prompts for the last sector.

```
Using default response e
Selected partition 4
First sector (9189376-12582911, default 9189376):
Using default value 9189376
Last sector, +sectors or +size{K,M,G} (9189376-12582911, default
12582911):
Using default value 12582911
Partition 4 of type Extended and of size 1.6 GiB is set
```

3. Now that the extended partition has been created, you can create a logical partition within it. Still from the fdisk interface, press **n** again. The utility will prompt that all primary partitions are in use now and by default suggests adding a logical partition with partition number 5.

```
Command (m for help): n
All primary partitions are in use
Adding logical partition 5
```

4. Press **Enter** to accept the default first sector. When asked for the last sector, enter **+100M** (or any other size you want to use).

```
First sector (9191424-12582911, default 9191424):
Using default value 9191424
Last sector, +sectors or +size{K,M,G} (9191424-12582911, default
12582911): +100M
Partition 5 of type Linux and of size 100 MiB is set

Command (m for help):
```

5. Now that the logical partition has been created, enter **w** to write the changes to disk and quit fdisk. To complete the procedure, enter **partprobe** to update the kernel partition table. The new partition is now ready for use.

TIP The **fdisk** utility writes changes to disk only when you enter **w**, which is the **fdisk** write command. If you have made a mistake and want to get out, press **q** to quit.

In Exercise 14.2, you have used the **partprobe** command to push changes in the partition table to the kernel partition table. This will normally work out well, but in some cases does not. If at any time you are getting an error using partprobe, just reboot your computer, using the **reboot** command. If partitions have not been written to your system correctly, you really do not want to continue modifying and managing partitions, because you risk creating severe problems on your server.

Creating GPT Partitions with gdisk

If a disk is configured with a GUID partition table (GPT), or if it is a new disk that does not contain anything yet and has a size that goes beyond 2 TiB, you need to use the gdisk utility to create partitions. This utility has a lot of similarities with fdisk but some differences as well. The following procedure shows how to create partitions in gdisk.

NOTE fdisk has some support for managing GPT partitions also. At the time of this writing, the GPT support in fdisk is not stable. For that reason, it is recommended to use gdisk on GPT partitions and fdisk on MBR partitions.

WARNING! Do not ever use gdisk on a disk that has been formatted with fdisk and already contains fdisk partitions. Gdisk will detect that an MBR is present and it will convert this to a GPT (see the following code listing). Your computer will most likely not be able to boot after doing this!

```
[root@localhost ~]# gdisk /dev/vda
GPT fdisk (gdisk) version 0.8.6

Partition table scan:
  MBR: MBR only
  BSD: not present
  APM: not present
  GPT: not present


***************************************************************
Found invalid GPT and valid MBR; converting MBR to GPT format.
THIS OPERATION IS POTENTIALLY DESTRUCTIVE! Exit by typing 'q' if
you do not want to convert your MBR partitions to GPT format!
***************************************************************

Command (? for help):
```

To save you the hassle of going through this, I verified it does what it says. After converting an MBR to a GPT your machine will not start anymore.

Now let's take a look at how to create partitions using gdisk.

Exercise 14.3 Creating GPT Partitions with gdisk

To apply the procedure in this exercise, you need a new disk device. Do *not* use a disk that contains data that you want to keep, because this exercise will delete all data on it. If you are using this exercise on a virtual machine, you may add the new disk through the virtualization software. If you are working on a physical machine, you can use a USB thumb drive as a disk device for this exercise. Note that this exercise works perfectly on a computer that starts from BIOS and not EFI, all you need is a dedicated disk device.

1. To create a partition with gdisk, type **gdisk /dev/vdb**. (Replace /dev/vdb with the exact device name used on your computer.) Gdisk will try to detect the current layout of the disk, and if nothing has been detected, it will create the GPT partition table and associated disk layout.

```
[root@localhost ~]# gdisk /dev/vdb
GPT fdisk (gdisk) version 0.8.6

Partition table scan:
  MBR: not present
  BSD: not present
  APM: not present
  GPT: not present

Creating new GPT entries.

Command (? for help):
```

2. Type **n** to enter a new partition. You can choose any partition number between 1 and 128, but it is wise to accept the default partition number that is suggested.

```
Command (? for help): n
Partition number (1-128, default 1):
```

3. You now are asked to enter the first sector. By default, the first sector that is available on disk will be used, but you can specify an offset as well. This does not make sense at all, so just press **Enter** to accept the default first sector that is proposed.

```
First sector (34-2097118, default = 2048) or {+-}size{KMGTP}:
```

4. When asked for the last sector, by default the last sector that is available on disk is proposed (which would create a partition that fills the entire hard disk). You can specify a different last sector, or specify the disk size using +, the size, and KMGTP. So to create a 2 TiB disk partition, use **+2TiB**.

```
Last sector (2048-2097118, default = 2097118) or {+-}size{KMGTP}:
+100M
```

5. You now are asked to set the partition type. If you do not do anything, the partition type is set to 8300, which is the Linux file system partition type. Other options are available as well. You can press **l** to show a list of available partition types.

```
Current type is 'Linux filesystem'
Hex code or GUID (L to show codes, Enter = 8300): l
0700 Microsoft basic data  0c01 Microsoft reserved    2700 Windows RE
4200 Windows LDM data      4201 Windows LDM metadata  7501 IBM GPFS
7f00 ChromeOS kernel      7f01 ChromeOS root         7f02 ChromeOS reserved

 Linux swap              8300 Linux filesystem      8301 Linux reserved
8e00 Linux LVM            a500 FreeBSD disklabel     a501 FreeBSD boot
a502 FreeBSD swap         a503 FreeBSD UFS           a504 FreeBSD ZFS
a505 FreeBSD Vinum/RAID   a580 Midnight BSD data     a581 Midnight BSD boot
a582 Midnight BSD swap    a583 Midnight BSD UFS      a584 Midnight BSD ZFS
a585 Midnight BSD Vinum   a800 Apple UFS             a901 NetBSD swap
a902 NetBSD FFS           a903 NetBSD LFS            a904 NetBSD
concatenated
a905 NetBSD encrypted     a906 NetBSD RAID           ab00 Apple boot
af00 Apple HFS/HFS+       af01 Apple RAID            af02 Apple RAID
offline
af03 Apple label          af04 AppleTV recovery      af05 Apple Core
Storage
be00 Solaris boot         bf00 Solaris root          bf01 Solaris /usr &
Mac Z
bf02 Solaris swap         bf03 Solaris backup        bf04 Solaris /var
bf05 Solaris /home        bf06 Solaris alternate se  bf07 Solaris Reserved
1
bf08 Solaris Reserved 2   bf09 Solaris Reserved 3    bf0a Solaris Reserved
4
bf0b Solaris Reserved 5   c001 HP-UX data            c002 HP-UX service
ed00 Sony system partition  ef00 EFI System            ef01 MBR partition
scheme
ef02 BIOS boot partition  fb00 VMWare VMFS           fb01 VMWare reserved
fc00 VMWare kcore crash p fd00 Linux RAID
Hex code or GUID (L to show codes, Enter = 8300):
```

The relevant partitions types are as follows:

- **8200:** Linux swap
- **8300:** Linux file system
- **8e00:** Linux LVM

Notice that these are the same partition types as the ones that are used in MBR, with two 0s added to their names. You can also just press **Enter** to accept the default partition type 8300.

6. The partition is now created (but not yet written to disk). Press **p** to show an overview, which allows you to verify that this is really what you want to use.

```
Command (? for help): p
Disk /dev/vdb: 2097152 sectors, 1024.0 MiB
Logical sector size: 512 bytes
Disk identifier (GUID): 870DF067-6735-482E-83CE-5123E20509E0
Partition table holds up to 128 entries
First usable sector is 34, last usable sector is 2097118
Partitions will be aligned on 2048-sector boundaries
Total free space is 1892285 sectors (924.0 MiB)

Number  Start (sector)    End (sector)  Size       Code  Name
   1    2048              206847   100.0 MiB  8300  Linux filesystem
```

7. If you are satisfied with the current partitioning, press **w** to write changes to disk and commit. This gives a warning, after which the new partition table is written to the GUID partition table.

```
Command (? for help): w

Final checks complete. About to write GPT data. THIS WILL
OVERWRITE EXISTING
PARTITIONS!!

Do you want to proceed? (Y/N): y
OK; writing new GUID partition table (GPT) to /dev/vdb.
The operation has completed successfully.
```

8. If at this point you get an error message indicating that the partition table is in use, type **partprobe** to update the kernel partition table.

Creating File Systems

At this point, you know how to create partitions. A partition all by itself is not very useful. It only becomes useful if you decide to do something with it. That often means that you have to put a file system on top of it. In this section, you learn how to do that.

Different file systems can be used on RHEL 7. Table 14.4 provides an overview of the most common file systems.

Table 14.4 File System Overview

Key Topic

File System	Description
XFS	The default file system in RHEL 7.
Ext4	The default file system in previous versions of RHEL. Still available and supported in RHEL 7.
Ext3	The previous version of Ext4. On RHEL 7, there is no real need to use Ext3 anymore.
Ext2	A very basic file system that was developed in the early 1990s. There is no need to use this file system on RHEL 7 anymore.
BtrFS	A relatively new file system that was not yet supported in RHEL 7.0 but will be included in later updates.
NTFS	Not supported on RHEL 7.
VFAT	A file system that offers compatibility with Windows and Mac, it is the functional equivalent of the FAT32 file system. Useful to use on USB thumb drives that are used to exchange data with other computers but not on a server's hard disks.

To format a partition with one of the supported file systems, you can use the **mkfs** command, using the option **-t** to specify which specific file system needs to be used. Alternatively, one of the file system specific tools can be used, such as mkfs.ext4 to format an Ext4 file system.

NOTE If you are using mkfs without any further specification of which file system you want to format, an Ext2 file system will be formatted. This is probably not what you want to use, so do not forget to specify which file system you want to use.

To format a partition with the default XFS file system, the command **mkfs -t xfs** is used. Listing 14.1 shows the output of this command.

Listing 14.1 Formatting a File System with XFS

```
[root@server3 ~]# mkfs -t xfs /dev/vda5
meta-data=/dev/vda5              isize=256    agcount=4, agsize=6400 blks
         =                       sectsz=512   attr=2, projid32bit=1
         =                       crc=0
data     =                       bsize=4096   blocks=25600, imaxpct=25
         =                       sunit=0      swidth=0 blks
```

```
naming    =version 2              bsize=4096   ascii-ci=0 ftype=0
log       =internal lo            bsize=4096   blocks=853, version=2
          =                       sectsz=512   sunit=0 blks, lazy-count=1
realtime =none                    extsz=4096   blocks=0, rtextents=0
```

Exercise 14.4 Creating a File System

In Exercise 14.1, you have created a partition /dev/vda3. In this exercise, you format it with an XFS file system. Notice that this exercise has one step only!

1. From a root shell, type **mkfs.xfs /dev/vda3**.

Changing File System Properties

When working with file systems, some properties can be managed as well. File system properties are specific for the file system you are using, so you work with different properties and different tools for the different file systems.

Managing Ext4 File System Properties

The generic tool for managing Ext4 file system properties is tune2fs. This tool was developed a long time ago for the Ext2 file system and is compatible with Ext3 and Ext4 also. When managing Ext4 file system properties, the **tune2fs -l** command is a nice command to start with. Listing 14.2 shows the output of this command where different file system properties are shown:

Listing 14.2 Showing File System Properties with **tune2fs -l**

```
[root@server1 ~]# tune2fs -l /dev/sdb1
tune2fs 1.42.9 (28-Dec-2013)
Filesystem volume name:   <none>
Last mounted on:          <not available>
Filesystem UUID:          2fbf3e73-166f-4a3d-8df6-ccfe727c1da5
Filesystem magic number:  0xEF53
Filesystem revision #:    1 (dynamic)
Filesystem features:      has_journal ext_attr resize_inode dir_index
filetype extent 64bit flex_bg sparse_super huge_file uninit_bg dir_
nlink extra_isize
Filesystem flags:         signed_directory_hash
Default mount options:    user_xattr acl
```

```
Filesystem state:            clean
Errors behavior:             Continue
Filesystem OS type:          Linux
Inode count:                 25688
Block count:                 102400
Reserved block count:        5120
Free blocks:                 93504
Free inodes:                 25677
First block:                 1
Block size:                  1024
Fragment size:               1024
Group descriptor size:       64
Reserved GDT blocks:         256
Blocks per group:            8192
Fragments per group:         8192
Inodes per group:            1976
Inode blocks per group:      247
Flex block group size:       16
Filesystem created:          Sat May 16 03:44:37 2015
Last mount time:             n/a
Last write time:             Sat May 16 03:44:37 2015
Mount count:                 0
Maximum mount count:         -1
Last checked:                Sat May 16 03:44:37 2015
Check interval:              0 (<none>)
Lifetime writes:             4447 kB
Reserved blocks uid:         0 (user root)
Reserved blocks gid:         0 (group root)
First inode:                 11
Inode size:                  128
Journal inode:               8
Default directory hash:      half_md4
Directory Hash Seed:         a87a5804-f7c6-4028-89ed-799c2bb47133
Journal backup:              inode blocks
```

As you can see, the **tune2fs -l** command shows many file system properties. One interesting property is the file system label, which shows as the Filesystem volume name. Labels are used to set a unique name for a file system, which allows the file system to be mounted, even if the underlying device name changes. Also interesting are the file system features and default mount options.

To change any of the default file system options, the **tune2fs** command enables you with other parameters. Some common usage examples are listed below:

- Use **tune2fs -o** to set default file system mount options. When set to the file system, the option does not have to be specified while mounting through /etc/fstab anymore. Use, for instance, **tune2fs -o acl,user_xattr** to switch on access control lists and user extended attributes. Use a ^ in front of the option to switch it off again, as in **tune2fs -o ^acl,user_xattr**.
- Ext file systems also come with file system features that may be enabled as a default. To switch on a file system feature, use **tune2fs -O** followed by the feature. To turn a feature off, use a ^ in front of the feature name.
- Use **tune2fs -L** to set a label on the file system. As described in the section "Mounting File Systems" later in this chapter, you can use a file system label to mount a file system based on its name instead of the device name. Instead of **tune2fs -L**, the **e2label** command enables you to do so.

Managing XFS File System Properties

The XFS file system is a completely different file system, and for that reason also has a completely different set of tools to manage its properties. It does not allow you to set file system attributes within the file system metadata. You can, however, change some XFS properties, using the **xfs_admin** command. For instance, use **xfs_admin -L mylabel** to set the file system label to mylabel.

Adding Swap Partitions

You use most of the partitions on a Linux server for regular file systems. On Linux, swap space is normally also allocated on a disk device. That can be a partition, or an LVM logical volume (discussed in Chapter 15. In case of emergency, you can even use a file to extend the available swap space.

Using swap on Linux is a convenient way to improve Linux kernel memory usage. If a shortage of physical RAM occurs, non-recently-used memory pages can be moved to swap, which makes more RAM available for programs that need access to memory pages. Most Linux servers for that reason are configured with a certain amount of swap. If swap starts being used intensively, you could be in trouble though, and that is why swap usage should be closely monitored.

It sometimes makes sense to allocate more swap. If a shortage of memory occurs, this shortage can be alleviated by allocating more swap space in some situations. (See Chapter 24, "Configuring Time Services," for more information about system performance optimization.) This is done through a procedure where first a partition is created with the swap partition type. Then this partition is formatted as swap. The following procedure describes how to do this.

Exercise 14.5 Creating a Swap Partition

1. Use **fdisk /dev/vda** to open your disk in fdisk. (Use gdisk if you are using a disk with a GUID partition table.)
2. Press **n** to add a new partition. Specify start and stop cylinders and size.
3. Type **t** to change the partition type. If you are using fdisk, use partition type 82. If you are using gdisk, use partition type 8200.
4. Use mkswap to format the partition as swap space. Use, for instance, **mkswap /dev/vda6** if the partition you have just created is /dev/vda6.
5. Type **free -m**. You see the amount of swap space that is currently allocated.
6. Use swapon to switch on the newly allocated swap space. If, for instance, the swap device you have just created is /dev/vda6, use **swapon /dev/vda6** to activate the swap space.
7. Type **free -m** again. You see that the new swap space has been added to your server.

Adding Swap Files

If you do not have free disk space to create a swap partition and you do need to add swap space urgently, you can use a swap file as well. From a performance perspective, it does not even make that much difference if a swap file is used instead of a swap device such as a partition or a logical volume, and it may help you fixing an urgent need in a timely manner.

To add a swap file, you need to create the file first. The **dd if=/dev/zero of=/swapfile bs=1M count=100** command would add 100 blocks with a size of 1 Mebibyte from the /dev/zero device (which generates 0s) to the /swapfile file. The result is a 100 MiB file that can be configured as swap. To do so, you can follow the same procedure as for swap partitions. First use **mkswap /swapfile** to mark the file as a swap file, after which you can use **swapon /swapfile** to active it.

Mounting File Systems

Just creating a partition and putting a file system on it is not enough to start using it. To use a partition, you have to mount it as well. By mounting a partition (or better, the file system on it), you make its contents accessible through a specific directory.

To mount a file system, some information is needed:

- **What to mount:** This information is mandatory and specifies the name of the device that needs to be mounted.
- **Where to mount it:** This is also mandatory information which specifies the directory on which the device should be mounted.
- **What file system to mount:** Optionally, you can specify the file system type. In most cases, this is not necessary. The **mount** command will detect which file system is used on the device and make sure the correct driver is used.
- **Mount options:** Many mount options can be used when mounting a device. Using options is optional and depends on the needs you may have with the file system.

Manually Mounting File Systems

To manually mount a file system, the **mount** command is used. To disconnect a mounted file system, the **umount** command is used. Using these commands is relatively easy. To mount the file system that is on /dev/vda5 on the directory /mnt, use the following command:

```
mount /dev/vda5 /mnt
```

To disconnect the mount, you can use **umount** with either the name of the device or the name of the mount point you want to disconnect. So, both of the following commands will work:

```
umount /dev/vda5
umount /mnt
```

Using Device Names, UUIDs, or Disk Labels

To mount a device, the name of the device can be used, as in the command /dev/vda5. If your server is used in an environment where a dynamic storage topology is used, this is not always the best approach. You may today have a storage device /dev/sda5, which after changes in the storage topology can be /dev/sdb5 after the next reboot of your server. This is why on a default RHEL 7 installation UUIDs are used instead of device names.

Every file system by default has a UUID associated to it, not just file systems that are used to store files but also special file systems such as the swap file system. You can use the **blkid** command to get an overview of the current file systems on your system and the UUID that is used by that file system.

Listing 14.3 Using **blkid** to Find Current File System UUIDs

```
[root@server3 ~]# blkid
/dev/vda1: UUID="02305166-840d-4f74-a868-c549b3229e65" TYPE="xfs"
/dev/vda2: UUID="Hasz5q-nZF3-XN94-L2fm-xUwz-3VEq-qVCAYi" TYPE="LVM2_
member"
/dev/vda5: UUID="42f419c4-633f-4ed7-b161-519a4dadd3da" TYPE="xfs"
/dev/mapper/centos-swap: UUID="5867ba02-fd89-475c-be56-7922febde43b"
TYPE="swap"
/dev/mapper/centos-root: UUID="b2022ac4-73c6-4e6b-a52f-703e3e2476b7"
TYPE="xfs"
```

Before the use of UUIDs was common, file systems were often configured to work with labels, which can be set using the **e2label** or the **xfs_admin -L** commands. This has become more uncommon in recent Linux versions. If a file system has a label, the **blkid** command will also show it.

To mount a file system based on a UUID, you use **UUID=nnnnn** instead of the device name. So if you want to mount /dev/vda5 from Listing 14.3 based on its UUID, the command becomes as follows:

```
mount UUID="42f419c4-633f-4ed7-b161-519a4dadd3da" /mnt
```

Manually mounting devices using the UUID is not exactly easier. If mounts are automated as discussed in the next section, however, it does make sense using UUIDs instead of device names.

To mount a file system using a label, you use the **mount LABEL=labelname** command. For example, use **mount LABEL=mylabel /mnt** to temporarily mount the file system with the name mylabel on the /mnt directory.

Automating File System Mounts Through /etc/fstab

Normally, you do not want to be mounting file systems manually. Once you are happy with them, it is a good idea to have them mounted automatically. The classical way to do this is through the /etc/fstab file. Listing 14.4 shows sample contents of this file.

Listing 14.4 Sample /etc/fstab file Contents

```
[root@server3 ~]# cat /etc/fstab

#
# /etc/fstab
# Created by anaconda on Fri Jan 16 10:28:41 2015
#
# Accessible filesystems, by reference, are maintained under '/dev/disk'
# See man pages fstab(5), findfs(8), mount(8) and/or blkid(8) for more info
#
/dev/mapper/centos-root /          xfs     defaults          1 1
UUID=02305166-840d-4f74 /          xfs     defaults          1 2
/dev/mapper/centos-swap swap       swap    defaults          0 0
```

In the /etc/fstab file, everything is specified to mount the file system automatically. For this purpose, every line has six fields, as summarized in Table 14.5.

Table 14.5 /etc/fstab Fields

Key Topic

Field	Description
Device	The device that must be mounted. A device name, UUID, or label can be used.
Mount Point	The directory or kernel interface where the device needs to be mounted.
File System	The file system type.
Mount Options	Mount options.
Dump Support	Use 1 to enable support to backup using the dump utility. This may be necessary for some backup solutions.
Automatic Check	Specifies if the file system should be checked automatically when booting. Use 0 to disable automated check, 1 if this is the root file system and it has to be checked automatically, and 2 for all other file systems that need automatic checking while booting. Network file systems should have this option set to 0.

Based on what has previously been discussed about the **mount** command, you should have no problem understanding the device, mount point, and file system fields in /etc/fstab. Notice that in the mount point not all file systems use a directory name. Some system devices such as swap are not mounted on a directory, but on a kernel interface. It is easy to recognize when a kernel interface is used; its name does not start with a / (and does not exist in the file system on your server).

The Mount Options field defines specific mount options that can be used. If no specific options are required, this line will just read "defaults." To offer specific functionality, a large number of mount options can be specified here. Table 14.6 gives an overview of some of the more common mount options.

Table 14.6 Common Mount Options

Key Topic

Option	Use
auto/ noauto	The file system will [not] be mounted automatically.
acl	Adds support for file system access control lists (see Chapter 7, "Configuring Permissions").
user_xattr	Add support for user extended attributes (see Chapter 7).
ro	mounts the file system in read-only mode.
atime / noatime	Disables or enables access time modifications.
noexec / exec	Denies or allows execution of program files from the file system.
_netdev	Use this to mount a network file system. This tells fstab to wait until the network is available before mounting this file system.

The fifth column of /etc/fstab specifies support for the dump utility. This is a utility that was developed to create file system backups. It is good practice to switch this feature on by specifying a 1 for all real file systems, and switch it off by specifying 0 for all system mounts.

The last column indicates if the file system integrity needs to be checked while booting. Put a 0 if you do not want to check the file system at all, a 1 if this is the root file system which needs to be checked before anything else, and a 2 if this is a nonroot file system that needs to be checked while booting.

> **WARNING** If a file system through /etc/fstab is flagged for automatic file system check and something prevents the file system to be checked correctly, your system stops booting and prompts "enter root password to enter maintenance mode." To prevent this from ever happening, you could choose to disable automated checks while booting. See Chapter 19, "Troubleshooting the Boot Procedure," for more information on how to fix this specific case.

Exercise 14.6 Mounting Partitions Through /etc/fstab

In this exercise, you mount the XFS formatted partition /dev/vda5 that you have created in previous exercises.

1. From a root shell, type **blkid**. Use the mouse to copy the UUID="nnnn" part for /dev/vda5.
2. Type **mkdir -p /mounts/data** to create a mount point for this partition.
3. Open /etc/fstab in an editor and add the following line:

```
UUID="nnnn"          /mounts/data        xfs        defaults  1 2
```

4. Before attempting an automatic mount while rebooting, it is a good idea to test the configuration. Type **mount -a**. This mounts everything that is specified in /etc/fstab and that has not been mounted already.
5. Type **df -h** to verify that the partition has been mounted correctly.

Summary

In this important chapter, you learned how to work with partitions and file systems on RHEL 7. You learned how to create partitions for MBR and GPT disks, and how to put a file system on top of the partition. You also learned how to mount these partitions manually and automatically through /etc/fstab.

Exam Preparation Tasks

Review All Key Topics

Review the most important topics in the chapter, noted with the Key Topic icon in the outer margin of the page. Table 14.7 lists a reference of these key topics and the page numbers on which each is found.

Table 14.7 Key Topics for Chapter 14

Key Topic Element	Description	Page
Table 14.2	Disk size specifications	324
Table 14.3	Common disk device types	325
Table 14.4	File system types	335
Table 14.5	/etc/fstab fields	342
Table 14.6	Common mount options	343

Complete Tables and Lists from Memory

Print a copy of Appendix B, "Memory Tables," (found on the disc), or at least the section for this chapter, and complete the tables and lists from memory. Appendix C, "Memory Tables Answer Key," also on the disc, includes completed tables and lists to check your work.

Define Key Terms

Define the following key terms from this chapter and check your answers in the glossary:

BIOS, MBR, GRUB 2, partition, primary partition, extended partition, logical partition, GPT, mount, umount, UUID, label, Ext2, Ext3, Ext4, XFS, BtrFS, VFAT, fstab

Review Questions

1. Which tool do you use to create GUID partitions?
2. Which tool do you use to create MBR partitions?
3. What is the default file system on RHEL 7?
4. What is the name of the file that is used to automatically mount partitions while booting?
5. Which mount option do you use if you want a file system not to be mounted automatically while booting?
6. Which command enables you to format a partition that has type 82 with the appropriate file system?
7. You have just added a couple of partitions for automatic mounting while booting. How can you safely test if this is going to work without actually rebooting?
8. Which file system is created if you use the **mkfs** command without any file system specification?
9. How do you format an Ext4 partition?
10. How do you find UUIDs for all devices on your computer?

End-of-Chapter Labs

In the exercises you have worked through in this chapter, you have already created partitions. Before working on these end-of-chapter labs, it is a good idea to start from a clean installation. In Exercise 14.1, you created some backup files. Before starting to work on these end-of-chapter labs, restore the original setup using the following three steps:

Lab 14.1

1. Type **dd if=/dev/diskfile of=/dev/vda**. (Use **of=/dev/sda** if your disk device is /dev/sda instead of /dev/vda.)
2. Copy the backup of the /etc/fstab file, using **cp /root/fstab /etc**.

This restores the original configuration. You are now ready to start the end-of-chapter labs. After successfully completing the end-of-chapter labs, repeat this procedure. This allows you to work on clean disks when creating LVM logical volumes as described in the next chapter.

Lab 14.2

1. Add two partitions to your server. If possible, put them on the primary disk that is in use on your server. If that is not possible, use a second (virtual or USB) disk to add these partitions. Create both partitions with a size of 100 MiB. One of these partitions must be configured as swap space; the other partition must be formatted with an Ext4 file system.
2. Configure your server to automatically mount these partitions. Mount the Ext4 partition on /mounts/data and mount the swap space as swap space.
3. Reboot your server and verify that all is mounted correctly. In case of problems, read Chapter 19 for tips on how to troubleshoot.

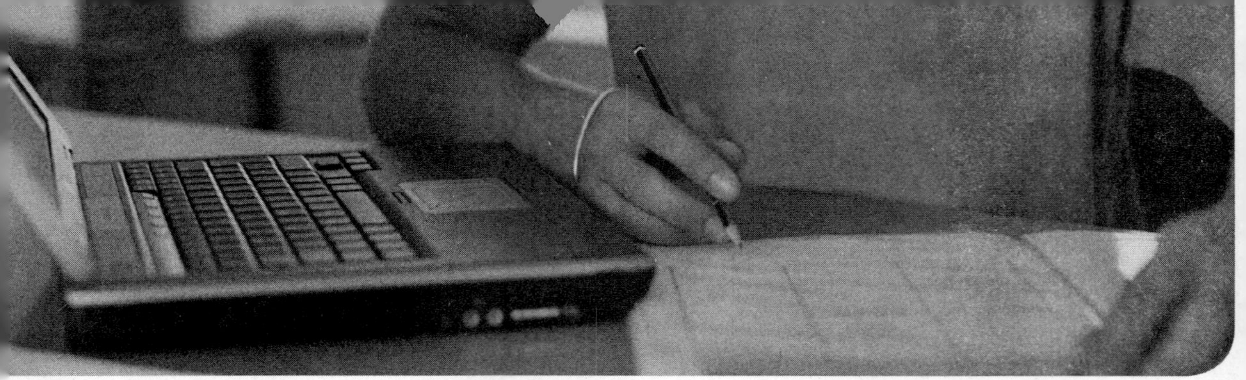

The following topics are covered In this chapter:

- Understanding LVM
- Creating LVM Logical Volumes
- Resizing LVM Logical Volumes

The following RHCSA exam objectives are covered in this chapter:

- Create and remove physical volumes, assign physical volumes to volume groups, and create and delete logical volumes
- Extend existing logical volumes

CHAPTER 15

Managing LVM Logical Volumes

In the preceding chapter, you learned how to manage partitions on a hard disk. Creating multiple partitions on a disk is useful because it allows you to separate between different data types, but it does not offer the flexibility that the Logical Volume Manager (LVM) does. In this chapter, you learn how to configure and manage LVM logical volumes.

"Do I Know This Already?" Quiz

The "Do I Know This Already?" quiz allows you to assess whether you should read this entire chapter thoroughly or jump to the "Exam Preparation Tasks" section. If you are in doubt about your answers to these questions or your own assessment of your knowledge of the topics, read the entire chapter. Table 15.1 lists the major headings in this chapter and their corresponding "Do I Know This Already?" quiz questions. You can find the answers in Appendix A, "Answers to the 'Do I Know This Already?' Quizzes and 'Review Questions.'"

Table 15.1 "Do I Know This Already?" Section-to-Question Mapping

Foundation Topics Section	Questions
Understanding LVM	1–2
Creating LVM Logical Volumes	3–9
Resizing LVM Logical Volumes	10

1. Which of the following is not a standard component in an LVM setup?
   a. Logical volume
   b. File system
   c. Volume group
   d. Physical volume

2. Which of the following is not an LVM feature?
   a. Volume resizing
   b. Hot replacement of failing disk
   c. Copy on write
   d. Snapshots

3. Which partition type do you need on a GPT partition to mark it with the LVM partition type?
   a. 83
   b. 8e
   c. 8300
   d. 8e00

4. Which of the following commands shows correctly how to create a logical volume that uses 50% of available disk space in the volume group?
   a. **vgadd -n lvdata -l +50%FREE vgdata**
   b. **lvcreate lvdata -l 50%FREE vgdata**
   c. **lvcreate -n lvdata -l 50%FREE vgdata**
   d. **lvadd -n lvdata -l 50% FREE /dev/vgdata**

5. Which command shows an overview of available physical volumes?
   a. **pvshow**
   b. **pvdisplay**
   c. **pvs**
   d. **pvlist**

6. Which of the following statements about physical volumes is/are true?
   a. Partitions should be flagged as LVM partition before assigning them as a physical volume.
   b. Raw disks can be flagged as a physical volume.
   c. Physical volumes can only be created on the Ext4 or XFS file system.
   d. Physical volumes *cannot* be created on LUNs.

7. Which of the following shows correct syntax for creating a volume group?
    a. **vgcreate /dev/vgdata sda1**
    b. **vgcreate sda1 /dev/vgdata**
    c. **vgcreate vgdata /dev/sda1**
    d. **vgcreate vgdata sda1**
8. Which of the following commands would set the extent size that is used when creating a logical volume to a default of 4 MiB?
    a. **pvcreate -s 4M /dev/sda4**
    b. **vgcreate -s 4M vgdata /dev/sda4**
    c. **lvcreate -s 4M -L 200M -n lvdata vgdata**
    d. **lvcreate -x 4M -L 200M -n lvdata vgdata**
9. Which of the following is not a likely correct name for the logical volume lvdata that was created in the volume group vgdata?
    a. /dev/vgdata-lvdata
    b. /dev/vgdata/lvdata
    c. /dev/dm-1
    d. /dev/mapper/vgdata-lvdata
10. Which of the following commands resizes the logical volume /dev/vgdata/lvdata as well as the file system that is used on top of it, and adds 1GB to the existing volume size?
    a. **lvresize -l +1G -r /dev/vgdata/lvdata**
    b. **lvresize -L +1G -r /dev/vgdata/lvdata**
    c. **lvresize -L 1G -r /dev/vgdata/lvdata**
    d. **lvresize -l 1G -f /dev/vgdata/lvdata**

Foundation Topics

Understanding LVM

In the early days of Linux servers, storage was handled by creating partitions on disks. Even if this approach does work, there are some disadvantages, the most important of which is that disks are inflexible. That is why the Logical Volume Manager was introduced. Where it is not possible to dynamically grow a partition that is running out of disk space, this is possible when working with LVM. LVM offers many other advantages, as well, which you learn about in this chapter.

LVM Architecture

In the LVM architecture, several layers can be distinguished. On the lowest layer, the storage devices are used. These can be any storage devices, such as complete disks, partitions, logical units (LUNs) on a storage-area network (SAN) and whatever else is made possible in modern storage topologies.

The storage devices need to be flagged as physical volumes, which makes them usable in an LVM environment, and which can also be used by other utilities trying to access to logical volume. A storage device that is a physical volume can be added to the volume group, which is the abstraction of all available storage. "The abstraction" means that the volume group is not something that is fixed, but that it can be resized when needed, which makes it possible to add more space on the volume group level when volumes are running out of disk space. The idea is simple: If you are running out of disk space on a logical volume, you take available disk space from the volume group. And if there is no available disk space in the volume group, you just add it by adding a physical volume.

On top of the volume group are the logical volumes. Logical volumes do not act on disks directly but get their disk space from available disk space in the volume group. That means that a logical volume may consist of available storage from multiple physical volumes, which does not really matter (as long as some level of redundancy is used on the disk layer).

NOTE It is a good idea to avoid logical volumes from spanning multiple physical volumes; if one of the physical volumes breaks, all files on the LVM file system will become inaccessible.

The actual file systems are created on the logical volumes. As the logical volumes are flexible with regard to size, that makes the file systems flexible as well. If a file system is running out of disk space, it is relatively easy to extend the file system, or to reduce it if the file system allows that.

Key Topic

Figure 15.1 gives an overview of the LVM architecture.

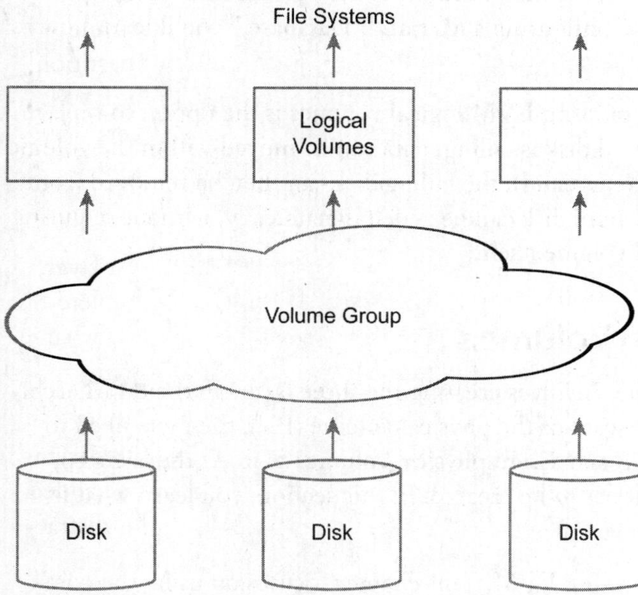

Figure 15.1 LVM architecture overview.

LVM Features

There are several reasons why LVM is great. The most important reason is that LVM offers a flexible solution for managing storage. Volumes are no longer bound to the restrictions of physical hard drives. If additional storage space is needed, the volume group can easily be extended so that disk space can be added to the logical volumes. It is also possible to reduce the size of a logical volume, but only if the file system that was created on that volume supports resizing. This is the case for the Ext4 file system but not for the XFS file system, which is used as the default file system on RHEL 7.

Another important reason why administrators like using LVM is the support for snapshots. A snapshot keeps the current state of a logical volume and can be used to revert to a previous situation or to make a backup of the file system on the logical volume if the volume is open.

LVM snapshots are created by copying the logical volume administrative data (the metadata) that describe the current state of files to a snapshot volume. As long as nothing changes, from the LVM snapshot metadata the original blocks in the original volume are addressed. When blocks are modified, the blocks containing the previous state of the file are copied over to the snapshot volume, which for that reason will grow. Using this method ensures that by accessing an LVM snapshot volume the exact state of the files as they were when the snapshot was created can be accessed. In Chapter 35, "Configuring a MariaDB Database," you'll learn how to create snapshots.

A third important advantage of using LVM logical volumes is the option to replace failing hardware easily. If a hard disk is failing, data can be moved within the volume group (through the **pvmove** command), the failing disk can then be removed from the volume group, and a new hard disk can be added dynamically, without requiring any downtime for the logical volume itself.

Creating LVM Logical Volumes

Creating LVM logical volumes involves creating the three layers in the LVM architecture. You first have to take care of the physical volume (PV), then you need to create the volume group (VG) and assign physical volumes to it. As the last step, the logical volume (LV) itself has to be created. In this section, you learn what is involved in creating these three layers.

Different utilities exist for creating LVM. This chapter focuses on using the command-line utilities. They are relatively easy to use, and they are available in all environments (whether you are running a graphical interface or not).

TIP You absolutely do not need to learn the commands discussed in this chapter by heart. All you really need to remember is **pv**, **vg**, **lv**. Open a command line, type **pv** and press the **Tab** key twice. This will show all commands that start with pv, which are all commands that are used for managing physical volumes. After you have found the command you need, run this command with the **--help** option. This shows a usage summary that lists everything that needs to be done to create the element you need. Listing 15.1 shows an example of the **pvcreate --help** command (which is explained in the next subsection).

Listing 15.1 Requesting help for the pvcreate command

```
[root@server1 ~]# pvcreate --help
  pvcreate: Initialize physical volume(s) for use by LVM

pvcreate
        [--norestorefile]
        [--restorefile file]
        [-d|--debug]
        [-f[f]|--force [--force]]
        [-h|-?|--help]
        [--labelsector sector]
        [-M|--metadatatype 1|2]
        [--pvmetadatacopies #copies]
        [--bootloaderareasize BootLoaderAreaSize[bBsSkKmMgGtTpPeE]]
        [--metadatasize MetadataSize[bBsSkKmMgGtTpPeE]]
        [--dataalignment Alignment[bBsSkKmMgGtTpPeE]]
        [--dataalignmentoffset AlignmentOffset[bBsSkKmMgGtTpPeE]]
        [--setphysicalvolumesize PhysicalVolumeSize[bBsSkKmMgGtTpPeE]
        [-t|--test]
        [-u|--uuid uuid]
        [-v|--verbose]
        [-y|--yes]
        [-Z|--zero {y|n}]
        [--version]
        PhysicalVolume [PhysicalVolume...]
```

Creating the Physical Volumes

Before the LVM tools can be used to create physical volumes, you need to create a partition marked as the LVM partition type. This is basically the same procedure as described in the preceding chapter, with the only difference that before writing changes to disk in fdisk or gdisk, you need to press **t** to change the partition type. (Exercise 15.1 shows exactly what you need to do.) If you are using an MBR disk, the partition type is 8e. If you are using a GUID disk, use the partition type 8300.

After creating the partition and flagging it as an LVM partition type, you need to use **pvcreate** to mark it as a physical volume. This writes some metadata to the partition, which allows it to be used in a volume group. The entire procedure is summarized in Exercise 15.1.

Exercise 15.1 Creating the Physical Volume

In this exercise, you create a physical volume. To do this exercise, you need a hard disk that has free (unpartitioned) disk space available. The recommended method to make disk space available is by adding a new hard disk in your virtual machine environment. In this exercise, I use a clean /dev/vdb device to create the partition. You may have to change the device name to match your configuration. If you do not have a dedicated hard disk available to create this configuration, you might want to consider attaching a USB key to your machine.

1. Open a root shell and type **fdisk /dev/vdb**.
2. Type **n** to create a new partition. Select **p** to make it a primary partition, and use the partition number that is suggested as a default. If you are using a clean device, this will be partition number 1.
3. Press **Enter** when asked for the first sector and type **+100M** to accept the last sector.
4. Once you are back on the fdisk prompt, type **t** to change the partition type. Because there is one partition only, fdisk does not ask which partition to use this partition type on. You may have to select a partition if you are using a different configuration.
5. The partitioner asks for the partition type you want to use. Type **8e**. Then, press **w** to write changes to disk and quit fdisk. Listing 15.2 shows an overview of all commands that have been used so far. If you are getting a message that the partition table could not be updated while writing the changes to disk, reboot your system.

Listing 15.2 Creating an LVM Partition in fdisk

```
[root@localhost ~]# fdisk /dev/vdb
Welcome to fdisk (util-linux 2.23.2).

Changes will remain in memory only, until you decide to write them.
Be careful before using the write command.

Device does not contain a recognized partition table
Building a new DOS disklabel with disk identifier 0xe39ca22b.

Command (m for help): n
```

```
Partition type:
   p   primary (0 primary, 0 extended, 4 free)
   e   extended
Select (default p):
Using default response p
Partition number (1-4, default 1):
First sector (2048-2097151, default 2048):
Using default value 2048
Last sector, +sectors or +size{K,M,G} (2048-2097151, default 2097151):
+100M
Partition 1 of type Linux and of size 100 MiB is set

Command (m for help): t
Selected partition 1
Hex code (type L to list all codes): 8e
Changed type of partition 'Linux' to 'Linux LVM'

Command (m for help): w
The partition table has been altered!

Calling ioctl() to re-read partition table.
Syncing disks.
```

6. Now that the partition has been created, you need to flag it as an LVM physical volume. To do this, type **pvcreate /dev/vdb1**. You should now get this prompt: Physical volume "/dev/vbd1" successfully created.
7. Now type **pvs** to verify that the physical volume has been created successfully. The output may look like Listing 15.3. Notice that in this listing another physical volume already exists; that is because RHEL uses LVM by default to organize storage.

Listing 15.3 Verifying the Physical Volume

```
[root@localhost ~]# pvs
  PV         VG     Fmt  Attr PSize   PFree
  /dev/vda2  centos lvm2 a--    3.51g       0
  /dev/vdb1         lvm2 a--  100.00m 100.00m
```

As an alternative to the **pvs** command, which shows a summary of the physical volumes and their attributes, you can also use the **pvdisplay** command to show some more details. Listing 15.4 shows an example of the output of this command.

Listing 15.4 Example **pvdisplay** Command Output

```
[root@server1 ~]# pvdisplay
  --- Physical volume ---
  PV Name               /dev/vda2
  VG Name               centos
  PV Size               3.51 GiB / not usable 3.00 MiB
  Allocatable           yes (but full)
  PE Size               4.00 MiB
  Total PE              898
  Free PE               0
  Allocated PE          898
  PV UUID               CILii7-DzOd-w4L0-yOxi-9NXg-D3nP-ZugJIj
```

If you want a very synthetic overview of the current storage configuration, you might also like the **lsblk** command. As can be seen in Listing 15.5, this command gives a hierarchical overview of which disks and partitions are used in what LVM volume groups and logical volumes.

Listing 15.5 Use **lsblk** for a Synthetic Overview of the Current Configuration of Storage on Your Server

```
[root@localhost ~]# lsblk
NAME                  MAJ:MIN RM  SIZE RO TYPE MOUNTPOINT
fd0                     2:0    1    4K  0 disk
sda                     8:0    0    8G  0 disk
├─sda1                  8:1    0  200M  0 part /boot
├─sda2                  8:2    0  6.9G  0 part
│ ├─centos-swap       253:0    0  256M  0 lvm  [SWAP]
│ └─centos-root       253:1    0  5.9G  0 lvm  /
├─sda3                  8:3    0  100M  0 part
└─sda4                  8:4    0  887M  0 part
  └─vgik-lvgroups     253:2    0  440M  0 lvm  /groups
sr0                    11:0    1 1024M  0 rom
```

Creating the Volume Groups

Now that the physical volume has been created, you can assign it to a volume group. It is possible to add a physical volume to an existing volume group (which is discussed later in this chapter), but you will now learn how to create a new volume group and add the physical volume to it. This is a simple one-command procedure. Just type **vgcreate** followed by the name of the volume group you want to create and the name of the physical device you want to add to it. So, if the physical volume name is /dev/vdb1, the complete command is **vgcreate vgdata /dev/vdb1**.

You are completely free in your choice of name for the volume group. I like to start all volume group names with vg, which makes it easy to find the volume groups if there are many, but you are free to choose anything you like.

In this procedure, you learned how to create a volume group in a two-step procedure where first the physical volume is created with the **pvcreate** command, after which the volume group is added using the **vgcreate** command. You can do this in a one-step procedure as well (where using a separate **pvcreate** command will not be necessary). If you are adding a partition to the volume group, however, it must be marked as partition type 8e already.

The one-step procedure is particularly useful for adding a complete disk device (which does not need to be marked as anything). If you want to add the disk /dev/sdc, for instance, just type **vgcreate vgdata /dev/sdc** to create a volume group vgdata that contains the /dev/sdc device. When you are doing this to add a device that has not been marked as a physical volume yet, the vgcreate utility will automatically flag it as a physical volume.

When creating volume groups, a physical extent size is used. The physical extent size defines the size of the building blocks used to create logical volumes. A logical volume always has a size that is a multiple of the physical extent size. If you need to create huge logical volumes, it is more efficient to use a big physical extent size. If you do not specify anything, a default extent size of 4.00 MiB is used. The physical extent size is always specified as a multiple of 2 MiB, with a maximum size of 128 MiB. Use the **vgcreate -s** option to specify the physical extent size you want to use.

NOTE When working with LVM, there is the physical extent size to consider. This is the size of the basic building blocks used in the LVM configuration. When working with an ext4 file system, logical extents are used. The extent size on LVM are in no way related to the extent sizes that are used on the file systems.

After creating the volume group, you can request details about the volume group using the **vgs** command for a short summary, or the **vgdisplay** command to get more information. Listing 15.6 shows an example of the output of the **vgdisplay** command.

Listing 15.6 Showing Current Volume Group Properties

```
[root@server1 ~]# vgdisplay
...

  --- Volume group ---
  VG Name               vgdata
  System ID
  Format                lvm2
  Metadata Areas        1
  Metadata Sequence No  2
  VG Access             read/write
  VG Status             resizable
  MAX LV                0
  Cur LV                1
  Open LV               0
  Max PV                0
  Cur PV                1
  Act PV                1
  VG Size               248.00 MiB
  PE Size               4.00 MiB
  Total PE              62
  Alloc PE / Size       31 / 124.00 MiB
  Free  PE / Size       31 / 124.00 MiB
  VG UUID               TutZ0F-Fe0q-VGR4-y0dO-O0RM-Mv7e-09zyar
```

Creating the Logical Volumes and File Systems

Now that the volume group has been created, you can start creating logical volumes from it. This procedure is slightly more complicated than the creation of physical volumes or volume groups because there are more choices to be made. While creating the logical volume, you must specify a volume name and a size.

The volume size can be specified as an absolute value using the **-L** option. Use, for instance, **-L 5G** to create an LVM volume with a 5GB size. Alternatively, you can use relative sizes using the **-l** option. For instance, use **-l 50%FREE** to use half of all available disk space. You'll further need to specify the name of the volume group that the logical volume is assigned to, and optionally (but highly recommended), you can use **-n** to specify the name of the logical volume. For instance, use **lvcreate -n lvvol1 -L 100M vgdata** to create a logical volume with the name lvvol1 and add that to the vgdata volume group.

Understanding LVM Device Naming

Now that the logical volume has been created, you can start using it. To do this, you need to know the device name. LVM volume device names can be addressed in multiple ways. The simple method is to address the device as /dev/vgname/lvname. So if you have created a volume with the name lvdata, which gets its available disk space from the vgdata volume group, the device name would be /dev/vgdata/lvdata.

For naming LVM volumes, another system plays a role: device mapper. The device mapper (abbreviated as dm) is a generic interface that the Linux kernel uses to address storage devices. Device mapper is used by multiple device types, such as LVM volumes, but also by software RAID and advanced network devices such as multipath devices. These devices are created in two locations: as devices that are sequentially numbered in the /dev directory, such as /dev/dm-0, /dev/dm-1, and further. Because these device names do not provide any information about the device and therefore are confusing, symbolic links are created in the /dev/mapper directory. These symbolic links use a name that uses the vgname-lvname pattern. So, the device /dev/vgdata/lvdata would also be known as /dev/mapper/vgdata-lvdata. When working with LVM logical volumes, you can use any of these device names. Listing 15.7 shows an overview of the different LVM device names as provided by the device mapper.

Listing 15.7 LVM Device Name Overview

```
[root@localhost ~]# \ls -l /dev/vgdata/lvdata
lrwxrwxrwx. 1 root root 7 Feb 11 05:00 /dev/vgdata/lvdata -> ../dm-2
[root@localhost ~]# \ls -l /dev/mapper/
total 0
lrwxrwxrwx. 1 root root       7 Feb 11 03:50 centos-root -> ../dm-1
lrwxrwxrwx. 1 root root       7 Feb 11 03:50 centos-swap -> ../dm-0
crw-------. 1 root root 10, 236 Feb 11 03:50 control
lrwxrwxrwx. 1 root root       7 Feb 11 05:00 vgdata-lvdata -> ../dm-2
[root@localhost ~]# \ls -l /dev/dm-2
brw-rw----. 1 root disk 253, 2 Feb 11 05:00 /dev/dm-2
```

Exercise 15.2 Creating the Volume Group and Logical Volumes

In Exercise 15.1, you created a physical volume. In this exercise, you continue working on that physical volume and assign it to a volume group. Then you add a logical volume from that volume group. You can work on this exercise only after successful completion of Exercise 15.1.

1. Open a root shell. Type **pvs** to verify the availability of physical volumes on your machine. You should see the /dev/vdb1 physical volume that was created previously.
2. Type **vgcreate vgdata /dev/vdb1**. This will create the volume group with the physical volume assigned to it.
3. Type **vgs** to verify that the volume group was created successfully. Also type **pvs**. Notice that this command now shows the name of the physical volumes, with the names of the volume groups they are assigned to.
4. Type **lvcreate -n lvdata -l 50%FREE vgdata**. This creates an LVM logical volume with the name lvdata, which will use 50% of available disk space in the vgdata volume group.
5. Type **lvs** to verify that the volume was added successfully.
6. At this point, you are ready to create a file system on top of the logical volume. Type **mkfs.xfs /dev/vgdata/lvdata** to create the file system.
7. Type **mkdir /files** to create a folder on which the volume can be mounted.
8. Add the following line to /etc/fstab:

```
/dev/vgdata/lvdata /files    xfs       defaults  1 2
```

9. Type **mount -a** to verify that the mount works and mount the file system.

Table 15.2 summarizes the relevant commands for creating logical volumes.

Table 15.2 LVM Management Essential Commands

Key Topic

Command	Explanation
pvcreate	Creates physical volumes
pvs	Shows a summary of available physical volumes
pvdisplay	Shows a list of physical volumes and their properties
vgcreate	Creates volume groups
vgs	Shows a summary of available volume groups

Command	Explanation
vgdisplay	Shows a detailed list of volume groups and their properties
lvcreate	Creates logical volumes
lvs	Shows a summary of all available logical volumes
lvdisplay	Shows a detailed list of available logical volumes and their properties

Resizing LVM Logical Volumes

One of the major benefits of using LVM is that LVM volumes are easy to resize, which is very useful if your file system is running out of available disk space. If the XFS file system is used, a volume can be increased, but not decreased, in size. Other file systems such as Ext4 and Btrfs support decreasing of the file system size also. Decreasing an Ext4 file system can be done offline only, which means that you need to unmount it before you can resize it. In this section, you learn how to increase the size of an LVM logical volume.

Resizing Volume Groups

The main part of LVM flexibility sits in the fact that it is so easy to resize the volume groups and the logical volumes that are using disk space from the volume group. The **vgextend** command is used to add storage to a volume group, and the **vgreduce** command is used to take physical volumes out of a volume group (which can lead to some additional complications). For the RHCSA test, you need to know how to extend the available storage in volume groups. This procedure is relatively easy:

1. Make sure that a physical volume or device is available to be added to the volume group.
2. Use **vgextend** to extend the volume group. The new disk space will show immediately in the volume group.

After extending a volume group, you can use the **vgs** command to verify that a physical volume has been added to the volume group. In Listing 15.8, you can see that the centos VG contains two physical volumes, as indicated in the #PV column.

Listing 15.8 Verifying VG Resize Operations with **vgs**

```
[root@server2 ~]# vgs
  VG      #PV #LV #SN Attr    VSize   VFree
  centos    2   3   0 wz--n-    7.00g 560.00m
  vgsan     1   2   0 wz--n- 496.00m  96.00m
```

Resizing Logical Volumes and File Systems

Like volume groups can be extended with the **vgextend** command, logical volumes can be extended with the **lvextend** command. This command has a very useful option to take care of extending the file systems on the logical volume at the same time; it is recommended to use this option and not the alternative approach where logical volumes and the file systems on top of the logical volumes are extended separately. When resizing a logical volume with the file system it contains, nothing will happen to the file system, and its data will remain intact. Most file system resizing operations can even be done online, without any need to unmount the file system.

To grow the logical volume size, use **lvresize**, followed by the **-r** option to resize the file system used on it. Then, specify the size you want the resized volume to be. The easiest and most intuitive way to do that is by using **-L** followed by a **+** sign and the amount of disk space you want to add, as in **lvresize -L +1G -r /dev/vgdata/lvdata**. An alternative way to resize the logical volume is by using the **-l** option. This option is followed by the number of extents that are added to the logical volume or by the absolute or relative percentage of extents in the volume group that will be used. You can, for example, use the following commands to resize the logical volume:

Key Topic

- **lvresize -r -l 75%VG /dev/vgdata/lvdata** This resizes the logical volume so that it will take 75% of the total disk space in the volume group.
- **lvresize -r -l +75%VG /dev/vgdata/lvdata** This tries to add 75% of the total size of the volume group to the logical volume. (Notice the difference with the previous command.)
- **lvresize -r -l +75%FREE /dev/vgdata/lvdata** This adds 75% of all free disk space to the logical volume.
- **lvresize -r -l 75%FREE /dev/vgdata/lvdata** This resizes the logical volume to a total size that equals 75% of the amount of free disk space. (Notice the difference with the previous command.)

While resizing a logical volume, you can also use the **-l** option, followed by the number of logical extents that you want to add or remove. A logical extent is the logical building block used when creating logical volumes, and it maps to a physical extent, the size of which can be specified when creating a volume group. All resize operations need to match complete logical extents. You will sometimes notice that the resize size is rounded up or down to the logical extent size. You can also specify the number of logical extents that need to be added or removed directly by using the **-l** option with the **lvresize** command.

As you can see, resizing a logical volume has many options, and you need to take care to use the right options because it is easy to make a mistake! In Exercise 15.3, you learn how to resize logical volumes and the file systems used on top of them.

NOTE The size of an XFS file system cannot be decreased; it can only be increased. If you need a file system that can be shrunk in size, use Ext4, not XFS.

Exercise 15.3 Resizing Logical Volumes

In Exercises 15.1 and 15.2, you have created a physical volume, volume group, and logical volume. In this exercise, you extend the size of the logical volume and the file system used on top of it.

1. Type **pvs** and **vgs** to show the current physical volume and volume group configuration.
2. Use **fdisk** to add another partition with a size of 100M. Do not forget to flag this partition with the LVM partition type. I'll assume this new partition is /dev/sdb2 for the rest of this exercise. Replace this name with the name used on your configuration.
3. Type **vgextend vgdata /dev/sdb2** to extend vgdata with the total size of the /dev/sdb2 device.
4. Type **vgs** to verify that the available volume group size has increased.
5. Type **lvs** to verify the current size of the logical volume lvdata.
6. Type **df -h** to verify the current size of the file system on lvdata.
7. Type **lvextend -r -l +50%FREE /dev/vgdata/lvdata** to extend lvdata with 50% of all available disk space in the volume group.
8. Type **lvs** and **df -h** again to verify that the added disk space has become available.
9. Type **lvreduce -r -L -150M /dev/vgdata/lvdata**. This shrinks the lvdata volume with 50MB. Notice that while doing this the volume is temporarily unmounted, which happens automatically.

Summary

In this chapter, you learned how to work with LVM logical volumes. First you learned how LVM provides features that are not available in normal partitioning, such as easy resizing or working with snapshots. You also learned how to create partitions that can be used in an LVM configuration, and you learned how to create physical volumes, volume groups, and logical volumes to create an LVM infrastructure. You also learned how to resize volume groups and logical volumes.

Exam Preparation Tasks

Review All Key Topics

Review the most important topics in the chapter, noted with the Key Topic icon in the outer margin of the page. Table 15.3 lists a reference of these key topics and the page numbers on which each is found.

Table 15.3 Key Topics for Chapter 15

Key Topic Element	Description	Page
Figure 15.1	LVM architecture overview	353
Table 15.2	LVM management essential commands	362
List	LVM resize commands	364

Define Key Terms

Define the following key terms from this chapter and check your answers in the glossary:

PV, physical volume, VG, volume group, LV, logical volume, device mapper, physical extent, logical extent, snapshot

Review Questions

1. Which partition type is used on a GUID partition that needs to be used in LVM?
2. Which command enables you to create a volume group with the name vggroup that contains the physical device /dev/sdb3 and uses a physical extent size of 4MiB?

3. Which command shows a short summary of the physical volumes on your system as well as the volume group to which these belong?
4. What do you need to do to add an entire hard disk /dev/sdd to the volume group vgroup?
5. Which command enables you to create a logical volume lvvol1 with a size of 6MiB?
6. Which command enables you to add 100MB to the logical volume lvvol1, assuming that the disk space is available in the volume group?
7. What is the first step to take to add another 200MB of disk space to a logical volume if the required disk space is not available in the volume group?
8. Which option do you use when using lvextend to make sure that the file system is also resized?
9. How do you show which logical volumes are available?
10. Which command do you use to check the file system integrity on the file system on /dev/vgdata/lvdata?

End-of-Chapter Labs

To complete the end-of-chapter labs with this chapter, you need a dedicated disk device. Use a USB thumb drive, or add a new virtual disk to your virtual environment before starting.

Lab 15.1

1. Create a 500MB logical volume lvgroup. Format it with the XFS file system and mount it persistently on /groups. Reboot your server to verify that the mount works.
2. After rebooting, add another 250MB to the lvgroup volume that you just created. Verify that the file system resizes as well while resizing the volume.
3. Verify that the volume extension was successful.

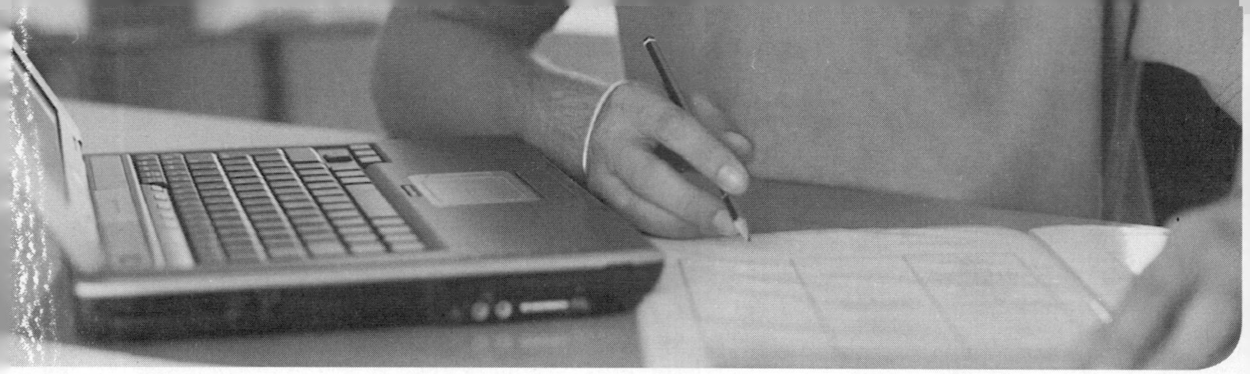

The following topics are covered in this chapter:

- Understanding the Role of the Linux Kernel
- Working with Kernel Modules
- Updating the Linux Kernel

The following RHCSA exam objectives are covered in this chapter:

- Update the kernel package appropriately to ensure a bootable system

CHAPTER 16

Basic Kernel Management

The Linux kernel is the heart of the Linux operating system. It takes care of many things, including hardware management. In this chapter, you learn all you need to know about the Linux kernel from an RHCSA perspective. In fact, you even learn a bit more. This chapter includes information about topics that are not on the current list of RHCSA objectives. I think it is good to know about these topics anyway. Any serious Linux administrator should be able to deal with issues related to the topics discussed in this chapter.

"Do I Know This Already?" Quiz

The "Do I Know This Already?" quiz allows you to assess whether you should read this entire chapter thoroughly or jump to the "Exam Preparation Tasks" section. If you are in doubt about your answers to these questions or your own assessment of your knowledge of the topics, read the entire chapter. Table 16.1 lists the major headings in this chapter and their corresponding "Do I Know This Already?" quiz questions. You can find the answers in Appendix A, "Answers to the 'Do I Know This Already?' Quizzes and 'Review Questions.'"

Table 16.1 "Do I Know This Already?" Section-to-Question Mapping

Foundation Topics Section	Questions
Understanding the Role of the Linux Kernel	1–4
Working with Kernel Modules	5, 9
Updating the Linux Kernel	10

1. What causes a tainted kernel?
   a. A kernel driver that is not available as open source driver
   b. A driver that was developed for a different operating system but has been ported to Linux
   c. A driver that has failed.
   d. An unsupported driver.

2. What is the name of the command that shows kernel events since booting?
   a. **logger**
   b. **dmesg**
   c. **klogd**
   d. **journald**
3. Which command enables you to find the actual version of the kernel that is used?
   a. **uname -r**
   b. **uname -v**
   c. **procinfo -k**
   d. **procinfo -l**
4. Which command shows the current version of RHEL you are using?
   a. **uname -r**
   b. **cat /proc/rhel-version**
   c. **cat /etc/redhat-release**
   d. **uname -k**
5. What is the name of the process that helps the kernel initializing hardware devices properly?
   a. systemd-udevd
   b. hwinit
   c. udev
   d. udevd
6. Where does your system find the default rules that are used for initializing new hardware devices?
   a. /etc/udev/rules.d
   b. /usr/lib/udev/rules.d
   c. /usr/lib/udev.d/rules
   d. /etc/udev.d/rules

7. Which command should you use to unload a kernel module, including all of its dependencies?
   a. **rmmod**
   b. **insmod -r**
   c. **modprobe -r**
   d. **modprobe**

8. Which command enables you to see whether the appropriate kernel modules have been loaded for hardware in your server?
   a. **lsmod**
   b. **modprobe -l**
   c. **lspci -k**
   d. **lspci**

9. Where do you specify a kernel module parameter to make it persistent?
   a. /etc/modules.conf
   b. /etc/modprobe.conf
   c. /etc/modprobe.d/somefilename
   d. /usr/lib/modprobe.d/somefilename

10. Which statements about updating the kernel is *not* true?
    a. The **yum update kernel** command will install a new kernel and not update it.
    b. The **yum install kernel** command will install a new kernel and keep the old kernel.
    c. The kernel package should be set as a yum protected package to ensure that after an update the old kernel is still available.
    d. After you have installed a new kernel version, you must run the **grub2-mkconfig** command to modify the GRUB 2 boot menu so that is shows the old kernel and the newly installed kernel.

Foundation Topics

Understanding the Role of the Linux Kernel

The Linux kernel is the heart of the operating system. It is the layer between the user who works with Linux from a shell environment and the hardware that is available in the computer on which the user is working. The kernel is doing so by managing the I/O instructions it receives from the software and translating those to processing instructions that are to be executed by the central processing unit and other hardware in the computer. The kernel also takes care of handling essential operating system tasks. One example of such a task is the scheduler that makes sure that processes that are started on the operating system are handled by the CPU.

Understanding the use of Kernel Threads and Drivers

The operating system tasks that are performed by the kernel are implemented by different kernel threads. Kernel threads are easily recognized with a command like **ps aux**. The kernel thread names are listed between square brackets (see Listing 16.1).

Listing 16.1 Listing Kernel Threads with **ps aux**

```
[root@server1 ~]# ps aux | head -n 20
USER     PID %CPU %MEM    VSZ   RSS TTY      STAT START   TIME COMMAND
root       1  1.8  0.6  52980  6812 ?        Ss   11:44   0:02 /usr/lib/
systemd/systemd --switched-root --system --deserialize 23
root       2  0.0  0.0      0     0 ?        S    11:44   0:00 [kthreadd]
root       3  0.0  0.0      0     0 ?        S    11:44   0:00 [ksoftirqd/0]
root       4  0.0  0.0      0     0 ?        S    11:44   0:00 [kworker/0:0]
root       5  0.0  0.0      0     0 ?        S<   11:44   0:00 [kworker/0:0H]
root       6  0.0  0.0      0     0 ?        S    11:44   0:00 [kworker/u128:0]
root       7  0.1  0.0      0     0 ?        S    11:44   0:00 [migration/0]
root       8  0.0  0.0      0     0 ?        S    11:44   0:00 [rcu_bh]
root       9  0.0  0.0      0     0 ?        S    11:44   0:00 [rcuob/0]
root      10  0.0  0.0      0     0 ?        S    11:44   0:00 [rcuob/1]
root      11  0.0  0.0      0     0 ?        S    11:44   0:00 [rcuob/2]
root      12  0.0  0.0      0     0 ?        S    11:44   0:00 [rcuob/3]
```

```
root        13  0.0  0.0      0      0 ?      S     11:44    0:00 [rcuob/4]
root        14  0.0  0.0      0      0 ?      S     11:44    0:00 [rcuob/5]
root        15  0.0  0.0      0      0 ?      S     11:44    0:00 [rcuob/6]
root        16  0.0  0.0      0      0 ?      S     11:44    0:00 [rcuob/7]
root        17  0.0  0.0      0      0 ?      S     11:44    0:00 [rcuob/8]
root        18  0.0  0.0      0      0 ?      S     11:44    0:00 [rcuob/9]
root        19  0.0  0.0      0      0 ?      S     11:44    0:00 [rcuob/10]
```

Another important task of the Linux kernel is hardware initialization. To make sure that this hardware can be used, the Linux kernel uses drivers. Every piece of hardware contains specific features, and to use these features, a driver must be loaded. The Linux kernel is modular, and drivers are loaded as kernel modules, about which you read more later in this chapter.

In some cases, the availability of drivers is an issue because hardware manufacturers are not always willing to provide open source drivers that can be integrated well with the Linux kernel. That can result in a driver that is not providing all the functionality that is provided by the hardware.

If a manufacturer is not willing to provide open source drivers, it can be an alternative to work with closed source drivers. Although these make it possible to use the hardware in Linux, the solution is not ideal. Because a driver performs privileged instructions within the kernel space, a badly functioning driver may crash the entire kernel. If this happens with an open source driver, the Linux kernel community can help debugging the problem and make sure that the issue is fixed. If it happens with a closed source driver, the Linux kernel community cannot do anything. But, a proprietary driver may provide access to features that are not provided by its open source equivalent.

To make it easy to see whether a kernel is using closed source drivers, the concept of the tainted kernel is used. A tainted kernel is a kernel that contains closed source drivers. The concept of tainted kernels helps in troubleshooting drivers. If your RHEL 7 kernel appears to be tainted, Red Hat support can identify it as a tainted kernel and recognize which driver is making it a tainted kernel. To fix the problem, they may ask you to take out the driver that is making it a tainted kernel.

Analyzing What the Kernel Is Doing

Key Topic

To help analyze what the kernel is doing, some tools are provided by the Linux operating systems:

- The **dmesg** utility
- The /proc file system
- The uname utility

The first utility to consider whether detailed information about the kernel activity is required is dmesg. This utility shows the contents of the kernel ring buffer, an area of memory where the Linux kernel keeps its recent log messages. An alternative method to get access to the same information in the kernel ring buffer is by using the **journalctl --dmesg** command, which is equivalent to **journalctl -k**. In Listing 16.2, you can see a part of the result of the **dmesg** command.

Listing 16.2 Analyzing Kernel Activity Using dmesg

```
[    8.153928] sd 0:0:0:0: Attached scsi generic sg0 type 0
[    8.154289] sd 0:0:1:0: Attached scsi generic sg1 type 0
[    8.154330] sd 0:0:2:0: Attached scsi generic sg2 type 0
[    8.154360] sd 0:0:3:0: Attached scsi generic sg3 type 0
[    8.154421] sr 4:0:0:0: Attached scsi generic sg4 type 5
[    8.729016] ip_tables: (C) 2000-2006 Netfilter Core Team
[    8.850599] nf_conntrack version 0.5.0 (7897 buckets, 31588 max)
[    8.939613] ip6_tables: (C) 2000-2006 Netfilter Core Team
[    9.160092] Ebtables v2.0 registered
[    9.203710] Bridge firewalling registered
[    9.586603] IPv6: ADDRCONF(NETDEV_UP): eno16777736: link is not
ready
[    9.587520] e1000: eno16777736 NIC Link is Up 1000 Mbps Full Duplex,
Flow Control: None
[    9.589066] IPv6: ADDRCONF(NETDEV_CHANGE): eno16777736: link becomes
ready
[   10.689365] Rounding down aligned max_sectors from 4294967295 to
4294967288
[ 5158.470480] Adjusting tsc more than 11% (6940512 vs 6913395)
[21766.132181] e1000: eno16777736 NIC Link is Down
[21770.391597] e1000: eno16777736 NIC Link is Up 1000 Mbps Full Duplex,
Flow Control: None
[21780.434547] e1000: eno16777736 NIC Link is Down
```

In the dmesg output, all kernel-related messages are shown. Each message starts with a time indicator that shows at which specific second the event was logged. This time indicator is relative to the start of the kernel, which allows you to see exactly how many seconds have passed between the start of the kernel and a particular event. (Notice that the **journalctl -k / --dmesg** commands show clock time, instead of time that is relative to the start of the kernel.) This time indicator gives a clear indication of what has been happening and at which time it has happened.

Another valuable source of information is the /proc file system. The /proc file system is an interface to the Linux kernel, and it contains files with detailed actual status information on what is happening on your server. Many of the performance-related tools mine the /proc file system for more information.

As an administrator, you will find that some of the files in /proc are very readable and contain actual status information about CPU, memory, mounts, and more. Take a look, for instance, at /proc/meminfo, which gives detailed information about each memory segment and what exactly is happening in these memory segments.

A last useful source of information that should be mentioned here is the **uname** command. This command gives different kinds of information about your operating system. Type, for instance, **uname -a** for an overview of all relevant parameters of **uname -r** to see which kernel version currently is used. This information also shows when using the **hostnamectl status** command.

> **TIP** On some occasions, you might need to know specific information about the RHEL version you are using. To get that information, display the contents of the **/etc/redhat-release** command; it will tell you which Red Hat version you are using and which update level is applied. In Listing 16.3, you can see the results of the **uname -r** command and the contents of the redhat-release file.

Listing 16.3 Getting More Information About the System

```
[root@server1 ~]# uname -r
3.10.0-123.el7.x86_64
[root@server1 ~]# cat /etc/redhat-release
Red Hat Enterprise Linux Server release 7.0 (Maipo)
```

Working with Kernel Modules

In the old days of Linux, kernels had to be compiled to include all drivers that were required to support computer hardware. Other specific functionality needed to be compiled into the kernel as well. Since the release of Linux kernel 2.0 in the mid 1990s, kernels are no longer compiled but modular. A modular kernel consists of a relatively small core kernel and provides driver support through modules that are loaded when required. Modular kernels are very efficient, as only those modules that really are needed are included.

TIP A kernel module implements specific kernel functionality. Kernel modules are used to load drivers that allow proper communications with hardware devices, but are not limited to loading hardware drivers alone. Other kernel features can be loaded as modules as well.

Understanding Hardware Initialization

The loading of drivers is an automated process that roughly goes like this:

1. During boot, the kernel probes available hardware.
2. Upon detection of a hardware component, the **systemd-udevd** process takes care of loading the appropriate driver and making the hardware device available.
3. To decide how the devices are initialized, systemd-udevd reads rules files in /usr/lib/udev/rules.d. These are system provided udev rules files that should not be modified.
4. After processing the system provided udev rules files, systemd-udevd goes to the /etc/udev/rules.d directory to read any custom rules if these are available.
5. As a result, required kernel modules are loaded automatically and status about the kernel modules and associated hardware is written to the sysfs file system which is mounted on the /sys directory.

The systemd-udevd process is not a one-time only process; it continuously monitors plugging and unplugging of new hardware devices. To get an impression of how this works, as root you can type the command **udevadm monitor**. This is all events that are processed while activating new hardware devices. Use Ctrl+C to close the udevadm monitor output.

Listing 16.4 shows output of the **udevadm monitor** command. In this command, you can see how features that are offered by the hardware are discovered automatically by the kernel and udev working together. Each phase of the hardware probing is concluded by the creation of a file in the /sys file system. Once the hardware has been fully initialized, you can also see that some kernel modules are loaded.

NOTE Although useful to know, hardware initialization is not included in the current RHCSA or RHCE objectives.

Listing 16.4 Output of the **udevadm monitor** Command

```
[root@server2 ~]# udevadm monitor
monitor will print the received events for:
UDEV - the event which udev sends out after rule processing
KERNEL - the kernel uevent

KERNEL[132406.831270] add      /devices/pci0000:00/0000:00:11.0/0000:02
:04.0/usb1/1-1 (usb)
KERNEL[132406.974110] add      /devices/pci0000:00/0000:00:11.0/0000:02
:04.0/usb1/1-1/1-1:1.0 (usb)
UDEV  [132406.988182] add      /devices/pci0000:00/0000:00:11.0/0000:02
:04.0/usb1/1-1 (usb)
KERNEL[132406.999249] add      /module/usb_storage (module)
UDEV  [132407.001203] add      /module/usb_storage (module)
KERNEL[132407.002559] add      /devices/pci0000:00/0000:00:11.0/0000:02
:04.0/usb1/1-1/1-1:1.0/host33 (scsi)
UDEV  [132407.002575] add      /devices/pci0000:00/0000:00:11.0/0000:02
:04.0/usb1/1-1/1-1:1.0 (usb)
KERNEL[132407.002583] add      /devices/pci0000:00/0000:00:11.0/0000:02
:04.0/usb1/1-1/1-1:1.0/host33/scsi_host/host33 (scsi_host)
KERNEL[132407.002590] add      /bus/usb/drivers/usb-storage (drivers)
UDEV  [132407.004479] add      /bus/usb/drivers/usb-storage (drivers)
UDEV  [132407.005798] add      /devices/pci0000:00/0000:00:11.0/0000:02
:04.0/usb1/1-1/1-1:1.0/host33 (scsi)
UDEV  [132407.007385] add      /devices/pci0000:00/0000:00:11.0/0000:02
:04.0/usb1/1-1/1-1:1.0/host33/scsi_host/host33 (scsi_host)
KERNEL[132408.008331] add      /devices/pci0000:00/0000:00:11.0/0000:02
:04.0/usb1/1-1/1-1:1.0/host33/target33:0:0 (scsi)
KERNEL[132408.008355] add      /devices/pci0000:00/0000:00:11.0/0000:02
:04.0/usb1/1-1/1-1:1.0/host33/target33:0:0/33:0:0:0 (scsi)
KERNEL[132408.008363] add      /devices/pci0000:00/0000:00:11.0/0000:02
:04.0/usb1/1-1/1-1:1.0/host33/target33:0:0/33:0:0:0/scsi_disk/33:0:0:0
(scsi_disk)
KERNEL[132408.008370] add      /devices/pci0000:00/0000:00:11.0/
0000:02:04.0/usb1/1-1/1-1:1.0/host33/target33:0:0/33:0:0:0/scsi_
device/33:0:0:0 (scsi_device)
KERNEL[132408.008921] add      /devices/pci0000:00/0000:00:11.0/0000:02
:04.0/usb1/1-1/1-1:1.0/host33/target33:0:0/33:0:0:0/bsg/33:0:0:0 (bsg)
UDEV  [132408.009408] add      /devices/pci0000:00/0000:00:11.0/0000:02
```

```
:04.0/usb1/1-1/1-1:1.0/host33/target33:0:0 (scsi)
UDEV  [132408.010073] add      /devices/pci0000:00/0000:00:11.0/0000:02
:04.0/usb1/1-1/1-1:1.0/host33/target33:0:0/33:0:0:0 (scsi)
UDEV  [132408.010937] add      /devices/pci0000:00/0000:00:11.0/
0000:02:04.0/usb1/1-1/1-1:1.0/host33/target33:0:0/33:0:0:0/scsi_
device/33:0:0:0 (scsi_device)
UDEV  [132408.011628] add      /devices/pci0000:00/0000:00:11.0/0000:02
:04.0/usb1/1-1/1-1:1.0/host33/target33:0:0/33:0:0:0/scsi_disk/33:0:0:0
(scsi_disk)
UDEV  [132408.013592] add      /devices/pci0000:00/0000:00:11.0/0000:02
:04.0/usb1/1-1/1-1:1.0/host33/target33:0:0/33:0:0:0/bsg/33:0:0:0 (bsg)
KERNEL[132408.636583] add      /devices/virtual/bdi/8:16 (bdi)
UDEV  [132408.637010] add      /devices/virtual/bdi/8:16 (bdi)
KERNEL[132408.648521] add      /devices/pci0000:00/0000:00:11.0/0000:02
:04.0/usb1/1-1/1-1:1.0/host33/target33:0:0/33:0:0:0/block/sdb (block)
KERNEL[132408.648540] add      /devices/pci0000:00/0000:00:11.0/0000:
02:04.0/usb1/1-1/1-1:1.0/host33/target33:0:0/33:0:0:0/block/sdb/sdb1
(block)
UDEV  [132409.000130] add      /devices/pci0000:00/0000:00:11.0/0000:02
:04.0/usb1/1-1/1-1:1.0/host33/target33:0:0/33:0:0:0/block/sdb (block)
UDEV  [132409.199109] add      /devices/pci0000:00/0000:00:11.0/0000:
02:04.0/usb1/1-1/1-1:1.0/host33/target33:0:0/33:0:0:0/block/sdb/sdb1
(block)
KERNEL[132409.381930] add      /module/fat (module)
KERNEL[132409.381951] add      /kernel/slab/fat_cache (slab)
KERNEL[132409.381958] add      /kernel/slab/fat_inode_cache (slab)
KERNEL[132409.381964] add      /module/vfat (module)
UDEV  [132409.385090] add      /module/fat (module)
UDEV  [132409.385107] add      /kernel/slab/fat_cache (slab)
UDEV  [132409.385113] add      /kernel/slab/fat_inode_cache (slab)
UDEV  [132409.386110] add      /module/vfat (module)
```

Managing Kernel Modules

Linux kernel modules normally are loaded automatically for the devices that need them, but you will sometimes have to load the appropriate kernel modules manually. A few commands are used for manual management of kernel modules. Table 16.2 provides an overview.

An alternative method of loading kernel modules is by doing this through the /etc/modules-load.d directory. In this directory, you can create files to load modules automatically that are not loaded by the udev method already.

Table 16.2 Linux Kernel Module Management Overview

Key Topic

Command	Use
lsmod	Lists currently loaded kernel modules
modinfo	Displays information about kernel modules
modprobe	Loads kernel modules, including all of their dependencies
modprobe -r	Unloads kernel modules, considering kernel module dependencies

The first command to use when working with kernel modules is **lsmod**. This command lists all kernel modules that currently are used, including the modules by which this specific module is used. Listing 16.5 shows the output of the first 10 lines of the **lsmod** command.

Listing 16.5 Listing Loaded Modules with **lsmod**

```
[root@server1 udev]# lsmod  | head
Module                    Size  Used by
ipt_MASQUERADE           12880  3
xt_CHECKSUM              12549  1
ip6t_rpfilter            12546  1
target_core_pscsi        18810  0
target_core_file         18030  0
target_core_iblock       18177  0
iscsi_target_mod        278732  1
target_core_mod         299412  5 target_core_iblock,target_core_
pscsi,iscsi_target_mod,target_core_file
ip6t_REJECT              12939  2
```

TIP Many Linux commands show their output in different columns, and it is not always clear which column is used to show which kind of information. Most of these commands have a header line on the first line of command output. So, if on any command you are not sure what you are seeing, pipe the output of the command through head to see whether there is a header file, or pipe the command output to less, which allows you to page up to the first line of command output easily.

If you want to have more information about a specific kernel module, you can use the **modinfo** command. This gives complete information about the specific kernel modules, including two interesting sections: the alias and the parms. A module alias is another name that can also be used to address the module. The parms lines refer to parameters that can be set while loading the module. (In the section "Managing Kernel Module Parameters" later in this chapter, you learn how to work with kernel module parameters.) Listing 16.6 shows partial output of the **modinfo e1000** command.

Listing 16.6 Showing Module Information with **modinfo**

```
[root@server1 udev]# modinfo e1000
filename:        /lib/modules/3.10.0-123.el7.x86_64/kernel/drivers/net/
ethernet/intel/e1000/e1000.ko
version:         7.3.21-k8-NAPI
license:         GPL
description:     Intel(R) PRO/1000 Network Driver
author:          Intel Corporation, <linux.nics@intel.com>
srcversion:      BB8DA267AB1A33D60457C03
alias:           pci:v00008086d00002E6Esv*sd*bc*sc*i*
...
depends:
intree:    Y
vermagic: 3.10.0-123.el7.x86_64 SMP mod_unload modversions
signer:   CentOS Linux kernel signing key
sig_key: BC:83:D0:FE:70:C6:2F:AB:1C:58:B4:EB:AA:95:E3:93:61:28:FC:F4
sig_hashalgo:    sha256
parm:      TxDescriptors:Number of transmit descriptors (array of int)
parm:      RxDescriptors:Number of receive descriptors (array of int)
parm:      Speed:Speed setting (array of int)
parm:      Duplex:Duplex setting (array of int)
parm:      AutoNeg:Advertised auto-negotiation setting (array of int)
parm:      FlowControl:Flow Control setting (array of int)
parm:      XsumRX:Disable or enable Receive Checksum offload (array of
int)
parm:      TxIntDelay:Transmit Interrupt Delay (array of int)
parm:      TxAbsIntDelay:Transmit Absolute Interrupt Delay (array of int)
parm:      RxIntDelay:Receive Interrupt Delay (array of int)
parm:      RxAbsIntDelay:Receive Absolute Interrupt Delay (array of int)
```

```
parm:    InterruptThrottleRate:Interrupt Throttling Rate (array of int)
parm:    SmartPowerDownEnable:Enable PHY smart power down (array of int)
parm:    copybreak:Maximum size of packet that is copied to a new buffer
on receive (uint)
parm:    debug:Debug level (0=none,...,16=all) (int)
```

To manually load and unload modules, you can use the **modprobe** and **modprobe -r** commands. On earlier Linux versions, you may have used the **insmod** and **rmmod** commands. These should be used no longer because they do not consider kernel module dependencies. In Exercise 16.1, you learn how to manage kernel modules using these commands.

Exercise 16.1 Managing Kernel Modules from the Command Line

In this exercise, you work with the basic commands that are used for managing Linux kernel modules from the command line.

1. Open a root shell and type **lsmod | head**. This shows all kernel modules currently loaded.
2. Type **modprobe ext4** to load the ext4 kernel module. Verify that it is loaded, using the **lsmod** command again.
3. Type **modinfo ext4** to get information about the ext4 kernel module. Notice that it does not have any parameters.
4. Type **modprobe -r ext4** to unload the ext4 kernel module again.
5. Type **modprobe -r xfs** to try to unload the xfs kernel module. Notice that you get an error message as the kernel module currently is in use.

Checking Driver Availability for Hardware Devices

On modern Linux servers, many hardware devices are supported. On occasion, you might find that some devices are not supported properly, though. The best way to find out whether this is the case for your hardware is by using the **lspci** command. If used without arguments, it shows all hardware devices that have been detected on the PCI bus. A very useful argument is **-k**, which lists all kernel modules that are used for the PCI devices that were detected. Listing 16.7 shows sample output of the **lspci -k** command.

Listing 16.7 Checking Kernel Module Availability

```
[root@server1 ~]# lspci -k
00:00.0 Host bridge: Intel Corporation 440BX/ZX/DX - 82443BX/ZX/DX Host
bridge (rev 01)
        Subsystem: VMware Virtual Machine Chipset
        Kernel driver in use: agpgart-intel
00:01.0 PCI bridge: Intel Corporation 440BX/ZX/DX - 82443BX/ZX/DX AGP
bridge (rev 01)
00:07.0 ISA bridge: Intel Corporation 82371AB/EB/MB PIIX4 ISA (rev 08)
        Subsystem: VMware Virtual Machine Chipset
00:07.1 IDE interface: Intel Corporation 82371AB/EB/MB PIIX4 IDE (rev
01)
        Subsystem: VMware Virtual Machine Chipset
        Kernel driver in use: ata_piix
00:07.3 Bridge: Intel Corporation 82371AB/EB/MB PIIX4 ACPI (rev 08)
        Subsystem: VMware Virtual Machine Chipset
00:07.7 System peripheral: VMware Virtual Machine Communication
Interface (rev 10)
        Subsystem: VMware Virtual Machine Communication Interface
        Kernel driver in use: vmw_vmci
00:0f.0 VGA compatible controller: VMware SVGA II Adapter
        Subsystem: VMware SVGA II Adapter
        Kernel driver in use: vmwgfx
00:10.0 SCSI storage controller: LSI Logic / Symbios Logic 53c1030
PCI-X Fusion-MPT Dual Ultra320 SCSI (rev 01)
        Subsystem: VMware LSI Logic Parallel SCSI Controller
        Kernel driver in use: mptspi
00:11.0 PCI bridge: VMware PCI bridge (rev 02)
...
02:00.0 USB controller: VMware USB1.1 UHCI Controller
        Subsystem: VMware Device 1976
        Kernel driver in use: uhci_hcd
02:01.0 Ethernet controller: Intel Corporation 82545EM Gigabit Ethernet
Controller (Copper) (rev 01)
        Subsystem: VMware PRO/1000 MT Single Port Adapter
        Kernel driver in use: e1000
02:02.0 Multimedia audio controller: Ensoniq ES1371 / Creative Labs
CT2518 [AudioPCI-97] (rev 02)
        Subsystem: Ensoniq AudioPCI 64V/128 / Creative Sound Blaster
CT4810
        Kernel driver in use: snd_ens1371
02:03.0 USB controller: VMware USB2 EHCI Controller
```

```
        Subsystem: VMware USB2 EHCI Controller
        Kernel driver in use: ehci-pci
02:05.0 SATA controller: VMware SATA AHCI controller
        Subsystem: VMware SATA AHCI controller
        Kernel driver in use: ahci
```

If you discover that PCI devices were found for which no kernel modules could be loaded, you are probably dealing with a device that is not supported. You can try to find a closed source kernel module, but you should realize that that might endanger the stability of your kernel. A much better approach is to check with your hardware vendor that Linux is fully supported before you purchase specific hardware.

Managing Kernel Module Parameters

You might sometimes want to load kernel modules with specific parameters. If this is the case, you first need to find out which parameter you want to use. If you have found the parameter you want to use, you can load it manually, specifying the name of the parameter followed by the value that you want to assign. To make this an automated procedure, you can create a file in the /etc/modprobe.d directory, where the module is loaded including the parameter you want to be loaded. In Exercise 16.2 you see how to do this using the cdrom kernel module.

Exercise 16.2 Loading Kernel Modules with Parameters

In this exercise, you learn how to work with kernel module parameters.

1. Type **lsmod | grep cdrom**. If you have used the optical drive in your computer, this module should be loaded, and it should also indicate that it is used by the sr_mod module.
2. Type **modprobe -r cdrom**. This will not work because the module is in use by the sr_mod module.
3. Type **modprobe -r sr_mod; modprobe -r cdrom**. This will unload both modules.
4. Type **modinfo cdrom**. This will show information about the cdrom module including the parameters that it supports. One of these is the debug parameter, that supports a Boolean as its value.
5. Now use the command **modprobe cdrom debug=1**. This will load the cdrom module with the debug parameter set to on.

6. Type **dmesg**. For some kernel module, load information is written to the kernel ring buffer which can be displayed using the **dmesg** command. Unfortunately this is not the case for the cdrom kernel module.
7. Create a file with the name /etc/modprobe.d/cdrom and give it the following contents:

```
options cdrom debug=1
```

This will enable the parameter every time the cdrom kernel module will be loaded.

Upgrading the Linux Kernel

From time to time, you need to upgrade the Linux kernel. When you upgrade the Linux kernel, a new version of the kernel is installed and used as the default kernel. The old version of the kernel file will still be available, though. This ensures that your computer can still boot if in the new kernel nonsupported functionality is included. To install a new version of the kernel, you can use the command **yum upgrade kernel**. The **yum install kernel** command also works. Both commands install the new kernel besides the old kernel.

The kernel files for the last four kernels that you have installed on your server will be kept in the /boot directory. The GRUB 2 boot loader automatically picks up all kernels that it finds in this directory.

Summary

In this chapter, you learned how to work with the Linux kernel. You learned that the Linux kernel is modular, and how working with kernel modules is important. You also learned how to manage kernel modules, and how kernel modules are managed automatically while working with new hardware.

Exam Preparation Tasks

Review All Key Topics

Review the most important topics in the chapter, noted with the Key Topic icon in the outer margin of the page. Table 16.3 lists a reference of these key topics and the page numbers on which each is found.

Table 16.3 Key Topics for Chapter 16

Key Topic Element	Description	Page
List	Overview of kernel-related tools	374
Table 16.2	Kernel module management overview	379

Define Key Terms

Define the following key terms from this chapter and check your answers in the glossary:

kernel, module, dmesg, udev, sysfs, proc, tainted kernel

Review Questions

1. Which command shows the current version of the kernel that is used on your computer?
2. Where do you find current version information about your RHEL 7 installation?
3. Which command shows a list of kernel modules that currently are loaded?
4. Which command enables you to discover kernel module parameters?
5. How do you unload a kernel module?
6. What can you do if you get an error message while trying to unload a kernel module?
7. How do you find which kernel module parameters are supported?
8. Where do you specify kernel module parameters that should be used persistently?
9. Assuming that the cdrom module has a parameter **"debug"**, which must be set to 1 to enable debug mode, which line would you include in the file that will automatically load that module?
10. How do you install a new version of the kernel?

End-of-Chapter Labs

In the end-of-chapter labs, you install a new version of the kernel and work with kernel modules.

Lab 16.1

1. Find out whether a new version of the kernel is available. If so, install it and reboot your computer so that it is used.
2. Use the appropriate command to show recent events that have been logged by the kernel.
3. Locate the kernel module that is used by your network card. Find out whether it has options. Try loading one of these kernel module options manually; if that succeeds, take the required measures to load this option persistently.

The following topics are covered in this chapter:

- Configuring a Basic Apache Server
- Understanding Apache Configuration files
- Creating Apache Virtual Hosts

The following RHCSA exam objectives are covered in this chapter:

- No RHCSA exam objectives relate directly to Apache

CHAPTER 17

Configuring a Basic Apache Server

This is the only chapter in this book that discusses a subject that is not even listed in the RHCSA objectives. However, for a Red Hat server administrator it is important to know how to deal with the Apache web server. In following chapters, you learn how to configure SELinux and installation servers. These are topics that are difficult to understand without knowing how to deal with the Apache web service. Also, in Chapter 18, "Managing and Understanding the Boot Procedure," you learn how to work with services in an RHEL 7 environment. Knowing how to configure a common service like the Apache web service will surely help doing so. That is why this chapter explains Apache web server basics. For more in-depth information about the Apache web service, you can read Chapter 33, "Managing Advanced Apache Services."

"Do I Know This Already?" Quiz

The "Do I Know This Already?" quiz allows you to assess whether you should read this entire chapter thoroughly or jump to the "Exam Preparation Tasks" section. If you are in doubt about your answers to these questions or your own assessment of your knowledge of the topics, read the entire chapter. Table 17.1 lists the major headings in this chapter and their corresponding "Do I Know This Already?" quiz questions. You can find the answers in Appendix A, "Answers to the 'Do I Know This Already?' Quizzes and 'Review Questions.'"

Table 17.1 "Do I Know This Already?" Section-to-Question Mapping

Foundation Topics Section	Questions
Configuring a Basic Apache Server	1–4
Understanding Apache Configuration files	5–7
Creating Apache Virtual Hosts	8–10

1. Which command installs the software packages that are needed to configure an Apache web server?
   a. **yum install httpd**
   b. **yum install web-server**
   c. **yum install apache**
   d. **yum install apache2**
2. What is the name of the main Apache configuration file?
   a. /etc/httpd/conf/httpd.conf
   b. /etc/httpd/httpd.conf
   c. /etc/apache2/apache.conf
   d. /etc/httpd/default-server.conf
3. Which parameter in the Apache configuration file is used to specify where Apache will serve its documents from?
   a. **ServerRoot**
   b. **ServerDocuments**
   c. **DocumentRoot**
   d. **DocumentIndex**
4. Which parameter in the main Apache configuration file defines the location where the Apache process looks for its configuration files?
   a. **ServerRoot**
   b. **ServerDocuments**
   c. **DocumentRoot**
   d. **DocumentIndex**
5. Which directory contains the main Apache configuration file?
   a. /etc/httpd
   b. /etc/htttpd/conf
   c. /etc/httpd/conf.d
   d. /etc/httpd/conf.modules.d

6. Which directory contains the configuration files for the different Apache modules?
    a. /etc/httpd
    b. /etc/htttpd/conf
    c. /etc/httpd/conf.d
    d. /etc/httpd/conf.modules.d

7. Which directory is used to drop configuration files that are installed from RPMs?
    a. /etc/httpd
    b. /etc/htttpd/conf
    c. /etc/httpd/conf.d
    d. /etc/httpd/conf.modules.d

8. Which virtual host type allows you to run multiple virtual hosts on the same IP address?
    a. NameBased
    b. IPBased
    c. ConfigurationBased
    d. Default

9. Which line is used to start the definition of a virtual host that listens on port 80 of all IP addresses on the current server?
    a. **<VirtualHost *:80>**
    b. **<VirtualHost *>**
    c. **<NameHost *:80**
    d. **<NameHost *>**

10. Which of the following statements about virtual hosts is not true?
    a. When virtual hosts are offered through an httpd process, the default configuration no longer works.
    b. The names of virtual hosts must be resolvable through /etc/hosts or DNS.
    c. To use virtual hosts, the mod_virt package must be installed.
    d. Virtual host configurations can be specified in httpd.conf.

Foundation Topics

Configuring a Basic Apache Server

Configuring a basic Apache server is not hard to do. It consists of a few easy steps:

1. Install the required software.
2. Identify the main configuration file.
3. Create some web server content.

Installing the Required Software

The Apache server is provided through some different software packages. The basic package is httpd; this package contains everything that is needed for an operational but basic web server. There are some additional packages, as well. For a complete overview, you can use the **yum search http** command and use **yum install httpd** to install the base package.

Notice that the **yum search http** command gives a lot of packages. This is because the Apache web server is modular and the different modules are provided through additional yum packages.

Instead of using the individual software packages, you can also use yum groups. The **yum groups list** command gives an overview of all yum groups that are available, and the Basic Web Server yum group provides all you need to install the Apache web server and its core requirements. Use **yum groups install "Basic Web Server"** to install it.

Identifying the Main Configuration File

The configuration of the Apache web server goes through different configuration files. The section "Understanding Apache Configuration Files" later in this chapter provides an overview of the way these files are organized. The main Apache configuration file is /etc/httpd/conf/httpd.conf. In this section, many parameters are specified. The most important parameter to understand for setting up a basic web server is the **DocumentRoot** parameter. This parameter specifies the default location where the Apache web server looks for its contents.

Another important configuration parameter is the **ServerRoot**. This defines the default directory where Apache will look for its configuration files. By default, the /etc/httpd directory is used for this purpose, but alternative directories can be used as well. You notice that in the httpd.cond many other configuration files are referred to. The use of additional configuration files makes it easy for applications to install snap-in files that will be included by the Apache server from RPM packages. The names of these configuration files are all relative to the **ServerRoot** /etc/httpd.

Listing 17.1 shows a part of the contents of the httpd.conf configuration file.

Listing 17.1 Partial Contents of the /etc/httpd/conf/httpd.conf Configuration File

```
[root@server1 ~]# cat /etc/httpd/conf/httpd.conf | grep -v '#'

ServerRoot "/etc/httpd"
Listen 80

Include conf.modules.d/*.conf

User apache
Group apache

ServerAdmin root@localhost

<Directory />
    AllowOverride none
    Require all denied
</Directory>

DocumentRoot "/web"

<Directory "/var/www">
    AllowOverride None
    Require all granted
</Directory>

<Directory "/web">
    Options Indexes FollowSymLinks
    AllowOverride None
    Require all granted
</Directory>

<IfModule dir_module>
    DirectoryIndex index.html
</IfModule>
```

```
<Files ".ht*">
    Require all denied
</Files>

ErrorLog "logs/error_log"

LogLevel warn

<IfModule log_config_module>
    LogFormat "%h %l %u %t \"%r\" %>s %b \"%{Referer}i\" \"%{User-
      Agent}i\"" combined
    LogFormat "%h %l %u %t \"%r\" %>s %b" common
    <IfModule logio_module>
      LogFormat "%h %l %u %t \"%r\" %>s %b \"%{Referer}i\" \"%{User-
        Agent}i\" %I %O" combinedio
    </IfModule>
    CustomLog "logs/access_log" combined
</IfModule>

<IfModule alias_module>
    ScriptAlias /cgi-bin/ "/var/www/cgi-bin/"
</IfModule>

<Directory "/var/www/cgi-bin">
    AllowOverride None
    Options None
    Require all granted
</Directory>

<IfModule mime_module>
    TypesConfig /etc/mime.types
    AddType application/x-compress .Z
    AddType application/x-gzip .gz .tgz
    AddType text/html .shtml
    AddOutputFilter INCLUDES .shtml
</IfModule>

AddDefaultCharset UTF-8

<IfModule mime_magic_module>
    MIMEMagicFile conf/magic
```

```
</IfModule>

EnableSendfile on
IncludeOptional conf.d/*.conf
```

Creating Web Server Content

After identifying the web server DocumentRoot, you know all you need to know to configure a basic web server. The Apache web server by default looks for a file with the name index.html and will present the contents of that document to clients using a browser to access the web server. It suffices to configure this file with very basic contents; just a line like "Welcome to my web server" will do.

To test the web server, you can launch a browser. The Firefox browser is installed by default on all graphical installations of RHEL 7. If your server does not run a graphical interface, use **yum install elinks** to install the text-based elinks browser. This browser does not allow you to load complicated web pages, but it does allow you to verify the working of the web server. Figure 17.1 shows what the elinks interface looks like. In Exercise 17.1, you learn how to set up a basic web server.

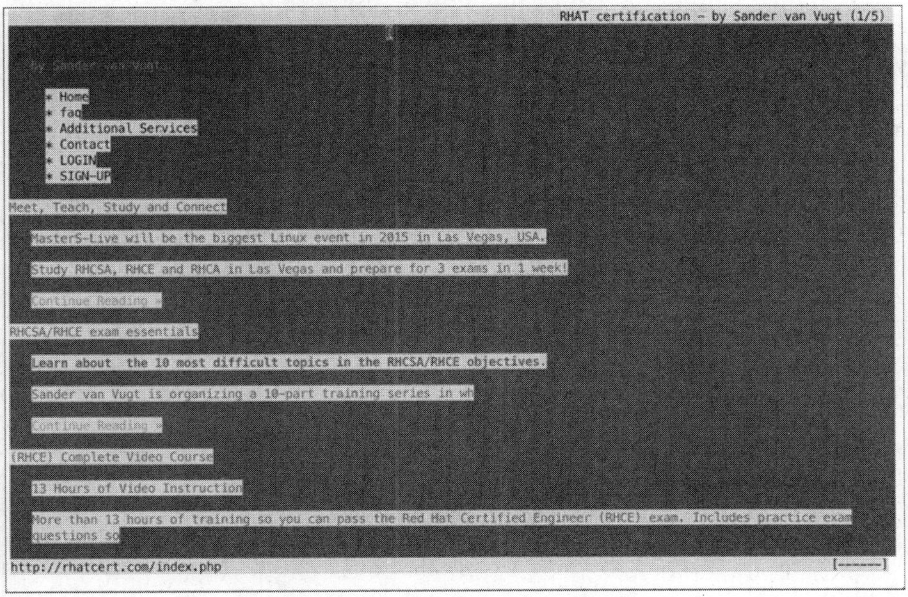

Figure 17.1 Testing web pages from a text-only console using elinks.

Exercise 17.1 Setting Up a Basic Web Server

In this exercise, you learn how to set up a basic Apache web server. Nothing fancy, just enough to get you going and test web server functionality.

1. Type **yum groups install "Basic Web Server"**. This installs the httpd package, and some of the most commonly used additional packages as well.
2. Open the main Apache configuration file with an editor, and look up the line that starts with DocumentRoot. This identifies the location where the Apache server will look for the contents it will service. Confirm that it is set to /var/www/html.
3. In the directory /var/www/html, create a file with the name index.html. In this file, type **"Welcome to my web server"**.
4. To start and enable the web server, type **systemctl start httpd; systemctl enable httpd**. This starts the web server and makes sure that it starts automatically after restarting the server. Use **systemctl status httpd** to check that the web server is up and running. In Listing 17.2 you can see what the result of this command should look like.
5. Type **yum install elinks** to install the elinks text-based browser. Type **elinks http://localhost** to connect to the web server and verify it is working.

Listing 17.2 Verifying the Availability of the Apache Web Server with **systemctl status**

```
[root@server2 ~]# systemctl status httpd
httpd.service - The Apache HTTP Server
   Loaded: loaded (/usr/lib/systemd/system/httpd.service; disabled)
   Active: active (running) since Sat 2015-05-16 04:27:49 PDT; 1s ago
 Main PID: 42997 (httpd)
   Status: "Processing requests..."
   CGroup: /system.slice/httpd.service
           ├─42997 /usr/sbin/httpd -DFOREGROUND
           ├─42998 /usr/sbin/httpd -DFOREGROUND
           ├─42999 /usr/sbin/httpd -DFOREGROUND
           ├─43000 /usr/sbin/httpd -DFOREGROUND
           ├─43001 /usr/sbin/httpd -DFOREGROUND
           └─43002 /usr/sbin/httpd -DFOREGROUND

May 16 04:27:49 server2.example.com systemd[1]: Started The Apache HTTP
Server.
```

Understanding Apache Configuration Files

A default installation of the Apache web server creates a relatively complex configuration tree in the /etc/httpd directory. Listing 17.3 shows the default contents of this directory. Notice that the contents of this directory may differ on your server if additional software has been installed. Apache is modular, and upon installation of additional Apache modules, different configuration files might be installed here.

Listing 17.3 Default Contents of the /etc/httpd Directory

```
[root@server1 httpd]# \ls -l
total 8
drwxr-xr-x. 2 root root   35 Feb 23 03:12 conf
drwxr-xr-x. 2 root root 4096 Feb 25 12:41 conf.d
drwxr-xr-x. 2 root root 4096 Feb 25 12:41 conf.modules.d
lrwxrwxrwx. 1 root root   19 Feb 17 13:26 logs -> ../../var/log/httpd
lrwxrwxrwx. 1 root root   29 Feb 17 13:26 modules -> ../../usr/lib64/
httpd/modules
lrwxrwxrwx. 1 root root   10 Feb 17 13:26 run -> /run/httpd
```

The first thing you notice is the presence of three symbolic links to logs, modules, and a run directory. These are created to allow Apache to be started in a chroot environment.

Key Topic

A chroot environment provides a fake root directory. This is a directory in the file system that is presented as the root directory for the process that is running in the chroot environment. This is done for security reasons: Processes that are running in a chroot environment can access files in that chroot environment only, which decreases the risk of security incidents to happen when intruders manage to get a login shell using the web server identity and try walking through the file system to do unauthorized things.

The main configuration files for the Apache web server is in the /etc/httpd/conf directory. To start, there is the httpd.conf file, which contains the most important configuration parameters. Apart from that, there is a file with the name magic. This file is used by browser to interpret how the contents of the web server should be interpreted. It makes sure that the web server content is shown correctly in different browsers.

The /etc/httpd/conf.d directory contains files that are included in the Apache configuration. This is done by the line **Include conf.modules.d/*.conf** in the httpd.conf file. This directory can be used by RPMs that include Apache snap-in files. As is the case for the ServerRoot, this approach makes it possible to add configuration files that define the different web pages without changing the contents of the /etc/httpd/conf/httpd.conf file.

The last configuration directory is /etc/httpd/conf.modules.d. Apache is a modular web server. Therefore, the functionality of the Apache web server can easily be extended by adding additional modules that enable many different features. If modules are used, they can use their own module specific configuration files, which will be dropped in the /etc/httpd/conf.modules.d directory. Again, the purpose of this approach is to keep the configuration in /etc/httpd/conf.d/httpd.conf as clean as possible and to make sure that module specific configuration is not overwritten if the Apache generic configuration is updated.

Creating Apache Virtual Hosts

Many companies host more than one website. Fortunately, it is not necessary to install a new Apache server for every website that you want to run. Apache can be configured to work with virtual hosts. A virtual host is a distinguished Apache configuration file that is created for a unique hostname. When working with virtual hosts, the procedure to access the host is roughly like the following:

1. The client starts a session to a specific virtual host, normally by starting a browser and entering the URL to the website the client wants to use.
2. DNS helps resolving the IP address of the virtual host, which is the IP address of the Apache server that can host different virtual hosts.
3. The Apache process receives requests for all the virtual hosts it is hosting.
4. The Apache process reads the HTTP header to analyze which virtual host this request needs to be forwarded to.
5. Apache reads the specific virtual host configuration file to find which document root is used by this specific virtual host.
6. The request is forwarded to the appropriate contents file in that specific document root.

When working with virtual hosts, there are a few things to be aware of:

Key Topic

- If your Apache server is configured for virtual hosts, all servers it is hosting should be handled by virtual hosts. To create a catch all entry for all HTTP requests that are directed to this host but that do not have a specific virtual host file, you can create a virtual host for _default_:80.
- Name-based virtual hosting is the most common solution. In this solution, virtual hosts are using different names but the same IP address.

- IP-based virtual hosts are less common, but are required if the name of a web server must be resolved to a unique IP address. IP-based virtual hosts do require several IP addresses on the same machine and are common in configuration where the Apache server uses TLS to secure connections.

TIP Configuring virtual hosts is not an RHCSA objective, but it is useful to know how to configure them anyway. If you are preparing for the RHCE exam, you absolutely do need to know how to configure virtual hosts. Exercise 17.2 walks you through the procedure. If you are interested in RHCSA exam-related contents only, you are welcome to skip this exercise.

Exercise 17.2 Installing Apache Virtual Hosts

In this exercise, you create two virtual hosts. To help you setting up virtual hosts, you first set up name resolution, after which you create the virtual hosts configuration as well. Because SELinux has not been discussed yet, you temporarily switch off SELinux.

NOTE I later tell you that you should never switch off SELinux. For once, I make an exception to this important security rule. To focus on what needs to be done on the Apache web server, it is easier to focus just on Apache and not to configure SELinux as well.

1. On both server1 and server2, open the file /etc/hosts with an editor and add two lines that make it possible to resolve the names of the virtual host you are going to create to the IP address of the virtual machine:

```
192.168.122.210    server1.example.com        server1
192.168.122.220    server2.example.com        server2
192.168.122.210    account.example.com        account
12.168.122.210     sales.example.com          sales
```

2. On server1, open a root shell and add the following to the /etc/httpd/conf/httpd.conf file. (You can leave all other settings as they are.)

```
<Directory/www/docs>
          Required all granted
          AllowOverride None
</Directory>
```

3. On server1, open a root shell and create a configuration file with the name **account.example.com.conf** in the directory /etc/httpd/conf.d. Give this file the following content:

```
<VirtualHost *:80>
        ServerAdmin webmaster@account.example.com
        DocumentRoot /www/docs/account.example.com
        ServerName account.example.com
        ErrorLog logs/account/example.com-error_log
        CustomLog logs/account.example.com-access_log common
</VirtualHost>
```

4. Close the configuration file and from the root shell use **mkdir -p /www/docs/account.example.com**.
5. Create a file with the name index.html in the account document root, and make sure its contents read "Welcome to account."
6. Temporarily switch off SELinux using **setenforce 0**.
7. Use **systemctl restart httpd** to restart the Apache web server.
8. Use elinks http://account.example.com. You should now see the account welcome page. (You may have to install elinks, using **yum install -y elinks**.)
9. Back on the root shell, copy the /etc/httpd/conf.d/account.example.com.conf file to a file with the name /etc/httpd/conf.d/sales.example.com.conf.
10. Open the sales.example.com.conf file in vi, and use the vi command **:%s/account/sales/g**. This should replace all instances of account with the text sales.
11. Create the /www/docs/sales.example.com document root, and create a file index.html in it, containing the text "Welcome to the sales server."
12. Restart httpd and verify that the account and the sales servers are both accessible.

Summary

In this chapter, you learned about Apache basics. The information in this chapter helps you configure a basic Apache web server, which helps testing advanced topics like firewall configuration or SELinux configuration that are covered in later chapters in this book.

Exam Preparation Tasks

Review All Key Topics

Review the most important topics in the chapter, noted with the Key Topic icon in the outer margin of the page. Table 17.2 lists a reference of these key topics and the page numbers on which each is found.

Table 17.2 Key Topics for Chapter 17

Key Topic Element	Description	Page
Paragraph	chroot explanation	397
List	Virtual host explanation	398

Define Key Terms

Define the following key terms from this chapter and check your answers in the glossary:

DocumentRoot, virtual hosts, chroot

Review Questions

1. Which yum group contains many useful Apache packages?
2. How do you enable the httpd service to be started automatically when booting?
3. What is the default location where RPMs can drop plug-in configuration files that should be considered by the Apache server?
4. Which command enables you to test a web server from a server that does not offer a graphical interface?
5. What is the name of the default Apache configuration file?
6. Which directory is used as the default Apache document root?
7. Which file is the Apache process looking for by default in the document root?
8. Which command enables you to see whether the Apache web server is currently running?

9. Which location is preferably used for storing virtual host configuration files?
10. Names of configuration files and directories in the main Apache configuration file are relative to the ServerRoot. To which directory is the ServerRoot set by default?

End-of-Chapter Labs

In this end-of-chapter lab, you install and configure a basic Apache server.

Lab 17.1

1. Install the required packages that allow you to run a basic web server. Make sure that the web server process is started automatically when your server reboots. Do *not* use any virtual server.
2. Make sure the web server presents a default page showing "Welcome to my web server."
3. Use elinks to test the working of your web server.
4. Use **yum install httpd-manual** to install the Apache documentation.
5. Use a browser to test access to the /manual web page on your server.

The following topics are covered in this chapter:

- Working with Systemd
- Working with GRUB 2

The following RHCSA exam objectives are covered in this chapter:

- Start and stop services and configure services to start automatically at boot
- Configure systems to boot into a specific target automatically
- Modify the system bootloader

Managing and Understanding the Boot Procedure

In this chapter, you learn how the boot procedure on Red Hat Enterprise Linux is organized. We first go through a section about systemd, the overall service that takes care of starting everything on your server. In this section, you also learn how systemd targets are used to group systemd units and come to a final operational environment.

The second part of this chapter discusses GRUB2 and how to apply changes to the GRUB 2 boot loader. Troubleshooting is not a topic in this chapter; it is covered in Chapter 19, "Troubleshooting the Boot Procedure."

"Do I Know This Already?" Quiz

The "Do I Know This Already?" quiz allows you to assess whether you should read this entire chapter thoroughly or jump to the "Exam Preparation Tasks" section. If you are in doubt about your answers to these questions or your own assessment of your knowledge of the topics, read the entire chapter. Table 18.1 lists the major headings in this chapter and their corresponding "Do I Know This Already?" quiz questions. You can find the answers in Appendix A, "Answers to the 'Do I Know This Already?' Quizzes and 'Review Questions.'"

Table 18.1 "Do I Know This Already?" Section-to-Question Mapping

Foundation Topics Section	Questions
Working with Systemd	1–7, 10
Working with GRUB 2	8, 9

1. Which command shows all service unit files on your system that are currently loaded?
   a. **systemctl --type=service**
   b. **systemctl --type=service --all**
   c. **systemctl --list-services**
   d. **systemctl --show-units | grep services**

2. Which statement about systemd wants is *not* true?
   a. You can create wants by using the **systemctl enable** command.
   b. The target to which a specific want applies is agnostic of the associated wants.
   c. Wants are always administered in the /usr/lib/systemd/system directory.
   d. Each service knows to which target its wants should be added.

3. What is the best solution to avoid conflicts between incompatible units?
   a. Nothing, the unit files have defined for themselves which units they are not compatible with.
   b. Disable the service using **systemctl disable.**
   c. Unmask the service using **systemctl unmask.**
   d. Mask the service using **systemctl mask.**

4. Which of the following is not a valid status for systemd services?
   a. Running(active)
   b. Running(exited)
   c. Running(waiting)
   d. Running(dead)

5. To allow targets to be isolated, you need a specific statement in the target unit file. Which of the following describes that statement?
   a. **AllowIsolate**
   b. **Isolate**
   c. **SetIsolate**
   d. **Isolated**

6. Which of the following is not a valid systemd unit type?
   a. service
   b. udev
   c. mount
   d. socket

7. You want to find out which other systemd units have dependencies to this specific unit. Which command would you use?
   a. **systemd list-dependencies --reverse**
   b. **systemctl list-dependencies --reverse**
   c. **systemctl status my.unit --show-deps**
   d. **systemd status my.unit --show-deps -r**

8. What is the name of the file where you should apply changes to the GRUB 2 configuration?
   a. /boot/grub/menu.lst
   b. /boot/grub2/grub.cfg
   c. /etc/sysconfig/grub
   d. /etc/default/grub

9. After applying changes to the GRUB 2 configuration, you need to write those changes. Which of the following commands will do that for you?
   a. **grub2 -o /boot/grub/grub.cfg**
   b. **grub2-mkconfig > /boot/grub2/grub.cfg**
   c. **grub2 > /boot/grub2/grub.cfg**
   d. **grub2-install > /boot/grub2/grub.cfg**

10. Which of the following is *not* a valid command while working with units in systemctl?
    a. **systemctl unit start**
    b. **systemctl status -l unit**
    c. **systemctl mask unit**
    d. **systemctl disable unit**

Foundation Topics

Working with Systemd

Systemd is the new service in Red Hat Enterprise Linux 7 that is responsible for starting all kinds of things. Systemd goes way beyond starting services; other items are started from systemd as well. In this chapter, you learn how systemd is organized and what items are started from systemd.

Understanding Systemd

To describe it in a generic way, the systemd System and Service Manager is used to start stuff. The stuff is referred to as *units*. Units can be many things. One of the most important unit types is the service. Typically, services are processes that provide specific functionality and allow connections from external clients coming in. Apart from services, other unit types exist, such as sockets, mounts, and others. To display a list of available units, type **systemctl -t help** (see Listing 18.1).

Key Topic

Lising 18.1 Unit Types in Systemd

```
[root@server1 ~]# systemctl -t help
Available unit types:
service
socket
target
device
mount
automount
snapshot
timer
swap
path
slice
scope
```

TIP For RHCSA, you need to know how to work with services. The other unit types do not matter that much.

Understanding Service Units

The major benefit of working with systemd, as compared to previous methods Red Hat used for managing services, is that it provides a uniform interface to start units. This interface is defined in the unit file. The system default unit files are in /usr/lib/systemd/system. System-specific modifications (overriding the defaults) are in /etc/systemd/system. Also, the runtime configuration that is generated automatically is stored in /run/systemd/system. Listing 18.2 gives an example of the vsftpd.service unit file.

Listing 18.2 Example of the Vsftpd Unit File

```
[Unit]
Description=Vsftpd ftp daemon
After=network.target

[Service]
Type=forking
ExecStart=/usr/sbin/vsftpd /etc/vsftpd/vsftpd.conf

[Install]
WantedBy=multi-user.target
```

From this unit file example, you can see that it is relatively easy to understand. Any systemd service unit file consists of three sections. (You'll find different sections in other types of unit files.)

Key Topic

- **[Unit]**, which describes the unit and defines dependencies. This section also contains the important **After** statement, and optionally the **Before** statement. These statements define dependencies between different units. The Before statement relates to another unit that is started after this unit. The after unit refers to a unit that needs to be started before this unit can be started.
- **[Service]**, in which there is a description on how to start and stop the service and request status installation. Normally, you can expect an ExecStart line, which indicates how to start the unit, or an ExecStop line, which indicates how to stop the unit.
- **[Install]**, in which the wants are taken care of. You'll read more about this in the next section, "Understanding Target Units."

Listing 18.3 shows another example of a unit file. This time it is the tmp.mount unit.

Listing 18.3 Example of a Mount Unit File

```
[Unit]
Description=Temporary Directory
Documentation=man:hier(7)
Documentation=http://www.freedesktop.org/wiki/Software/systemd/
  APIFileSystems
DefaultDependencies=no
Conflicts=umount.target
Before=local-fs.target umount.target

[Mount]
What=tmpfs
Where=/tmp
Type=tmpfs
Options=mode=1777,strictatime

# Make 'systemctl enable tmp.mount' work:
[Install]
WantedBy=local-fs.target
```

The tmp.mount unit file in Listing 18.3 shows some interesting additional information. In the Unit section, you can see the **Conflicts** statement. This is used to list units that cannot be used together with this unit. Use this for mutually exclusive units. Next, there is the Mount section, which is specific for this unit type and defines where exactly the mount has to be performed. You'll recognize the arguments that are typically used in any **mount** command. Last, there is the WantedBy section, which defines where the unit has to be started.

Another type of unit that is interesting to look at is the socket. A socket creates a method for applications to communicate with one another. Some services create their own sockets while starting, whereas other services need a socket unit file to create sockets for them. It is also the other way around: Every socket needs a corresponding service file. The socket file example in Listing 18.4 shows how this happens for virtlockd, a systemd socket that tracks activity for virtual machines.

Listing 18.4 Socket Unit File Example

```
[root@server202 system]# cat virtlockd.socket
[Unit]
Description=Virtual machine lock manager socket

[Socket]
ListenStream=/var/run/libvirt/virtlockd-sock

[Install]
WantedBy=multi-user.target
```

When working with systemd unit files, you risk getting overwhelmed with options. Every unit file can be configured with different options. To figure out which options are available for a specific unit, use the **systemctl show** command. For instance, the **systemctl show sshd** command shows all systemd options that can be configured in the sshd.service unit, including their current default values. Listing 18.5 shows the output of this command.

Listing 18.5 Showing Available Options with **systemctl show**

```
Id=sshd.service
Names=sshd.service
Requires=basic.target
Wants=sshd-keygen.service system.slice
WantedBy=multi-user.target
ConsistsOf=sshd-keygen.service
Conflicts=shutdown.target
ConflictedBy=sshd.socket
Before=shutdown.target multi-user.target
After=network.target sshd-keygen.service systemd-journald.socket
basic.target system.slice
Description=OpenSSH server daemon
LoadState=loaded
ActiveState=active
SubState=running
FragmentPath=/usr/lib/systemd/system/sshd.service
UnitFileState=enabled
InactiveExitTimestamp=Sat 2015-05-02 11:06:02 EDT
InactiveExitTimestampMonotonic=2596332166
```

```
ActiveEnterTimestamp=Sat 2015-05-02 11:06:02 EDT
ActiveEnterTimestampMonotonic=2596332166
ActiveExitTimestamp=Sat 2015-05-02 11:05:22 EDT
ActiveExitTimestampMonotonic=2559916100
InactiveEnterTimestamp=Sat 2015-05-02 11:06:02 EDT
InactiveEnterTimestampMonotonic=2596331238
CanStart=yes
CanStop=yes
CanReload=yes
CanIsolate=no
StopWhenUnneeded=no
RefuseManualStart=no
RefuseManualStop=no
AllowIsolate=no
DefaultDependencies=yes
OnFailureIsolate=no
IgnoreOnIsolate=no
```

Understanding Target Units

Key Topic

The unit files are used to build the functionality that is needed on your server. To make it possible to load them in the right order and at the right moment, a specific type of unit is used: the target unit. A simple definition of a target unit is "a group of units." Some targets are used as the equivalents to the old run levels, which on earlier versions of RHEL were used to define the state a server should be started in. A run level was a collection of services that were needed for a server to be started in multi-user mode or in graphical mode. Targets go beyond that. A good starting point to understanding targets is to see them as a group of units.

Targets by themselves can have dependencies to other targets, which are defined in the target unit. Let's take a look at Listing 18.6, where you can see the definition of the multi-user.target, which defines the normal operational state of an RHEL server.

Listing 18.6 The Multi-user.target File

```
[root@server202 system]# cat multi-user.target
...

[Unit]
Description=Multi-User System
```

```
Documentation=man:systemd.special(7)
Requires=basic.target
Conflicts=rescue.service rescue.target
After=basic.target rescue.service rescue.target
AllowIsolate=yes

[Install]
Alias=default.target
```

You can see that by itself the target unit does not contain much. It just defines what it requires and which services and targets it cannot coexist with. It also defines load ordering, by using the **After** statement in the Unit section. And you can see that in the Install section it is defined as the default.target, so this is what your server starts by default. The target file does not contain any information about the units that should be included; that is in the individual unit files and the wants (explained in the upcoming section "Understanding Wants").

Even if a systemd target looks a bit like the old run levels, it is more than that. A target is a group of units, and there are multiple different targets. Some targets, such as the multi-user.target and the graphical.target, define a specific state that the system needs to enter. Other targets just bundle a group of units together, such as the nfs.target and the printer.target. These targets are included from other targets, like the multi-user or graphical targets.

Understanding Wants

To understand the concept of a want, let's start looking at the verb *want* in the English language, as in "I want a cookie." Wants in systemd define which units systemd wants when starting a specific target. Wants are created when systemd units are enabled, and this happens by creating a symbolic link in the /etc/systemd/system directory. In this directory, you'll find a subdirectory for every target, containing wants as symbolic links to specific services that are to be started.

Managing Units Through Systemd

As an administrator, you need to manage systemd units. It starts by starting and stopping units. You use the **systemctl** command to do that. In Exercise 18.1, you walk start, stop, and manage a unit. After you have configured a unit so that it can be started without problems, you need to make sure that it restarts automatically upon reboot. You do this by enabling or disabling the unit.

TIP Memorizing all the different arguments that can be used with the **systemctl** command might seem hard, but you don't have to do that. Instead, just type **systemctl** and press the **Tab** key twice to use command autocompletion. This will show you all available commands.

Key Topic

Exercise 18.1 Managing Units with systemctl

1. Type **yum -y install vsftpd** to install the Very Secure FTP service.
2. Type **systemctl start vsftpd**. This activates the FTP server on your machine.
3. Type **systemctl status vsftpd**. You'll get an output as in Listing 18.7 and see that the vsftpd service is currently operational. You can also see in the Loaded line that it is currently disabled, which means that it will not be activated on a system restart.
4. Type **systemctl enable vsftpd**. This creates a symbolic link in the wants directory for the multi-user target to ensure that the service gets back after a restart.
5. Type **systemctl status vsftpd** again. You'll now see that the unit file has changed from being disabled to enabled.

Listing 18.7 Requesting Current Unit Status with **systemctl status**

```
[root@server202 system]# systemctl status vsftpd
vsftpd.service - Vsftpd ftp daemon
   Loaded: loaded (/usr/lib/systemd/system/vsftpd.service; disabled)
   Active: active (running) since Sun 2014-09-28 08:42:59 EDT; 2s ago
  Process: 34468 ExecStart=/usr/sbin/vsftpd /etc/vsftpd/vsftpd.conf
(code=exited, status=0/SUCCESS)
 Main PID: 34469 (vsftpd)
   CGroup: /system.slice/vsftpd.service
           └─34469 /usr/sbin/vsftpd /etc/vsftpd/vsftpd.conf

Sep 28 08:42:59 server202.example.com systemd[1]: Starting Vsftpd ftp
daemon...
Sep 28 08:42:59 server202.example.com systemd[1]: Started Vsftpd ftp
daemon.
Hint: Some lines were ellipsized, use -l to show in full.
```

When requesting the current status of a systemd unit as in Listing 18.6, you can see different kinds of information about it. Table 18.2 shows the different kinds of information that you can get about unit files when using the **systemctl status** command:

Table 18.2 Systemd Status Overview

Status	Description
Loaded	The unit file has been processed and the unit is active.
Active(running)	Running with one or more active processes.
Active(exited)	Successfully completed a one-time configuration.
Active(waiting)	Running and waiting for an event.
Inactive	Not running.
Enabled	Will be started at boot time.
Disabled	Will not be started at boot time.
Static	This unit can not be enabled but may be started by another unit automatically.

As an administrator, you'll also often need to get a current overview of the current status of systemd unit files. Different commands can help you to get this insight, some of which are shown in Table 18.3.

Table 18.3 Systemctl Unit Overview Commands

Key Topic

Command	Description
systemctl --type=service	Shows only service units
systemctl list-units --type=service	Shows all active service units (same result as the previous command)
systemctl list-units --type=service --all	Shows inactive service units as well as active service units
systemctl --failed --type=service	Shows all services that have failed
systemctl status -l your.service	Shows detailed status information about services

Managing Dependencies

Systemctl units in many cases have dependencies. Some units will be started as a dependency of other units, and an event where one specific unit is requested may trigger the start of another unit. An example is the cups.service service. This service can be started by itself, but it can also be started by activity on the cups.path and cups.socket units, which may trigger the service to be started again. As an administrator, you can request a list of unit dependencies. Type **systemctl list-dependencies** followed by a unit name to find out which dependencies it has, and add the **--reverse** option to find out which units are dependent of this unit. Listing 18.8 shows an example of this command.

Listing 18.8 Showing Unit Dependencies

```
[root@server1 ~]# systemctl list-dependencies vsftpd
 vsftpd.service
├─system.slice
└─basic.target
  ├─alsa-restore.service
  ├─alsa-state.service
  ├─firewalld.service
  ├─microcode.service
  ├─rhel-autorelabel-mark.service
  ├─rhel-autorelabel.service
  ├─rhel-configure.service
  ├─rhel-dmesg.service
  ├─rhel-loadmodules.service
  ├─paths.target
  ├─slices.target
  │ ├─-.slice
  │ └─system.slice
  ├─sockets.target
  │ ├─avahi-daemon.socket
  │ ├─cups.socket
  │ ├─dbus.socket
  │ ├─dm-event.socket
  │ ├─iscsid.socket
  │ ├─iscsiuio.socket
  │ ├─lvm2-lvmetad.socket
  │ ├─rpcbind.socket
  │ ├─systemd-initctl.socket
  │ ├─systemd-journald.socket
  │ ├─systemd-shutdownd.socket
  │ ├─systemd-udevd-control.socket
  │ └─systemd-udevd-kernel.socket
```

```
├─sysinit.target
│ ├─dev-hugepages.mount
│ ├─dev-mqueue.mount
│ ├─dmraid-activation.service
│ ├─iscsi.service
```

Apart from dependencies, some units have conflicts with other units. Examples of these include the following:

- Mount and umount units that cannot be loaded together
- The network and NetworkManager service
- The iptables and the firewalld service
- The cronyd and ntpd service

If units have conflicts with other units, this is described in the unit file. As an administrator, you can also make sure that conflicting units will never be loaded at the same time on the same system. To do this, you can use the **systemctl mask** command, which basically makes a unit no longer a candidate for being started. Apply the following procedure to find out how it works:

1. Open a root shell and type **systemctl status firewalld**. Next type **systemctl status iptables**. If one of the services is active, do not load it again in the next step.
2. Type **systemctl start firewalld** and **systemctl start iptables** to load both services. You will see that iptables refuses to start; this is because the firewalld service is already activated.
3. Type **cat /usr/lib/systemd/system/firewalld.service**. Notice the conflicts setting. Type **cat /usr/lib/systemd/system/iptables.service**. Notice that this unit does not have a conflicts line.
4. Unload both services by using **systemctl stop firewalld** followed by **systemctl stop iptables**. Notice that it is not really necessary to stop the iptables service because it has failed to load, but we really need to make sure that it is not loaded at all before continuing.
5. Type **systemctl mask iptables** and look at what is happening: A symbolic link to /dev/null is created for /etc/systemd/system/iptables.service (as you can see in the output of the following command example). Because the unit files in

/etc/systemd have precedence over the files in /usr/lib/systemd, this makes it impossible to start the iptables service by accident:

```
[root@server202 system]# systemctl mask iptables
ln -s '/dev/null' '/etc/systemd/system/iptables.service'
```

6. Type **systemctl start iptables**. You'll see an error message indicating that this service is masked and for that reason cannot be started.

7. Type **systemctl enable iptables**. Notice that no error message is shown and it looks as if it is working all right. Restart your server using **systemctl reboot** (or just **reboot**).

8. After restart, type **systemctl status -l iptables**. You'll see that it is inactive and that the loaded status is indicated as masked:

```
[root@server202 ~]# systemctl status -l iptables
iptables.service
    Loaded: masked (/dev/null)
    Active: inactive (dead)
```

Managing Systemd Targets

Key Topic

As an administrator, you need to make sure that the required services are started when your server boots. To do this, use the **systemctl enable** and **systemctl disable** commands. You do not have to think about the specific target a service has to be started in. The services know for themselves in which targets they need to be started and a want is created automatically in that target. The following procedure walks you through the steps of enabling a service:

1. Type **systemctl status vsftpd**. If the service has not yet been enabled, the Loaded line will show that it currently is disabled:

```
[root@server202 ~]# systemctl status vsftpd
vsftpd.service - Vsftpd ftp daemon
    Loaded: loaded (/usr/lib/systemd/system/vsftpd.service;
   disabled)
    Active: inactive (dead)
```

2. Type **ls /etc/systemd/system/multi-user.target.wants**. You'll see symbolic links that are taking care of starting the different services on your machine. You can also see that the vsftpd.service link does not exist.

3. Type **systemctl enable vsftpd**. The command shows you that it is creating a symbolic link for the file /usr/lib/systemd/system/vsftpd.service to the directory /etc/systemd/system/multi-user.target.wants. So basically, when you enable a systemd unit file, on the background a symbolic link is created.

TIP On both the RHCSA and the RHCE exams, you are likely to configure a couple of services. It is a good idea to read through the exam questions, identify the services that need to be enabled, and enable them all at once to make sure that they are started automatically when you restart. This prevents your being so focused on configuring the service that you completely forget to enable it as well.

Isolating Targets

As already discussed, on systemd machines there are a couple of targets. You also know that a target is a collection of units. Some of those targets have a special role because they can be isolated. By isolating a target, you start that target with all of its dependencies. Not all targets can be isolated, but only targets that have the isolate option enabled. We'll explore the **systemctl isolate** command in a while. Before doing that, let's take a look at the default targets on your computer.

To get a list of all targets currently loaded, type **systemctl --type=target**. You'll see a list of all the targets currently active. If your server is running a graphical environment, this will include all the dependencies required to install the graphical.target also. However, this list does not show all the targets, but only the active targets. Type **systemctl --type=target --all** for an overview of all targets that exist on your computer. You'll now see inactive targets also.

Of the targets on your system, a few have an important role because they can be started (isolated) to determine the state your server starts in. These are also the targets that can be set as the default target. These targets also roughly correspond to run levels as they were used on earlier versions of RHEL. These are the following targets:

- poweroff.target - runlevel 0
- rescue.target - runlevel 1
- multi-user.target - runlevel 3
- graphical.target - runlevel 5
- reboot.target - runlevel 6

If you look at the contents of each of these targets, you'll also see that they contain the AllowIsolate=yes line. That means that you can switch the current state of your computer to either one of these targets using the **systemctl isolate** command. Exercise 18.2 shows you how to do this.

Key Topic

Exercise 18.2 Isolating Targets

1. From a root shell, go to the directory /usr/lib/systemd/system. Type **grep Isolate *.target**. This shows a list of all targets that allow isolation.
2. Type **systemctl isolate rescue.target**. This switches your computer to rescue. target. You need to type the root password on the console of your server to log in.
3. Type **systemctl isolate reboot.target**. This restarts your computer.

Setting the Default Target

Setting the default target is an easy procedure that can be accomplished from the command line. Type **systemctl get-default** to see the current default target and use **systemctl set-default** to set the desired default target.

To set the graphical target as the default target, you need to make sure that the required packages are installed. If this is not the case, you can use the **yum group list** command to show a list of all RPM package groups. The "server with gui" and "GNOME Desktop" package groups both apply. Use **yum group install "server with gui"** to install all GUI packages on a server where they have not been installed yet.

Working with GRUB 2

The GRUB 2 boot loader is one of the first things that needs to be working well to boot a Linux server. As an administrator, you will sometimes need to apply modifications to the GRUB 2 boot loader configuration. This section explains how to do so. The RHEL 7 boot procedure is discussed in more detail in Chapter 19, where troubleshooting topics are covered as well.

Understanding GRUB 2

The GRUB 2 boot loader makes sure that you can boot Linux. GRUB 2 is installed in the boot sector of your server's hard drive and is configured to load a Linux kernel and the initramfs:

Key Topic

- The kernel is the heart of the operating system, allowing users to interact with the hardware that is installed in the server.
- The initramfs contains drivers that are needed to start your server. It contains a mini file system that is mounted during boot. In it are kernel modules that are needed during the rest of the boot process (for example, the LVM modules and SCSI modules for accessing disks that are not supported by default).

Normally, GRUB 2 works just fine and does not need much maintenance. In some cases, though, you might have to change its configuration. To apply changes to the GRUB 2 configuration, the starting point is the /etc/default/grub file. In this file, you'll find options that tell GRUB what to do and how to do it. Listing 18.9 shows the contents of this file after an installation with default settings of CentOS 7.

Listing 18.9 Contents of the /etc/default/grub File

Key Topic

```
[root@server202 grub.d]# cat /etc/default/grub
GRUB_TIMEOUT=5
GRUB_DISTRIBUTOR="$(sed 's, release .*$,,g' /etc/system-release)"
GRUB_DEFAULT=saved
GRUB_DISABLE_SUBMENU=true
GRUB_TERMINAL_OUTPUT="console"
GRUB_CMDLINE_LINUX="rd.lvm.lv=centos/swap vconsole.font=latarcyrheb-
  sun16 rd.lvm.lv=centos/root crashkernel=auto  vconsole.keymap=us
  rhgb quiet"
GRUB_DISABLE_RECOVERY="true"
```

As you can see, the /etc/default/grub file does not contain much information. The most important part that it configures is the GRUB-CMDLINE_LINUX option. This line contains boot arguments for the kernel on your server.

> **TIP** For the RHCSA exam, make sure that you understand the contents of the /etc/default/grub file. That is the most important part of the GRUB 2 configuration anyway.

Apart from the configuration in /etc/default/grub, there are a few configuration files in /etc/grub.d. In these files, you'll find rather complicated shell code that tells GRUB what to load and how to load it. You typically do not have to modify it. You also will not need to modify anything if you want to make it possible to select from different kernels while booting. GRUB 2 picks up new kernels automatically and adds them to the boot menu automatically, so nothing has to be added manually.

Based on the configuration files mentioned previously, the main configuration file /boot/grub2/grub.cfg is created. Even if this looks like a configuration file that can be manually modified, you should never do that, because it will get overwritten at some point. This will happen, for instance, after updating the kernel. The RPM from which the kernel is updated will run a post-installation script that regenerates the kernel. In the next section, you learn how to make changes to the GRUB 2 configuration.

If you enter the GRUB 2 boot prompt to add kernel startup parameters, the contents of the /boot/grub2/grub.cfg file display. From here, you add one-time-only startup options. Listing 18.10 shows the relevant part of the grub.cfg file that takes care of loading the Linux kernel. In this listing, you see the part of the configuration file that takes care of loading the default kernel. Notice the line that starts with linux16; this line specifies all kernel boot parameters.

Listing 18.10 Partial Contents of the /boot/grub2/grub.cfg Configuration File

```
menuentry 'CentOS Linux (3.10.0-229.1.2.el7.x86_64) 7 (Core)' --class
centos --class gnu-linux --class gnu --class os --unrestricted
$menuentry_id_option 'gnulinux-3.10.0-123.el7.x86_64-advanced-50faa2a1-
01d3-430b-8114-4a98daf5bdb9' {
      load_video
      set gfxpayload=keep
      insmod gzio
      insmod part_msdos
      insmod xfs
      set root='hd0,msdos1'
      if [ x$feature_platform_search_hint = xy ]; then
        search --no-floppy --fs-uuid --set=root --hint-bios=hd0,msdos1
--hint-efi=hd0,msdos1 --hint-baremetal=ahci0,msdos1 --hint='hd0,msdos1'
057ba3d8-bfe7-4676-bb99-79e9980a1966
     else
       search --no-floppy --fs-uuid --set=root 057ba3d8-bfe7-4676-bb99-
79e9980a1966
     fi
     linux16 /vmlinuz-3.10.0-229.1.2.el7.x86_64 root=/dev/mapper/
centos-root ro rd.lvm.lv=centos/swap vconsole.font=latarcyrheb-sun16
rd.lvm.lv=centos/root crashkernel=auto  vconsole.keymap=us rhgb quiet
LANG=en_US.UTF-8
     initrd16 /initramfs-3.10.0-229.1.2.el7.x86_64.img
}
```

One of the most important differences between GRUB 2 and its previous version is the availability of GRUB 2 modules. In GRUB 2, a large number of modules are available. By default, you can find them in /boot/grub2/i386-pc. The modules determine what you can and what you cannot do from the GRUB 2 boot loader. If some hardware or file system is not supported in what you want to do, check here to make sure that a supporting GRUB 2 module is available. In Listing 18.10, you can see examples of the code used to load specific GRUB 2 modules.

Modifying Default GRUB 2 Boot Options

To apply modifications to the GRUB 2 boot loader, the file /etc/default/grub is your entry point; do not change the contents of the /boot/grub2/grub.cfg configuration file directly. The most important line in this file is GRUB_CMDLINE_LINUX, which defines how the Linux kernel should be started. In this line, you can apply permanent fixes to the GRUB 2 configuration. Some likely candidates for removal are the options **rhgb** and **quiet**. These options tell the kernel to hide all output while booting. That is nice to hide confusing messages for end users, but if you are a server administrator, you probably just want to remove these options.

> **TIP** On the exam, you want to know immediately if something does not work out well. To accomplish this, it is a good idea to remove the **rhgb** and **quiet** boot options. Without these you will not have to guess why your server takes a long time after a restart; you'll just be able to see.

Another interesting parameter is GRUB_TIMEOUT. This defines the amount of time your server waits for you to access the GRUB 2 boot menu before it continues booting automatically. If your server runs on physical hardware that takes a long time to get through the BIOS checks, it may be interesting to increase this time a bit.

While working with GRUB 2, you need to know a bit about kernel boot arguments. There are many of them, and most of them you'll never use, but it is good to know where you can find them. Type **man 7 bootparam** for a man page that contains an excellent description of all boot parameters that you may use while starting the kernel.

In Exercise 18.3, you learn how to apply modifications to GRUB 2.

> **TIP** You should know how to apply changes to the GRUB configuration, but you should also know that the default GRUB 2 configuration works fine as it is for almost all computers. So, you will probably never have to apply any changes at all!

Key Topic

Exercise 18.3 Applying Modifications to GRUB2

In this exercise you'll apply some changes to the GRUB2 boot configuration and write them to the /boot/grub2/grub.cfg configuration file.

1. Open the file /etc/default/grub with an editor and remove the **rhgb** and **quiet** options from the GRUB_CMDLINE_LINUX line.
2. From the same file, set the GRUB_TIMEOUT parameter to 10 seconds. Save changes to the file and close the editor.
3. From the command line, type **grub2-mkconfig > /boot/grub2/grub.cfg** to write the changes to GRUB 2. (Note that instead of using the redirector > to write changes to the grub.cfg file, you could use the **-o** option. Both methods have the same result.)
4. Reboot and verify that while booting you see boot messages scrolling by.

Summary

In this chapter you learned how systemd and GRUB 2 are used to bring your server into the exact state you desire at the end of the boot procedure. You also learned how systemd is organized, and also how units can be configured for automatic start with the use of targets. You also read how to apply changes to the default GRUB 2 boot loader. In the next chapter, you learn how to troubleshoot the boot procedure and fix some common problems.

Exam Prep Tasks

Review All Key Topics

Review the most important topics in the chapter, noted with the Key Topic icon in the outer margin of the page. Table 18.4 lists a reference of these key topics and the page numbers on which each is found.

Table 18.4 Key Topics for Chapter 18

Key Topic Element	Description	Page Number
Listing 18.1	Unit types in systemd	408
List	Three sections of a systemd unit file	409
Paragraph	Understanding Target Units	412
Exercise 18.1	Managing units with **systemctl**	414

Key Topic Element	Description	Page Number
Table 18.3	Systemctl unit overview commands	415
Section	Managing systemd targets	418
Exercise 18.2	Isolating targets	420
Bullet list	Explanation of the role of kernel and initramfs	420
Listing 18.9	Contents of the /etc/default/grub file	421
Exercise 18.3	Applying modifications to GRUB 2	424

Complete Tables and Lists from Memory

Print a copy of Appendix B, "Memory Tables" (found on the disc), or at least the section for this chapter, and complete the tables and lists from memory. Appendix C, "Memory Tables Answer Key," also on the disc, includes completed tables and lists to check your work.

Define Key Terms

Define the following key terms from this chapter and check your answers in the glossary:

unit, wants, target, systemd, dependencies, initramfs, kernel, boot loader, GRUB

Review Questions

1. What is a unit?
2. Which command enables you to make sure that a target is no longer eligible for automatic start on system boot?
3. Which configuration file should you modify to apply common changes to GRUB 2?
4. Which command should you use to show all service units that are currently loaded?
5. How do you create a want for a service?
6. How do you switch the current operational target to the rescue target?
7. Why can it happen that you get the message that a target cannot be isolated?

8. You want to shut down a systemd service, but before doing that you want to know which other units have dependencies to this service. Which command would you use?
9. What is the name of the GRUB 2 configuration file where you apply changes to GRUB 2?
10. After applying changes to the GRUB 2 configuration, which command should you run?

End-of-Chapter Labs

You have now learned how to work with systemd units and the GRUB 2 boot loader. Before continuing, it is a good idea to work on some labs that help you ensure that you can apply the skills that you acquired in this chapter.

Lab 18.1

Make sure that the firewalld service is started on boot. Also make sure that the iptables service can never be started at the same time.

Lab 18.2

Change your GRUB 2 boot configuration so that you will see boot messages upon startup.

The following topics are covered in this chapter:

- Understanding the RHEL 7 Boot Procedure
- Passing Kernel Boot Arguments
- Using a Rescue Disk
- Fixing Common Issues
- Recovering Access to a Virtual Machine

The following RHCSA exam objectives are covered in this chapter:

- Boot systems into different targets manually
- Interrupt the boot process in order to gain access to a system

CHAPTER 19

Troubleshooting the Boot Procedure

In the preceding chapter, you learned how an RHEL 7 server boots and which role the boot loader GRUB 2 and systemd play in that. In this chapter, you learn what you can do when common problems occur while booting your server. This chapter teaches general approaches that help to fix some of the most common problems that may occur while booting. Make sure to master the topics discussed in this chapter well; they might save your (professional) life one day!

"Do I Know This Already?" Quiz

The "Do I Know This Already?" quiz allows you to assess whether you should read this entire chapter thoroughly or jump to the "Exam Preparation Tasks" section. If you are in doubt about your answers to these questions or your own assessment of your knowledge of the topics, read the entire chapter. Table 19.1 lists the major headings in this chapter and their corresponding "Do I Know This Already?" quiz questions. You can find the answers in Appendix A, "Answers to the 'Do I Know This Already?' Quizzes and 'Review Questions.'"

Table 19.1 "Do I Know This Already?" Section-to-Question Mapping

Foundation Topics Section	Questions
Understanding the RHEL 7 Boot Procedure	1
Passing Kernel Boot Arguments	2–6
Using a Rescue Disk	7
Fixing Common Issues	8–9
Recovering Access to a Virtual Machine	10

1. Which of the following comes first in the Red Hat Enterprise Linux 7 boot procedure?
   a. Systemd
   b. Kernel
   c. GRUB 2
   d. Initramfs

2. You have just entered a kernel argument on the GRUB 2 boot prompt. Which key(s) enables you to start with this boot argument?
   a. **ZZ**
   b. **Ctrl+X**
   c. **Esc**
   d. **Enter**

3. Your initramfs seems faulty and cannot initialize the LVM volumes on your disk. Which configuration file should you check for options that are used?
   a. /etc/dracut.d/dracut.conf
   b. /etc/dracut.conf
   c. /etc/sysconfig/dracut
   d. /etc/mkinitrd.conf

4. You do not have the root password and want to reset it. Which kernel argument offers the recommended way to reset it?
   a. **init=/bin/bash**
   b. **init=/bin/sh**
   c. **systemd.unit=emergency.target**
   d. **rd.break**

5. You want to see exactly what is happening on system boot. Which two boot options should you remove from the GRUB 2 boot prompt? (Choose two.)
   a. **rhgb**
   b. **logo**
   c. **quiet**
   d. **silent**

6. You want to enter the most minimal troubleshooting mode where as few services as possible are loaded. Which boot argument should you use?
   a. **systemd.unit=break.target**
   b. **systemd.unit=emergency.target**
   c. **systemd.unit=rescue.target**
   d. **1**

7. Which of the following situations can be resolved only by using a rescue disk?
   a. The kernel stops loading.
   b. The initramfs stops loading.
   c. You never get to a GRUB 2 boot prompt.
   d. You are prompted to enter the root password for maintenance mode.

8. You have entered a troubleshooting mode, and disk access is read-only. What should you do?
   a. Restart the troubleshooting mode and pass the **rw** boot option to the kernel.
   b. Use the **rd.break** boot argument to manually start into the initramfs mode.
   c. Use **mount -o remount,rw /**.
   d. Use **mount /**.

9. Your server shows a blinking cursor only while booting. No GRUB 2 menu is available. What is the first step in troubleshooting this issue?
   a. From a rescue disk, try the boot from local disk option.
   b. Start a rescue environment and reinstall GRUB.
   c. Start a rescue environment and re-create the initramfs.
   d. Use the **rd.break** boot argument.

10. When recovering access to a virtual machine, you need to make the storage devices in the image file available. Which of the following commands would do that, assuming that the name of the image file is /home/user/lab1.img??
    a. **partx -ax /home/user/lab1.img**
    b. **kpartx -ax /home/user/lab1.img**
    c. **kpartx -av /home/user/lab1.img**
    d. **partx -av /home/user/lab1.img.**

Foundation Topics

Understanding the RHEL 7 Boot Procedure

To fix boot issues, it is essential to have a good understanding of the boot procedure. If issues occur during boot, you need to be able to judge in which phase of the boot procedure the issue occurs so that you can select the appropriate tool to fix the issue.

The following steps summarize how the boot procedure happens on Linux.

Key Topic

1. **Performing POST:** The machine is powered on. From the system firmware, which can be the modern Universal Extended Firmware Interface (UEFI) or the classical Basic Input Output System (BIOS), the Power-On Self-Test (POST) is executed, and the hardware that is required to start the system is initialized.
2. **Selecting the bootable device:** Either from the UEFI boot firmware or from the Master Boot Record, a bootable device is located.
3. **Loading the boot loader:** From the bootable device, a boot loader is located. On Red Hat, this is usually GRUB 2.
4. **Loading the kernel:** The boot loader may present a boot menu to the user, or can be configured to automatically start a default operating system. To load Linux, the kernel is loaded together with the initramfs. The initramfs contains kernel modules for all hardware that is required to boot, as well as the initial scripts required to proceed to the next stage of booting. On RHEL 7, the initramfs contains a complete operational system (which may be used for troubleshooting purposes).
5. **Starting /sbin/init:** Once the kernel is loaded into memory, the first of all processes is loaded, but still from the initramfs. This is the /sbin/init process, which on Red Hat is linked to systemd. The udev daemon is loaded as well to take care of further hardware initialization. All this is still happening from the initramfs image.
6. **Processing initrd.target:** The systemd process executes all units from the initrd.target, which prepares a minimal operating environment, where the root file system on disk is mounted on the /sysroot directory. At this point, enough is loaded to pass to the system installation that was written to the hard drive.
7. **Switching to the root file system:** The system switches to the root file system that is on disk and at this point can load the systemd process from disk as well.

8. **Running the default target:** Systemd looks for the default target to execute and runs all of its units. In this process, a login screen is presented, and the user can authenticate. Notice that the login prompt can be prompted before all systemd unit files have been loaded successfully. So, seeing a login prompt does not necessarily mean that your server is fully operational yet.

In each of the phases listed, issues may occur because of misconfiguration or other problems. Table 19.2 summarizes where a specific phase is configured and what you can do to troubleshoot if things go wrong.

TIP Troubleshooting has always been a part of the RHCSA exam. If you encounter an issue, make sure that you can identify in which phase of the boot procedure it occurs and what you can do to fix it.

Table 19.2 Boot Phase Configuration and Troubleshooting Overview

Key Topic

Boot Phase	Configuring It	Fixing It
POST	Hardware configuration (F2, Esc, F10, or another key)	Replace hardware.
Selecting the bootable device	BIOS/UEFI configuration or hardware boot menu	Replace hardware or use rescue system.
Loading the boot loader	**grub2-install** and edits to /etc/defaults/grub	GRUB boot prompt and edits to /etc/defaults/grub, followed by grub2-mkconfig.
Loading the kernel	Edits to the GRUB configuration and /etc/dracut.conf.	GRUB boot prompt and edits to /etc/defaults/grub, followed by grub2-mkconfig.
Starting /sbin/init	Compiled into initramfs	**init= kernel** boot argument, **rd.break** kernel boot argument.
Processing initrd.target	Compiled into initramfs	Not typically required.
Switch to the root file system	/etc/fstab	/etc/fstab.
Running the default target	/etc/systemd/system/default.target	Start the rescue.target as a kernel boot argument.

In the next section you learn how to apply the different troubleshooting techniques described in this table.

Passing Kernel Boot Arguments

If your server does not boot normally, the GRUB boot prompt offers a convenient way to stop the boot procedure and pass specific options to the kernel while booting. In this section, you learn how to access the boot prompt and how to pass specific boot arguments to the kernel while booting.

Accessing the Boot Prompt

When your server boots, you briefly see the GRUB 2 menu. Look fast because it will only last for a few seconds. From this boot menu you can type **e** to enter a mode where you can edit commands, or **c** to enter a full GRUB command prompt, as shown in Figure 19.1. To pass boot options to a starting kernel, use **e**.

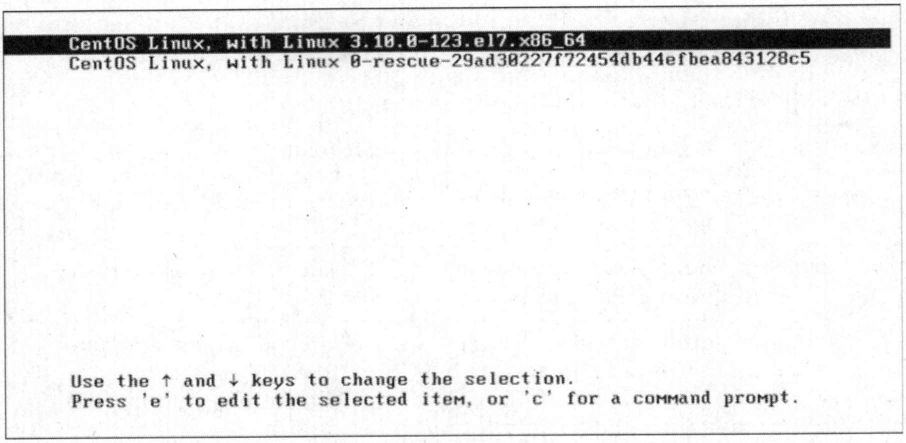

Figure 19.1 Entering the GRUB boot prompt.

After passing an **e** to the GRUB boot menu, you'll see the interface that is in Figure 19.2. From this interface, scroll down to locate the section that begins with linux16 /vmlinuz followed by a lot of arguments. This is the line that tells GRUB how to start a kernel, and by default it looks like this:

```
linux16 /vmlinuz-0-rescue-5dea58df1a3b4cb5947ddb6c78a6773f
root=UUID=432d640e-3339-45fa-a66d-89da9c869550 ro rd.lvm.lv=centos/
swap vconsole.font=latarcyrheb-sun16 rd.lvm.lv=centos/root
crashkernel=auto  vconsole.keymap=us rhgb quiet
```

To start, it is a good idea to remove the **rhgb** and **quiet** parts from this line; these arguments hide boot messages for you, and typically you do want to see what is happening while booting. In the next section you learn about some troubleshooting options that you can enter from the GRUB boot prompt.

```
        set root='hd0,msdos1'
        if [ x$feature_platform_search_hint = xy ]; then
          search --no-floppy --fs-uuid --set=root --hint-bios=hd0,msdos1 --hin\
t-efi=hd0,msdos1 --hint-baremetal=ahci0,msdos1 --hint='hd0,msdos1'  6b994d14-d\
1a8-44c8-a427-a7cb7efa0c83
        else
          search --no-floppy --fs-uuid --set=root 6b994d14-d1a8-44c8-a427-a7cb\
7efa0c83
        fi
        linux16 /vmlinuz-0-rescue-29ad30227f72454db44efbea843128c5 root=UUID=5\
077d04a-0928-4ef0-ba05-dc3ee9878df7 ro rd.lvm.lv=centos/swap vconsole.font=lat\
arcyrheb-sun16 rd.lvm.lv=centos/root crashkernel=auto  vconsole.keymap=us rhgb\
 quiet
        initrd16 /initramfs-0-rescue-29ad30227f72454db44efbea843128c5.img
_

      Press Ctrl-x to start, Ctrl-c for a command prompt or Escape to
      discard edits and return to the menu. Pressing Tab lists
      possible completions.
```

Figure 19.2 Enter boot arguments on the line that starts with linux16.

After entering the boot options you want to use, press **Ctrl+X** to start the kernel with these options. Notice that these options are used one time only and are not persistent. To make them persistent you must modify the contents of the /etc/default/grub configuration file and use **grub2-mkconfig -o /boot/grub2/grub.cfg** to apply the modification.

Starting a Troubleshooting Target

When you are in trouble, you have a few options that you can enter on the GRUB boot prompt:

- **rd.break** This stops the boot procedure while still in the initramfs stage. This option is useful if you do not have the root password available. The complete procedure for recovering a missing root password follows later in this chapter.
- **init=/bin/sh** or **init=/bin/bash** This specifies that a shell should be started immediately after loading the kernel and initrd. This is a useful option, but not the best option, because in some cases you'll lose console access or miss other functionality.
- **systemd.unit=emergency.target** This enters in a bare minimal mode where a minimal number of systemd units is loaded. It requires a root password. To see that only a very limited number of unit files have been loaded, you can type the **systemctl list-units** command.
- **systemd.unit=rescue.target** This starts some more systemd units to bring you in a more complete operational mode. It does require a root password. To see that only a very limited number of unit files have been loaded, you can type the **systemctl list-units** command.

In Exercise 19.1, you learn how to enter the rescue.target mode. The other modes listed here are discussed in the following sections.

Exercise 19.1 Exploring troubleshooting targets.

1. (Re)start your computer. When the GRUB menu shows, select the first line in the menu and press **e**.
2. Scroll down to the line that starts with linux16 /vmlinuz. At the end of this line, type **systemd.unit=rescue.target**. Also remove the options **rhgb quit** from this line.
3. Enter the root password when you are prompted for it.
4. Type **systemctl list-units**. This shows all unit files that are currently loaded. You can see that a basic system environment has been loaded.
5. Type **systemctl show-environment**. This shows current shell environment variables.
6. Type **systemctl reboot** to reboot your machine.
7. When the GRUB menu shows, press **e** again to enter the editor mode. At the end of the line that loads the kernel, type **systemd.unit=emergency.target**.
8. When prompted for it, enter the root password to log in.
9. After successful login, type **systemctl list-units**. Notice that the number of unit files loaded is reduced to a bare minimum.

Using a Rescue Disk

If you are lucky when you are in trouble, you'll still be able to boot from hard disk. If you are a bit less lucky, you'll just see a blinking cursor on a system that does not boot at all. If that happens, you need a rescue disk. The default rescue image for Red Hat Enterprise Linux is on the installation disk. When booting from the installation disk, you'll see a Troubleshooting menu item. Select this item to get access to the options you need to repair your machine (see Figure 19.3).

Restoring System Access Using a Rescue Disk

After selecting the troubleshooting option, you'll notice that some specific options show:

- **Install Red Hat 7 in Basic Graphics Mode:** This option reinstalls your machine. Do not use it unless you want to troubleshoot a situation where a normal installation does not work and you need a basic graphics mode.

Normally, you should not ever need to use this option to troubleshoot a broken installation.

- **Rescue a Red Hat System:** This is the most flexible rescue system. In Exercise 19.2, you can explore it in detail. This should be the first option of choice when using a rescue disk.
- **Run a Memory Test:** Run this option if you encounter memory errors. It allows you to mark bad memory chips so that your machine can boot normally.
- **Boot from Local Drive:** If you cannot boot from GRUB on your hard disk, try this option first. It offers a boot loader that tries to install from your machine's hard drive, and as such is the least intrusive option available.

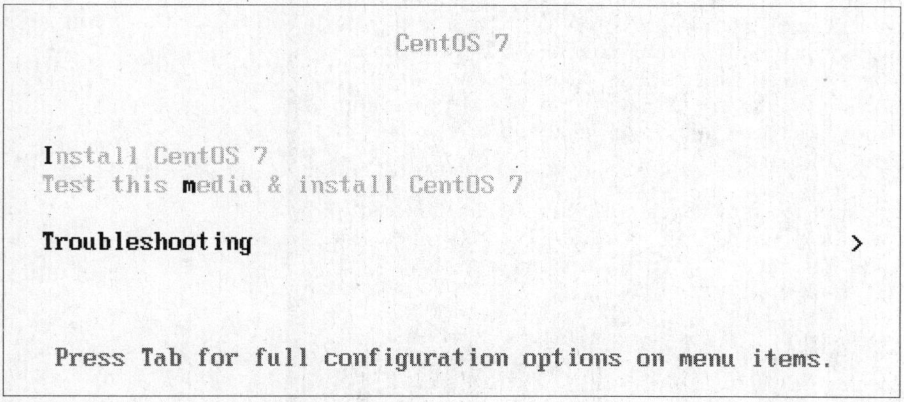

Figure 19.3 Starting from a rescue disk.

After starting a rescue system, you usually need to enable full access to the on-disk installation. Typically, the rescue disk detects your installation and mounts it on the /mnt/sysimage directory. To fix access to the configuration files and their default locations as they should be available on disk, use the **chroot /mnt/sysimage** command to make the contents of this directory your actual working environment. If you do not use this **chroot** command, many utilities will not work, because if they write to a configuration file that would be the version of the configuration file that exists on the rescue disk (and for that reason is read-only). Using the **chroot** command ensures that all path references to configuration files are correct.

In Exercise 19.2 you learn how to use the Rescue a Red Hat System option to troubleshoot a system that does not boot anymore.

Exercise 19.2 Using the Rescue Option

1. Restart your server from the installation disk. Select the **Troubleshooting** menu option.
2. From the Troubleshooting menu, select **Rescue a Red Hat System**. This prompts you to press **Enter** to start the installation. Do not worry: This option does not overwrite your current configuration; it just loads a rescue system.
3. The rescue system now prompts you that it will try to find an installed Linux system and mount on /mnt/sysimage. Press **Continue** to accept this option (see Figure 19.4).

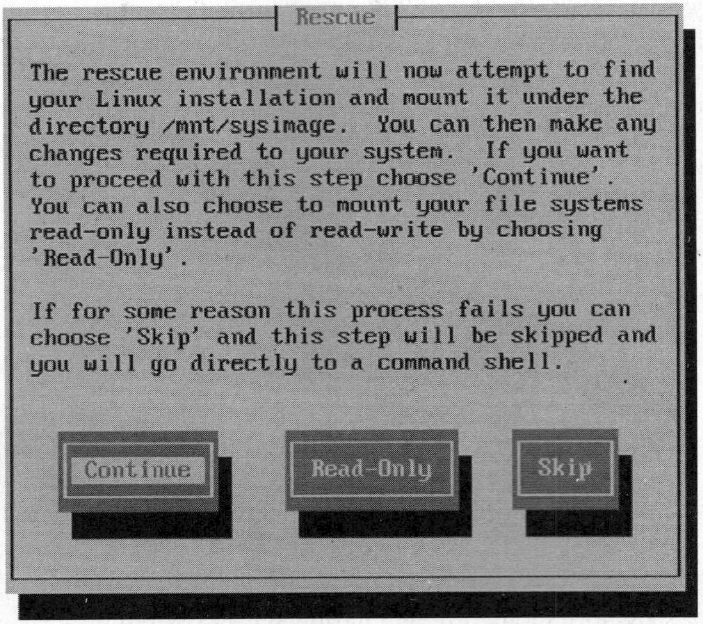

Figure 19.4 The rescue system looks for an installed system image and mount it for you.

4. If a valid Red Hat installation was found, you are prompted that your system has been mounted under /mnt/sysimage. At this point, you can press **Enter** twice to access the rescue shell.
5. Your Linux installation at this point is accessible through the /mnt/sysimage directory. Type **chroot /mnt/sysimage**. At this point, you have access to your root file system and you can access all tools that you need to repair access to your system.
6. Type **exit** and **reboot** to restart your machine in a normal mode.

Reinstalling GRUB Using a Rescue Disk

One of the common reasons you need to start a rescue disk is because the GRUB 2 boot loader is broken. If that happens, you might need to install it again. After you have restored access to your server using a rescue disk, reinstalling GRUB 2 is not hard to do and consists of two steps:

- Make sure that you have made the contents of the /mnt/sysimage directory to your current working environment.
- Use the **grub2-install** command, followed by the name of the device on which you want to reinstall GRUB 2. So on a KVM virtual machine, the command to use is **grub2-install /dev/vda**, and on a physical server or a VMware or Virtual Box virtual machine, it is **grub2-install /dev/sda**.

Re-Creating the Initramfs Using a Rescue Disk

Occasionally, the initramfs image may get damaged as well. If this happens, you cannot boot your server into normal operational mode. To repair the initramfs image after booting into the rescue environment, you can use the **dracut** command. If used with no arguments, this command creates a new initramfs for the kernel currently loaded.

Alternatively, you can use the **dracut** command with several options to make an initramfs for specific kernel environments. There is also a configuration file with the name /etc/dracut.conf that you can use to include specific options while re-creating the initramfs. The **dracut** configuration is dispersed over different locations:

- /usr/lib/dracut/dracut.conf.d/*.conf contains the system default configuration files.
- /etc/dracut.conf.d contains custom dracut configuration files.
- /etc/dracut.conf is used as the master configuration file.

Listing 19.1 shows an example of the default dracut.conf configuration file.

Listing 19.1 /etc/dracut.conf Default Contents

```
[root@server1 ~]# cat /etc/dracut.conf
# PUT YOUR CONFIG HERE OR IN separate files named *.conf
# in /etc/dracut.conf.d
# SEE man dracut.conf(5)
```

```
# Sample dracut config file

#logfile=/var/log/dracut.log
#fileloglvl=6

# Exact list of dracut modules to use.  Modules not listed here are
not going
# to be included.  If you only want to add some optional modules use
# add_dracutmodules option instead.
#dracutmodules+=""

# dracut modules to omit
#omit_dracutmodules+=""

# dracut modules to add to the default
#add_dracutmodules+=""

# additional kernel modules to the default
#add_drivers+=""

# list of kernel filesystem modules to be included in the generic
initramfs
#filesystems+=""

# build initrd only to boot current hardware
#hostonly="yes"
#

# install local /etc/mdadm.conf
#mdadmconf="no"

# install local /etc/lvm/lvm.conf
#lvmconf="no"

# A list of fsck tools to install. If it is not specified, module's
hardcoded
# default is used, currently: "umount mount /sbin/fsck* xfs_db xfs_
check
# xfs_repair e2fsck jfs_fsck reiserfsck btrfsck". The installation is
# opportunistic, so non-existing tools are just ignored.
#fscks=""
```

```
# inhibit installation of any fsck tools
#nofscks="yes"

# mount / and /usr read-only by default
#ro_mnt="no"

# set the directory for temporary files
# default: /var/tmp
#tmpdir=/tmp
```

TIP According to the Red Hat objectives, you should not have to work with a rescue disk on the exam. However, as an RHCSA and also as an RHCE, you should expect the unexpected, which it why it is a good idea to ensure that you can handle common as well as a bit less common troubleshooting scenarios.

Fixing Common Issues

In one small chapter such as this, it is not possible to consider all the possible problems one might encounter when working with Linux. There are some problems, though, that are more likely to occur than others. In this section you learn about some of the more common problems.

Reinstalling GRUB 2

Boot loader code does not disappear just like that, but on occasion it can happen that the GRUB 2 boot code gets damaged. In that case, you better know how to reinstall GRUB 2. The exact approach depends on whether your server is still in a bootable state. If it is, it is fairly easy to reinstall GRUB 2. Just type **grub2-install** followed by the name of the device to which you want to install it. The command has many different options to fine-tune what exactly will be installed, but you probably will not need them because, by default, the command installs everything you need to make your system bootable again.

It becomes a little bit more complicated if your machine is in a nonbootable state. If that happens, you first need to start a rescue system and restore access to your server from the rescue system. (See Exercise 19.2 for the exact procedure how to do that.) After mounting your server's file systems on /mnt/sysimage and using **chroot /mnt/sysimage** to make the mounted system image your root image, it is as easy as described previously: Just run **grub2-install** to install GRUB 2 to the desired installation device. So if you are in a KVM virtual machine, run **grub2-install /dev/vda**, and if you are on a physical disk, run **grub2-install /dev/sda**.

Fixing the Initramfs

In rare cases, it might happen that the initramfs gets damaged. If you analyze the boot procedure carefully, you will learn that you have a problem with the initramfs because you'll never see the root file system getting mounted on the root directory, nor will you see any systemd units getting started. If you suspect that you are having a problem with the initramfs, it is easy to re-create it. To re-create it using all default settings (which is fine in most cases), you can just run the **dracut --force** command. (Without **--force**, the command will refuse to overwrite your existing initramfs.)

When running the **dracut** command, you can use the /etc/dracut.conf configuration file to specify what exactly is written to the initramfs. In this configuration file, you can see options like **lvmconf="no"** that can be used to switch specific features on or off. Use these options to make sure that you have all the required functionality in your initramfs.

Recovering from File System Issues

If you make a misconfiguration to your file system mounts, the boot procedure may just end with the message "Give root password for maintenance." This message is, in particular, generated by the **fsck** command that is trying to verify the integrity of the file systems in /etc/fstab while booting. If **fsck** fails, manual intervention is required which may result in this message during boot. Make sure that you know what to do when this happens to you!

> **TIP** Make sure to master this topic very well. File system-related topics have a heavy weight in the RHCSA objectives, and it is likely that you will need to create partitions and/or logical volumes and put them in /etc/fstab for automatic mounting. That makes it also likely that something will go wrong, and if that happens on the exam, you better make sure that you know how to fix it!

If a device is referred to that does not exist, or if there is an error in the UUID that is used to mount the device, for example, systemd waits first to see whether the device comes back by itself. If that does not happen, it gives the message "Give root password for maintenance" (see Figure 19.5). If that happens, you should by all means first enter the root password. Then you can type **journalctl -xb** as suggested to see whether relevant messages providing information about what is wrong are written to the journal. If the problem is file system oriented, type **mount -o remount,rw /** to make sure the root file system is mounted read-only and analyze what is wrong in the /etc/fstab file and fix it.

```
[    1.981729] sd 2:0:0:0: [sda] Assuming drive cache: write through
[    1.982607] sd 2:0:0:0: [sda] Assuming drive cache: write through
[    1.983393] sd 2:0:0:0: [sda] Assuming drive cache: write through
[    3.262839] piix4_smbus 0000:00:07.3: Host SMBus controller not enabled!
[    3.430005] end_request: I/O error, dev fd0, sector 0
[    3.450991] end_request: I/O error, dev fd0, sector 0
Welcome to emergency mode! After logging in, type "journalctl -xb" to view
system logs, "systemctl reboot" to reboot, "systemctl default" to try again
to boot into default mode.
Give root password for maintenance
(or type Control-D to continue): _
```

Figure 19.5 If you see this, you normally have an /etc/fstab issue.

Resetting the Root Password

A common scenario for a Linux administrator is that the root password has gone missing. If that happens, you need to reset it. The only way to do that is by booting into minimal mode, which allows you to log in without entering a password. To do so, follow these steps:

Key Topic

1. On system boot, press **e** when the GRUB 2 boot menu is shown.
2. Enter **rd.break** as boot argument to the line that loads the kernel and press **Ctrl+X** to boot with this option.
3. You'll now be dropped at the end of the boot stage where initramfs is loaded, just before a mount of the root file system on the directory /.
4. Type **mount -o remount,rw /sysroot** to get read/write access to the system image.
5. At this point, make the contents of the /sysimage directory your new root directory by typing **chroot /sysroot**.
6. Now you can enter **passwd** and set the new password for the user root.
7. Because at this very early boot stage SELinux has not been activated yet, the context type on /etc/shadow will be messed up. If you reboot at this point, no one will be able to log in. So you must make sure that the context type is set correctly. To do this, at this point you should load the SELinux policy by using **load_policy -i**.

8. Now you can manually set the correct context type to /etc/shadow. To do this, type **chcon -t shadow_t /etc/shadow**.
9. Reboot. You can now log in with the changed password for user root.

> **NOTE** In the preceding procedure you have read how to use the **load_policy -i** and **chcon** commands to correct the labels on the /etc/shadow file. An alternative (and easier) method is to create a file with the name /.autorelabel which will force SELinux to restore labels that are set on the entire file system.

Recovering Access to a Virtual Machine

A special case of troubleshooting is a situation that involves a virtual machine. If you have a problem in the virtual machine, and you cannot access it using Virtual Machine Manager or **virsh console** as described in Chapter 10, "Working with Virtual Machines," you also can't connect to it using SSH. However, there is still an option. The technique described here is a bit advanced, but because it might someday help you reestablish access to a virtual machine that would otherwise have been lost, it is worth knowing about.

> **TIP** The procedure that is described here is relatively complicated, and you should not have to apply it unless you mess up severely during the exam. So instead of memorizing this procedure, just be very careful to prevent issues like this from happening!

1. To start, open a root shell on the KVM host. From that host file, make sure that the virtual machine is stopped by using **virsh destroy** *vmname*. (Use the name of the virtual machine as listed by the **virsh list** command.).
2. Find the disk image file. It normally is stored in the /var/lib/libvirt/images directory. If you cannot find it there, use **virsh dumpxml vmname | grep "source file="** to find the name of the source file:

```
[root@lab ~]# virsh dumpxml sander-vm1 | grep "source file="
      <source file='/home/sander/lab1.img'/>
      <source file='/var/lib/libvirt/images/sander-vm1.img'/>
```

3. Now that you know the name of the virtual machine image file, you can mount it into the host environment by using the **kpartx -a** command. This command

analyzes the disk layout on the virtual machine and creates storage devices that allow you to mount devices in the virtual machine in the host file system:

```
[root@lab ~]# kpartx -av /home/sander/lab1.img
add map loop0p1 (253:5): 0 1024000 linear /dev/loop0 2048
add map loop0p2 (253:6): 0 7362560 linear /dev/loop0 1026048
```

4. The **kpartx** command has created devices that enable you to access the two partitions in the virtual machine. If this is a typical RHEL 7 setup, the first partition is the /boot partition, and the second partition is normally used for LVM logical volumes. You can mount the /boot partition easily by using **mount /dev/mapper/loop0p1 /mnt**.

5. To access the logical volumes that exist within the virtual machine's second partition, use the **pvscan** command:

```
[root@lab mapper]# pvscan /dev/mapper/loop0p2
  PV /dev/sda3          VG centos    lvm2 [48.83 GiB / 0 free]
  PV /dev/sda4          VG centos    lvm2 [50.00 GiB / 20.00 GiB
free]
  PV /dev/sda5          VG vglvm     lvm2 [347.32 GiB / 329.32 GiB
free]
  PV /dev/mapper/loop0p2  VG centosvm   lvm2 [3.51 GiB / 0
free]
  Total: 4 [449.65 GiB] / in use: 4 [449.65 GiB] / in no VG: 0
[0   ]
```

6. You now have activated the LVM setup within the virtual machine. If you type the **lvs** command, you should show the logical volumes listed as well, but in an active state. To activate them, use the **vgchange** command on the volume group that was found in the virtual machine disk image file. So for this exam, you type **vgchange -a y centosvm** to activate all logical volumes. After doing so, you can mount them also to directly access all files in the virtual machine file system and fix all issues that prevented the virtual machine from booting normally.

WARNING This procedure works well unless within the virtual machine the same LVM volume group name is used as on the host machine. This will normally not be the case because the VG name by default is the same as the hostname (and you normally want hostnames to be unique). If the VG names are not unique, though, you risk mixing them up and working on the wrong logical volume.

7. After you have fixed all issues in the virtual machine, you first need to unmount all file systems currently mounted. Next, you need to remove the device files that have been created based on the contents of the virtual machine image file by using the **kpartx -dv /home/sander/lab1.img** command. (Make sure to use the filename of the image file that is actually used on your computer.)

Summary

In this chapter, you learned how to troubleshoot the Red Hat Enterprise Linux 7 boot procedure. You learned in general what happens when a server boots and at which specific points you can interfere to fix things that go wrong. You also learned what to do in some specific cases. Make sure that you know these procedures well; you are likely to encounter them on the exam.

Exam Prep Tasks

Review All Key Topics

Review the most important topics in the chapter, noted with the Key Topic icon in the outer margin of the page. Table 19.3 lists a reference of these key topics and the page numbers on which each is found.

Table 19.3 Key Topics for Chapter 19

Key Topic Element	Description	Page
List	Summary of phases processed while booting	432
Table 19.2	Boot phase configuration and troubleshooting overview	433
List	Summary of relevant GRUB 2 boot options for troubleshooting	435
List	Resetting the root password	443

Complete Tables and Lists from Memory

Print a copy of Appendix B, "Memory Tables" (found on the disc), or at least the section for this chapter, and complete the tables and lists from memory. Appendix C, "Memory Tables Answer Key," also on the disc, includes completed tables and lists to check your work.

Define Key Terms

Define the following key terms from this chapter and check your answers in the glossary:

target, GRUB, initramfs, dracut

Review Questions

1. Which key do you need to press to enter the GRUB boot menu editor mode?
2. During startup, the boot procedure is not completed and the server asks for the root password instead. What is likely to be the reason of this?
3. You want to enter troubleshooting mode, but you do not know the root password. Which argument would you pass to the kernel to enter a mode that provides access to most of the machine's functionality?
4. You start your server and nothing happens. You just see a blinking cursor and that's all. What is the first step to troubleshoot this issue?
5. You want to find out which units are available in a specific troubleshooting environment. Which command would you use?
6. You want to start troubleshooting a lost root password. Which argument would you pass to the GRUB 2 boot loader?
7. From the shell that you have started to troubleshoot a lost password for user root, you want to load the SELinux policy. Which command enables you to do that?
8. While troubleshooting the root password, what do you need to do to make sure the SELinux labels are set correctly?
9. You have applied changes to the GRUB 2 boot loader and want to save them. How do you need to do that?
10. You do know the root password on a machine where you want to enter the most minimal troubleshooting mode. Which GRUB 2 boot argument would you use?

End-of-Chapter Labs

Lab 19.1 shows you how to troubleshoot some common problems.

Lab 19.1

1. Restart your server and change the root password from the appropriate troubleshooting mode.
2. In /etc/fstab, change one of the device names so that on next reboot the file system on it cannot be mounted. Restart and fix the issue that you encounter.
3. Use a rescue disk to bring your server up in full troubleshooting mode from the rescue disk.
4. Re-create the initramfs.

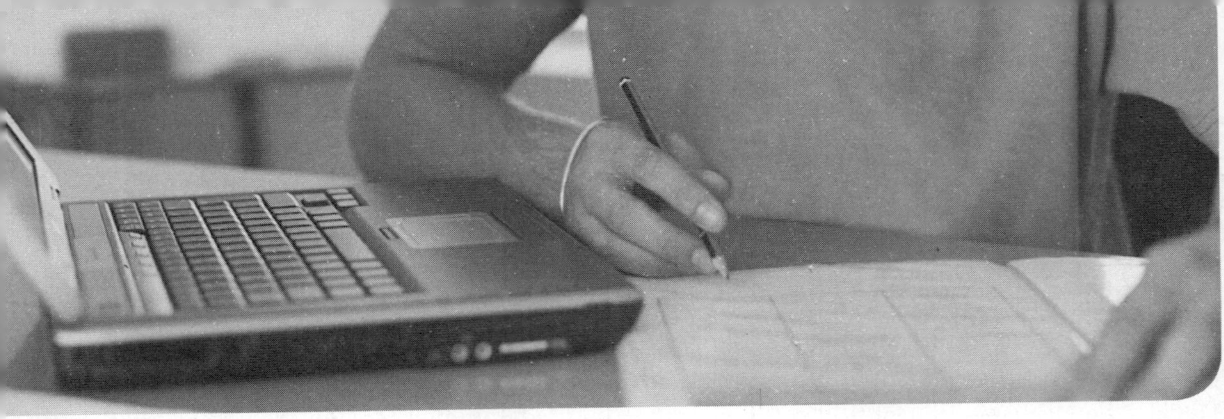

The following topics are covered in this chapter:

- Setting Up an Installation Server
- Setting Up a TFTP and DHCP Server for PXE Boot
- Creating a Kickstart File

The following RHCSA exam objectives are covered in this chapter:

- Installing Red Hat Enterprise Linux automatically using Kickstart

CHAPTER 20

Using Kickstart

In this chapter, you learn how to install RHEL 7 automatically using Kickstart. Kickstart by itself is simple to understand and configure: It is just a configuration file that needs to be used by the installer to specify how exactly the installation is to be performed (and that is also what the RHCSA objective seems to refer to).

Using Kickstart in an environment where you are still installing from an optical disk is not that useful, though, which is why in this chapter you learn how to set up a complete environment where an installation server is providing access to the repository that is used, and a PXE boot server is configured to provide access to a boot image that can be used to start a fully automated installation. This may go way beyond the RHCSA objectives, but at least it provides you with useful information that you can use to set up a fully automated installation environment.

"Do I Know This Already?" Quiz

The "Do I Know This Already?" quiz allows you to assess whether you should read this entire chapter thoroughly or jump to the "Exam Preparation Tasks" section. If you are in doubt about your answers to these questions or your own assessment of your knowledge of the topics, read the entire chapter. Table 20.1 lists the major headings in this chapter and their corresponding "Do I Know This Already?" quiz questions. You can find the answers in Appendix A, "Answers to the 'Do I Know This Already?' Quizzes and 'Review Questions.'"

Table 20.1 "Do I Know This Already?" Section-to-Question Mapping

Foundation Topics Section	Questions
Setting Up An Installation Server	1
Setting up a TFTP and DHCP Server for PXE Boot	2–6
Creating a Kickstart File	7–10

1. Which of the following installation server types is *not* supported?
   a. NFS
   b. CIFS
   c. HTTP
   d. FTP
2. What can you use if you want a minimal boot image to be available to the servers you want to install, but you do not want to provide that through a network PXE server?
   a. Use the boot.iso image that is provided by Red Hat at RHN.
   b. Use the installation disk.
   c. Copy the bootloader to the server you want to install before starting the installation.
   d. Copy the boot image on the HTTP installation server.
3. Which service needs to be enabled to provide TFTP services?
   a. tftp
   b. tftpd
   c. httpd
   d. xinetd
4. In which file do you specify the name of the PXE boot image that needs to be handed out to installable clients?
   a. /etc/ftpt.conf
   b. /etc/xinetd.d/tftp
   c. /etc/dhcpd.conf
   d. /etc/pxe.conf
5. In which file do you specify the name of the TFTP server root directory?
   a. /etc/ftpt.conf
   b. /etc/xinetd.d/tftp
   c. /etc/dhcpd.conf
   d. /etc/pxe.conf

6. Which RPM package contains the boot loader that is used in a PXE environment to provide all available boot options to the clients?
   a. syslinux
   b. lilo
   c. grub
   d. grub2

7. Which boot argument must be used on the GRUB 2 boot prompt that is provided from the installation DVD to refer to a Kickstart file?
   a. **install=**
   b. **ks=**
   c. **kickstart=**
   d. **anaconda=**

8. What is the name of the default Kickstart file that is created after installing an RHEL server?
   a. /root/kickstart.cfg
   b. /root/anaconda.cfg
   c. /root/anaconda-ks.cfg
   d. /root/anaconda-kickstart.cfg

9. What is the name of the utility that provides a menu-driven interface to create Kickstart files?
   a. kickstart-config
   b. system-config-kickstart
   c. config-kickstart
   d. system-config-install

10. Which of the following *cannot* be specified using system-config-kickstart?
    a. LVM logical volumes
    b. Individual RPM packages
    c. Firewalld services
    d. All of the above

Foundation Topics

Setting Up an Installation Server

In this chapter, you learn how to set up an installation server. This is useful if you need to install many instances of Red Hat Enterprise Linux. Using an installation server means that you can avoid installing every physical server by inserting a DVD in that server. You'll install new servers over the network instead. Also, it allows you to install servers that do not have an optical drive, such as blades.

Setting up an installation server involves different steps.

Key Topic

- To start, you need to make the installation files available. To do this, you configure a network server. This can be an NFS, FTP, or HTTP server.
- Then you need to deliver a boot image to the clients that need to be installed. For a fully automated network installation, you need to set up PXE boot that provides a boot image to your client by working together with the DHCP server.
- As the last step to set up an installation server, you create a Kickstart file. This is an answer file that contains all settings that are needed to install your servers and the final step in setting up a completely automated installation. The Kickstart file can be provided through an installation server to provide a fully automated installation, but it can also be offered on a USB device.

Configuring a Network Server as Installation Server

The first step to set up an installation server is to configure a network server as installation server. This comes down to copying the entire installation DVD to a share on a network server, which makes the installation server an online repository. After doing this, you can use a client computer to access the installation files. After setting it up, you test it. You boot from a regular installation DVD or image and refer to the network path for installation. Once the entire installation server has been completely set up, the procedure will be much more useful because a boot image will be provided by the TFTP server. Because there is no TFTP server yet, you'll have to use the installation DVD instead. Exercise 20.1 walks you through this procedure.

Exercise 20.1 Setting Up the Network Installation Server

In this exercise, you set up the network installation server by copying over all files required for installation to a directory that is offered by an HTTP server. After doing this, you test the installation from a virtual machine. To perform this exercise, you need the account.example.com virtual Apache web server that you created in Chapter 17, "Configuring a Basic Apache Server."

1. Insert the Red Hat Enterprise Linux installation DVD in the optical drive of your server and navigate to the Packages directory on the installation disk.
2. Use **mkdir /www/docs/account.example.com/install** to create a subdirectory in the Apache document root for account.example.com.
3. Use **cp -R * /www/docs/account.example.com/install** from the directory where the Red Hat Enterprise Linux installation DVD is mounted to copy all files on the DVD to the install directory in your web server document root.
4. Modify the configuration file for the server1 virtual host in /etc/httpd/conf.d/account.example.com and make sure that it includes the line Options Indexes. Without this line, the virtual host will only show contents of a directory if it contains an index.html file.
5. Use service httpd restart to restart the Apache web server.
6. Start a browser and browse to http://account.example.com/install. You should now see the contents of the installation DVD.
7. Start Virtual Machine Manager and create a new virtual machine. Give the virtual machine the name **testnetinstall** and select Network Install when asked how to install the operating system.
8. When asked for the installation URL, enter http://account.example.com/install (and verify that this URL can be resolved). The installation should now be started.
9. You can now interrupt the installation procedure and remove the virtual machine. You have now seen that the installation server is operational, and it is time to move on to the next phase in the procedure.

Setting Up a TFTP and DHCP Server for PXE Boot

Key Topic

Now that you have set up a network installation server, it is time to configure PXE boot. This allows you to boot a server you want to install from the network card of the server. (You normally have to change default boot order, or press a key while booting, to activate PXE boot.) The PXE server next hands out a boot image that the server you want to install uses to start the initial phase of the boot.

There are two steps involved: You need to install a TFTP server and have it provide a boot image to PXE clients, and you need to configure DHCP to talk to the TFTP server to provide the boot image to PXE clients.

NOTE In this section, you learn how to set up a network based installation server that delivers a boot image to the clients as well. As an alternative, you could choose to set up a simpler environment, where the clients that need to be installed boot from a local boot image and from there refer to the installation files on the network installation server. For this purpose, Red Hat provides the boot.iso image on RHN.

Installing the TFTP Server

The first part of the installation is easy: You need to install the tftp-server package using **yum -y install tftp-server**. The tftpd service is managed by the xinetd service, and to tell xinetd that it should allow access to TFTP, you need to open the /etc/xinetd.d/tftp file (see Listing 20.1) and change the disabled parameter from yes to no.

NOTE The xinetd service is also know as the Internet super service. It comes from a time where memory resources were limited, and to use memory as efficient as possible, xinetd could be configured to listen on many ports, making it possible to access many different services. Using xinetd can still be helpful, particularly for services that are not accessed very often. The xinetd service will make sure that the service is started when some processes access its port, and will also shut it down after a specific period of inactivity.

After enabling the tftp service, complete the following steps to make it available:

1. Restart the xinetd service using **systemctl start xinetd**.
2. Make sure to include xinetd in your startup procedure, using **systemctl enable xinetd**.
3. Make sure to permit tftp in your firewall configuration, using **firewall-cmd --permanent --add-service=tftp**.
4. Reload the firewall configuration to make the firewall modification effective, using **firewall-cmd --reload**.

Listing 20.1 The xinetd File for TFTP

```
[root@server1 ~]# cat /etc/xinetd.d/tftp
# default: off
# description: The tftp server serves files using the trivial file
# transfer \
#         protocol.  The tftp protocol is often used to boot diskless \
#         workstations, download configuration files to network-aware
# printers, \
#         and to start the installation process for some operating
# systems.
service tftp
{
        socket_type                     = dgram
        protocol                        = udp
        wait                            = yes
        user                            = root
        server                          = /usr/sbin/in.tftpd
        server_args                     = -s /var/lib/tftpboot
        disable                         = no
        per_source                      = 11
        cps                             = 100 2
        flags                           = IPv4
}
```

At this point the Trivial File Transfer Protocol (TFTP) server is operational. You now have to configure Dynamic Host Configuration Protocol (DHCP) to communicate to the TFTP server to hand out a boot image.

Configuring DHCP for PXE Boot

On an installation server, the TFTP server cannot exist without a DHCP server. When making a PXE boot, the DHCP server is the first to answer with all the required IP-related configuration and information about the DHCP server that is to be used. Therefore, you now have to install a DHCP server. Use **yum install -y dhcp** to install the server. You then have to create a subnet and modify the DHCP server configuration so that it can hand out a boot image to PXE clients. To do this, make sure to include the following (see Listing 20.2) in your dhcpd.conf and restart the DHCP server.

Listing 20.2 Adding PXE Boot Lines to the dhcpd.conf

```
subnet 192.168.1.0 netmask 255.255.255.0 {
        option routers 192.168.1.1 ;
        range 192.168.1.200 192.168.1.250 ;
        next-server 192.168.1.70;
        filename "pxelinux/pxelinux.0";
}
```

In the DHCP configuration file, a subnet is specified. This is the subnet where the PXE server should offer its services. In most configurations, this would be a dedicated network, which is a good idea, because you do not want workstations that perform a PXE boot to get installed with Red Hat Enterprise Linux by accident. If you want to offer PXE-based installation services on a network where also clients are in use that rely on PXE boot, it is recommended to define a **class** statement to define which machines should be allowed to use PXE boot and which should not.

> **TIP** On the exam, it will not be a problem making no further specification to define which machines should be using the PXE server and which should not. You will not have anything that relies on a PXE boot to get started anyway.

Within the subnet definition, the **next-server** statement gives the IP address of the server that is configured with TFTP. Even if it is on the same server that is offering DHCP, you should still specify the next-server IP address. The **filename** statement defines the file that should be offered to workstations that are making a PXE boot. Notice that this filename is relative to the TFTP server root as defined in the TFTP configuration file.

Creating the TFTP PXE Server Content

You have now prepared the DHCP server with the appropriate settings, but so far it has nothing to offer yet. This section describes how to create the TFTP PXE server content that is going to be offered through DHCP.

The role of the PXE server is to deliver an image to the client that performs a PXE boot. In fact, it replaces the task that is normally performed by GRUB 2 and the contents of the boot directory and provides a bootloader over the network. Therefore, to configure a PXE server, you need to copy everything that is needed to boot your server to the /var/lib/tftpboot/pxelinux directory. You also need to create a

PXE boot file that performs the task that is normally handled by the grub.conf file. In Exercise 20.2, you copy all required content to the TFTP server root directory.

A special role in the PXE boot configuration is played by the file **default**. This file contains the boot information for all PXE clients. If you create a file with the name default, that is used by all clients that are allowed to PXE boot. You can also create a configuration file for a specific host by using the IP address in the name of the file. There is one restriction, though; it has to be the IP address in a hexadecimal notation. To help you a bit with that, a host that is performing a PXE boot always shows its hexadecimal IP address on the console while booting.

Alternatively, you can calculate the hexadecimal IP address yourself. If you do so, make sure to calculate the hexadecimal value for the four parts of the IP address of the target host; the calculator on your computer can help you with that. If the IP address is 192.168.0.200, for instance, the hexadecimal value is C0.A8.0.C8. So, if you create a file with the name C0A80C8, this file will only be read by that specific host. For your RHCSA exam preparation, you certainly do not have to go that deep. Just make sure that you offer a default configuration that can be used by all hosts performing a PXE boot.

Exercise 20.2 Configuring the TFTP Server for PXE Boot

To set up a TFTP server, you configure a DHCP server and the TFTP server. Notice that the configuration of a DHCP Server on your network can cause problems. An additional complicating factor is that the KVM virtual network environment probably already runs a DHCP server. Therefore, you cannot use the DHCP server that you'll configure to serve virtual machines. To make this exercise a success, make sure your Red Hat Enterprise Linux server is disconnected from the network and connect it to one PC only that is capable of performing a PXE boot. Every modern PC should be capable of making a PXE boot. You do not have to reinstall the computer you are using for this purpose. You just have to test that it can make a PXE boot.

1. Use yum **install -y tftpserver** to install the TFTP server. Because TFTP is managed by xinetd, use **systemctl enable xinetd** to have xinetd started automatically.
2. Open the configuration file /etc/xinetd.d/tftp with an editor and change the line **disabled = yes** to **disabled = no**.
3. If not installed yet, install a DHCP server. Open the configuration file /etc/dhcp/dhcpd.conf and give it the contents of Listing 20.2. Make sure the IP address ranges you are using match the IP configuration that is used on your network.

4. Copy the syslinux<version>.rpm from the Packages directory on the RHEL installation disc to /tmp. You'll need to extract the file pxelinux.0 from it, which is an essential file for setting up the PXE boot environment. To extract the RPM file, use **cd /tmp** to go to the /tmp directory, and from there, use **rpm-2cpio syslinux<version>.rpm | cpio -idmv** to extract the file.

NOTE You can also perform this part of the procedure in an easier way: Just install the syslinux package, and after installing it, copy the file to the right location as described here.

5. Copy the /usr/share/syslinx/pxelinux.0 file to /var/lib/tftpboot/pxelinux.
6. Use **mkdir /var/lib/tftpboot/pxelinux/pxelinux.cfg** to create the directory in which you'll store the pxelinux configuration file.
7. In /var/lib/tftpboot/pxelinux/pxelinux.cfg, create a file with the name default that contains the following lines:

```
default Linux
prompt 1
timeout 10
display boot.msg
label Linux
          menu label ^Install RHEL
          menu default
          kernel vmlinuz
          append initrd=initrd.img
```

8. If you want to use a splash image file while doing PXE boot, copy the /boot/grub/splash.xpm.gz file to /var/lib/tftptboot/pxelinux/.
9. On the Red Hat installation disc, in the directory images/pxeboot, you can find the files vmlinuz and initrd.img. Copy these to the directory /var/lib/tftpboot/pxelinux/.
10. Use systemctl restart dhcpd and systemctl restart xinetd to (re)start the required services.
11. On the server, use **tail -f /var/log/messages** to trace what is happening. Connect a computer directly to the server, and from that computer, choose PXE boot in the boot menu. You will see that the computer starts the PXE boot and loads the installation image that you have prepared for it.

12. If you want to continue the installation, when the installation program asks what type of media contains the installation media, select URL. Then, enter the URL to the web server installation image that you created in Exercise 20.1: http://account.example.com/install.

13. Finally, you need to instruct the firewall to enable the traffic using the following four commands:

```
firewall-cmd --permanent --add-service=dhcp
firewall-cmd --permanent --add-service=tftp
firewall-cmd --permanent --add-service=http
firewall-cmd --reload
```

In Exercise 20.2, you set up a PXE server to start an installation. You can use the same server to add some additional sections as well. A useful section, for instance, is the rescue system, and it might also be useful to add a section that allows you to boot from local disk. The example contents for the default file from Listing 20.3 shows how you can do that.

If you are adding more options to the PXE menu, it also makes sense to increase the timeout to allow users to make a choice. In Listing 20.3, this is done by using the timeout 600 value. Notice, however, that this is not typically what you want if you want to use the PXE server for automated installations using a Kickstart file, as described in the following section.

Listing 20.3 Adding More Options to the PXE Boot Menu

```
default Linux
prompt 1
timeout 600
display boot.msg
label Linux
        menu label ^Install RHEL
        menu default
        kernel vmlinuz
        append initrd=initrd.img
label Rescue
        menu label ^Rescue system
        kernel vmlinuz
        append initrd=initrd.img rescue
```

```
label Local
        menu label Boot from ^local drive
localboot 0xffff
```

Creating a Kickstart File

You have now created an environment where everything you need to install your server is available on another server. Therefore, you do not have to work with optical disks anymore to perform an installation. Red Hat offers an excellent solution for this challenge: the Kickstart file. In this section, you learn how to use a Kickstart file to perform a completely automated installation and how you can optimize the Kickstart file to fit your needs.

Using a Kickstart File to Perform an Automated Installation

When you install a Red Hat system, a file with the name anaconda-ks.cfg is created in the home directory of the root user. This file contains most settings that were used while installing your computer. It is a good starting point if you want to try out an automated Kickstart installation.

To specify that you want to use a Kickstart file to install a server, you need to tell the installer where it can find the file. If you want to perform an installation from a local Red Hat installation disc, while installing add the **ks= boot** parameter. As an argument to this parameter, add a complete link to the file. If you have copied the Kickstart file to the account.example.com web server Document root, for example, add the following line as a boot option while installing from a DVD:

Key Topic

```
ks=http://account.example.com/anaconda-ks.cfg
```

To use a Kickstart file in an automated installation from a TFTP server, you need to add the Kickstart file to the section in the TFTP default file that starts the installation. The section that you need to install the server would in that case look like the following:

```
label Linux
        menu label ^Install RHEL
        menu default
        kernel vmlinuz
        append initrd=initrd.img \
        ks=http://account.example.com/anaconda-ks.cfg
```

In this file, make sure that the title of the menu label starts with a ^, which identifies it as a menu label title. Also make sure that the **append** line is one line only that starts with append and ends with the URL to the Kickstart file.

You can also use a Kickstart file while installing a virtual machine using Virtual Machine Manager. In Exercise 20.3, you learn how to perform a network installation without PXE boot and configure this installation to use the anaconda-ks.cfg file.

Exercise 20.3 Performing a Virtual Machine Network Installation Using a Kickstart File

In this exercise, you perform a network installation of a virtual machine that uses a Kickstart file. You use the network installation server that you have created in Exercise 20.1. This network server is used to access the installation files but also to provide access to the Kickstart file.

NOTE In this exercise, you are using the DNS name of the installation server. If installation fails with the message "unable to retrieve http://account.example.com/install/images/install.img," that is because account.example.com cannot be resolved with DNS. Use the IP address of the installation server instead.

1. On the installation server, copy the anaconda-ks.cfg file from the /root directory to /www/docs/account.example.com directory. You can just copy it straight to the root directory. After copying the file, set the permissions to mode 644; otherwise, the Apache user cannot read it.
2. Start Virtual Machine Manager and click the Create Virtual Machine button. Enter a name for the virtual machine, and select Network Install.
3. In the second screen of the Create a New Virtual Machine Wizard, enter the URL to the web server installation directory: http://account.example.com/install. Open the URL Options and enter the following Kickstart URL: http://account.example.com/anaconda-ks.cfg (see Figure 20.1).
4. Accept all default options in the remaining windows of the Create a New Virtual Machine Wizard, which will start the installation. In the beginning of the procedure, you'll see the message "Retrieving anaconda-ks.cfg." If that message disappears and you do not see an error message, the Kickstart file has loaded correctly.
5. Stop the installation after the Kickstart file has loaded. The Kickstart file was not made for virtual machines, so it will ask lots of questions anyway. (The only purpose of this exercise was to show that including a Kickstart file actually works.) After stopping the installation, remove the Kickstart file from the Virtual Machine Manager configuration.

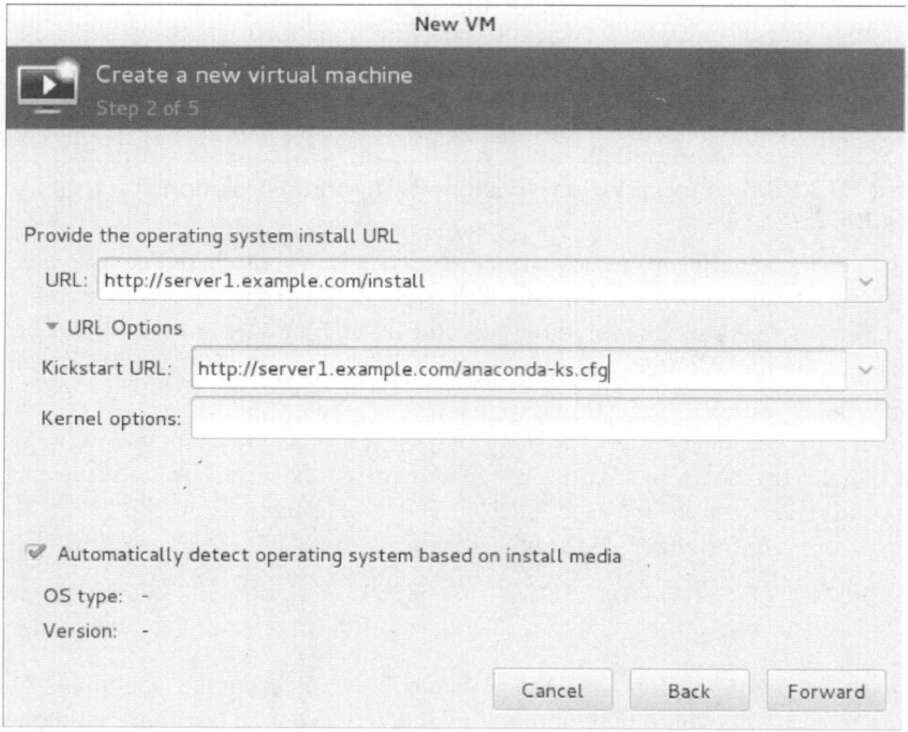

Figure 20.1 Specifying required options to use a Kickstart file.

Modifying the Kickstart File with system-config-kickstart

In the previous exercise, you started a Kickstart installation based on the Kickstart file that was created after the installation of your server was finished. You might have noticed that still many questions were asked anyway. That is because your Kickstart file did not fit the hardware of the virtual machine you were trying to install. In many cases, you need to fine-tune the Kickstart configuration file. To do this, you can use the system-config-kickstart graphical interface (see Figure 20.2).

Using system-config-kickstart, you can create new Kickstart files, but you can also read an existing Kickstart file and make all modifications you need without the risk of making syntax errors that could cause your Kickstart file to fail.

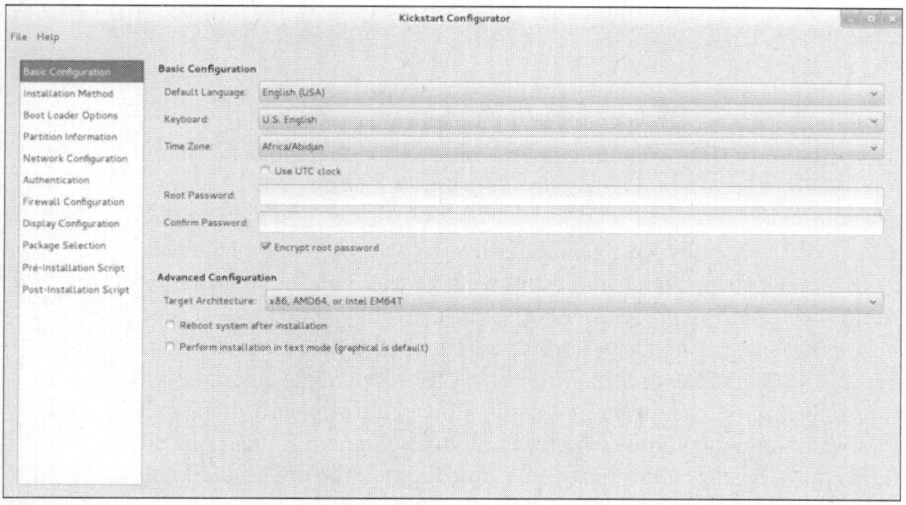

Figure 20.2 Use system-config-kickstart to create or tune Kickstart files.

NOTE In earlier versions of RHEL, many system-config tools were available to make configuring RHEL easy. In RHEL 7, the operating system itself has gone through a major revision, and most of the system-config tools have been replaced. The system-config-kickstart utility is one of the few remaining utilities. If you have worked with previous versions of RHEL, you'll notice that its interface still looks a lot like the RHEL 6 installation interface and that a few items have changed in it. You'll also notice that many new features, in particular those that are new to RHEL 7, are not supported in this interface. For instance, you cannot create firewalld configurations through system-config-kickstart; neither is it possible to configure LVM or install individual RPM packages using this tool.

Under the Basic Configuration option, you can find basic options like the keyboard and time zone that your server will be installed in. Here, you'll also find an interface to set the root password. Under Installation Method, you'll find (among other things) the installation source. For a network installation, you need to select the type of network installation server and the directory used on that server. In Figure 20.3, you can see what this would look like for the installation server you created in Exercise 20.1.

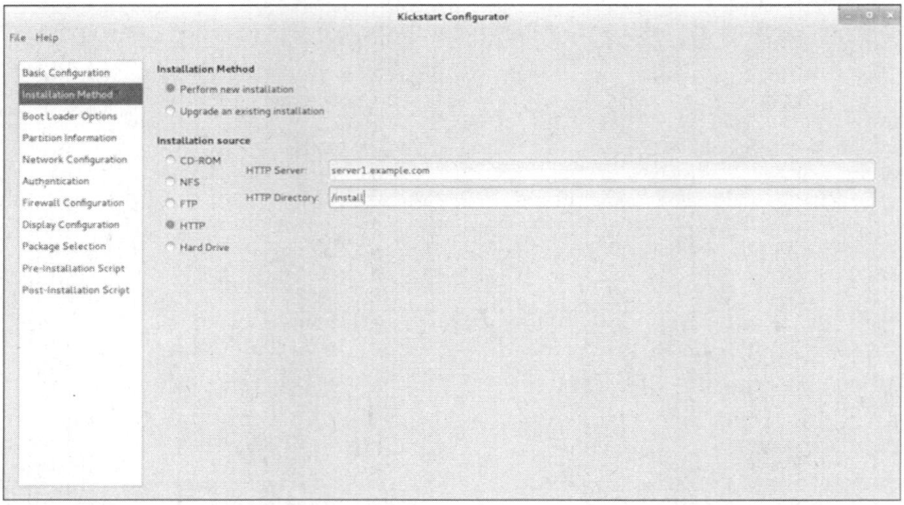

Figure 20.3 Specifying the network installation source.

Under Boot Loader Options, you can specify that you want to install a new bootloader and where you want to install it. If specific kernel parameters are needed while booting, you can specify them here as well. An important option is Partition Information (see Figure 20.4). Here, you can tell Kickstart which partitions you want to create on the server. Unfortunately, the interface does not allow you to create logical volumes. So if you need these, you need to add them manually, which is explained in the following section.

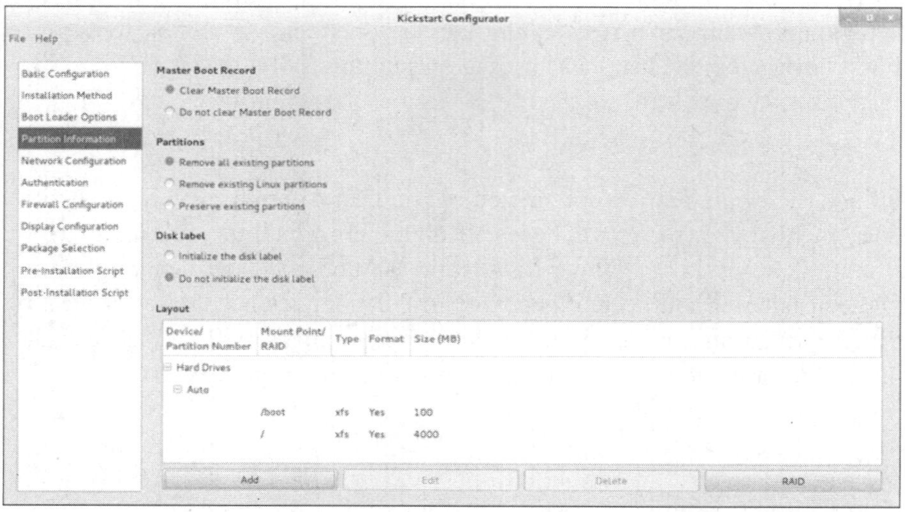

Figure 20.4 Creating partitions.

The Network Configuration option by default is empty. If you want networking on your server, you need to use the Add Network Device option to indicate the name of the device and how you want the device to get its network configuration. The Authentication option offers tabs to specify external authentication services, such as NIS, LDAP, Kerberos, and some others. If you do not specify any of these, you just use the local authentication mechanism that goes through /etc/passwd, which is fine for many servers.

If you do not like SELinux and firewalls, activate the Firewall Configuration option. SELinux is on by default (which is good in most cases), and the firewall by default is switched off. If your server is connected directly to the Internet, turn it on and select all trusted services that you want to allow. On the Display Configuration option, you can tell the installer whether your server should install a graphical environment.

An interesting option is Package Selection. This option allows you to select Package categories but not individual packages. If you need individual packages, you need to create a manual configuration. Finally, there are the Pre-Installation Script and Post-Installation Script options that allow you to add scripts to the installation procedure to execute specific tasks while installing the server.

Making Manual Modifications to the Kickstart File

There are some modifications that you cannot make to a Kickstart file using the graphical interface. Fortunately, a Kickstart file is an ASCII text file that can easily be edited by hand. By making manual modifications, you can configure features like LVM logical volumes, or individual packages, tasks that cannot be accomplished from the system-config-kickstart interface. In Listing 20.4, you can see the contents of the anaconda-ks.cfg file that is generated upon installation of a server. Studying this file is interesting because it shows examples of everything that cannot be done from the graphical interface.

Listing 20.4 Contents of the anaconda-ks.cfg File

```
[root@server1 ~]# cat anaconda-ks.cfg
#version=RHEL7
# System authorization information
auth --enableshadow --passalgo=sha512

# Use CDROM installation media
cdrom
# Run the Setup Agent on first boot
firstboot --enable
```

```
ignoredisk --only-use=sda
# Keyboard layouts
keyboard --vckeymap=us --xlayouts='us'
# System language
lang en_US.UTF-8

# Network information
network  --bootproto=dhcp --device=eno16777736 --ipv6=auto --activate
network  --hostname=localhost.localdomain
# Root password
rootpw --iscrypted $6$w.otIj7Fjqpr4Gmy$Uwo6TCHDf8TzI98nyy3zagSi6HVrs4Ur
8JI7J90.q5PtYi236k0Zo4rQp4kDyOY8zXS1dMbJadMNvSQ9Ul9SS1
# System timezone
timezone America/New_York --isUtc
user --name=user
password=$6$CwZOJIdBeiVJmte0$cYFoDfuucuIzSOeS3FIQvhxl1T02mrfeo
BCAvybP9719/HN9qY7ZtWVJ5iKXdKTBgbFz8o3gBCAIKI4j4HrQD. --iscrypted
--gecos="user"
# X Window System configuration information
xconfig  --startxonboot
# System bootloader configuration
bootloader --location=mbr --boot-drive=sda
autopart --type=lvm
# Partition clearing information
clearpart --none --initlabel

%packages
@base
@core
@desktop-debugging
@dial-up
@fonts
@gnome-desktop
@guest-agents
@guest-desktop-agents
@input-methods
@internet-browser
@multimedia
@print-client
@x11

%end
```

The anaconda-ks.cfg file starts with some generic settings. The first line that needs attention is the network line. As you can see, it contains the device name `--device eno16777736`. This device name is related to the specific hardware configuration of the server the file was created on, and it will probably not work on many hardware platforms. So, it is better to replace it with **--device eth0**.

The next interesting parameter is the line that contains the root password. As you can see, it contains the encrypted root password that was used while installing this server. If you want the installation process to prompt for a root password, you can just remove this line completely; everything that the installer cannot get directly from the Kickstart file will be prompted for.

In this example Kickstart file, you can see that the disk is partitioned automatically, using the **autopart --type=lvm** option. Then, the repository that is to be used is specified. This is also a parameter for which it is likely that it needs to be changed. The **--baseurl** parameter contains a URL that refers to the installation URL that you want to use. It can, for instance, read **--baseurl=http://account.example.com/install** to refer to an http installation server.

In the next section, the packages that are to be installed are specified. Everything that starts with a @ (such as @base) refers to an RPM package group. Individual packages can be specifically added by just mentioning the name of the packages.

> **TIP** If you do not get any errors, but the server seems to stall or will not provide the installation files, you can switch over to other virtual terminals on the server that you are installing to check whether it shows any error messages. To do so, you can use the **Ctrl+Alt-F2** up to **Ctrl+Alt-F7** key sequences. To get back to the graphical installation screen, use **Ctrl+Alt-F1**.

Summary

In this chapter, you learned how to set up an installation server. You learned how a typical installation server consists of a few different parts. First you need to have the installation files available online, which in this chapter was done by using a web server. Then, you need a mechanism to deliver a boot image. You learned how to configure DHCP and TFTP for this purpose. Lastly, for fully automated installations, you need an answer file. This answer file is provided by Kickstart. Putting all of these together allows you to work with a fully functional installation server.

Exam Preparation Tasks

Review All Key Topics

Review the most important topics in the chapter, noted with the Key Topic icon in the outer margin of the page. Table 20.2 lists a reference of these key topics and the page numbers on which each is found.

Table 20.2 Key Topics for Chapter 20

Key Topic Element	Description	Page
List	Steps involved in creating an installation server	454
Paragraph	Explanation of the way how TFTP, PXE, and DHCP are related	455
Sample code	Sample usage of a Kickstart file during installation	462

Define Key Terms

Define the following key terms from this chapter and check your answers in the glossary:

xinetd, tftp, installation server, Kickstart, anaconda

Review Questions

1. What is the name of the default Kickstart file that is created after installing an RHEL server?
2. What is the name of the utility that can be used to generate Kickstart files?
3. Which three features cannot be configured using system-config-kickstart?
4. You want to install a server using the installation disk and a Kickstart file that is available at http://server.example.com/kickstart.cfg. How do you specify to the installer that this file should be used?
5. Which services do you need to install to create a fully automated installation environment?
6. After installing the TFTP server, which service must be enabled and started to give access to the TFTP server?
7. When you are creating a PXE boot server, the boot menu must be created in a file. What is the name of that file?

8. Which RPM package contains the bootloader that can be used while doing a PXE boot?
9. You are looking for a minimal ISO image that can be used to boot a server before accessing the online repository that that server should be using. Where can you find it?
10. What is the default home directory for the TFTP server?

End-of-Chapter Labs

In the end-of-chapter labs, you set up an installation server consisting of an HTTP installation source, a DHCP server with a TFTP server, and a Kickstart installation file. To complete this exercise successfully, it is important that you work in a network that does not have any operational DHCP servers.

Lab 20.1

1. Set up an HTTP installation server that provides access to the installation files over the network.
2. Configure DHCP and TFTP so that the boot image can be provided to the clients that need to be installed.
3. Create a Kickstart file that provides all settings for a basic installation. Use the minimal installation pattern, but do make sure it meets at least the following requirements:
   - Put /home on a dedicated partition or logical volume.
   - Install the nmap package as well.
4. Install a virtual machine using the installation server you have just created.

The following topics are covered in this chapter:

- Understanding SELinux Working Modes
- Understanding Context Settings and Policy
- Restoring Default File Contexts
- Using Boolean Settings to Modify SELinux Settings
- Diagnosing and Addressing SELinux Policy Violations

The following RHCSA exam objectives are covered in this chapter:

- Set enforcing and permissive modes for SELinux
- List and identify SELinux file and process context
- Restore default file contexts
- Use Boolean settings to modify system SELinux settings
- Diagnose and address routine SELinux policy violations

CHAPTER 21

Managing SELinux

Since the earliest days of Linux, file permissions have been the standard method of securing Linux systems. In some cases, file permissions are just not enough for getting a secured server. Let's take a look at an example:

One morning I found out that my server was hacked. An intruder had broken through a bad script on my web server and had obtained shell access as the httpd user. Using this file access, he managed to create thousands of little PHP scripts that were involved in a massive DDoS attack.

From a security perspective, it is interesting that nothing really was wrong with the security settings on this server. All permissions were set in a decent way, and the httpd user, like any other user on a Linux server, does have permissions to create files in /var/tmp, as in /tmp. So, what would have been a good solution to prevent this kind of problem?

You could, of course, argue that the administrator of the web server should have been doing a better job and should have been watching what the scripts on the server were doing. But that is not how Linux servers are normally used. The Linux server administrator does not know all the applications running on his server, and the application administrator does not understand enough about Linux to ensure that something like this can never happen.

Another solution is to apply further security measures. For instance, this specific situation would have been prevented if the permission to run program files from the /tmp and /var/tmp directory would have been taken away by using the **noexec mount** option. But even if that would have worked for this specific situation, it is not a good overall security solution that prevents applications from doing things they are not supposed to be doing.

That is why SELinux was invented. SELinux provides mandatory access control to a Linux server, where every system call is denied unless it has been specifically allowed. This chapter explains how to use SELinux to make sure that serious security incidents will never happen on your server.

> **TIP** By any means, make sure that at the end of the exam SELinux is working on your server. If it is not, it will cost you many points!

"Do I Know This Already?" Quiz

The "Do I Know This Already?" quiz allows you to assess whether you should read this entire chapter thoroughly or jump to the "Exam Preparation Tasks" section. If you are in doubt about your answers to these questions or your own assessment of your knowledge of the topics, read the entire chapter. Table 21.1 lists the major headings in this chapter and their corresponding "Do I Know This Already?" quiz questions. You can find the answers in Appendix A, "Answers to the 'Do I Know This Already?' Quizzes and 'Review Questions.'"

Table 21.1 "Do I Know This Already?" Section-to-Question Mapping

Foundation Topics Section	Questions
Understanding SELinux Working Modes	1–2
Understanding Context Settings and Policy	3–6
Restoring Default File Contexts	7
Using Boolean Settings to Modify SELinux Settings	8
Diagnosing and Addressing SELinux Policy Violations	9–10

1. Which of the following is not a valid SELinux mode?
   a. Enforcing
   b. Permissive
   c. Disabled
   d. Enabled

2. Which of the following commands enables you to see the current SELinux mode?
   a. **sestatus**
   b. **lsmode**
   c. **semode**
   d. **getenforce**

3. Which of the following items in the context label is the most significant for SELinux system administration tasks?
   a. Type
   b. User
   c. Role
   d. Mission

4. To which of the following can SELinux security *not* be applied?
   a. Users.
   b. Files.
   c. Ports.
   d. It can be applied to all of the above.

5. Which command-line switch is used with many commands to display SELinux-related information?
   a. **-S**
   b. **-X**
   c. **-Z**
   d. **-D**

6. Which of the following commands should be used to set the context type of the directory /web to httpd_sys_content_t?
   a. **chcon -t httpd_sys_content_t /web**
   b. **semanage -t httpd_sys_content_t "/web(/.*)?"**
   c. **semanage fcontext -t httpd_sys_content_t "/web(/.*)?"**
   d. **semanage fcontext -a -t httpd_sys_content_t "/web(/.*)?"**

7. Which command must you run to ensure that it has the appropriate SELinux context after moving a file to another location?
   a. **reboot**
   b. **restorecon /new/filename**
   c. **chcon**
   d. **restorecon -R /etc/selinux -v**

8. Which command enables you to change a Boolean in a way that it survives a reboot?
    a. **chcon boolean -P**
    b. **setsebool -P**
    c. **setsebool**
    d. **semanage boolean**

9. Which file contains all information you need to troubleshoot SELinux messages?
    a. /var/log/audit/audit.log
    b. /var/log/selinux/selinux.log
    c. /var/log/messages
    d. /var/log/selinux.log

10. You want to grep the log file for SELinux log messages. Which of the following strings should you grep upon?
    a. selinux
    b. deny
    c. violatino
    d. avc

Foundation Topics

Understanding SELinux Working and Modes

If SELinux is enabled and nothing else has been configured, all system calls are denied. To specify what exactly is allowed, a policy is used. In this policy, rules define which source domain is allowed to access which target domain. The source domain is the object that is trying to access something. Typically, this is a process or a user. The target domain is the object that is accessed. Typically, that is a file, directory, or a network port to define exactly what is allowed; context labels are used. Using these labels is the essence of SELinux because these labels are used to define access rules. Table 21.2 summarizes it all.

Key Topic

Table 21.2 SELinux Core Elements

Element	Use
Policy	A collection of rules that define which source has access to which target.
Source domain	The object that is trying to access a target. Typically a user or a process.
Target domain	The thing that a source domain is trying to access. Typically a file or port.
Context	A security label that is used to categorize objects in SELinux.
Rule	A specific part of the policy that determines which source domain has which access permissions to which target domain.
Labels	Same as context label, defined to determine which source domain has access to which target domain.

On a Linux system, you can choose to enable or disable SELinux. When SELinux is enabled, kernel support for SELinux is loaded, and some applications that are SELinux aware change their behavior, because specific libraries are used on a system that has SELinux enabled. If SELinux is disabled, no SELinux activity will be happening at all. Changing between SELinux enabled and SELinux disabled mode requires a reboot of your system. This is because SELinux is a feature that is deeply interwoven with the Linux kernel.

If on a system SELinux is enabled, you can select to put SELinux in enforcing mode or in permissive mode. In enforcing mode, SELinux is fully operational and enforcing all SELinux rules in the policy. If SELinux is in permissive mode, all SELinux-related activity is logged, but no access is blocked. This makes SELinux permissive mode an excellent mode to do troubleshooting. Permissive mode is also a great way to do something and see the result from an SELinux perspective. That can help in building new and more efficient policies.

To set the default SELinux mode while booting, use the file /etc/sysconfig/selinux. Listing 21.1 shows the content of this file.

Listing 21.1 Content of the /etc/sysconfig/selinux File

```
[root@server1 ~]# cat /etc/sysconfig/selinux

# This file controls the state of SELinux on the system.
# SELINUX= can take one of these three values:
#     enforcing - SELinux security policy is enforced.
#     permissive - SELinux prints warnings instead of enforcing.
#     disabled - No SELinux policy is loaded.
SELINUX=enforcing
# SELINUXTYPE= can take one of these two values:
#     targeted - Targeted processes are protected,
#     minimum - Modification of targeted policy. Only selected
processes are protected.
#     mls - Multi Level Security protection.
SELINUXTYPE=targeted
```

As you can see, in this file, which is read while booting, you can choose to put SELinux in enforcing, permissive, or disabled mode.

On a server that currently has SELinux enabled, you can use the **getenforce** command to see whether it currently is in enforcing or in permissive mode. To switch between permissive and enforcing mode, you can use **setenforce**. The command **setenforce 0** puts SELinux in permissive mode, and **setenforce 1** puts SELinux in enforcing mode.

Another useful command is **sestatus**. If used with the option **-v**, this command shows detailed information about the current status of SELinux on a server. Listing 21.2 shows the output of the **sestatus -v** command. It not only shows you which parts of SELinux are enabled but also shows the current version of the policy that is loaded and the context labels for some critical parts of the system.

Listing 21.2 Using **sestatus -v** to get Detailed Information About the Current Protection Status

```
[root@server1 log]# sestatus -v
SELinux status:                 enabled
SELinuxfs mount:                /sys/fs/selinux
SELinux root directory:         /etc/selinux
Loaded policy name:             targeted
Current mode:                   enforcing
Mode from config file:          enforcing
Policy MLS status:              enabled
Policy deny_unknown status:     allowed
Max kernel policy version:      28

Process contexts:
Current context:
unconfined_u:unconfined_r:unconfined_t:s0-s0:c0.c1023
Init context:                   system_u:system_r:init_t:s0
/usr/sbin/sshd                  system_u:system_r:sshd_t:s0-s0:c0.c1023

File contexts:
Controlling terminal:           unconfined_u:object_r:user_devpts_t:s0
/etc/passwd                     system_u:object_r:passwd_file_t:s0
/etc/shadow                     system_u:object_r:shadow_t:s0
/bin/bash                       system_u:object_r:shell_exec_t:s0
/bin/login                      system_u:object_r:login_exec_t:s0
/bin/sh                         system_u:object_r:bin_t:s0 ->
system_u:object_r:shell_exec_t:s0
/sbin/agetty                    system_u:object_r:getty_exec_t:s0
/sbin/init                      system_u:object_r:bin_t:s0 ->
system_u:object_r:init_exec_t:s0
/usr/sbin/sshd                  system_u:object_r:sshd_exec_t:s0
```

In Exercise 21.1, you practice working with these different modes.

Exercise 21.1 Manipulating SELinux Modes

1. Open a root console on your server and type **getenforce**. You'll normally see that SELinux is in enforcing mode.
2. Type **setenforce 0** and type **getenforce** again. SELinux now switches to permissive mode.

3. Open the file /etc/sysconfig/selinux with an editor and change the line SELINUX= so that it reads **SELINUX=disabled**. Reboot your server.
4. After rebooting, log in to a root shell again and type **getenforce**. You'll see that SELinux is now in disabled mode.
5. Try using the command **setenforce 1**. You'll see the message "setenforce: SELinux is disabled." You cannot switch between disabled and enforcing mode without rebooting your server.
6. Open the file /etc/sysconfig/selinux again and change the line SELINUX=disabled back to **SELINUX=enforcing**. Reboot your system again.
7. After rebooting, type **sestatus -v** and read current status information about SELinux.

TIP Whatever you do, do not change the contents of the /etc/sysconfig/selinux file. Your exam system must be configured with SELinux in enforcing mode. To troubleshoot SELinux, you can put it temporarily in permissive mode by using **setenforce 0**. In this mode, you can troubleshoot any SELinux problem, but at least you'll be sure that after a reboot your server is started in a mode where SELinux is enabled, which is an essential requirement if you want to pass the exam.

Notice that on real Red Hat servers SELinux on occasion is set to be disabled. Putting SELinux in disabled mode certainly makes it easier for administrators to run their applications. However, it also makes it less secure. Often, there is no reason but the ignorance of the system administrator to put SELinux in disabled mode, even if the vendors of some applications tell you the application is supported only if SELinux is set to be disabled.

On the other end, a fully enforcing system is especially important if your server is accessed directly by users from the Internet. If your server cannot be reached directly from the Internet, but is in a safe internal network, it is not strictly necessary to have SELinux enabled. On both the RHCSA and the RHCE exams, however, you must make sure that SELinux is enabled and fully protecting your server.

NOTE SELinux is often disabled on servers because of laziness and because application vendors just do not know how to deal with it. On many occasions, even applications that do not know how to work with SELinux can be fully functional on a server with SELinux. It just takes a bit more work to figure out the additional rules in the policy that need to be created to use the application on an SELinux-enabled system.

Understanding Context Settings and the Policy

Key Topic

Context settings are an important part of SELinux operations. The context is a label that can be applied to different elements:

- Files and directories
- Ports
- Processes
- Users

Context labels define the nature of the item, and SELinux rules are created to match context labels of source objects to the context labels of target objects. So, setting correct context labels is a very important skill for system administrators. You learn how to do that later in this chapter.

Monitoring Current Context Labels

To see current context settings on these objects, many commands offer support for the **-Z** option. Listing 21.3 shows how **ls -Z** shows context settings for some directories in the / file system. Other commands also support the **-Z** option to show current context label settings. Some examples are **ps Zaux**, which shows a list of all processes, including their context label, or **netstat -Ztulpen**, which shows all network ports and the current context label associated with each port.

Listing 21.3 Displaying Context Labels on Files with **ls -Z**

```
[root@server1 /]# ls -Z
lrwxrwxrwx. root root system_u:object_r:bin_t:s0       bin -> usr/bin
dr-xr-xr-x. root root system_u:object_r:boot_t:s0      boot
drwxr-xr-x  root root ?                                dev
drwxr-xr-x. root root system_u:object_r:etc_t:s0       etc
drwxr-xr-x. root root system_u:object_r:home_root_t:s0 home
```

```
lrwxrwxrwx. root root system_u:object_r:lib_t:s0            lib -> usr/lib
lrwxrwxrwx. root root system_u:object_r:lib_t:s0            lib64 -> usr/
lib64
drwxr-xr-x. root root system_u:object_r:mnt_t:s0            media
drwxr-xr-x. root root system_u:object_r:mnt_t:s0            mnt
drwxr-xr-x. root root system_u:object_r:usr_t:s0            opt
dr-xr-xr-x  root root ?                                     proc
dr-xr-x---. root root system_u:object_r:admin_home_t:s0 root
drwxr-xr-x  root root ?                                     run
lrwxrwxrwx. root root system_u:object_r:bin_t:s0            sbin -> usr/sbin
drwxr-xr-x. root root system_u:object_r:var_t:s0            srv
dr-xr-xr-x  root root ?                                     sys
drwxrwxrwt. root root system_u:object_r:tmp_t:s0            tmp
drwxr-xr-x. root root system_u:object_r:usr_t:s0            usr
drwxr-xr-x. root root system_u:object_r:var_t:s0            var
drwxr-xr-x. root root unconfined_u:object_r:httpd_sys_content_t:s0 web
```

Every context label always consists of three different parts:

Key Topic

- **User:** The user can be recognized by _u in the context label; it is set to system_u on most directories in Listing 21.3. SELinux users are not the same as Linux users, and they are not important on the RHCSA or RHCE exams.
- **Role:** The role can be recognized by _r in the context label. In Listing 21.3, most objects are labeled with the object_r role. In advanced SELinux management, specific SELinux users can be assigned permissions to specific SELinux roles. For the RHCSA and RHCE exams, you do not have to know how to configure these.
- **Type:** The type context can be recognized by _t in the context label. In Listing 21.3, you can see that a wide variety of context types is applied to the directories in the / file system. Make sure that you know how to work with context types, because they are what it is all about on the exams.

TIP Just to make sure that you are focusing on the parts that really matter, on the RHCSA as well as the RHCE exams, you need to work with context types only. You can safely ignore the user and role parts of the context label.

Setting Context Types

As an administrator, it is important that you know how to set context types. You can set these context types on files and directories (RHCSA requirement) and other objects such as network ports (RHCE requirement). Because setting context types on files is what you really need to know for RHCSA, let's focus on that task first.

You can use two commands to set context type:

- **semanage:** This is the command you want to use. The **semanage** command writes the new context to the SELinux policy, from which it is applied to the file system.
- **chcon:** This command is for use in specific cases only and normally should be avoided. The **chcon** command writes the new context to the file system and not to the policy. Everything that is applied with **chcon** is overwritten when the file system is relabeled, or the original context is restored from the policy to the file system. Do *not* use this command!

NOTE You might want to know why, if you should not use it, that I mention it. Well, you'll often see the **chcon** command still being referred to in the documentation, which might give the impression that it is a useful command. It is not, because if your file system is relabeled, all changes applied with **chcon** are lost. File system relabeling actions can take you by surprise if you are new to SELinux, and you will fail your exam if by accident a file system relabeling is happening on a file system where you have applied SELinux context with **chcon**. So, I repeat: Do *not* use it.

TIP The **semanage** command is not installed by default. Fortunately, there is **yum whatprovides**. Type **yum whatprovides */semanage** to find the RPM containing **semanage**, and then install it. Do not learn the names of all relevant RPMs by heart; just remember **yum whatprovides**. It will find any RPM you need. See Chapter 11, "Managing Software," for more information about the use of the **yum** command and package management in general.

To set context using **semanage**, you first need to find the appropriate context (a topic covered in more depth in the next section, "Finding the Context Type You Need"). An easy way to find the appropriate context is by looking at the default context settings on already existing items. If you want to change the context for a web server, for example, type **ls -Z /var/www** to see the context settings:

```
[root@server1 /]# ls -Z /var/www
drwxr-xr-x. root root system_u:object_r:httpd_sys_script_exec_t:s0
  cgi-bin
drwxr-xr-x. root root system_u:object_r:httpd_sys_content_t:s0 html
```

As you can see, the context settings on /var/www/html are set to httpd_sys_content_t. (We're looking only at the context type because the user and role are for advanced use only.) To set this context type to any new directory that you want to be accessible by the Apache web server, use the following command:

```
semanage fcontext -a -t httpd_sys_content_t "/mydir(/.*)?"
```

In this command, the option **-a** is used to add a context type. This is what you need to do for all directories that you have created manually yourself. Then, you use **-t** to change the context type (as opposed to user and role). The last part of the command is a regular expression, which is used to refer to the directory /mydir and anything that might exist below this directory.

Setting the context in this way is not enough, though, because you'll write it only to the policy and not to the file system. To complete the command, you now need to apply the policy setting to the file system, as follows:

```
restorecon -R -v /mydir
```

You'll see that the new context is now applied, which allows the httpd process to access the directory.

TIP The **semanage** command is not the easiest command to remember. Fortunately, it has some excellent man pages. Type **man semanage** and use **G** to go all the way down to the bottom of the man page. You'll now see the "see also" section, which mentions **semanage-fcontext**. Open this man page using **man semanage-fcontext**, type **/examples**, and you'll see some pretty examples that mention exactly what you need to know (see Listing 21.4).

Listing 21.4 semanage fcontext Usage Example from the man Page

```
EXAMPLE
       remember to run restorecon after you set the file context
       Add file-context for everything under /web
       # semanage fcontext -a -t httpd_sys_content_t "/web(/.*)?"
       # restorecon -R -v /web

       Substitute /home1 with /home when setting file context
```

```
       # semanage fcontext -a -e /home /home1
       # restorecon -R -v /home1

       For home directories under top level directory, for example /
disk6/home,
       execute the following commands.
       # semanage fcontext -a -t home_root_t "/disk6"
       # semanage fcontext -a -e /home /disk6/home
       # restorecon -R -v /disk6

SEE ALSO
       selinux (8), semanage (8)

AUTHOR
       This man page was written by Daniel Walsh <dwalsh@redhat.com>

                                   20130617                semanage-
fcontext(8)
```

Now it is time for an exercise. In Exercise 21.2, you learn how to change the document root for the Apache web server and label the new document root in the right way.

Exercise 21.2 Setting a Context Label on a Nondefault Apache Document Root

1. Open a root shell and type **yum install httpd elinks –y**.
2. Still from the root shell, type **mkdir /web**.
3. Type **vim /web/index.html** and put the following contents in the file: **welcome to my web server**.
4. Type **vim /etc/httpd/conf/httpd.conf** to open the Apache configuration file and find the **DocumentRoot** parameter. Change it so that it reads **DocumentRoot "/web"**.
5. In the same httpd.conf configuration file, add the following section:

```
<Directory "/web">
    AllowOverride None
    Require all granted
</Directory>
```

6. Type **systemctl restart httpd; systemctl enable httpd** to start and enable the httpd service.
7. Type **elinks http://localhost**. You'll see the default Red Hat web page and not the contents of the index.html file you have just created.
8. Type **setenforce 0** to switch SELinux to permissive mode.
9. Repeat Step 7. You'll now get access to your custom web page, which proves that SELinux was doing something to block access.
10. Type **semanage fcontext -a -t httpd_sys_content_t "/web(/.*)?"** to apply the new context label to /web.
11. Type **restorecon -R -v /web**. The **-v** (verbose) option ensures that you see what is happening and that you will see the new context being applied to /web.
12. Set SELinux back in enforcing mode, using **setenforce 1**.
13. Type **elinks http://localhost**. You'll now get access to your custom web page.

Finding the Context Type You Need

One of the challenging parts of setting SELinux contexts is finding the context you need. Roughly, there are three approaches:

- Look at the default environment
- Read the configuration files
- Use **man -k _selinux** to find SELinux-specific man pages for your service

The most powerful way of getting the SELinux information you need is by using **man -k _selinux**, which searches the database of man pages for man pages that match _selinux in the name or description of the man page. On RHEL 7, however, these man pages are not installed by default. To install them, you need to install the policycoreutils-devel package, after which you can use the command **sepolicy manpage -a -p /usr/share/man/man8 to** install the SELinux man pages. Exercise 21.3 guides you through the procedure you need to apply to install the application-specific SELinux man pages.

TIP Exercise 21.3 shows an essential skill. Make sure that you master this procedure before going to the exam.

Exercise 21.3 Installing SELinux-Specific Man Pages

1. Type **man -k _selinux**. You'll probably see just one or two man pages.
2. Type **yum whatprovides */sepolicy**. This shows you the name of the RPM that contains the sepolicy binary, which is policycoreutils-devel.
3. Type **yum -y install policycoreutils-devel** to install this package.
4. Type **sepolicy manpage -a -p /usr/share/man/man8** to install the man pages.
5. Type **man -k _selinux**. You'll see no changes yet.
6. Type **mandb** to update the database that contains names and descriptions of all man pages that are installed.
7. Once the **mandb** command has finished (this can take a few minutes), type **man -k _selinux**. You'll now see a long list of man pages scrolling by.
8. Type **man -k _selinux | grep http** to find the man page that documents SELinux settings for the httpd service and scroll through it. Notice that it is a complete list of all that you can do with SELinux on the httpd service.

Restoring Default File Contexts

In the previous section, you learned how to apply context types using **semanage**. You also applied the context settings from the policy to the file system using **restorecon**. The **restorecon** command is a useful command because in the policy the default settings are defined for most files and directories on your computer. If the wrong context setting is ever applied, you just have to type **restorecon** to reapply if from the policy to the file system.

Using **restorecon** this way can be useful to fix problems on new files. Before explaining how to do it, let's take a look at how new context settings are applied:

Key Topic

- If a new file is created, it inherits the context settings from the parent directory.
- If a file is copied to a directory, this is considered a new file, so it inherits the context settings from the parent directory.
- If a file is moved, or copied while keeping its properties (by using **cp -a**), the original context settings of the file are applied.

Especially the latter of these three situations is easily fixed by using **restorecon**. In Exercise 21.4, we simulate this problem, and you fix it using **restorecon**.

It is also possible to relabel the entire file system. Doing so applies all context settings as defined in the policy to the file system. Because the policy should always be leading and contain correct context settings, relabeling a file system may be a good idea. To relabel the file system, you can either use the command **restorecon -Rv /** or you can create a file with the name **/.autorelabel.** The next time your server is restarted, the file system will automatically be relabeled.

A relabeling action will sometimes occur spontaneously. If while troubleshooting a server you have started the server in a mode where SELinux was disabled, and you have applied modifications to the file system, SELinux will detect that the file system has changed without SELinux monitoring it. This will result in an automatic relabeling of the entire file system. Notice that on large file systems relabeling the file system can take a significant amount of time. Figure 21.1 shows what you should see when your file system is automatically relabeled.

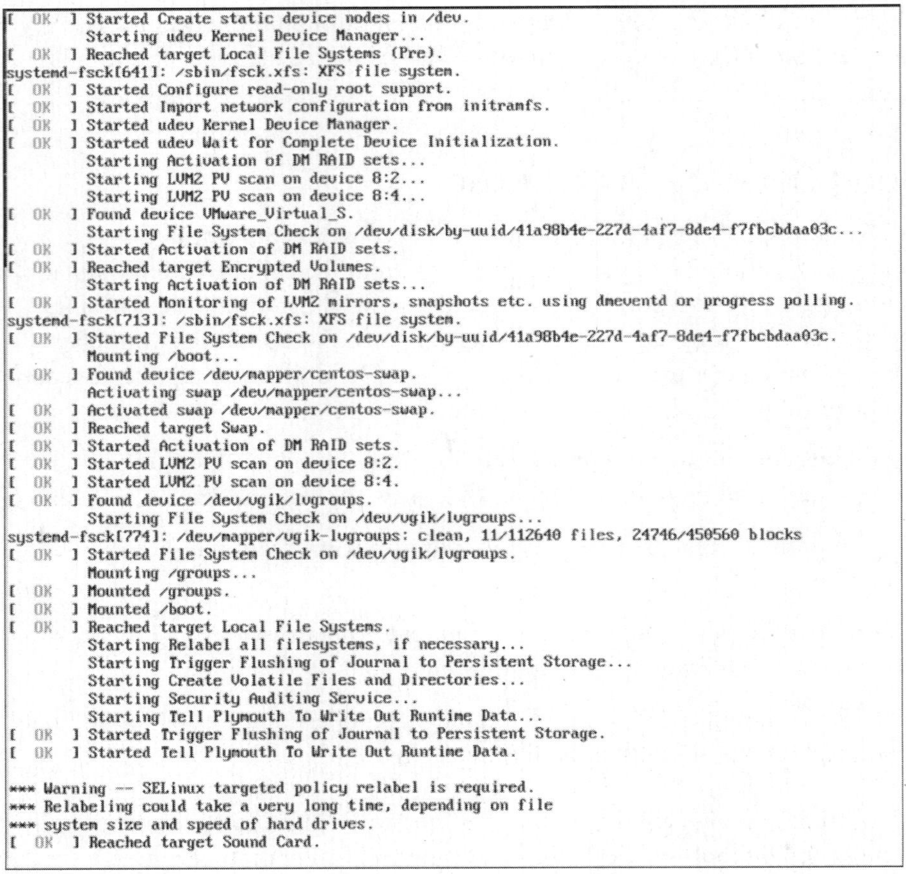

```
[  OK  ] Started Create static device nodes in /dev.
         Starting udev Kernel Device Manager...
[  OK  ] Reached target Local File Systems (Pre).
systemd-fsck[641]: /sbin/fsck.xfs: XFS file system.
[  OK  ] Started Configure read-only root support.
[  OK  ] Started Import network configuration from initramfs.
[  OK  ] Started udev Kernel Device Manager.
[  OK  ] Started udev Wait for Complete Device Initialization.
         Starting Activation of DM RAID sets...
         Starting LVM2 PV scan on device 8:2...
         Starting LVM2 PV scan on device 8:4...
[  OK  ] Found device VMware_Virtual_S.
         Starting File System Check on /dev/disk/by-uuid/41a98b4e-227d-4af7-8de4-f7fbcbdaa03c...
[  OK  ] Started Activation of DM RAID sets.
[  OK  ] Reached target Encrypted Volumes.
         Starting Activation of DM RAID sets...
[  OK  ] Started Monitoring of LVM2 mirrors, snapshots etc. using dmeventd or progress polling.
systemd-fsck[713]: /sbin/fsck.xfs: XFS file system.
[  OK  ] Started File System Check on /dev/disk/by-uuid/41a98b4e-227d-4af7-8de4-f7fbcbdaa03c.
         Mounting /boot...
[  OK  ] Found device /dev/mapper/centos-swap.
         Activating swap /dev/mapper/centos-swap...
[  OK  ] Activated swap /dev/mapper/centos-swap.
[  OK  ] Reached target Swap.
[  OK  ] Started Activation of DM RAID sets.
[  OK  ] Started LVM2 PV scan on device 8:2.
[  OK  ] Started LVM2 PV scan on device 8:4.
[  OK  ] Found device /dev/vgik/lvgroups.
         Starting File System Check on /dev/vgik/lvgroups...
systemd-fsck[774]: /dev/mapper/vgik-lvgroups: clean, 11/112640 files, 24746/450560 blocks
[  OK  ] Started File System Check on /dev/vgik/lvgroups.
         Mounting /groups...
[  OK  ] Mounted /groups.
[  OK  ] Mounted /boot.
[  OK  ] Reached target Local File Systems.
         Starting Relabel all filesystems, if necessary...
         Starting Trigger Flushing of Journal to Persistent Storage...
         Starting Create Volatile Files and Directories...
         Starting Security Auditing Service...
         Starting Tell Plymouth To Write Out Runtime Data...
[  OK  ] Started Trigger Flushing of Journal to Persistent Storage.
[  OK  ] Started Tell Plymouth To Write Out Runtime Data.

*** Warning -- SELinux targeted policy relabel is required.
*** Relabeling could take a very long time, depending on file
*** system size and speed of hard drives.
[  OK  ] Reached target Sound Card.
```

Figure 21.1 Autorelabeling the file system.

Exercise 21.4 Using *restorecon* to Relabel Files

1. From a root shell, type **ls -Z /etc/hosts**. You'll see the file has the net_config_t context label.
2. Type **cp /etc/hosts ~** to copy the file to the root home directory. Because copying is considered the creation of a new file, the context setting on the ~/hosts file is set as admin_home_t. Use **ls -Z ~/hosts** to verify this.
3. Use **mv ~/hosts /etc** and confirm that you want to overwrite the existing file.
4. Type **ls -Z /etc/hosts** to confirm that the context type is still set to admin_home_t.
5. Use **restorecon -v /etc/hosts** to reapply the correct context type. The **-v** option shows you what is happening.
6. Type **touch /.autorelabel** and restart your server. While restarting, make sure to press the **Escape** key on your keyboard so that you'll see boot messages. You'll see that the file system is automatically relabeled.

Using Boolean Settings to Modify SELinux Settings

In the SELinux policy, there are many rules. Some of these rules allow specific activity, whereas other rules deny that activity. Changing rules is not easy, and that is why SELinux Booleans are provided to easily change the behavior of a rule.

An example of a Boolean is ftpd_anon_write, which by default is set to off. That means that even if you have configured your FTP server to allow anonymous writes, the Boolean will still deny it, and the anonymous user cannot upload any files. If a conflict exists between the setting of a parameter in a service configuration file and in a Boolean, the Boolean always takes precedence. But Booleans are easy to change.

To get a list of Booleans on your system, use **getsebool -a**. If you are looking for Booleans that are set for a specific service, use **grep** to filter down the results. In Listing 21.5, you can see how this command is used to show current Booleans that match FTP.

An alternative way to show current Boolean settings is by using the **semanage boolean -l** command. This command provides some more details, because it shows the current Boolean setting and the default Boolean setting.

Listing 21.5 Displaying Boolean Settings

```
root@server1 ~]# getsebool -a | grep ftp
ftp_home_dir --> off
ftpd_anon_write --> off
ftpd_connect_all_unreserved --> off
ftpd_connect_db --> off
ftpd_full_access --> off
ftpd_use_cifs --> off
ftpd_use_fusefs --> off
ftpd_use_nfs --> off
ftpd_use_passive_mode --> off
httpd_can_connect_ftp --> off
httpd_enable_ftp_server --> off
sftpd_anon_write --> off
sftpd_enable_homedirs --> off
sftpd_full_access --> off
sftpd_write_ssh_home --> off
tftp_anon_write --> off
tftp_home_dir --> off
```

To change a Boolean, you can use **setsebool**. If you want to switch the ftpd_anon_write boolean to allow anonymous writes, for example, use **setsebool ftpd_anon_write on**. This changes the runtime value of the Boolean, but does not change it permanently. To apply permanent changes to a Boolean, use **setsebool -P**. Notice that this takes longer, because parts of the policy need to be recompiled to apply the modification. In Exercise 21.5, you apply these commands to see how Booleans are working.

Exercise 21.5 Working with SELinux Booleans

1. From a root shell, type **getsebool -a | grep ftp**. You'll see the ftpd_anon_write boolean, with its current value off.
2. Type **setsebool ftpd_anon_write on**. This changes the value in runtime.
3. Type **getsebool ftpd_anon_write**. It shows the value of the Boolean as on.
4. Type **semanage boolean -l | grep ftpd_anon**. Notice that this command shows the runtime configuration set to on, but the permanent setting is still set to off.

5. Use **setsebool -P ftpd_anon_write on** to switch the runtime and the default setting for the Boolean to on.
6. Repeat **semanage boolean -l | grep ftpd_anon**. Notice that it is now set to on, on.

Diagnosing and Addressing SELinux Policy Violations

Configuring a system with SELinux can be a challenging task. To make it easier to understand what is happening, SELinux logs everything it is doing. The primary source to get logging information is the audit log, which is in /var/log/audit/audit.log. SELinux messages are logged with type=AVC in the audit log. So, to see what SELinux is doing, you can use the command **grep AVC /var/log/audit/audit.log**. If SELinux messages have been logged, this command shows a result as in Listing 21.6.

Listing 21.6 Getting SELinux Messages from Audit.log

```
[root@server1 audit]# grep AVC audit.log
type=USER_AVC msg=audit(1414933364.949:11): pid=1 uid=0 auid=4294967295
ses=4294967295
subj=system_u:system_r:init_t:s0 msg='avc:  received setenforce notice
(enforcing=0)
exe="/usr/lib/systemd/systemd" sauid=0 hostname=? addr=? terminal=?'
type=AVC msg=audit(1414933365.304:13): avc:  denied  { read } for
pid=1330 comm="alsactl"
name="asound.state" dev="dm-1" ino=72731037 scontext=system_u:system_
r:alsa_t:s0-s0:c0.c1023
tcontext=system_u:object_r:file_t:s0 tclass=file
type=AVC msg=audit(1414933365.304:13): avc:  denied  { open } for
pid=1330 comm="alsactl"
path="/var/lib/alsa/asound.state" dev="dm-1" ino=72731037 scontext=
system_u:system_r:alsa_t:
s0-s0:c0.c1023 tcontext=system_u:object_r:file_t:s0 tclass=file
type=AVC msg=audit(1414933365.304:14): avc:  denied  { getattr } for
pid=1330 comm="alsactl"
path="/var/lib/alsa/asound.state" dev="dm-1" ino=72731037 scontext=
system_u:system_r:alsa_t:
s0-s0:c0.c1023 tcontext=system_u:object_r:file_t:s0 tclass=file
```

At first sight, the SELinux log messages look complicated. If you look a bit closer, though, they are not that hard to understand. Let's take a closer look at the last line in the log file:

```
type=AVC msg=audit(1414933365.304:14): avc:  denied  { getattr } for
pid=1330
comm="alsactl" path="/var/lib/alsa/asound.state" dev="dm-1"
ino=72731037
scontext=system_u:system_r:alsa_t:s0-s0:c0.c1023 tcontext=system_u:obj
ect_r:file_t:s0
tclass=file
```

The first relevant part in this line is the text **avc: denies { gettattr }**. That means that a **getattr** request was denied, so some process has tried to read attributes of a file and that was denied. Following that message, we can see **comm=alsactl**, which means that the command trying to issue the **getattr** request was **alsactl**, and we can see **path="/var/lib/alsa/asound.state"**, which is the file that this process has tried to access.

In the last part of the log line, we can get information about the source context and the target context. The source context (which is the context setting of the **alsactl** command) is set to **alsa_t**, and the target context (which is the context setting of the asound.state file) is set to **file_t**. And apparently, SELinux did not like that too much.

Making SELinux Analyzing Easier

Based on the information you find in the audit.log, you may be able to decide what you need to do to fix the problem. If you do not, there is **sealert**. First, you need to install sealert by using **yum -y install setroubleshoot-server**. Then, it is a good idea to restart your server to make sure that all processes that are involved are restarted correctly. The next time an SELinux message is written to the audit log, an easier-to-understand message is written to syslog and by default can be read in /var/log/messages. Listing 21.7 shows an output example.

Listing 21.7 sealert Makes Analyzing SELinux Logs Easier

```
Nov  2 10:01:40 server1 setroubleshoot: Plugin Exception restorecon
Nov  2 10:01:40 server1 setroubleshoot: SELinux is preventing /usr/
sbin/httpd from getattr access on the file. For complete SELinux
messages. run sealert -l 0ed02423-1149-4561-b6a0-8ea2957329ea
Nov  2 10:01:40 server1 python: SELinux is preventing /usr/sbin/httpd
from getattr access on the file.
```

```
*****  Plugin catchall_labels (83.8 confidence) suggests
*******************

If you want to allow httpd to have getattr access on the  file
Then you need to change the label on $FIX_TARGET_PATH
Do
# semanage fcontext -a -t FILE_TYPE '$FIX_TARGET_PATH'
where FILE_TYPE is one of the following: NetworkManager_exec_t,
NetworkManager_log_t,
--removed 5 pages of the "one of the following" output --
Then execute:
restorecon -v '$FIX_TARGET_PATH'


*****  Plugin catchall (17.1 confidence) suggests
**************************

If you believe that httpd should be allowed getattr access on the  file
by default.
Then you should report this as a bug.
You can generate a local policy module to allow this access.
Do
allow this access for now by executing:
# grep httpd /var/log/audit/audit.log | audit2allow -M mypol
# semodule -i mypol.pp
```

The useful thing about **sealert** is that it is trying to analyze what has happened and based on the analysis, it suggests what you need to do to fix the problem. The not-so-useful part is that in some cases (as was the case in this example), hundreds of possible context types are shown and the administrator has to choose the right one. (I removed five pages of output in Listing 21.6 to keep it readable.) So, if you do not know what you are doing, you risk getting completely lost.

When working with **sealert**, you can see that different plug-ins are called, and every plug-in has a confidence score. If, as in the example in Listing 21.6, one plug-in gives an 83.8 % confidence score, while the other only is giving a 17.1% confidence score, it may be obvious that the former approach is what you should be doing. Unfortunately, however, it is not always that readable.

TIP If you are not sure what SELinux is trying to tell you, install setroubleshoot-server and analyze what **sealert** shows. The information that is shown by **sealert** is often a lot more readable. Sometimes it will not help you at all, whereas sometimes the information can prove quite helpful.

Summary

This chapter provided an RHCSA-level introduction to SELinux. Based on the information in this chapter, you learned how to fix common SELinux situations. Make sure that you master the topics discussed in this chapter before taking the RHCSA exam.

To be prepared for RHCE-level SELinux tasks, you need to know how to apply SELinux security settings for specific services. That involves some more advanced tasks, as well. In the chapters about service configuration that are in the RHCE part of this book, you also learn how to perform these advanced tasks.

Exam Prep Tasks

Review All Key Topics

Review the most important topics in the chapter, noted with the Key Topic icon in the outer margin of the page. Table 21.3 lists a reference of these key topics and the page numbers on which each is found.

Table 21.3 Key Topics for Chapter 21

Key Topic Element	Description	Page Number
Table 21.1	SELinux core elements	477
List	Elements a context label can be applied to	481
List	Three parts of a context label	482
List	How new context settings are applied	487

Complete Tables and Lists from Memory

Print a copy of Appendix B, "Memory Tables" (found on the disc), or at least the section for this chapter, and complete the tables and lists from memory. Appendix C, "Memory Tables Answer Key," also on the disc, includes completed tables and lists to check your work.

Define Key Terms

Define the following key terms from this chapter and check your answers in the glossary:

policy, enforcing, permissive, context, context type, source context, target context, audit log

Review Questions

1. You want to put SELinux temporarily in permissive mode. Which command do you use?
2. You need a list of all available Booleans. Which command do you use?
3. You do not see any service-specific SELinux man page. What solution do you need to apply?
4. What is the name of the package you need to install to get easy-to-read SELinux log messages in the audit log?
5. What commands do you need to run to apply the httpd_sys_content_t context type to the directory /web?
6. When would you use the **chcon** command?
7. Which file do you need to change if you want to completely disable SELinux?
8. Where does SELinux log all of its messages?
9. You have no clue which context types are available for the ftp service. What command enables you to get more specific information?
10. Your service does not work as expected and you want to know whether it is due to SELinux or something else. What is the easiest way to find out?

End-of-Chapter Labs

You have now learned how SELinux works. To practice managing this essential service, you can now work through the end-of-chapter labs about SELinux.

Lab 21.1

1. Change the Apache document root to /web. In this directory, create a file with the name index.html and give it the contents "welcome to my web server". Restart the httpd process and try to access the web server. This will not work. Fix the problem.

2. In the home directory of the user root, create a file with the name hosts and give it the following contents:

   ```
   192.168.122.200    labipa.example.com
   192.168.122.210    server1.example.com
   192.168.122.220    server2.example.com
   ```

   Move the file to the /etc directory and do what is necessary to give this file the correct context.

The following topics are covered in this chapter:

- Understanding Linux Firewalling
- Working with Firewalld

The following RHCSA exam objectives are covered in this chapter:

- Configure firewall settings using **firewall-config**, **firewall-cmd**, or iptables

CHAPTER 22

Configuring a Firewall

If a server is connected to the Internet, it needs to be protected against unauthorized access. SELinux is one part of this protection, and a firewall is the second part. The Linux kernel implements firewalling via the netfilter framework. To configure which packets are allowed and which are not, firewalld is the default solution in RHEL 7. In this chapter, you learn how firewalld is configured in an RHEL 7 environment. This chapter covers basic functionality. Advanced (RHEL level) functionality is discussed in Chapter 32, "Advanced Firewall Configuration."

"Do I Know This Already?" Quiz

The "Do I Know This Already?" quiz allows you to assess whether you should read this entire chapter thoroughly or jump to the "Exam Preparation Tasks" section. If you are in doubt about your answers to these questions or your own assessment of your knowledge of the topics, read the entire chapter. Table 22.1 lists the major headings in this chapter and their corresponding "Do I Know This Already?" quiz questions. You can find the answers in Appendix A, "Answers to the 'Do I Know This Already?' Quizzes and 'Review Questions.'"

Table 22.1 "Do I Know This Already?" Section-to-Question Mapping

Foundation Topics Section	Questions
Understanding Linux Firewalling	1–3, 7
Working with Firewalld	4–6, 8–10

1. Which of the following is not a standard firewalld zone?

   a. Untrusted

   b. Trusted

   c. External

   d. Internal

2. Which of the following is the name of firewalling as implemented in the Linux kernel?
   a. iptables
   b. firewalld
   c. netfilter
   d. firewall-mod
3. Which of the following is *not* an advantage of firewalld?
   a. Rules can be modified through dbus.
   b. It has an easy to use command-line interface.
   c. It has an easy to use graphical interface.
   d. It can be used as an enhancement to iptables.
4. Which command enables you to list all available firewalld services?
   a. **firewall-cmd --list-services**
   b. **firewall-cmd --list-all**
   c. **firewall-cmd --get-services**
   d. **firewall-cmd --show-services**
5. What is the name of the GUI tool that enables you to easily manage firewalld configurations?
   a. system-config-firewall
   b. firewall-gtk
   c. **firewall-config**
   d. firewall-gui
6. Which of the following shows correct syntax for adding a port persistently to the current firewalld configuration?
   a. **firewall-cmd --addport=2022/tcp --permanent**
   b. **firewall-cmd --add-port=2022/tcp --permanent**
   c. **firewall-cmd --addport=2022/tcp --persistent**
   d. **firewall-cmd --add port=2022/tcp --persistent**

7. Which zones should you use for an interface that is on a network where you need minimal firewall protection because every other computer on that same network is trusted?
   a. Trusted
   b. Home
   c. Work
   d. Private

8. Which of the following statements is true about the **--permanent** command-line option when used with **firewall-cmd**?
   a. Configuration that is added using **--permanent** is activated immediately and will be activated automatically after (re)starting firewalld.
   b. Configuration that is added using **--permanent** is activated immediately.
   c. Configuration that is added using **--permanent** is not activated immediately and can be activated only by using **systemctl restart firewalld**.
   d. To activate configuration that has been added with the **--permanent** option, you need to reload the firewall configuration by using **firewall-cmd –reload**.

9. Which command enables you to get an overview of all the current firewall configurations for all zones?
   a. **firewall-cmd --show-current**
   b. **firewall-cmd --list-all**
   c. **firewall-cmd --list-current**
   d. **firewall-cmd --show-all**

10. Which of the following statements is *not* true about the **firewall-config** GUI tool?
   a. All configuration that is created in **firewall-config** is automatically activated and stored permanently.
   b. The **firewall-config** tool provides an easy interface to add ports to zones.
   c. In its default screen, **firewall-config** shows all zones.
   d. **firewall-config** connects to the firewalld service. If this service is not running, you may have problems working with **firewall-config**.

Foundation Topics

Understanding Linux Firewalling

Key Topic

You can use a firewall to limit traffic coming in to a server or going out of the server. Firewalling is implemented in the Linux kernel by means of the netfilter subsystem. Netfilter allows kernel modules to inspect every incoming, outgoing, or forwarded packet and act upon such a packet by either allowing it or blocking it. So, the kernel firewall allows for inspection of incoming packets, outgoing packets, and packets that are traversing from one interface to another if the RHEL server is providing routing functionality.

Understanding Previous Solutions

To interact with netfilter, different solutions can be used. On earlier versions of Red Hat Enterprise Linux, iptables was the default solution to configure netfilter packet filtering. This solution worked with the command-line utility **iptables**, which provided a sophisticated and detailed way of defining firewall rules, but that also was challenging to use for the occasional administrator because of the complicated syntax of **iptables** commands and because the ordering rules could become relatively complex. The iptables service is still offered on Red Hat Enterprise Linux 7. It is not recommended as the default service, though, and it cannot be used on a server where firewalld is used as well.

Understanding Firewalld

Key Topic

In Red Hat Enterprise Linux 7 a new method was introduced: Firewalld is a system service that can configure firewall rules by using different interfaces. Administrators can manage rules in a firewalld environment, but even more important is that applications can request ports to be opened using the DBus messaging system, which means that rules can be added or removed without any direct action required of the system administrator.

Firewalld was developed as a complete new solution for managing Linux firewalls. It uses the firewalld service to manage the netfilter firewall configuration. The firewalld service is incompatible with the iptables service. Do not ever use firewalld and iptables on the same system; they are mutually exclusive.

> **TIP** The RHCSA objective does *not* define which tool you should use to create firewall rules. It just mentions that you should be able to create firewall rules by using iptables, **firewall-config**, or **firewall-cmd**. So, you do not have to be able to work with each of these tools; you just have to be able to configure a firewall with the tool that works best for you.

Understanding Firewalld Zones

Key Topic

Firewalld is making firewall management easier by working with zones. A zone is a collection of rules that are applied to incoming packets matching a specific source address or network interface. Firewalld applies to incoming packets only by default, and no filtering is happening on outgoing packets.

The use of zones is particularly important on servers that have multiple interfaces. On such servers, zones allow administrators to easily assign a specific set of rules. On servers that have just one network interface, you might very well do with just one zone, which is the default zone. Every packet that comes into a system is analyzed for its source address, and based on that source address, firewalld analyzes to see whether the packet belongs to a specific zone. If that is not the case, the zone for the incoming network interface is used. If no specific zone is available, the packet is handled by the settings in the default zone.

Firewalld works with some default zones. Table 22.2 describes these default zones.

Table 22.2 Firewalld Default Zones

Key Topic

Zone name	Default Settings
Block	Incoming network connections are rejected with an "icmp-host-prohibited" message. Only network connections that were initiated on this system are allowed.
Dmz	For use on computers in the demilitarized zone. Only selected incoming connections are accepted, and limited access to the internal network is allowed.
Drop	Any incoming packets are dropped and there is no reply.
External	For use on external networks with masquerading (Network Address Translation [NAT]) enabled, used especially on routers. Only selected incoming connections are accepted.
Home	For use with home networks. Most computers on the same network are trusted, and only selected incoming connections are accepted.
Internal	For use in internal networks. Most computers on the same network are trusted, and only selected incoming connections are accepted.

Zone name	Default Settings
Public	For use in public areas. Other computers in the same network are not trusted, and limited connections are accepted. This is the default zone for all newly created network interfaces.
trusted	All network connections are accepted.
work	For use in work areas. Most computers on the same network are trusted, and only selected incoming connections are accepted.

Understanding Firewalld Services

Key Topic

The second key element while working with firewalld is the service. Note that a service in firewalld is *not* the same as a service in systemd. In firewalld, some default services are defined, which allows administrators to easily allow or deny access to specific ports on a server.

Behind each service is a configuration file that explains which UDP or TCP ports are involved, and if so required, which kernel modules must be loaded. To get a list of all services available on your computer, you can use the command **firewall-cmd --get-services**. (see Listing 22.1).

> **TIP** You can find more in-depth information about the configuration of firewalld services in Chapter 32.

Listing 22.1 Use **firewall-cmd --get-services** for a List of All Available Services

```
[root@localhost sssd]# firewall-cmd --get-services
amanda-client bacula bacula-client dhcp dhcpv6 dhcpv6-client dns ftp
high-availability http https imaps ipp ipp-client ipsec kerberos
kpasswd ldap ldaps libvirt libvirt-tls mdns mountd ms-wbt mysql nfs ntp
openvpn pmcd pmproxy pmwebapi pmwebapis pop3s postgresql proxy-dhcp
radius rpc-bind samba samba-client smtp ssh telnet tftp tftp-client
transmission-client vnc-server wbem-https
```

In essence, what it comes down to when working with firewalld is that the right services need to be added to the right zones. In special cases, the configuration may be enhanced with more specific settings. In the next section, you learn which tools you can use for that purpose.

Service files are stored in the directory /usr/lib/firewalld/services or /etc/firewalld/services. Listing 22.2 shows what the contents of a service file looks like.

Listing 22.2 Contents of the ftp Service File

```
[root@server1 services]# cat ftp.xml
<?xml version="1.0" encoding="utf-8"?>
<service>
  <short>FTP</short>
  <description>FTP is a protocol used for remote file transfer. If you
plan to make your FTP
server publicly available, enable this option. You need the vsftpd
package installed for this
option to be useful.</description>
  <port protocol="tcp" port="21"/>
  <module name="nf_conntrack_ftp"/>
</service>
```

Working with Firewalld

In the next sections, you learn how to configure a firewall with firewalld. Two tools are available for this purpose: the command-line tool **firewall-cmd**; and the **firewall-config** tool, which has a graphical interface. It is a good idea to focus your efforts on the **firewall-cmd** tool. This easily accessible tool enables uncomplicated configuration. If you prefer working with the graphical **firewall-config** tool, that is possible, too. You can do everything with the graphical tool that you can do with the command-line tool.

When working with either of these tools, be aware of where exactly modifications are made. Both tools work with an in-memory state of the configuration in addition to an on-disk state (permanent state) of the configuration. While using either of these tools, make sure to commit changes to disk before proceeding.

> **TIP** When working with firewalld, make sure that it is not possible that someone by accident uses iptables to configure the firewall. Using iptables will severely mess up your firewall configuration, especially if the iptables service is loaded on a system where the firewalld service is already loaded. To make sure that this can never happen, use the **systemctl mask iptables** command. This command ensures that the iptables service cannot be started by accident.

Working with Firewall-cmd

The **firewall-cmd** tool is an easily accessible tool that enables administrators to change the runtime configuration of the firewall and to write this configuration to disk. Before learning all the options available with this versatile command, in Exercise 22.1 you work with some of the most important options **firewall-cmd** offers.

Exercise 22.1 Managing the Firewall with Firewall-cmd

1. Open a root shell. Type **firewall-cmd --get-default-zone**. This shows the current default zone. You'll see the current default zone, which is by default set to public.
2. To see which zones are available, type **firewall-cmd --get-zones**.
3. Now show the services that are available on your server by using **firewall-cmd --get-services**. Notice that the **firewall-cmd --get** options show what is available on your server.
4. To see which services are available in the current zone, type **firewall-cmd --list-services**. You'll see a short list containing a Dynamic Host Configuration Protocol (DHCP) client as well as Secure Shell (SSH).
5. Now type **firewall-cmd --list-all**. Look at the output and compare the output to the result of **firewall-cmd --list-all --zone=public**. Both commands show a complete overview of the current firewall configuration, as shown in Listing 22.3. Notice that you see much more than just the zone and services that are configured in that zone; you also see information about the interfaces and more advanced items.

Listing 22.3 Showing Current Firewall Configuration

```
[root@localhost ~]# firewall-cmd --list-all
public (default, active)
  interfaces: eno16777736
  sources:
  services: dhcpv6-client ssh
  ports:
  masquerade: no
  forward-ports:
  icmp-blocks:
  rich rules:
```

6. Type **firewall-cmd --add-service=vnc-server** to add the VNC server to the configuration of the firewall. Verify using **firewall-cmd --list-all**.
7. Type **systemctl restart firewalld** and repeat **firewall-cmd --list-all**. Notice that the vnc-server service is no longer listed.
8. Add the vnc-server service again, but make it permanent this time, using **firewall-cmd --add-service vnc-server --permanent**.
9. Type **firewall-cmd --list-all** again to verify. You'll see that VNC server is not listed. Services that have been added to the on-disk configuration are not added automatically to the runtime configuration. Type **firewall-cmd --reload** to reload the on-disk configuration into runtime configuration.
10. Type **firewall-cmd --addport=2022/tcp --permanent**, followed by **firewall-cmd --reload**. Verify using **firewall-cmd --list-all**. You'll see that a port has now been added to the firewalld configuration.

TIP On the exam, work with services as much as possible. Only use specific ports if no services contain the ports that you want to open.

In the preceding exercise, you worked with zones and services and you learned how to add services and ports to the default zone. The **firewall-cmd** interface offers many more options. Table 22.3 describes some of the most important command-line options.

Table 22.3 Common **firewall-cmd** Options

Key Topic

Firewall-cmd Options	Explanation
--get-zones	Lists all available zones
--get-default-zone	Shows the zone currently set as default zone
--set-default-zone=<ZONE>	Changes the default zone
--get-services	Shows all available services
--list-services	Shows services currently in use
--add-service=<service-name> [--zone=<ZONE>]	Adds a service to the current default zone or the zone that is specified
--remove-service=<service-name>	Removes a service from the configuration
--list-all [--zone=<ZONE>]	Lists all configurations in a zone

Firewall-cmd Options	Explanation
--add-port=<port/protocol> [--zone=<ZONE>]	Adds a port and protocol
--remove-port=<port/protocol> [--zone=<ZONE>]	Removes a port from the configuration
--add-interface=<INTERFACE> [--zone=<ZONE>]	Adds an interface to the default zone or a specific zone that is specified
--remove-interface=<INTERFACE> [--zone=<ZONE>]	Removes an interface from a specific zone
--add-source=<ipaddress/netmask> [--zone=<ZONE>]	Adds a specific IP address
--remove-source=<ipaddress/netmask> [--zone=<ZONE>]	Removes an IP address from the configuration
--permanent	Writes configuration to disk and not to run-time
--reload	Reloads the on-disk configuration

Working with Firewall-config

If you want to make firewall configuration really easy, you can use the GUI utility **firewall-config** instead.

NOTE To use this utility, you need to update your server. Type **yum update -y** before starting it. Without the updates, you will not be able to start it. If you still have trouble starting **firewall-config**, try (re)starting the firewalld service by using **systemctl restart firewalld**. This often fixes connection problems.

After starting **firewall-config**, you'll see the interface that is in Figure 22.1. In this interface, you get easy access to most of the features required for firewall configuration.

When working with **firewall-config**, it is important to notice the Configuration drop-down box in the upper part of the window. By default, all configuration that you'll do is added to the runtime environment. This makes the configuration effective immediately, but it will not be persistent between reboots. When using **firewall-config**, it is a good idea to select the Permanent option. This will allow added configuration to be written to the configuration so that it is persistent.

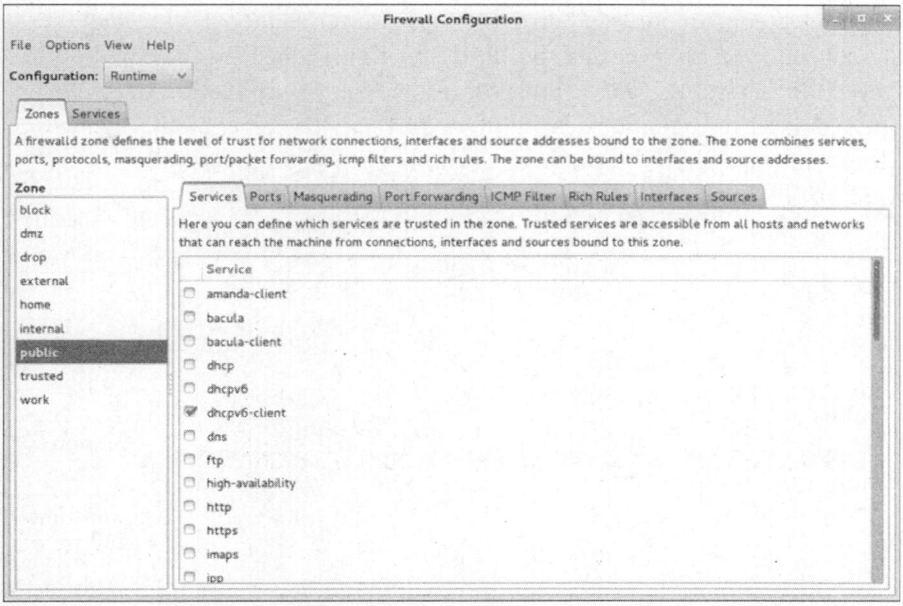

Figure 22.1 The **firewall-config** opening screen.

In the **firewall-config** tool, different interfaces are available. The default interface enables you to add services to specific zones, but there are tabs as well that allow you to add ports, port forwarding, and many other advanced configuration options. If you want to open a specific port in the firewall (for which no service exists), for instance, you can just activate the **Ports** tab and click **Add** to specify the specific port information that is required (see Figure 22.2).

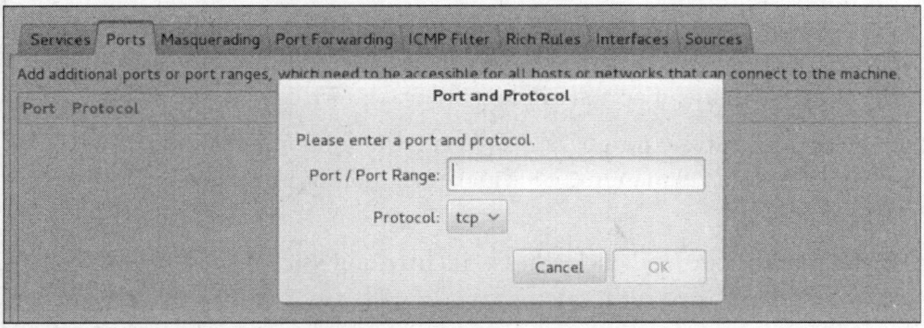

Figure 22.2 Adding specific ports to the firewall.

Another useful interface in **firewall-config** is offered through the Services tab. On this tab, you can define what should be included in a service file. Each service can be configured to contain ports and protocols, specific kernel modules through the Modules tab, and you can even add specific destinations, which are IP addresses that are allowed for this service. Take a look, for instance, at the ftp service, which not only opens port 21 tcp but also adds the **nf_conntrack_ftp** kernel module, which is needed to allow passive FTP traffic to be allowed through the firewall (see Figure 22.3).

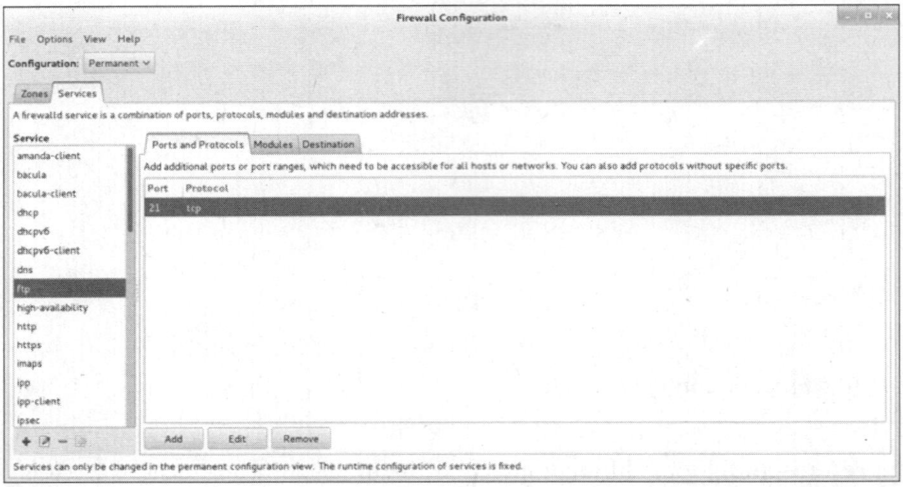

Figure 22.3 Configuring Services using **firewall-config**.

Exercise 22.2 introduces the most common configuration steps in **firewall-config**.

Exercise 22.2 Using Firewall-config

1. Open a terminal and type the command **firewall-config** to start the **firewall-config** GUI interface. Alternatively, you can access it from the **Applications > Sundry > Firewall** menu option in the graphical interface.
2. Click the word **Runtime** next to the Configuration option. Open the drop-down list and select **Permanent**. This makes all modifications you apply permanent.
3. Select the **public** zone, and click at least the **http** and **ssh** service to enable them.
4. Select the **Ports** tab, and from this tab, click **Add**. Type port **2022** and protocol **tcp** and click OK to add them to the list.
5. Activate the **Services** tab and select the **Kerberos** service. Notice that it shows protocols and ports, but no specific modules or destinations. Do the same for the **ftp** service and notice that it includes a kernel module as well.

6. Close the **firewall-config** utility by clicking the **X** in the upper-right corner.
7. From a terminal window, type **firewall-cmd --list-all**. Notice that the changes you have just made are not applied yet. That is because you have configured them as permanent changes, not as runtime changes.
8. Type **firewall-cmd --reload** and **firewall-cmd --list-all** again. You'll see that the changes have now been applied.

As you can see while browsing through the interface, **firewall-config** is a complete tool. It has just one disadvantage: It needs a graphical environment. For that reason, you are probably better off focusing on the command-line interface **firewall-cmd**, which is easy to use and does not have any specific requirements.

Summary

In this chapter, you learned how to set up a basic firewall environment, where firewalld services are added to firewalld zones to allow access to specific services on your computer. You also learned how to set up a base firewall by using the **firewall-cmd** command-line tool or the **firewall-config** graphical interface. The topics discussed in this chapter cover all the RHCSA objectives. Firewalld configuration is also an RHCE topic. You can read about the RHCE level objectives in Chapter 32.

Exam Prep Tasks

Key Topics

Review the most important topics in the chapter, noted with the Key Topic icon in the outer margin of the page. Table 22.4 lists a reference of these key topics and the page numbers on which each is found.

Table 22.4 Key Topics for Chapter 22

Key Topic Element	Description	Page
Paragraph	Introduces firewalling in the Linux kernel	502
Paragraph	Introduces netfilter as opposed to other firewalling tools	502
Paragraph	Introduces how firewalld zones are used	503

Key Topic Element	Description	Page
Table 22.2	Firewalld default zones	503
Paragraph	Introduces the concept of a firewalld service	504
Table 22.3	Common **firewall-cmd** options	507

Define Key Terms

Define the following key terms from this chapter and check your answers in the glossary:

firewall, netfilter, iptables, firewalld, zones, services

Complete Tables and Lists from Memory

Print a copy of Appendix B, "Memory Tables" (found on the disc), or at least the section for this chapter, and complete the tables and lists from memory. Appendix C, "Memory Tables Answer Key," also on the disc, includes completed tables and lists to check your work.

Review Questions

1. Which service should be running before you try to create a firewall configuration with **firewall-config**?
2. Which command adds UDP port 2355 to the firewall configuration in the default zone?
3. Which command enables you to list all firewall configuration in all zones?
4. Which command enables you to remove the vnc-server service from the current firewall configuration?
5. Which **firewall-cmd** command enables you to activate a new configuration that has been added with the **--permanent** option?
6. Which **firewall-cmd** option enables you to verify that a new configuration has been added to the current zone and is now active?
7. Which command enables you to add the interface eno1 to the public zone?
8. If you add a new interface to the firewall configuration while no zone is specified, which zone will it be added to?

9. Which command enables you to add the source IP address 192.168.0.0/24 to the default zone?
10. Which command enables you to list all services that are currently available in firewalld?

End-of-Chapter Labs

You have now learned how to work with firewalld on a Red Hat Enterprise Linux 7 server. Make sure to master these skills by working through the following end-of-chapter labs.

1. Create a firewall configuration that allows access to the following services that may be running on your server:
   - web
   - ftp
   - ssh
2. Make sure the configuration is persistent and will be activated after a restart of your server.

The following topics are covered in this chapter:

- Mounting NFS Shares
- Mounting SMB File Systems
- Mounting Remote File Systems Through fstab
- Using Automount to Mount Remote File Systems
- Configuring an FTP Server

The following RHCSA exam objectives are covered in this chapter:

- Mount CIFS and NFS network file systems

CHAPTER 23

Configuring Remote Mounts and FTP

This chapter focuses on some minor topics that have always had their place in the list of RHCSA and RHCE exam objectives. For some reason, at the time of this writing, of all topics discussed in this chapter, only the mounting of CIFS and NFS network file systems is listed in the objectives. Let's just assume that you want these mounts to happen automatically as well, which is why I am discussing how to set automatic mounting through fstab and automount also. And just to be sure, you can also read how to configure an FTP server (just because it seems weird that someone can become an RHCSA or an RHCE without even knowing how to set up an FTP server).

"Do I Know This Already?" Quiz

The "Do I Know This Already?" quiz allows you to assess whether you should read this entire chapter thoroughly or jump to the "Exam Preparation Tasks" section. If you are in doubt about your answers to these questions or your own assessment of your knowledge of the topics, read the entire chapter. Table 23.1 lists the major headings in this chapter and their corresponding "Do I Know This Already?" quiz questions. You can find the answers in Appendix A, "Answers to the 'Do I Know This Already?' Quizzes and 'Review Questions.'"

Table 23.1 "Do I Know This Already?" Section-to-Question Mapping

Foundation Topics Section	Questions
Mounting NFS Shares	1–4
Mounting SMB File Systems	5
Mounting Remote File Systems Through fstab	6
Using Automount to Mount Remote File Systems	7, 8, 10
Configuring an FTP Server	9

1. You want to enable an NFS share where all access to files in the share is anonymous. Which of the following security options should you use?
   a. You do not have to specify anything; the default setting is based on anonymous access to files.
   b. **none**
   c. **sys**
   d. **krb5**

2. You need to configure a Kerberos-enabled NFS mount. Which of the following is *not* a requirement to do so?
   a. Copy the keytab file to /etc/krb5.keytab
   b. Start the nfs-secure service
   c. Use the **sec=krb5** (or **krb5i** or **krb5p**) mount option in the mount
   d. Enable the Kerberos service on the client

3. You want to use a Kerberos-enabled NFS mount. Which of the following mount options should you use to guarantee that a message has not been tampered with while transmitted. There is no need to encrypt message contents as well.
   a. **krb5**
   b. **krb5i**
   c. **krb5p**
   d. **krb5ip**

4. You type the command **showmount -e** to display available mounts on an NFS server, but you do not get any result. Which of the following is the most likely explanation?
   a. The NFS client software is not running.
   b. You are using a UID that does not exist on the server.
   c. SELinux is not configured properly.
   d. The firewall does not allow showmount traffic.

5. You want to log in to an SMB share. Which of the following commands shows correct syntax for doing so?

   a. **mount -o username=sambauser1 //server/share /somewhere**

   b. **mount -o uname=sambauser1 //server/share /somewhere**

   c. **mount sambauser1@//server/share /somewhere**

   d. **mount -o username=sambauser1@//server/share /somewhere**

6. Which of the following statements about authentication is true when configuring automatic mounts of SMB shares through fstab?

   a. You need to specify the username; while the share is mounted, you'll see a prompt for a password.

   b. You can only specify username and password by using mount options in /etc/fstab.

   c. You do not have to specify username or password in fstab; you are prompted for them when accessing the share.

   d. A secure way to specify username and password is by using a credentials file while mounting the share.

7. Which of the following is not a required step in configuring automount?

   a. Create a master map file in /etc/auto.master.d.

   b. In the master map file, specify the automount directory and the name of the automount file that contains the required configuration.

   c. In the automount file, specify the name of the subdirectory on which the remote file system has to be mounted, the mount options, and the name of the remote file systems.

   d. On the local mount point, set the appropriate permissions.

8. Which of the following statements is *not* true about direct mounts in automount?

   a. A direct mount mounts on an existing directory.

   b. Direct mounts can be performed for the root user only.

   c. There is no difference in mount options that are used on a direct mount or on an indirect mount.

   d. A direct file contains the name of an existing directory in the master map file.

9. Which of the following is not a requirement for setting up an anonymous FTP drop box?
   a. Set the **ftpd_allow_anon_upload** Boolean.
   b. Remote the read permission on the Linux file system from the shared directory.
   c. Create an anonymous user.
   d. Set the SELinux context type to **public_content_rw_t**.

10. Which of the following lines should be used in the /etc/auto.something file to mount a CIFS share with the name data on the server lab on the directory lab?
    a. **lab -fstype=cifs,credentials=/root/creds ://lab/data**
    b. **lab -fstype=smb,credentials=/root/creds //lab/data**
    c. **lab -fstype=cifs,credentials=/root/creds //lab:/data**
    d. **lab -fstype=smb,credentials=/root/creds ://lab/data**

Foundation Topics

Mounting NFS Shares

In previous chapters, you learned how to work with local file systems and mount them into the file system structure. In this chapter, you learn how to work with network file systems. The classic network file system is NFS (which stands for Network File System). It is a protocol that was developed for UNIX by Sun in the early 1980s, and it has been available on Linux forever. Its purpose is to make it possible to mount remote file systems into the local file system hierarchy.

An NFS share is exported by the NFS server. The format of the share is servername:/sharename. So, if on server labipa.example.com the directory /data is shared, the NFS client can mount it as labipa.example.com:/data. The complete command to temporarily mount the share on the /mnt directory in this case is **mount labipa.example.com:/data /mnt**.

On Red Hat Enterprise Linux 7, NFS 4 is the default NFS version. This NFS version provides a feature known as the *pseudo root mount*. That is best explained using an example. So, suppose that the NFS server labipa.example.com exports three different directories: /data, /srv, and /home. Further suppose that you have access permissions to all three of them. If that is the case, you can mount all three of them individually. The pseudo root mount, however, allows you to mount the root directory on the NFS server, which would give access to all three of the exported shares. The command to make the pseudo root mount is **mount labipa.example.com:/ /mnt**. So, you would mount the root directory, even if it has not been shared specifically. In Exercise 23.1, you learn how to work with pseudo root mounts in NFS 4.

Understanding NFS Security Options

By default, NFS security is limited. On the NFS share, security is allowed or denied based on the hostname that wants to access the share. If the hostname is allowed, the share can be mounted and accessed by users from the NFS client. When a client accesses an NFS share, the NFS server by default maps the UID of the client user to the same UID on the NFS server. This can lead to unexpected results.

If on the NFS server user linda has UID 505, and on the client user bob has UID 505, for example, bob will access the NFS share as UID 505, which is mapped to UID linda on the server. So, bob will have access to all files that linda has access to on the server.

To prevent unexpected surprises from happening when NFS is used to enable user access to files, it is a good idea to use a central mechanism to take care of authentication. That can be a Lightweight Directory Access Protocol (LDAP) server, such as the FreeIPA service that is available in the Red Hat Enterprise Linux 7 repositories. If all servers that are part of the NFS configuration are using the same LDAP server, you know for sure that UID mapping problems are prevented.

To specify how security is handled, different security options can be used when making the mount, using the **sec=*method*** mount option. Table 23.2 summarizes the default security options.

Table 23.2 Default NFS Security Options

Key Topic

Option	Explanation
none	Access to files is anonymous and mapped to the UID and GID of the user nfsnobody. Writes are permitted only if nfsnobody has write access.
sys	File access is based on UID and GID values on the client and the matching of these to the IDs used on the server. This is the default setting.
krb5	Client users must prove identity using Kerberos. After that, Linux permissions apply. See Chapter 36, "Configuring NFS," to learn more about the RHCE objective of setting up Kerberized NFS servers and mounts.
krb5i	Like **krb5**, but adds the guarantee that data in a request has not been tampered with.
krb5p	Like **krb5i**, but adds encryption to each request. This has the highest level of protection, but does have a negative impact on performance.

Understanding Kerberos Requirements

Key Topic

To configure a Kerberos mount, some additional services are needed:

- A keytab file with the name /etc/krb5.keytab. This is a file that contains the client credentials that the NFS client can use to join the Kerberos environment. This keytab needs to be configured for the client and contain the host principal, the NFS principal, or even better, both.
- The nfs-secure service must be running on the client.

For more details about setting up a Kerberos-enabled NFS environment, see Chapter 36.

TIP Creating Kerberos principals and keytabs is not part of the RHCSA and RHCE exam objectives. If you need to set up a Kerberos-enabled NFS share on the exam, Red Hat will provide you with the location of the keytab file. So, you'll just have to download it to the appropriate location. To enable the Kerberos mount, you just have to know how to add the **sec=krb5[ip]** option to the mount and make sure that the nfs-secure service is started.

RHEL 7 NFS Support

On Red Hat Enterprise Linux 7, NFS 4 is the default version of NFS. If when making an NFS mount the NFS server offers a previous version of NFS, the client falls automatically back to that version. From a client, you can also force a specific NFS version to be used for the mount, by using the **nfsvers= mount** option. This can prove useful if you are connecting to a server or a device that offers NFS 3 only.

Mounting the NFS Share

To mount an NFS share, you first need to find the names of the shares. This information can be provided by the administrator, but it is also possible to find out yourself. To discover which shares are available, you have multiple options:

- If NFSv4 is used on the server, you can use a root mount. That means that you just mount the root directory of the NFS server, and under the mount point you'll only see the shares that you have access to.
- Use **netstat -an | grep your.nfs.server.ip:port** to verify the availability of the mount.
- Use the **showmount -e nfsserver** command to find out which shares are available.

WARNING The **showmount** command may have issues with NFSv4 servers that are behind a firewall. This is because showmount relies on the portmapper service, which uses random UDP ports while making a connection, and the firewalld nfs service opens port 2049 only, which does not allow portmapper traffic. If the firewall is set up correctly, the mountd and rpc-bind services need to be added to the firewall as well. It is very well possible that shares have been set up correctly on the server but you cannot see them because showmount does not get through the firewall. If you suspect that this is the case, use the NFS root mount as explained in Exercise 23.1, or just try mounting the NFS share.

Exercise 23.1 Mounting an NFS Share

This exercise assumes the availability of an NFS server. It is recommended to use the free lab environment that is offered at http://www.rhatcert.com. This environment contains a server with the name labipa that is configured to offer NFS, Samba, and LDAP services. See Appendix D for more details on setting up this lab environment.

1. On server1, use **yum install -y nfs-utils** to install the RPM package that contains the showmount utility.
2. Type **showmount -e 192.168.122.200**. Notice that you get a "port mapper failure - Unable to receive: errno 113 (No route to host)" error.
3. Log in as root to the labipa machine. Use **ssh root@192.168.122.200**. Type **systemctl stop firewalld** and repeat Step 2 of this exercise. Notice that you now have access. Type **systemctl start firewalld** again to enable the firewall.
4. On server1, type **mount 192.168.122.200:/ /mnt**. (Notice the space between the slashes in the command.) This performs an NFSv4 pseudo root mount of all NFS shares.
5. Type **mount | grep 122** to verify the mount has succeeded.
6. Still on server1, use **ls /mnt**. This shows the subdirectories data and home, which correspond to the mounts offered by the labipa server.

Mounting SMB File Systems

To ensure the best possible compatibility for file exchange between different operating systems, Samba is a common solution. On Red Hat Enterprise Linux, you can configure the Samba server to provide access to clients using the Server Message Block (SMB) or Common Internet File System (CIFS) protocols to access these shares. In Chapter 38, "Setting up an SMTP Server," you can read how to set up such a Samba server. You can also set up Red Hat Enterprise Linux as a client to servers that are offering SMB or CIFS shares, which allows Red Hat servers to access Windows shares directly. In this section, you learn how to mount a remote SMB file system. This procedure can be applied to mount SMB-compatible shares that are offered from any platform, so it works on Windows shares and on Linux shares.

> **NOTE** Different terminology is used when talking about SMB-based services. The standard protocol that is offered by Windows servers is known as the Server Message Block (SMB) protocol. This protocol on Linux is implemented by the Samba server. CIFS is a dialect of SMB, and it is rather common that SMB and CIFS are used interchangeably.

Discovering SMB Shares

Before an SMB share can be mounted, make sure that the cifs-utils and the samba-client RPM packages are installed on the client. Also, you need to add the samba-client service to the firewall configuration on the client by using **firewall-cmd --add-service samba-client --permanent; firewall-cmd --reload**. After installing this, you can use the **smbclient -L** command to discover available SMB shares.

The **smbclient** command asks for the password of the current user. This is because **smbclient** is a very generic utility that allows you to list shares but also to log in to Samba shares on remote servers and fetch files from the remote server. To list shares, however, no credentials are required. So, when the command asks for the password, you may just press **Enter**. Alternatively, you can use the **-Uusername** option with **smbclient**, to authenticate using a valid Samba user account. You'll read more about this in Chapter 38. Listing 23.1 shows the result of the **smbclient -L** command.

Listing 23.1 Discovering SMB Shares

```
[root@localhost ~]# smbclient -L 192.168.122.201
Enter root's password:
Anonymous login successful
Domain=[MYGROUP] OS=[Unix] Server=[Samba 4.1.1]

        Sharename       Type      Comment
        ---------       ----      -------
        data            Disk      Demo data directory
        homedirs        Disk      LDAP user home directories
        IPC$            IPC       IPC Service (Samba Server Version
                                  4.1.1)
Anonymous login successful
Domain=[MYGROUP] OS=[Unix] Server=[Samba 4.1.1]
```

```
        Server               Comment
        ---------            -------
        LABIPA               Samba Server Version 4.1.1

        Workgroup            Master
        ---------            -------
        MYGROUP              LABIPA
```

In Listing 23.1, you can see how the smbclient utility is used to discover available shares on IP address 192.168.122.201. (To bypass possible problems in name resolution, the IP address of the host is used instead of the name.) The command then prompts for the password of the current user. Because the option **-L** requests a list of available shares only and nothing else, you can just press **Enter** to ignore this question. Next, the current domain or workgroup of the Samba server is shown, as well as the available shares.

Alternatively, you may use the **net share -l** command. This command lists just the shares that are available on the Samba server and does not display the additional configuration that is shown when using **smbclient -L**. Notice that the **net share -l** command lists shared printers as well, whereas **smblcient -L** just lists shared directories. The **net** command is available on Linux to provide a command-line interface that is more familiar to Windows administrators who want to configure file sharing from a Linux server. Listing 23.2 shows what the result of the **net share -l** command looks like.

Listing 23.2 Listing Samba Shares with **net share**

```
[root@server1 ~]# net share -l
Enter root's password:
Anonymous login successful

Enumerating shared resources (exports) on remote server:


Share name    Type     Description
----------    ----     -----------
sambashare    Disk     Sambashare
IPC$          IPC      IPC Service (Samba Server Version 4.1.12)
textprinter   Print    textprinter
DummyPrinter  Print    DummyPrinter
```

NOTE For discovery based on SMB hostnames to be working, the nmbd service must be running on the Samba server. This is not always the case, which is why using IP addresses instead of hostnames might be a safe choice.

Mounting SMB Shares

To mount an SMB share, you can use the **mount** command. You can use the **-t cifs** option to specify that the mount is to an SMB share, but without this option it will also work because the **mount** command is smart enough to discover by itself that it is an SMB share you want to connect to. If guest access is allowed on the share, you can specify the **-o guest** option to authenticate as the guest user without a password. Alternatively, use the **-o user=guest** option for the same purpose. The complete **mount** command looks like this:

```
mount -t cifs -o user=guest //192.168.122.200/data /mnt
```

This command mounts the /data share that is available on 192.168.122.200 on the local /mnt directory. Notice that you'll be able to access files in the share, but not to write any files in the share, which is because you are authenticated as the guest user who has limited access permissions to the share.

Authenticating to SMB Shares

In the preceding section, you read how to mount a share with guest credentials. If you want to do something with the share, you should authenticate as a valid Samba user. This is a specific user account that has the credentials required to connect to a Samba share. (An ordinary Linux user cannot do that.) For this purpose, a Samba user must have been created, as discussed in Chapter 38.

To specify the Samba username you want to use, you can add the **-o username=someone** mount option:

```
mount -o username=sambauser1 //server/share /somewhere
```

When you do this, the **mount** command prompts for a password. In Exercise 23.2, you learn how to discover and mount Samba shares from the command line.

Exercise 23.2 Discovering and Mounting SMB Shares

This exercise assumes that you are using the test environment that is available at http://www.rhatcert.com.

1. Log in to server1 and open a root shell; mounts need to be performed as the root user.
2. Type **yum install -y cifs-utils samba-client** to install the required RPM packages.
3. Type **smbclient -L 192.168.122.200** to list available shares on the labipa server.
4. Type **mount -t cifs -o guest //192.168.122.200/data /mnt** to mount the /data share as guest on the /mnt directory.
5. Type **mount** to verify that the mount has succeeded.

Accessing Samba Shares Through the Graphical Interface

While preparing for the RHCSA exam, it is a good idea to focus on accessing Samba shares from the command line. There are other options, though. Samba shares can be accessed from the GNOME 3 graphical interface on a Linux server as well. To do this, complete these steps:

1. From the graphical interface, click **Places > Browse Network**. If Samba naming services have been configured and are allowed in the firewall, you'll see the Samba server listed.
2. Alternatively, select **Network > Connect to Server** and add the name of the server followed by the share name. You need to do this in the format **smb://servername/sharename**, such as **smb://ipa.example.com/data** (see Figure 23.1).
3. You'll now see a window where you'll have to enter the user credentials you want to authenticate with (see Figure 23.2). After successful authentication, the share will be added to the graphical interface. Click the **Eject** button if you want to disconnect it.

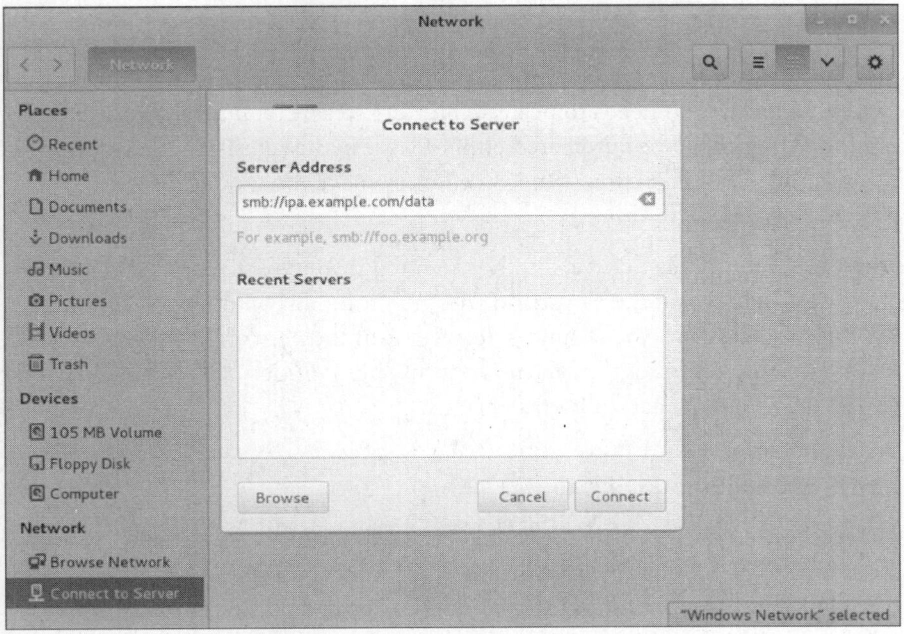

Figure 23.1 Entering the share name you want to connect to.

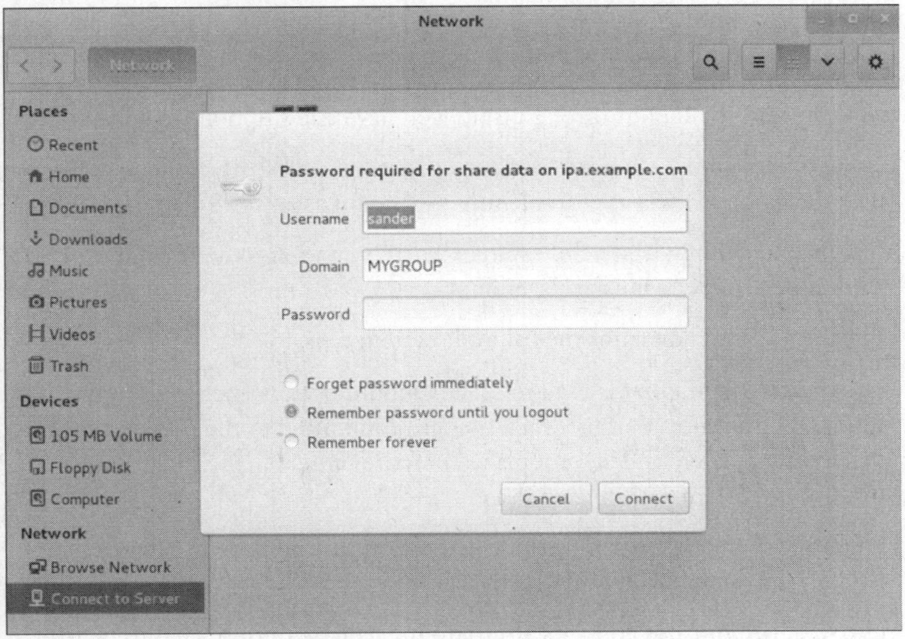

Figure 23.2 Entering Samba user credentials.

Mounting Remote File Systems Through fstab

You now know how to manually mount NFS and SMB file systems from the command line. If a file system needs to be available persistently, you need to use a different solution. Mounts can be automated either by using the /etc/fstab file or by using the autofs service. In this section, you learn how to make the mount through /etc/fstab.

For all remote file systems that need to be mounted through /etc/fstab, make sure to include the _netdev and the x-systemd.automount mount options. The _netdev mount option ensures that the mount is delayed until the network is fully available. The x-systemd.automount option ensures optimal integration with systemd and will ensure that the mount is made a lot faster.

Mounting NFS Shares Through fstab

As you have learned in earlier chapters, the /etc/fstab file is used to mount file systems that need to be mounted automatically when a server restarts. Only the user root can add mounts to this configuration file, thus providing shares that will be available for all users. The /etc/fstab file can be used to mount the NFS file system as well as Samba. To mount an NFS file system through /etc/fstab, make sure that the following line is included:

```
server1:/share      /nfs/mount/point   nfs,_netdev,x-systemd.
  automount,        sync        0 0
```

When making an NFS mount through fstab, you have a few options to consider:

Key Topic

- In the first column, you need to specify the server and share name. Use a colon after the name of the server to identify the mount as an NFS share.
- The second column has the file system where you want to do the mount; this is not different from any regular mount.
- The third column contains the NFS file system type.
- The fourth column that is used to specify mount options includes the sync option. This ensures that modified files are committed to the remote file system immediately and are not placed in write buffers first (which would increase the risk of data getting lost).
- The fifth column contains a zero, which means that no backup support through the dump utility is requested.
- The sixth column also contains a zero, to indicate that no fsck has to be performed on this file system while booting to check the integrity of the file system. The integrity of the file system would need to be checked on the server, not on the client.

Mounting SMB Shares Through fstab

When mounting SMB file systems through /etc/fstab, you need to consider a specific challenge: You need to specify the user credentials that are needed to issue the mount. On an NFS share, this is not necessary because the user who accesses the shared file system by default does so using his own credentials. While mounting a Samba share through /etc/fstab, these user credentials are normally specified with the **username=** and **password=** mount options, but it is not a good idea to put these in clear text in the /etc/fstab file.

> **EXAM TIP!** Make sure to include the _netdev mount option in /etc/fstab as well for anything that involves networking for the mount to be completed. This ensures that the mount will be made a lot faster. Also make sure to include the x-systemd.automount option, which guarantees optimal integration with systemd and makes the mount a lot faster.

As an alternative to specifying credentials in the /etc/fstab file directly, you can consider using a credentials file. When using a credentials file, the credentials file itself contains the username, password, and (optionally) the domain you want to connect to. When using a credentials file, it is mandatory to secure the file. The best way to secure it is by putting it in the home directory of the root user, set the owners to root:root, and set the permission mode 600. The contents of the creds file can look like Listing 23.3.

Listing 23.3 Example of a Credentials File

```
username=linda
password=secret
domain=mydomain
```

> **TIP** The layout of the credentials file is described in man mount.cifs.

To use a credentials file when mounting from the command line, you can include the **-o credentials=***filename* option, as in the following:

```
mount -t cifs -o credentials=/root/creds //server1/data /mnt/data
```

To do the same from the /etc/fstab file, the following line needs to be included in /etc/fstab:

```
//server1/data     /mnt/data cifs      _netdev,, x-systemd.
automount,credentials=/root/creds      0 0
```

TIP You can find more information about advanced mount options in Chapter 38.

Using Automount to Mount Remote File Systems

As an alternative to using /etc/fstab, you can configure automount to mount the share automatically. Automount can be used for SMB as well as NFS mounts, and the big difference is that mounts through automount are affected on demand and not by default. So, using automount ensures that no file systems are mounted that are not really needed.

Understanding Automount

Automount is implemented by the autofs service that takes care of mounting a share when it is attempted to be accessed. That means it is mounted on demand and that it does not have to be mounted permanently. An important benefit of using automount is that it works completely in user space, and contrary to mounts that are made through the **mount** command, no root permissions are required.

TIP On previous versions of RHEL, the auto.master file was used to define the file systems to be automounted. On RHEL 7, you can work with snippet files in the /etc/auto.master.d directory as an alternative. You can still use the old method, though.

To configure automount, the autofs package has to be installed. After you install that, a master-map file needs to be created in the directory /etc/auto.master.d. The name of this file does not matter, but it needs to end in autofs. In the master map file, the directory is specified that should be monitored by the autofs service. From this file, a second file is referred to that contains the setting with which the automount is performed. In Exercise 23.3, you create this configuration yourself.

When using automount, you can use two different kinds of automount maps:

- An indirect map contains a directory that should be created by automount. Indirect mounting allows for alteration without the need to restart the autofs service, which makes it completely accessible from user space.
- A direct file does not involve creation of a directory, it has to exist before automount can mount the (remote) file system.

Configuring Automount for NFS

Configuring an automount solution is a complicated multistep procedure. To show how it works, Exercise 23.3 lists all steps involved. Follow the steps in this exercise to see for yourself how to configure automount.

Exercise 23.3 Configuring Direct and Indirect Maps to Mount NFS Shares

This exercise is performed on server1. It uses the NFS shares that are provided through the labipa server.

1. Type **yum install -y autofs** to install the autofs package.
2. Create the master map file that contains further instructions that tell the autofs service how to automount the remote file systems. Type **vim /etc/auto.master.d/demo.autofs** to create and open the file.
3. Add the master map entry for indirect mapped mounts by adding the following line:

   ```
   /shares    /etc/auto.demo
   ```

   This uses the /shares directory as the starting point for all indirect mounts. The auto.demo file is referred to as the file that contains the instructions that further complete the automount.
4. In the same file, include the following line for directly mapped mount points:

   ```
   /-         /etc/auto.direct
   ```

   Direct mounts always have **/-** as the starting point for the direct mounts in the master map file. Further instructions on how to perform the mount are in the auto.direct file. Notice that the names of these secondary files do not really matter. The only requirement is that they need to be created in the path that is indicated.
5. In the indirect mount file auto.demo, include the following line to mount labipa:/data on the directory /shares/data using the **rw** and **sync** NFS mount options:

   ```
   data       -rw,sync  labipa:/data
   ```

   Notice that the first field as a relative directory name contains the name of the mount point, which is followed by the mount options, which are followed by the name of the NFS server and share on that server. Notice that in this indirect mount, the /shares directory as well as its data subdirectory, will be automatically created by automount at the moment that the indicated file system is mounted.

6. Now create the direct mounts configuration in the file /etc/auto.direct. Give this file the following contents:

```
/mnt        -rw,sync   labipa:/home
```

Notice that in a direct mount, the directory that is used as the mount point should already exist before the automount can be done.

7. Type **systemctl enable autofs; systemctl start autofs** to start the autofs service.

8. At this point, you can test the automount configuration. Type **cd /shares**. This should automatically do the automount of the labipa:/data share in /shares/data. Now type **cd /mnt**. This should automatically mount the labipa:/home share on the /mnt directory.

Using Wildcards in Automount

In Exercise 23.3, you have read how to perform automounts based on fixed directory names. In some cases, this is not very useful and you are better off using dynamic directory names. This is, for example, the case for automounting home directories.

Consider the labipa:/home directory, which contains several user home directories. When a user logs in to a system, you may want to mount the corresponding home directory on labipa:/home. To make this happen, you use the following configuration:

1. To configure an indirect mount, where home directories are mounted on /home/guests, create the master map file /etc/auto.master.d/home.autofs and give it the following contents:

```
/home/guests          /etc/auto.homes
```

2. Create the /etc/auto.homes file and give it the following contents:

```
*            -rw,sync   labipa:/home/ldap/&
```

3. Restart the autofs service, using **systemctl restart autofs**.

By applying this procedure, you'll make sure that if a user logs in who has the local home directory location set to /home/guests/$USER, an automount of the corresponding subdirectory name is automatically done from the /home/ldap/$USER directory on labipa.

NOTE If you have worked with automount on previous versions of RHEL, you have probably configured the first step of the procedure directly in /etc/auto.master. This is still possible, which means that instead of creating a master map entry in /etc/auto.master.d as described in Exercise 23.3, you could directly put the line **/shares -rw,sync labipa:/data** in the auto.master file. This solution still works but is deprecated. On RHEL 7, the auto.master file is considered a part of the RPM, and it might be overwritten while updating RPMs on your server. For that reason, the approach described in Exercise 23.3 is preferred, as in that exercise; the system-managed part of the configuration is clearly distinguished from the user-managed part of the configuration.

TIP If you think the new method where master map entries are created in /etc/auto.master.d is complicated, you are welcome to use the old method. All that counts on the exam is that your solution works; it does not really matter how you accomplished that.

Using Automount to Mount SMB Shares

The procedure for mounting SMB shares with automount is roughly the same as the procedure that is described in the previous section to mount NFS shares with automount. There are a few items to consider:

- If you want to use a credentials file, make sure to include the absolute path to that file (such as /root/filename.cre) in the mount options.
- The name of the share that should be mount should start with a colon (:). All devices that are mounted in automount and have a name that starts with a / should be prepended by a colon.

Configuring an FTP Server

FTP has always been a common service in Linux environments. It is no longer in the RHCSA or RHCE objectives. However, because every system administrator should know at least how to configure an FTP server, in Exercise 23.4 you learn how to configure an FTP server and set it up as an anonymous drop box, where users can put files in, but after putting them in, cannot read them anymore.

NOTE In this exercise I'll just walk you through the procedure of setting up an FTP server as an anonymous user drop box. If you ever want to do this on a real server, make sure to put the FTP server document root on a dedicated storage device, or use quota to maximize the amount of data that can be stored in the drop box.

Exercise 23.4 Configuring an FTP Anonymous Drop Box

1. On server1, type **yum install -y vsftpd**.
2. The FTP server uses the directory /var/ftp as the default document root. In this directory, create a subdirectory with the name uploads, using **mkdir /var/ftp/uploads**. Type **chmod 0730 /var/ftp/uploads** to set the correct permissions, and set the group owner to the group ftp by using **chgrp ftp /var/ftp/uploads**. On an anonymous drop box, users can write files, but they cannot read them.
3. Open the file /etc/vsftpd/vsftpd.conf in an editor and make sure that it includes the following parameters. Do not change anything else:

```
anon_upload_enable=YES
anon_mkdir_write_enable=YES
anon_mask = 077
chown_uploads = yes
chown_username = root
```

4. Type **systemctl enable vsftpd; systemctl start vsftpd** to enable and start the FTP server.
5. Type **firewall-cmd --add-service ftp --permanent** followed by **firewall-cmd --reload**.
6. From server2, type **yum install -y lftp** to install the lftp command-line client.
7. Type **lftp server1** and type **ls**. You'll see the pub and uploads directories.
8. Type **put /etc/hosts**. You'll fail.
9. Type **grep AVC /var/log/audit/audit.log**. You'll see a message indicating that this action has been denied.
10. Type **semanage fcontext -a -t public_content_rw_t "/var/ftp/uploads(/.*)?"** followed by **restorecon -Rv /var/ftp/uploads** and try Steps 7 and 8 again. You'll still fail.

TIP Step 10 fails if the **semanage** commands are not yet installed. You do not want to learn a long list of all required RPM packages. As discussed in Chapter 11, "Managing Software," use **yum whatprovides */semanage** to find the name of the RPM you need to install to be able to use this command.

11. Type **getsebool -a | grep ftp**. You'll see the **ftpd_anon_write** Boolean, which is currently off.
12. Type **setsebool -P ftpd_anon_write on** to switch on the Boolean.
13. Try to upload the file again. You'll now succeed and have created an anonymous user file-upload drop box.

Summary

In this chapter, you learned how to mount remote file systems and how to set up an FTP server. You first learned how to manually mount either an NFS or an SMB file system from the command line. Then you learned how these mounts can be automated through /etc/fstab or automount. In the last section in this chapter, you learned how to set up an FTP server to allow for anonymous file uploads.

Exam Preparation Tasks

Review All Key Topics

Review the most important topics in the chapter, noted with the Key Topic icon in the outer margin of the page. Table 23.3 lists a reference of these key topics and the page numbers on which each is found.

Table 23.3 Key Topics for Chapter 23

Key Topic Element	Description	Page
Table 23.2	Default NFS security options	520
List	Configuring a Kerberos mount	520
List	Options to consider when making an NFS mount through fstab	528

Complete Tables and Lists from Memory

Print a copy of Appendix B, "Memory Tables" (found on the disc), or at least the section for this chapter, and complete the tables and lists from memory. Appendix C, "Memory Tables Answer Key," also on the disc, includes completed tables and lists to check your work.

Define Key Terms

Define the following key terms from this chapter and check your answers in the glossary:

SMB, CIFS, NFS, portmap, automount, mount map file, direct mount, indirect mount, credentials file, pseudo root mount

Review Questions

1. Which file must be present to create a Kerberized NFS mount?
2. Which command enables you to show available NFS mounts on server1?
3. Which command enables you to mount an NFS share that is available on server1:/share?
4. Which command can you use to discover SMB mounts on a specific server?
5. Which package must be installed on an SMB client before you can make an SMB mount?
6. How do you mount the Samba share data on server1 with guest access on the local directory /mnt?
7. How would you mount a Samba mount through fstab while avoiding putting the username and password in /etc/fstab?
8. Which requirements are there for the automount file that you create in /etc/auto.master.d?
9. In which case is using a direct mount in automount recommended?
10. What is the name of the configuration file that contains the vsftpd configuration?

End-of-Chapter Labs

In this chapter, you learned how to mount remote file systems and automate those mounts using /etc/fstab or automount. You have also learned how to set up an FTP server and saw the essential parts of a typical FTP server. In the end-of-chapter labs, you practice these skills in a way that is similar to how you need to do it on the exam.

Lab 23.1

1. Create an automount configuration that mounts the labipa:/data directory on the directory /labdata on server1.
2. Configure a permanent Samba mount through /etc/fstab that mounts the data share on the 192.168.122.200 test VM permanently on the directory /srv/samba/guest.
3. Install an FTP server from which anonymous users can download files. Do *not* allow file upload to this server.

The following topics are covered in this chapter:

- Understanding Local Time
- Using Network Time Protocol
- Managing Time on Red Hat Enterprise Linux
- Using Graphical Tools to Manage Time

The following RHCSA exam objectives are covered in this chapter:

- Configure a system to use time services

CHAPTER 24

Configuring Time Services

An increasing number of services offered through Linux servers depend on the correct configuration of time on the server. Think of services such as database synchronization, Kerberos authentication, and more. In this chapter, you learn how time is configured on a Linux server.

"Do I Know This Already?" Quiz

The "Do I Know This Already?" quiz allows you to assess whether you should read this entire chapter thoroughly or jump to the "Exam Preparation Tasks" section. If you are in doubt about your answers to these questions or your own assessment of your knowledge of the topics, read the entire chapter. Table 24.1 lists the major headings in this chapter and their corresponding "Do I Know This Already?" quiz questions. You can find the answers in Appendix A, "Answers to the 'Do I Know This Already?' Quizzes and 'Review Questions.'"

Table 24.1 "Do I Know This Already?" Section-to-Question Mapping

Foundation Topics Section	Questions
Understanding Local Time	1–2
Using Network Time Protocol	4–5
Managing Time on Red Hat Enterprise Linux	3, 6–9
Using Graphical Tools to Manage Time	10

1. When a system is started, where does it initially get the system time?
   a. NTP
   b. Software time
   c. The hardware clock
   d. Network time

2. Which of the following statements is *not* true about local time?
   a. Local time is the current time in the current time zone.
   b. In local time, DST is considered.
   c. System time typically should correspond to the current local time.
   d. Hardware time typically corresponds to the current local time.

3. Which is the recommended command in RHEL 7 to set the local time zone?
   a. **hwclock**
   b. **tz**
   c. **date**
   d. **timedatectl**

4. Which clock type would you recommend on a server that is *not* connected to any other server but needs to be configured with the most accurate time possible?
   a. RTC
   b. UTC
   c. An atomic clock
   d. NTP

5. Which configuration file contains the default list of NTP servers that should be contacted on RHEL 7?
   a. /etc/ntp/ntp.conf
   b. /etc/ntp.conf
   c. /etc/chrony/chronyd.conf
   d. /etc/chrony.conf

6. Which of the following shows correct syntax to set the current system time to 9:30 p.m.?
   a. **date 9:30**
   b. **date --set 9.30 PM**
   c. **date -s 21:30**
   d. **date 2130**

7. Which command correctly translates epoch time into human time?

  a. **time --date '@1420987251'**

  b. **time --date '$1420987251'**

  c. **time --date '#1420987251'**

  d. **time --date '1420987251'**

8. Which command enables you to monitor the difference between the hardware clock and system clock?

  a. **tail -f /var/lib/time/drift**

  b. **date -h**

  c. **hwclock -c**

  d. **hwclock -d**

9. Which command enables you to show current information that includes the local time, hardware time, and the time zone the system is in?

  a. **timedatectl --all**

  b. **timedatectl --tz**

  c. **timedatectl -ht**

  d. **timedatectl**

10. Which command starts the graphical utility that you can use to manage time?

  a. **timedatectl**

  b. **system-config-time**

  c. **timedatectl-gtk**

  d. **system-config-date**

Foundation Topics

Understanding Local Time

Key Topic

When a Linux server boots, the hardware clock, also referred to as real-time clock, is read. This clock typically resides in the computer hardware. Generally, it is an integrated circuit on the system board that is completely independent of the current state of the operating system and keeps running even when the computer is shut down. From the hardware clock, the system gets its initial time setting.

The time on the hardware clock on Linux servers is usually set to universal time coordinated (UTC). UTC is a time that is the same everywhere on the planet, and based on UTC, the current local time is calculated. (Later in this chapter you learn how this works.)

Key Topic

System time is a time maintained by the operating system. Once the system has booted, the system clock is completely independent of the hardware clock. Therefore, when system time is changed, the new system time is not automatically synchronized with the hardware clock.

System time is a time that is maintained by the operating system and it is kept in UTC. Applications running on the server are converting system time into local time. Local time is the actual time in the current time zone. In local time, daylight savings time (DST) is considered so that it always shows an accurate time for that system. Table 24.2 gives an overview of the different concepts that play a role in Linux time.

Key Topic

Table 24.2 Understanding Linux Time

Concept	Explanation
Hardware clock	The hardware clock that resides on the main card of a computer system
Real-time clock	Same as the hardware clock
System time	The time that is maintained by the operating system
Software clock	Similar to system time
Universal time coordinated	A worldwide standard time
Daylight savings time	Calculation that is made to change time automatically when daylight savings time changes occur.
Local time	The time that corresponds to the time in the current time zone

Using Network Time Protocol

As you learned, the current system time is based on a hardware clock. This hardware clock is typically a part of the computer's motherboard, and it might be unreliable. Because of its unreliability, it is a good idea to use time from a more reliable source. Generically speaking, two solutions are available.

One option is to buy a more reliable hardware clock. This may be, for instance, a very accurate atomic clock connected directly to your computer. When such a very reliable clock is used, an increased accuracy of the system time is guaranteed. Using an external hardware clock is a common solution to guarantee that datacenter time is maintained, even if the connection to external networks for time synchronization temporarily is not available.

Another and more common solution is to configure your server to use Network Time Protocol (NTP). NTP is a method of maintaining system time that is provided through NTP servers on the Internet. It is an easy solution to provide an accurate time to servers, because most servers are connected to the Internet anyway.

Key Topic

Setting up a server to use NTP time on RHEL 7 is easy if the server is already connected to the Internet. If this is the case, the /etc/chrony.conf file is configured with a standard list of NTP servers on the Internet that should be contacted. The only thing the administrator has to do is switch on NTP, by using **timedatectl set-ntp 1**. In Chapter 40, "Managing Time Synchronization," you can read more about the RHCE requirement of setting up time synchronization using NTP.

Managing Time on Red Hat Enterprise Linux

Different commands are involved in managing time on Red Hat Enterprise Linux. Table 24.3 provides an overview.

Key Topic

Table 24.3 Commands Related to RHEL 7 Time Management

Command	Short description
date	Manages local time
hwclock	Manages hardware time
timedatectl	Developed to manage all aspects of time on RHEL 7

Key Topic

On a Linux system, time is calculated as an offset of epoch time. Epoch time is the number of seconds since January 1, 1970, in UTC. In some logs (such as /var/log/audit/audit.log), you'll find time stamps in epoch time and not in human time. To convert such an epoch time stamp to human time, you can use the **--date** option, followed by the epoch string that is starting with an @:

```
date --date '@1420987251'
```

The use of epoch time is also creating a potential timing problem on Linux. On a 32-bit system, the number of seconds that can be counted in the field that is reserved for time notation is finished in 2037. (Try setting the time to somewhere in 2050 if you are on a 32-bit kernel; it will not work.) 64-bit systems can address time until far into the twenty-second century.

Using date

The **date** command enables you to manage the system time. You can also use it to show the current time in different formats. Some common usage examples of **date** are listed here:

- **date** Shows the current system time
- **date +%d-%m-%y** Shows the current system day of month, month, and year
- **date -s 16:03** Sets the current time to 3 minutes past 4 p.m.

Using hwclock

The **date** command enables you to set and show the current system time. Using the **date** command will not change the hardware time that is used on your system. To manage hardware time, you can use the **hwclock** command. The **hwclock** command has many options, some of which are of particular interest:

- **hwclock -c** shows the difference between hardware time and system time. The output of this command is refreshed every 10 seconds. Listing 24.1 shows the output of this command.
- **hwclock --systohc** synchronizes current system time to the hardware clock.
- **hwclock --hctosys** synchronizes current hardware time to the system clock.

Listing 24.1 Monitoring Differences Between Hardware and System Time

```
[root@server1 ~]# hwclock -c
hw-time        system-time           freq-offset-ppm   tick
1428584002     1428584002.011018
1428584012     1428584012.033019                2200      22
```

```
1428584022    1428584022.054953          2197      22
1428584032    1428584032.083572          2418      24
1428584042    1428584042.111683          2517      25
```

Using timedatectl

A new command in RHEL 7 that enables you to manage many aspects of time is **timedatectl**. As shown in Listing 24.2, when used without any arguments, this command shows detailed information about the current time and date. It also displays the time zone your system is in, in addition to information about the use of NTP network time and information about the use of DST.

Listing 24.2 Using **timedatectl** to Get Detailed Information About Current Time Settings

```
[root@localhost ~]# timedatectl
      Local time: Sun 2015-01-11 10:02:41 EST
  Universal time: Sun 2015-01-11 15:02:41 UTC
        RTC time: Sun 2015-01-11 15:02:51
        Timezone: America/New_York (EST, -0500)
     NTP enabled: n/a
NTP synchronized: no
 RTC in local TZ: no
      DST active: no
 Last DST change: DST ended at
                  Sun 2014-11-02 01:59:59 EDT
                  Sun 2014-11-02 01:00:00 EST
 Next DST change: DST begins (the clock jumps one hour forward) at
                  Sun 2015-03-08 01:59:59 EST
                  Sun 2015-03-08 03:00:00 EDT
```

The **timedatectl** command works with commands to perform time operations. Table 24.4 provides an overview of the relevant commands.

Table 24.4 **timedatectl** Command Overview

Key Topic

Command	Explanation
status	Show current time settings
set-time TIME	Set the current time
set-timezone ZONE	Set the current time zone

Command	Explanation
list-timezone	Show a list of all time zones
set-local-rtc [0|1]	Control whether RTC (the Real Time Clock—this normally refers to the hardware clock) is in local time
set-ntp [0|1]	Control whether NTP is enabled

The **timedatectl** command was developed as a generic solution to manage time on RHEL 7. It has some functions that are offered through other commands, but the purpose of the command is that eventually it will replace other commands used for managing time and date settings. When **timedatectl** is used to switch on NTP time, it talks to the **chronyd** process. In Chapter 40, you'll learn more about managing NTP time by using chrony. Exercise 24.1 walks you through some common options to manage time on a RHEL 7 server.

TIP On RHEL 7, chrony is the default solution to manage network time. NTP can still be implemented through **ntpd**, though. If you have services that need **ntpd**, you are free to use it, but you should realize that in that case you cannot use the **timedatectl** command.

Exercise 24.1 Managing Local Time

1. Open a root shell and type **date**.
2. Now type **hwclock** and see whether both commands are showing more or less the same time.
3. Type **hwclock -c**. Notice that this shows differences between system time and hardware time in much more detail. Use **Ctrl+C** to interrupt.
4. You have just seen that the current time displayed by **hwclock -c** is in epoch time.
5. Use **date -d '@12345678'** (in which you replace 12345678 with the epoch time **hwclock -c** has just shown) to translate the current epoch time to human-readable time.
6. Type **timedatectl show** to show current time settings.
7. Use **timedatectl list-timezones** to show a list of all time zone definitions.
8. Use **timedatectl set-timezone Europe/Amsterdam** to set the current time zone to Amsterdam.

9. Type **timedatectl show** and notice the differences with the previous output.
10. Type **timedatectl set-ntp 1** to switch on NTP use. You might see the error "failed to issue method call." If you get this message, type **yum -y install chrony** and try again.
11. Open the configuration file /etc/chrony.conf and look up the server lines. These are used to specify the servers that should be used for NTP time synchronization.
12. Type **systemctl status chronyd** and verify that the chrony service is started and enabled. If this is not the case, use **systemctl start chronyd; systemctl enable chronyd** to make sure that it is operational.
13. Type **systemctl status -l chronyd** and read the status information. Listing 24.3 shows you what the output of the command should look like.

Listing 24.3 Monitoring Current Time Synchronization Status

```
[root@localhost system]# systemctl status -l chronyd
chronyd.service - NTP client/server
   Loaded: loaded (/usr/lib/systemd/system/chronyd.service; enabled)
   Active: active (running) since Sun 2015-01-11 10:20:15 EST; 2min 14s
ago
  Process: 13938 ExecStartPost=/usr/libexec/chrony-helper add-dhclient-
servers (code=exited, status=0/SUCCESS)
  Process: 13935 ExecStart=/usr/sbin/chronyd -u chrony $OPTIONS
(code=exited, status=0/SUCCESS)
 Main PID: 13937 (chronyd)
   CGroup: /system.slice/chronyd.service
           └─13937 /usr/sbin/chronyd -u chrony

Jan 11 10:20:15 localhost.localdomain chronyd[13937]: chronyd version
1.29.1 starting
Jan 11 10:20:15 localhost.localdomain chronyd[13937]: Linux kernel
major=3 minor=10 patch=0
Jan 11 10:20:15 localhost.localdomain chronyd[13937]: hz=100 shift_hz=7
freq_scale=1.00000000 nominal_tick=10000 slew_delta_tick=833 max_tick_
bias=1000 shift_pll=2
Jan 11 10:20:15 localhost.localdomain chronyd[13937]: Generated key 1
Jan 11 10:20:15 localhost.localdomain systemd[1]: Started NTP client/
server.
Jan 11 10:20:20 localhost.localdomain chronyd[13937]: Selected source
178.21.23.127
```

```
Jan 11 10:20:20 localhost.localdomain chronyd[13937]: System clock
wrong by 11.256802 seconds, adjustment started
Jan 11 10:20:31 localhost.localdomain chronyd[13937]: System clock was
stepped by 11.257 seconds
   Jan 11 10:20:33 localhost.localdomain chronyd[13937]: Selected
   source 87.195.109.207
```

Managing Time Zone Settings

Between Linux servers, time is normally communicated in UTC. This allows servers across different time zones to all use the same time settings, which makes managing time in large organizations a lot easier. To make it easier for end users, though, the local time must also be set. To do this, the appropriate time zone needs to be selected.

On Red Hat Enterprise Linux 7, you have four approaches to setting the correct local time zone:

- Use the system-config-date utility as discussed in the next section of this chapter.
- Go to the directory /usr/share/zoneinfo. In this directory, you'll find different subdirectories containing files for each of the time zones that has been defined. To set the local time zone on a server, you can create a symbolic link with the name /etc/localtime to the time zone file that is involved. If you want to set local time to Los Angeles time, for instance, use **ln -sf /usr/share/zoneinfo/America/Los_Angeles /etc/localtime**.
- Use the **tzselect** utility. This tool starts the interface shown in Listing 24.4, from which the appropriate region and locale can be selected.
- Use **timedatectl** to set the time zone information.

Listing 24.4 Selecting the Time Zone Using **tzselect**

```
[root@server1 ~]# tzselect
Please identify a location so that time zone rules can be set
correctly.
Please select a continent or ocean.
 1) Africa
 2) Americas
 3) Antarctica
 4) Arctic Ocean
```

```
 5) Asia
 6) Atlantic Ocean
 7) Australia
 8) Europe
 9) Indian Ocean
10) Pacific Ocean
11) none - I want to specify the time zone using the Posix TZ
format.
#? 2
Please select a country.
 1) Anguilla                  28) Haiti
 2) Antigua & Barbuda         29) Honduras
 3) Argentina                 30) Jamaica
 4) Aruba                     31) Martinique
 5) Bahamas                   32) Mexico
 6) Barbados                  33) Montserrat
 7) Belize                    34) Nicaragua
 8) Bolivia                   35) Panama
 9) Brazil                    36) Paraguay
10) Canada                    37) Peru
11) Caribbean Netherlands     38) Puerto Rico
12) Cayman Islands            39) St Barthelemy
13) Chile                     40) St Kitts & Nevis
14) Colombia                  41) St Lucia
15) Costa Rica                42) St Maarten (Dutch part)
16) Cuba                      43) St Martin (French part)
17) Curacao                   44) St Pierre & Miquelon
18) Dominica                  45) St Vincent
19) Dominican Republic        46) Suriname
20) Ecuador                   47) Trinidad & Tobago
21) El Salvador               48) Turks & Caicos Is
22) French Guiana             49) United States
23) Greenland                 50) Uruguay
24) Grenada                   51) Venezuela
25) Guadeloupe                52) Virgin Islands (UK)
26) Guatemala                 53) Virgin Islands (US)
27) Guyana
#?
```

Using Graphical Tools to Manage Time

If your server is configured with a graphical interface, you can use the graphical tool to manage time. To do so, follow these steps:

1. On the graphical display, click the current time that is shown in the upper-right corner.
2. On the screen that opens, click **Date & Time Settings**.
3. A new screen opens. To get access to the options that allow you to change time, click **Unlock**.
4. From the screen you see now, you can switch network time on and off and change the current time zone setting as well as the current time.

Alternatively, you can start the graphical utility to manage time by using the **system-config-date** command. Figure 24.1 shows the interface of this utility.

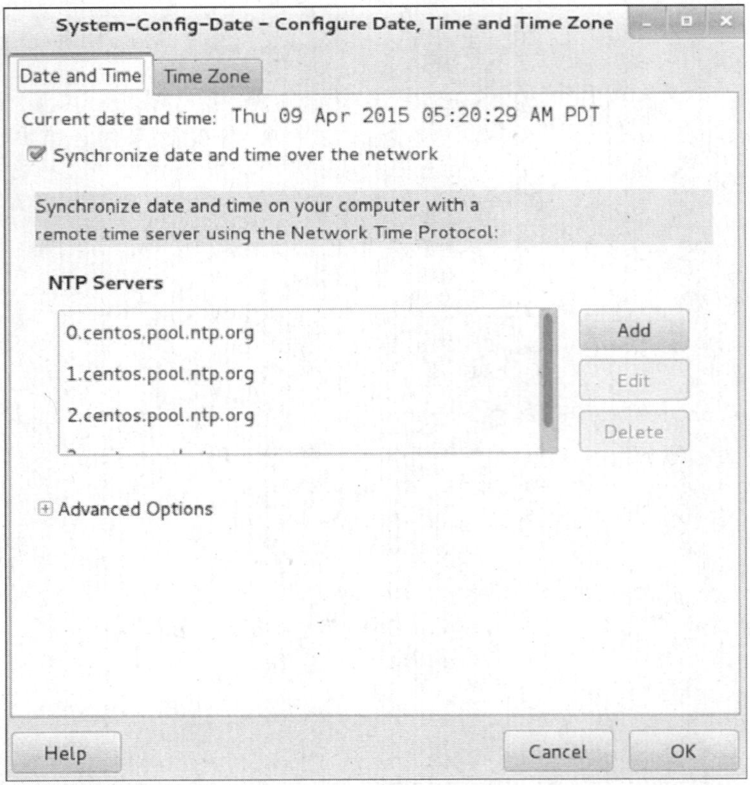

Figure 24.1 Managing Date and Time Using system-config-date

Summary

In this chapter, you learned how time works on Linux. You read how your operating system can get its time by using hardware time, system time, and local time. You also learned how to manage time using the **date**, **hwclock**, and **timedatectl** commands.

Exam Prep Tasks

Review All Key Topics

Review the most important topics in the chapter, noted with the Key Topic icon in the outer margin of the page. Table 24.5 lists a reference of these key topics and the page numbers on which each is found.

Table 24.5 Key Topics for Chapter 24

Key Topic Element	Description	Page Number
Paragraph	Definition of hardware time	542
Paragraph	Definition of system time	542
Table 24.2	Understanding Linux time	542
Paragraph	Using NTP time	543
Table 24.3	Commands related to RHEL 7 time management	543
Paragraph	Explanation of epoch time	543
Table 24.4	**Timedatectl** command overview	545

Complete Tables and Lists from Memory

Print a copy of Appendix B, "Memory Tables" (found on the disc), or at least the section for this chapter, and complete the tables and lists from memory. Appendix C, "Memory Tables Answer Key," also on the disc, includes completed tables and lists to check your work.

Define Key Terms

Define the following key terms from this chapter and check your answers in the glossary:

hardware time, rtc, system time, network time, UTC, epoch time, time synchronization

Review Questions

1. Which command enables you to set the system time to 4:24 p.m.?
2. How do you synchronize the current system time with the hardware time?
3. Which command enables you to show epoch time as human-readable time?
4. Which command enables you to synchronize the system clock with hardware time?
5. Which service is used to manage NTP time on RHEL 7?
6. Which command enables you to use NTP time on your server?
7. Which configuration file contains the list of NTP servers to be used?
8. Which command enables you to list time zones?
9. Which command enables you to set the current time zone?
10. How do you use chrony to set system time?

End-of-Chapter Labs

In this chapter, you read how to manage time. Because it is very important for a server to use the correct time, you can now practice some of the most essential skills you have acquired in this chapter.

Lab 24.1

1. Compare the current hardware time to the system time. If there is a difference, make sure to synchronize time.
2. Set the time zone to correspond to the current time in Boston.

PART 2

RHCE

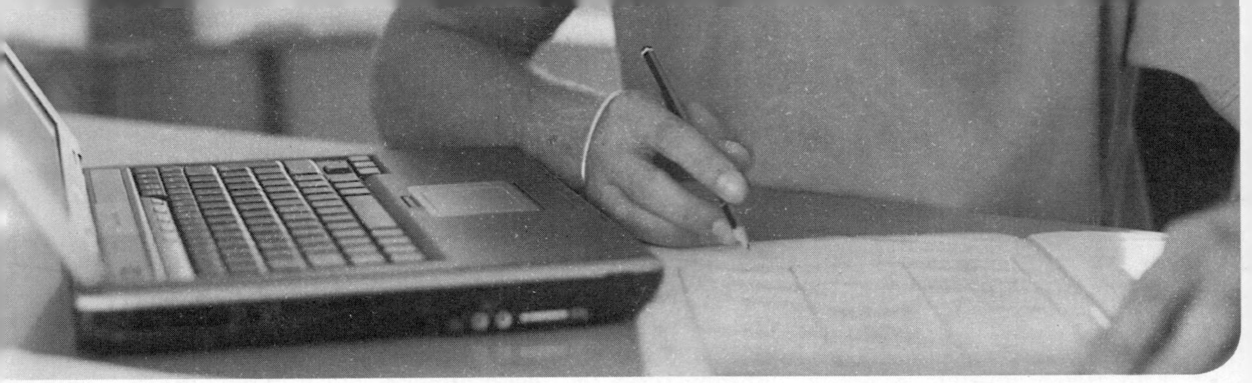

The following topics are covered in this chapter:

- Understanding Remote Authentication
- Understanding Kerberos Basics
- Configuring LDAP Authentication with Kerberos Authorization
- Using an IPA Server or Active Directory

The following RHCE exam objectives are covered in this chapter:

- Configure a system to authenticate using Kerberos

CHAPTER 25

Configuring External Authentication and Authorization

If you have many servers to manage, you probably do not want to set up user accounts on every single server. In that case, it makes sense to configure your server for external authentication and authorization. This chapter teaches you how to configure a server to use either Lightweight Directory Access Protocol (LDAP) or Kerberos for this purpose.

"Do I Know This Already?" Quiz

The "Do I Know This Already?" quiz allows you to assess whether you should read this entire chapter thoroughly or jump to the "Exam Preparation Tasks" section. If you are in doubt about your answers to these questions or your own assessment of your knowledge of the topics, read the entire chapter. Table 25.1 lists the major headings in this chapter and their corresponding "Do I Know This Already?" quiz questions. You can find the answers in Appendix A, "Answers to the 'Do I Know This Already?' Quizzes and 'Review Questions.'"

Table 25.1 "Do I Know This Already?" Section-to-Question Mapping

Foundation Topics Section	Questions
Understanding Remote Authentication	4–5
Understanding Kerberos Basics	1–3
Configuring LDAP Authentication with Kerberos Authorization	6–9
Using an IPA Server or Active Directory	10

1. Which statement about Kerberos authentication is *not* true?
   a. A user receives a Kerberos ticket after authenticating to the server. This ticket is next decrypted with the user password and will be sent back to the KDC server.
   b. To authenticate, the user password is sent to the KDC, which checks the password and based on that hands out an authentication ticket.

c. The Kerberos ticket is used each time a Kerberized service is accessed.

d. Kerberos passwords are used as a symmetric key to encrypt and decrypt Kerberos tickets.

2. A Kerberos principal name normally contains three parts. Which of the following is not among these?

   a. Primary

   b. Domain

   c. Instance

   d. Realm

3. Kerberos enable services need to store their password in a file so that they can start up automatically. If default names are used, which of the following files would be used for that purpose?

   a. /etc/krb5.keytab

   b. /etc/krb5.conf

   c. /etc/krb.principal

   d. /etc/krbpasswd

4. Which of the following services is *not* used for account information storage?

   a. LDAP

   b. NIS

   c. /etc/passwd

   d. Kerberos

5. Which of the following is *not* commonly used as a remote authentication-related service that runs on RHEL 7?

   a. OpenLDAP

   b. Kerberos

   c. NIS

   d. IdM

6. Which configuration file can you use to specify that the sssd service should be used as the authentication backend service?
    a. /etc/authconfig.conf
    b. /etc/sssd/authconfig.conf
    c. /etc/sysconfig/authconfig
    d. /etc/sssd/sssd.conf
7. Where does the LDAP client look for the CA certificate to connect to the LDAP server?
    a. /etc/ldap.conf
    b. /etc/ldap/certs
    c. /etc/ldap/cacerts
    d. /etc/openldap/cacerts
8. Which of the following variables in /etc/sysconfig/authconfig is not required to set up authentication using the sssd backend?
    a. USESSSDAUTH
    b. USESSSD
    c. USEPAMACCESS
    d. FORCELEGACY
9. You are on a server that does not have an /etc/sssd/sssd.conf file with authentication settings. In which file would you expect to find the settings that tell your server to authenticate on LDAP?
    a. /etc/ldap.conf
    b. /etc/openldap/openldap.conf
    c. /etc/krb5.conf
    d. /etc/nslcd.conf
10. Which command allows you to join an AD domain from the command line?
    a. **join**
    b. **ipa-client-install**
    c. **realm**
    d. **adjoin**

Foundation Topics

Understanding Remote Authentication

By default, authentication and security are handled locally. When a user enters a username and password, these are checked against the users in the /etc/passwd and /etc/shadow file. This works fine if you are dealing with one single Linux server, or just a few Linux servers. It is different if you have many Linux servers to deal with. In that case, it makes sense to use a centralized identity management server. With such a centralized identity management server, users get an option to use single sign-on (SSO) as well. This means that a user authenticates once, and after authenticating receives a ticket or cookie that can be used to authenticate to other services on all other participating servers automatically.

A centralized identity management system normally provides two services at least:

- **Account information:** This is information such as username, home directory location, and so on. It is the information that identifies the user on a Linux system. Typically, the Lightweight Directory Access Protocol (LDAP) is used to provide the account information.
- **Authentication information:** This is what is needed to validate that a user is who he claims to be. This can be done by using an encrypted password that is stored on an LDAP server, or by using an advanced authentication protocol such as Kerberos.

Table 25.2 provides an overview of the services an identity management system provides and the servers used to implement these services.

Key Topic

Table 25.2 Account Information and Authentication Services Overview

Service	Used for	Description
LDAP	Account information and authentication	Generic network service used for authentication. Implemented in products such as Active Directory and IPA server.
NIS	Account information and authentication	Legacy UNIX method to provide centralized account information and authentication.
NIS+	Account information and authentication	An update on the legacy NIS service that was mentioned previously.
Kerberos	Authentication	Protocol developed for secure authentication of users and services.

Service	Used for	Description
/etc/passwd	Account information	Default file that contains account information.
/etc/shadow	Authentication	Default file that contains authentication information.

On RHEL 7, three services are generally involved in setting up centralized account information and authentication:

- **LDAP:** LDAP was started as a protocol to get information from hierarchical directory servers such as X.500-based directory servers. Currently, LDAP is available on Linux through several projects such as OpenLDAP and 389, the latter of which is used by FreeIPA.
- **Kerberos:** Kerberos is available as a service that can be used for authorization, on top of an LDAP directory server.
- **Identity management:** Red Hat identity management (IdM) is based on the FreeIPA project. IdM was developed to provide an easy solution to set up an LDAP/Kerberos server. It also includes a Domain Name System (DNS) server, in addition to a Network Time Protocol (NTP) time server. If you use IdM, you no longer need to separately configure LDAP and Kerberos servers.

To connect to these services, Red Hat provides different solutions as well. To meet the RHCSA and RHCE objectives, you must be able to connect to an LDAP server and handle authorization through Kerberos. You can do so by using the IPA client or the LDAP/Kerberos client. Configuring the IPA client is *not* an RHCSA/RHCE objective. For that reason, in this chapter you learn how to configure authentication through the generic LDAP client that is available on RHEL 7. The section "Configuring LDAP Authentication with Kerberos Authorization" explains how to do this. Before we can move on to that section, let's first discuss some Kerberos basics.

Understanding Kerberos Basics

As one of the RHCE objectives, you have to configure Kerberos authentication. Before taking a look at the software configuration options, let's first see how Kerberos is organized.

Understanding Kerberos Authentication

Kerberos is an authentication protocol designed for secure network login without the need for users to reauthenticate when accessing new services. Also, the service is designed to minimize the amount of time a user password has to be sent over the network (which makes it vulnerable). Kerberos authentication is based on credentials called *tickets*. These tickets are secured with encryption. Tickets are used as an alternative to transmitting passwords across the network. Instead of passwords, tickets are sent over the network, and these tickets are encrypted with the user password.

In Kerberos, tickets are issued by a central key server, which is known as the Key Distribution Center (KDC). In Kerberos, a realm is used, which consists of all hosts that use the same KDC to get tickets; so, the realm is like a group of hosts. A Kerberos realm can be compared to a Windows domain or an LDAP suffix. As a default, the DNS domain of the Kerberos site written in all caps is used as the Kerberos realm name. So for hosts residing in example.com, the realm name is EXAMPLE.COM.

Kerberos is not just used for user authentication. Applications running on hosts can also use Kerberos for secure access. Such a host is referred to as an *application server*. Each application server and each server has an identity in Kerberos, with a password associated with it. The KDC (Key Distribution Center) knows the passwords of all users and servers. Later in this book, you learn how to configure Network File System (NFS) and Samba as Kerberized applications.

When a user logs in, the user (locally) enters his password. The login program then converts the user name to a Kerberos principal name. The login program then sends the request to the KDC authentication service, which answers with a ticket granting ticket for that principal.

Upon receiving the login request, the KDC generates a secret session key that is used as the ticket granting ticket (TGT). It keeps one copy and encrypts a second copy with the user password used as the encryption key. The encrypted copy is sent back to the login program.

Upon receiving the encrypted copy, the login program attempts to decrypt it with the password that the user has entered. If this succeeds, the user is authenticated and has a current TGT. Based on that current TGT, the user can authenticate on Kerberos-enabled network services as well. Because the TGT at that moment is current, the user does not need to enter the password again, which really makes Kerberos an SSO system.

When connecting to Kerberos-enabled services, time stamps play an important role. This is why in a Kerberos environment it is essential that time between all servers is synchronized. A deviance of more than a few minutes may lead to authentication problems.

Understanding Kerberos Principals

To identify the participants in Kerberos authentication, principals are used by users and by network services. Principal names have the form primary/instance@REALM, in which the instance part is optional. An example of a principal name is nfs/server1.example.com@EXAMPLE.COM. In this name, the following parts are used:

- nfs is the primary.
- server1.example.com is the name of the host the principal belongs to.
- EXAMPLE.COM refers to the realm the principal belongs to.

In service names, the three parts of the principal name are normally used. This is not the case for usernames. In usernames, the instance part is normally omitted; so, a common Kerberos username is lisa@EXAMPLE.COM, for instance.

Users and services have Kerberos principals. Services usually store their password in the keytab file, which allows the server to log in to Kerberos without human intervention. If a server is hosting Kerberized services, it will usually have the file /etc/krb5.keytab, which contains the names of all service principals on that server, in addition to the password. The name of the keytab file can be different, but normally should end in .keytab.

> **TIP** Even if it is not meant to be a readable file, you can use the **strings** command to see the contents of the keytab file. Listing 25.1 shows the result of the command **strings /etc/krb5.keytab**, and clearly shows that principals are stored for the NFS service and for the Samba service. (The **klist** command can do the same for you.)

Listing 25.1 Using **strings** to Show the Contents of the /etc/krb5.Keytab File

```
[root@server1 ~]# strings /etc/krb5.keytab
EXAMPLE.COM
host
server1.example.com
P~      4
EXAMPLE.COM
host
server1.example.com
EXAMPLE.COM
host
```

```
server1.example.com
b[X4
EXAMPLE.COM
host
server1.example.com
I:Bs5d
EXAMPLE.COM
host
server1.example.com
EXAMPLE.COM
host
server1.example.com
EXAMPLE.COM
cifs
server1.example.com
EXAMPLE.COM
cifs
server1.example.com
EXAMPLE.COM
cifs
server1.example.com
EXAMPLE.COM
cifs
server1.example.com
EXAMPLE.COM
cifs
server1.example.com
FqHG
EXAMPLE.COM
cifs
server1.example.com
```

Configuring LDAP Authentication with Kerberos Authorization

In this section, you learn how to configure LDAP authentication with Kerberos authorization. The first subsection explains which utilities and configuration files are involved in this procedure. The second subsection discusses two important back-end services: nslcd and sssd. In the third subsection, you learn how to actually set up external authentication.

TIP The information in this section covers the RHCE exam objectives. In Chapter 6, "User and Group Management," you can read how to set up your server for authentication against an LDAP server where only LDAP passwords are used.

RHEL 7 provides the authconfig utilities to configure LDAP authentication with optional Kerberos authorization. The authconfig utility comes in three versions:

Key Topic

- **authconfig** A command-line utility that enables administrators to set up authentication by using command-line options. **authconfig** commands will be long, but they have the benefit that it can be scripted easily. Listing 25.2 shows some of the command-line switches that you can use with **authconfig** and shows how rich this utility really is and that it offers options to specify any item that is important while authenticating.
- **authconfig-tui** The menu-driven interactive interface that makes setting up authentication a bit easier.
- **authconfig-gtk** A graphical interface that you can use to set up authentication. This tool is not part of a typical installation of RHEL. To use it, make sure that the authconfig-gtk package is installed.

Listing 25.2 Partial Listing of **authconfig** Command-Line Options

```
[root@server1 ~]# authconfig --help
Usage: authconfig [options] {--update|--updateall|--test|--probe|--
restorebackup <name>|--savebackup <name>|--restorelastbackup}

Options:
  -h, --help              show this help message and exit
  --enableshadow, --useshadow
                        enable shadowed passwords by default
  --disableshadow         disable shadowed passwords by default
  --enablemd5, --usemd5
                        enable MD5 passwords by default
  --disablemd5            disable MD5 passwords by default
  --passalgo=<descrypt|bigcrypt|md5|sha256|sha512>
                        hash/crypt algorithm for new passwords
  --enablenis             enable NIS for user information by default
  --disablenis            disable NIS for user information by default
  --nisdomain=<domain>    default NIS domain
```

```
    --nisserver=<server>    default NIS server
    --enableldap            enable LDAP for user information by default
    --disableldap           disable LDAP for user information by default
    --enableldapauth        enable LDAP for authentication by default
    --disableldapauth       disable LDAP for authentication by default
    --ldapserver=<server>
                        default LDAP server hostname or URI
    --ldapbasedn=<dn>       default LDAP base DN
    --enableldaptls, --enableldapstarttls
                        enable use of TLS with LDAP (RFC-2830)
    --disableldaptls, --disableldapstarttls
                        disable use of TLS with LDAP (RFC-2830)
    --enablerfc2307bis      enable use of RFC-2307bis schema for LDAP user
information lookups
    --disablerfc2307bis     disable use of RFC-2307bis schema for LDAP user
information lookups
    --ldaploadcacert=<URL>
                        load CA certificate from the URL
    --enablesmartcard       enable authentication with smart card by
default
    --disablesmartcard      disable authentication with smart card by
default
    --enablerequiresmartcard
                        require smart card for authentication by default
    --disablerequiresmartcard
                        do not require smart card for authentication by
default
    --smartcardmodule=<module>
                        default smart card module to use
    --smartcardaction=<0=Lock|1=Ignore>
                        action to be taken on smart card removal
    --enablefingerprint     enable authentication with fingerprint readers
by default
    --disablefingerprint    disable authentication with fingerprint readers
by default
    --enableecryptfs        enable automatic per-user ecryptfs
    --disableecryptfs       disable automatic per-user ecryptfs
    --enablekrb5            enable kerberos authentication by default
    --disablekrb5           disable kerberos authentication by default
    --krb5kdc=<server>      default kerberos KDC
    --krb5adminserver=<server>
                        default kerberos admin server
```

```
--krb5realm=<realm>       default kerberos realm
--enablekrb5kdcdns        enable use of DNS to find kerberos KDCs
--disablekrb5kdcdns       disable use of DNS to find kerberos KDCs
--enablekrb5realmdns      enable use of DNS to find kerberos realms
```

While using either of these utilities, several configuration files are involved. Knowing the names of these files proves useful for troubleshooting purposes:

Key Topic

- **/etc/ldap.conf:** Contains the configuration of the LDAP client. This file is needed to indicate which LDAP server should be used.
- **/etc/krb5.conf:** Contains Kerberos-specific information.
- **/etc/sssd/sssd.conf:** Contains information used by the system security services daemon (sssd). This daemon is used in most configurations for retrieving and caching user information and authentication information.
- **/etc/nslcd.conf:** Depending on the packages that are installed on your server, the nslcd service might be used for retrieving and caching user information as an alternative to the sssd.conf configuration file. This is not a default configuration but in some situations will be used.

TIP Red Hat has spent a lot of effort in integrating the sssd service in the previous version of RHEL, and it sure looks like they are still focusing on using sssd as the primary service that is used for managing login attempts toward external servers. However, you might find yourself in a situation where sssd is not available and nslcd is. This situation occurs if on configuration of user authentication, the sssd package was not installed. So, make sure that you understand both of these backend services and their configuration files! Or make sure that the sssd package is installed before you start configuring external authentication.

- **/etc/nsswitch.conf:** Indicates which service should be contacted to retrieve authentication and authorization related information. It contains lines like **passwd: files sss** that specify that the local configuration files should be used first, after which the sssd service should be used.
- **/etc/pam.d/*:** Contains configuration files that define how authentication should be handled for various services.
- **/etc/openldap/cacerts:** Stores the root certificate authorities that are used for validating SSL certificates and identifying LDAP services.

- **/etc/sysconfig/authconfig:** Contains variables that specify how the authconfig utilities should do their work.

Using nslcd or sssd as the Authentication Backend Service

Depending on the configuration you are using to set up authentication services, you might get different results. If the sssd RPM package was installed before you started configuring authentication, the sssd service is used as the authentication backend. In other cases, you might find that the nslcd service is taking care of authentication. In Chapter 6, you learned how to work with both backend services to configure external authentication.

Red Hat has included the sssd service in RHEL to take care of authentication. So, you best make sure that the sssd package is installed when you start configuring authentication, so that all authentication is handled by sssd. To enforce the usage of sssd, there are some additional tips to be considered also:

- On a minimal installation of RHEL, the packages needed by sssd are not available. Make sure that at least the sssd packages are installed before you start using the authconfig utilities.
- To avoid problems, it is a good idea to use the server with a graphical user interface (GUI) installation pattern (which is the case for the free test environment that you can download from http://www.rhatcert.com). On this configuration, sssd is used by default.
- Make sure that the sssd packages are installed before using the authconfig utilities.
- Make sure the sssd service is running before using the authconfig utilities.
- If using authconfig, set up LDAP authentication *without Kerberos authorization* first, and then open the utility again and configure Kerberos if required.
- Make sure that the file /etc/sysconfig/authconfig contains the following parameters before you run any of the authconfig utilities. These parameters enforce SSSD to be used for authentication. The **FORCELEGACY** parameter refers to nslcd. By setting it to no, you switch off nslcd use:
  - **USESSSD=yes**
  - **FORCELEGACY=no**
  - **USESSSDAUTH=yes**

Setting Up External Authentication

To set up external authentication, you can use either the authconfig-tui or authconfig-gtk utilities. In this section, you learn how to create the configuration using authconfig-tui. Exercise 25.1 walks you through the different parts that are involved in setting up the configuration.

Exercise 25.1 Setting Up External Authentication

In this exercise, you set up server1 for external authentication on the labipa.example.com server. This exercise assumes you are using the labipa server that is described in Appendix D, "Setting Up Identity Management," or that you are using the lab virtual machines (VMs) available for download at http://www.rhatcert.com. All steps in this exercise are performed on server1.

1. Verify that you can reach the labipa.example.com server by name, by using **ping labipa.example.com**. If this does not work, fix before proceeding by either including an entry in DNS that resolves labipa.example.com to its hostname or by using the DNS server that is available through the labipa server.
2. Type **yum install -y sssd sssd-tools nss-pam-ldapd**.
3. Type **mkdir /etc/openldap/cacerts**.
4. Copy the certificate from the IPA server to your local server by using **scp labipa.example.com:/root/cacert.p12 /etc/openldap/cacerts**.
5. Type **vim /etc/sysconfig/authconfig**. Make sure that this file contains the following configuration options:
```
USESSSDAUTH=yes
USESSSD=yes
FORCELEGACY=no
```
6. As root, start authconfig-tui. In User Information, select **Cache Information**, **Use LDAP**, and under Authentication, select **Use LDAP Authentication**.
7. In the LDAP Settings screen, select **Use TLS** and specify the following:
```
Server:   labipa.example.com
Base DN: dc=example,dc=com
```
8. Open the file /etc/sssd/sssd.conf and add the following line, which will still use TLS encrypted sessions, but ease up the integrity checks of the certificate. This proves useful in an environment where self-signed certificates are used, as is the case in this setup, but should normally not be necessary while working with certificates that have been obtained from external certificate authorities:
```
ldap_tls_reqcert = never
```

9. Type **systemctl restart sssd** to restart the sssd service.
10. From a shell, type **su - lisa**. You should now see the message "cannot change to /home/lisa: No such file or directory," which is fine because we have not configured any home directory automounting.
11. Type **id**. This will show that you are currently logged in as user lisa.

TIP Because the authentication backend that is used really depends on the software that is installed on the server you are using, make sure on the exam that you know how to handle nslcd as well as sssd. Also read the last section in Chapter 6 for more details about the configuration of both of these services.

After configuring LDAP authentication as described in Exercise 25.1, you can now enable Kerberos authorization as well. The easiest way to do so is by running authconfig-tui again. Exercise 25.2 describes the procedure.

Exercise 25.2 Configuring Kerberos Authorization

This exercise continues from Exercise 25.1 and can be completed only after successful completion of Exercise 25.1.

1. On server1, open a root shell and start **authconfig-tui**.
2. Type **yum install -y pam_krb5 krb5-workstation** to install the RPM packages that add Kerberos support to all applications that support it.
3. On the authentication Configuration screen, under Authentication, select **Use Kerberos** to enable Kerberos authorization.
4. On the LDAP Settings screen, do not change anything; you configured this in the previous exercise.
5. In the Kerberos Settings screen, enter the following parameters:

```
Realm:     EXAMPLE.COM
KDC: labipa.example.com
Admin Server: labipa.example.com
```

   Alternatively, you can check the options **Use DNS to Resolve Hosts to Realms** and **Use DNS to Locate KDCs for Realms** to fill these fields automatically. This option is going to use the SRV resource records that Kerberos creates in DNS, and that are used to register services in DNS, and make it easy to find information about these services as well.

6. When you are back on the shell prompt, type **kinit -k** as root. This verifies that the host can authenticate and shows that Kerberos authentication configuration is correct.
7. Now that you know that the host can authenticate, type **kinit lisa**. Enter the password for user lisa. This proves that Kerberos authentication works correctly.

At this point, external authentication should be working, based on the sssd service. So, the /etc/sssd/sssd.conf file should have been created. In this file, you'll find all the configuration settings that you have entered through the authconfig utilities. Listing 25.3 shows the content of the file as it should be at this point:

Listing 25.3 Sample /etc/sssd/sssd.conf Content

```
[root@server1 ~]# cat /etc/sssd/sssd.conf
[domain/example.com]

cache_credentials = True
krb5_store_password_if_offline = True
ipa_domain = example.com
id_provider = ipa
auth_provider = ipa
access_provider = ipa
ipa_hostname = server1.example.com
chpass_provider = ipa
ipa_server = _srv_, ipa.example.com
ldap_tls_cacert = /etc/ipa/ca.crt
[sssd]
services = nss, pam, ssh
config_file_version = 2

domains = example.com
[nss]

[pam]

[sudo]
```

```
[autofs]

    [ssh]

    [pac]
```

Using an IPA Server or Active Directory

Red Hat provides the IPA server (see Appendix D) to provide authentication services. To use these services in an easy way, you can use the ipa client. You can configure the ipa client by using authconfig, but it can also be set up using the ipa-client-install utility. Before using this utility, make sure that the server on which you run it has DNS configured to use the IPA server. The ipa-client-install utility will get almost all information from the DNS server.

An alternative external authentication source is Active Directory. This can also be accomplished through the authconfig utility. An alternative approach is to install sssd and run the **realm** command to connect to AD. To do this, complete these steps:

1. Use **yum install -y realmd**.
2. Discover settings for the AD domain you want to join by using **realm discover mydomain.example.com**.
3. Use **realm join mydomain.example.com** to join the AD domain. This command creates all required configuration. While doing this, the Active Directory administrator account is used to join the domain. To use another user, add the **--user** option to the command.
4. At this point, AD user accounts are usable but cannot log in yet. To allow login to AD, use **realm permit --realm mydomain.example.com --all**.

NOTE Currently, realmd is still at a very early development stage and not quite ready for production yet.

Summary

In this chapter, you learned how to set up your server for external authentication. You learned the difference between authentication and authorization, and you learned which backend services can be used to set up both. You also learned how to configure a server to use sssd or nslcd for authentication and authorization.

Exam Preparation Tasks

Review All Key Topics

Review the most important topics in the chapter, noted with the Key Topic icon in the outer margin of the page. Table 25.3 lists a reference of these key topics and the page numbers on which each is found.

Table 25.3 Key Topics for Chapter 25

Key Topic Element	Description	Page Numbers
Table 25.2	Account information and authentication services overview	560
Bulleted List	authconfig utilities overview	565
Bulleted List	authconfig related configuration files	567

Complete Tables and Lists from Memory

Print a copy of Appendix B, "Memory Tables" (found on the disc), or at least the section for this chapter, and complete the tables and lists from memory. Appendix C, "Memory Tables Answer Key," also on the disc, includes completed tables and lists to check your work.

Define Key Terms

Define the following key terms from this chapter and check your answers in the glossary:

LDAP, NIS, Kerberos, Realm, KDC, TGT, primary, principal, keytab, application server, sssd, nslcd

Review Questions

1. Which command would you use if you are looking for a graphical tool that enables you to set up external authentication?
2. You are expecting to find the authentication configuration in the file /etc/sssd/sssd.conf. This file does not exist, but yet your server can authenticate against an LDAP server. What is the most likely explanation?

3. Your server is using sssd, and you are seeing messages in the logs telling you that the LDAP CA certificate is causing errors. What is an easy way to fix this?
4. Which configuration file do you modify before running the authconfig tools to make sure that sssd is used as the authentication backend?
5. Which command enables you to register your server to the AD domain mydomain.example.com?
6. Which file would you look in for the current Kerberos client configuration settings?
7. Which command enables you to initiate a Kerberos session from the command line?
8. Which file would you check to make sure that client utilities are using the sssd authentication backend service?
9. Which file contains the configuration of the LDAP client?
10. Which file contains the login credentials for services that are using Kerberos?

End-of-Chapter Labs

Lab 25.1

1. Configure server1 to use LDAP authentication and Kerberos authorization using the nslcd authentication backend service.
2. Configure server2 to use LDAP authentication and Kerberos authorization using the sssd authentication backend service.
3. Verify that both servers are working by logging in as LDAP user lisa. Use **kinit** to verify credentials.

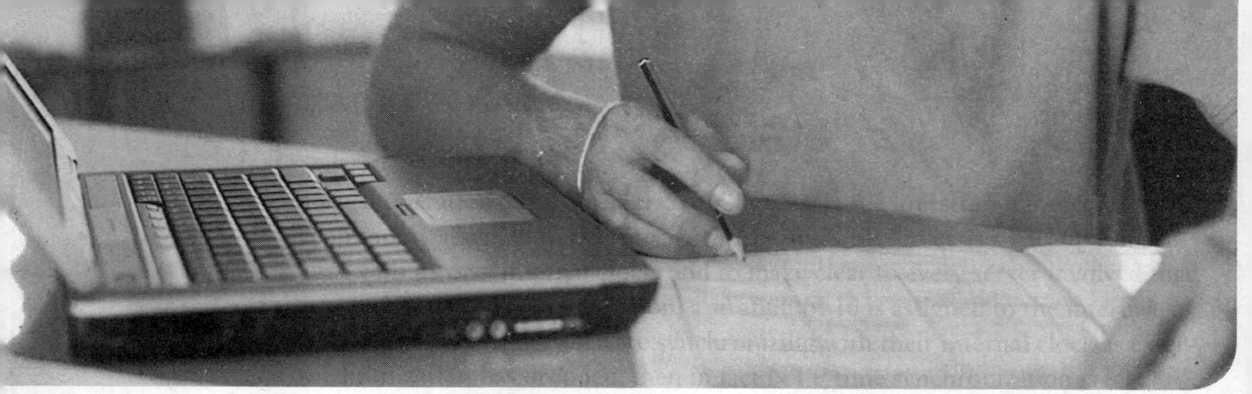

The following topics are covered in this chapter:

- Understanding iSCSI
- Setting up the iSCSI Target
- Setting up the iSCSI Initiator
- Troubleshooting iSCSI

The following RHCE exam objectives are covered in this chapter:

- Configuring a system as either an iSCSI target or initiator that persistently mounts an iSCSI target

CHAPTER 26

Configuring an iSCSI SAN

In the old days of computing, every computer and every server had its own hard drive. Storage was local, and sharing files between servers could only happen by using network protocols such as Network File System (NFS) or Samba. In modern datacenter environments, it is becoming increasingly common to separate disk storage from the computer where the actual computing is happening. This allows for a more flexible datacenter where another server can easily be attached to the external storage in case something goes wrong. This way of working in essence is what all storage-area networks (SANs) are doing.

When using SAN solutions, two scenarios are common. First, there is the type of SAN that just has the purpose of separating storage from the physical server. Another approach for using a SAN is in environments where high-availability clusters are used. In a high-availability cluster, two nodes can access the same storage simultaneously. Using a high-availability cluster needs to be supported by the file system on the shared storage, though. If multiple computers are going to write to the same XFS file system simultaneously, things will go wrong for sure because the nodes will not be aware of what is happening on the other node.

To use SAN storage in a clustered environment, where multiple nodes are writing to the storage at the same time, you need a clustered file system such as GFS2. When you are using a clustered file system, the different nodes that are accessing the storage are aware of operations happening on the other node, which prevents errors from happening. Configuring such a clustered file system is beyond the requirements for the RCHSA or RHCE exams and for that reason is not covered in this chapter.

In this chapter, you learn how to set up a solution where one server provides access to the shared storage device, and the other server provides access to the shared storage.

TIP A SAN offers shared block devices. Another common solution to offer shared storage is the NAS (network-attached storage). In a NAS, file systems are shared, such as NFS of Server Message Block (SMB). In general, a SAN solution is preferred because it is faster and it offers more flexibility. The user of the SAN can decide for himself what he wants to do on the SAN because it is offering shared block devices, whereas a NAS user can just mount the shared file system. Some SAN appliances offer NAS access as well so that the storage administrator can choose which solution he wants to offer.

"Do I Know This Already" Quiz

The "Do I Know This Already?" quiz allows you to assess whether you should read this entire chapter thoroughly or jump to the "Exam Preparation Tasks" section. If you are in doubt about your answers to these questions or your own assessment of your knowledge of the topics, read the entire chapter. Table 26.1 lists the major headings in this chapter and their corresponding "Do I Know This Already?" quiz questions. You can find the answers in Appendix A, "Answers to the 'Do I Know This Already?' Quizzes and 'Review Questions.'"

Table 26.1 "Do I Know This Already?" Section-to-Question Mapping

Foundation Topics Section	Questions
Understanding iSCSI	2–4
Setting up the iSCSI Target	5–7
Setting up the iSCSI Initiator	8–9
Troubleshooting iSCSI	10

1. Which of the following statements about SAN storage is correct?
   a. Storage on the SAN can be shared between nodes without taking any additional measures.
   b. To access SAN storage, you need a Fibre Channel infrastructure.
   c. To allow shared simultaneous access from different servers to a SAN volume simultaneously, you need a special file system.
   d. To configure SAN storage, you need to configure an iSCSI initiator.

2. Which of the following *cannot* be shared as SAN storage using an iSCSI target?
   a. A file
   b. A disk
   c. An LVM volume
   d. All of the above can be shared.

3. Which statement about iSCSI network topology is true?
   a. You need at least a 100Mb network.
   b. The iSCSI traffic cannot be mixed with other network traffic.
   c. To configure a redundant topology, it is recommended to create a multipath configuration.
   d. Only fiber media is supported in iSCSI SAN solutions.

4. Which of the following is the name for the backend storage that is shared through the iSCSI target?
   a. LUN
   b. ACL
   c. IQN
   d. Backend storage

5. What is the name of the utility you use to configure the LIO iSCSI target?
   a. lioconfig
   b. iscsiadm
   c. targetcli
   d. ietadm

6. When setting up an LIO iSCSI target, different steps need to be performed. Which of the following commands comes first?
   a. **create iqn.2014-11.com.example:target**
   b. **tgp1/acls/ create iqn.2014-11.com.example:server1**
   c. **fileio/ create file /root/diskfile1 1G**
   d. **luns/ create /backstores/block/block1**

7. Which firewall port must be opened on the iSCSI target server to allow access to the shared storage device?
    a. 3128
    b. 2160
    c. 3260
    d. 3821

8. What is the name where you would configure the iSCSI initiator name?
    a. /etc/iscsi/iscsid.conf
    b. /etc/iscsi/iscsi-initiator.conf
    c. /etc/iscsi/initiatorname.iscsi
    d. /etc/initiatorname.conf

9. Which statement about iSCSI initiator discovery is *not* true?
    a. If you know the initiatorname already, you do not have to perform a discovery.
    b. The results of the isicsi discovery are stored in /var/lib/iscsi.
    c. Discovery results are stored persistent.
    d. The iSCSI discovery process shows the IQN of the iSCSI target.

10. Which of the following commands shows correct syntax for getting as many details as possible about a current session?
    a. **iscsiadm -m session -P 3**
    b. **iscsiadm --mode -P 1**
    c. **iscsiadm --mode node -P 2**
    d. **iscsiadm --mode session -P 4**

Foundation Topics

To perform the tasks described in this chapter, you need two servers: one that is configured as the iSCSI SAN, and the other one that is configured as the node that is accessing the storage devices shared by the SAN. In the exercises in this chapter, two servers are used:

- Server1 is iSCSI target. On this server, you need disk space to set up an LVM volume and a file. 100MB is enough for setting these up.
- Server2 is the iSCSI initiator and does not need to meet any specific requirements.

Understanding iSCSI

In this section, you learn about iSCSI as a SAN solution. You'll read how it compares to Fibre Channel SAN and how software iSCSI targets relate to hardware iSCSI solutions. You also learn what is needed to set up an iSCSI SAN.

Comparing SAN Solutions

When setting up a SAN, you need to make sure that shared disks are made available to the servers that are connecting to the SAN. There are two leading technologies for providing such a solution. Fibre Channel uses a dedicated high-speed network topology to access SAN storage. In Fibre Channel, a dedicated network infrastructure is used with hardware that is set up to offer the best possible performance while accessing the shared storage devices. This network topology can use optical fiber in the network infrastructure as well as classical network cables where signals are sent over copper wires. Fibre Channel is the more popular solution for environments where the best possible performance is needed on the storage network. Also, Fibre Channel was developed as a solution where security is well developed, and it guarantees delivery at the lower levels of the protocol stack.

As an alternative to relatively expensive Fibre Channel SAN solutions, iSCSI was developed by IBM in 1994. Originally, they were looking for a storage protocol over Ethernet, but the developers found out that the overhead for TCP was not as big as feared, which is why the iSCSI protocol was developed over TCP/IP. In iSCSI, the SCSI protocol is used for storage. This protocol defines the topology and electrical specifications for accessing disks. It has been used from the early days of computing to provide storage in servers. Whereas the SCSI protocol was used to connect local disks to a server, the iSCSI protocol was developed to encapsulate SCSI commands in IP packets, using TCP to guarantee the delivery of packets. This does not change a lot to the working of the SCSI protocol itself; it just changes the way that disks are connected to a server.

Because iSCSI was designed to be used on commodity networks, it has the reputation of being slower than Fibre Channel SAN. This does not have to be true, though; it all depends on the infrastructure that is used. When designing a dedicated iSCSI network that is using 10 Gigabit Ethernet, it can be as fast as any Fibre Channel topology.

Software Versus Hardware iSCSI SAN

In this chapter, you learn how to configure an iSCSI SAN based on Red Hat Enterprise Linux. We explore setting up a software iSCSI SAN solution. Apart from software SAN solutions as described in this section, hardware iSCSI SAN solutions are available as well.

No fundamental difference exists in the operation of software or hardware iSCSI SAN. The main difference is that in a hardware iSCSI SAN, the hardware is optimized to deliver the best possible performance. That does not necessarily mean that a hardware iSCSI SAN is performing better than its software-based counterpart. It all depends on the way it is optimized.

When installing a software-based iSCSI SAN, you may build a well-performing solution. It all starts by selecting high-end hardware such as a fast network infrastructure and fast disks to ensure that data can be written fast. Also, special iSCSI optimized network cards can be used, often referred to as *host bus adapters* (HBAs). These often include a hardware TCP offload engine that allows the iSCSI packets to be handled on the HBA.

The software also plays an important role in optimizing iSCSI. There are many ways to optimize the Linux iSCSI processes. This, in fact, can be a benefit as compared to a hardware-based SAN solution. In a hardware SAN, you might have to purchase additional license to be able to use advanced features or features that are offering a better performance. In a software-based iSCSI SAN, all you need to create the best possible SAN is just available as free software.

iSCSI SAN Architecture

When setting up an iSCSI SAN, you configure one server as the iSCSI target. This is the server that offers access to the shared storage devices. When you configure Red Hat Enterprise Linux as an iSCSI target, the shared storage devices typically are LVM logical volumes, but they can be complete disks or partitions as well. You can even configure the SAN to provide access to an image file (as you'll see when setting up the iSCSI SAN in the first exercise). This image file is just an empty file used as the iSCSI storage backend, and it does not have to adapt to any specific standard.

The other server is going to be used as the iSCSI initiator. This is the server that connects to the SAN. After connecting to the SAN, the iSCSI initiator sees an additional disk device.

When setting up an iSCSI SAN, you typically want to use a dedicated network architecture. That means that on the SAN network you want to have just SAN network traffic and nothing else. On that network, you might also want to set up redundancy to make sure that if your primary SAN switch fails, a redundant network path is available. Every iSCSI initiator should have a secondary connection to the iSCSI target, so that if one connection completely drops, the other connection can take over.

When using a redundant network connection, the iSCSI initiator will see the SAN device twice, once over each different path to the SAN. This might lead to a situation where the same shared disk device is presented twice as well. To make sure that in such a setup where redundant paths are available the SAN device is addressed correctly, the iSCSI initiator should be configured to run the multipath driver. The driver provides one interface that the initiator can talk through, which is set up for redundancy and will ensure that the connection to the storage can just continue, even if one of the paths to the SAN drops completely. Figure 26.1 provides an overview of a typical iSCSI SAN architecture.

iSCSI SAN Terminology

When working with iSCSI on Red Hat Enterprise Linux 7, you need to be familiar with some specific terminology. Table 26.2 introduces the relevant terminology.

Table 26.2 iSCSI Terminology

Key Topic

Item	Description
IQN	The iSCSI qualified name. A unique name that is used for identifying targets as well as initiators.
Backend storage	The storage devices on the iSCSI target that the iSCSI target component is providing access to.
Target	The service on an iSCSI server that gives access to backend storage devices.
Initiator	The iSCSI client that connects to a target and is identified by an IQN.
ACL	The access control list that is based on the iSCSI initiator IQNs and used to provide access to a specific target. While setting up the iSCSI target on RHEL 7, creating an ACL is mandatory. This ACL is based on the IQN of the iSCSI initiator that should be granted access.

Item	Description
LUN	A logical unit number. The backend storage devices that are shared through the target. This can be any device that supports read/write operations, such as disks, partitions, logical volumes, files, or tape drives.
Portal	The IP address and port that a target or initiator uses to establish connections. Also referred to as node.
TPG	The target portal group. This is the collection of IP address and TCP ports to which a specific iSCSI target will listen.
Discovery	The process whereby an initiator finds the targets that are configured on a portal and stores this information locally for future reference. Discovery is done by using the **iscsiadm** command.
Login	Authentication that gives an initiator access to LUNs on the target. After successful login, the login information is stored on the initiator automatically. Login is performed using the **iscsiadm** command.

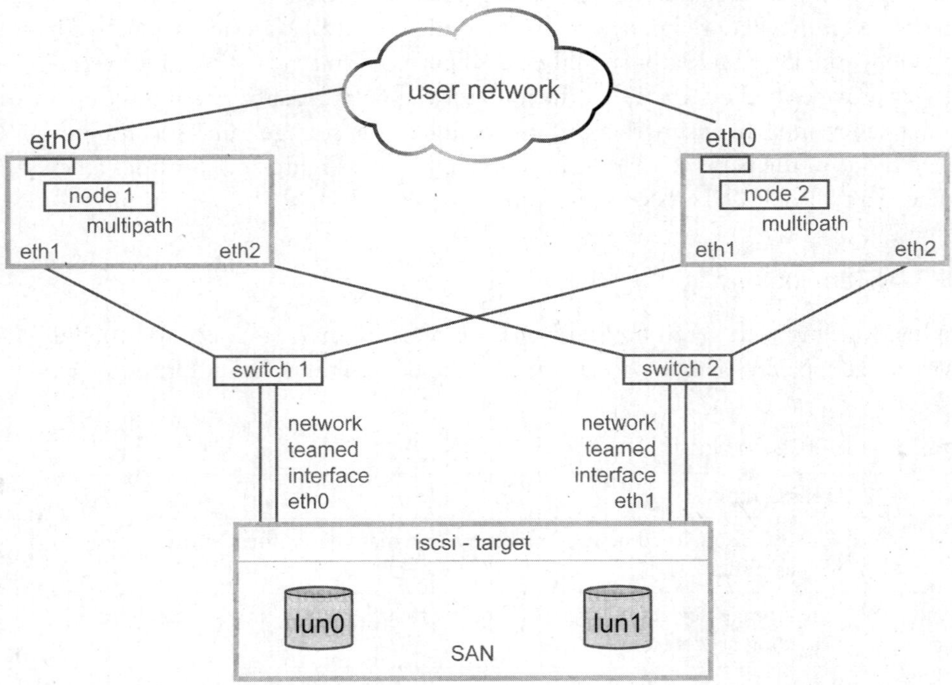

Figure 26.1 iSCSI SAN schematic overview.

Setting Up the iSCSI Target

Throughout different versions of Linux, different iSCSI target packages have been used. In Red Hat Enterprise Linux 7, the LIO (Linux I/O) target is used. LIO is the standard iSCSI target solution since Linux kernels 2.6.38, and because of its native support in OpenStack Cloud, it has become an attractive storage solution that has rapidly replaced alternative iSCSI target solutions in many Linux distributions. The default interface to manage the LIO target is the **targetcli** command. This command uses familiar Linux commands, such as **cd**, **ls**, **pwd**, and **set** to configure the target.

The **targetcli** command was developed as a very intuitive command. Working with it is like working in a directory structure where items need to be created in the different directories. It has excellent command completion as well as a very good help function, which makes working with the iSCSI target very intuitive.

When using the targetcli utility, you'll go through a few steps to set up the target as follows:

Key Topic

1. Create the backing storage devices.
2. Create the IQN and default target portal group (TGP).
3. Configure one or more ACLs for the TPG.
4. Create LUNs to provide access to the backing storage devices.
5. Create a portal to provide a network interface that iSCSI initiators can connect to.
6. Verify and commit the configuration.

Exercise 26.1 walks you through the procedure of setting up an iSCSI target using **targetcli**.

Exercise 26.1 Setting Up the Target with the targetcli Utility

In this exercise, you set up an iSCSI target on server1. This exercise assumes that on server1 that you have an LVM volume group available with the name vgsan. Within the volume group, you need free disk space that allows you to create two LVM logical volumes.

1. Open a root shell on server1. Type **vgs** to verify the name of the LVM volume group and the amount of available disk space. If you do not have a volume group with available disk space, you should create a volume group first.

2. Type **lvcreate -L 200M -n lvsan1 /dev/vgsan** and **lvcreate -L 200M -n lvsan2 /dev/vgsan** to provide the backing storage needed for setting up your iSCSI target.
3. Enter **yum -y install targetcli**.
4. Type **targetcli**. This opens the targetcli interface, which looks like a shell prompt. Type **ls** to show the default interface (see Figure 26.2)

```
ING shell — root@server1:~ — ssh — bash — ttys003
  Verifying  : targetcli-2.1.fb34-1.el7.noarch                                    3/7
  Verifying  : python-ethtool-0.8-5.el7.x86_64                                    4/7
  Verifying  : 1:python-configshell-1.1.fb11-3.el7.noarch                         5/7
  Verifying  : pyparsing-1.5.6-9.el7.noarch                                       6/7
  Verifying  : python-kmod-0.9-4.el7.x86_64                                       7/7

Installed:
  targetcli.noarch 0:2.1.fb34-1.el7

Dependency Installed:
  pyparsing.noarch 0:1.5.6-9.el7               python-configshell.noarch 1:1.1.fb11-3.el7
  python-ethtool.x86_64 0:0.8-5.el7            python-kmod.x86_64 0:0.9-4.el7
  python-rtslib.noarch 0:2.1.fb46-1.el7        python-urwid.x86_64 0:1.1.1-3.el7

Complete!
[root@server1 ~]# targetcli
Warning: Could not load preferences file /root/.targetcli/prefs.bin.
targetcli shell version 2.1.fb34
Copyright 2011-2013 by Datera, Inc and others.
For help on commands, type 'help'.

/> ls
o- / ........................................................................ [...]
  o- backstores ............................................................. [...]
  | o- block ................................................. [Storage Objects: 0]
  | o- fileio ................................................ [Storage Objects: 0]
  | o- pscsi ................................................. [Storage Objects: 0]
  | o- ramdisk ............................................... [Storage Objects: 0]
  o- iscsi ........................................................... [Targets: 0]
  o- loopback ........................................................ [Targets: 0]
/>
```

Figure 26.2 The targetcli interface.

5. The first step in setting up an iSCSI target is configuring the backstore. Type **cd /backstores** to enter the backstores branch of targetcli, which allows you to specify which backing storage is going to be used.
6. Type **block/ create block1 /dev/vgsan/lvsan1**. This assigns the LVM logical volume that you have created earlier as the backstore in the iSCSI target. Repeat for lvsan2 by typing **block/ create block2 /dev/vgsan/lvsan2**. Notice the way the command works; it starts with **block/**, which brings you to the contents of the directory /block, and from there the **create** commands are issued. Also notice that despite the fact that you are using the **create** command, it does not really create the backing storage device; it assigns an already existing storage device as the backing storage.
7. Now let's create a file-backed block device as well: **fileio/ create file1 /root/diskfile1 100M**. This command creates a sparse file with a size of 100 MiB and assigns it as a backing storage device.

8. At this time, type **ls** to get an overview of the current configuration. It should look like Figure 26.3 and show you two block devices and one file-backed storage device.

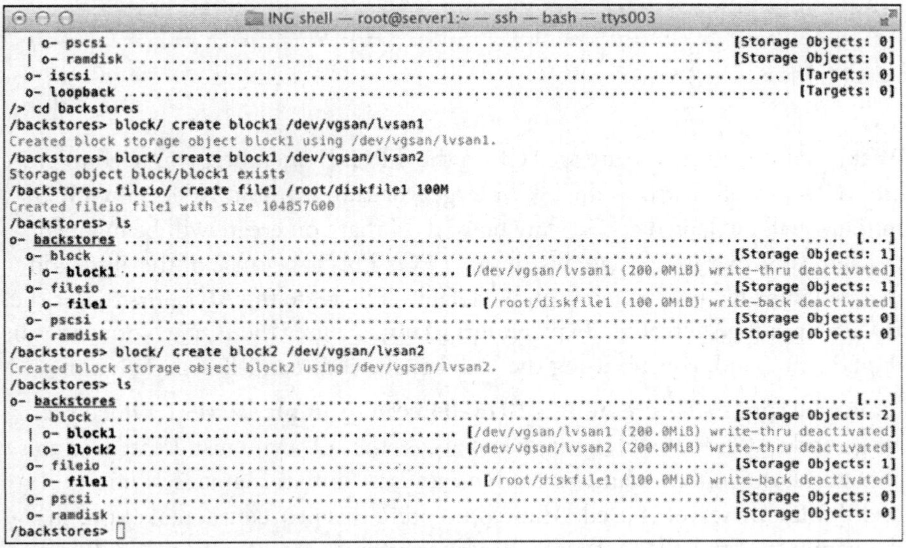

Figure 26.3 Block backstores overview.

9. Now that the block backstores are taken care of, you can start configuring the unique identifier for your iSCSI target, the iSCSI IQN, which will also create the default TGP. To start, use **cd /iscsi/** to get to the iscsi branch of the configuration.
10. Now type **create iqn.2015-04.com.example:target** to create the IQN. Notice that the name of the IQN starts with year-month (in YY-MM notation) and is followed by the inversed DNS domain name. Make sure you respect this naming standard; otherwise, the IQN will not be created.

> **TIP** Notice that the IQN naming standard is very strict. If you specify the month as one digit instead of two, for instance, you'll get a "WWN not valid" message, and creation will fail!

11. Type **ls**. This shows the contents of the iscsi branch, where you now see the IQN you just created, as well as the TPG tpg1 that was created automatically while creating the IQN (see Figure 26.4).

```
/iscsi> create iqn.2014-11.com.example.target1
Created target iqn.2014-11.com.example.target1.
Created TPG 1.
/iscsi> ls
o- iscsi ....................................................................... [Targets: 1]
  o- iqn.2014-11.com.example.target1 ............................................... [TPGs: 1]
    o- tpg1 ........................................................... [no-gen-acls, no-auth]
      o- acls ........................................................................ [ACLs: 0]
      o- luns ........................................................................ [LUNs: 0]
      o- portals .................................................................. [Portals: 0]
/iscsi> 
```

Figure 26.4 The iscsi overview.

12. At this point, you can create an ACL in the TPG. Remember, you need to create ACLs as well to access the iSCSI target, because without ACLs, any iSCSI initiator will be denied access. Any new LUN that you create will be mapped to each ACL that is associated with the TPG. This is because of the auto_add_mapped_luns feature, which is on by default. To create the ACL, first enter the IQN that you just created. Type **cd iqn.[Tab]** to enter the IQN. Notice that in the **cd** command, you are using the Tab key for command-line completion.
13. Now type **tpg1/acls/ create iqn.2015-04.com.example:server1**, which creates a node ACL that allows server1 to access the IQN you just created. In this command, the initiatorname as used in /etc/iscsi/initiatorname.iscsi on the iSCSI initiator server is used. After completing this procedure, make sure that the contents of this file on the iSCSI initiatorname matches. (See also the section "Setting the Initiatorname" later in this chapter for more details.) If so required, repeat this command for all other iSCSI initiators that need access to this iSCSI target.
14. Now that you have created the ACL, you need to create the LUNs. The LUNs are needed to associate a block device with a specific TPG. To do this, type the following commands:

```
tpg1/luns/ create /backstores/block/block1
tpg1/luns/ create /backstores/block/block2
tpg1/luns/ create /backstores/fileio/file1
```

TIP While creating LUNs, you can specify additional parameters. For instance, from the **tpg1/luns/** context, type **create lun=10 storage_object=/backstores/block/block1** to assign the LUN number 10 to the backing storage device that is specified.

15. Type **ls** to verify what you have created so far. The result should look like Figure 26.5.

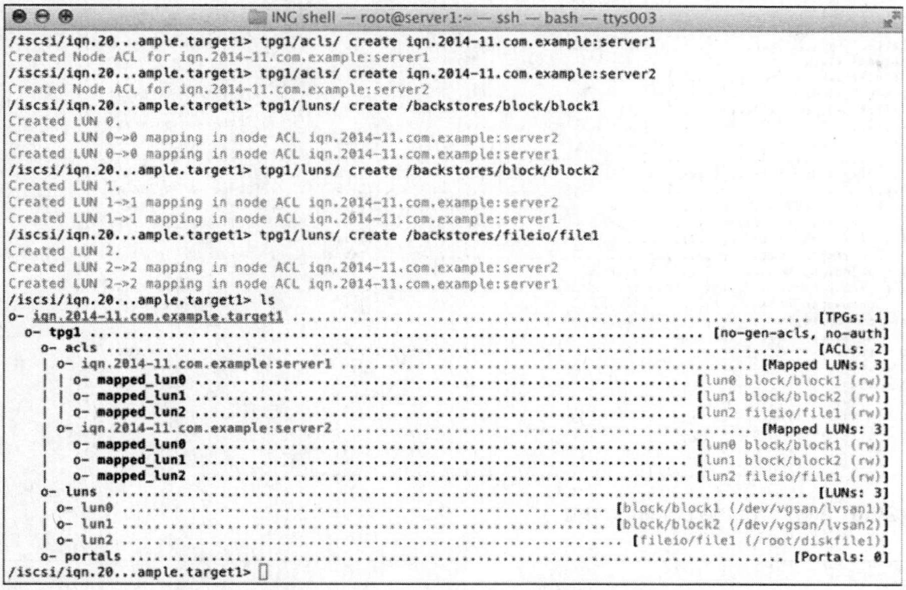

Figure 26.5 While you are creating LUNs, the configured ACLs automatically get access.

16. At this point, you can create the portal. This connects the iSCSI configuration to the specific IP address on the iSCSI target server. To make this work, you need to ensure that the iSCSI target is on a fixed IP address. If that IP address is 192.168.4.210, the command to use is **tpg1/portals/ create 192.168.4.210**. Notice that this step is required only if you want to have the iSCSI target offering its services on only a specific IP address. If you do not create a portal, a default portal is used that binds to the IP address 0.0.0.0, which represents all IP addresses on your server.

17. The configuration has now completed. Get back to the root of the configuration tree by using **cd /** and type **ls** to get a complete overview of the configuration. It should look like Figure 26.6. You can now type **exit** to close the configuration interface. This automatically writes the configuration file.

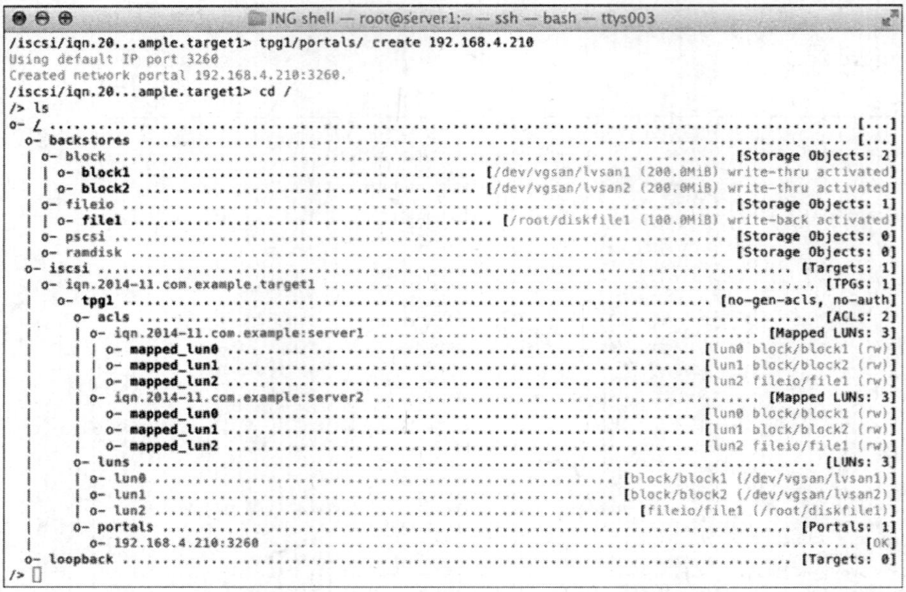

Figure 26.6 Verifying the configuration.

At this point, the iSCSI target configuration is written, but the target is not yet operational. The configuration is written to the file /etc/target/saveconfig.json. This is a file in the Java JSON format and is not really meant to be edited directly. While you are saving the configuration, the iSCSI target service is also started automatically and listening on port 3260 of the specified portal IP address. Listing 26.1 shows partial contents of the JSON file.

Listing 26.1 The iSCSI Target Configuration as Stored in the Saveconfig.json File

```
[root@server2 ~]# cat /etc/target/saveconfig.json
{
  "fabric_modules": [],
  "storage_objects": [
    {
      "attributes": {
        "block_size": 512,
        "emulate_dpo": 0,
        "emulate_fua_read": 0,
        "emulate_fua_write": 1,
```

```
          "emulate_model_alias": 1,
          "emulate_rest_reord": 0,
          "emulate_tas": 1,
          "emulate_tpu": 0,
          "emulate_tpws": 0,
          "emulate_ua_intlck_ctrl": 0,
          "emulate_write_cache": 1,
          "enforce_pr_isids": 1,
          "fabric_max_sectors": 8192,
          "is_nonrot": 0,
          "max_unmap_block_desc_count": 1,
          "max_unmap_lba_count": 8192,
          "max_write_same_len": 4096,
          "optimal_sectors": 8192,
          "queue_depth": 128,
          "unmap_granularity": 1,
          "unmap_granularity_alignment": 0
        },
        "dev": "/dev/vgsan/lvsan1",
        "name": "block1",
        "plugin": "block",
        "readonly": false,
        "write_back": false,
        "wwn": "2dafba09-b611-4cd5-802c-6ab2afa85bfb"
      }
    ],
    "targets": [
      {
        "fabric": "iscsi",
        "tpgs": [
          {
            "attributes": {
              "authentication": 0,
              "cache_dynamic_acls": 0,
              "default_cmdsn_depth": 16,
              "demo_mode_write_protect": 1,
              "generate_node_acls": 0,
              "login_timeout": 15,
              "netif_timeout": 2,
              "prod_mode_write_protect": 0
            },
```

```
        "enable": true,
        "luns": [
          {
            "index": 2,
            "storage_object": "/backstores/fileio/file1"
          },
          {
            "index": 1,
            "storage_object": "/backstores/block/block2"
          },
          {
            "index": 0,
            "storage_object": "/backstores/block/block1"
          }
        ],
        "node_acls": [
          {
            "attributes": {
              "dataout_timeout": 3,
              "dataout_timeout_retries": 5,
              "default_erl": 0,
              "nopin_response_timeout": 30,
              "nopin_timeout": 15,
              "random_datain_pdu_offsets": 0,
              "random_datain_seq_offsets": 0,
              "random_r2t_offsets": 0
            },
            "mapped_luns": [
              {
                "index": 2,
                "tpg_lun": 2,
                "write_protect": false
              },
              {
                "index": 1,
                "tpg_lun": 1,
                "write_protect": false
              },
              {
                "index": 0,
                "tpg_lun": 0,
                "write_protect": false
```

```
                    }
                ],
                "node_wwn": "iqn.2015-04.com.example:server1"
            }
        ],
        "parameters": {
            "AuthMethod": "CHAP,None",
            "DataDigest": "CRC32C,None",
            "DataPDUInOrder": "Yes",
            "DataSequenceInOrder": "Yes",
            "DefaultTime2Retain": "20",
            "DefaultTime2Wait": "2",
            "ErrorRecoveryLevel": "0",
            "FirstBurstLength": "65536",
            "HeaderDigest": "CRC32C,None",
            "IFMarkInt": "2048~65535",
            "IFMarker": "No",
            "ImmediateData": "Yes",
            "InitialR2T": "Yes",
            "MaxBurstLength": "262144",
            "MaxConnections": "1",
            "MaxOutstandingR2T": "1",
            "MaxRecvDataSegmentLength": "8192",
            "MaxXmitDataSegmentLength": "262144",
            "OFMarkInt": "2048~65535",
            "OFMarker": "No",
            "TargetAlias": "LIO Target"
        },
        "portals": [
            {
                "ip_address": "0.0.0.0",
                "iser": false,
                "port": 3260
            }
        ],
        "tag": 1
      }
    ],
    "wwn": "iqn.2015-04.com.example:target"
  }
 ]
}
```

TIP As you have noticed, the procedure to configure an iSCSI target is a long procedure that involves many steps. You might be wondering how to memorize all of these steps for the exam. The secret is that you should not try to memorize all the individual steps. Instead, you want to see the global overview of what you have been doing. You started by creating the backstores that provide the storage that the iSCSI target is sharing. Next you created an IQN, which automatically created the TPG also. The third step was to create ACLs to allow nodes to access the target, following which you created the LUNs. While you were creating the LUNs, ACLs were assigned automatically. The last step was to configure the portal and write the configuration. There is not much to memorize here, because if you type **ls** in the targetcli interface, all of these steps are listed in the order that you should execute them.

TIP You can also study the man page of the targetcli command to get some help on the iSCSI configuration on the exam. Notice, however, that the QuickStart in this man page does not use authentication, so no ACLs are created here. So if you want to use this man page on the exam, make sure to study it well so that you know which information is available and which is not available through this man page.

Opening the Firewall

Now that the iSCSI target has been configured, you need to make sure that it can be accessed through the firewall and that the service is started automatically. To start, type **systemctl enable target; systemctl start target**. To open port 3260 in the firewall, type **firewall-cmd --add-port=3260/tcp --permanent; firewall-cmd --reload**. No further action is required to run the iSCSI target. You practice these commands in Exercise 26.2.

Exercise 26.2 Finalizing the iSCSI Target Configuration

1. On server1, type **systemctl start target** followed by **systemctl enable target**.
2. Type **systemctl status target** and verify that the target currently is active and that the status is set to enabled (see Listing 26.2).

Listing 26.2 Make Sure That the Service Is Active and Enabled

```
[root@server1 ~]# systemctl enable target; systemctl start target
ln -s '/usr/lib/systemd/system/target.service' '/etc/systemd/system/
  multi-user.target.wants/target.service'
[root@server1 ~]# systemctl status target
target.service - Restore LIO kernel target configuration
   Loaded: loaded (/usr/lib/systemd/system/target.service; enabled)
   Active: active (exited) since Sun 2014-11-09 05:24:24 EST;
  2min 20s ago
  Process: 45549 ExecStart=/usr/bin/targetctl restore (code=exited,
  status=0/SUCCESS)
 Main PID: 45549 (code=exited, status=0/SUCCESS)

Nov 09 05:24:24 server1.example.com systemd[1]: Started Restore LIO
  kernel target configuration.
```

3. Open the firewall, using **firewall-cmd --add-port=3260/tcp --permanent**, followed by **firewall-cmd --reload**.
4. Type **firewall-cmd --list-all** to verify the firewall configuration. The results should look like Listing 26.3.

Listing 26.3 Verifying the Firewall Configuration

```
[root@server1 ~]# firewall-cmd --list-all
public (default, active)
  interfaces: eno16777736
  sources:
  services: dhcpv6-client ssh
  ports: 3260/tcp
  masquerade: no
  forward-ports:
  icmp-blocks:
  rich rules:
```

Setting Up the iSCSI Initiator

Now that the iSCSI target server is configured and operational, you can move on to the next step and configure the iSCSI initiator. You can see this as the ISCSI client because it will request access to storage offered by the iSCSI target server. To do this, you need to go through a few steps:

1. Set the iSCSI initiatorname.
2. Use **iscsiadm** to discover available targets.
3. Use **iscsiadm** to log in to the target.

Setting the iSCSI Initiatorname

Access to the iSCSI target is based on the initiatorname. The initiatorname is configured on iSCSI nodes where the iscsi-initiator-utils RPM package has been installed. The initiatorname is stored in the file /etc/iscsi/initiatorname.iscsi.

After you install the iscsi-initiator-utils package, your nodes will have a default initiatorname that is based on the Red Hat IQN and used as a UUID number. It may look like InitiatorName=iqn.1994-05.com.redhat:76f76a97c56e224. There is nothing wrong with using this default initiatorname, unless it is hard to read. That is why you may consider using an initiatoname that is easier to read, such as iqn.2015-04.com.example:server1.

While setting an initiatorname manually, make sure that you respect the syntax restrictions. Initiatornames must start with iqn, followed by a four-digit year, followed by a two-digit month and the inversed DNS name of your domain, which is followed by a unique identifier for the initiator.

After changing the iSCSI initiatorname, do not forget to restart the iscsid service by using **systemctl restart iscsid**!

> **TIP** Notice that on the iSCSI initiator two services are needed. The iscsid service is the main service that accesses all configuration files involved. The iscsi service is the service that establishes the iSCSI connections.

Performing the Discovery

To connect to an iSCSI SAN, you start by exploring which configuration is available. The iscsiadm command has different modes, and in discovery mode the command shows available connections. When using iSCSI discovery, you need three different arguments:

- **--type sendtargets** This tells the discovery mode how to find the iSCSI targets. In some configurations, an iSNS service can be configured to make discovery easier, but setting up iSNS is not an RHCE requirement. Therefore, you'll find the targets you need using --type sendtargets.
- **--portal** This argument tells the **iscsiadm** command which IP address and port to address to perform the discovery. You can use an IP address or node name as the argument, and optionally, you can specify a port as well. If no port is specified, the default port 3260 is used.
- **--discover** This argument tells the iscsid service to perform a discovery.

Using these command arguments, you can perform an iSCSI discovery with the following command:

```
iscsiadm --mode discovery --type sendtargets --portal 192.168.4.210
--discover
```

Note that instead of the **--mode discovery** option, you can also use **--mode discoverydb**. This discovery mode uses a database and allows for some additional commands to be used. For the RHCE objectives, you can consider the discovery and discoverydb modes as more or less equivalent to one another.

After a successful discovery, you can request more information about the target that was discovered, using the **-P** option. This option can be used in any iscsiadm mode, and it will show details about the current mode. In all modes, the print levels 0 and 1 are supported. In some modes, you can go beyond that to display more additional information. Listing 26.4 shows the result of the **iscsiadm --mode discovery -P 1** command.

Listing 26.4 Showing iSCSI Discovery Details

```
[root@server2 ~]# iscsiadm --mode discovery -P 1
SENDTARGETS:
DiscoveryAddress: 192.168.4.210,3260
Target: iqn.2014-11.com.example.target1
          Portal: 192.168.4.210:3260,1
                    Iface Name: default
iSNS:
No targets found.
STATIC:
```

```
No targets found.
FIRMWARE:
No targets found.
[root@server2 ~]# man iscsiadm
[root@server2 ~]# iscsiadm --mode discovery -P 1
SENDTARGETS:
DiscoveryAddress: 192.168.4.210,3260
Target: iqn.2014-11.com.example.target1
          Portal: 192.168.4.210:3260,1
                   Iface Name: default
iSNS:
No targets found.
STATIC:
No targets found.
FIRMWARE:
No targets found.
```

Making the Connection

Based on the name that you found when performing the iSCSI discovery and assuming that you have set the initiatorname correctly, you can now log in to the iSCSI target and make the actual connection. To do this, use a command that looks like the following:

```
iscsiadm --mode node --targetname iqn.2014-11.com.exaple:target1
--portal 192.168.4.21-:3260 --login
```

In this command, a few options are used:

- **--mode node** This specifies iscsiadm to enter "node" mode. This is the mode in which the actual connection with the target can be established.
- **--targetname** This specifies the name of the target as discovered when using the iSCSI discovery process.
- **--portal** This is the IP address and port on which the target is listening.
- **--login** This authenticates to the target and will store credentials as well to ensure that on reboot the connection can be reestablished again.

After logging in, a session with the iSCSI target is established. Both the session and the node connection can be monitored, using the **-P** option. Use **iscsiadm --mode node -P 1** to see node connection details, and **iscsiadm --mode session -P [1-3]** to get information about the current iSCSI session (see Listing 26.5).

Listing 26.5 Listing iSCSI Node and Session Information

```
[root@server2 ~]# iscsiadm --mode node -P 1
Target: iqn.2014-11.com.example:target1
        Portal: 192.168.4.210:3260,1
                Iface Name: default
[root@server2 ~]# iscsiadm --mode node -P 2
iscsiadm: Invalid info level 2. Try 0 or 1.
[root@server2 ~]# iscsiadm --mode node -P 1
Target: iqn.2014-11.com.example:target1
        Portal: 192.168.4.210:3260,1
                Iface Name: default
[root@server2 ~]# iscsiadm --mode session -P 1
Target: iqn.2014-11.com.example:target1 (non-flash)
        Current Portal: 192.168.4.210:3260,1
        Persistent Portal: 192.168.4.210:3260,1
                **********
                Interface:
                **********
                Iface Name: default
                Iface Transport: tcp
                Iface Initiatorname: iqn.2014-11.com.
example:server2
                Iface IPaddress: 192.168.4.220
                Iface HWaddress: <empty>
                Iface Netdev: <empty>
                SID: 3
                iSCSI Connection State: LOGGED IN
                iSCSI Session State: LOGGED_IN
                Internal iscsid Session State: NO CHANGE

[root@server2 ~]#
```

After making the connection to the iSCSI target, you'll see the new SCSI devices as offered by the target. A convenient command to list these commands is **lsscsi**. Listing 26.6 shows the output of this command where you can clearly see the origins of the devices as well.

Listing 26.6 Showing Available Disk Devices with **lsscsi**

```
[root@server2 ~]# lsscsi
[0:0:0:0]     disk     VMware,   VMware Virtual S 1.0    /dev/sda
[2:0:0:0]     cd/dvd   NECVMWar VMware SATA CD01 1.00   /dev/sr0
[35:0:0:0]    disk     LIO-ORG   block1              4.0    /dev/sdb
[35:0:0:1]    disk     LIO-ORG   block2              4.0    /dev/sdc
[35:0:0:2]    disk     LIO-ORG   file1               4.0    /dev/sdd
```

Making iSCSI Connections Persistent

After configuring an iSCSI connection, you need to make sure that it comes back after a restart. You also need to make sure that iSCSI disks can be mounted automatically on reboot. In this section, you learn how to do that.

Managing iSCSI Connection Persistency

After logging in to an iSCSI target server, the connections are persistent automatically. That means that on reboot, the **iscsid** and **iscsi** services are started on the iSCSI client, and these services will read the iSCSI configuration that is locally stored to automatically reconnect. Therefore, there is no need to put anything in configuration files if you have successfully connected once to the iSCSI server.

All the relevant iSCSI configuration is stored in the directory /var/lib/iscsi. This directory contains several subdirectories, of which the nodes subdirectory is the most important one. In the nodes subdirectory, all previous connections are stored. If you go into this directory, you can see a subdirectory that has the name of the iSCSI target IQN. In this IQN subdirectory, you'll find a subdirectory for each known portal, which contains the file default that contains all session parameters.

If you need an iSCSI connection not to be restored after reboot, you first have to log out to disconnect the actual session by using **iscsiadm --mode node --targetname iqn.2014-11.com.example:target1 --logout**.

Next you need to delete the corresponding IQN subdirectory and all of its contents. You can do this with the **rm** command or by using **iscsiadm --mode node --targetname iqn.2014-11.com.example:target1 --op=delete**. This ensures that all configuration is wiped and that you can make a clean restart.

TIP Stop the iscsi.service and remove all files under /var/lib/iscsi/nodes to clean up all current configuration. After doing that, restart the iscsi.service and start the discovery and login again.

Mounting iSCSI Devices

To mount an iSCSI device, you need to take care of a few things. First, the iSCSI disk that now appears as /dev/sdb might appear as a different device name the next time it is connected due to a topology change in your SAN configuration. For that reason, it is not a smart idea to put a reference to /dev/sdb in the /etc/fstab file. You should instead use a file system UUID. Every file system automatically gets a UUID. To request the value of that UUID, you can use the **blkid** command. Notice that this command shows results only if you have first created a file system on the device that you want to use.

TIP Still confused as to whether you need to configure mounts through /etc/fstab or systemd? Don't be. On RHEL 7, /etc/fstab is still the preferred method to make file system mounts persistent.

The second issue when making persistent iSCSI mounts is that normally the /etc/fstab file is processed before the network is available. To make sure the iSCSI disk can be mounted, you need to use the **_netdev** mount option in /etc/fstab.

So to ensure that an iSCSI mount is configured persistently, put an entry in /etc/fstab that looks like this:

```
UUID-XXXXXXXX-XXXX-XXXX-XXXXXXXX /iscsi        xfs       _netdev    0 2
```

In Exercise 26.3, you learn how to create the iSCSI connection.

Exercise 26.3 Making an iSCSI Connection

1. On server 2, open a root shell and type **yum -y install iscsi-initiator-utils lsscsi** to install the software that you need to perform this exercise.
2. Type **iscsiadm --mode discovery --type sendtargets --portal 192.168.4.210 --discover**. This should return the name of the iSCSI target as you have configured it in the previous exercise.
3. Next, type **iscsiadm --mode node --targetname iqn.2014-11.com.example:target1 --portal 192.168.4.210:3260 --login**.

4. The iSCSI devices should now be available. Type **lsscsi** to show them. You should see three LIO devices. Use **iscsiadm -m session -P3**, which also shows all disks.
5. On the first iSCSI device (I'll assume that it is /dev/sdb in this exercise, but it can be a different device on your server depending on the configuration that is used), type **mkfs.xfs /dev/sdb**.
6. Use **blkid /dev/sdb** to get the UUID that is set for the XFS file system that you have just created on /dev/sdb.
7. Create a mount point for the iSCSI disk, using **mkdir /mnt/iscsi**.
8. Type **vim /etc/fstab** to open the /etc/fstab file in an editor and add a line that looks like the following. (Make sure to replace the UUID with the UUID you have found in Step 6 of this exercise.)

```
UUID=XXXXXXXX-XXXX-XXXX-XXXXXX /mnt/iscsi        xfs          _
netdev    0 2
```

9. Type **mount -a**. This should mount the iSCSI disk. Type **mount** without any arguments to verify.

TIP If you want to make it easy to create an iSCSI configuration, study **man 8 iscsiadm**. It contains some great examples that help you go through the basic steps of configuring an iSCSI connection. Do realize, though, that on the RHCE exam, you need to expect the unexpected, and you might have to perform some tasks that you cannot get that easily from the man page.

Troubleshooting iSCSI

As you have read in this chapter, setting up an iSCSI configuration is a complex task where many things can go wrong. So it might prove helpful to do a bit of troubleshooting when the iSCSI connection does not work. The following tips may help with that:

- On the iSCSI target, use **systemctl status target** to verify that the target is operational.
- On the iSCSI initiator, use **systemctl status iscsi** to verify the working of the iscsid process.
- On the target, type **targetcli** and then type **ls** to verify the configuration.

- On the iSCSI initiator, use **iscsiadm -m session -P 3** to get current connection information about your iSCSI disk. Grep on the word *attached* to see which disk device currently is attached.
- If you are getting an "iSCSI login failed due to authorization failure" message, check that you have changed the initiatorname in /etc/iscsi/initiatorname.iscsi. Also make sure that you have restarted the iscsid process.

Summary

In this chapter, you learned how to set up an iSCSI SAN. The first part of this chapter explained how to configure the SAN part of iSCSI using the iSCSI LIO target software. In the second part, you learned how to configure the iSCSI initiator to connect to the iSCSI SAN. You also learned how to analyze the current iSCSI configuration and what you can do if it does not work as expected.

Exam Preparation Tasks

Review All Key Topics

Review the most important topics in the chapter, noted with the Key Topic icon in the outer margin of the page. Table 26.3 lists a reference of these key topics and the page numbers on which each is found.

Table 26.3 Key Topics for Chapter 26

Key Topic Element	Description	Page Number
Table 26.2	iSCSI terminology	583
Step list	Setting up the target for using the targetcli utility	585

Complete Tables and Lists from Memory

Print a copy of Appendix B, "Memory Tables" (found on the disc), or at least the section for this chapter, and complete the tables and lists from memory. Appendix C, "Memory Tables Answer Key," also on the disc, includes completed tables and lists to check your work.

Define Key Terms

Define the following key terms from this chapter and check your answers in the glossary:

iSCSI, target, initiator, LIO, LUN, storage backend, portal, multipath, host bus adapter, fiber channel

Review Questions

1. Which command enables you to see currently connected iSCSI disks?
2. When mounting an iSCSI disk persistently through fstab, which two considerations should be made?
3. Which command enables you to open the interactive shell where you can create iSCSI targets?
4. Why do you need to perform an iSCSI discovery?
5. Which directory on an iSCSI client machine is used to store all connection information?
6. What is the name of the file where you'll configure the iSCSI initiatorname?
7. Which daemon must be running on the iSCSI client server?
8. What command enables you to get very detailed information about currently existing iSCSI connections?
9. What is the name for the collection of IP addresses and ports on which an iSCSI target will listen?
10. What is wrong in the following IQN: iqn.2014-11.com.example.myserver?

End-of-Chapter Labs

Now that you have learned how to set up the iSCSI target and the initiator, you can prepare for these tasks at an RHCE exam level. In the end-of-chapter labs here, you set up an iSCSI target and an iSCSI initiator.

Lab 26.1

1. Configure server1 as an iSCSI target server with two LUNs. Both LUNs need to be based on a 1GB LVM logical volume as the storage backend. Configure everything to make this LUN operational. Make sure that both LUNs can be accessed by server1 and server2.

Lab 26.2

1. Configure the iSCSI initiator on both server1 and server2. (Normally it does not make sense to run an iSCSI initiator on a server that also is an iSCSI target, but it makes it easier to configure iSCSI without installing an additional server.)

Lab 26.3

1. On server2, create an XFS file system on LUN1 and mount it persistently through /etc/fstab.

The following topics are covered in this chapter:

- Understanding Top Performance Data
- Using iostat, vmstat, and pidstat
- Configuring sar

The following RHCE exam objectives are covered in this chapter:

- Produce and deliver reports on system utilization (processor, memory, disk, and network)

CHAPTER 27

System Performance Reporting

An important part of the responsibilities of a system administrator consists of making sure that performance on a server is healthy. On Linux, a wide scope of tools is available for this purpose. This chapter gives an overview of some of the most important tools that can be used for monitoring and reporting on performance data. Performance optimization is not covered in this chapter; this is the subject of the next chapter.

"Do I Know This Already?" Quiz

The "Do I Know This Already?" quiz allows you to assess whether you should read this entire chapter thoroughly or jump to the "Exam Preparation Tasks" section. If you are in doubt about your answers to these questions or your own assessment of your knowledge of the topics, read the entire chapter. Table 27.1 lists the major headings in this chapter and their corresponding "Do I Know This Already?" quiz questions. You can find the answers in Appendix A, "Answers to the 'Do I Know This Already?' Quizzes and 'Review Questions.'"

Table 27.1 "Do I Know This Already?" Section-to-Question Mapping

Foundation Topics Section	Questions
Understanding top Performance Data	1–2
Using iostat, vmstat, and pidstat	6–8
Configuring sar	9–10

1. Which of the following top parameters shows the time the CPU spends handling processes in user space?
   a. sy
   b. us
   c. hi
   d. wa

2. By default, top shows one line that summarizes CPU performance data for all CPUs in the system. How can you tell top to show one line for each CPU (core) in your system instead of the summary line?
   a. Start top with the option **--all**.
   b. From the top interface, press A.
   c. Open the top field selection interface and select All CPUs.
   d. From the top interface, press 1.

3. Which of the following statements is true about (page) cache memory?
   a. Your server can do perfectly without it.
   b. Cache memory ensures that registers that are often accessed on the CPU are stored close to the CPU cores.
   c. Memory pages in cache will be freed automatically if a memory shortage occurs.
   d. Cache is used to store recently used file system metadata.

4. Which key is used to show columns that can be shown in top?
   a. f
   b. c
   c. w
   d. j

5. You have modified top settings quite a bit and you want to make sure that the current display configuration is automatically opened after restarting top. How do you do that?
   a. Modify the contents of ~/.toprc.
   b. Use w to write the settings to ~/.toprc.
   c. Use W to write the settings to ~/.toprc.
   d. Type D to write the top settings as the defaults.

6. Which utility would you use to show detailed performance statistics for specific processes?
   a. iostat
   b. vmstat
   c. mpstat
   d. pidstat

7. Which command shows usage information about the /dev/sda device only and does that 10 times with a 2 second interval?
   a. **iostat -c /dev/sda 2 10**
   b. **iostat -c /dev/sda 10 2**
   c. **iostat -d /dev/sda 2 10**
   d. **iostat -d /dev/sda 10 2**

8. Which tool would you use if you want to know if swap space currently is being used actively?
   a. iostat
   b. mpstat
   c. memstat
   d. vmstat

9. You are typing **sar -P 0** to show CPU usage statistics, but you get no results. Which of the following is the most likely explanation?
   a. You are typing the wrong command.
   b. The sysstat service hasn't been started.
   c. You have just installed the sysstat package and not enough data has been gathered yet to show results.
   d. The sar database hasn't been built yet.

10. Which file do you need to change if you want to store performance data for usage in sar for longer than the 28 days?
   a. /etc/sysstat.conf
   b. /etc/sysstat/sar.conf
   c. /etc/sysconfig/sysstat
   d. /etc/cron.d/sysstat

Foundation Topics

Understanding top Performance Data

The **top** utility is among the best tools to monitor performance data. It provides a real-time overview of what is happening on a server, and it has many options for tuning which specific performance data should be monitored.

Understanding Load Average

The first parameter to look at when analyzing performance through top is the load average in the upper-right corner of the top output (see Figure 27.1).

```
root@localhost:~                                   root@server2:~

top - 04:27:46 up 10:23,  3 users,  load average: 0.00, 0.01, 0.05
Tasks: 291 total,   2 running, 289 sleeping,   0 stopped,   0 zombie
%Cpu(s):  0.0 us,  0.3 sy,  0.0 ni, 99.3 id,  0.0 wa,  0.0 hi,  0.3 si,  0.0 st
KiB Mem:   1011104 total,   848920 used,   162184 free,      180 buffers
KiB Swap:  1023996 total,     2192 used,  1021804 free.   178232 cached Mem

  PID USER      PR  NI    VIRT    RES    SHR S %CPU %MEM     TIME+ COMMAND     P
  766 root      20   0  267148   4204   3360 S  0.3  0.4   0:47.36 vmtoolsd    0
13064 root      20   0  123780   1776   1156 R  0.3  0.2   0:01.43 top         0
    1 root      20   0   54960   6804   3768 S  0.0  0.7   0:03.44 systemd     0
    2 root      20   0       0      0      0 S  0.0  0.0   0:00.04 kthreadd    0
    3 root      20   0       0      0      0 S  0.0  0.0   0:00.92 ksoftirqd+  0
    5 root       0 -20       0      0      0 S  0.0  0.0   0:00.00 kworker/0+  0
    7 root      rt   0       0      0      0 S  0.0  0.0   0:00.00 migration+  0
    8 root      20   0       0      0      0 S  0.0  0.0   0:00.00 rcu_bh      0
    9 root      20   0       0      0      0 S  0.0  0.0   0:00.00 rcuob/0     0
   10 root      20   0       0      0      0 S  0.0  0.0   0:00.00 rcuob/1     0
   11 root      20   0       0      0      0 S  0.0  0.0   0:00.00 rcuob/2     0
   12 root      20   0       0      0      0 S  0.0  0.0   0:00.00 rcuob/3     0
   13 root      20   0       0      0      0 S  0.0  0.0   0:00.00 rcuob/4     0
   14 root      20   0       0      0      0 S  0.0  0.0   0:00.00 rcuob/5     0
   15 root      20   0       0      0      0 S  0.0  0.0   0:00.00 rcuob/6     0
   16 root      20   0       0      0      0 S  0.0  0.0   0:00.00 rcuob/7     0
   17 root      20   0       0      0      0 S  0.0  0.0   0:00.00 rcuob/8     0
   18 root      20   0       0      0      0 S  0.0  0.0   0:00.00 rcuob/9     0
   19 root      20   0       0      0      0 S  0.0  0.0   0:00.00 rcuob/10    0
   20 root      20   0       0      0      0 S  0.0  0.0   0:00.00 rcuob/11    0
   21 root      20   0       0      0      0 S  0.0  0.0   0:00.00 rcuob/12    0
   22 root      20   0       0      0      0 S  0.0  0.0   0:00.00 rcuob/13    0
   23 root      20   0       0      0      0 S  0.0  0.0   0:00.00 rcuob/14    0
   24 root      20   0       0      0      0 S  0.0  0.0   0:00.00 rcuob/15    0
   25 root      20   0       0      0      0 S  0.0  0.0   0:00.00 rcuob/16    0
   26 root      20   0       0      0      0 S  0.0  0.0   0:00.00 rcuob/17    0
   27 root      20   0       0      0      0 S  0.0  0.0   0:00.00 rcuob/18    0
```

Figure 27.1 Monitoring load average.

To understand load average, you need to know that every process that needs to be served enters a run queue before the kernel scheduler can allocate it to run on a CPU core. The load average indicates the average number of processes that is waiting to be served at any given moment. Because any CPU core can only handle one process, the load average should always be related to the number of CPU cores in the server. As a rough guideline, the number indicated as the load average should not be much higher than the total number of CPU cores. So if your server has four cores, four processes can be handled at the same time, and the CPU load should not be higher than four. If it is, you need to find out why this is the case and make sure that your server is not currently overloaded.

CPU Performance Data

A second performance indicator is in the third line of top, it shows the percentage of CPU usage. By default, this line summarizes performance data for all CPUs in the system. If you press 1, you can see one line for each CPU core. On modern servers, where often multiple CPU cores are used, it is important to see the per CPU usage. When looking at the load average, you may think that 7% of wait time (wa) is not too bad, but on your 16 core server it may very well be that one CPU is occupied for 100% waiting for I/O, which means that you have got a process that is causing trouble. Table 27.2 summarizes the different values in the CPU load line.

Table 27.2 CPU Performance Parameters

Key Topic

Performance Indicator	Explanation
us	Percentage of time the CPU spends handling processes in user mode. These often are processes that have been started without root privileges and do not do any direct interaction with the Linux kernel.
sy	Percentage of time the CPU spends in kernel mode. This is globally the time that is spent handling system calls and accessing drivers.
ni	The percentage of time the server spends handling processes of which the nice value has been adjusted.
id	Percentage of time the processor spends in the idle loop. This is time the CPU is available without taking time away from other processes.
wa	Time the processor spends waiting for noninterruptible I/O, such as requests to disks, hard-mounted NFS, and tape units. A high value in this parameter indicates slow-performing storage and may need further optimization, which would normally be applied to the storage channel.

Performance Indicator	Explanation
hi	Time the processor spends handling hardware interrupts. A high value may indicate faulty hardware.
si	Time the processor spends handling software interrupts.
st	Percentage of stolen time. This parameter shows in a virtualization environment, where virtual machines are "stealing" processor time from the hypervisor.

Memory Usage

Another important performance indicator that top shows is memory usage. Information about usage of RAM and usage of swap space is shown. By reading these statistics, you can ensure that your server has enough RAM for the tasks it has to run. Table 27.3 summarizes the RAM usage statistics:

Table 27.3 Memory Usage Parameters

Key Topic

Usage Indicator	Explanation
KiB Mem	Total amount of physical memory in KiB (1 KiB = 1024 bytes)
used	Total amount of RAM that is used for any purpose
free	Total amount of RAM that is not used for anything
buffers	Total amount of used memory that is used for storing unstructured data
cached Mem	Total amount of memory that is used to cache files that have recently been fetched from disk

To understand memory usage parameters, you should know that the Linux kernel uses physical memory as efficiently as possible. Normally, a part of RAM is used for loading programs. If there is enough memory, another part of it will be used for caching recently read files. This is the part that shows up as cached Mem in top. Because of this feature of caching memory, a system can get a lot faster. What is displayed in top as cache is what accelerates disk access. If frequently accessed files are stored in cache, they do not have to be fetched from disk the next time they are needed, and that makes the overall performance of your server better.

> **NOTE** While top shows the cache parameter, it is better to talk about page cache. This makes it clear to distinguish between the different types of cache that are used. Cache is used on different levels, like the L1, L2, and L3 cache on the CPU, or the cache on the disk controller. In these three cache levels, a lower number indicates that the cache is closer to the CPU and therefore is faster (and more expensive). In this chapter, I follow top terminology, where the word *cache* is equivalent to the term *page cache*.

On a Linux server that has been up and running for a long period, you notice that only a small percentage of free memory is available and a relatively large amount of memory is in cache. As mentioned, that is good for performance, and it does not have any negative impact on the performance of your server. When more memory needs to be allocated, the kernel can easily dump caches and make memory in cache available for loading programs.

You should notice, though, that at all times sufficient memory should be available for caching files. Files that are not in cache need to be fetched from disk, and fetching files from disk really is a lot slower and will have negative impact on the overall performance of your server. As a rough guideline, approximately 25% of memory should be available as free memory, or used by cache. (Note that there are exceptions to this rough guideline; it really depends on what your server is doing!)

The buffer memory is comparable to cache memory. Buffers are used for unstructured data, such as file system tables, inode tables, and others. In general, the number of buffers that is used should not be as high as the amount of cache that is in use, but there are exceptions to this generic guideline. Try for example the **find / > /dev/null** command and see the impact it has on the use of buffers. Because many file system metadata structures have to be accessed, they will be loaded in memory and increase the amount of buffer cache that is allocated.

Understanding Swap Usage

On many Linux systems, you will see memory that is available as swap. Swap is emulated RAM on disk. Because the Linux kernel uses swap in a very efficient way, it is no problem if swap is actively being used. When allocating swap, the Linux kernel makes a difference between active and inactive memory. This difference is made for anonymous memory pages (typically application memory) and file memory (memory in buffers and cache). You can observe current usage statistics in /proc/meminfo (see Listing 27.1).

Listing 27.1 Memory Usage Information in /proc/meminfo

```
Active:              450832 kB
Inactive:            259008 kB
Active(anon):        358196 kB
Inactive(anon):      173332 kB
Active(file):         92636 kB
Inactive(file):       85676 kB
```

If a shortage of memory occurs, the Linux kernel can do two things:

- Drop caches: This immediately makes more memory available, but the next time the files that were in cache are requested, they need to be read from disk and put in cache again. If the kernel drops only Inactive(file) memory, it does not really matter, because these are memory pages that were not used recently anyway.
- Use swap: All inactive(anon) memory is an excellent candidate to move to swap. These are memory pages that are used by applications but have not been used recently. Therefore, it does not really matter if they're used to swap and the performance penalty will be minimal.

Notice that the free utility also gives an overview of current memory usage statistics. Listing 27.2 shows the output of this command.

Listing 27.2 Output of the **free -m** Command

```
[root@server2 ~]# free -m
             total     used      free    shared  buff/cache   available
Mem:         1833      632       6       10      548          1002
Swap:        611       0         611
```

In its output, the **free -m** command gives an overview of the total amount of memory, the amount of memory that is used, and the amount of memory that is available. Notice that the total memory is shown as used + free + buff/cache memory. When the **free** command got updated in RHEL 7.1, the **available** parameter was introduced. This parameter shows the amount of memory that is available as free memory, plus the inactive file memory (which refers to cached files that have not been used recently). The second line of the **free -m** command shows information about swap usage.

If more details are required about the composition of swap space, you can use the **swapon -s** command. As shown in Listing 27.3, this command shows which swap devices are currently allocated as swap files. You can see that swap space on the system where this command was used is composed of dm-0 and dm-4, which are LVM logical volumes, which by the **swapon -s** command are falsely identified as partition devices.

Listing 27.3 Using **swapon -s** to Get an Overview of Current Swap Usage

```
[root@server2 ~]# swapon -s
Filename                        Type          Size      Used      Priority
/dev/dm-0                      partition     524284     0          -1
/dev/dm-4                      partition     102396     0          -2
```

Process Memory Usage

The name of the top utility is **top** because processes are sorted by resource usage. Normally, they are sorted on CPU usage. You can sort on other performance parameters as well by using the > and < keys. If, for instance, you want to sort on memory usage, press the > key once, and press < again to get back to sorting on %CPU. For each process, top shows current usage of virtual memory, resident memory, and shared memory.

Virtual memory is not real memory; it is a set of pointers that set to memory addresses in the virtual address space. The total available virtual address space on a modern 64-bit system is 32TB, and the only purpose of this virtual address space is that each process when starting can set uniquely reserved memory pointers. The amount of virtual memory that a process has reserved is indicated in the top column VIRT. Normally this amount of memory is quite large.

When a process starts becoming active, it will allocate resident memory. This memory shows in top in the RES column. Resident memory is real memory that needs to be allocated in RAM.

Customizing top Display

When you are working with top, many performance parameters can be displayed. For an overview of available parameters, press **f**. This shows all fields that are available in top. To add specific fields to the default display, navigate to the field using the arrow keys on your keyboard and select the field you want to show using the space bar. After making your selection, press **q** to quit and show the top interface with the new field selection. Figure 27.2 shows the interface where you can do this.

```
Fields Management for window 1:Def, whose current sort field is %CPU
   Navigate with Up/Dn, Right selects for move then <Enter> or Left commits,
   'd' or <Space> toggles display, 's' sets sort.  Use 'q' or <Esc> to end!

* PID     = Process Id             nMaj    = Major Page Faults
* USER    = Effective User Name    nMin    = Minor Page Faults
* PR      = Priority               nDRT    = Dirty Pages Count
* NI      = Nice Value             WCHAN   = Sleeping in Function
* VIRT    = Virtual Image (KiB)    Flags   = Task Flags <sched.h>
* RES     = Resident Size (KiB)    CGROUPS = Control Groups
* SHR     = Shared Memory (KiB)    SUPGIDS = Supp Groups IDs
* S       = Process Status         SUPGRPS = Supp Groups Names
* %CPU    = CPU Usage              TGID    = Thread Group Id
* %MEM    = Memory Usage (RES)     ENVIRON = Environment vars
* TIME+   = CPU Time, hundredths   vMj     = Major Faults delta
* COMMAND = Command Name/Line      vMn     = Minor Faults delta
  PPID    = Parent Process pid     USED    = Res+Swap Size (KiB)
  UID     = Effective User Id      nsIPC   = IPC namespace Inode
  RUID    = Real User Id           nsMNT   = MNT namespace Inode
  RUSER   = Real User Name         nsNET   = NET namespace Inode
  SUID    = Saved User Id          nsPID   = PID namespace Inode
  SUSER   = Saved User Name        nsUSER  = USER namespace Inode
  GID     = Group Id               nsUTS   = UTS namespace Inode
  GROUP   = Group Name
  PGRP    = Process Group Id
  TTY     = Controlling Tty
  TPGID   = Tty Process Grp Id
  SID     = Session Id
  nTH     = Number of Threads
* P       = Last Used Cpu (SMP)
  TIME    = CPU Time
* SWAP    = Swapped Size (KiB)
  CODE    = Code Size (KiB)
  DATA    = Data+Stack (KiB)
```

Figure 27.2 Selecting top display fields.

After selecting the display fields in top, you can make them permanent. To do this, press **W**. This writes the new settings to ~/.toprc. This activates the settings again after restarting top.

Using iostat, vmstat, and pidstat

The **top** utility offers an overall interface that shows many aspects of Linux performance, but some other performance monitoring utilities are available as well, many of which come from the sysstat package. Table 27.4 describes these utilities.

Table 27.4 Performance Monitoring Utilities Overview

Key Topic

Tool	Description
cifsiostat	Shows performance statistics for the CIFS file sharing service
nfsiostat	Shows performance statistics for the NFS file sharing service
iostat	Generic utility that shows I/O performance statistics
mpstat	Used to show CPU utilization information in a multi-CPU environment
pidstat	Shows process ID (PID)-related performance statistics
vmstat	Generic utility that shows detailed information about memory usage

Using iostat

The iostat utility is useful if you want to find out which I/O devices have been used intensively and what amount of I/O has been happening on these devices. If you run the utility without any arguments, if gives the output that you can see in Listing 27.4.

Listing 27.4 iostat Default Output

```
[root@localhost ~]# iostat
Linux 3.10.0-123.13.2.el7.x86_64 (localhost.localdomain)  12/26/2014
_x86_64_  (1 CPU)

avg-cpu:  %user   %nice %system %iowait  %steal   %idle
           0.18    0.00    0.32    0.00    0.00   99.50

Device:     tps    kB_read/s    kB_wrtn/s    kB_read    kB_wrtn
sda         0.45       10.48         1.17     439818      49314
dm-0        0.02        0.03         0.05       1184       2192
dm-1        0.44       10.31         1.07     432822      45073
```

The iostat output shows per device statistics. The first column lists the devices. In Listing 27.4, three devices are listed: the hard disk /dev/sda and two LVM logical volumes dm-0 and dm-1. For each of these devices, the average number of transactions per second is shown fist. You then see how many kilobytes have been read and written per second, and how many kilobytes have been written in total.

With iostat, you can show different performance parameters also. Read the man page for a detailed overview. Two interesting parameters are **-c**, which displays

CPU usage information, and **-d**, which shows device usage information. You can also use iostat in continues mode, where an interval and a counter are used. For instance, the command **iostat -d /dev/sda 2 10** shows usage statistics for the /dev/sda device only, with 10 polling loops in total at a 2-second interval.

When using iostat in this mode, you notice that the values for the amount of data that has been read and written is significantly higher in the first line. That is because the first line summarizes totals since startup, while the other lines summarize usage in each polling loop.

Using vmstat

The vmstat utility shows information about virtual memory usage. Like iostat, you can use this utility in polling mode, using commands like **vmstat 2 5** to show 5 polling loops with a 2-second interval (see Listing 27.5).

Listing 27.5 Showing System Usage Information with **vmstat**

```
[root@localhost ~]# vmstat 2 5
procs ----------memory----- ---swap-- ---io---- -system-- ---cpu-----
 r  b   swpd   free  buff  cache  si   so  bi    bo   in   cs us sy id wa
st
 3  0  2192 167664   180 181148  0   0  10   1  48   89  0  0 100  0  0
 0  0  2192 167640   180 181180  0   0   0   0  73  107  0  1 100  0  0
 0  0  2192 167640   180 181180  0   0   0   0  69  107  0  0 100  0  0
 0  0  2192 167640   180 181180  0   0   0   0  55   94  0  0 100  0  0
 0  0  2192 167640   180 181180  0   0   0   0  68  127  2  1  98  0  0
```

The information that is shown with vmstat is displayed in different categories:

- **procs:** Provides information about the number of processes that were active in the last polling loop, or were waiting for I/O devices
- **memory:** Gives information about important memory usage parameters such as the amount of swapped memory, free memory, and the memory that is currently allocated to buffers or cache
- **swap:** Shows swap activity
- **io:** Shows I/O activity
- **system:** Provides information about the number of interrupts and context switches that have happened on your system

- **cpu:** Gives information about CPU usage, such as the amount of time the CPU has spent in user space, system space, the idle loop, waiting for I/O, and dealing with stolen time

An important statistic that can be obtained from vmstat is the number of blocks that have been swapped in and swapped out. On Linux, it is not bad per se if swap is used. Swap usage is only bad if a large number of blocks is moved from memory to swap and back. This is indicated by the si and so parameters that you can see below the swap line in the vmstat output.

Another common way to use vmstat is by issuing the command **vmstat -s**. This displays a summary of all parameters that are important for performance in relation to memory use (see Listing 27.6).

Listing 27.6 Use **vmstat -s** for an Overview of Memory-Related Performance Parameters

```
[root@localhost ~]# vmstat -s
      1011104 K total memory
       810348 K used memory
       361844 K active memory
       262040 K inactive memory
       200756 K free memory
          180 K buffer memory
       181400 K swap cache
      1023996 K total swap
         2192 K used swap
      1021804 K free swap
         8100 non-nice user cpu ticks
           28 nice user cpu ticks
        10735 system cpu ticks
      4732129 idle cpu ticks
          213 IO-wait cpu ticks
            5 IRQ cpu ticks
         3818 softirq cpu ticks
            0 stolen cpu ticks
       441354 pages paged in
        52237 pages paged out
            0 pages swapped in
          548 pages swapped out
      2268772 interrupts
      4180999 CPU context switches
   1419548648 boot time
        15996 forks
```

Using pidstat

To monitor application performance, the **pidstat** command is useful. The most interesting part that is shown by this utility is about the context switches that have occurred. To enable multitasking, the Linux kernel uses context switches. A context switch occurs when a CPU moves over to handling another task. Context switches are relatively expensive in terms of performance and should for that reason be avoided if possible.

Typically, there are two different types of context switches: voluntary context switches and nonvoluntary context switches. A voluntary context switch occurs when an application for the moment has no more active threads and can move control over to another application. A nonvoluntary context switch occurs when an application has used its time slice on the scheduler and the scheduler moves it away to make space for another thread. Voluntary context switches are just a part of normal operation; nonvoluntary context switches should be avoided if possible (but that will not always work).

When there are more threads that want to run then there are cores in the system, the kernel spreads CPU availability over the threads that need attention; this is the way time sharing works, and by doing so, nonvoluntary context switches will occur.

To check the number of context switches that has happened on an application, you can use the **pidstat** command. This command also works with arguments that specify how many polling loops should occur and how often they should occur. In Listing 27.7, you see an example of the output of the **pidstat** command.

Listing 27.7 Showing Context Switches with **pidstat**

```
[root@localhost ~]# pidstat -w -p 3446 2 5
Linux 3.10.0-123.13.2.el7.x86_64 (localhost.localdomain)  12/26/2014
_x86_64_  (1 CPU)

07:23:38 AM   UID       PID   cswch/s nvcswch/s  Command
07:23:40 AM     0      3446      0.50      0.00  sshd
07:23:42 AM     0      3446      0.50      0.00  sshd
07:23:44 AM     0      3446      0.50      0.00  sshd
07:23:46 AM     0      3446      0.50      0.00  sshd
07:23:48 AM     0      3446      0.50      0.00  sshd
Average:        0      3446      0.50      0.00  sshd
```

Configuring sar

The name sar stands for System Activity Reporter. Whereas tools such as vmstat, iotstat, and pidstat are used to show live performance statistics, the sar utility uses processes that gather and store performance data. The result is that you can analyze this performance data, even over a period that has happened in the past.

To use sar, two different processes need to be started. If the sysstat RPM package is installed, this happens automatically through cron. The processes are sa1 and sa2, and they are started through /etc/cron.d/sysstat; Listing 27.8 shows its configuration.

Listing 27.8 Starting the sa Services Through cron

```
[root@localhost cron.d]# cat sysstat
# Run system activity accounting tool every 10 minutes
*/10 * * * * root /usr/lib64/sa/sa1 1 1
# 0 * * * * root /usr/lib64/sa/sa1 600 6 &
# Generate a daily summary of process accounting at 23:53
53 23 * * * root /usr/lib64/sa/sa2 -A
```

As you can see, the sa1 process collects data every 10 minutes and the sa2 process does so every day. This can be tuned according to your specific needs.

These sa processes collect data and write the data to the /var/log/sa directory. When the **sar** command is used, it uses this directory for data. By default, performance data for the last 28 days is kept, but this can be configured through the HISTORY variable, which is set in the /etc/sysconfig/sysstat file.

Once enough data has been gathered, the **sar** command enables you to get information from this data. Notice that you may not succeed in getting the same results, because not enough data may be gathered yet on your server.

TIP To filter sar data that has been logged between specific times, make sure that military time is used, and not time that is noted in AM/PM notation. A common way to do this is by starting sar with the LANG=C variable definition, as in **LANG=C sar -q**. To make sure that sar is always started this way, it is a good idea to define an alias in the shell startup script /etc/bashrc or ~/.bashrc:

```
alias sar='LANG=C sar'
```

In Exercise 27.1, you work with sar to show some data from the sar logs.

Exercise 27.1 Using sar to Display System Activity Information

1. Open a root shell. Enter the following command to make sure that the time indication in sar output is correct: **echo "alias sar='LANG=C sar'" >> /etc/bashrc**.
2. Open the file /etc/sysconfig/sysstat with an editor and change the HISTORY variable to keep a history of 60 days. Make sure it reads HISTORY=60.
3. Show network statistics, using **sar -n DEV**.
4. Report I/O statistics and information about transfer rates, using **sar -b**. This command allows you to identify peek I/O throughput over a longer period of time.
5. Type **sar -P 0** to show CPU usage statistics.
6. Type **sar 1 10** to show sar output 10 times, with a 1-second interval.

Summary

In this chapter, you learned about some solutions to analyze performance on a Linux server. You have learned how to get a generic overview of performance parameters using the top utility. Then, you learned how to get more detailed performance statistics using the different tools from the sysstat RPM package, and vmstat. In the next chapter, you learn how based on this information you can optimize your server performance.

Exam Preparation Tasks

Review All Key Topics

Review the most important topics in the chapter, noted with the Key Topic icon in the outer margin of the page. Table 27.5 lists a reference of these key topics and the page numbers on which each is found.

Table 27.5 Key Topics for Chapter 27

Key Topic Element	Description	Page
Table 27.2	CPU performance parameters	611
Table 27.3	Memory usage parameters	612
Paragraph	Definition of virtual memory	615
Paragraph	Definition of resident memory	615
Table 27.4	Performance monitoring tools overview	617

Complete Tables and Lists from Memory

Print a copy of Appendix B, "Memory Tables" (found on the disc), or at least the section for this chapter, and complete the tables and lists from memory. Appendix C, "Memory Tables Answer Key," also on the disc, includes completed tables and lists to check your work.

Define Key Terms

cache, buffers, virtual memory, resident memory, scheduler, queue, context switches

Review Questions

1. How do you sort on memory usage in top?
2. Current load average as displayed by top shows a value of 5. Does this indicate bad performance?
3. Your server has a total of 1GB of RAM and you want to load a program that needs 300MB. You have only 200MB of free memory. Can this program load?
4. When starting top, you do not get the result you get normally when working with this utility. What is the easiest way to restore top so that it shows default performance parameters, as on a system that has just been installed?
5. Which tool would you use to analyze if swap usage is not slowing down your computer too much?
6. Which tool would you use to show information about context switches for one specific process?
7. You want to identify the most busy hard disk on your server. Which tool would you use?

8. You are using sar but do not see any data. You have verified syntax and you are sure there is nothing wrong with that. What could be the reason it does not work as expected?

9. You need to sort data that sar has logged between 10 a.m. and 2 p.m. Which setting will make it easier to sort this data?

10. Which tool should you use if you need detailed information on I/O for your Samba server?

End-of-Chapter Labs

In the end-of-chapter labs, you modify top data display and work with the sar utility to get information out of your system. As an RHCE, you need to be able to improvise, and that is why the second end-of-chapter lab contains a task that was not explained in this chapter.

1. Modify the default parameters that are displayed when using top. Add the following information to the top interface, and make sure top gets back with this information the next time it is started.

    - Processes should be sorted based on memory usage not CPU usage.
    - Add a column to show swap statistics.
    - Add information about the last used CPU.
    - Show the number of page faults that have been issued by the processes listed in top.

2. Configure sar so that performance data can be gathered over the last year. Use sar to show swapping statistics for processes that have been running yesterday between 11 a.m. and 2 p.m.

The following topics are covered in this chapter:

- Understanding System Optimization Basics
- Understanding the /proc File System
- Using sysctl to Automate System Optimization Parameters

The following RHCE exam objectives are covered in this chapter:

- Use /proc/sys and sysctl to modify and set kernel runtime parameters

CHAPTER 28

System Optimization Basics

An RHEL kernel is optimized for generic purposes. Therefore, most RHEL servers perform quite well without any further optimization. If you really want to get the best possible performance out of your RHEL 7 server, however, you need to apply some system optimization skills. In this chapter, you learn how it works.

"Do I Know This Already?" Quiz

The "Do I Know This Already?" quiz allows you to assess whether you should read this entire chapter thoroughly or jump to the "Exam Preparation Tasks" section. If you are in doubt about your answers to these questions or your own assessment of your knowledge of the topics, read the entire chapter. Table 28.1 lists the major headings in this chapter and their corresponding "Do I Know This Already?" quiz questions. You can find the answers in Appendix A, "Answers to the 'Do I Know This Already?' Quizzes."

Table 28.1 "Do I Know This Already?" Section-to-Question Mapping

Foundation Topics Section	Questions
Understanding the System Optimization Basics	1
Understanding the /proc File System	2–6
Using sysctl to Automate System Optimization Parameters	7–10

1. There are a few generic recommendations that should be followed when trying to optimize system performance. Which of the following is *not* one of them?
   a. Do not try out performance optimization on a production server. Using a wrong parameter may crash the server and you do not want that to happen on production.
   b. Use one tool only to analyze system performance data. Using another tool may give different results, which does not help.

c. Change one setting at a time and verify it's working.

d. Make a plan before you start and do not just modify random parameters.

2. Which file do you need to change to enable packet forwarding between network cards on your server?

a. /proc/net/router

b. /proc/net/ipv4/ip_forward

c. /proc/sys/net/ipv4/ip_forward

d. /proc/sys/net/ipv4/router

3. Where in the /proc file system do you find the settings that can be used to optimize memory usage?

a. /proc/sys/mem

b. /proc/sys/vm

c. /proc/sys/kern

d. /proc/sys/vfs

4. Which file would you look at to get detailed information on system memory usage?

a. /proc/meminfo

b. /proc/memory

c. /proc/iomem

d. /proc/kcore

5. Which parameter would you change to block ping packets while still allowing other ICMP packets?

a. /proc/sys/net/ipv4/icmp_echo_ignore_all

b. /proc/sys/net/ipv4/icmp_echo_ignore_broadcasts

c. /proc/sys/net/ipv4/icmp_ignore_ping

d. /proc/sys/net/ipv4/tcp_block_icmp_ping

6. Which tunable would you change to increase the willingness of the Linux kernel to swap?
   a. /proc/sys/kernel/swap
   b. /proc/sys/kernel/swappiness
   c. /proc/sys/vm/swap
   d. /proc/sys/vm/swappiness
7. Where would you specify the tunables that have to be activated automatically when booting?
   a. /etc/sysctl.conf
   b. /usr/lib/sysctl.d
   c. /etc/sysctl.d
   d. /etc/lib/sysctl.d
8. What is the most efficient way to get an overview of sysctl tunables?
   a. **sysctl -p**
   b. **sysctl -a**
   c. **sysctl -l**
   d. **sysctl -v**
9. After making changes to the sysctl configuration, which command enables you to read the modifications and execute them in an easy way?
   a. **sysctl -p**
   b. **sysctl -a**
   c. **sysctl -l**
   d. **sysctl -v**
10. Which **sysctl** command can you use to write a setting to a sysctl configuration parameter, without updating the configuration files?
    a. **sysctl -w**
    b. **sysctl -p**
    c. **sysctl -n**
    d. **sysctl -v**

Foundation Topics

Understanding System Optimization Basics

The Linux kernel offers a complicated framework to have your server behave in the best possible way. By default, it comes tuned for an average workload. On many servers, an average workload just is not good enough, which is why some advanced Linux tunables are available.

By making modifications to the Linux tunables, you can greatly improve the performance of your server. There is a risk involved as well, though. It is also relatively easy to tune your server in a way that performance will get worse, not better. That is why Linux performance tuning should be done by experts who know what they are doing. To become skilled in Linux performance tuning takes a lot more than one chapter in an RHCE book. That is why in the RHCA curriculum Red Hat has dedicated an entire course to it. In this chapter, you learn about the bare basics of Linux performance tuning.

Even if in this chapter we just cover performance tuning basics, it is good to start discussing a few generic guidelines (just to keep you from becoming too enthusiastic, which may lead to accidents later).

To start, performance tuning involves a lot of research. You've read about this earlier in this book. After doing the research, you can quietly start optimizing performance. Some rules apply, though:

- **1:** Do not ever try out settings on a production server. Use a test system for trials, and apply only those settings that you have verified to production servers.
- **2:** Change one setting at a time and test it thoroughly. Good testing normally means repeating the same test three times. If after doing three tests you still see significant improvement, you know that this was good modification.
- **3:** Make a plan before you start. Too much performance optimization happens without a good plan, with the result that the administrator is not really working on performance improvements but changing random settings hoping something good comes out of it.

If you are ready to play by these rules, you are allowed to move on and read the next section.

Understanding the /proc File System

The key to Linux performance tuning is in the /proc file system. This file system offers an interface to the Linux kernel and it can be used to analyze the current state of the kernel and make modifications to different settings. In the next subsections, you learn how to get performance optimization information out of the /proc file system and how to optimize performance through it.

> **NOTE** Many, if not all, the system utilities (including **lscpu**, **uname**, **top**, **ps**, **lsmod**, and many more) are getting the information they show from the /proc file system. So, if you do not like reading from the /proc file system too much, just make sure that you find the appropriate tool.

Using /proc to Analyze Performance

The /proc file system contains many files that provide information about the current performance state of a Linux server. Most of the performance analyzing utilities that you learned about in the previous chapter are getting their information from the / proc file system. Table 28.2 provides an overview of important performance-related files.

Table 28.2 /proc Performance Related Files

Key Topic

File	Use
meminfo	Detailed information about memory usage.
cmdline	The line that was used to boot the current kernel image. Useful to find out which boot options were specified on the GRUB 2 boot loader prompt, which allows you to identify boot options that were entered manually.
cpuinfo	Detailed information about the CPU and its features.
partitions	Lists all storage devices and partitions on those storage devices.
sysrq-trigger	A potentially dangerous file that can be used to send low-level instructions to the kernel.
modules	Lists all kernel modules that are currently loaded.
kcore	Points to the current state of system memory.

Apart from the configuration files mentioned in Table 28.2, there are also the process ID (PID) directories. Every process that runs on Linux has a unique PID, and each of these processes builds its own environment. Although not easy to read, this environment is available through the PID directories. In these directories, you'll find, for instance, the status file containing detailed information about memory usage, or the environ file that gives an overview of all the environment variables that are used by the process. Listing 28.1 shows what the contents of the status file could look like. Notice that it contains information that cannot be shown easily in any other way, including the number of context switches that was made regarding this specific process.

Listing 28.1 Analyzing the Status of Memory Allocated by Processes Through the PID Directory

```
[root@server2 34644]# cat status
Name:      gconfd-2
State:      S (sleeping)
Tgid:      34644
Ngid:      0
Pid:      34644
PPid:      1
TracerPid:      0
Uid:      1000      1000      1000      1000
Gid:      1000      1000      1000      1000
FDSize:      128
Groups:      10 1000
VmPeak:        149816 kB
VmSize:        149784 kB
VmLck:              0 kB
VmPin:              0 kB
VmHWM:           2408 kB
VmRSS:           2408 kB
VmData:           360 kB
VmStk:            136 kB
VmExe:             44 kB
VmLib:           6596 kB
VmPTE:            112 kB
VmSwap:             0 kB
Threads:      1
SigQ:      0/7258
SigPnd:      0000000000000000
ShdPnd:      0000000000000000
SigBlk:      0000000000000000
SigIgn:      0000000000000002
```

```
SigCgt:      0000000180004201
CapInh:      0000000000000000
CapPrm:      0000000000000000
CapEff:      0000000000000000
CapBnd:      0000001fffffffff
Seccomp:      0
Cpus_allowed:      ffffffff,ffffffff
Cpus_allowed_list:     0-63
Mems_allowed:      00000000,00000000,00000000,00000000,00000000,0000
0000,00000000,00000000,00000000,00000000,00000000
,00000000,00000000,00000000,00000000,00000000,00000000,00000000,000
00000,00000000,00000000,0000000
0,00000000,00000000,00000000,00000000,00000000,00000000,00000000,00
000000,00000000,00000001
Mems_allowed_list:     0
voluntary_ctxt_switches:      1477
nonvoluntary_ctxt_switches:      1
```

Using /proc/sys to Tune Linux Performance

Key to optimizing Linux performance is the /proc/sys directory. In this directory, you'll find tunables, divided in different categories. Table 28.3 provides an overview.

Table 28.3 /proc/sys Tunable Directories

Key Topic

Tunable	Explanation
abi	This is the application binary interface. It is used to provide an interface to applications, in particular to non-open source applications. You'll probably never use this for optimization.
crypto	The cryptographic interface that provides cryptography for specific services such as IPsec and dm-crypt. Used rarely for Linux performance optimization.
debug	When debugging features are switched on in the Linux kernel, this directory contains tunables. Not used often for regular sysadmin tasks.
dev	Contains a few tunables that are related to devices.
fs	The interface to the virtual file system. Contains a few useful tunables, such as file-max, which specifies the maximum number of files that can be opened simultaneously.
kernel	The kernel interface. Contains many useful tunables.
net	The network interface. Contains many useful tunables.

Tunable	Explanation
sunrpc	The sunrpc interface. Contains a few useful tunables that are related to NFS file sharing.
vm	The virtual memory interface. Contains many useful tunables.

To optimize a Linux system, the /proc/sys directory contains many parameters. Most parameters should be changed only when fully understanding the subsystem that is behind it. For that reason, in this chapter you deal with not-so-impressive parameters only. Optimizing a Linux server is the topic of an entire course by its own in the Red Hat Certified Architecture (RHCA) curriculum.

To change a parameter, there are two methods:

- Use **echo** to write the new parameter to the kernel tunable file.
- Use **sysctl -w** to write the parameter to the kernel tunable.

When optimizing the Linux kernel, you should always first write the parameter to the /proc/sys file system in a nonpersistent way. Then, you test whether it works. After you have confirmed the workings, you can make it permanent, as explained in the next section. In Exercise 28.1, you learn how to temporarily change the hostname value as maintained by the kernel. Notice that this is just an example of how to change the system hostname as currently known by the Linux kernel. Use **hostnamectl** to make persistent changes to the hostname.

Exercise 28.1 Temporarily Changing /proc Settings

In this exercise, you temporarily change a setting in the /proc file system.

1. Open a root shell and type the command **uname -a**. This shows the current host name that is set for this machine.
2. Type **cat /proc/sys/kernel/hostname**. This shows the same hostname.
3. Type **echo something.example.com > /proc/sys/kernel/hostname**. This writes the new hostname to the kernel settings without making it persistent.
4. Type **uname -a**. You'll see that the hostname as displayed with **uname -a** has changed as well.
5. Reboot your server to revert to the default settings.

Using sysctl to Automate System Optimization Parameters

To change kernel settings persistently, you need to write them to sysctl. Sysctl is a service that reads a couple of configuration files which are applied while your system is booting. In this section, you learn how to work with sysctl.

During boot, the systemd-sysctl service is started. This service reads the sysctl configuration. This configuration is offered through different files:

- /etc/sysctl.conf is the default configuration file. On RHEL 7, this file should be used no longer.
- The /usr/lib/sysctl.d directory is used for default optimization options. The content of this directory is intended to be managed through RPMs and not manually, so do not make any changes to it.
- The /etc/sysctl.d directory is used for custom options. If you have any modifications to make, it should be done here.

The parameters that you put in the sysctl configuration files are directly related to the contents of the /proc/sys file system. The sysctl tunables are filenames related to the /proc/sys directory, but instead of a slash as a directory separator, a dot is used. So, the file /proc/sys/vm/swappiness is referred to as vm.swappiness in sysctl.

To get an idea of all available tunables, you can use the **sysctl -a** command. This command lists all available tunables. It offers an easy way to find specific tunables, especially when combined with **grep** or when piped through **less**. After you have found the tunable you want to set, you need to put it in a sysctl configuration file. Listing 28.2 shows partial output of the **sysctl -a** command.

Listing 28.2 Analyzing sysctl Parameters with **sysctl -a**

```
[root@server2 ~]# sysctl -a | head -15
abi.vsyscall32 = 1
crypto.fips_enabled = 0
debug.exception-trace = 1
debug.kprobes-optimization = 1
dev.cdrom.autoclose = 1
dev.cdrom.autoeject = 0
dev.cdrom.check_media = 0
dev.cdrom.debug = 0
dev.cdrom.info = CD-ROM information, Id: cdrom.c 3.20 2003/12/17
dev.cdrom.info =
dev.cdrom.info = drive name:          sr0
```

```
dev.cdrom.info = drive speed:        1
dev.cdrom.info = drive # of slots:   1
dev.cdrom.info = Can close tray:        1
dev.cdrom.info = Can open tray:        1
```

The default location for all tunables is the directory /etc/sysctl.d. In this directory, you should create a file with a name that ends in .conf. In that file, you'll put the tunable with the value you want to set for the tunable. In the lines where you put these, you first enter the name of the tunable, then a space, followed by an = sign, followed by another space and the intended value.

You should not put any contents in the /etc/sysctl.conf file or in the /usr/lib/sysctl.d directory; both locations are considered to be managed by the system.

The **sysctl** command also offers a few useful options. Table 28.4 provides an overview. In Exercise 28.2, you learn how to apply some options.

Key Topic

Table 28.4 sysctl Command-Line Options

Option	Value
-a	Shows all tunables.
--system	Shows all tunables that have been changed through sysctl.
-p <filename>	Loads values from the <filename> that is specified. Use this to activate changes that you have just entered in a sysctl file. If no filename is specified, etc/sysctl.conf is used.
-w	Write a new value to a tunable. This has the same effect as using echo to write the value to the variable.
-x	Does nothing. This information does not help you; I just wanted to share that this command has a defined option that does not do anything.

Exercise 28.2 Modifying Kernel Tunables Through sysctl

In this exercise, you learn how to apply sysctl options. The purpose of this exercise is not to teach you how to optimize your server; it is just to show you how sysctl works.

1. Type **ping localhost**. You should get an answer from localhost.
2. Type **sysctl -a | grep icmp**. This shows all sysctl tunables and filters out the tunables that have icmp in their name. It includes the **net.ipv4.icmp_echo_ignore_all** parameter, which can be used to ignore all ping requests.

3. Type **echo 1 > /proc/sys/net/ipv4/icmp_echo_ignore_all**. This temporarily sets the value of the tunable to 1, which tells your server not to react to any ping packet.
4. Type **ping localhost** to verify that ping no longer works.
5. Use **sysctl -w "net.ipv4.icmp_echo_ignore_all=0"** and ping localhost again. It should now work again.
6. Reboot and test. You'll notice that the setting was not persistent.
7. Use an editor to create the file /etc/sysctl.d/ping.conf and give this file the following contents:

```
net.ipv4.icmp_echo_ignore_all = 1
```

8. Reboot again and test whether you can ping your server. You'll notice that it no longer works.

TIP Optimizing system performance is a science all by itself, and you are not supposed to know how to do this on the exam. You are supposed to set some common parameters, though. Table 28.5 shows my personal pick of useful parameters, I recommend that you memorize them before taking the test; they are so common that you might see them on the exam as well.

Table 28.5 Most Useful sysctl Tunables

Key Topic

Tunable	Use
net.ipv4.ip_forward	Set to 1 to enable packet forwarding between network interfaces.
net.ipv4.icmp_echo_ignore_all	Set to 1 to disable all ping.
net.ipv4.icmp_echo_ignore_broadcasts	Set to 1 to disable broadcast ping.
vm.swappiness	Use a value between 0 and 100 to increase the willingness of your server to swap data.
kernel.hostname	Set the hostname of this system.

Summary

In this chapter, you learned how to optimize your server using sysctl. You learned how the /proc file system is organized and how to set kernel tunables manually by echoing new values to the /proc/sys file system. You also learned how to optimize your server using the **sysctl** command and make settings persistent by working with the related configuration files.

Exam Preparation Tasks

Review All Key Topics

Review the most important topics in the chapter, noted with the Key Topic icon in the outer margin of the page. Table 28.6 lists a reference of these key topics and the page numbers on which each is found.

Table 28.6 Key Topics for Chapter 28

Key Topic Element	Description	Page
Table 28.2	Important /proc files	631
Table 28.3	/proc/sys tunables	633
Table 28.4	sysctl command-line options	636
Table 28.5	Most useful sysctl tunables	637

Complete Tables and Lists from Memory

Print a copy of Appendix B, "Memory Tables," (found on the disc), or at least the section for this chapter, and complete the tables and lists from memory. Appendix C, "Memory Tables Answer Key," also on the disc, includes completed tables and lists to check your work.

Define Key Terms

Define the following key terms from this chapter and check your answers in the glossary:

sysctl, swappiness

Review Questions

1. Where in /proc would you look to find process specific information about the environment variables the process is using?
2. Which /proc file would you check to find out information about currently available disk devices?
3. Where in /proc would you look for detailed information about memory usage?
4. Which command enables you to enable IP packet forwarding on your server?
5. How would you permanently enable IP packet forwarding on your server?
6. Which command shows all kernel tunables?
7. Which tunable can you use to tell your server not to react to any ping requests?
8. Which service is started on boot to read sysctl tunables?
9. Which sysctl tunable sets the hostname of this server?
10. Which command enables you to read and activate settings you have just made to the /etc/sysctl.d/net.conf file?

End-of-Chapter Labs

In these end-of-chapter labs, you apply sysctl tunables. Make sure that all settings survive a reboot.

Lab 28.1

1. Use sysctl tunables to set your hostname to host1.example.com. Figure out how this modification relates to the **hostnamectl** command.
2. Use sysctl tunables to enable IP packet forwarding on your server.
3. Use sysctl tunables to make sure your server does not answer to any ping request.

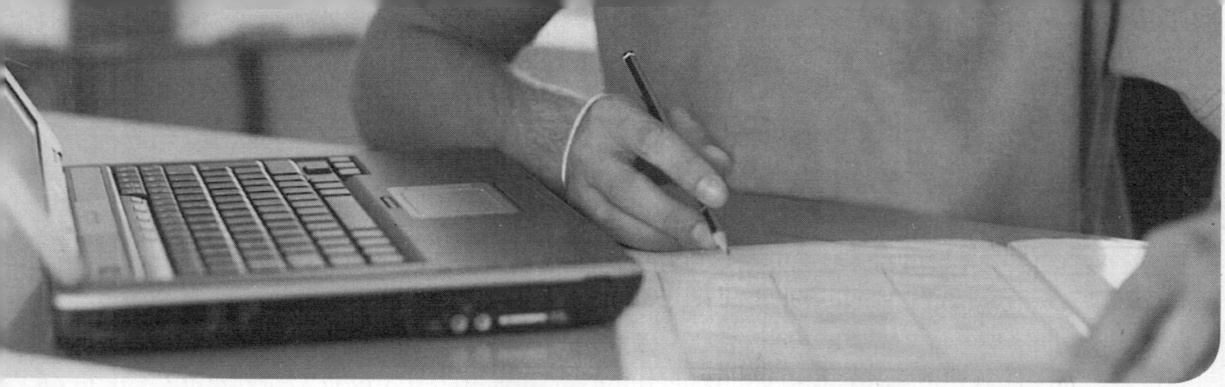

The following topics are covered in this chapter:

- Understanding rsyslogd Modules
- Connecting journald to rsyslog
- Configuring Remote Logging

The following RHCE exam objectives are covered in this chapter:

- Configure remote logging

## CHAPTER 29

Configuring Advanced Log Features

In Chapter 13, "Configuring Logging," you learned about the basics of log file management and analysis. As an RHCE, you need to be aware of some advanced configurations as well. In this chapter, you learn how to work with modules in rsyslogd. You also learn how the integration between rsyslogd and journald is organized and how to configure remote logging.

"Do I Know This Already?" Quiz

The "Do I Know This Already?" quiz allows you to assess whether you should read this entire chapter thoroughly or jump to the "Exam Preparation Tasks" section. If you are in doubt about your answers to these questions or your own assessment of your knowledge of the topics, read the entire chapter. Table 29.1 lists the major headings in this chapter and their corresponding "Do I Know This Already?" quiz questions. You can find the answers in Appendix A, "Answers to the 'Do I Know This Already?' Quizzes and 'Review Questions.'"

Table 29.1 "Do I Know This Already?" Section-to-Question Mapping

Foundation Topics Section	Questions
Understanding rsyslogd Modules	1–4
Connecting journal to rsyslog	5–6
Configuring Remote Logging	7–10

1. Which of the following is not a default rsyslogd module type?
   a. input
   b. output
   c. parser
   d. firewall

2. Which input file module parameter would you use to define the priority of messages that come from the input file?
   a. **InputPriority**
   b. **InputFilePriority**
   c. **InputSeverity**
   d. **InputFileSeverity**

3. Which of the following uses correct syntax for loading the input file module?
   a. **$ModLoad iminputfile**
   b. **$ModLoad imfile**
   c. **$ModLoad inputfile**
   d. **$ModLoad file**

4. Which of the following is missing in configuration of the ommysql module shown here?

```
$ModLoad ommysql
*.*      :ommysql:...,rsyslog,dbuser,password
```

   a. The name of the server
   b. The port where MySQL is listening on
   c. The name of the database
   d. The name of the table

5. What is the name of the module that is used in rsyslogd to receive messages that are generated by journald?
   a. imuxsock
   b. imjournal
   c. omuxsock
   d. omjournal

6. You want to switch off the feature that sends messages from journald to rsyslogd. How do you do this?
   a. Switch off the imuxsock module in rsyslog.conf.
   b. Switch off the imjournal module in rsyslog.conf.
   c. Set **ForwardToSyslog=no** in /etc/systemd/journald.conf.
   d. Set **UseSyslog=no** in /etc/systemd/journald.conf.

7. Which of the following is *not* among the typical benefits of using a central log server?
   a. When using a remote log server, you do not have to run rsyslogd locally.
   b. Messages that are stored on a remote log server cannot be accessed by intruders anymore.
   c. On a remote log server, logrotate can be configured to keep messages for a longer period.
   d. On a remote log server, lots of disk space can be allocated for storing log files.
8. What is the default port that is used for communication between log servers?
   a. 514
   b. 524
   c. 1024
   d. 1514
9. What would be a valid reason to send messages to a remote log server using UDP and not TCP?
   a. By using UDP a significant reduction of network bandwidth use can be obtained.
   b. UDP is more secure than TCP.
   c. Using UDP ensures that your log server can also receive messages from legacy servers or devices that are supporting UDP only.
   d. UDP does not require the loading of additional modules in rsyslog.conf.
10. Apart from loading the imtcp module in rsyslog.conf on the log server, which configuration line is required to allow for log reception over TCP?
   a. **$TCPServerRun 514**
   b. **$InputTCPServerRun 514**
   c. **@TCPServerRun 514**
   d. **@InputTCPServerRun 514**

Foundation Topics

Understanding rsyslogd Modules

In Chapter 13, you learned how to configure rules in rsyslogd, which enables you to send messages to specific destinations based on the facilities and priorities that you have previously configured. In this section, you learn about another feature that is used in rsyslogd: modules. Modules make rsyslogd extensible and allow you to include functionality that is not included by default.

In rsyslogd, different types of modules can be used:

- **Input modules:** These are modules that have a name starting with im. Input modules are used to specify from where rsyslogd will receive messages.
- **Output modules:** These are modules that have a name starting with om. By default, log messages are sent to the destinations as specified in /etc/rsyslog.conf. By using output modules, messages can be sent elsewhere, like to a database or to the journal.
- **Other module types:** Different other module types exist, such as parser modules, message modification modules, and more.

As an RHCE, you need to have a good understanding of the working of input modules and output modules because they are used for many purposes, such as including log messages from nondefault sources and handling logging to nondefault log destinations.

Understanding the Need for Modules

The original syslog was developed a long time ago, when UNIX systems were used for limited purposes, and the number of services was more restricted than it is today. Rsyslog is an enhancement to the original syslog service. This means that backward compatibility needs to be kept, while at the same time new features need to be introduced. To reach this goal, modules are used.

The two most important module types are input modules and output modules. An input module allows reception from services that are not included in the original list of facilities. Input modules, for example, are used to enable rsyslogd to receive messages from journald, or from plain-text files that are generated by services incapable of logging to rsyslogd directly.

Output modules are used to add to the default destinations. In the original design, the number of destinations that could be used was limited and for instance, writing to a database was not supported. To open rsyslogd for other log destinations, output modules can be used. An example of a useful output module is the mysql database module, which allows messages to be written directly to a database. Another example of an output module is usrmsg, which allows syslog to write messages to users.

Using Modules in rsyslog Configuration

Because you are an administrator of rsyslog, you should have a generic understanding of how modules are used. Let's take a look at an example, where the imfile (input module file) module is used to monitor an input file and write new events to rsyslogd (see Listing 29.1).

Listing 29.1 Using the imfile Module

```
$ModLoad imfile

$InputFileName /var/log/httpd/access_log
$InputFileTag apache-access:
$InputFileStateFile state-apache-access
$InputRunFileMonitor
$InputFileFacility local1
$InputFileSeverity info
$InputFilePollInterval 30
```

In Listing 29.1, several parameters are used. Table 29.2 provides an overview of these parameters and their use.

Table 29.2 imfile Module Parameters Overview

Key Topic

Module	Use
InputFileName	Name of the file that the module is monitoring
InputFileTag	Tag that is used when writing log messages
InputFileStateFile	Name of the file that rsyslog is using internally to track changes
InputRunFileMonitor	Parameter that is used to trigger continuous monitoring of the input file
InputFileFacility	Name of the facility that rsyslog will be using
InputFileSeverity	The priority that will be used when logging messages through this file
InputFilePollInterval	The interval that should be used for polling the input file

Another common module that is often used with rsyslog is the ommysql module, an output module that makes it possible to log messages to a MySQL or MariaDB database. The createDB.sql file (which by default is installed to the /usr/share/doc/rsyslog directory) ensures that all the right settings are available in the mysql database. Because you are an rsyslog administrator, you only have to configure the output module in rsyslog. This would look like the following.

```
$ModLoad ommysql
*.*     :ommysql:myservername,rsyslog,dbuser,password
```

As you can see, not much is needed to send log messages to MySQL. You just have to load the output module ommysql and add a line that sends all messages with all priorities to the ommysql module, which is configured on the second line. While doing so, different parameters need to be specified, as you can see in the second example line:

- The name of the database server
- The name of the database
- The username used to connect to the database
- The password used by that user

Make sure to set the appropriate owner and permissions for the configuration file; otherwise, the whole world will be able to read the database username and password!

Connecting journald to rsyslog

By default, journald send messages to rsyslogd. In this section, you learn how this connection is configured, which allows you to further tune it according to your needs.

The journal sends messages to syslog by default. There are two parts of configuration that take care of that. First, the file /etc/systemd/journald.conf contains the line ForwardToSyslog, which by default is set to yes. Listing 29.2 shows the contents of this file. Then, rsyslog.conf contains the configuration needed to receive messages coming from the journal.

Listing 29.2 Use the /etc/systemd/journald.conf to Forward Information to rsyslog

```
[root@server2 ~]# cat /etc/systemd/journald.conf
#  This file is part of systemd.
#
```

```
#  systemd is free software; you can redistribute it and/or modify it
#  under the terms of the GNU Lesser General Public License as
published by
#  the Free Software Foundation; either version 2.1 of the License, or
#  (at your option) any later version.
#
# See journald.conf(5) for details

[Journal]
#Storage=auto
#Compress=yes
#Seal=yes
#SplitMode=login
#SyncIntervalSec=5m
#RateLimitInterval=30s
#RateLimitBurst=1000
#SystemMaxUse=
#SystemKeepFree=
#SystemMaxFileSize=
#RuntimeMaxUse=
#RuntimeKeepFree=
#RuntimeMaxFileSize=
#MaxRetentionSec=
#MaxFileSec=1month
#ForwardToSyslog=yes
#ForwardToKMsg=no
#ForwardToConsole=no
#TTYPath=/dev/console
#MaxLevelStore=debug
#MaxLevelSyslog=debug
#MaxLevelKMsg=notice
#MaxLevelConsole=info
```

The first solution to receive messages from the journal was through the imuxsock module. This module enables reception of messages through UNIX sockets, which are direct connections made between Linux processes using file descriptors. This method is now deprecated and replaced with the imjournal module, a module that was specially developed for integration of rsyslogd and journald. In rsyslog.conf, two lines are needed to further handle log reception correctly:

```
$OmitLocalLogging on
$IMJournalStateFile imjournal.state
```

The first of these lines disables log reception through the imuxsocks module. The second line defines the name of the state file that rsyslogd is using to keep track of the synchronization status between rsyslogd and journald.

Configuring Remote Logging

There are several reasons why it makes sense to configure a remote log server. In this section, you learn why it is recommended to work with remote log servers. You also learn how to set up rsyslogd to send messages to a remote log server, and how to configure rsyslogd to allow for reception of messages from a remote log server.

Understanding the Need for Remote Log Servers

It makes sense to use a central log server for several reasons:

Key Topic

- Messages that are stored on a remote log server cannot be accessed by intruders unless they have also breached the remote server.
- On a remote log server, more storage can be dedicated for storing log messages, with the result that logrotate can be configured to keep messages for a longer period than the default period of 5 weeks that is used for most files by default.
- On a remote log server, lots of disk space can be allocated for storing log files.
- It is easier to check log files on one server than having to connect to multiple servers to analyze the information that has been logged.

Apart from the security argument to configure a remote log server, logrotate is another important reason why it makes sense doing so. By default, logrotate rotates log files every week, and it keeps compressed message files for the last 4 weeks. Therefore, if ever you need information about events that have happened over 5 weeks ago, logrotate has already rotated them away. If you are using a remote log server, you can configure the log server to keep messages for a significantly longer period of time.

Another important reason to use remote logging is security. If your server gets hacked, the first thing the hacker probably wants to do is to wipe his traces. This is doable if log files are stored on the compromised server. It becomes a lot harder when the messages have been written to a remote log server, because that server would have to be breached as well.

Configuring Remote Logging

Configuring a remote log server involves two parts. You need to open the remote log server for reception of log files, and you have to tell the local server to forward messages to the remote log server. Setting up a remote log server can be summarized by the following:

- Configure rsyslogd to receive messages coming from remote servers, using the imudp or imtcp rsyslogd input modules.
- Configure the firewall to accept incoming traffic on port 514.
- Add rules on the client servers to send messages to the remote log server.

The detailed procedure for setting up a remote log server is described in Exercise 29.1.

TIP Setting up a remote log server by itself is not so hard. The challenge is in the details, such as setting up the firewall correctly to allow log messages to be received as well on the remote log server. On the RHCE exam, it is a good idea to read all questions first, and after reading the questions, set up the firewall to allow network traffic on all ports that are needed on your servers.

Exercise 29.1 Setting Up Remote Logging

In this exercise, you configure server2 to receive messages from remote rsyslogd processes. You define the rsyslogd configuration on server1 to forward messages to server2 and open a firewall port on server2 that allows for log file message reception.

1. Open a root shell on server2. Then, open the configuration file /etc/rsyslog.conf.
2. In rsyslog.conf enable the following two lines to enable log reception on TCP port 514:

   ```
   $ModLoad imtcp
   $InputTCPServerRun 514
   ```

3. Close the configuration file and type **systemctl restart rsyslogd** to restart the rsyslogd service. This allows the rsyslogd process on the log server to receive messages from others.

4. Still on server2, open the firewall to accept messages on TCP port 514, using the following two lines:

```
firewall-cmd --add-port=514/tcp
firewall-cmd --add-port=514/tcp --permanent
```

5. Open a root shell on server1, and scroll down to the end of the configuration file. Here, you find the following example configuration line:

```
#*.* @@remote-host:514
```

This line shows how to configure your server to forward messages to a remote server. Change this line to read like the following to forward messages to rsyslogd on server2:

```
*.*        @@server2.example.com:514
```

6. Use **systemctl restart rsyslogd** to restart the rsyslogd process and start logging to the remote server.

While setting up a remote log server, you can enable log reception over TCP and UDP. Because UDP is a connectionless protocol, message delivery is not guaranteed. This is an important reason to prefer log handling over TCP. If you want to set up a server that can receive log messages from legacy syslog compatible devices, however, you should enable UDP log reception as well. As you saw in Exercise 29.1, enabling log reception is easy; example lines for log reception over TCP or UDP are already present. You just have to remove the hash signs in front of the lines:

```
# Provides UDP syslog reception
#$ModLoad imudp
#$UDPServerRun 514

# Provides TCP syslog reception
#$ModLoad imtcp
#$InputTCPServerRun 514
```

To send messages to the log server, you can use the example line near the end of /etc/rsyslog.conf. In this line, you use a single @ to send logs over UDP, and a double @ to send logs using TCP. Notice that by default messages generated through all facilities with all priorities are sent to the remote server; you can change this as needed. For instance, use the following line to send messages with a priority of error and higher to the remote log server log.example.com using TCP:

```
*.err     @@log.example.com
```

Summary

In this chapter, you learned how to configure advanced rsyslog features. You learned how to work with modules in rsyslogd, how to connect journald to rsyslogd, and how to set up remote logging as well.

Exam Preparation Tasks

Review All Key Topics

Review the most important topics in the chapter, noted with the Key Topic icon in the outer margin of the page. Table 29.3 lists a reference of these key topics and the page numbers on which each is found.

Table 29.3 Key Topics for Chapter 29

Key Topic Element	Description	Page
Table 29.2	imfile parameters	645
List	Understanding the need for remote log servers	648

Complete Tables and Lists from Memory

Print a copy of Appendix B, "Memory Tables" (found on the disc), or at least the section for this chapter, and complete the tables and lists from memory. Appendix C, "Memory Tables Answer Key," also on the disc, includes completed tables and lists to check your work.

Define Key Terms

Define the following key terms from this chapter and check your answers in the glossary:

input module, output module, journald

Review Questions

1. Which rsyslogd module should you use to enable reception of journald log messages?
2. What is the name of the deprecated module that can be used to enable receiving journald messages in rsyslogd?
3. To make sure that the legacy method for receiving messages from journald in rsyslogd is not used, which additional parameter should be used?
4. Which configuration file contains settings that allow you to further tune the working of journald?
5. Which parameter takes care of forwarding messages from journald to rsyslogd?
6. Which rsyslogd module can you use to include messages from a specific non-rsyslog generated log file?
7. Which rsyslogd module do you need to use to forward messages to a MariaDB database?
8. Which two lines do you need to include in rsyslog.conf to allow the current log server to receive messages over TCP?
9. How do you configure the local firewalld firewall to allow for log message reception over TCP port 514?
10. Which line do you include on a server where you want to forward rsyslog messages to logserver.example.com, which is configured to receive messages using UDP and the default port?

End-of-Chapter Labs

Lab 29.1

1. Configure server2 as a log server. It should be configured to receive messages from server1 only, using TCP. Also make sure that journald-generated messages are received.

The following topics are covered in this chapter:

- Configuring Network Teaming
- Configuring IPv6 Addresses
- Routing IP Traffic

The following RHCE exam objectives are covered in this chapter:

- Configure teaming or bonding to configure aggregated network links between two Red Hat Enterprise Linux systems
- Configure IPv6 addresses and perform basic IPv6 troubleshooting
- Route IP traffic and create static routes

CHAPTER 30

Configuring Routing and Advanced Networking

In Chapter 8, "Configuring Networking," you learned how to configure network interfaces using NetworkManager and associated utilities. In this chapter, you learn how to configure advanced networking features. The chapter starts with an explanation of the configuration of the team interface, a modern alternative that replaces the bonding driver to create network interfaces for redundancy, throughput, or both. The second part of this chapter shows how to configure IPv6 addresses, and in the last part of this chapter, you learn how to configure custom routes on RHEL 7.

"Do I Know This Already?" Quiz

The "Do I Know This Already?" quiz allows you to assess whether you should read this entire chapter thoroughly or jump to the "Exam Preparation Tasks" section. If you are in doubt about your answers to these questions or your own assessment of your knowledge of the topics, read the entire chapter. Table 30.1 lists the major headings in this chapter and their corresponding "Do I Know This Already?" quiz questions. You can find the answers in Appendix A, "Answers to the 'Do I Know This Already?' Quizzes and 'Review Questions.'"

Table 30.1 "Do I Know This Already?" Section-to-Question Mapping

Foundation Topics Section	Questions
Configuring Aggregated Network Interfaces	1–5
Configuring IPv6 Addresses	6–9
Routing IP Traffic	10

1. Which runner should you use if you want a simple solution that balances load across different interfaces, where no additional protocol support is needed on the switches that are involved?
   a. roundrobin
   b. activebackup
   c. loadbalance
   d. lacp
2. Which of the following approaches cannot be used to create a teaming configuration?
   a. Edit the configuration files in /etc/sysconfig/network-scripts manually
   b. The graphical NetworkManager applet
   c. nmtui
   d. nmcli
3. Which configuration file contains the IP configuration that is used by a team device?
   a. ifcfg-team
   b. ifcfg-team-slave
   c. ifcfg-device-interface
   d. ifcfg-device
4. Different configuration files are used in setting up a teaming configuration. Which of the following is not a part of them?
   a. ifcfg-team
   b. ifcfg-team-slave
   c. ifcfg-device-interface
   d. ifcfg-device
5. Which of the following statements about the network team interface is *not* true?
   a. Starting a team interface automatically starts all port interfaces.
   b. Starting a port interface will start the team interface.
   c. A team interface without any associated ports can start static IP connections.
   d. A team interface without any associated ports cannot start DHCP connections.

6. What would be the IPv6 link local address for an interface that has the MAC address 02:0c:29:e4:71:4a?
   a. 20c:29ff:fee4:714a
   b. fe80::20c:29ff:fee4:714a
   c. 2000::20c:29ff:fee4:714a
   d. 2000:fffe:20c:29e4:714a

7. Which command enables you to ping all IPv6 nodes that are on the local network that is connected through the eth0 interface?
   a. **ping6 fe80::1%eth0**
   b. **ping6 fe80::1 eth0**
   c. **ping6 ff02::1%eth0**
   d. **ping6 ff02::1 eth0**

8. Which items are wrong in the following command (choose multiple)?

   nmcli con add con-name eno16777736 type ethernet ifname eno16777736 ipv6 2002:db:0:1::100/64 gw6 2002:db:0:1::1 ipv4 192.168.4.122/24 gw4 192.168.4.1?

   a. **gw6** should be **gwv6.**
   b. **gw4** should be **gwv4.**
   c. **ipv6** should be **ip6.**
   d. **ipv4** should be **ip4.**

9. After setting an IPv6 address, which command enables you to make sure that the interface does not try to get an address using DHCP anymore?
   a. **nmcli con mod ifname method manual**
   b. **nmcli mod ifname manual**
   c. **nmcli con ifname method manual**
   d. **nmcli con mod ifname ipv6.method manual**

10. How do you enable packet forwarding on interfaces on an RHEL 7 host?
    a. There need to be static entries for all routes that packets have to be forwarded to.
    b. Use **echo 1 > /proc/sys/net/ipv4/ip_forward** to enable kernel-level IP forwarding.
    c. Make sure that the radvd service is started to route packets.
    d. Use **echo 1 > /proc/sys/net/routing.**

Foundation Topics

Configuring Aggregated Network Interfaces

On network servers, it is an important requirement to ensure that the network interface is available at all times. On Red Hat Enterprise Linux 7, you can create aggregated network interfaces. Use network teaming or network bonding to accomplish this goal.

In earlier versions of RHEL, network bonding was the default method for creating aggregated network interfaces. In RHEL 7, network teaming has been added as a solution. The main difference between these two is that network bonding happened completely in user space, whereas in network teaming, the teamd daemon is added to allow interaction in user space as well. Even if both methods are still valid, network teaming is the preferred method.

TIP On the exam, you can decide for yourself which method you want to use. The RHCE objectives clearly indicate that you have to be able to create aggregated network interfaces using teaming or bonding. So, you can select the method that suits you best. If you are comfortable with the network bonding method, use this method. If you have never created aggregated network interfaces before, you had better select the network teaming approach because this is going to be the more significant method in the future.

Using Bonding

To create a bonded network interface, you can use either the nmtui or the nmcli utilities. This section describes how to use the nmcli utility, which is relatively easy because there is a good man page that describes in a clear way how to set up a bonded network interface. Make sure that if you use this method on the exam, you are very familiar with **man 5 nmcli-examples**. Example 6 shows everything you have to do to set up a bonded network interface (see Listing 30.1).

Listing 30.1 man nmcli-examples Shows Exactly What You Have to Do to Set Up a Bonded Interface

```
Example 6. Adding a bonding master and two slave connection profiles

           $ nmcli con add type bond ifname mybond0 mode active-backup
           $ nmcli con add type bond-slave ifname eth1 master mybond0
           $ nmcli con add type bond-slave ifname eth2 master mybond0

       This example demonstrates adding a bond master connection and
two slaves. The first command adds a master bond connection, naming
       the bonding interface mybond0 and using active-backup mode. The
next two commands add slaves connections, both enslaved to mybond0.
       The first slave will be bound to eth1 interface, the second to
eth2.
```

Let's take a detailed look at what the example in the man page explains. To start, the command **nmcli con add type bond ifname mybond0 mode active-backup** is used. In this command, a connection is added, and the type of this connection is set as **bond**. The interface that will be created for this connection will be known as **mybond0**, and the mode is set to **active-backup**. Because no name is assigned to the connection, nmcli will set that name automatically, which you can verify using **nmcli con show**. The default name is bond-mybond0.

When setting up a bonded interface, you have seven different modes available. Table 30.2 gives an overview of these modes, but you are fine in general using the active-backup mode, which is one of the more common modes for creating bonded interfaces.

Table 30.2 Bonding Modes Overview

Mode	Explanation
balance-rr (0)	This mode transmits packets in sequential order between slaves. This mode provides load balancing and fault tolerance.
active-backup (1)	One slave is active and other slave only becomes active if this slave fails. The MAC address of the bond is available on one interface only. This method provides fault tolerance, not load balancing.
balance-xor (2)	A mode that provides load balancing and fault tolerance by using all slaves, and using the same slave for the same destination address.
broadcast (3)	Everything is transmitted on all slave devices. Provides fault tolerance, not load balancing.

Mode	Explanation
802.3ad (4)	In this method, aggregation groups are created that share the same speed and duplex settings. 802.3ad support on the switches is required, as is additional configuration on the switch.
balance-tlb (5)	Adaptive transmit load balancing. Outgoing traffic is distributed between slaves according to the current load, and incoming traffic is received by the current slave. This mode is not used often.
balance-alb (6)	Like method 5, but adds receive load balancing for IPv4 traffic. This mode is not used often.

After setting up the bonded connection, you need to add physical interfaces to it. To do this, you need the following command on each of the physical interfaces that you want to assign to the bond: **nmcli con add type bond-slave ifname eth1 master mybond0**. (Make sure to replace the uncommon device name eth1 with the name of the device as it is used on your hardware.) This creates a new connection on top of the physical device that you want to use and assigns it to the previously created bond master mybond0.

After you create the bond in this way, the associated configuration files are created. After creating the bonded interface using these commands, you can show its current status by using **nmcli dev show mybond0**. The result of this command is shown in Listing 30.2.

Listing 30.2 Verifying the Status of the Bond Device

```
[root@server1 ~]# nmcli dev show mybond0
GENERAL.DEVICE:                                   mybond0
GENERAL.TYPE:                                     bond
GENERAL.HWADDR:                                   DE:8A:A4:7E:DC:05
GENERAL.MTU:                                      1500
GENERAL.STATE:                                    70 (connecting (getting IP
configuration))
GENERAL.CONNECTION:                               bond-mybond0
GENERAL.CON-PATH:                                 /org/freedesktop/
NetworkManager/ActiveConnection/2
```

At this point, you need to create the IP address configuration that you want to use on the bonded device. To do this, use **nmcli con mod bond-mybond0 ipv4.addresses 192.168.4.210/24**. Then, use **nmcli con up bond-mybond0** to bring the connection up, and you'll have a working bonding interface.

The result of your work so far will be saved to the /etc/sysconfig/network-scripts directory, where you should now see three different configuration files:

- ifcfg-bond-mybond0
- ifcfg-bond-slave-eno16777736
- ifcfg-bond-slave-eno33554992

If you still see a configuration file that refers to the old connection that was used on the physical network card (such as ifcfg-eno16777736), you can safely remove that. In Listing 30.3, you can see what the contents of the bond configuration file looks like, and Listing 30.4 shows the contents of one of the bond slave interface files.

Listing 30.3 Verifying the Contents of the bond0 Configuration File

```
[root@server1 network-scripts]# cat ifcfg-bond-mybond0
DEVICE=mybond0
TYPE=Bond
BONDING_MASTER=yes
BOOTPROTO=none
DEFROUTE=yes
IPV4_FAILURE_FATAL=no
IPV6INIT=yes
IPV6_AUTOCONF=yes
IPV6_DEFROUTE=yes
IPV6_FAILURE_FATAL=no
NAME=bond-mybond0
UUID=98e61443-cd2a-4eb6-9a9f-c652d95c22fa
ONBOOT=yes
BONDING_OPTS=mode=active-backup
IPADDR=192.168.4.210
PREFIX=24
IPV6_PEERDNS=yes
IPV6_PEERROUTES=yes
```

Listing 30.4 Verifying the Contents of the bond-slave Configuration File

```
[root@server1 network-scripts]# cat ifcfg-bond-slave-eno16777736
TYPE=Ethernet
NAME=bond-slave-eno16777736
UUID=7621cc16-86eb-408a-afbf-3ca4d56c1752
DEVICE=eno16777736
ONBOOT=yes
MASTER=mybond0
SLAVE=yes
```

On an operational bond, you can verify the current status through the /proc/net/bonding interface, where a configuration file will be created for each bonding connection that has been added to the configuration. Through this file, you can easily see the current status of the interface, including MAC addresses that are used and the current status of interfaces. Listing 30.5 shows what the contents of this file could look like.

Listing 30.5 Monitoring the Current State of a Bond Connection Through /proc

```
[root@server1 ~]# cat /proc/net/bonding/mybond0
Ethernet Channel Bonding Driver: v3.7.1 (April 27, 2011)

Bonding Mode: fault-tolerance (active-backup)
Primary Slave: None
Currently Active Slave: eno33554992
MII Status: up
MII Polling Interval (ms): 100
Up Delay (ms): 0
Down Delay (ms): 0

Slave Interface: eno33554992
MII Status: up
Speed: 1000 Mbps
Duplex: full
Link Failure Count: 0
Permanent HW addr: 00:0c:29:46:f3:fc
Slave queue ID: 0
```

Using Teaming

Network teaming is another method to combine different physical network devices into one logical interface to allow for failover or higher throughput. As mentioned before, you can use either of them to accomplish the same goal of using an aggregated network interface.

Key Topic

On earlier versions of Red Hat Enterprise Linux, network bonding was used to accomplish the same goals. In the previous section, you learned how to configure network bonding. Network teaming is new in Red Hat Enterprise Linux 7. The solution consists of a small kernel driver and a daemon that is available in userspace: teamd. The kernel takes care of handling network packets, while the teamd driver handles logic and interface processing. To determine how exactly this is happening, different runners are used. Runners in teaming are equivalent to the bonding modes as listed in Table 30.1. They are used to define the logic of traffic handling between the interfaces that are involved in the configuration. Table 30.2 gives a summary of available runners.

Table 30.2 Teaming Runners Overview

Key Topic

Runner	Working
broadcast	All packets are transmitted on all ports.
roundrobin	Packets are transmitted in a round-robin fashion from each port in the team.
activebackup	A failover runner that watches for link changes and selects an active interface.
loadbalance	A runner that uses a hash function to reach optimal load balancing when selecting network interfaces for packet transmission.
lacp	A runner that is doing load balancing based on the Lightweight Access Control Protocol (LACP), which is also known as 802.3ad. Make sure that it is supported on your switches before selecting this runner. If this runner is used, you'll probably have to do some additional configuration on your switches as well.

Configuring Network Teams

A team interface can be created with either the **nmcli** or the **nmtui** utilities. For the exam it does not matter at all which utility you are using, only the result counts. For that reason you might consider using the easiest tool for you!

Creating a team interface involves a couple of steps:

1. Create the team interface.
2. Add IP address configuration.
3. Assign the port interfaces.
4. Bring the team and port interfaces up.

As mentioned, on the exam it does not matter which utility you are using to configure the team interface. Because it provides more insight doing it through the nmcli utility, you learn in this section how to configure a team interface using that utility. Based on your understanding of the working of the nmcli utility, you'll find configuring a team interface through the nmtui utility easy.

The first step in the procedure consists of creating the team interface. The following command gives an example on how to do this:

```
nmcli con add type team con-name team0 config '{ "runner":  {"name":
"loadbalance"}}'
```

This command looks complicated, and it is, because several tasks are performed from one single command:

- The **nmcli con add** command is used to add an interface of the type **team**.
- The **con-name** part of the command is used to set the name of the connection to **team0**.
- The **config** part of the command is used to specify additional configuration. There are many quotes used in this part of the command, but that is just because it is a very organized command:
  - The entire **config** argument is between single quotes.
  - Every element of the configuration is between curly braces and double quotes.
  - Every element that is assigned to a configuration element is between curly braces and double quotes as well.

After creating the team connection, use **nmcli con show** to show the current configuration.

TIP Are you lost already? I was the first time I got this far. If on the exam you want to configure a team interface using the **nmcli** command, take a look at **man 5 nmcli-examples**. You'll find some nice examples in that man page, also on how to create a team interface.

Now that the connection has been created, you can assign IP address information to the connection. The following two commands add an IPv4 address to the interface:

```
nmcli con mod team0 ipv4.addresses 192.168.4.220/24
```

Notice that with this command you have assigned an IPv4 address configuration, which is not functional yet. At this moment, it does not make much sense bringing it up, because no network devices are assigned to the team interface yet. To do this, use the **nmcli con add type team-slave ifname <DEVICE> master <TEAM>** command. In this command, you need to replace the <DEVICE> part with the name of the network device you want to add, and the <TEAM> part with the name of the team interface you have just created. So, the following command adds two network devices to the team interface:

```
nmcli con add type team-slave ifname eno16777736 master team0
nmcli con add type team-slave ifname eno33554960 master team0
```

After doing this, you can put the team0 interface up:

```
nmcli con up team0
```

Listing 30.6 shows a summary of all commands that have been issued so far.

Listing 30.6 Creating a Team Interface Command Overview

```
nmcli con add type team con-name team0 config '{ "runner": {"name":
"loadbalance"}}'
nmcli con show
nmci con mod team0 ipv4.addresses 192.168.4.220/24
ip a
nmcli con add type team-slave ifname eno16777736 master team0
nmcli con add type team-slave ifname eno33554960 master team0
nmcli con up team0
ip a
```

To monitor the availability of the team0 interface, you can use the **nmcli con show** command. Alternatively, you can query the **teamd** user space process, using the **teamdctl** command. Notice that this command uses the name of the team device, not the team interface. Use **ip addr show** to get an overview of currently used device names. Listing 30.7 shows the output of this command.

Listing 30.7 Monitoring the Team Interface Configuration with teamdctl

```
[root@localhost ~]# teamdctl team0 state
setup:
  runner: loadbalance
ports:
  eno33554960
    link watches:
      link summary: up
      instance[link_watch_0]:
        name: ethtool
        link: up
  eno16777736
    link watches:
      link summary: up
      instance[link_watch_0]:
        name: ethtool
        link: up
```

Looking Behind the Teaming Configuration

The teaming configuration is stored in three different levels of files. On top of the hierarchy is the team interface file shown in Listing 30.8.

> **NOTE** You can modify the contents of the configuration files in /etc/sysconfig/network-scripts directly. After modifying, use **nmcli con reload** so that NetworkManager reads the configuration changes.

Listing 30.8 Contents of the Team Interface File

```
[root@localhost network-scripts]# cat ifcfg-team0
DEVICE=nm-team
TEAM_CONFIG="{ \"runner\": {\"name\": \"loadbalance\"}}"
DEVICETYPE=Team
BOOTPROTO=dhcp
DEFROUTE=yes
IPV4_FAILURE_FATAL=no
IPV6INIT=yes
IPV6_AUTOCONF=yes
IPV6_DEFROUTE=yes
IPV6_FAILURE_FATAL=no
NAME=team0
UUID=679b70f9-1445-4e25-9f66-93b358974627
ONBOOT=yes
IPADDR0=192.168.4.220
PREFIX0=24
PEERDNS=yes
PEERROUTES=yes
IPV6_PEERDNS=yes
IPV6_PEERROUTES=yes
```

As you can see, the content of this file is very similar to the content of a regular network configuration file, with the exception that it includes a TEAM_CONFIG section. The team interface itself does not include any information about the individual interfaces that are assigned to it.

The second level of configuration file is for the teaming slave. Listing 30.9 shows what the typical content of this file looks like.

Listing 30.9 Teaming Slave Configuration

```
[root@localhost network-scripts]# cat ifcfg-team-slave-eno16777736
BOOTPROTO=none
DEFROUTE=yes
PEERDNS=yes
PEERROUTES=yes
IPV4_FAILURE_FATAL=no
IPV6INIT=yes
IPV6_AUTOCONF=yes
```

```
IPV6_DEFROUTE=yes
IPV6_PEERDNS=yes
IPV6_PEERROUTES=yes
IPV6_FAILURE_FATAL=no
NAME=team-slave-eno16777736
UUID=6ffc4eff-adde-474b-8ddc-1e6de1c5b3b5
DEVICE=eno16777736
ONBOOT=yes
TEAM_MASTER=679b70f9-1445-4e25-9f66-93b358974627
DEVICETYPE=TeamPort
```

As you can see, there are two specific lines for the teaming configuration. The TEAM_MASTER line includes the UUID of the team master, and the DEVICETYPE line identifies the device type as a team device. In this file, the DEVICE line identifies the device this interface is connected to.

The third tier consists of the device file (see Listing 30.10). This is just the regular contents of a device file and from nothing can be seen that this device is associated to a team interface. The only difference with regular device file contents is that the **ONBOOT** parameter is set to **no**. That is because the device is not managed as an individual device, but through the team driver.

Listing 30.10 Team Member Device Configuration

```
[root@localhost network-scripts]# cat ifcfg-eno16777736
HWADDR=00:0C:29:88:D5:53
TYPE=Ethernet
BOOTPROTO=dhcp
DEFROUTE=yes
PEERDNS=yes
PEERROUTES=yes
IPV4_FAILURE_FATAL=no
IPV6INIT=yes
IPV6_AUTOCONF=yes
IPV6_DEFROUTE=yes
IPV6_PEERDNS=yes
IPV6_PEERROUTES=yes
IPV6_FAILURE_FATAL=no
NAME=eno16777736
UUID=e94fe839-6fdf-4fc5-bf33-3c2a1cfbb90e
ONBOOT=no
```

Table 30.3 provides an overview of the significant configuration parameters for the team devices and interfaces. In Exercise 30.1, you learn how to set up an aggregated network interface on your server using teaming.

Table 30.3 Teaming Configuration Files Parameter Overview

Key Topic

Device File	Parameter	Use
ifcfg-team	**TEAM_CONFIG**	Used to identify the significant parameters to use such as the runner type.
ifcfg-team	**DEVICETYPE**	Team.
ifcfg-team	**IPADDR0**	IP address configuration is set on the team interface.
ifcfg-team	**UUID**	Contains the UUID that is used by the team slaves to identify which team masters they belong to.
ifcfg-team-slave	**BOOTPROTO**	Set to none and do not include an IPv4 configuration.
ifcfg-team-slave	**TEAM_MASTER**	Contains the UUID of the team interface.
ifcfg-team-slave	**DEVICE**	Identifies the device this interface connects to.
ifcfg-devicename	**NAME**	Sets the name of this specific device.

Exercise 30.1 Configuring Network Teaming

In this exercise, you create a teaming interface on server1. In the previous section, you learned in detail how to set up a team device using nmcli. To show the alternative approach as well, you learn in this exercise how to set up the team device using the nmtui utility. To perform this exercise, you need a virtual machine that has been configured with two network devices.

1. Open a root terminal and type **ip link show**. Note the names of the devices you'll find; you need them later. In this exercise I use the device names eno16777736 and eno33554960 as examples. Change according to your specific configuration.
2. Type **nmtui** to start the nmtui utility.
3. Select Edit a connection. You'll now see the connections for all devices in your setup.
4. Highlight the first Ethernet interface that is listed and select Edit.
5. Behind IPv4 Configuration, make sure that <Disabled> is selected. Also deselect the Automatically Connect option and apply the configuration by selecting OK.

6. Repeat this procedure for the other interface as well.
7. Restart the nmtui utility and select Edit a Connection. Then select Add to add a new connection. From the drop-down list, select the Team connection type.
8. In the Edit Connection window, set the device name to team0. Then, select Add to add a slave (see Figure 30.1).

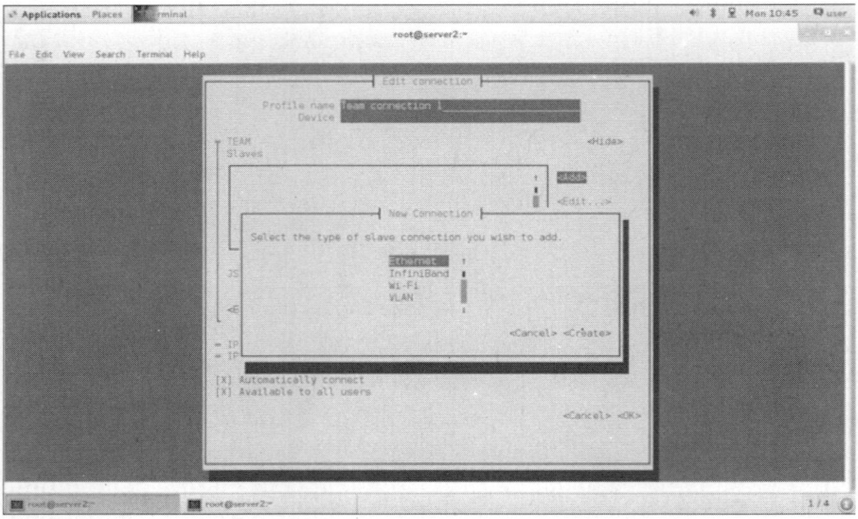

Figure 30.1 Adding a new team slave.

9. In the New Connection window, select Ethernet to add an Ethernet connection.
10. In the Device field, enter the name of the network connection (eno16777736).
11. Repeat this procedure to add the other interface as well.
12. Quit the nmtui utility and start it again. From the menu, select Activate a Connection.
13. Highlight the team connection you have just created. Select Deactivate. Highlight it again and now select Activate. (On occasion, this might hang the utility. If that happens, just reboot.)
14. Type **teamdctl team0 state view** to verify the current state of your new team connection.
15. Start nmtui again, and select Edit a Connection. Select the team connection you just created and scroll down to the IPv4 configuration option. Set this option to Manual and enter the IP address **192.168.4.220/24**. Save the configuration and reboot your virtual machine. You should now be able to make a network connection on the specified IP address.

In Exercise 30.1, you learned how to create a teamed network connection. As you have seen, many steps are involved in doing so. The procedure may seem confusing, but it comes down to five essential steps that should be applied in that specific order:

Key Topic

- Note the local device names.
- Set local interfaces to *not* start automatically.
- Set IP configuration to be disabled on local interfaces and enable it on the team connection.
- Create the team device, specify a name.
- Add device types based on their names.

Troubleshooting Network Teaming

As you have previously read, the team interface is composed of multiple network ports. When troubleshooting network team interfaces, you must keep the following particularities in mind:

- The team interface is started when one of its port interfaces is started, but this does not start all other port interfaces as well.
- Starting a team interface does not automatically start all port interfaces.
- Stopping a team interface does stop all involved port interfaces.
- Static IP connections can be started on a team interface that does not have any ports currently active.
- DHCP connections can only be started when ports are available.

A useful utility to debug network teaming is teamnl. For instance, type **teamnl team0 ports** to see the ports in the team device and their current state. Another useful **teamnl** command is **teamnl team0 options**, which dumps the options that are currently set for the teaming interface. Listing 30.11 shows what the result of this command looks like.

Listing 30.11 Dumping Current Teaming Options

```
[root@localhost ~]# teamnl team0 options
     queue_id (port:eno33554960) 0
 priority (port:eno33554960) 0
 user_linkup_enabled (port:eno33554960) false
 user_linkup (port:eno33554960) true
 enabled (port:eno33554960) true
```

```
queue_id (port:eno16777736) 0
priority (port:eno16777736) 0
user_linkup_enabled (port:eno16777736) false
user_linkup (port:eno16777736) true
enabled (port:eno16777736) true
mcast_rejoin_interval 0
mcast_rejoin_count 0
notify_peers_interval 0
notify_peers_count 0
mode roundrobin
```

You can also dump the configuration of devices in a team interface. To do so, use **teamdctl team0 config dump**. This dumps the configuration in the JSON format that is used by the teaming driver. When the configuration is getting more complex, you can redirect the output of this command to a file so that is can be easily applied to other configurations. Listing 30.12 shows the output of the **teamdctl team0 config dump** command.

Listing 30.12 Dumping Current Configuration in the JSON Format

```
[root@localhost ~]# teamdctl team0 config dump
{
    "device": "team0",
    "ports": {
        "eno16777736": {
            "link_watch": {
                "name": "ethtool"
            }
        },
        "eno33554960": {
            "link_watch": {
                "name": "ethtool"
            }
        }
    },
    "runner": {
        "name": "roundrobin"
    }
}
```

Configuring IPv6 Addresses

Experts have been telling the world for many years that IPv4 addresses are almost all handed out and that administrators need to start thinking about alternatives. It appears that with advanced networking solutions such as Network Address Translation (NAT) companies can still use their IT infrastructure based on IPv4 for a long time yet to come. Nevertheless, it is a fact that there is a shortage of IPv4 addresses, and every administrator should have at least some knowledge about the working of IPv6.

Understanding IPv6 Addresses

In IPv4 addresses, 32 bits were used for configuring network addresses. That allows a theoretical maximum of about 4 billion unique network addresses. As the number of available IPv4 addresses currently is exhausted, when IPv6 was designed a total of 128 bits was reserved for creating IPv6 addresses.

To make it easier to manage IPv6 addresses, the standard notation of an IPv6 address is as a hexadecimal number. The hexadecimal numbering plan is based on 16 numbers in a range from 0 to 9, followed by a to f. Because hexadecimal numbers are not easy to read, the IPv6 address is noted as 8 groups of 16 bits (which equals 4 hexadecimal numbers, such as in the following example):

```
fe80:0000:0000:0010:29ff:fee4:714a:0001
```

To make it a bit easier to read, leading 0s do not have to be written, and long strings of all 0s can be summarized as ::. Therefore, the previous example address can be rewritten as follows:

```
fe80::10:29ff:fee4:714a:1
```

As the available range of IPv6 addresses is so large, IPv6 uses a standard subnet mask of /64. Therefore, for each subnet, 64 bits are available for addressing hosts, which means that a subnet can hold as many hosts as necessary. If an organization needs to assign a specific subnet, it should request a shorter network prefix, like /48 instead of /64, which would leave 16 bits for subnet allocation.

In IPv6, a few specific IP addresses and address ranges are reserved. Table 30.4 provides an overview.

Key Topic

Table 30.4 Common IPv6 Addresses and Networks

Address	Purpose	Description
::1/128	localhost	The IPv6 equivalent for 127.0.0.1/8.
::	All addresses	The IPv6 equivalent to IPv4 0.0.0.0.
::/0	The default router	Used in routing tables to indicate the default gateway.
2000::/3	Global unicast address	The pool of addresses that are currently allocated.
fc00::/7	Unique local addresses	IPv6 addresses that are available for use in private networks and cannot be routed on the global IPv6 network (comparable to the 192.168.0.0/16 and so on addresses in IPv4).
fe80::/64	Link-local addresses	The link-local address, an IP address that is automatically configured on each IPv6 interface but does not allow for globally unique addressing.
ff00::/8	Multicast	The IPv6 multicast address, which is particularly important because IPv6 does not use broadcast addresses.
2001:db8/32	Addresses reserved for use in documentation	In IPv6 address examples, 2001:db8 addresses should be used. These will normally not be assigned directly to interfaces.

A specific IPv6 address is the link-local address. This is an unroutable address what is assigned to IPv6 interfaces automatically. The link-local address is created automatically based on the network prefix fe80::/64 followed by the MAC address on the network card, where fffe is inserted in the middle of the MAC address part. So, if the MAC address were 02:0c:29:04:71:4a, the link-local address would be fe80::20x:29ff:fee4:714a/64.

If you need IPv6 addresses for internal use only, and want to make sure that these addresses cannot be reached (either by accident or on purpose) by anyone on an external network, consider using unique local addresses. Like the private addresses in IPv4, these addresses can be used to connect to nodes on the Internet only if Network Address Translation (NAT) is used.

In IPv6, there is no broadcast anymore. For that reason, multicast plays a much larger role in IPv6 than it did in IPv4. An important multicast address is ff02::1, which is the all-nodes link-local address. If you would ping this address, traffic is sent to all nodes on that specific link. To avoid confusion, you need to add the interface you want to use while using this address, so you use **ping6 ff02::1%eth0** to ping all nodes on the local network connected to the eth0 interface.

Managing IPv6 Address Configurations

IPv6 addresses can be assigned manually or through DHCP. When you use DHCP, an IPv6 host uses the multicast address ff02::1:2 to port 547/UDP, which belongs to the all-dhcp-servers link-local multicast group. The DHCPv6 server sends an answer to port 546 on the client to provide it with an IPv6 address.

As an alternative to using DHCP, IPv6 also supports stateless address autoconfiguration (SLAAC). Using SLAAC, the host brings up its interface with a link-local fe80::/64 address. Then it sends a router solicitation request to ff02::2, which is the all-routers link-local multicast group. An IPv6 router on that link then replies on the link-local address with a network prefix. The host then appends its MAC address with the fffe padding to create a unique IPv6 address.

A third option to provide IPv6 addresses is through manual configuration. When using this approach, the following node parts cannot be used:

- The all-0s identifier 0000:0000:0000:0000, which is used as the subnet router anycast address by all routers on the link
- The identifiers fdff:ffff:ffff:ff80 through fdff:ffff:ffff:ffff

To assign IPv6 addresses, the nmtui and the nmcli utilities can be used. Most commands work just like how IPv4 is configured. Let's take a look at some nmcli examples:

Key Topic

- **nmcli con add con-name eno16777736 type ethernet ifname eno16777736 ip6 2001:db8:0:1::100/64 gw6 2001:db8:0:1::1 ip4 192.168.4.122/24 gw4 192.168.4.1** This command adds IPv4 and IPv6 address configuration to the interface at the same time.
- **nmcli con show eno1 | grep ipv6** This command shows IP configuration on eno16777736, filtering out only the IPv6-related information (see Listing 30.13).

Listing 30.13 Showing IPv6 Information for an Interface

```
[sander@lab ~]$ nmcli con show eno1 | grep ipv6
ipv6.method:                                auto
ipv6.dns:
```

```
ipv6.dns-search:
ipv6.addresses:
ipv6.routes:
ipv6.ignore-auto-routes:                no
ipv6.ignore-auto-dns:                   no
ipv6.never-default:                     no
ipv6.may-fail:                          yes
ipv6.ip6-privacy:                       -1 (unknown)
ipv6.dhcp-hostname:                     --
```

- **nmcli con mod eno16777736 ipv6.address "2001:db8:0:1::1"** This command modifies the statically assigned IPv6 address.
- **nmcli con mod eno16777736 +ipv6.dns 2001:4860:4860::8888** This command adds the Google DNS server to the current list of DNS servers. Notice the use of the +, which adds a value to the current configuration.

After setting IP address configuration, you can verify it using common tools like **ip addr show** and **ip route show**. These show the configuration for IPv4 and IPv6. To monitor IPv6 configuration only, you can use the **-6** argument to the **ip** command. So, **ip -6 addr show** shows IPv6 addresses only, and **ip -6 router show** shows IPv6 routing configuration only.

Troubleshooting IPv6

To troubleshoot IPv6, you can use a few commands. To start, there is the **ping6** command, which can be used to ping IPv6 addresses. Use for instance **ping6 2001:db8:0:1::1** to ping a specific address, or **ping6 ff02::%eth0** to ping all multicast addresses on the link connected to eth0.

To analyze routing information in an IPv6 network, use the **tracepath6** command. This command shows all hops between the current node and the destination node. For information about ports and services that are in use, you can use either the **ss** or the **netstat** command, which by default show IPv6-related information.

In Exercise 30.2, you learn how to work with IPv6 on RHEL 7.

Exercise 30.2 Working with IPv6 Addresses

In this exercise, you work with IPv6 addresses. To do this exercise, use the server1 and server2 machines. It is recommended not to use the servers with the teaming interface that you have used in the previous exercise because this makes configuration a bit more difficult.

1. On server1, open a root shell and type the command **nmcli con show**. Note the name of the network connection that is used on the server. In this exercise, I'll assume the name eno16777736; replace according to your configuration.
2. Type **ip addr show eno16777736** and notice the current IPv6 configuration.
3. Type **nmcli con show eno16777736 | grep -i ipv6**. This shows the current configuration for your interface.
4. Assign the ipv6 address fddb:fe2a:badb:abe::1 to the interface using **nmcli con mod eno16777736 ipv6.addresses 'fddb:fe2a:badb:abe::1/64'**.
5. Set the IP configuration to a static IP address using **nmcli con mod eno16777736 ipv6.method manual**.
6. Restart the interface, using **nmcli con down eno16777736; nmcli con up eno16777736**.
7. Verify the current IPv6 configuration, using **ip addr show dev eno16777736**.
8. Repeat the procedure on server2 to assign the IP address fddb:fe2a:badb:abe::2/64.
9. From server2, type **ping6 fddb:fe2a:badb:abe::1** to verify that server1 can be reached based on its IPv6 address.
10. Type **ip -6 route** to show the IPv6 routing table.
11. Ping the link-local addresses that can be reached through interface eno16777736, using **ping6 ff02::1%eno16777736**.

Routing IP Traffic

On an RHEL 7 system that has multiple network interfaces, you'll occasionally need to configure routing. To do this, you first have to switch on routing. Then, custom routes can be created to specify where packets need to be sent to.

Enabling Routing

Every RHEL 7 system can be configured as a router. The only requirement is that multiple network devices are available to route network traffic through. To configure a server as a router, you first have to set the value in the /proc/sys/net/ipv4/ip_forward to 1. This can be done manually using **echo 1 > /proc/sys/net/ipv4/ip_forward**. To make the configuration persistent, you need to create a file in the /etc/sysctl.d directory. You are free to select a name for the file you want to create, but the filename must have .conf in the end of it. Also, make sure it contains the following contents:

```
net.ipv4.ip_forward = 1
```

When you restart your server, this command makes the setting persistent.

Configuring Custom Routes

On most servers, the only route that is set is the default gateway. This specifies the IP address of the router that takes care of all traffic that needs forwarding to external networks. The **ip route show** command shows to which IP address the default route is currently set (see Listing 30.14).

Listing 30.14 Monitoring the Current Default Route Setting

```
[root@server2 sysctl.d]# ip route show
default via 192.168.4.2 dev eno16777736  proto static  metric 1024
10.0.0.0/24 via 192.168.4.1 dev eno16777736  proto static  metric 10
192.168.4.0/24 dev eno16777736  proto kernel  scope link  src
192.168.4.220
```

Apart from the default route, specific routes can be required as well. This is needed in particular for networks that cannot be reached through the default route. To set a custom route, a few parameters need to be specified:

- The network IP address.
- The netmask that should be used.
- The IP address of the router that is addressed to reach the specific network.
- The metric, which indicates the relative price of a route. The lower the metric, the more likely that a specific route is used if multiple paths exist to the same destination.

The easiest way to configure custom routes is to use the graphical NetworkManager utility or the nmtui text-driven utility. Using this utility, you can specify custom routes by entering the network address, the associated netmask, the gateway that needs to be addressed, and the metric associated with that route.

The results are written to a file with the name /etc/sysconfig/network-scripts/route-interface. Listing 30.15 shows sample contents of this file.

Listing 30.15 Sample Contents of the Route Configuration File

```
[root@server2 network-scripts]# cat route-eno16777736
ADDRESS0=10.0.0.0
NETMASK0=255.255.255.0
GATEWAY0=192.168.4.1
METRIC0=10
```

Summary

In this chapter, you learned how to configure advanced networking features. In the first part of this chapter, you learned how to enable network link aggregation. You learned how to do this using teaming and bonding. You learned that teaming is the modern alternative to using the bond driver in previous versions of RHEL, which allows network devices to be bundled in one interface to provide for higher redundancy, throughput, or both. The second part of this chapter showed how to configure IPv6 addresses, and in the last part of this chapter, you learned how to configure custom routes on RHEL 7.

Exam Preparation Tasks

Review All Key Topics

Review the most important topics in the chapter, noted with the Key Topic icon in the outer margin of the page. Table 30.5 lists a reference of these key topics and the page numbers on which each is found.

Table 30.5 Key Topics for Chapter 30

Key Topic Element	Description	Page
Paragraph	Definition of network teaming	663
Table 30.2	Teaming runners overview	663
Table 30.3	Teaming configuration files parameter overview	669
List	How to create a teamed network connection	671
Table 30.4	Common IPv6 addresses overview	674
List	IPv6 configuration examples	674

Complete Tables and Lists from Memory

Print a copy of Appendix B, "Memory Tables" (found on the disc), or at least the section for this chapter, and complete the tables and lists from memory. Appendix C, "Memory Tables Answer Key," also on the disc, includes completed tables and lists to check your work.

Define Key Terms

Define the following key terms from this chapter and check your answers in the glossary:

teaming, bonding, runners, IPv6, hexadecimal, default route, static route, dynamic route

Review Questions

1. Which runner do you use if you want to use the 802.3ad link aggregation protocol on a teamed link?
2. Which command enables you to see current states in a teamed network interface?
3. Which man page would you consult to get an overview of nmcli examples that include examples on how to create a teamed interface?
4. Which parameter is used in the team port configuration file to indicate which team this interface is a part of?
5. Which command enables you to see the current state of ports in a team interface?
6. Which IP address is used by default for link local IP addresses?
7. Which command shows all nodes configured with an IPv6 address that are reachable through the network device eth0?
8. Which four elements are required in a routing configuration file?
9. Which file would you expect to contain the routing configuration for the eno1 interface?
10. How can you configure your server's kernel for packet forwarding?

End-of-Chapter Labs

To perform the exercises in this lab, you need two installations of RHEL 7 that are configured with two network interfaces each. The exercise assumes that these machines are using the names server1 and server2. Change the names according to your setup.

Lab 30.1

1. Create both servers with a team interface. The servers should not use a regular network interface anymore but just the two team interfaces for all of their communications. Use a runner protocol configuration that ensures that no additional configuration has to be used on the networking infrastructure.
2. Configure both interfaces with an IPv6 address and verify that both hosts can ping one another.
3. Configure both servers to enable package forwarding.

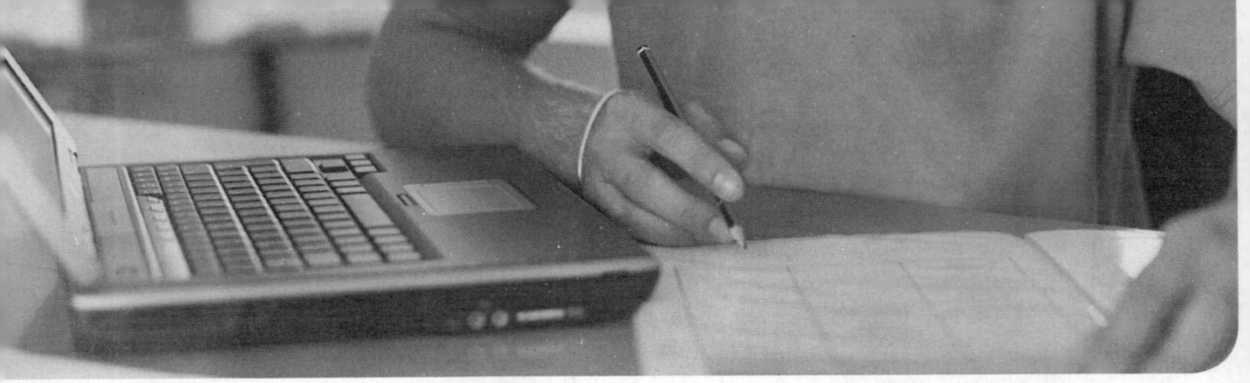

The following topics are covered in this chapter:

- Understanding Shell Scripting Core Elements
- Using Variables and Input
- Using Conditional Loops

The following RHCE exam objectives are covered in this chapter:

- Use shell scripting to automate system maintenance tasks

CHAPTER 31

An Introduction to Bash Shell Scripting

Shell scripting is a science all by itself. You do not learn about all the nuts and bolts related to this science in this chapter. Instead, you learn how to apply basic shell scripting elements, which allows you to write a simple shell script and analyze what is happening in a shell script.

"Do I Know This Already?" Quiz

The "Do I Know This Already?" quiz allows you to assess whether you should read this entire chapter thoroughly or jump to the "Exam Preparation Tasks" section. If you are in doubt about your answers to these questions or your own assessment of your knowledge of the topics, read the entire chapter. Table 31.1 lists the major headings in this chapter and their corresponding "Do I Know This Already?" quiz questions. You can find the answers in Appendix A, "Answers to the 'Do I Know This Already?' Quizzes and 'Review Questions.'"

Table 31.1 "Do I Know This Already?" Section-to-Question Mapping

Foundation Topics Section	Questions
Understanding Shell Scripting Core Elements	1–2
Using Variables and Input	3–5
Using Conditional Loops	6–10

1. Which line should every bash shell script start with?
   a. **/bin/bash**
   b. **#!/bin/bash**
   c. **!#/bin/bash**
   d. **!/bin/bash**

2. What is the purpose of the **exit 0** command that can be used at the end of a script?
   a. It informs the parent shell that the script could be executed without any problems.
   b. It makes sure the script can be stopped properly.
   c. It is required only if a for loop has been used to close the for loop structure.
   d. It is used to terminate a conditional structure in the script.

3. How do you stop a script to allow a user to provide input?
   a. **pause**
   b. **break**
   c. **read**
   d. **stop**

4. Which line stores the value of the first argument that was provided when starting a script in the variable NAME?
   a. **NAME = $1**
   b. **$1 = NAME**
   c. **NAME = $@**
   d. **NAME=$1**

5. What is the best way to distinguish between different arguments that have been passed into a shell script?
   a. **$?**
   b. **$#**
   c. **$***
   d. **$@**

6. What is used to close an **if** loop?
   a. **end**
   b. **exit**
   c. **stop**
   d. **fi**

7. What is missing in the following script at the position of the dots?

```
if [ -f $1 ]
then
        echo "$1 is a file"
..... [ -d $1 ]
then
        echo "$1 is a directory"
else
        echo "I do not know what \$1 is"
fi
```

   a. **else**
   b. **if**
   c. **elif**
   d. **or**

8. What is missing in the following script at the position of the dots?

```
for (( counter=100; counter>1; counter-- )); ......
                echo $counter
done
exit 0
```

   a. **in**
   b. **do**
   c. **run**
   d. **start**

9. Which command is used to send a message with the subject "error" to the user root if something didn't work out in a script?
   a. **mail error root**
   b. **mail -s error root**
   c. **mail -s error root .**
   d. **mail -s error root < .**

10. In a **case** statement, it is a good idea to include a line that applies to all other situations. Which of the following would do that?
   a. *)
   b. *
   c. else
   d. or

Foundation Topics

Understanding Shell Scripting Core Elements

Basically, a shell script is a list of commands that is sequentially executed, with some scripting logics in it that allows code to be executed under specific conditions only. To understand complex shell scripts, it is a good idea to start with some basic script. Listing 31.1 shows a very basic script.

Listing 31.1 Basic Script Example

```
#!/bin/bash
#
# This is a script that greets the world
# Usage: ./hello

clear
echo hello world

exit 0
```

This basic script contains a few elements that should be used in all scripts. To start, there is the *shebang*. This is the line #!/bin/bash. When a script is started from a parent shell environment, it opens a subshell. In this subshell, different commands are executed. These commands can be interpreted in any way, and to make it clear how they should be interpreted, the shebang is used. In this case, the shebang makes clear that the script is a bash shell script. Other shells can be specified as well. For instance, if your script contains Perl code, the shebang should be #!/usr/bin/perl. It is good practice to start a script with a shebang; if it is omitted, the script code will be executed by the shell that is used in the parent shell as well.

Right after the shebang, there is a part that explains what the script is about. It is a good idea in every script to include a few comment lines. In a short script, it is often obvious what the script is about. If the script is becoming longer, and as more people get involved in writing and maintaining the script, it will often become less clear what the writer of the script intended to do. To avoid that, make sure that you include comment lines, starting with a #. Do not only put them in the beginning of the script but also at the start of every subsection of the script. It will surely help if you read your script a few months later! You can also use comments within lines.

No matter on which position it is used, everything from the # until the end of the line is comment.

Then, there is the body of the script. In the example script from Listing 31.1, it is just a simple script containing a few commands that are sequentially executed. You learn that the body may grow bigger as the script develops.

At the end of the script I have included the statement **exit 0**. An **exit** statement tells the parent shell whether the script was successful. The exit status of the last command in the script is the exit status of the script itself, unless the **exit 0** command is used at the end of the script. But it is good to know that you can work with **exit** to inform the parent shell how it all went. To request the exit status of the last command, from the parent shell, the command **echo $?** can be used.

After creating a script, make sure that it can be executed. The most common way to do this is by applying the execute bit to it. So, if the name of the script is hello, use **chmod +x hello** to make it executable. The script can also be executed as an argument of the **bash** command, for instance. Use **bash hello** to run the hello script. If started as an argument of the bash command, the script does not need to be executable.

You can basically store the script anywhere you like, but if you are going to store it in a location that is not included in the $PATH, you need to execute it with a ./ in front of the script name. So just typing **hello** is not going to be enough to run your script; type **./hello** to run it. Or put it in a standard directory that is included in the $PATH variable, like /usr/local/bin. In Exercise 31.1 you apply these skills and write a simple shell script.

Exercise 31.1 Writing a Simple Shell Script

In this exercise, you write a simple shell script and apply basic shell scripting elements.

1. Use vim to create a file with the name hello in your home directory.
2. Give this file the contents that you see in Listing 31.1 and close it.
3. Use **./hello** to try to execute it. You get a "permission denied" error message.
4. Type **chmod +x hello** and try to execute it again. You see that it now works.

Using Variables and Input

Linux bash scripts are much more than just a list of commands that is sequentially executed. One of the nice things about scripts is that they can work with variables and input to make the script flexible. In this section, you learn how to work with these.

Using Positional Parameters

When starting a script, arguments can be used. An argument is anything that you put behind the script command. Arguments can be used to make a script more flexible. Take, for instance, the command **useradd lisa**. In this example, the command is **useradd**, and the argument **lisa** is specifying what needs to be done. In this case, a user with the name lisa has to be created. In this example, **lisa** is the argument to the command **useradd**. In a script, the first argument is referred to as **$1**, the second argument is referred to as **$2**, and so on. The example script in Listing 31.2 shows how an argument can be used. Go ahead and try it using any username you want to use!

Listing 31.2 Example Script That Is Using Arguments

```
#!/bin/bash
# run this script with a few arguments
echo The first argument is $1
echo The second argument is $2
echo the third argument is $3
```

If you tried to run the sample code from Listing 31.2, you might have noticed that its contents are not perfect. If you use three arguments while using the previous script, it will work perfectly. If you only use two arguments, the third echo prints with no value for $3. If you use four arguments, the fourth value (which would be stored in $4) is never used. So, if you want to use arguments, you are better off using a more flexible approach. Listing 31.3 shows an example of a script that is using a more flexible approach.

Listing 31.3 Using Arguments in a Flexible Way

```
#!/bin/bash
# run this script with a few arguments
echo you have entered $# arguments
for i in "$@"
do
        echo $i
done
exit 0
```

In Listing 31.3, two new items that relate to the arguments are introduced:

- $# is a counter that shows how many arguments were used when starting the script.
- $@ refers to all arguments that were used when starting the script.

To evaluate the arguments that were used when starting this script, a conditional loop with **for** is used. In conditional loops with **for**, commands are executed as long as the condition is true. In this script, the condition is **for i in "$@"**, which means "for each argument." Each time the script goes through the loop, a value from the $@ variable is assigned to the $i variable. So, as long as there are arguments, the body of the script is executed. The body of a **for** loop always starts with **do** and is closed with **done**, and between these two, the commands are listed that need to be executed. So, the example script in Listing 31.3 will use **echo** to show the value of each argument and stop when no more arguments are available. In Exercise 31.2, you can try this for yourself.

Exercise 31.2 Working with Positional Parameters

In this exercise, you learn how to write a script that works with positional parameters.

1. Open an editor to create the file ex312a and copy the contents from Listing 31.2 into this file.
2. Save the file and make it executable.
3. Run the command **./ex312a a b c**. You see that three lines are echoed.
4. Run the command **./ex312a a b c d e f**. You see that still three lines are echoed.
5. Open an editor to create the file ex312 and copy the contents from Listing 31.3 into this file.
6. Save the file and make it executable.
7. Run the command **./ex312 a b c**. You see that three lines are echoed.
8. Run the command **./ex312** without arguments. You see that it does not echo anything.

Working with Variables

A variable is a label that is used to refer to a specific location in memory which contains a specific value. Variables can be defined statically by using NAME=value or in a dynamic way. There are two solutions to define a variable dynamically: **Key Topic**

Key Topic

- Use **read** in the script to ask the user who runs the script for input
- Use command substitution to use the result of a command and assign that to a variable. For example, the **date +%d-%m-%y** command shows the current date in day-month-year format. To assign that to a script, you could use **TODAY=$(date +%d-%m-%y)**. In command substitution, you just have to put the command whose result you want to use between a dollar and braces.

In the previous section about positional parameters, you learned how to provide arguments when starting a script. In some cases, it can be more efficient to ask for information when you find out that something essential is missing. The script in Listing 31.4 shows how to do this.

Listing 31.4 Example of a Script That Uses the **read** Command

```
#!/bin/bash
if [ -z $1 ]; then
        echo enter a name
        read NAME
else
        NAME=$1
fi
echo you have entered the text $NAME
exit 0
```

In the example script from Listing 31.4, an **if ... then ... else ... fi** statement is used to check whether the argument **$1** exists. This is done by using a **test**. (**test** is a command by its own.) The **test** command can be written in two ways: **test** or **[...]**. In Listing 31.4, the line **if [-z $1] ...** executes to see of the test **-z $1** is true. The **-z test** checks to see whether $1 is nonexistent. So stated otherwise, the line **if [-z $1]** checks to see whether $1 is empty, which means that no argument was provided when starting this script. If this is the case, the commands after the **then** statement are executed. Notice that when writing the **test** command with the square brackets, it is essential to use spaces after the opening bracket and before the closing bracket, without spaces the command will not work.

Notice that the **then** statement immediately follows the test. This is possible because a semicolon is used (;). A semicolon is a command separator and can replace a new line in a script. In the **then** statement, two commands are executed: an **echo** command that displays a message on screen, and a **read** command.

The **read** command stops the script so that user input can be processed and stored in the variable NAME. So **read NAME** puts all user input in the variable NAME, which will be used later in the script.

In the example script in Listing 31.4, the next part is introduced by the **else** statement. The commands after the **else** statement are executed in all other cases, which in this case means "if an argument was provided." If that is the case, the variable NAME is defined and the current value of $1 is assigned to it.

Notice how the variable is defined: directly after the name of the variable there is an = sign, which is followed by $1. Notice that you should never use spaces when defining variables.

Then, the if loop is closed with a **fi** statement. Once the if loop has been completed, you know for sure that the variable NAME is defined and has a value. The last line of the script reads the value of the variable NAME and displays this value to STDOUT via the **echo** command. Notice that to request the current value of a variable, the variable name is referred to, starting with a $ sign in front of it.

In Exercise 31.3, you can practice working with input.

Exercise 31.3 Working with Input

In this script, you practice working with input.

1. Open an editor and create a file with the name ex313. Enter the contents of Listing 31.2 in this file.
2. Write the file to disk and use **chmod +x ex313** to make it executable.
3. Run the script using **./ex313** and no further arguments. You see that it prompts for input.
4. Run the script using **"hello"** as its argument. It will echo "you have entered the text hello" to the STDOUT.

Using Conditional Loops

As you have already seen, in a script conditional loops can be used. These conditional loops are only executed if a certain condition is true. In bash there are a few conditional loops that are often used.

Key Topic

- **if .. then .. else**—Used to execute codes if a specific condition is true
- **for**—Used to execute commands for a range of values
- **while**—Used to execute code as long as a specific condition is true

- **until**—Used to execute code until a specific condition is true
- **case**—Used to evaluate specific values, where beforehand a limited number of values is expected

Working with if then else

The **if then else** construction is common to evaluate specific conditions. You have already seen an example with it in Listing 31.4. This conditional loop is often used together with the test command. This command enables you to test many things, not just if a file exists, but it can compare files, compare integers, and much more.

TIP Take a look at the man page of the test command.

The basic construction with **if** is **if ... then ... fi**. This evaluates one single condition, as in the following:

```
if [ -z $1 ]
then
        echo no value provided
fi
```

In Listing 31.4 you have seen how two conditions can be evaluated, including an **else** in the statement. Listing 31.5 shows how multiple conditions can be evaluated, contracting **else** with **if** to **elif**. This is useful if many different values need to be checked. Notice that in this sample listing, multiple test commands are used as well.

Listing 31.5 Example with **if then else**

```
#!/bin/bash
# run this script with one argument
# the goal is to find out if the argument is a file or a directory
if [ -f $1 ]
then
     echo "$1 is a file"
elif [ -d $1 ]
then
     echo "$1 is a directory"
```

```
else
    echo "I do not know what \$1 is"
fi
exit 0
```

Using || and &&

Instead of writing full **if ... then** statements, you can use the logical operators || and &&. || is a logical OR and will execute the second part of the statement only if the first part is not true; && is the logical AND and will execute the second part of the statement only if the first part it true. Consider these two one-liners:

```
[ -z $1 ] && echo no argument provided
ping -c 1 10.0.0.20 2>/dev/null || echo node is not available
```

In the first example, a test is performed to see whether $1 is empty. If that test is true (which basically means that the command exits with the exit code 0), the second command is executed.

In the second example, a **ping** command is used to check the availability of a host. The logical OR is used in this example to echo the text "node is not available" in case the **ping** command was not successful. You often find that instead of fully written if then statements, the && and || constructions are used. In Exercise 31.4 you can practice some if then else skills, using either **if ... then ..else** or && and ||.

Exercise 31.4 Using if ... then ... else

In this exercise, you work on a script that checks the availability of the Apache web server.

1. Start an editor and create a script with the name filechk.
2. Copy the contents from Listing 31.5 to this script.
3. Run a couple of tests with it, as in **./filechk /etc/hosts**, **./filechck /usr**, **./filechk non-existing-file**.

Applying for

The **for** conditional provides an excellent solution for processing ranges of data. In Listing 31.6, you can see the first example with for, where a range is defined and processed as long as there are unprocessed values in that range.

Listing 31.6 Example with for

```
#!/bin/bash
#
for (( COUNTER=100; COUNTER>1; COUNTER-- )); do
        echo $COUNTER
done
exit 0
```

A **for** conditional statement always starts with **for**, which is followed by the condition that needs to be checked. Then comes a **do**, which is followed by the commands that need to be executed if the condition is true, and the conditional statement is closed with a **done**.

In the example in Listing 31.6, you can see that the condition is a range of numbers assigned to the variable COUNTER. The variable first is initialized with a value of 100, and as long as the value is bigger than 1, in each iteration 1 is subtracted. As long as the condition is true, the value of the $COUNTER variable is displayed, using the **echo** commands.

In Listing 31.7, you can see one of my favorite one-liners with **for**. The range is defined this time as a series of numbers, starting with 100 and moving up to 104.

Listing 31.7 Example One-Liner with **for**

```
for i in {100..104}; do ping -c 1 192.168.4.$i >/dev/null && echo
192.168.4.$i is up; done
```

Notice how the range is defined: You first specify the first number, followed by two dots and closed with the last number in the range. With **for i in**, each of these numbers is assigned to the variable **i**. For each of these numbers, a **ping** command is executed, where the option **-c 1** makes sure that one ping request only is sent.

In this **ping** command, it is not the result that counts, which is why the result is redirected to the /dev/null device. Based on the exit status of the **ping** command, the part behind the && is executed. So, if the host could be reached, a line is echoed indicating that it is up.

Understanding while and until

Where the **for** statement that you have just read about is useful to work through ranges of items, the **while** statement is useful if you want to monitor something like the availability of a process. The counterpart of **while** is **until**, which keeps the iteration open until a specific condition is true. In Listing 31.8 you can read how while is used to monitor process activity.

Listing 31.8 Monitoring Processes with **while**

```
#!/bin/bash
#
# usage: monitor <processname>
while ps aux | grep $1 | grep -v grep  > /dev/tty11
do
    sleep 5
done

clear
echo your process has stopped
logger $1 is no longer present
mail -s "process $1 has stopped" root < .
```

The script in Listing 31.8 consists of two parts. First, there is the **while** loop. Second, there is everything that needs to be executed when the **while** loop no longer evaluates to true. The core of the **while** loop is the **ps** command, which is grepped for the occurrence of $1. Notice the use of **grep -v grep**, which excludes lines containing the **grep** command from the result. Keep in mind that the **ps** command will include all running commands, including the **grep** command that the output of the **ps** command is piped to. This can result in a false positive match. The results of the **ps aux** command is redirected to /dev/tty11. That makes it possible to read the results later from tty11 if that is needed, but they do not show by default.

After the **while** statements follow the commands that need to be executed if the statement evaluates to true. In this case, the command is **sleep 5**, which will basically pause the script for 5 seconds. As long as the **while** command evaluates to true, it keeps on running. If it does no longer (which in this case means that the process is no longer available), it stops and the commands that follow the **while** loop can be executed.

You should be familiar with all of these commands, except on the last one. In the line **mail -s "process $1 has stopped" root < .**, a message is sent to the user root, using the internal mail system that runs on RHEL 7 by default. The **mail** command takes as its first argument the subject, specified using the **-s** option. Notice the **< .** at the end of the command.

Normally, when using the **mail** command in an interactive mode, it will open an editor in which the message body can be written. This editor is closed by providing a line that has only a dot. In this command, the dot is provided through redirection of the STDIN. This allows the message to be processed without any further requirement for user activity.

The counterpart of **while** is **until**, of which an example is in Listing 31.9. **until** opens an iteration that lasts until the condition is true. In Listing 31.9, it is used to filter the output of the **users** command for the occurrence of $1, which would be a username. Until this command is true, the iteration continues. When the username has been found in the output of **users**, the iteration closes and the commands after the **until** loop are executed.

Listing 31.9 Monitoring User Login with **until**

```
#!/bin/bash
#
until users | grep $1 > /dev/null
do
     echo $1 is not logged in yet
     sleep 5
done
echo $1 has just logged in
mail -s "$1 has just logged in" root < .
```

Understanding case

The last of the important iteration loops is case. The **case** statement is used to evaluate a number of expected values. The **case** statement in particular is important in Linux startup scripts that on previous versions of RHEL were used to start services. In a **case** statement, you define every specific argument that you expect, which is followed by the command that needs to be executed if that argument was used. In Listing 31.10, you can see the blueprint of the case statement that was used on RHEL 6 to start almost any service.

Listing 31.10 Evaluating Specific Cases with **case**

```
case "$1" in
  start)
          start;;
  stop)
          rm -f $lockfile
          stop;;
  restart)
          restart;;
  reload)
          reload;;
  status)
          status
          ;;
  *)
          echo "Usage: $0 (start|stop|restart|reload|status)"
          ;;
esac
```

The **case** statement has a few particularities. To start, the generic syntax is **case *item-to-evaluate* in**. Then follows a list of all possible values that need to be evaluated. Each item is closed with a). Then follows a list of commands that need to be executed if the specific argument was used. The list of commands is closed with a double semicolon. This ;; can be used directly after the last command, and it can be used on a separate line. Also notice that the *) refers to all other options not previously specified. It is a "catchall" statement. The **case** iteration loop is closed by an **esac** statement.

Notice that the evaluations in **case** are performed in order. When the first match is made, the **case** statement will not evaluate anything else. Within the evaluation, wildcard-like patterns can be used. This shows in the *) evaluation, which matches everything. But you could as well use evaluations like start|Start|START) to match the use of a different case.

Bash Shell Script Debugging

When a script does not do what you expect it to do, it is useful to do some debugging. If a script does not do what you expect it to do, try staring it as an argument to the **bash -x** command. This will show you line by line what the script is trying to do, and it will show you specific errors if it does not work as well. Listing 31.11

shows an example of using **bash -x** where it becomes immediately clear that the **grep** command does not know what it is expected to do, which is because it misses an argument to work on.

Listing 31.11 Using **bash -x** to Debug Scripts

```
[root@server1 ~]# bash -x 319.sh
+ grep
Usage: grep [OPTION]... PATTERN [FILE]...
Try 'grep --help' for more information.
+ users
+ echo is not logged in yet
is not logged in yet
+ sleep 5
```

Summary

In this chapter you learned how to write shell scripts. You've worked through a few examples and are now familiar with some of the basic elements that are required to create a successful script.

Exam Preparation Tasks

Review All Key Topics

Review the most important topics in the chapter, noted with the Key Topic icon in the outer margin of the page. Table 31.2 lists a reference of these key topics and the page numbers on which each is found.

Table 31.2 Key Topics for Chapter 31

Key Topic Element	Description	Page
Paragraph	Definition of variable	689
List	Dynamically defining variables	690
List	Conditional loops overview	691

Define Key Terms

Define the following key terms from this chapter and check your answers in the glossary:

shebang, parent shell, subshell, variable, iteration, conditional loop, OR, AND

Review Questions

1. What is the effect if a script does *not* start with a shebang?
2. How can you check if a variable VAR has no value?
3. What would you use in a script to count the number of arguments that has been used?
4. What would you use to refer to all arguments that have been used when starting the script?
5. How do you process user input in a script?
6. What is the simplest way to test if a file exists and execute the command "echo file does not exist" if it does not?
7. Which test would you perform to find out if an item is a file or a directory?
8. Which construction would you use to evaluate a range of items?
9. How do you close an **elif** statement in a script?
10. In a **case** statement, you evaluate a range of items. For each of these items you execute one or more commands. What do you need to use after the last command to close the specific item?

End-of-Chapter Labs

In the end-of-chapter labs, you apply your scripting skills to write two simple scripts.

Lab 31.1

1. Write a script that works with arguments. If the argument **one** is used, the script should create a file /tmp/one. If the argument **two** is used, the script should send a message containing the subject two to the root user.

2. Write a countdown script. The script should use one argument (and not more than one). This argument specifies the number of minutes to count down. It should start with that number of minutes and count down second by second, writing the text "there are nn seconds remaining" at every iteration. Use **sleep** to define the seconds. When there is no more time left, the script should echo "time is over" and quit.

The following topics are covered in this chapter:

- Excluding Iptables Services
- Creating Firewalld Services
- Creating Firewalld Rich Rules
- Configuring Network Address Translation

The following RHCE exam objectives are covered in this chapter:

- Use firewalld and associated mechanisms such as rich rules, zones, and custom rules to implement packet filtering and configure Network Address Translation

CHAPTER 32

Advanced Firewall Configuration

In Chapter 22, "Configuring a Firewall," you read how to configure firewalld on RHEL 7 to add firewalld services to zones to allow access to network services through the firewall. For the RHCE exam, you need to be able to handle some advanced configurations as well. These include custom service files and working with rich rules and Network Address Translation. This chapter explains how to perform these tasks.

"Do I Know This Already?" Quiz

The "Do I Know This Already?" quiz allows you to assess whether you should read this entire chapter thoroughly or jump to the "Exam Preparation Tasks" section. If you are in doubt about your answers to these questions or your own assessment of your knowledge of the topics, read the entire chapter. Table 32.1 lists the major headings in this chapter and their corresponding "Do I Know This Already?" quiz questions. You can find the answers in Appendix A, "Answers to the 'Do I Know This Already?' Quizzes and 'Review Questions.'"

Table 32.1 "Do I Know This Already?" Section-to-Question Mapping

Foundation Topics Section	Questions
Excluding Iptables Services	1
Creating Firewalld Services	10
Configuring Firewalld Rich Rules	2–6
Configuring Network Address Translation	7–9

1. When the firewalld service is used for managing the firewall, a couple of services should never be running on your server. What services should not be running when you are using firewalld?

   a. iptables

   b. ebtables

   c. ip6tables

   d. network

2. Which of the following cannot be configured using firewalld rich rules?
   a. Logging
   b. Filtering based on one specific IP address instead of all IP addresses assigned to a zone
   c. Custom port allocations
   d. Rate limiting

3. In a firewalld configuration, you can use different building blocks. These building blocks are processed in a specific order, and are shown in the following list. Which answer lists their correct order?
   1. Deny rules
   2. Logging rules
   3. Direct rules
   4. Allow rules
   5. Port forwarding and masquerading rules
      a. 3, 5, 2, 4, 1
      b. 5, 3, 2, 4, 1
      c. 3, 5, 4, 1, 2
      d. 2, 1, 5, 3, 4

4. Which man page has examples about the syntax of firewalld rich rules?
   a. (1) firewall-cmd
   b. (5) firewalld.conf
   c. (5) firewalld.richlanguage
   d. (5) firwalld.zones

5. Which of the following shows the correct syntax for adding a rich rule that blocks access for one specific IP address?
   a. **firewall-cmd --zone=dmz --add-rich-rule='rule family=ipv4 source address=10.0.0.100/32 reject'**
   b. **firewall-cmd --zone=dmz --add-rich-rule='rule family=ip4 source address=10.0.0.100/32 reject'**
   c. **firewall-cmd --zone=dmz --add-rich-rule='family=ipv4 source address=10.0.0.100/32 reject'**
   d. **firewall-cmd --zone=dmz --add-rich-rule='rule family=ipv4 source=10.0.0.100/32 reject'**

6. Which of the following shows the correct syntax for writing log messages to syslog, where all log messages are prefixed with **SSH ATTEMPT**, the log priority is set to **notice**, and a maximum of two packets per minute is logged?
   a. **firewall-cmd --zone=dmz --add-rich-rule='rule service name="ssh" log prefix="SSH ATTEMPT:" level="notice" limit value="2/m" accept**
   b. **firewall-cmd --zone=dmz --add-rich-rule='rule service name="ssh" log prefix="SSH ATTEMPT:" facility="notice" limit="2/m" accept**
   c. **firewall-cmd --zone=dmz --add-rich-rule='rule service name="ssh" log prefix="SSH ATTEMPT:" level="notice" limit="2/m" accept**
   d. **firewall-cmd --zone=dmz --add-rich-rule='rule service name="ssh" log prefix="SSH ATTEMPT:" facility="notice" limit value="2/m" accept**

7. Which statement about port forwarding is true?
   a. To configure port forwarding, rich rules must be used.
   b. Port forwarding can be configured only on a router.
   c. To configure port forwarding to another host, masquerading must be configured as well for the return packets.
   d. To configure port forwarding, the **--add-port** option must be used in **firewall-cmd**.

8. Which of the following shows the correct syntax for masquerading?
   a. **firewall-cmd --permanent --zone=<ZONE> --add-rich-rule='rule family=ipv4 source address=10.0.0.0/24 masquerade'**
   b. **firewall-cmd --permanent --add-rich-rule='rule family=ipv4 source address=10.0.0.0/24 masquerade'**
   c. **firewall-cmd --permanent --zone=<ZONE> --addrule='rule family=ipv4 source address=10.0.0.0/24 masquerade'**
   d. **firewall-cmd --permanent --zone=<ZONE> --add-rich-rule='rule family=ip4 source address=10.0.0.0/24 masquerade'**

9. Which statement about masquerading is true?
   a. Masquerading must be configured on the public zone.
   b. Masquerading can be configured for IPv4 as well as IPv6.
   c. Masquerading requires a public IP address to be set on the external interface.
   d. Masquerading requires the masquerading host to be configured as a router.

10. Which of the following is the typical location for custom firewalld service files?

    a. /etc/systemd/system

    b. /usr/lib/firewalld/services

    c. /etc/firewalld/services

    d. /etc/firewalld

Foundation Topics

NOTE This chapter assumes your familiarity with all the RHCSA topics described in Chapter 22. If you have doubts about anything here, it might be wise to review the topics described in Chapter 22.

Excluding Iptables Services

When working with firewalld, you should no longer use iptables and related services. That is because these services are incompatible to one another, and making changes to the iptables configuration will affect firewalld as well, so they must be avoided. On a server where multiple administrators are working, you risk that a less-knowledgeable administrator wants to create a firewall configuration and notices that the iptables service is not running and wants to start the iptables service anyway. This might mess up your firewalld-based firewall configuration.

Systemd provides a nice solution to make sure that unwanted services are not started by accident: You can use **systemctl mask** to exclude them from ever being started.

To exclude all iptables-based services from ever being started, type **for i in iptables ip6tables ebtables; do systemctl mask $i; done**. This command creates a symbolic link to /dev/null for the related service files in /etc/systemd/system. The following example shows what happens. By using the **systemctl mask** command, the symbolic links are created. (You do not have to use the **ln** commands yourself.)

```
[root@localhost ~]# for i in iptables ip6tables ebtables; do
  systemctl mask $i; done
ln -s '/dev/null' '/etc/systemd/system/iptables.service'
ln -s '/dev/null' '/etc/systemd/system/ip6tables.service'
```

Notice that this is an elegant way to disable services. Service files in /etc/systemd/system always take precedence over the configuration files in /usr/lib/systemd/system. By linking the iptables-related service scripts in /etc/systemd/system to /dev/null, they will never start, but it is easy to enable them again by just removing these symbolic links or by using the command **for i in iptables ip6tables ebtables; do systemctl unmask $i; done**.

NOTE The ebtables service is used to manage firewalling on Linux software bridges.

TIP If you are very comfortable with iptables, you can use iptables on the exam. Because firewalld is the new direction that Red Hat is taking for firewall configuration, in this chapter you learn how to configure a firewall using firewalld. But on the exam, Red Hat expects you to create a configuration. They will not usually tell you how to do that but only expect that it works. So, if you can do it with iptables, that is fine.

Creating Firewalld Services

In Chapter 22, you read how to add service files to zones in firewalld. Firewalld comes with a number of default services, not to be confused with services in systemd, which are something completely different. You can list these services using **firewall-cmd --get-services**. This command shows all firewalld services, which are stored as XML files in the directories /usr/lib/firewalld/services and /etc/firewalld/services.

TIP On RHEL 7, many services (such as systemd, firewalld, modprobe, and others) have default configuration files that should not be modified. These default configuration files are stored in the /usr/lib directory. Do not ever change them, because they may be overwritten when the RPM where the configuration file comes from is updated. Custom configuration files should be stored in the /etc directory, as is the case for firewalld, which stores custom configuration files in /etc/firewalld. These custom files may have the same name as the default files in /usr/lib/firewalld but will always take precedence. This is true not only for firewalld but also for all other services that store their service files in this way.

In some cases, you need to add ports to the firewall configuration that are not included by default. If that is the case, you can use the **--add-port** option with the **firewall-cmd** command, but you can create a service configuration file as an alternative. In Exercise 32.1, you learn how to create a custom service file that allows the ssh service to be accessed on port 2022.

NOTE Firewalld services are not related to systemd services. The only purpose of the firewalld service is to open a port in the firewall; it will not start the process, nor will it change the configuration of the process as managed with the systemd service. Note that in Exercise 32.1 you only create the firewalld service and do not modify the process configuration. So, at the end of the exercise, there will be no service listening on port 2022! (Of course, you are free to reconfigure your ssh service to offer services on port 2022.)

NOTE In the following exercise, you create a service file by editing the XML code. As an alternative, you can use **firewall-cmd --new-service** to do this. See man firewall-cmd for more information.

Exercise 32.1 Creating a Custom Firewalld Service

1. Because it is much easier to base new service files on existing service files, use the command **cp /usr/lib/firewalld/services/ssh.xml /etc/firewalld/services**.
2. Open the file /etc/firewalld/services/ssh with an editor. It should show the following contents (see Listing 32.1).

Listing 32.1 Firewalld ssh Service File Contents

```
[root@localhost services]# cat ssh.xml
<?xml version="1.0" encoding="utf-8"?>
<service>
  <short>SSH</short>
  <description>Secure Shell (SSH) is a protocol for logging into
and executing commands on remote machines. It provides secure
encrypted communications. If you plan on accessing your machine
remotely via SSH over a firewalled interface, enable this option.
You need the openssh-server package installed for this option to be
useful.</description>
  <port protocol="tcp" port="22"/>
</service>
```

3. In the service file, change the port that is set to 22 to a new port (2022).
4. Modify the description setting to show that this is a modified service file.
5. Save changes to disk and use **mv /etc/firewalld/services/ssh /etc/firewalld/services/ssh-custom**.
6. Type **firewall-cmd --get-services**. Notice that you do not see the new service file listed yet.
7. Type **firewall-cmd --reload** and repeat **firewall-cmd --get-services**. You'll see the new service file listed now.
8. Type **firewall-cmd --add-service ssh-custom --permanent**, followed by **firewall-cmd --reload**.
9. Type **firewall-cmd --list-services**. You'll see the new service file added to the default zone.

10. Notice that this exercise has shown how to create a firewall service. To make the process available on the new port, modify the process configuration also. Read Chapter 39, "Managing SSH," for more details on how to do this for the ssh service.

Configuring Firewalld Rich Rules

Up to now, you have worked with firewalld services. Although convenient, the options that are offered by firewalld services are sometimes a bit limited. That is why firewalld offers alternative solutions for allowing traffic as well. Currently, there are two solutions:

Key Topic

- Direct rules allow administrators to add detailed hand code rules into the firewall configuration. They offer advanced features and are somewhat hard to manage. They use a syntax that looks a lot like iptables syntax and allow administrators to work with firewalld in an iptables-like way. For the RHCE exam, you do not have to know how to create direct rules.
- Rich rules give administrators an easy-to-use expressive language to define custom rules that cannot be created using the default firewalld syntax.

TIP Do not waste time on direct rules; you only have to know how to configure rich rules on the RHCE exam.

Rich Rule Syntax

Rich rules are used to create allow/deny rules, but with advanced options, such as the following:

- Logging configuration
- Port forwarding
- Masquerading
- Rate limiting
- Allow/deny connections for one specific zone

The basic syntax of a rich rule is as follows:

- Rule
  - [source] [destination]
  - {service | port | protocol | icmp-block | masquerade | forward-port}
  - [log] [audit]
  - [accept | reject | drop]

TIP Before you start trying to memorize rich rule syntax, take a look at man 5 firewalld.richlanguage. This man page contains some good examples of how to create rich rules, which will help you find the right syntax easily while taking the exam.

Ordering

When working with rich rules, it is easy to create conflicting rules. For instance, you may deny access to an entire network but want to allow access to one specific node in that network. Because it is possible to create conflicting rules, ordering becomes important as well when working with rich rules. The basic ordering rules within zones are as follows:

1. Direct rules
2. Port forwarding and masquerading rules
3. Logging rules
4. Allow rules
5. Deny rules

Typically, a rule that will not be matched by anything will be denied, but that depends on the default zone configuration as well. If the trusted zone is used, for instance, packets that are not matching anything are allowed.

Managing Rich Rules

There are four basic manipulations when working with rich rules. Table 32.2 describes these manipulations.

Key Topic

Table 32.2 Rich Rules Basic Manipulations

Manipulation	Explanation
--add-rich-rule='<RULE>'	Adds <RULE> to the default zone or to the zone that is specified.
--remove-rich-rule='<RULE>'	Removes <RULE> from the default zone or from the zone that is specified.
--query-rich-rule='<RULE>'	Queries if <RULE> has been added to a zone. Returns 0 if the rule is present and 1 if it is not and does not give any further details.
--list-rich-rules	Lists all rich rules for the default zone or for the zone that is specified as an argument.

> **TIP** To make testing of rich rules easier, you can add rich rules to the runtime configuration with a timeout. Once the timeout has passed, the rich rule is automatically removed. This ensures that you will not be locked out after making an error to the configuration of rich rules, which is useful when configuring a firewall on a remote server. To add a timeout to a rich rule, add the **--timeout=XX** to the end of the **firewall-cmd** rule.

To help you learning the rich rule syntax, Exercise 32.2 walks you through the procedure to add some rich rules to a zone. Notice that none of the rules is set to **--permanent**, because this exercise is to demonstrate rich rule workings only.

Exercise 32.2 Using Rich Rules

1. From a root shell, type **firewall-cmd --zone=dmz --add-rich-rule= 'rule family=ipv4 source address=10.0.0.100/32 reject' --timeout=60**.
2. Type **firewall-cmd --list-all --zone=dmz** to verify that the rule has been added successfully.
3. Now enter **firewall-cmd --add-rich-rule='rule service name=http log limit value=3/m accept' --zone=dmz**.
4. Type **firewall-cmd --list-all --zone=dmz** again to verify that the new rule was added successfully. Also notice that the rule you have added in step 1 of this exercise is now gone.
5. Type **firewall-cmd --add-rich-rule='rule protocol value=icmp accept' --zone=dmz**. This rule allows all Internet Control Message Protocol (ICMP) traffic toward the demilitarized zone (DMZ).

6. Type **firewall-cmd --add-rich-rule='rule family=ipv4 source address=10.0.0.0/24 port port=7900-7905 protocol=tcp accept' --zone=dmz**.
7. Verify that all rich rules have successfully been added, by using **firewall-cmd --list-all --zone=dmz**.

Logging with Rich Rules

In the commands in Exercise 32.2, you saw how a log line was added for rules that are sent to the hpptd service, with a rate limitation of three per minute. In rich rules, you can enter more specifically what should be logged and how it should be logged. You can add the log prefix and the level options as well. The log prefix is used when writing messages to syslog, and the level determines the log level (known as *priority* in the different log systems). Here is an example of such a rich rule:

```
firewall-cmd --zone=dmz --add-rich-rule='rule service name="ssh" log
  prefix="SSH ATTEMPT: " level="notice" limit value="3/m" accept
```

TIP Avoid problems configuring firewalls on the exam by creating all firewall configurations from the console and not from Secure Shell (SSH). If you do something wrong, at least you will not lose connectivity.

Configuring Network Address Translation

Network Address Translation (NAT) is a common firewalld functionality. To use NAT, the RHEL 7 machine needs to be configured as a router. Therefore, it needs to have at least two network interfaces and forward incoming packets from one interface to the other interface. To configure a server as a router, make sure to set the sysctl tuneable **net.ipv4.ip_forward = 1**. See Chapter 28, "System Optimization Basics," for more information about how to do this.

While packets are forwarded from one interface to another in a NAT configuration, the packet headers are modified. There are two types of NAT:

- In masquerading, the IP address of a node on the internal network is changed by the IP address of the NAT router. The goal is to ensure that the host on the private network can communicate on the Internet but that it cannot be accessed directly. Key Topic

- In port forwarding, the NAT router redirects all traffic that is addressed to a public port on the NAT router to another port, and often another host, on the private network. Port forwarding makes services on the private network available on the Internet, even if they are not running on a host that directly interfaces the Internet.

Configuring Masquerading

Masquerading is a common technique that is applied on IPv4 networks. Masquerading cannot be used with IPv6 firewalld. In masquerading, the IP address of a host on the private network is replaced with the public IP address on the NAT router. The NAT router then forwards the packet to its destination on the Internet. While this happens, the NAT router also changes the source port address of the outgoing packet. When the answer comes back from the host on the Internet, the NAT router uses the port address to which the answer is sent to forward the packet to the host the packet originally originated from.

To configure masquerading for hosts in a specific zone, use the following command:

```
firewall-cmd --permanent --zone=<ZONE> --add-masquerade
```

This command masquerades packets coming from all hosts in that specific zone. If you need some more control over which packets exactly are masqueraded, you can add a rich rule that matches packets coming from specific source addresses only:

```
firewall-cmd --permanent --zone=<ZONE> --add-rich-rule='rule
  family=ipv4 source address=10.0.0.0/24 masquerade'
```

IP masquerading can be configured from the command line. You can also create basic masquerading configurations from the firewall-config interface. To do this in firewall-config, you just have to specify the zone and click the **Masquerading** tab. Then click the option **Masquerade Zone** to enable it. Figure 32.1 shows what the interface looks like.

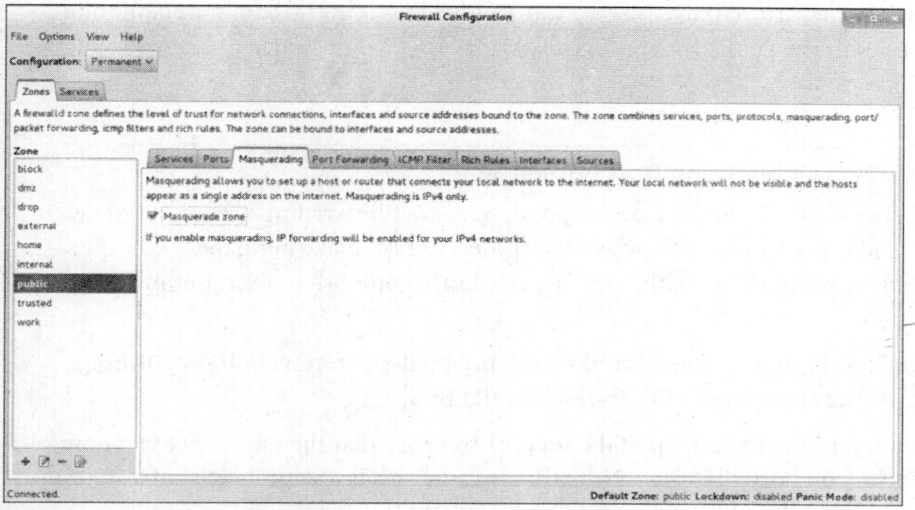

Figure 32.1 Enabling masquerading from the firewall-config interface.

Configuring Port Forwarding

Port forwarding is an excellent way to make services on the private network available on a public port on the NAT router. All packets that are addressed to that specific port will be forwarded to the private host. When port forwarding is configured, you also need to take care of packets going in the opposite direction. For the hosts on the private network to send packets back to the original source on the public network, masquerading must be configured as well. So, when configuring port forwarding, two configurations are needed:

- Port forwarding is required to make services on private hosts available.
- Unless you are using NAT on the local host, masquerading is required to be able to send back an answer from these hosts on the private network.

To configure port forwarding, you need the **--add-forward-port** option, followed by the source and destination port configuration. If you want to forward all packets coming in at port 2022 on the NAT router to an SSH process on internal host 10.0.0.10, for example, you need the following command:

```
firewall-cmd --permanent --zone=public --add-forward-
  port=port=2022:proto=tcp:toport=22:toaddr=10.0.0.10
```

Do not forget that to make this work masquerading must be configured on the interfaces in the public zone, too. In Exercise 32.3, you practice port forwarding configuration.

Exercise 32.3 Configuring Port Forwarding

To complete this exercise, you need two servers. Port forwarding is configured on server1, and server2 is used for testing purposes. Do *not* make permanent configurations; they might interfere with tasks you need to accomplish in exercises in upcoming chapters.

1. On server1, type **firewall-cmd --add-forward-port=port=4404:proto:tcp: toport=22:toaddr=<YOUR-IP-ADDRESS>**.
2. From server2, use **ssh -p 4044 server1** to verify that the ssh service can now be reached on port 4044 also. Note that because this is a same-host configuration, no additional masquerading rules are needed.

As is the case for masquerading, you can configure port forwarding easily from the firewall-config utility. To do this, select the zone to which you want to apply it and click the **Port Forwarding** tab. This brings up the interface that you see in Figure 32.2. In this interface, start by selecting the source protocol and port. Then specify the destination. Select **Local Forwarding** to forward incoming traffic on the specified port to another port on the same host. Use **Forward to Another Port** if you want to forward traffic to a port on another machine. If masquerading has not been enabled yet, the interface prompts and asks whether you want to enable masquerading as well. Answer **Yes** to this question, because without masquerading the answers to packets addressed to the forwarded port cannot be sent to the originator of the request.

When creating firewall configuration using firewall-config, do not forget to select the **Permanent** option.

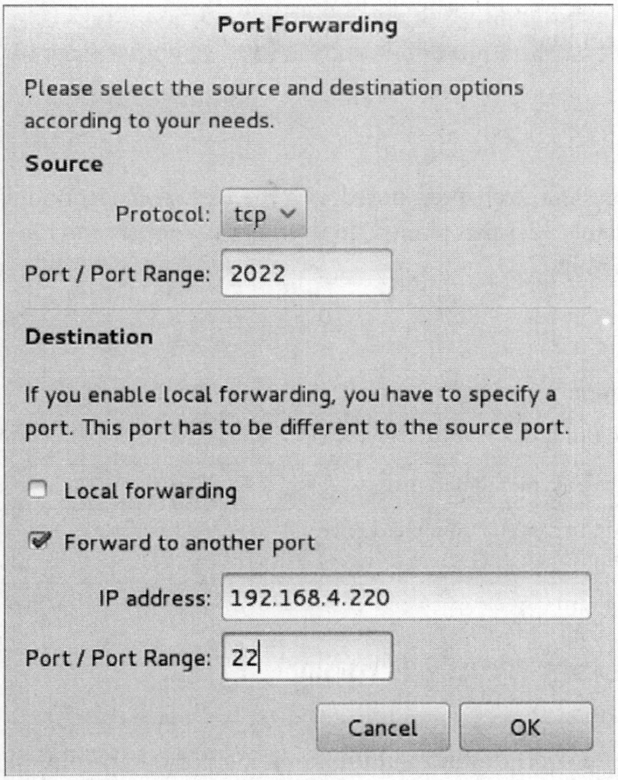

Figure 32.2 Configuring port forwarding from the firewall-config interface.

Summary

In this chapter, you learned about advanced firewall configurations. You have read how to work with rich rules that allow you to be more specific about which types of traffic you want to allow and which you do not. You have also read about NAT and how that technique can be used to configure IP masquerading and to configure port forwarding.

Exam Preparation Tasks

Review All Key Topics

Review the most important topics in the chapter, noted with the Key Topic icon in the outer margin of the page. Table 32.3 lists a reference of these key topics and the page numbers on which each is found.

Table 32.3 Key Topics for Chapter 32

Key Topic Element	Description	Page
List	Definition of direct rules and rich rules	708
Table 32.2	Rich rules base manipulations	710
List	Definition of masquerading and port forwarding	711

Complete Tables and Lists from Memory

Print a copy of Appendix B, "Memory Tables" (found on the disc), or at least the section for this chapter, and complete the tables and lists from memory. Appendix C, "Memory Tables Answer Key," also on the disc, includes completed tables and lists to check your work.

Define Key Terms

Define the following key terms from this chapter and check your answers in the glossary:

services, Network Address Translation, rich rules, masquerading, port forwarding

Review Questions

1. How would you make sure when using firewalld that the iptables service cannot be started by accident?
2. Where would you store custom firewalld service files?
3. Which line would you include in a custom service file to specify TCP port 2022?

4. Which command enables you to list all services currently available on your server?
5. What type of firewalld rules would you use if rich rules do not offer the solution you need?
6. Which command enables you to add a rich rule that allows all hosts with a source IP address coming from the 10.0.0.0/24 network to access ports 7900 up to 7905?
7. Which rich rule enables you to configure a maximum of three packets per minute to be logged for the http service?
8. What is the difference between Network Address Translation and masquerading?
9. Which command enables you to allow incoming traffic on port 4404 and forward it to the ssh service on IP address 10.0.0.10?
10. Which command is used to enable IP masquerading for all packets going out on the public zone?

End-of-Chapter Labs

For the RHCE exam, be prepared to work with rich rules, in addition to NAT and port forwarding. In the end-of-chapter labs, you'll be able to practice all of these. To complete these end-of-chapter labs, you need two servers.

Lab 32.1

1. Create a permanent rich rule configuration in the DMZ that matches the following requirements:
   - All packets coming in from the 10.0.1.0/24 network should be blocked.
   - All packets that are addressed to the SSH services should be logged with a maximum of two packets per minute. The messages should be logged with the "debug" log level, and the prefix "SSH: ".
   - If packets are coming from the host with IP address 10.0.1.1 and are addressed to port 80 or 22, they should be accepted.
2. On server1, configure SSH to listen on port 2022. Verify from server2 that SSH is available on this port. After verifying, on server1 configure port forwarding that forwards all packets addressed to port 2222 on server1 to port 2022 on server1.

The following topics are covered In this chapter:

- Revising Apache Basics
- Configuring TLS Security
- Deploying CGI Applications
- Configuring Private Directories

The following RHCE exam objectives are covered In this chapter:

- Configure a virtual host
- Configure private directories
- Deploy a basic CGI application
- Configure group-managed content
- Configure TLS security

CHAPTER 33

Managing Advanced Apache Services

In Chapter 17, "Configuring A Basic Apache Server," you learned about configuring a basic Apache web server. This chapter continues on the skills that you acquired in Chapter 17 and assumes that you are familiar with anything that has been explained in Chapter 17. You have to be familiar with those topics anyway because they cover some of the Apache-related RHCE exam objectives. In this chapter, you learn more about the configuration of private directories, deploying CGI applications, and configuring TLS security.

"Do I Know This Already?" Quiz

The "Do I Know This Already?" quiz allows you to assess whether you should read this entire chapter thoroughly or jump to the "Exam Preparation Tasks" section. If you are in doubt about your answers to these questions or your own assessment of your knowledge of the topics, read the entire chapter. Table 33.1 lists the major headings in this chapter and their corresponding "Do I Know This Already?" quiz questions. You can find the answers in Appendix A, "Answers to the 'Do I Know This Already?' Quizzes and 'Review Questions.'"

Table 33.1 "Do I Know This Already?" Section-to-Question Mapping

Foundation Topics Section	Questions
Revising Apache Basics	1–4
Configuring TLS Security	5–7
Deploying CGI Applications	8–9
Configuring Private Directories	10

1. What specifically is the AllowOverride directive used for?
   a. If set to yes, the contents of a directory can be changed.
   b. This setting is specifically for user home directories. If set to yes, these will be included in the Apache configuration.
   c. If set to yes, the .htaccess file in Apache directories will be considered, which will have a performance price.
   d. Set to yes if you want to allow users to create additional configuration files in directories.
2. Which directive do you need if you want to see a list of files in a directory where the default DirectoryIndex file does not exist?
   a. AllowIndexes
   b. RequireIndex no
   c. AllowFileList
   d. Options Indexes
3. Which directory by default is used for Apache module files to drop additional configuration files?
   a. /etc/httpd/conf.d
   b. /etc/httpd/modules.conf.d
   c. /etc/modules.d
   d. /etc/sysconfig/include
4. Since RHEL 7, an Apache boolean that was previously enabled is now off by default. This boolean switches Apache to a more restricted configuration, where directories need to be configured with specific SELinux context labels to allow Apache to work. What is the name of this Boolean?
   a. http_restricted
   b. http_confined
   c. httpd_unified
   d. httpd_secure

5. Which utility enables you to generate a TLS certificate and key for setting up a TLS security Apache web server?
   a. genkey
   b. openssl
   c. createkey
   d. sslkey

6. What is the default directory where the TLS private key is stored?
   a. /etc/ssl/certs/servername.key
   b. /etc/pki/tls/private/servername.key
   c. /etc/tls/keys/servername.key
   d. /etc/ssl/certs/private/servername.key

7. When configuring an Apache server for use of TLS, some directives are generally changed. Which of the following is not typically among them?
   a. SSLEngine
   b. SSLCertificateFile
   c. SSLCertificateKeyFile
   d. ServerName

8. Which of the following are not valid ways for including PHP scripts in Apache?
   a. Run the scripts as embedded code.
   b. Use mod_php which allows Apache to run those scripts using an internal interpreter.
   c. Run the PHP script as CGI script.
   d. Compile the script to a secure context so that is can be executed directly by the httpd process.

9. Which SELinux configuration must be applied to an Apache web server that needs to access a database that is running on the same server?
   a. None, this works by default.
   b. Set the httpd_can_network_connect_db Boolean to enabled.
   c. Set the httpd_can_network_connect Boolean to enabled.
   d. Apply both Answers B and C.

10. On a freshly installed Apache server, which command enables you to add a web server user lisa to allow for setting up protected content that is available to authenticated users only?

a. htpasswd2 /etc/httpd/htpasswd lisa

b. htpasswd -c /etc/httpd/htpasswd lisa

c. htpasswd2 /etc/httpd/htpasswd lisa

d. htpasswd -c lisa

Foundation Topics

Revising Apache Basics

In Chapter 17, you learned about a basic Apache configuration. In this section, we revise the most important Apache basic settings you need to be familiar with. You first read how to set essential Apache parameters, followed by an overview of essential Apache SELinux-related settings.

Essential Apache Parameters

So that we can discuss the important parameters (referred to as *directives* in the Apache documentation), Listing 33.1 gives an overview of the most significant configuration parameters in the /etc/httpd/conf/httpd.conf configuration file. (Notice that to focus on the essential parameters, some parts of the configuration file have been removed.).

Listing 33.1 Essential httpd.conf Configuration File Settings

```
[root@server1 ~]# cat /tmp/httpd.conf
ServerRoot "/etc/httpd"
Listen 80
Include conf.modules.d/*.conf

User apache
Group apache

ServerAdmin root@localhost

<Directory />
    AllowOverride none
    Require all denied
</Directory>
DocumentRoot "/var/www/html"

<Directory "/var/www">
    AllowOverride None
    # Allow open access:
    Require all granted
</Directory>
```

```
# Further relax access to the default document root:
<Directory "/var/www/html">
    Options Indexes FollowSymLinks
    AllowOverride None
    Require all granted
</Directory>

<IfModule dir_module>
    DirectoryIndex index.html
</IfModule>

<Files ".ht*">
    Require all denied
</Files>

ErrorLog "logs/error_log"
LogLevel warn
<IfModule alias_module>
    ScriptAlias /cgi-bin/ "/var/www/cgi-bin/"
</IfModule>

<Directory "/var/www/cgi-bin">
    AllowOverride None
    Options None
    Require all granted
</Directory>

IncludeOptional conf.d/*.conf
```

Table 33.2 gives an overview of the most significant settings in code example from Listing 33.1.

Key Topic

Table 33.2 httpd.conf Essential Configuration Parameters Overview

Parameter	Explanation
ServerRoot	The directory that contains all server configuration. Names of other configuration files are relative to this directory.
Listen	The port that the httpd process listens on.
Include	Used to refer to directories that contain additional configuration files that need to be included.

Parameter	Explanation
ServerAdmin	The name of the server administrator.
Directory	Used as a block of parameters to specify parameters that are specific for one directory. Often used to determine which kind of content is allowed. A directory block often contains AllowOverride, Require, and Options as common directives.
AllowOverride	If set to None, httpd will not read the contents of the .htaccess file that can be used for per-directory settings.
Options	Used to specify several options. A common option is Indexes, which will show a directory listing if no index.html exists in the directory that access is requested to.
Require all	Set to Granted to allow the contents of the directory to be accessed. Set to Denied to deny access to all contents of this specific directory.
DirectoryIndex	Specifies the name of the file in which the contents should be shown when accessing a directory. index.html is used by default for this purpose.
ErrorLog	Used to name the file where errors are logged to.
LogLevel	Indicates which type of messages (and higher) should be logged.
ScriptAlias	Defines an alias that is relative to the DocumentRoot where Apache looks for scripts that are allowed for execution.
IncludeOptional	Lists optional configuration files that can be included as well.

Revising Apache SELinux-Related Settings

Many SELinux-related security settings exist for the Apache web server. That is because it is one of the most vulnerable servers and also one of the most often used servers on Linux. It often uses scripts to allow content to be generated dynamically. Because of these scripts, higher security risks do exist. To mitigate these risks, different Apache-related SELinux security contexts and Booleans exist. Table 33.3 summarizes the most significant Apache-related SELinux settings.

Table 33.3 Apache-Related SELinux Settings

Key Topic

Setting	Type	Use
httpd_sys_content_t	Context type	Set on directories that Apache is allowed access to.
httpd_sys_content_rw_t	Context type	Set on directories that Apache is allowed read/write access to.
httpd_sys_script_exec_t	Context type	Used for directories that contain executable scripts.

Setting	Type	Use
httpd_unified	Boolean	Defines Apache restricted policy. It is off by default, or simplified/unified policy when set to on.
httpd_enable_cgi	Boolean	Switched on by default to allow Apache to run scripts.
httpd_tty_comm	Boolean	Used to determine if Apache is allowed access to a TTY. Make sure to switch on if you are using TLS private keys that prompt for a password on startup.

Configuring Write Access to the DocumentRoot

By default, only the root user has write access to the DocumentRoot. If you have a group of web developers who need to be able to write files to the DocumentRoot also, you need to take additional measures. Two common solutions exist:

- Configure a file system access control list (ACL; see Chapter 7, "Configuring Permissions") that grants members of the group's web developers all necessary rights to the directory.
- Make the DocumentRoot group-owned by the web developers and set the sticky bit permission on the directory to set default file ownership to the group owner on new items that are added to the directory.

To set an ACL that allows members of the webdev group write access to the DocumentRoot, you can use the following commands:

```
setfacl -R -m g:webdev:rwX /var/www/html
setfacl -R -m d:g:wevdev:rwx /var/www/html
```

Notice that in the first of these commands an uppercase *X* is used to set the execute bit only to directories and not to files.

Exercise 33.1 Enhancing Virtual Server Configuration

In Exercise 17.2, you have configured two virtual servers: account.example.com and sales.example.com. For that exercise, you have switched off SELinux. In this exercise, you continue working on the configuration created in Exercise 17.2. If you do not have that configuration anymore, you should start this exercise by performing the steps described in Exercise 17.2. At the start of this exercise, the virtual servers are supposed to be available.

1. Open a root shell and type **getenforce** to request the current SELinux state. If it is not set to Enforcing, use **setenforce Enforcing** to switch on SELinux. Also make sure that the default SELinux state is set to enforcing in the file /etc/sysconfig/selinux.
2. Use **elinks http://sales.example.com**. You should not get access to the virtual web server. This is expected because the correct SELinux context settings have not been applied yet.
3. Use **semanage fcontext -a -t httpd_sys_content_t "/www/docs(/.*)?"** to set the correct context type in the custom SELinux document root that has been used for the servers.
4. Type **restorecon -Rv /www/docs** to apply the context that you have just set to the file system.
5. Create a group for web developers, using **groupadd webdev**.
6. Set ACLs to make sure that members of the group webdev have access to the document root of the virtual users, using the following two commands:

```
setfacl -R -m g:webdev:rwX /www/docs
setfacl -R -m d:g:webdev:rwx /www/docs
```

7. Use **elinks http://sales.example.co**m to verify access to the sales virtual web server. You should now get access.
8. Type **usermod -aG webdev lisa.**
9. Use **su - lisa** to become lisa and verify write access to the /www/docs/sales directory using **touch /www/docs/sales/lisa.html**.

TIP The procedure that you have applied in this exercise is important, and on the exam you must make sure that you can apply it as well. Notice that a very good example is in the "Examples" section at the end of man 8 semanage-fcontext.

Configuring TLS Security

By default, the identity of a web server is not verified. This opens your web server for man-in-the-middle attacks, where someone else is assuming your web server's identity. If additional security is required, the server can be configured with Transport Layer Security (TLS). In this section, you learn how to do this. When secured with TLS, the web server is configured with public/private key certificates to guarantee the identity of the web server. Using these keys makes it possible to verify the server identity but also to send data that is encrypted and therefore not readable while in transit.

> **TIP** The advanced Apache topics look complicated, and to some extent they are. However, good configuration examples are available for everything discussed in this chapter. Install the httpd-manual RPM package, and after installing it, access the complete Apache manual at http://localhost/manual. It is a good idea to use this manual for each of the exercises in this chapter so that you are used to working with the contents and will not lose too much time looking up specific items.

Understanding TLS Security

TLS is the successor of SSL (Secure Sockets Layer). Its main purpose is that it allows the client to verify the identity of the server. To do this, certificates are used. The certificate contains the server identity and the public key of the server. A client uses the certificate to send encrypted data back to the server.

To guarantee the authenticity of the certificate, it normally is signed by a certificate authority (CA). The CA is an external trusted party that has signed the certificate. Related to the certificate is the server's private key. Data encrypted with the public key can be decrypted only with the private key.

The TLS connection is established as follows:

1. The client initiates a connection, using a ClientHello message. This message contains a list of the encryption protocols and ciphers that the client supports.
2. The server responds with a ServerHello message, indicating the encryption ciphers it supports. The server also sends the server certificate, containing the public key, general server information like the fully qualified domain name (FQDN), and a signature from a CA.
3. The client verifies the server certificate by checking whether the supplied information matches the request, and also by verifying all signatures.
4. If the certificate is verified, the client creates a session key. This session key is encrypted with the public key of the server and sent back to the server.
5. The server decrypts the session key, after which it can be used to encrypt and decrypt all data that is sent between client and server.

Configuring Apache for Using TLS Certificates

To configure Apache for using TLS certificates, three steps must be accomplished:

1. A certificate must be obtained.
2. The required Apache TLS modules must be installed.
3. The Apache (virtual) host must be configured to use the certificates.

The following procedure describes how these steps are applied to create a certificate for the sales.example.com server:

1. Type **yum install crypto-utils mod_ssl** to install the required packages.
2. Type **genkey sales.example.com**. This opens the genkey utility, which tells you where the key and the certificate will be stored (see Figure 33.1). From the first screen, select **Next**.

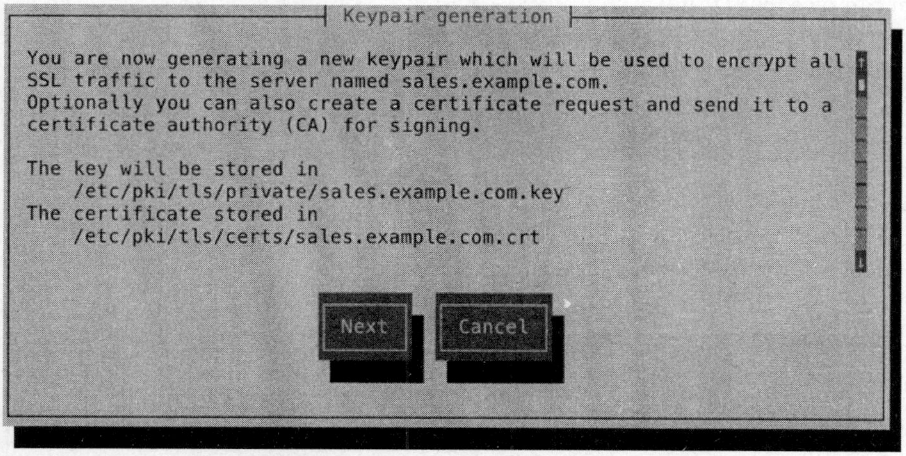

Figure 33.1 Creating certificates with genkey.

3. In the second step, the size of the key needs to be specified. A bigger size is higher security but slower. It is a good idea to accept the default of 2048 bits. Only in exceptional situations does it make sense to use more secure keys.
4. After selecting the key size, some random bits are generated. This takes some time. You can decrease the time it takes by performing some random activity on the server you are working on (like moving the mouse) or run the command **rngd -r /dev/urandom** which creates the entropy for you.

5. After generating the certificate and key, you can configure a virtual host with TLS. Configuring a virtual host with TLS is not much different from configuring a regular virtual host, you just have some additional parameters to deal with. A good starting point is the file /etc/httpd/conf.d/ssl.conf (see Listing 33.2).

Listing 33.2 Contents of the /etc/httpd/conf.d/ssl.conf File

```
[root@server2 /]# grep -v '^#' /etc/httpd/conf.d/ssl.conf
Listen 443 https
SSLPassPhraseDialog exec:/usr/libexec/httpd-ssl-pass-dialog
SSLSessionCache         shmcb:/run/httpd/sslcache(512000)
SSLSessionCacheTimeout  300
SSLRandomSeed startup file:/dev/urandom  256
SSLRandomSeed connect builtin
SSLCryptoDevice builtin

<VirtualHost _default_:443>
ErrorLog logs/ssl_error_log
TransferLog logs/ssl_access_log
LogLevel warn
SSLEngine on
SSLProtocol all -SSLv2
SSLCipherSuite HIGH:MEDIUM:!aNULL:!MD5
SSLCertificateFile /etc/pki/tls/certs/localhost.crt
SSLCertificateKeyFile /etc/pki/tls/private/localhost.key

<Files ~ "\.(cgi|shtml|phtml|php3?)$">
    SSLOptions +StdEnvVars
</Files>

<Directory "/var/www/cgi-bin">
    SSLOptions +StdEnvVars
</Directory>

BrowserMatch "MSIE [2-5]" \
         nokeepalive ssl-unclean-shutdown \
         downgrade-1.0 force-response-1.0

CustomLog logs/ssl_request_log \
          "%t %h %{SSL_PROTOCOL}x %{SSL_CIPHER}x \"%r\" %b"
</VirtualHost>
```

6. To configure a virtual host, start by changing the **VirtualHost _default_:443** line to **VirtualHost *:443**. Then, change the ServerName to match the name of the server you are going to be using.
7. After changing the ServerName, you need to change the SSLCertificateFile and the SSLCertificateKeyFile to match the names of the files that you have just created.
8. If you want all traffic that comes in on the regular HTTP port 80 to be redirected to the TLS secured host, include the following block in the definition of the /etc/httpd/conf.d/sales.example.com.conf file you have created previously:

```
<VirtualHost *:80>
            ServerName sales.example.com
            RewriteEngine on
            RewriteRule ^(/.*)$  https://%{HTTP_POST}$1
              [redirect=301]
</VirtualHost>
```

9. Restart the httpd service, using **systemctl start httpd.service** and make sure it is enabled by using **systemctl enable httpd.service**.

TIP Setting up a web server that uses TLS for enhanced security may seem difficult. It is not. Once you have access to the public/private key pair, you only need to configure the **SSLCertificateFile** and the **SSLCertificateKeyFile** directives to tell Apache where these files can be found. You do not need to remember any syntax specifics either because everything you need is in the mod_ssl package that needs to be installed to use TLS.

Deploying CGI Applications

Not many current websites serve static content only. Most web servers are using scripting in some way to provide access to content that is generated dynamically. This allows the web server to show exactly that content that is needed by the user, in the way that it can be interpreted by the browser the user is using. Most modern web servers are using some kind of CGI applications. There are several ways to provide dynamic content, some of which are discussed here.

Using Common Gateway Interface

Common Gateway Interface (CGI) is among the oldest methods to serve dynamic content. When a CGI resource is accessed, the Apache server executes that resource as a program and uses the output of that process. The advantage of using CGI is that it is very flexible; it does not define which scripting language is needed to generate the dynamic content. Therefore, a script such as a Perl script can be used, but compiled C programs or Java executables can be used as well.

To serve CGI contents, a few requirements exist:

- The ScriptAlias **ScriptAlias /cgi-bin/ "/var/www/cgi-bin/"** must exist. (Of course, it can be changed to refer to any other directory on the file system.)
- The ScriptAlias directory (that is, the directory where the scripts are stored) must be provided with the httpd_sys_script_exec_t SELinux context type.

Serving Dynamic PHP Content

PHP scripts are often used in an Apache environment. PHP scripts can be included using CGI, but a much better way is to install the mod_php Apache module which enables an internal PHP interpreter, which is much more efficient. Installing mod_php adds the configuration file /etc/httpd/conf.d/php.conf, which contains a few lines that allow PHP scripts to be executed (see Listing 33.3).

Listing 33.3 /etc/httpd/conf.d/php.conf Contents

```
[root@server2 conf.d]# grep -v '^#' php.conf
<FilesMatch \.php$>
    SetHandler application/x-httpd-php
</FilesMatch>

AddType text/html .php

DirectoryIndex index.php


php_value session.save_handler "files"
php_value session.save_path    "/var/lib/php/session"
```

This configuration file ensures that any file that has a .php extension will be executed by the httpd server as well, which makes a pretty easy solution to allow PHP scripts to be executed.

Using Dynamic Python Content

As is the case for PHP script, Python scripts can also be executed in two ways. They can be included as a CGI script, or the Web Server Gateway Interface (WSGI) can be used. This interface provides a new directive in the Apache configuration files to refer to the names of specific scripts. To deploy WSGI scripts, use the following approach:

1. Install the mod_wsgi package.
2. Add a **WSGIScriptAlias** line to a virtual host definition. This directive takes two arguments, the first of which refers to the alias on the Apache server, and the second of which refers directly to the Python script. So, the line could look like the following:

   ```
   WSGIScriptAlias /webapp/ /opt/webapp/app.py
   ```

3. Ensure that the WSGI application is executable by the Apache user and group and that the SELinux context is set to httpd_sys_content_t.

Connecting to Databases

Most web servers are connected to databases to store and fetch dynamic data. The MariaDB is often used for this purpose, as is the case for its predecessor MySQL. When the database is running on the same host, no additional configuration is required to access the database. If the database is running on a remote host, you must make sure that the **httpd_can_network_connect_db** Boolean is enabled. If it is not obvious that the target is a database, you also need to set the **httpd_can_network_connect** Boolean. In Chapter 35, "Configuring a Maria Database," you learn how to set up a MariaDB database.

TIP Are you already getting afraid for the exam and wondering how on earth you are ever going to remember all this? There is no need to! Just install the httpd-manual package and make sure that you know how to find all topics discussed in this chapter. Exercise 33.2 gives an impression, and Figure 33.2 shows what it looks like.

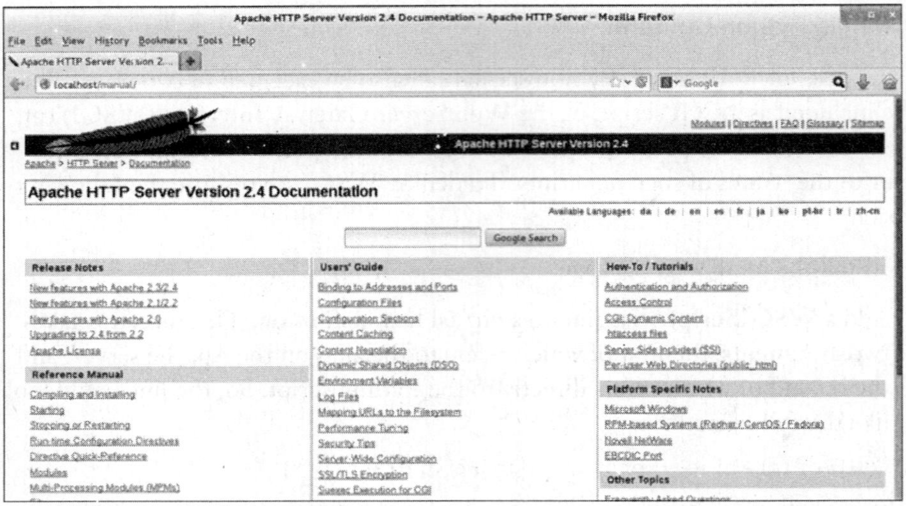

Figure 33.2 The Apache manual contains tons of very useful information.

Exercise 33.2 Surviving Advanced Apache Topics on the RHCE Test

In this exercise, you learn how to use the httpd-manual RPM package. The information is the most accessible when accessed from a graphical environment, but you can also read its contents using a text-based browser, such as elinks.

1. Type **yum install -y httpd-manual** to install the Apache manual.
2. Type **systemctl restart httpd**, followed by **systemctl status httpd**. (It is always a good idea to verify that a service came up without problems after restarting it.)
3. Start the Firefox browser and enter the URL **http://localhost/manual**.
4. Particularly, take a look at the following how-to / tutorials:
   - **Authentication and Authorization:** All you need to know about authenticated access to the webserver (discussed in the next section)
   - **CGI: Dynamic Content:** More information about working with dynamic content
5. Also take a look at the SSL/TLS encryption parts.
6. Make sure that you know where to find all other topics discussed in this chapter. It really will make the Apache-related topics on the RCHE test a lot easier for you!

TIP Do not wait until the exam to find out what the httpd-manual RPM has to offer. Do it now; on the exam you will not have the time to do it.

Configuring Private Directories

Some web servers need content to be secured and accessible for authorized users only. To do this, you need to create web server users and add all the required elements in the web server configuration.

The first time you are adding a web server user, use **htpasswd -c /etc/httpd/htpasswd username**. For all subsequent users, do *not* use the **-c** option; it will create a new file overwriting the old one every time you are using it again! Also notice that the users will be written in clear text to the configuration file, so make sure to store it in a secure location.

After creating one or more Apache users, you need to include the following block in the virtual host configuration:

```
<Directory /var/www/html/secret>
        AuthType Basic
        AuthName "secret files"
        AuthUserFile /etc/httpd/htpasswd
        Require user valid-user
</Directory>
```

In theory, you could also create a file with the name .htaccess and put that in the directory to which you want to allow access for authenticated users only. On a default Apache web server that does not make too much sense, though, because the AllowOverride none directive is set as a default for the Apache DocumentRoot.

Apache access restrictions can also be configured for group access. This method is pretty similar to configuring user-based access restrictions. The following procedure summarizes how to set up group-based Apache access limitations:

1. Create a file that contains the group information. This can be a file with the name .htgroup in the directory to which you want to restrict access, but you can also create a specific group file in a common location, like /etc/httpd/htgroup.
2. In the htgroup file, define the group name and the users that are members. This looks as in the following line:

```
sales: lisa bob linda jamie
```

3. In the directory specification, use the **AuthGroupFile** and the **Require** directives as in the following lines:

```
AuthGroupFile /etc/httpd/htgroup
Require group sales
```

4. Make sure that the users that are a member of the group are created, using the **htpasswd** command, as explained earlier in this section. Remember that if you do not want to overwrite any currently existing htpasswd file, you should *not* use the **-c** option while using the **htpasswd** command.

Table 33.4 Commonly Used Options for Apache Access Restrictions.

Key Topic

Directive	Use
AuthType	Specifies the type of authentication that will be used. Set to Basic in most cases. More advanced authentication types are beyond the RHCE objectives.
AuthName	Defines a name for the authenticated directory.
AuthUserFile	Defines which file is used to check for users.
AuthGroupFile	Refers to the file that contains group names that are used for HTTP access restrictions.
Require	Specifies which users or groups have access. Three common ways exist to use this parameter: ■ Require valid user: Allows access to all users that are defined ■ Require user lisa bob: Allows access to users lisa and bob ■ Require group admin: allows access to members of the admin group

Summary

In this chapter, you learned how to work with advanced Apache configurations. You revised your skills to set up virtual hosts in Apache, and you learned how to apply the correct SELinux settings. Following that, you learned how to manage TLS settings, configure access to dynamic web applications, and configure access for authenticated users or groups only.

Exam Preparation Tasks

Review All Key Topics

Review the most important topics in the chapter, noted with the Key Topic icon in the outer margin of the page. Table 33.5 lists a reference of these key topics and the page numbers on which each is found.

Table 33.5 Key Topics for Chapter 33

Key Topic Element	Description	Page
Table 33.2	httpd.conf essential configuration parameters overview	724
Table 33.3	Essential SELinux settings overview	725
Table 33.4	Apache authentication-related directives	736

Complete Tables and Lists from Memory

Print a copy of Appendix B, "Memory Tables," (found on the disc), or at least the section for this chapter, and complete the tables and lists from memory. Appendix C, "Memory Tables Answer Key," also on the disc, includes completed tables and lists to check your work.

Define Key Terms

Define the following key terms from this chapter and check your answers in the glossary:

directive, DocumentRoot, ServerRoot, TLS, SSL, certificate, public key, private key, certificate authority, CGI, WSGI

Review Questions

1. Which directive should you use for a directory that has contents that should never be accessed by the Apache web server?
2. Which Boolean should be set to ease the SELinux rules for Apache a bit?
3. Which SELinux context type do you need to set on a directory that is used as the DocumentRoot?

4. In which directory would you typically find the TLS certificate file and the TLS key?
5. Which parameter is used to identify the private key that a TLS secured virtual host should use?
6. What is the default configuration file for configuring TLS secured web servers?
7. Which command enables you to create a TLS certificate?
8. How do you configure Apache to run the Python script /opt/webapp/app.py?
9. What is wrong with using the command **htpasswd -c /etc/httpd/htpasswd lisa** if you have already created some Apache users?
10. How do you configure a directory "secret" that is accessible for authenticated users only?

End-of-Chapter Labs

In these end-of-chapter labs, you practice with your newly acquired advanced Apache configuration skills. Make sure that you master the topics here because it is very likely that you have to work on Apache assignments on the exam!

Lab 33.1

1. Set up a TLS secured Apache web server for the virtual host secure.example.com. It should also listen on port 80, but all requests that are directed to port 80 should be forwarded to port 443 immediately.
2. Use the virtual host sales.example.com that you have created earlier. Make sure that the entire contents of this server are accessible to authenticated users only. Only users who are a member of the sales group should get access. Make users linda and lara a member of the sales group and verify the working of this configuration.

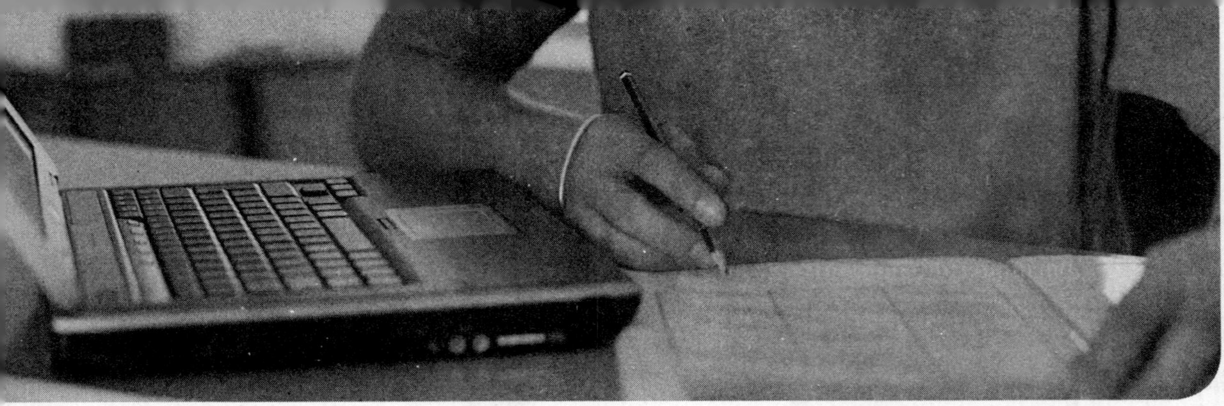

The following topics are covered in this chapter:

- Understanding DNS
- Setting Up a Cache-Only DNS Server
- Troubleshooting DNS Issues

The following RHCE exam objectives are covered in this chapter:

- Configure a caching-only name server
- Troubleshoot DNS client issues

CHAPTER 34

Configuring DNS

The Domain Name System (DNS) is used to translate hostnames into IP addresses, and when reversed, DNS zones are used to translate IP addresses into hostnames. It is also used to deliver additional types of information to DNS clients. An increasing number of services depend on DNS, which is why configuring DNS is an important task for Linux administrators. This chapter teaches you how to set up a cache-only DNS server. It also explains how to troubleshoot DNS client issues.

"Do I Know This Already?" Quiz

The "Do I Know This Already?" quiz allows you to assess whether you should read this entire chapter thoroughly or jump to the "Exam Preparation Tasks" section. If you are in doubt about your answers to these questions or your own assessment of your knowledge of the topics, read the entire chapter. Table 34.1 lists the major headings in this chapter and their corresponding "Do I Know This Already?" quiz questions. You can find the answers in Appendix A, "Answers to the 'Do I Know This Already?' Quizzes and 'Review Questions.'"

Table 34.1 "Do I Know This Already?" Section-to-Question Mapping

Foundation Topics Section	Questions
Understanding DNS	1–3
Setting up a Cache-Only DNS Server	4–8
Troubleshooting DNS Issues	9–10

1. Which of the following statements is *not* true about DNS lookups?
   a. Every host should be configured with at least 2 DNS name servers.
   b. If the requested data was not found locally on the DNS name server, a name server of the root domain is contacted.
   c. After retrieving information from another DNS server, the DNS server stores the requested information in its cache.
   d. Information in the cache of a DNS server expires once the TTL is reached.

2. Which of the following is not a default part of a resource record?
   a. Type
   b. Data
   c. Nameserver
   d. TTL

3. Which resource record is used to look up the hostname for a specific IPv4 address?
   a. A
   b. PTR
   c. AA
   d. AAAA

4. Which of the following is not a package that can be used on RHEL 7 as a caching name server?
   a. unbound
   b. bind
   c. unreal
   d. dnsmasq

5. Which command enables you to check for errors in the unbound configuration file?
   a. **checkconf**
   b. **unbound-checkconf**
   c. **testparm**
   d. **unbound-testparm**

6. When you are configuring the unbound cache-only DNS name server, a few parameters are very important to configure. Which of the following is *not* one of them?
   a. **forward-zone**
   b. **trust-anchor**
   c. **interface**
   d. **access-control**
7. Which parameter enables you to specify the name of a DNS domain for which DNSSEC validation can be skipped?
   a. **domain-insecure**
   b. **skip-option**
   c. **anchor**
   d. **trust-anchor**
8. Which of the following commands gives the information that needs to be specified with the **trust-anchor** option in unbound.conf?
   a. **dig +dnssec DNSKEY example.com**
   b. **dig +dnssec DNSSEC example.com**
   c. **dig dnssec +DNSKEY example.com**
   d. **dig dnssec example.com**
9. Which of the following commands enables you to dump the contents of the unbound cache and write the results to a file cache.txt?
   a. **unbound dump_cache**
   b. **systemctl dump unbound**
   c. **unbound-control --dump**
   d. **unbound-control dump_cache**
10. Which of the following messages would you expect in the dig output if the DNS name that was requested could not be found?
   a. ERROR
   b. DOMAIN_NOT_FOUND
   c. NXDOMAIN
   d. SRVFAIL

Foundation Topics

Understanding DNS

Key Topic

The Domain Name System is a hierarchical naming system used to get information about networked computers and other resources. The hierarchical structure is organized in domains, which contain resource records that hold information about the hosts and other resources in the DNS hierarchy. In modern network environments, DNS contains much more than just mappings between hosts and IP addresses. In a Kerberized environment, it is also used to store information about the services that are available in the network.

The DNS Hierarchy

On top of the DNS hierarchy is the root domain (.). Under the root domain are the top-level domains. These top-level domains are domains such as com, net, org, and many more (especially since the default top-level domains have recently been extended with new domain names). There are also top-level domains for each recognized country on the planet, such as cn for China, in for India, and de for Germany. Within the top-level domains, people and organizations can register their own domain. The complete name of the DNS domain always includes the path up to the top-level domain (and on some specific occasions, it includes a dot at the end of the path to refer to the DNS root domain). An example of such a domain name is redhat.com or rhatcert.com. (Notice that the domain names end in a dot to refer to the root domain.)

NOTE In applications, it is not common to include the dot at the end of the DNS name. In DNS configurations, it is important to make that difference. The name rhatcert.com could be interpreted as existing in the current DNS domain, whereas the name rhatcert.com is very specific about the location and beyond any doubt refers to a domain that exists in the DNS root domain.

Within these second-level domains, the owner of the second-level domain is free to do whatever he wants to organize the resource records in the most efficient way, as long as he also takes the responsibility of updating the DNS database with whatever resource records have been added. It is common to relate the resource records directly to the second-level domain, which gives names like www.rhatcert.com or ftp.redhat.com, but on many occasions an additional layer of subdomains is added.

DNS Terminology

When working with DNS, it is important to use correct terminology. This terminology is used when configuring services, and a misunderstanding of terminology may lead to errors in the DNS configuration. Some terms are particularly common:

Key Topic

- **Domain:** The collection of resource records that ends in a common name. A domain can contain subdomains.
- **Top-level domain:** The highest hierarchy in DNS names, containing domain names such as .com, .org., the ISO 3166-1 two-letter country code domain names, and the later additions like .aero, .bank, and more (see http://data.iana.org/TLD/tlds-alpha-by-domain.txt).
- **Subdomain:** A domain that is a branch within another domain, such as rhatcert within com or redhat within co.uk.
- **Name server:** The server that is responsible for the resource records in a zone. For redundancy purposes, normally more than one name server is available for each domain.
- **Resource record:** A database record that contains specific types of information that are managed by DNS. Different types of resource records exist.
- **Zone:** A domain minus all that has been delegated to subdomain servers. Basically, the zone refers to the branch of the DNS tree for which a specific name server is responsible.

Understanding DNS Lookups

Each computer and other device connected to the Internet is configured with a DNS resolver. The DNS resolver normally contains the IP addresses of one and up to three DNS name servers that are contacted when looking up DNS information on the Internet. If the first is not available, the second one is contacted, then the third one. If a DNS name server can be reached, it is the only DNS name server that is used. Therefore, if this DNS name server does not know the answer to a query, the request will not be tried again on another name server that is configured in the DNS resolver.

On a Linux system, the DNS resolver is in the configuration file /etc/resolv.conf, which on Red Hat is managed through NetworkManager and should not be edited directly; use **nmcli** or **nmtui** to set the DNS servers in the configuration for your network connections. When you request data from a DNS server, three types of answers can be given. In all of these, the adjective *authoritative* plays an important role. The status of the answer is shown in the output of a utility like the dig utility (see Listing 34.1). In the command output in Listing 34.1, the AUTHORITY: 13

part shows that no less than 13 different name servers were contacted to verify the authority of the answer.

An authoritative answer comes from a name server that is responsible for a zone and its records:

Key Topic

- **Local authoritative data:** An answer that is provided by a DNS server that is responsible for the requested data. This means that the answer is in resource records in the local zone.
- **Remote non-authoritative data via recursion:** If the DNS server cannot give the answer from its own database or cache, it contacts the responsible DNS server on the Internet via recursion. DNS recursion is the process where first a name server of the root domain is contacted to find the top-level domain that is needed. Then, a DNS server of the top-level domain is contacted to find the name server of the subdomain that is requested. Normally, the name server of the subdomain will be able to send the requested data. After receiving the answer, the DNS name server that originated the request will store the answer in its cache, after which the answer will be sent to the client that the request originally came from.
- **Local cached nonauthoritative data:** Once a DNS server has built up a cache that contains a number of records, answers can be provided directly from the cache. This makes the process of recursion unnecessary and therefore speeds up the procedure. The time that a record can be kept in cache is not infinite and is determined by the Time To Live (TTL). Once the TTL has expired, the cached entry becomes invalid, and the DNS server needs to start the recursion process again when the same data is requested once more.

> **NOTE** Different protocols are using a Time To Live (TTL). On DNS, the TTL refers to the amount of time that an answer can be kept in cache. In the IPv4 stack, the TTL refers to the number of routers that can be passed before an IPv4 packet is considered undeliverable.

Listing 34.1 Using **dig** to Verify the Authority of an Answer

```
[root@server1 ~]# dig rhatcert.com

; <<>> DiG 9.9.4-RedHat-9.9.4-18.el7_1.1 <<>> rhatcert.com
;; global options: +cmd
;; Got answer:
```

```
;; ->>HEADER<<- opcode: QUERY, status: NOERROR, id: 43963
;; flags: qr rd ra; QUERY: 1, ANSWER: 1, AUTHORITY: 13, ADDITIONAL: 1

;; OPT PSEUDOSECTION:
; EDNS: version: 0, flags:; udp: 4096
;; QUESTION SECTION:
;rhatcert.com.                IN      A

;; ANSWER SECTION:
rhatcert.com.          21599     IN      A      213.124.112.43

;; AUTHORITY SECTION:
.               6184      IN      NS      f.root-servers.net.
.               6184      IN      NS      m.root-servers.net.
.               6184      IN      NS      l.root-servers.net.
.               6184      IN      NS      c.root-servers.net.
.               6184      IN      NS      k.root-servers.net.
.               6184      IN      NS      e.root-servers.net.
.               6184      IN      NS      b.root-servers.net.
.               6184      IN      NS      a.root-servers.net.
.               6184      IN      NS      i.root-servers.net.
.               6184      IN      NS      d.root-servers.net.
.               6184      IN      NS      h.root-servers.net.
.               6184      IN      NS      j.root-servers.net.
.               6184      IN      NS      g.root-servers.net.

;; Query time: 108 msec
;; SERVER: 192.168.4.200#53(192.168.4.200)
;; WHEN: Sun May 17 10:27:37 EDT 2015
;; MSG SIZE  rcvd: 268
```

Understanding Resource Records

DNS resource records are the entries in the DNS zone that contain the information that is requested. Each resource record contains four different types of data:

- **Type:** This is the sort of information in this resource record. An example is an A resource record, which is used to map a hostname to an IP address.
- **Data:** The specific data that is stored in this record.

- **Class:** In theory, different resource record classes can be used; in practice, this is almost IN, which stands for Internet. Originally, DNS was intended not only to be available for Internet networks but also as a lookup system for other networks, such as CHAOSnet (class=CH) and Hesiod (class=HS). The class tells the DNS server what network the resource record is for.
- **TTL:** The Time To Live in seconds. It is useful to set a TTL on resource records that are cached to ensure that it does not happen that expired information is provided to the client. At the other end, once the TTL has expired, the authoritative name server needs to be contacted again, which is why it shouldn't be set too strict.

There are several important resource record types. Table 34.2 provides an overview of the types that matter most.

Key Topic

Table 34.2 Important Resource Record Types

Resource Record Type	Use
A (IPv4 address)	Maps a hostname to an IPv4 address.
AAAA (IPv6 address)	Maps a hostname to an IPv6 address.
CNAME (canonical name)	An alias for one name to another name that should have an A or AAAA record.
PTR (pointer)	Maps an IP address (v4 or v6) to a hostname.
NS (name server)	Maps a domain name to a DNS name server that is authoritative for the DNS zone.
SOA (start of authority)	Contains generic information about how a DNS zone works. It contains information about who is responsible for administration of the domain.
MX (mail exchange)	Indicates which MTA mail servers are used within a DNS domain.
TXT (text)	Maps a name to human readable text. This type of resource record is for instance used by protocols like Send Policy Framework, which in email is used to verify the name of the domain an email message was received from.
SRV (service)	Indicates which host to contact for specific services such as LDAP and Kerberos.

Setting Up a Cache-Only DNS Server

In the preceding section, you saw that a DNS resolver (be it standalone or built in in a recursive name server) has to send quite a few packets to get the information it needs. To make the process more efficient, it is quite common to install a cache-only DNS server. Using such a server makes DNS requests much more efficient, because many requests can be handled locally.

Using a cache-only DNS name server is common for smaller sites or departments of a larger organization, where it does make sense to handle DNS queries locally, but it does not make sense to keep a copy of the DNS database locally as well. In this section, you learn how to set up a cache-only DNS server.

Understanding the Need for DNSSEC

When setting up a cache-only DNS server, security is also important. Because a DNS request is mostly connectionless (the TCP protocol is used in special cases only, like when a UDP packet is too small to contain the response), DNS servers can be easily spoofed. A specific security problem for cache-only DNS servers is known as *DNS cache poisoning*, which is a process where the DNS server cache is filled with faulty data. Once the DNS cache is poisoned, clients that are using the cache can easily be directed to fake servers, which poses an important threat to security. To prevent against DNS cache spoofing, it is highly recommended to protect the DNS server with Domain Name System Security Extensions (DNSSEC) validation. This allows the DNS server to validate data before it is placed in cache.

Configuring the Unbound Caching Name Server

Different packages are available on RHEL 7 to configure a caching-only DNS name server, including bind, dnsmasq, and unbound. In RHEL 7, unbound is the recommended package, and in this chapter you learn how to configure unbound as a caching-only DNS name server. The reason that unbound is the recommended name server is because it is more secure than any of the other DNS name server packages. In Exercise 34.1, you learn how to configure the unbound caching name server.

TIP Unbound is the preferred package in RHEL 7, but it is not the only package. If you are an expert on any of the other caching-only DNS name server solutions, feel free to configure that on the exam.

Exercise 34.1 Installing and Configuring the Unbound Caching Name Server

1. On server1, install the unbound RPM package, using **yum install -y unbound**.
2. Start and enable the service, using **systemctl start unbound; systemctl enable unbound**.
3. By default, unbound only listens on the localhost network interface. That is not very useful. Open the configuration file /etc/unbound/unbound.conf with an editor, locate the interface parameter, and configure it as follows to allow it to accept incoming connections on any interface:
   ```
   interface: 0.0.0.0
   ```
4. Also by default, unbound does not accept any client connections. To accept incoming client connections, change the **access-control** parameter in unbound.conf to accept requests from the IP addresses that are specified by adding a line that looks like the following:
   ```
   access-control: 192.168.1.0/24 allow
   ```
5. When setting up a caching-only DNS name server, it also is a good idea to configure a forwarder. This makes sure that the caching-only name server forwards all DNS requests, instead of doing the name resolving for itself. In DNS, you configure forwarders per zone. To forward all requests to another DNS server, you need to configure a forward zone for the root (.) domain. Assuming that you have set up an IPA server as described in Appendix D, "Setting Up Identity Management," you will have a DNS server available at 192.168.122.200, so make sure to configure the forwarder as follows:
   ```
   forward-zone:
               name: "."
               forward-addr: 192.168.122.200
   ```
6. Save the changes to /etc/unbound/unbound.conf and run the command **unbound-checkconf** to verify that you have made no syntax errors.
7. Restart the unbound service using **systemctl restart unbound**.
8. Open the firewall for DNS traffic using **firewall-cmd --permanent --add-service=dns**, followed by **firewall-cmd --reload**.
9. On server2, start nmtui, select your network connection, and configure the DNS server that is now listening on server1 as the only DNS server on server 2.
10. Use **dig example.com** and verify that the answer is provided by the unbound server.

> **TIP** By default, unbound requires DNSSEC validation on all DNS responses it receives. For internal DNS domains that have not been configured with DNSSEC, you may want to bypass this. To do that, include the **domain-insecure** parameter in the unbound.conf file, followed by the name of the DNS domain you do not want to do DNSSEC validation for:
>
> ```
> domain-insecure: example.com
> ```
>
> If you are getting errors about server-keys that do not exist, you can fix those using the **unbound-control-setup** command, which creates all required keys automatically.

Configuring Trust Anchors

In modern DNS configurations, the use of DNSSEC is very important. Not all DNS domains are completely configured with DNSSEC, which may give problems if these domains have not been configured for exclusion of DNSSEC security by using he **domain-insecure** parameter. For these domains, a trust anchor can be used as a replacement for a complete chain of trust for the domain.

To get the trust anchor for a domain, you need to use the command **dig +dnssec DNSKEY yourdomain.com** on that domain. Use the complete output of that command as the argument for the **trust-anchor** parameter in unbound.conf. If multiple keys are shown in the output, you just have to use one of them. Listing 34.2 shows sample output of the **dig +dnssec DNSKEY** command.

Listing 34.2 Sample Output of the **dig +dnssec DNSKEY** Command

```
[sander@lab ~]$ dig +dnssec DNSKEY rhatcert.com

; <<>> DiG 9.9.4-RedHat-9.9.4-14.el7 <<>> +dnssec DNSKEY rhatcert.com
;; global options: +cmd
;; Got answer:
;; ->>HEADER<<- opcode: QUERY, status: NOERROR, id: 15565
;; flags: qr rd ra; QUERY: 1, ANSWER: 5, AUTHORITY: 0, ADDITIONAL: 1

;; OPT PSEUDOSECTION:
; EDNS: version: 0, flags: do; udp: 1400
;; QUESTION SECTION:
;rhatcert.com.                  IN      DNSKEY

;; ANSWER SECTION:
rhatcert.com.           86400   IN      DNSKEY      257 3 7
```

```
AwEAAf7hGmbiDxTt/ZU7yZNXvyyQbTpI1nHxujaCc3tymK2QI4DFEXjw
WwzZbO/UP1J45SwFJrUyylyhIMwZPdi/eSnS7dej3smfZiplLFbPGULQ
8YlDydybJcp0mOY3wNp1LCek6G25t+r7eeQlWyqphx91g9JcdUhrRkt7
iUiI7Vi7U39gmz/775R1RM6qpDasx8Dr1PDkk4xyDgz2RZAJbv8PiyHy
3Ilu1c3juDF66A3nEneZf7T4L2AL2YuSrp1JCc/Bhbjqxy1mShgeTsPr
Wyt8EI25AGXgc0UnmIVu7yV+/ujqNRNVuGpE9YvqQozoZonPIdyRz9ag OaG/A2iZx3c=
rhatcert.com.            86400      IN      DNSKEY      256 3 7
AwEAAdnA+3bY6JIyshZLrpImhTdVTMs/NM/tGH0gre+znPPJ72j1CVtP
l7y8dl+fEab5+0LJ0PWuQ+uavmaMDiqMNV1dEISEQV9ViX7RelLXXnjv
oa8rqoLREJX4mrcwMSitt/GDGTSBEaUqzVh9sO/n7ql18KV6y/p+PfKm lbQV/SeN
rhatcert.com.            86400      IN      DNSKEY      256 3 7
AwEAAbdYi5tz8UJ/T0X+R0+cXkq5/+UYX1JX4EzKkw/QIyCN8XKMuwf0
zSl5xiHRizNC1iqSV1RUlkH8dJiEplCZz/gH2jpioswuCxt3lmZ1GfxD
7nDjAZX0fCUTB7xdhwEHD2N12nCb1S+3XrB5+xJTuu9NrvKtgM48gDnO sTa4Lq37
rhatcert.com.            86400      IN      RRSIG      DNSKEY 7 2 86400
20150705140130 20150103140130
21600 rhatcert.com. diXlU+A/
d4XULjIlx7mm9thc2we9f9AIO1h75TqWVkb97TbOzoeRBiR+
HQ7J7hfz5kYa3EKxoal/C7GB6uqdt111njSu1OYDOV5dUD3+CB/j/hxo
eKcXknYDU/utKHe8qF+diIjVMJ4HEZTWzpZH08YVj7kwVWfvqnqFJI+v
DlfgfbKtO0GzZ3OQxizHaCRsJWAi4LnNL8MmPk7FjfjaS74sNilJY40N
4vMUOXivsme74h1wFHmjXe6xgZmBAAypoE/YYE1AGwmvsW/UOlWW6G/e
YBWtTzfd6t71NmCn9inR+zGWJqrCzY9c7iNelu1/Vab/KDhzzEyCrfSq l8Mzwg==
rhatcert.com.            86400      IN      RRSIG      DNSKEY 7 2 86400
20150705140130 20150103140130
61457 rhatcert.com.
u7x3AyA7rjEIHUtVb0esUsqVbkZ65yeqI1by5iOMrBK2muqjmvncLLf9
z21ff1JME4IjurjR4jK3VRBqK2NPRIGKo/5x0I1Di5oL8BSrce7nEfID
MUSVkmeyanKJBfCkRXmq6SlH8DGHygTSMuzKRyBu/S6GtpuL31ahRerk pv4=

;; Query time: 21 msec
;; SERVER: 212.54.35.25#53(212.54.35.25)
;; WHEN: Mon Jan 05 15:33:01 EST 2015
;; MSG SIZE  rcvd: 1085
```

Troubleshooting DNS Issues

Sometimes your DNS configuration might not work. If that happens, there are some approaches to troubleshoot. You dump the DNS cache that unbound keeps to fix issues such as stale resource records. If the DNS issues are related to the client configuration, the **dig** command may provide valuable information.

Dumping and Changing the Unbound Cache

The unbound service caches DNS records. On some occasions, these records may become outdated. If needed, you can use the **unbound-control dump_cache** command to dump the contents of the cache (which may be huge!). By default, the results of this command are printed to STDOUT; you may want to use redirection to write the results of the command to a file. In this file, you can make modifications, such as removing records that are no longer valid. After doing this, you can write the contents of the file back to the unbound server cache to update what is currently kept in the cache.

If while analyzing the unbound cache you notice that there are outdated records in the cache, you can use the **unbound-control flush myhost.zone.com** command to purge the outdated record. Alternatively, you can purge the current entries for an entire zone from cache, using **unbound-control flush somezone.com**.

To dump the contents of the unbound cache, use **unbound-control dump_cache > unbound-cache.txt**. To load the contents of the unbound-cache.txt file after making modifications in it, use **unbound-control load_cache < unbound-cache.txt**.

Using dig

If DNS is not working, you can use the **dig** command on a client computer to analyze what is going wrong. The **dig** command offers many options that tell you how information is obtained from DNS. In its most basic use, you can use **dig** to test that information about a specific domain can be resolved. To do this, type, for instance, **dig rhatcert.com**. It shows the results that you see in Listing 34.3.

Listing 34.3 Analyzing DNS Data with **dig**

```
[root@server ~]# dig rhatcert.com

; <<>> DiG 9.9.4-RedHat-9.9.4-14.el7 <<>> rhatcert.com
;; global options: +cmd
;; Got answer:
;; ->>HEADER<<- opcode: QUERY, status: NOERROR, id: 37234
;; flags: qr rd ra; QUERY: 1, ANSWER: 1, AUTHORITY: 0, ADDITIONAL: 1

;; OPT PSEUDOSECTION:
; EDNS: version: 0, flags:; udp: 1400
;; QUESTION SECTION:
;rhatcert.com.                  IN      A
```

```
;; ANSWER SECTION:
rhatcert.com.              86400     IN      A         213.124.112.43

;; Query time: 36 msec
;; SERVER: 212.54.35.25#53(212.54.35.25)
;; WHEN: Wed Jan 07 13:20:09 CET 2015
;; MSG SIZE  rcvd: 57
```

In the dig output, much information is provided. The **global options** line shows which dig parameters have been set. Normally, you are fine using the default parameters. Then there is the **Got answer** section, which gives information about the answer that was received. This part contains technical information about the DNS server, and also the status of the answer, which in this case is **NOERROR**. Therefore, resolving the DNS name was successful. Table 34.3 gives a short overview of common dig status information indicators.

Key Topic

Table 34.3 Common dig Status Indicators

Indicator	Meaning
NOERROR	DNS resolving was successful.
NXDOMAIN	The DNS information that was requested was not found.
SERVFAIL	There was an error contacting a vital DNS server.

In the question section, dig shows what the original query was. In this case, it was for an A resource record, of the IN record type, for the domain rhatcert.com. The answer section gives information about the actual answer that was received and in this case shows that the domain is reachable on IP address 213.124.112.43. Finally, the last four lines show a summary of query details.

Using dig, you can also request specific information about a DNS domain. Use, for instance, **dig MX rhatcert.com** to find the mail exchange that has been configured for the requested domain, or **dig NS rhatcert.com** to find which is the responsible name server for the domain. Another very useful example of dig usage is **dig -x 213.124.112.43**. This command shows you which name is configured in DNS for the requested IP address.

Also very useful is that dig can be used to query a specific DNS server. Use, for instance, **dig @server1.example.com MX rhatcert.com** to request the mail exchange server for rhatcert.com specifically from server1.example.com.

Analyzing Client Issues

If for any reason dig does not provide the answers that you expect, you need to do some basic troubleshooting. The following steps in general will help you finding the reason why DNS is not working as expected:

1. Use **cat /etc/resolv.conf** to verify the contents of the DNS resolver.
2. If the contents of resolv.conf looks right, try to ping the name server(s) mentioned. If the name server(s) do answer, make sure that you have not made a mistake in the name server address. You might have used a server that just is not a name server.
3. If the information in /etc/resolv.conf is wrong, use nmcli to verify the NetworkManager information to see which DNS name servers have been set. Do not modify the contents of /etc/resolv.conf manually; this information is managed through NetworkManager.

Summary

In this chapter, you learned how to set up DNS. The chapter started with an introduction of the working of DNS and which components are used in DNS. You next learned how to set up the unbound service as a DNS name server. Toward the end of the chapter, you learned how you can use dig to verify DNS issues, and how you can check the current DNS resolver workings to ensure that DNS is functioning properly.

Exam Preparation Tasks

Review All Key Topics

Review the most important topics in the chapter, noted with the Key Topic icon in the outer margin of the page. Table 34.4 lists a reference of these key topics and the page numbers on which each is found.

Table 34.4 Key Topics for Chapter 34

Key Topic Element	Description	Page Number
Paragraph	Definition of DNS	744
List	DNS terminology	745
List	DNS answer types	746

Key Topic Element	Description	Page Number
Table 34.2	Important resource record types	748
Table 34.3	Common dig status indicators	754

Complete Tables and Lists from Memory

Print a copy of Appendix B, "Memory Tables" (found on the disc), or at least the section for this chapter, and complete the tables and lists from memory. Appendix C, "Memory Tables Answer Key," also on the disc, includes completed tables and lists to check your work.

Define Key Terms

Define the following key terms from this chapter and check your answers in the glossary:

domain, zone, resource record, name server, resolver, top-level domain, subdomain, recursion, TTL, unbound, DNSSEC

Review Questions

1. Which resource record would you use to set up resolving for names to IPv6 addresses?
2. Mail servers do not succeed in delivering messages to your domain. Which resource record is probably not configured correctly?
3. Which command enables you to verify the current mail server setting for example.com?
4. Which command enables you to find the name that is configured in DNS for IP address 192.168.4.122?
5. Which setting do you configure in unbound.conf to make sure that all requests your caching server receives are forwarded to the DNS server with IP address 10.0.0.100?
6. What do you need to do to make sure that all clients on the 192.168.122.0/24 network can use your unbound DNS server?
7. Which parameter do you need to use to exclude a zone that is not signed with DNSSEC keys?

8. Which parameter do you configure in unbound.conf to make sure the unbound name server is listening on real interfaces and not just the localhost interface?
9. Which command enables you to verify that you have not made any typos in the unbound configuration?
10. Which command enables you to dump the unbound DNS cache so that it can be further analyzed?

End-of-Chapter Labs

In the end-of-chapter labs, you need three different servers. You need one server configured as a real DNS sever. If you are using the virtual machines that are provided with this book, you can use the labipa.example.com server for this purpose. Alternatively, you can set up your own DNS server according to the instructions in Appendix D.

Lab 34.1

1. Configure server1 as a cache-only DNS server. It should be configured to forward all requests to the central DNS server.
2. Configure server2 to be using the cache-only DNS server you have running on server1.

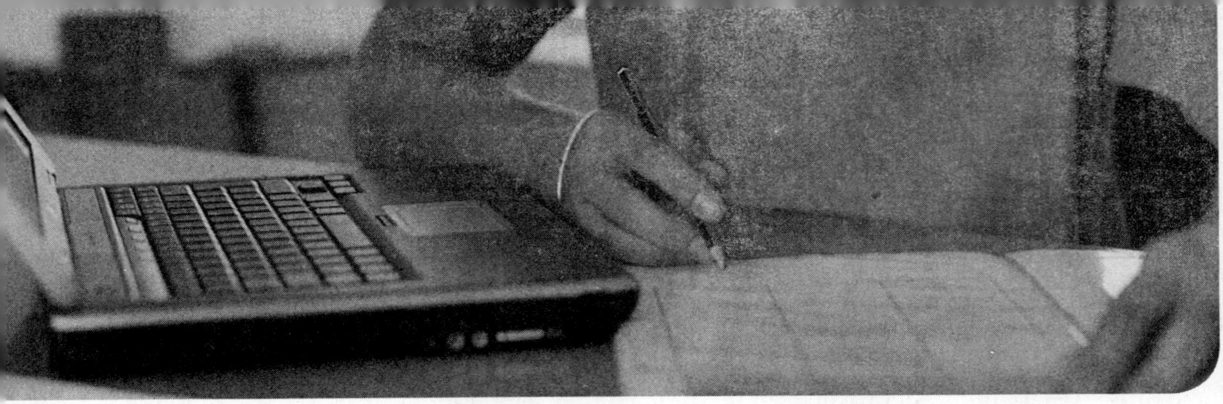

The following topics are covered in this chapter:

- MariaDB Base Configuration
- Performing Simple Database Administration Tasks
- MariaDB Backup and Restore

The following RHCE exam topics are covered in this chapter:

- Install and configure MariaDB
- Back up and restore a database
- Create a simple database schema
- Perform simple SQL queries against a database

## CHAPTER 35

Configuring a MariaDB Database

Databases are an essential element of a typical LAMP (Linux, Apache, MySQL, PHP) stack. In RHEL 7, MariaDB is the default database solution. In this chapter, you learn how to install a MariaDB database and perform essential database management tasks.

"Do I Know This Already?" Quiz

The "Do I Know This Already?" quiz allows you to assess whether you should read this entire chapter thoroughly or jump to the "Exam Preparation Tasks" section. If you are in doubt about your answers to these questions or your own assessment of your knowledge of the topics, read the entire chapter. Table 35.1 lists the major headings in this chapter and their corresponding "Do I Know This Already?" quiz questions. You can find the answers in Appendix A, "Answers to the 'Do I Know This Already?' Quizzes and 'Review Questions.'"

Table 35.1 "Do I Know This Already?" Section-to-Question Mapping

Foundation Topics Section	Questions
MariaDB Base Configuration	1–2
Performing Simple Database Administration Tasks	3–7
MariaDB Backup and Restore	8–10

1. Which command provides the easiest solution to apply basic security settings to MariaDB after installing it?
   a. Modify settings in the my.cnf configuration file
   b. Modify /etc/sysconfig/mariadb and set the parameter **CHROOT=yes**
   c. Run the mysql_secure_installation command after installation
   d. Enable the SELinux mysql policy module using **semodule -i mysql**

2. Which of the following parameters in my.cnf should you modify to enable full network access to MariaDB databases?
   a. Set the bind address to ::.
   b. Set skip-networking to 1.
   c. Disable connections through sockets.
   d. Use **firewall-cmd --enable mysql** to open the firewall.

3. Which command should you use to log in to the database using administrative permissions?
   a. **mariadb -u admin -p**
   b. **mysql -u root**
   c. **mysql -u root -p**
   d. **mysql admin@localhost -p**

4. You want to add a user account to the current database. To do so, you need to find out the current attributes for users, which are created in a table with the name users. Which command can you use to show these attributes?
   a. **describe users;**
   b. **show attributes for users;**
   c. **list users;**
   d. **select users;**

5. Which of the following shows correct syntax to add a user into the users table?
   a. **INSERT INTO user (Host,User,Password) VALUES (localhost,linda,password)**
   b. **INSERT INTO user (Host,User,Password) VALUES (localhost,linda,password);**
   c. **INSERT INTO user (Host,User,Password) VALUES ('localhost', 'linda','password');**
   d. **INSERT INTO user (Host,User,Password) VALUES ('localhost', 'linda','password';)**

6. Which command enables you to find all users who have the last name Johnson, assuming that the last name is stored in the name field?
   a. **select * from user where name = johnson;**
   b. **select user where name = johnson;**

c. **select * where name = johnson;**
d. **select * from user name = johnson;**

7. Which command shows correct syntax for adding a user lisa with the password password on the current database?
   a. **create user lisa@localhost identified by password;**
   b. **create user lisa identified by 'password';**
   c. **create lisa@localhost identified by 'password'**
   d. **create user lisa@localhost identified by 'password';**

8. Which of the following is not true about physical database backups?
   a. The physical backup stores a raw copy of the database files.
   b. The physical backup contains the database structure that is retrieved by using a query on the database.
   c. To make a physical database, the database must be stopped temporarily.
   d. For creating physical database backups, it is recommended to use LVM snapshots.

9. Which command shows correct syntax for making a logical database backup of the videos database?
   a. **mysqldump -u root -p videos -X --databases > /root/videos-db.dump**
   b. **mysqldump -u root -p videos -X --databases /root/videos-db**
   c. **mysqldump -u root videos --databases > /root/videos-db.dump**
   d. **mysqldump -u root -p videos --databases > /root/videos-db.dump**

10. Which command shows how to create a snapshot of the LVM logical volume /dev/vgdata/lvmariadb, which is needed to create a physical backup of your databases?
   a. **lvcreate -s -n lvmariadb-snap -L 2G /dev/vgdata/lvmariadb**
   b. **lvcreate -n lvmariadb-snap -L 2G lvmariadb**
   c. **lvcreate -s -n lvmariadb-snap 2G /dev/vgdata/lvmariadb**
   d. **lvcreate -s -n lvmariadb-snap -L 2G lvmariadb**

Foundation Topics

MariaDB Base Configuration

To start, you need to install MariaDB and apply basic settings. In this section, you learn how to do that by installing the software, securing it, and making small changes to the database configuration file /etc/my.cnf. Notice that many of the components of MariaDB have names that refer to MySQL. That is normal because MariaDB is a derivative from the MySQL database software.

Key Topic

To install MariaDB, complete the following steps:

1. Use **yum install mariadb mariadb-server mariadb-test -y** on the server where you want to install the software.
2. Type **systemctl start mariadb** followed by **systemctl enable mariadb** to start and enable the database service.
3. Verify that mariadb is running by using **systemctl status mariadb.** This should show the current status, including recent messages that have been logged. Listing 35.1 shows what this looks like.

Listing 35.1 Checking Mariadb Status Using **systemctl**

```
[root@server1 system]# systemctl status mariadb -l
mariadb.service - MariaDB database server
   Loaded: loaded (/usr/lib/systemd/system/mariadb.service; enabled)
   Active: active (running) since Thu 2015-03-26 04:44:32 PDT; 2 days
ago
 Main PID: 1663 (mysqld_safe)
   CGroup: /system.slice/mariadb.service
           ├─1663 /bin/sh /usr/bin/mysqld_safe --basedir=/usr
           └─2220 /usr/libexec/mysqld --basedir=/usr --datadir=/var/
lib/mysql --plugin-dir=/usr/lib64/mysql/plugin --log-error=/var/log/
mariadb/mariadb.log --pid-file=/var/run/mariadb/mariadb.pid --socket=/
var/lib/mysql/mysql.sock

Mar 26 04:44:24 server1.example.com systemd[1]: Starting MariaDB
database server...
Mar 26 04:44:27 server1.example.com mysqld_safe[1663]: 150326 04:44:27
mysqld_safe Logging to '/var/log/mariadb/mariadb.log'.
Mar 26 04:44:28 server1.example.com mysqld_safe[1663]: 150326 04:44:28
mysqld_safe Starting mysqld daemon with databases from /var/lib/mysql
Mar 26 04:44:32 server1.example.com systemd[1]: Started MariaDB
database server.
```

After installing MariaDB, it is a good idea to secure it as well. To do this, run the **mysql_secure_installation** command. This will apply a few security settings. Listed here are the questions that are asked, with a short explanation for each. Listing 35.2 shows the output of the command, with all the questions highlighted in a bold typeface font:

Key Topic

- **Enter current password for root (enter for none):** As stated, if the database root user has a password already, enter it here. If not, just press **Enter** to continue.
- **Set root password? [Y/n]:** Answer **y** to set the root password and enter the password that you want to use twice.
- **Remove anonymous users? [Y/n]:** Answer **y** to remove the anonymous users who by default exist in the database.
- **Disallow root login remotely? [Y/n]:** Answer **y** to ensure that the root user can do local login only. For root users who want to access remotely, it is still possible to connect to the server using Secure Shell (SSH) first.
- **Remove test database and access to it? [Y/n]:** Upon installation, a test database is created. For security reasons, it is a good idea to remove this test database, but because in this chapter the purpose is to learn working with the database, you should keep it. Therefore, answer **n** to this question.
- **Reload privilege tables now? [Y/n]:** Answer **y** to save and apply the changes you made.

Listing 35.2 Running mysql_secure_installation

```
[root@server1 system]# mysql_secure_installation

NOTE: RUNNING ALL PARTS OF THIS SCRIPT IS RECOMMENDED FOR ALL MariaDB
      SERVERS IN PRODUCTION USE!  PLEASE READ EACH STEP CAREFULLY!

In order to log into MariaDB to secure it, we'll need the current
password for the root user.  If you have just installed MariaDB, and
you haven't set the root password yet, the password will be blank,
so you should just press enter here.

Enter current password for root (enter for none):
OK, successfully used password, moving on...

Setting the root password ensures that nobody can log into the MariaDB
```

```
root user without the proper authorisation.

By default, a MariaDB installation has an anonymous user, allowing
anyone
to log into MariaDB without having to have a user account created for
them.  This is intended only for testing, and to make the installation
go a bit smoother.  You should remove them before moving into a
production environment.

Remove anonymous users? [Y/n] y
 ... Success!

Normally, root should only be allowed to connect from 'localhost'.
This
ensures that someone cannot guess at the root password from the
network.

Disallow root login remotely? [Y/n] y
 ... Success!

By default, MariaDB comes with a database named 'test' that anyone can
access.  This is also intended only for testing, and should be removed
before moving into a production environment.

Remove test database and access to it? [Y/n] n
 ... skipping.

Reloading the privilege tables will ensure that all changes made so far
will take effect immediately.

Reload privilege tables now? [Y/n] y
 ... Success!

Cleaning up...

All done!  If you have completed all of the above steps, your MariaDB
installation should now be secure.

Thanks for using MariaDB!
```

MariaDB can be used locally only, or it can be accessed over the network. There are advantages to both. If MariaDB is accessible over the network, it is easy to set up a service stack where the database is running on one server and related services are running somewhere else. This offers the maximum possible performance for the database, but it also increases the risk that things go wrong, because the database is accessible over the network. If you want to maximize security, consider switching off network access completely. That implies that all services that are using the database are available on the same server.

To determine whether MariaDB is going to use networking, you'll modify a few parameters in the /etc/my.cnf configuration file (which is the MariaDB main configuration file). Listing 35.3 shows sample contents of this file.

Listing 35.3 My.cnf Sample Contents

```
[root@server1 ~]# cat /etc/my.cnf
[mysqld]
datadir=/var/lib/mysql
socket=/var/lib/mysql/mysql.sock
# Disabling symbolic-links is recommended to prevent assorted security
risks
symbolic-links=0
# Settings user and group are ignored when systemd is used.
# If you need to run mysqld under a different user or group,
# customize your systemd unit file for mariadb according to the
# instructions in http://fedoraproject.org/wiki/Systemd

[mysqld_safe]
log-error=/var/log/mariadb/mariadb.log
pid-file=/var/run/mariadb/mariadb.pid

#
# include all files from the config directory
#
!includedir /etc/my.cnf.d
```

In the [mysqld] section, you can set a lot of parameters, including the following:

Key Topic

- **bind-address** The address on which the database service will be listening. Set to :: if you want to enable access through all IP addresses (IPv4 as well as IPv6), or leave blank to enable access over IPv4 only. Alternatively, you can specify the IP addresses of specific interfaces where the database should bind to.

- **skip-networking** Set to 1 to disable all networking. Communications with other local processes in that case will go through sockets, which by default are in /var/lib/mysql/mysql.sock. When you use this approach, the client software also needs to access the database through sockets and cannot use localhost and IP for local database access.
- **port** Specifies the port to listen on for TCP/IP connections.

For more information about the settings that you can configure, see the output of the command **/usr/libexec/mysqld --help --verbose**.

If the database needs to be accessed remotely, the firewall needs to be opened as well. MariaDB uses the firewalld mysql service file, which is in /usr/lib/firewalld/services/mysql.xml, so the firewall can easily be opened with the standard port 3306 using the following two commands:

firewall-cmd --permanent --add-service=mysql

firewall-cmd --reload

In Exercise 35.1, you learn how to install a MariaDB database.

Exercise 35.1 Installing MariaDB

In Exercise 35.1, you perform a base installation of MariaDB. You also disable network access and apply security settings. You then verify that some default system databases are available.

1. Type **yum install -y mariadb mariadb-server mariadb-test** to install the database software.
2. Use **systemctl start mariadb; systemctl enable mariadb** to start and enable the mariadb software.
3. Verify that mariadb is listening, using **ss -tulpen | grep mysql**. You should see a mysqld process listening on port 3306.
4. Disable networking by adding the line **skip_networking=1** to /etc/my.cnf and restart mariadb, using **systemctl restart mariadb**.
5. Start securing mariadb, using **mysql_secure_installation.** Set the password for the database root user to **password**, disable remote root access, and remove the test database and any anonymous users.
6. Type **mysql -u root -p** to log in to the database as root, and have the database prompt for a password.

7. From the MariaDB interactive shell prompt, type **show databases;** to display databases that are currently available. The result should look like Listing 35.4.
8. Type **exit;** to quit the MariaDB interactive shell interface.

Listing 35.4 After Logging In as Root, Type **show databases;** to See Which Databases Are Currently Available

```
MariaDB [(none)]> show databases;
+--------------------+
| Database           |
+--------------------+
| information_schema |
| mysql              |
| performance_schema |
+--------------------+
4 rows in set (0.00 sec)
```

When working with MariaDB, it is important to know the difference between databases, tables, and records. Table 35.2 summarizes them.

Table 35.2 Database Elements

Key Topic

Name	Description
Database	The totality of data that consists of different tables. Employees can be the name of a database.
Table	Classes of items that are used in a database. In an employee's database, you can have tables such as employment status and addressbook. Within the database, the tables can be interrelated. In each database, you must have at least one table.
Fields	The type of information that is created in a table. In an addressbook table, you have fields such as name, street, city, for example.
Record	The specific dataset stored in a table. Every customer, for example, has a record in the addressbook database where the name and street records contain specific values for that customer.
Value	Specific values that are stored in a field. For instance, the name field in the addressbook table may have Linda Jones as its value.

Performing Simple Database Administration Tasks

Even if you are a Linux administrator, it is useful to have basic knowledge of database administration commands. That does not make you a database administrator, but it does help you perform basic configuration tasks.

To start working with databases, you need to connect to the database service first. To do this, you use the **mysql** command, as in **mysql -u root -h localhost -p**. (Even if you are using MariaDB, many commands are still **mysql** commands.) This command logs you in as user root to server localhost and then prompts for a password. After logging in, as seen in Exercise 35.1, you enter the MySQL interactive shell where you will work with databases. You have already seen the command **show databases;**, which displays a list of available databases. Notice that in the MySQL shell commands are not case sensitive (but names of databases and tables are case sensitive). Also notice that all commands are terminated with a semicolon (;).

Working with databases looks a little like working with directories. The database administrator creates a database, then starts using the database, and then enters the contents of the database. The **USE** command is used like the **cd** command from a bash shell. Where **cd** allows you to switch between directories easily, the **USE** command allows you to switch between databases. Try for instance the following commands (after logging in to the MySQL shell environment as root):

1. Type **CREATE DATABASE addressbook;** to create a database with the name addressbook.
2. Type **USE addressbook;** to start using the addressbook database.
3. Type **SHOW TABLES;** to show its current tables. You should see none.
4. Now type **USE mysql;** to switch to the mysql database.
5. Type **SHOW TABLES;**, which will show many tables, including a table with the name user.
6. Type **describe user;** to get record names from the user table. This gives a detailed description, as you can see in Listing 35.5. It tells you which records or fields are available in a table, what type of data is expected in a field, and gives some more attributes on the table contents.

Listing 35.5 Showing Table Contents

```
MariaDB [mysql]> describe user;
+-----------------+---------------------+-----+-----+---------+-------+
| Field           | Type                | Null | Key | Default | Extra
+-----------------+---------------------+-----+-----+---------+-------+
| Host            | char(60)            | NO  | PRI |         |       |
| User            | char(16)            | NO  | PRI |         |       |
| Password        | ch                  | NO  |     |         |       |
...             |
| max_connections | int(11) unsigned | NO  |     | 0       |       |
| max_user_connect| int(11)          | NO  |     | 0       |       |
| plugin          | char(64)         | NO  |     |         |       |
| authent_string  | text             | NO  |     | NULL    |       |
+-----------------+------------------+-----+-----+---------+-------+
42 rows in set (0.00 sec)
```

In MariaDB, as well as in MySQL, you'll be using Structured Query Language (SQL) to manipulate data in the database. The basic commands allow you to create, read, update, and delete. These commands are also referred to as the CRUD operations: **create**, **select**, **update**, and **delete**. Before inserting data in a database, you need to create at least one table. Use **CREATE TABLE** to do that, followed by the name of the table you want to add, such as **CREATE TABLE addressbook(name VARCHAR(40), street VARCHAR(40));**. While defining a table, you also define the records that you want to add to the table, in addition to the data type that will be stored in that table. In this example, that's just the VARCHAR type, which allows you to store 40 bytes of variable data.

If you are working on a database that has already been defined, or if you need to verify what you have just created, you need to find out which are the attributes of a table. Use **DESCRIBE** to do this, as in the **DESCRIBE addressbook;**. This gives a result that looks like Listing 35.6, which first shows how to create a table, and next shows how to get information about the fields stored in that table.

Listing 35.6 Requesting Table Contents

```
MariaDB [addressbook]> CREATE TABLE addressbook(name VARCHAR(40),street
VARCHAR(40));
Query OK, 0 rows affected (0.00 sec)


MariaDB [addressbook]> DESCRIBE addressbook;
```

```
+--------+-------------+------+-----+---------+-------+
| Field  | Type        | Null | Key | Default | Extra |
+--------+-------------+------+-----+---------+-------+
| name   | varchar(40) | YES  |     | NULL    |       |
| street | varchar(40) | YES  |     | NULL    |       |
+--------+-------------+------+-----+---------+-------+
2 rows in set (0.01 sec)
```

After you have found out which fields are needed to create data in a table, you can use the **INSERT** command to add them: **INSERT INTO addressbook (name,street) VALUES ('linda jones','state street');**. In this command, you first refer to the name of the table where data has to be added, list the specific attributes you want to fill, and then list the values that you want to enter in those specific attributes. Notice that it is essential to put the values that you want to insert into the records between single quotes. Without these, the commands will not work. To verify that the command to insert data has worked, use **SELECT * from addressbook;**.

To delete data, use the **DELETE** command, as in **DELETE FROM addressbook WHERE name = 'lucy ball';**. Notice that in this command it is important not to forget the **WHERE** part. If you omit it, all records in the table will be erased. Also notice that in this command (as in any other command that you use in this example) you need to specify which table you want to apply the changes to.

To change data, use the **UPDATE** command: **UPDATE addressbook SET street='main street' WHERE name = 'linda jones';**. Notice that in this command you need to use the **WHERE** statement to tell MariaDB which record to use, and the **SET** command to specify the attribute you want to change, with its new value.

To read records, use the **SELECT** command: **SELECT name,street FROM addressbook;**. Alternatively, you can select to show all attributes, using *: **SELECT * FROM addressbook;** and using **where**, you can create simple queries, filtering on specific results: **SELECT * FROM addressbook WHERE street='state street';**.

When using **WHERE** clauses, you can use different operators:

=	Equal
<>	Not equal
>	Greater than
>=	Greater than or equal

<	Less than
>=	Less than or equal
BETWEEN	Between a range
LIKE	Search for a pattern
IN	Specify multiple possible values in a column

Managing Users

In MariaDB, you can create users and groups to provide specific access permissions to specific users on the databases and tables. Alternatively, MariaDB can use the Linux PAM (Pluggable Authentication Modules) system for authentication. For RHCE, you only have to know how to manage users using **mysql** commands. PAM is beyond the scope of RHCE.

When managing users from within MySQL, users by default are stored in the user table in the mysql database. To create new users, you'll use **CREATE USER;**. As the user who creates the new user, you need the CREATE USER or INSERT privilege in the mysql database. While creating a user, you typically include @hostname to the username (so that the result would be username@hostname). That allows you to make a difference between users who can log in from localhost only and users who can log in from other hosts.

If you want to create a user lisa, for example, use **CREATE USER lisa@localhost IDENTIFIED BY 'password';**. This creates a user with the name lisa and the password password. Passwords are stored encrypted in the MariaDB database. In the hostname specification, you have multiple options. You can use hostname or IP address and the % sign as a wildcard. For instance, lisa@% refers to user lisa who can log in from any host. When the user is no longer needed, use **DROP USER user@host;** to remove the user. Notice that users who are currently active on the system are not deleted immediately.

When you are creating a user, the user by default is created with no privileges. So the user can connect but will not be able to use any command. The privileges can be granted on specific tables but also on the entire database. As root, for instance, use **GRANT SELECT, UPDATE, DELETE, INSERT on addressbook.names to lisa@localhost;** to grant user lisa the basic permissions to the names table in the addressbook database. Let's take a look at some more examples where privileges are granted:

- **GRANT SELECT ON database.table TO user@host;** Gives SELECT privilege on a specific table in a specific database

- **GRANT SELECT ON database.* TO user@host;** Gives SELECT to all tables in database
- **GRANT SELECT ON *.* TO user@host;** Gives privileges to all tables in all databases
- **GRANT CREATE, ALTER, DROP ON database.* to user@ host;** Gives privilege to create, alter, and drop databases
- **GRANT ALL PRIVILEGES ON *.* to user@host;** Creates a superuser

When working with privileges, it is important to reload all privileges after changing them. To do that, use the **FLUSH PRIVILEGES;** command. To show privileges assigned to a specific user, you can use **SHOW GRANTS FOR user@host;**.

In Exercise 35.2, you create a simple database and work with user privileges on it.

Exercise 35.2 Creating a Database

1. Type **mysql -u root -p** to log in as root.
2. Type **create database videos;** to create a database with the name videos.
3. Type **USE videos;** to switch to the videos database.
4. Now let's enter some columns: **CREATE TABLE videos(title VARCHAR(40), actor VARCHAR(40), year INT, registration INT);**
5. Let's enter some data: **INSERT INTO videos (registration,title,actor,year) VALUES(1,'Basic Instinct','Sharon Stone', 1992);**
6. Repeat this to enter the following videos as well:

```
2,Pretty Woman, Julia Roberts, 1990
3,Terminator, Arnold Schwarzenegger, 1984
4,Jurassic Park, Harrison Ford, 1992
```

7. Type **SELECT * from videos;** to show an overview of the entire database. You should see a result as in Listing 35.7.

Listing 35.7 SELECT * result

```
MariaDB [videos]> INSERT INTO videos (registration, title,
actor,year) VALUES (1,'Basic Instinct', 'Sharon Stone', 1992);
Query OK, 1 row affected (0.01 sec)

MariaDB [videos]> INSERT INTO videos (registration, title,
actor,year) VALUES (2, 'Pretty Woman', 'Julia Roberts', 1990);
Query OK, 1 row affected (0.00 sec)
```

```
MariaDB [videos]> INSERT INTO videos (registration, title,
actor,year) VALUES (3, 'Terminator', 'Arnold Schwarzenegger', 1984);
Query OK, 1 row affected (0.01 sec)

MariaDB [videos]> INSERT INTO videos (registration, title,
actor,year) VALUES (4, 'Jurassic Park', 'Harrison Ford', 1992);
Query OK, 1 row affected (0.00 sec)

MariaDB [videos]> select * from videos;
+----------------+-----------------------+------+--------------+
| title          | actor                 | year | registration |
+----------------+-----------------------+------+--------------+
| Basic Instinct | Sharon Stone          | 1992 |            1 |
| Pretty Woman   | Julia Roberts         | 1990 |            2 |
| Terminator     | Arnold Schwarzenegger | 1984 |            3 |
| Jurassic Park  | Harrison Ford         | 1992 |            4 |
+----------------+-----------------------+------+--------------+
4 rows in set (0.00 sec)
```

8. Create a user using **CREATE USER julia@'%' IDENTIFIED BY 'secret';**.
9. Grant permissions to user julia using GRANT SELECT,INSERT,UPDATE,DELETE ON videos.* TO julia@'%';.
10. Type **FLUSH PRIVILEGES;** to update the privileges.
11. Type **DESCRIBE videos;** to show an overview of records in the videos database.
12. Insert another new video: **INSERT INTO videos(registration,title,actor, year) VALUES (5,'The Last Stand', 'Arnold Schwarzenegger', 2013);**.
13. Show a list of all records where the value of the actor field is set to Arnold Schwarzenegger: **SELECT * FROM videos WHERE actor = 'Arnold Schwarzenegger';**.
14. Type **quit** to close the MySQL shell interface.

MariaDB Backup and Restore

When making backups of MariaDB, you can take two approaches. You can create a physical backup. In a physical backup, you have a raw copy of the database directories and folders. This backup is fast and it is portable but only to machines using similar hardware and software. To make a physical backup, the database service should be offline, or the tables in the database should be locked to prevent data from changing during the backup.

As an alternative, you can make a logical backup. In a logical backup, the database structure is retrieved by querying the database. Such a backup is relatively slow because the database must be accessed and converted into a logical format. It does have two huge benefits though: (1) You can create a logical backup on an operational database, and (2) logical database backups are portable to other database providers as well. In a logical backup, though, log and configuration files are not included. So you might even want to consider creating both a physical as well as a logical backup.

To restore a backup, the first step would be to get the name of the database from the backup file (in case it is unknown). You can open the file with less, because it's a readable file. Next, make sure that the database you want to restore, and if it does not, uses mysql create databasename. To restore the logical backup, you can next run the command **mysqldump -u root -p databasename < /root/databasename.dump**.

To make a logical database backup, you can use the **mysqldump** (shell) command. If you want to create a backup of the videos database and write that to the file /root/videos-db.dump, for instance, you use the following command: **mysqldump -u root -p videos --databases > /root/videos-db.dump**. You can also use the **mysqldump** command to create a backup of all databases, using **mysqldump -u root -p --all-databases --databases > /root/all-db.dump**.

To create physical backups, it is a good idea to use LVM volumes. In LVM, you can create a snapshot, which contains the actual state of the LVM volume at the moment the snapshot was created. The physical backup itself will then be made from the snapshot and not from the actual open LVM volume.

An LVM snapshot is like a photo of an LVM logical volume. By making a backup of the snapshot, you'll be sure to have a stable backup of an environment where no files currently are open. To create a snapshot of a database volume, the database temporarily needs to be stopped. Roughly, the procedure to create a snapshot of a database volume is as follows:

Key Topic

1. From within the mariadb database, use the **FLUSH TABLES WITH READ LOCK;** command. This ensures that no files are in use while creating the snapshot. This command closes all tables and locks all tables for all databases with a global read lock. This is a convenient way to make sure that nothing is written to the database while the snapshot is being created in the next step of this procedure. An alternative solution is to stop the mariadb service completely by using **systemctl stop mariadb** and start it again after the snapshot has been created.

2. From another terminal window, type **lvcreate -s -n lvdatabase-snap -L 1G /dev/vgname/lvdatabase**. In this command, make sure to use the correct names of the volume and volume group. Also, consider the size of the snapshot volume. In general, 10% of the size of the original volume is considered large enough, assuming that the snapshot volume will be removed at the end of the procedure.
3. Now that the snapshot has been created, type **UNLOCK TABLES;** to start the database again.
4. Start the backup job.
5. After the backup job has finished, use **lvremove** to remove the snapshot volume.

In Exercise 35.3, you can read how to create a physical database backup.

Exercise 35.3 Creating a Physical MySQL Database Backup

1. To start, confirm where the actual database is stored. To do this, use **mysqladmin -u root -p variables | grep datadir**. This command shows the directory in the file system where data is stored. Typically, the result is the directory /var/lib/mysql.
2. Use the command **df /var/lib/mysql** to find out which LVM volume is used to host this location. (This will, of course, only work if during installation an LVM volume was created to host the physical database.)

NOTE To use snapshots in an efficient way, make sure that /var/lib/mysql is on a dedicated logical volume. If it is not, the backup risks being unnecessarily big. In this exercise, it is assumed that this is the case and that the mariadb database is on /dev/vgdata/lvmariadb.

3. Verify that within the volume group hosting the database volume, unallocated disk space is still available, using **vgs vgname**.
4. At this point, you need to temporarily freeze the database so that no modifications can be applied while the snapshot is created. To do this, connect to the database as root using **mysql -u root -p**, and type **FLUSH TABLES WITH READ LOCK;**. Do *not* close this session, because it will remove the lock!
5. In *another* terminal session, create the LVM snapshot. The following command assumes that the name of the volume group is **vgdata** and the name of the LVM

volume hosting the database is **lvmariadb**: **lvcreate -L 2G -s -n lvmariadb-snapshot /dev/vgdata/lvmariadb**. Make sure that the snapshot size is large enough to hold the backup.

6. Get back to the MariaDB session and type **UNLOCK TABLES;** to remove the locks.
7. Get back to the other session and mount the snapshot **mkdir /mnt/snapshot; mount -o nouuid /dev/vgdata/lvmariadb-snapshot /mnt/snapshot**.
8. Use **tar -cvf /root/mariadb.tar /mnt/snapshot/lib/mysql** to create the backup.
9. Once the backup has been created successfully, you have to unmount and remove the snapshot: **umount /mnt/snapshot; lvremove /dev/vgdata/lvmariadb-snapshot**.

To restore a backup, it depends which kind of backup you have. To restore a logical backup, you use a command like **mysql -u root -p videos < /root/videos-db.dump**. To restore a physical backup, you must first stop the mariadb service, after which you can use tar to restore the backup:

1. **systemctl stop mariadb**
2. **rm -rf /var/lib/mysql/***
3. **tar xvf /root/mariadb.tar -C /**

Make sure that you do verify the contents of the archive file before restoring the backup!

Summary

In this chapter, you learned the basics about MariaDB databases. You learned how to create a simple database with different tables and records in that database, and you learned how to operate basic query operations on that database. You also learned how to create users for the database and how to make physical as well as logical backups.

Exam Preparation Tasks

Review All Key Topics

Review the most important topics in the chapter, noted with the Key Topic icon in the outer margin of the page. Table 35.3 lists a reference of these key topics and the page numbers on which each is found.

Table 35.3 Key Topics for Chapter 35

Key Topic Element	Description	Page
List	How to install MariaDB	762
Paragraph	How to secure MariaDB	763
List	Some of the available parameters that can be set in [mysqld]	765
Table 35.2	Database elements	767
List	Create a snapshot of a database volume	774

Complete Tables and Lists from Memory

Print a copy of Appendix B, "Memory Tables" (found on the disc), or at least the section for this chapter, and complete the tables and lists from memory. Appendix C, "Memory Tables Answer Key," also on the disc, includes completed tables and lists to check your work.

Define Key Terms

SQL, table, database, fields, record, column, value, crud operations, values, backup, physical backup, logical backup

Review Questions

1. After installing the mariadb packages, which command do you need to run to set up basic security settings?
2. How do you configure MariaDB to be accessible through the network?
3. Which command enables you to get information about the settings that can be used in my.cnf?

4. After logging in to the MariaDB shell environment as root, which command enables you to get an overview of databases that are available?
5. Which command enables you to make addressbook your active database?
6. To find out which tables are available in the addressbook database, which command would you use?
7. To find out which fields are available in the addressbook table, which command would you use?
8. To find out which records are available in the addressbook table, which command would you use?
9. What command enables you to create a snapshot?
10. How can you temporarily prevent the database from writing modifications to the database files?

End-of-Chapter Labs

At this point, you know how to install MariaDB and how to create databases. You have also learned how to perform simple queries on a MariaDB database. In the following end-of-chapter labs, you apply these newly acquired skills and create a database as well as a logical backup of the database.

Lab 35.1

1. Create a database with the name customers. In this database, create two simple tables: one table with the name products that allows you to store products and their prices, another table with the name customers that allows you to store names and cities of the customers. Enter two products and two customers to the database.
2. After creating the database, make a logical backup of the database.
3. Install MariaDB. Set the password of user root to **secret**. Create a database with the name **addressbook**. In this database, make sure you can see the following fields:
   - first name
   - last name
   - street
   - number
   - city
   - zip
   - telephone

4. Enter the following records:

first name	last name	Street	number	city	zip	telephone
Linda	**Thomsen**	**State Street**	**14578**	**Provo**	**48261**	**651 555 432**
Lori	**Smith**	**Main Street**	**11**	**Sunnyvale**	**78025**	**453 555 667**
Marlet	**Joanes**	**Ocean Boulevard**	**124**	**Honolulu**	**99301**	**108 999 555**
Marsha	**Smith**	**Long Street**	**7812**	**Honolulu**	**99303**	**108 555 431**

5. Make a logical backup of the database and write it to /tmp/address-db.dump.

This following topics are covered in this chapter:

- Setting Up a Basic NFSv4 Server
- Setting Up a Kerberized NFS Server
- Understanding NFSv4 SELinux Transparency

The following RHCE exam objectives are covered in this chapter:

- Provide network shares to specific clients
- Provide network shares suitable for group collaboration
- Use Kerberos to control access to NFS network shares

CHAPTER 36

Configuring NFS

Network File System (NFS) is a very old protocol that was invented to share files between Linux hosts in an easy and convenient way. NFS has developed through the years, though, and it is still a very important protocol that is often used to share files between Linux and UNIX machines. In this chapter, you learn how to configure it.

To start, you learn how to create an NFS share on an NFS server and mount that share from an NFS client. You also learn how to create such a mount persistently. Then you learn about some advanced features, of which the Kerberization of the NFS share is the most important.

"Do I Know This Already?" Quiz

The "Do I Know This Already?" quiz allows you to assess whether you should read this entire chapter thoroughly or jump to the "Exam Preparation Tasks" section. If you are in doubt about your answers to these questions or your own assessment of your knowledge of the topics, read the entire chapter. Table 36.1 lists the major headings in this chapter and their corresponding "Do I Know This Already?" quiz questions. You can find the answers in Appendix A, "Answers to the 'Do I Know This Already?' Quizzes and 'Review Questions.'"

Table 36.1 "Do I Know This Already?" Section-to-Question Mapping

Foundation Topics Section	Questions
Setting Up a Basic NFSv4 Server	3, 5–7, 9
Configuring NFSv4 Kerberos Authentication	1, 2, 4, 10
Understanding NFSv4 SELinux Transparency	8

1. You want to connect an NFS client to a Kerberized NFS server. The mount can be made, but users do not get access to the share. Which of the following is the most likely explanation?
   a. The client is not using the same Kerberos mount option as the server.
   b. The nfs-secure process is not running on the client.
   c. The user did not get a Kerberos ticket.
   d. The nfs-secure-server process is not running on the server.

2. Which statement about the keytab file is correct?
   a. A Kerberized NFS server needs to have a keytab file containing the Kerberos credentials of the NFS server.
   b. A client that wants to access a Kerberized NFS server needs to have access to a keytab file containing the Kerberos credentials of the NFS server.
   c. The keytab file must be created from the NFS server.
   d. A keytab file is not necessary provided that all users are working from Kerberized sessions.

3. What is the name of the file where you create NFS exports?
   a. /etc/sysconfig/nfs
   b. /etc/nfs/nfs.conf
   c. /etc/exports
   d. /etc/shares

4. Which statement about user access to shares is *not* true?
   a. To set up a Kerberized connection, it is enough if the NFS server has access to a keytab file.
   b. By default users will have read-only access to NFS shares.
   c. If you want to synchronize user accounts between NFS server and client, you need to run the rpc.idmap process.
   d. The user nfsnobody can be used in a minimal security scenario.

5. Which port should be open in the firewall to allow access to an NFSv4 server?
   - a. 2049
   - b. Dynamic ports that have to be specified in /etc/sysconfig/nfs on the server
   - c. 2048 and Kerberos port 416
   - d. The entire dynamic port range
6. Which command enables you to check the availability of NFS shares behind a firewall that has the nfs-server service enabled, assuming that you are using a standard NFSv4 setup?
   - a. **showmount -e nfsserver**
   - b. **showmount -e nfsserver -p 2049**
   - c. **mount nfsserver:/share /mnt**
   - d. None. You cannot test NFS servers through the firewall.
7. You want to make sure that it can never happen that NFS clients have read/write access to shares. Which of the following is the most secure method to guarantee that?
   - a. Mount all shares read-only
   - b. Set the permission mode on all shares to 555
   - c. Make nfsnobody the owner of all shares and set permission mode to 500
   - d. Set the SELinux Boolean **nfs_export_all_rw=off**
8. Which NFS version do you need if you want SELinux context labels on the NFS server to be transparent on the NFS client?
   - a. 3 or higher
   - b. 4 or higher
   - c. 4.2
   - d. 4.3

9. Which mount option do you need in /etc/fstab to mount NFS shares on an NFS client?

- **a.** None. **mount** will recognize that it is an NFS share and retard the mount of it.
- **b.** None, but you need to enable the remote-fs.target systemctl service.
- **c.** **_netdev**
- **d.** None, as long as the **nfs** file system type is set. Just make sure that the **defaults** mount option is set.

10. Which file must exist on the NFS server to enable Kerberized NFS?

- **a.** /etc/nfs.keytab
- **b.** /etc/krb5.conf
- **c.** /etc/krb5.nfs
- **d.** /etc/krb5.keytab

Foundation Topics

Setting Up the Basic NFSv4 Server

NFS (Network File System) provides the classical way of sharing files between UNIX and Linux hosts. The protocol was developed a long time ago to work in an environment where Network Information System (NIS) is used to provide centralized user information, ensuring that all machines in a domain have access to similar usernames. NFS was developed as a light protocol to enable file sharing easily, with hostnames as the only restriction to be applied. User-specific settings were never introduced because NFS was used in an environment where all users came from the same authentication source anyway.

Even if NFS is a very old protocol, it has seen many developments, and its development continues, making it a relevant protocol even as the twenty-first century proceeds. In NFS, an NFS server is offering shares, which are also referred to as *exports*, and the NFS client mounts the share into its local file system. That is also what makes NFS an efficient protocol: Shares are mounted in the local file system, which provides one tree structure providing access to files, no matter where these files physically are. Because it is such a simple protocol with relatively low overhead, NFS is still commonly used, in two cases in particular:

- To provide access to home directories for Lightweight Directory Access Protocol (LDAP) users
- To easily access shared file systems on other Linux servers, which makes transferring files between servers easier

In this section, you learn how to install a basic NFS server.

Configuring the NFSv4 Server

On Red Hat Enterprise Linux 7, NFS 4 is the default version that is used. This version offers some interesting enhancements as compared to earlier versions of the protocol:

- **Pseudo root mounts:** A client that has access to several NFS shares no longer has to mount every individual mount but may perform a root mount. Thus, the client can mount the root directory on the NFS server, which provides access to all shares exported to the client on that server.

- **Kerberos security:** NFS was designed to use host-based security only. Once the host is authenticated, user-based restrictions are limited. Kerberos security is added to add encryption but also to give access to users only after their Kerberos credentials have been verified.
- **Simplified firewalling:** In old versions of NFS, the rpc.portmap process was used. This process generated random ports on which the NFS processes offered their services. This made it hard to provide access to NFS shares through a firewall. NFSv4 offers simplified firewalling, where TCP port 2049 is opened in the firewall to allow access to all NFS processes, and ports 111 as well as 20049 are opened for full client access.

Even if NFSv4 offers interesting enhancements as compared to earlier versions of the protocol, backward compatibility is also available. This might be useful to offer support to NFS clients that support previous versions only. By default, even if your NFS server is running NFSv4, it will be able to communicate with clients using a previous version of the protocol.

To create an export, the /etc/exports file has to include the name of the directory that is exported, the NFS clients to whom it is exported, and the options used to create the export. This export definition can be created in the /etc/exports file, but also as a file with the extension .exports in the directory /etc/exports.d. An export line might look like this:

```
/srv/nfsexport      vm[1-10].example.com(rw,no_root_squash)
```

To define which hosts will get access to the share, you can refer to those hosts in the second part of the export definition. In this example, access is granted to the hosts vm1 through vm10. Other approaches used as well, including * for all hosts, specific hostnames, specific IP addresses, and complete network addresses such as 10.50.0.0/16.

While creating the export, specific export options can be used as well, including the following:

- **ro** The share is exported as read-only, which ensures that no matter which permissions a user has on the share, no files can be created or modified.
- **rw** The share is exported as read/write, which enables writes, but only if the user has write permissions on the Linux file system of the exported directory as well.
- **no_root_squash** By default, the user root is mapped to the user nfsnobody on the NFS server. This ensures that a user who comes in as root from an NFS client has minimal permissions on the NFS server. If you want to grant

full access to the user root from an NFS client, use the **no_root_squash** option. Realize, though, that this is a very unsecure option.

To create an NFSv4 export, follow these steps:

1. Use **systemctl start nfs-server** to start the NFS server.
2. Use **systemctl enable nfs-server** to make sure that it is started automatically on boot.
3. Type **mkdir /srv/nfsexport** to create the directory that needs to be shared.
4. Add the following line to /etc/exports:

   /srv/nfsexport   server2(rw)
5. Type **exportfs -r** to make all changes to /etc/exports effective.
6. Open the firewall by using **firewall-cmd --permanent --add-service=nfs; firewall-cmd –reload**.

Accessing NFS Shares

Now that you have created an NFS share on the server, it is time to access it. This is relatively easy; you just need to mount the NFS share into the local file system of the NFS client computer. You do not need anything special to mount an NFS share. Just type a command using the structure **mount nfsserver:/sharename / mountpoint** to create the mount. The mount will now be integrated in the local file system.

Testing Client Access with showmount

Key Topic

To test whether a mount is available, you can use the **showmount** command. The command **showmount -e hostname** shows all mounts that are available on *hostname*. This command works fine and can be a great help, but there is a caveat: It does not get through the firewall if only port 2049 has been opened. If the firewall on the NFS server has been configured to let NFS traffic get in, it will still block the **showmount** command. So, if you want to test the availability of the NFS share, make sure that the firewall on the NFS server is temporarily disabled.

On earlier versions of RHEL, this was the only way to test access to the NFSv4 server. On RHEL 7, you can access the NFS server if ports 20049 and 111 have been opened in the firewall. You can accomplish this using the following commands:

```
firewall-cmd --add-service rpc-bind --permanent
firewall-cmd --add-service mountd --permanent
firewall-cmd --reload
```

TIP If you do not know that **showmount** has issues with the firewall, you'll risk losing valuable time on the exam. You might as well switch off the firewall on a temporary basis to test NFS share availability. Your shares will work fine if just port 2049 is open in the firewall.

Making NFS Mounts Persistent

If you want the mount to be created automatically on system boot, make sure to add the following line to /etc/fstab, as well:

```
nfsserver:/sharename        /mountpoint        nfs        _netdev  0 0
```

Key Topic

The **_netdev** mount option is used to tell the **mount** command to temporarily skip file systems using this mount option until the network has been started completely. On RHEL 7, this mount option is obsolete and replaced by the remote-fs.target systemd unit. Just make sure this service is enabled and network file systems will be mounted only once the network has been activated.

Configuring the Firewall for NFSv4

After creating an NFS share, you need to open the firewall on the NFS server for NFS traffic. When using NFSv4, this is done easily: Just type **firewall-cmd --permanent --add-service nfs; firewall-cmd --reload**. This opens port 2049 in the firewall, which is enough to allow for NFS traffic to come through.

Because some commands are not fully NFSv4 compatible, it is a good idea to open ports 111 and 20049 in the firewall as well. To do this, make sure that the mountd and rpc-bind firewalld services are added to the firewall configuration as well.

Configuring SELinux for NFSv4

At this point, your NFS server is almost operational. One important thing is still missing: You need to configure SELinux to allow the NFS server to access the shared file system. If you have just created the directory you want to share manually, the SELinux context type will be set to **default_t**, which denies the NFS server access to the contents of the directory. To allow the NFS server to access files, you want to remember three important context labels:

Key Topic

- **nfs_t** This context type will allow the NFS server to access the share.
- **public_content_t** This generic context type will allow the NFS server to read the contents of the directory. Other services such as Samba, FTP, and web services will be allowed read-only access to the share also.

- **public_content_rw_t** This context type allows read/write access to NFS and other services also. Use this if you also want other services to access files in the share.

Apart from these three context types, two Booleans can be used to restrict NFS server access: **nfs_export_all_ro** and **nfs_export_all_rw**. By default, both of these Booleans are enabled. If you want to make sure that NFS servers can offer read-only shares only, use **setsebool -P nfs_export_all_rw off** to switch off read/write access.

Now that you know all that needs to be done to operate an NFS server, it is time to practice these skills in Exercise 36.1, where you set up a base NFSv4 server.

Exercise 36.1 Setting Up a Base NFSv4 Server

In this section, you set up a basic NFSv4 server and open the firewall for client access to this server.

1. On server1, use **yum install nfs-utils policycoreutils-python -y** to install the required utilities.
2. Open the file /etc/exports with an editor and add the following line:

```
/srv/nfsexport      *(rw)
```

3. Type **mkdir /srv/nfsexport** to create the shared directory.
4. Set the NFS context on the share: **semanage fcontext -a -t nfs_t "/srv/nfsexport(/.*)?"**. Type **restorecon -Rv /srv/nfsexport** to apply the setting to the file system.
5. Launch and enable the NFS server by using **systemctl start nfs-server; systemctl enable nfs-server**.
6. Open the firewall for the nfs-server by using **firewall-cmd --permanent --add-service nfs; firewall-cmd --reload**.
7. From server2, type **showmount -e server1**. Notice that this command stalls.
8. From server1, type **systemctl stop firewalld**.
9. Repeat Step 7. Notice that the **showmount** command now works.
10. Add the rpc-bind and mountd firewall services to the firewall on server1 by using **firewall-cmd --permanent --add-service mountd --add-service rpc-bind; firewall-cmd --reload** and try Step 7 again. It will now work.
11. On server2, type **mkdir /mnt/nfs; mount server1:/srv/nfsexport /mnt/nfs**.
12. Type **mount** to verify that the NFS share has mounted correctly.

13. Still on server2, open the file /etc/fstab and add the following line to make the mount persistent:

```
server1.example.com:/srv/nfsexport  /mnt/nfs  nfs  _netdev  0 0
```

14. Type **systemctl status remote-fs.target** and verify that this systemd unit is enabled.

15. Restart server2 and verify that the mount is activated automatically.

TIP In the preceding exercise, you learned how to make a mount persistent through /etc/fstab. This is still how you want to do it on the RHCE exam if you are asked to create such a mount, and it is still how Red Hat recommends doing it.

You can create mounts through systemd, as well. To create such a mount, it is important that you create a systemd mount unit file that reflects the name of the mount point. To automate the mount on /mnt/nfs, the name of the systemd file has to be /etc/systemd/system/mnt-nfs.mount, and it needs the content shown in Listing 36.1

Listing 36.1 Creating Mounts Through Systemd

```
[root@server2 ~]# cat /etc/systemd/system/mnt-nfs.mount
#  This file is part of systemd.
#
#  systemd is free software; you can redistribute it and/or modify it
#  under the terms of the GNU Lesser General Public License as
published by
#  the Free Software Foundation; either version 2.1 of the License, or
#  (at your option) any later version.

[Unit]
Description=nfs mount on server1
After=nfs.target
Requires=nfs.target

[Mount]
What=server1.example.com:/nfsexport
Where=/mnt/nfs
```

```
Type=nfs
Options=

# Make 'systemctl enable mnt-nfs.mount' work:
[Install]
WantedBy=multi-user.target
```

Next, type **systemd enable nfs.target** and **systemd enable mnt-nfs.mount**. If you had configured the mount through /etc/fstab, remove the line that mounts the share through /etc/fstab. Restart your computer to make sure that this mount is started automatically.

Configuring NFS Kerberos Authentication

NFS was never designed to be secure. By default, access restrictions can be enforced based on IP addresses or Domain Name System (DNS) names only, and that is very easy to forge. If you want to make it secure, you need to use security features that are provided externally. In RHEL 7, Kerberos adds an additional range of security features to NFS. To add security to an NFS share, you need to add the **sec=*method*** option while defining the share in /etc/exports. The following security methods are available:

Key Topic

- **none** Anonymous access to files is allowed. All access is based on the permissions of the user nfsnobody on the NFS server. So, you must make sure that this user has the appropriate permissions to files and directories. If the user nobody needs write access as well, you need to make sure that the **nfsd_anon_write** SELinux Boolean is active also. Notice that you should never do this, because you'll be granting any user access to the share with full write permissions.
- **sys** This is the default security option, where user access to files is based on UID and GID values. A UID coming from the NFS client will be mapped to the same UID on the NFS server (even if the user names associated to that UID do not match).
- **krb5** NFS clients (that means machines, not users) prove their identity using a Kerberos keytab file. To access files in the NFS share, the user needs to initialize a Kerberos setting as well; otherwise, no access is allowed to files. That means that the authentication session of a user needs to be Kerberized, and if this is not the case, the user must initiate a session using **kinit** *username*.

- **krb5i** Same as **krb5** with the addition that a cryptographic guarantee is added to make sure that data in the request has not been tampered with.
- **krb5p** Same as **krb5i** but also adds encryption to all requests between server and client. This does have a performance impact, but it offers the best possible protection.

> **TIP** Configuring Kerberized NFS often goes wrong. If it does, this is often because no Kerberized user session was initiated. So, to make sure that you pass this topic on the exam, you'll first have to configure external authentication for your users so that users are authenticated against the Kerberos server, after which you can set up NFS Kerberized shares as well.

To establish a Kerberized session between NFS client and host, a few items are required:

Key Topic

- **/etc/krb5.keytab:** This file contains the security principals for both the NFS server as the NFS client, and it is required to join the Kerberos realm. In the /etc/krb5.keytab file, the host principal, the NFS principal, or both principals are contained. To verify the contents of the keytab file, use the **klist -k** command.
- **A Kerberized user session:** After configuring remote authentication against a Kerberos server, as described in Chapter 25, "Configuring External Authentication and Authorization," the login procedure is already Kerberized, and no additional action is required. You can use the **klist** command to verify that this is the case; this command shows all current Kerberos credentials on your machine. If **klist** does not show any Kerberos credentials, a Kerberized session can be established manually.
- The **sec=*method*** option, both in the share definition and in the mount options. This enables the desired Kerberos method.
- The nfs-server as well as the nfs-secure-server services must be active on the NFS server. On RHEL 7.0 you had to manually load this service and enable them, since RHEL 7.1 they are automatically loaded if shares with any of the Kerberos options are offered.
- The nfs-secure service must be loaded on the client. On RHEL 7.0 you had to manually load and enable this service. Since RHEL 7.1, it is loaded automatically if a Kerberized share is accessed.

The Kerberos keytab file plays an essential role in the entire process. It is created from the Kerberos Ticket Granting Server, and it contains the Kerberos principals that the NFS server needs to authenticate against Kerberos. It will also contain credentials for the server on which NFS services are offered. Just consider these credentials to be similar to a username and password that are used by services and servers. Every network service to which a user authenticates needs a service principal (that is, a keytab file) with a corresponding key. As an administrator, you can use the **klist -k** command to view and verify the contents of the keytab file. In Listing 36.2, you can see sample contents of the /etc/krb5.keytab file on a server that is using Kerberized NFS.

Listing 36.2 Sample Contents of a Keytab File

```
[root@server1 ~]# klist -k
Keytab name: FILE:/etc/krb5.keytab
KVNO Principal
---- --------------------------------------------------------------------------
   2 host/server1.example.com@EXAMPLE.COM
   2 host/server1.example.com@EXAMPLE.COM
   2 host/server1.example.com@EXAMPLE.COM
   2 host/server1.example.com@EXAMPLE.COM
   2 host/server1.example.com@EXAMPLE.COM
   2 host/server1.example.com@EXAMPLE.COM
   1 nfs/server1.example.com@EXAMPLE.COM
   1 nfs/server1.example.com@EXAMPLE.COM
   1 nfs/server1.example.com@EXAMPLE.COM
   1 nfs/server1.example.com@EXAMPLE.COM
   1 nfs/server1.example.com@EXAMPLE.COM
   1 nfs/server1.example.com@EXAMPLE.COM
```

TIP Creating Kerberos keytabs and principals is *not* an exam objective. That means that you will be provided with a keytab file containing all the Kerberos principals required for the service to run with Kerberos security added to it, and you can safely assume that this keytab file is okay. Exercise 36.2 gives a good explanation of what to expect on the exam.

Exercise 36.2 Configuring a Kerberized NFS Server

The configuration for this exercise is very strict. In this exercise, you use three different machines. server1.example.com is going to be configured as the NFS server, server2.example.com is going to be configured as the NFS client, and you need access to labipa.example.com, which is configured as the IPA server that is used in this exercise as the Kerberos server. See the Lab Setup Instructions earlier in this book for specific instructions on how to set up this environment. For your convenience, a VMware workstation image of labipa.example.com is provided on my website, http://www.rhatcert.com. In Appendix D, "Setting Up Identity Management," you'll find instructions on how to set up an IPA server that matches the environment that is described in this chapter. This exercise also assumes that you have a Kerberos user with the name lisa. See Appendix D for more details about creating such a Kerberos user. Finally, you need to ensure that on server2 remote login has been configured, as described in Chapter 25.

1. On the IPA server labipa.example.com, an FTP share is configured. In this share, you'll find the server1.keytab and the server2.keytab files, containing all security principals that are required to setup this environment. Download the server1.keytab file to server1:/etc/krb5.keytab and install the server2.keytab file to server2:/etc/krb5.keytab.
2. On both servers, use **restorecon -v /etc/krb5.keytab** to ensure that the SELinux labels are set correctly.
3. On the NFS server server1, type **systemctl status nfs-server** to verify that the nfs-server service which you have enabled in exercise 36.1 is indeed operational.
4. On the NFS server server1, type **mkdir /srv/secureshare** to create a directory that is going to be shared. Set SELinux context labels, using **semanage fcontext -a -t nfs_t "/srv/secureshare(/.*)?"** and use **restorecon -R /srv/secureshare** to apply. Type **chown lisa /srv/secureshare** to make user lisa the owner of this share.
5. Open the file /etc/exports with an editor and give it the following contents:

   ```
   /srv/secureshare    *(sec=krb5p,rw)
   ```

6. Type **exportfs -rv** to export the newly created share.
7. Type **showmount -e localhost** to verify the availability of the share.
8. Now that the NFS server server1 is configured, you can configure server2 as the NFS client.
9. On server2, type **mkdir -p /mnt/securenfs** to create a mount point to be used by the NFS secure server.

10. Manually mount the NFS share, using **mount -o sec=krb5p server1.example.com:/srv/secureshare /mnt/securenfs**.
11. Type **su - lisa** to access the share as lisa and browse the share.
12. Use **kinit lisa** to make sure that lisa has established a Kerberos session.
13. Type **touch lisa** to create a file in the share. You should be allowed to do this.

NOTE When writing this exercise on RHEL 7.1 software, on one configuration I got a crash in the **nfs-utils** package while the mount command was issued. In another test environment it worked smoothly. I consider the software unstable in RHEL 7.1 and hope this will get fixed in an upcoming update on the nfs-utils packages.

Understanding NFSv4 SELinux Transparency

By default, all NFS mounts on NFS clients have the **nfs_t** SELinux context type, no matter which context is set on the server. (Well, you need to set a context that allows the NFS server to access the share, of course.) One way to change this is by using the **context="context"** mount option, as in **mount -o context="system_u,object_r:public_content_rw_t:s0" server1:/srv/nfsexport /mnt/nfs**. This approach works for NFS versions prior to NFS version 4.2.

If you are configuring NFS 4.2, the SELinux context from the server can be made transparent to the client as well. If you want to use this relatively new functionality, you need to switch it on specifically. To do this, specify the **RPCNFSDARGS="-V 4.2"** option in /etc/sysconfig/nfs. After doing this, restart the nfs-server process (and also the nfs-secure-server process if that is used).

On the NFS client, you need the v4.2 mount option as well to make sure the mount point on the client gets the same SELinux context as the shared directory on the server:

```
mount -o v4.2 server1.example.com:/srv/nfsexport /mnt/nfsexport.
```

NOTE The man page that is shown when using **man 8 nfsd** talks about NFS up to version 4.1 as being the newer version. So, be aware that you probably will not be able to get relevant information from the man pages on the exam, as all 4.2 related information is not included in the man page.

In Exercise 36.3, you test this functionality.

Exercise 36.3 Enabling NFS SELinux Transparency

1. On the NFS server, you have already exported the directory /srv/nfsexport and provided it with the public_content_rw_t NFS context label.
2. Mount the share on the /mnt/nfsexport directory on the client, using **mount server1.example.com:/srv/nfsexport /mnt/nfs**.
3. Check the current context label: **ls -Zd /mnt/nfs**. You'll see it is set to **nfs_t**.
4. Back on server1 open the file /etc/sysconfig/nfs and give it the following contents:

   ```
   RPCNFSDARGS="-V 4.2"
   ```

5. Type **systemctl restart nfs-server; systemctl restart nfs-secure-server** to make the changes effective.
6. On the client, type **mount -o v4.2 server1.example.com:/myshare /mnt/nfsexport**.
7. On server1, use **touch /myshare/myfile** and use **ls -Z** to check its security label.
8. On server2, verify the context label using **ls -Z**. You will see that the client has inherited the context settings from the server.

Summary

In this chapter, you learned how to configure NFS. This chapter has provided more depth than just creating an NFS export and mounting it from the client. You learned how to create an environment where NFS shares can be offered in a context where security is added through SELinux, the firewall, and Kerberos. On the RHCE exam, you need to be prepared to offer the complete solution, as described in this chapter.

Exam Prep Tasks

Review All Key Topics

Review the most important topics in the chapter, noted with the Key Topic icon in the outer margin of the page. Table 36.2 lists a reference of these key topics and the page numbers on which each is found.

Table 36.2 Key Topics for Chapter 36

Key Topic Element	Description	Page Number
Section	Testing client access with **Showmount**	787
Paragraph	The **_netdev** mount option	788
List	Three context labels that allow the NFS server to access files	788
List	Available security methods for NFS	791
List	Required items for establishing a Kerberized session between NFS client and host	792

Define Key Terms

Define the following key terms from this chapter and check your answers in the glossary:

NFS, Kerberos, keytab, share, export, RPC

Review Questions

1. What is the name of the configuration file that contains NFS shares?
2. Which services must be started on an NFS client to enable the mounting of Kerberized shares from an NFS server?
3. Which services must be started on an NFS server to offer Kerberos security?
4. Which ports need to be open in the firewall to allow full access to the NFS server?
5. You want to create an NFS share where the web server can read documents as well. Write access is not necessary. Which SELinux context label enables you to set access as tight as possible?
6. Which option must be used in /etc/fstab to make sure NFS shares can be mounted automatically when rebooting?
7. You want to set up an NFS server for an environment where only the lightest form of Kerberos protection on the share is supported. Which **sec=** option should you use on the export?
8. Your NFS server does not have access to the same user accounts as your NFS clients. Which approach is recommended to set security?
9. Which file needs to be modified on the NFS server to allow transparency of SELinux context type to the client?

10. Which NFS version offers transparency of SELinux context types set on the server to the NFS client as well?

End-of-Chapter Labs

Now that you have read this chapter, you should be able to set up an NFS server and fully integrate it in a working environment. That's exactly what you have to do in Lab 36.1.

Lab 36.1

1. On server1, create an NFS share with the name /secureshare. Make sure that it can be mounted using maximal Kerberos security only. On server2, create a configuration that mounts the share automatically on the directory /mnt/secure while rebooting.

The following topics are covered in this chapter:

- Setting Up SMB File Sharing
- Securing Samba
- Accessing SMB Shares

The following RHCE exam objectives are covered in this chapter:

- Provide network shares to specific clients
- Provide network shares suitable for group collaboration
- Use Kerberos to authenticate access to shared directories

CHAPTER 37

Configuring Samba File Services

In many networks, Windows clients are used to access services on servers that are running on Linux more and more often. To allow these clients to use native file access protocols to access file shares, you can configure the Samba service on Linux. Samba is using the Server Message Block (SMB) protocol to offer access to shares. In this section, you learn how to set up a Samba server for such file access. You also learn how to access SMB file shares from Linux computers.

"Do I Know This Already?" Quiz

The "Do I Know This Already?" quiz allows you to assess whether you should read this entire chapter thoroughly or jump to the "Exam Preparation Tasks" section. If you are in doubt about your answers to these questions or your own assessment of your knowledge of the topics, read the entire chapter. Table 37.1 lists the major headings in this chapter and their corresponding "Do I Know This Already?" quiz questions. You can find the answers in Appendix A, "Answers to the 'Do I Know This Already?' Quizzes and 'Review Questions.'"

Table 37.1 "Do I Know This Already?" Section-to-Question Mapping

Foundation Topics Section	Questions
Setting Up SMB File Sharing	1–6
Securing Samba	7–8
Accessing SMB Shares	9–10

1. Which of the following is *not* a standard package used to set up an SMB client/server environment?
   a. samba
   b. samba-server
   c. cifs-utils
   d. samba-client

2. Which of the following would you configure to specify the domain your Samba server is configured in?
   a. **domain**
   b. **domain-server**
   c. **ads**
   d. **workgroup**

3. Which of the following statements about write access to a share is true?
   a. The **write list** parameter is used to specify the names of users and groups that have write access to a share, even if the share is not marked as writable.
   b. The **write list** parameter is required to specify which users and groups have write access to a share if the share is marked as writable.
   c. If the share is marked as read only, no one can write to it.
   d. The setting **read only = no** requires administrators to configure a write list to specify which users can write to the share.

4. Which of the following statements about user access to shares is true?
   a. The **valid groups** parameter is used to list groups that have access to the share.
   b. If a user is listed in the **valid users** parameter, he must have user or group Linux permissions to the share.
   c. The **valid users** parameter can be used to grant users access to a share. It can also be used to grant groups access to a share by prepending the group name with a @ or +.
   d. If nothing is set, no users have access to the share.

5. Which security setting is used as the default on RHEL 7 Samba?
   a. security = share
   b. security = user
   c. security = server
   d. security = ads

6. Which statement about Samba users is true?
   a. If you are adding users using smbpasswd, you need to use the **-a** option.
   b. When using Samba users as added with smbpasswd, you must disable the Linux password for that user.

c. Samba user passwords will be synchronized automatically with Linux user passwords.

d. To change the Samba password of a Samba user, use smbpasswd **-c**.

7. Which of the following context types do you use to allow the Samba service full access to a share but no other services?

    a. **samba_share_t**

    b. **samba_rw_t**

    c. **samba_content_t**

    d. **samba_content_rw_t**

8. You want to configure your Linux server to use Samba-shared home directories on another server. Which of the following SELinux Booleans do you need to configure?

    a. **user_samba_homedirs**

    b. **enable_samba_homedirs**

    c. **use_samba_home_dirs**

    d. **allow_samba_access**

9. Which command enables you to discover Samba shares that are available on a Samba server?

    a. **smbclient --browse**

    b. **smbclient -L**

    c. **cifs -L**

    d. **cifs-browse --list**

10. Which of the following mount options would you *not* typically use when setting up a multiuser Samba mount?

    a. **user=**

    b. **sec=ntlmssp**

    c. **cifscreds**

    d. **multiuser**

Foundation Topics

Setting Up SMB File Sharing

Key Topic

Setting up a Samba file server involves a few steps:

1. Install Samba packages.
2. Prepare directories on Linux.
3. Prepare permissions on Linux.
4. Create the share in /etc/samba/smb.conf.
5. Create Samba user accounts.
6. Secure the Samba share.

These steps are discussed in detail in the following subsections.

Installing Samba

Depending on the kind of server installation you have performed, the Samba server packages may not be installed yet. You will often find an /etc/samba/smb.conf on your system, but this comes from the samba-common package, which does not contain enough to start configuring the Samba server.

Key Topic

To install the Samba server packages and the client tools, make sure to install the following RPMs:

- **samba:** Contains the Samba daemons and related configuration files
- **cifs-utils:** Contains the Samba client packages, including the command you need to mount remote SMB shares
- **samba-client:** Contains some utilities that are required to set up Samba shares

You can do this by executing **yum install smba cifs-utils samba-client**.

Preparing Shared Directories on Linux

To configure a server to share directories with the Samba server, you first need to set up the Linux part of the configuration. When a user authenticates to the Samba server, a Samba user account is used, but the Samba user account is mapped to a Linux user account, and that user account needs access permissions.

Therefore, you have to create a directory and set appropriate permissions on that directory. You can do that in several ways: the easy way, where you just set permission mode 777 on the shared directory, or the more sophisticated way, where you set up directories with group owners and the permissions that members of that group need to access the directory. You can also work with access control lists (ACLs; see Chapter 7, "Configuring Permissions,") for more sophisticated access control to the shared directories.

TIP Typically on the exam you are requested to perform very specific configurations, and often security is an important topic. Be prepared to create Samba shares that are accessible only for specific users. So, if you want to set the permission mode to 777 on the Linux file system, make sure that you know how to tighten security at the share level.

Configuring /etc/samba/smb.conf

The main part of the Samba configuration itself is set in the file /etc/samba/smb.conf. This file contains two parts. The first part is the [global] section, where generic properties of the Samba service are defined. The second part contains the share definitions, where share specific settings are defined. Two special shares may be enabled as well:

- [homes] contains default values for accessing home directories that are shared through Samba.
- [printers] is used to provide access to printers that are shared using the CUPS printing system.

Listing 37.1 shows how these shares are defined in a default smb.conf file.

Listing 37.1 Definition of the [homes] and [printer] Shares

```
#======================= Share Definitions ==========================

[homes]
        comment = Home Directories
        browseable = no
        writable = yes
;       valid users = %S
;       valid users = MYDOMAIN\%S
```

```
[printers]
    comment = All Printers
    path = /var/spool/samba
    browseable = no
    guest ok = no
    writable = no
    printable = yes
```

Understanding the [global] Section

In the [global] section, you define basic Samba parameters. Table 37.2 summarizes some of the most important of these parameters.

Key Topic

Table 37.2 Samba Global Parameters

Samba Parameter	Use
workgroup	Specifies the Windows workgroup that the Samba server is a member of. This setting is also used to specify the Samba domain.
security	Indicates how security is handled. The default is set to **security = user**, which requires users to have a valid username that is managed by the Samba server and mapped to a Linux user account name.
host allow	A comma, space, or tab-delimited list of hosts that are allowed access to the Samba service. See man 5 hosts_access for details on the format that needs to be used.
load printers	This option, which by default is set to yes, ensures that printers from the CUPS print subsystem are shared through Samba.
cups options	This option is used to specify that print driver processing is handled by CUPS and at the Samba level no interpretation of print jobs has to happen.
log file	Specifies the name of the file that Samba writes log messages to.

While browsing through the contents of the smb.conf file, you'll see that many other configuration parameters exist. Many of these parameters are old and no longer required. Options such as the browser control options and the name resolution options were mainly used to guarantee compatibility with pre-Windows 2000 Windows environments.

Creating Shares

To create a directory share, you need to add a section near the end of the smb.conf file. The share name is placed in brackets and is followed by the directives that further define the share. Table 37.3 lists some of the most common share options.

Table 37.3 Common Directory Share Options

Key Topic

Directive	Use
path	The path on the Linux file system of the shared directory.
writable	Enables write access on a share. If set to yes, all authenticated users have write access (if also permitted by Linux permissions). If set to no, a comma-separated write list of users or groups can be used to specify names of users and groups that have write permissions on the share. (See also read only.)
read only	Setting the **read only** parameter to no has the same effect as setting **writable** to yes.
write list	Contains a comma separated list of users or groups that have write access, even if writable is set to no. To use groups, put a @ or + in front of the group name.
valid users	Use to limit access to the share to listed users only. By default all users have access to the share.
comment	Use to specify a comment. This comment is displayed to users before connecting to the share.
guest ok	Allows access to the guest account. Be careful using this, because it basically bypasses all security settings. This parameter is required on some administrative shares though.
browseable	Allows browse access to shares, which means that users can navigate through the share structure to see items available in the share. Make sure to disable on the [home] share.

A topic that often creates confusion is how to enable write access to a Samba share. The following list summarizes what it comes down to:

- At all times, users with no write permissions on the Linux file system will not have write permissions on the share.
- If **writable** is set to yes, all users with write permissions on the Linux file system have write access to the share.
- Setting **read only** to no has the same effect as setting **writable** to yes.
- If a share is set as read only, users that are listed in the write list still have write access to the share.

TIP To create a share on the exam, you can use the example that is in the public share definition, which is in smb.conf by default. Just make sure how to enable/disable write access and access to specific users or groups.

TIP Before testing the share settings, use the **testparm** command. This command tells you whether any syntax errors exist in the smb.conf file. It will not test for any logical errors, though, so it does not complain if you are trying to provide access to a share for users that do not exist.

Using Samba Users

When the **security = user** setting is used, you need to create two accounts to enable access to shared files and directories:

- A Linux account that has the appropriate Linux permissions on the share
- A Samba account that has a name that matches the Linux account and on which the SMB-compatible NTLM password is set

Typically, on a Samba server, you'll only have Samba-only users who need to access it (apart from the local root user which is used for administration of the server). These Samba-only users are user accounts that are used by Windows users who are connecting to a Samba share but that do not require login to a Linux terminal as well. For these Samba-only users, you do not have to set a Linux password. Even better, while creating the user, set the login shell to /sbin/nologin, which prevents the user from ever logging in to a terminal on your server.

Key Topic

To create Samba users, complete the following steps:

1. Create the Linux user (if it is not existing already) using **useradd -s /sbin/nologin lara**.
2. Add the samba user account, using **smbpasswd -a lara**. Enter the password twice when prompted.

Notice that if the **smbpasswd** command is used without the **-a** option, the command tries to change the password for existing Samba users. So, make sure to create new users that use the **-a** option.

TIP Another tool to manage Samba accounts is **pdbedit**. This command has many options to add Samba accounts and Samba-specific properties. If you are looking for options to specify times that login is allowed, or to add machine accounts, for example, pdbedit is an excellent tool. For the exam, you do not have to know how to use it. You might like the option **–L**, though, which lists all currently existing Samba users on your server.

In Exercise 37.1, you apply all that you learned so far in an exercise where you create a share and make it available to some users.

Exercise 37.1 Configuring a Samba Server

Perform all tasks in this exercise on server1. Server2 is used in a subsequent exercise for accessing this Samba share.

1. Open a root shell.
2. Make sure all required RPM packages are installed: **yum install -y samba samba-client cifs-utils.**
3. Create four Linux users that are going to be used as Samba users: **for i in bill melissa lara lisa; do useradd -s /sbin/nologin $i; done.**
4. Add the Linux users to the group sambagroup. Create the Linux group using **groupadd sambagroup** and make three Linux users (but *not* the user lisa!) members of this group, using **for i in bill melissa lara; do usermod -aG sambagroup $i; done**.
5. Create the Samba users as well: **for i in bill melissa lara lisa; do smbpasswd -a $i; done**. When prompted for a password, enter the password **password**.
6. Create a shared directory on the Linux file system: **mkdir -p /data/sambashare.**
7. Set Linux permissions on the share: **chgrp sambagroup /data/sambashare** followed by **chmod g=rwx /data/sambashare.**
8. Open the configuration file /etc/samba/smb.conf with an editor and change the **workgroup** parameter to read **workgroup = mysamba.**
9. Add the share section and make sure it looks like the following:

```
[sambashare]
comment = My Samba Share
path = /data/sambashare
write list = @sambagroup
```

10. Type **testparm** to verify that you have not made any syntax errors in the smb.conf file.
11. Start and enable the Samba daemons using **systemctl start smb** followed by **systemctl enable smb.**
12. Verify that the share is available by typing **smbclient -L.**
13. Temporarily switch off SELinux and firewalld using **setenforce 0** and **systemctl stop firewalld** — we'll focus on SELinux later.
14. From server2, access the share using **mount -o username=lara //localhost/sambashare /mnt**. You should be able to access the share.

TIP The big challenge configuring Samba on the exam is that there are so many things to consider. If it does not work as expected, it can be hard to find why exactly it does not work. To make troubleshooting a bit easier, it is a good idea to temporarily switch off firewalld and selinux using **setenforce 0** and **systemctl stop firewalld**. *Never* switch off these services permanently; if you do and forget to switch them on again at the end of the exam, you fail the exam. Also, it is a good idea to switch these services on immediately after completing a specific task so that you can verify that your configuration does also work with firewalld and is SELinux enabled and fully functional.

Securing Samba

In the previous section, you have temporarily switched off firewalld and SELinux, which has allowed you to focus on the Samba configuration. At the end of the exam, you must make sure that both firewall and SELinux are enabled. Also, you must be able to configure Kerberos authentication on Samba shares. This section shows you how to do this.

Samba-Related SELinux Parameters

If you do not configure SELinux, Samba share access will not work. There are a couple of SELinux context types and Booleans to consider when working with Samba. These are summarized in Table 37.4.

Table 37.4 Samba-Related SELinux Settings

Key Topic

SELinux Setting	Use
samba_share_t	Gives Samba read and write access to this directory and everything below.
public_content_t	Gives Samba and other services read-only access to this directory and everything below it.
public_content_rw_t	Gives Samba and other services read/write access to this directory and everything below it. Needs an additional Boolean setting.
smbd_anon_write	Allows write access for Samba anonymous users. Required when using the **public_content_rw_t** context type.
samba_enable_home_dirs	Allows Linux home directories to be shared through Samba.
use_samba_home_dirs	Allows remote SMB file shares to be mounted and shared as local Linux home directories.

The first three items in Table 37.4 are context settings. To apply them, use **semanage fcontext -a -t samba_share_t "/data/sambashare(/.*)?"** and apply the context setting using **restorecon -Rv /data/sambashare**. Concerning the Booleans, to permanently set the value 1 to the **smbd_anon_write** Boolean, use **setsebool -P smbd_anon_write 1**.

Samba Firewalling

After configuring SELinux to allow Samba traffic, you need to open the firewall as well. As you learned in earlier chapters, opening the firewall for Samba traffic is easy. In firewalld, a Samba service is available. You can see its contents in Listing 37.2.

Listing 37.2 Firewalld Samba Service

```
[root@localhost services]# cat samba.xml
<?xml version="1.0" encoding="utf-8"?>
<service>
  <short>Samba</short>
  <description>This option allows you to access and participate in
Windows file and printer sharing networks. You need the samba package
installed for this option to be useful.</description>
  <port protocol="udp" port="137"/>
  <port protocol="udp" port="138"/>
```

```
  <port protocol="tcp" port="139"/>
  <port protocol="tcp" port="445"/>
  <module name="nf_conntrack_netbios_ns"/>
</service>
```

As you can see, the service opens four different ports in the firewall. It also loads the nf_conntrack_netbios_ns kernel module, which takes care of NetBIOS name service connection tracking. The following ports need to be open to access all Samba services. Depending on what exactly your Samba service is doing, some of these ports may be omitted.

- **137:** netbios name services
- **138:** netbios datagram
- **139:** netbios ssn
- **445:** Microsoft Directory Services

> **TIP** On the exam, do not try to be smart and try to work with rich rules, just add the firewalld samba service to ensure full functionality.

To add the Samba service to the firewall, use the following two commands:

- **firewall-cmd --permanent --add-service=samba**
- **firewall-cmd --reload**

In Exercise 37.2, you learn how to apply SELinux and firewall security to your Samba server.

Exercise 37.2 Configuring Samba Server firewalling and SELinux

1. On server1, open a root shell.
2. Type **semanage fcontext -a -t samba_share_t "/data/sambashare(/.*)?"** to write the correct context label to the SELinux policy.
3. Apply the newly configured context label using **restorecon -R -v /data/sambashare**.
4. Open the firewall for Samba traffic, using **firewall-cmd --add-service samba --permanent**.

5. Apply the new firewalld configuration, using **firewall-cmd --reload**.
6. From server2, verify that you can access the Samba share using **mount -o username=lara //server1/sambashare /mnt**. You need to type the password for user lara to mount this share.

Setting Up Kerberized Samba Shares

To set up Kerberized Samba shares, make sure that the required keytab files are created. In this section, you learn how to do this. After that, you learn how to configure Samba to use Kerberized shares. Notice that on the exam you do *not* have to set up the IPA server-related tasks.

Creating the Kerberos Keytab Files

To create the required key material, you set up the Samba server as an IPA client. This allows for an easy method to create keytab files and modify existing keytab files on your server. Run the following procedure on server1 and make sure the IPA server is up and running:

1. Open a root shell on the client and type **yum install -y ipa-client ipa-admintools**.
2. Type **ipa-client-install** to start setting up this server as an IPA client.
3. Type **kinit admin** to obtain Kerberos credentials on the client.
4. At the IPA server, add the Samba service and add principals using the following commands:

```
ipa service-add cifs/server1.example.com
ipa service-add cifs/server2.example.com
```

5. Type **ipa-getkeytab -s ipa.example.com -p cifs/server1.example.com -k /etc/krb5.keytab** to add the CIFS principal to the local keytab.
6. Verify that the principals are in the keytab file by using the **klist -k** command. The result should look like Listing 37.3.

Listing 37.3 Verifying the Contents of the Keytab File

```
[root@server1 ~]# klist -k
Keytab name: FILE:/etc/krb5.keytab
KVNO Principal
---- --------------------------------------------------------------------------
   3 host/server1.example.com@EXAMPLE.COM
   3 host/server1.example.com@EXAMPLE.COM
   3 host/server1.example.com@EXAMPLE.COM
   3 host/server1.example.com@EXAMPLE.COM
   3 host/server1.example.com@EXAMPLE.COM
   3 host/server1.example.com@EXAMPLE.COM
   1 cifs/server1.example.com@EXAMPLE.COM
   1 cifs/server1.example.com@EXAMPLE.COM
   1 cifs/server1.example.com@EXAMPLE.COM
   1 cifs/server1.example.com@EXAMPLE.COM
   1 cifs/server1.example.com@EXAMPLE.COM
   1 cifs/server1.example.com@EXAMPLE.COM
```

At this point, server1 has the right keytab file.

Configure Samba to Use the Keytab File

On the exam, it is likely that Red Hat is providing the keytab file. You might have to download it from a central server and copy it to the /etc/krb5.keytab file. In this procedure, you do not have to do this because you just created your own keytab file:

1. Set the permission mode on the /etc/krb5.keytab file to 600 and ensure that it is owned by user and group root.
2. In the /etc/samba/smb.conf file, add the following sections:

```
security = ADS
realm = KERBEROS_REALM
encrypt passwords = yes
kerberos method = secrets and keytab
password server = ipa.example.com
```

3. After adding these, type **systemctl restart smb** to restart the Samba service.

4. To add new Samba users, you must add them in the IDM server; see Appendix D, “Setting Up Identity Management,” for more details. After adding these users, type the following commands from any Kerberized client and type the following commands to test:

```
kinit username
smbclient -k -L //sambaserver
```

This should show a list of active shares that are now usable for the Samba users.

Accessing SMB Shares

There are different ways that users can access SMB shares from a Linux computer. This allows users to connect to shares that are offered by other SMB servers, including Windows file servers, and it also allows administrators to preconfigure connections to SMB shares for all users on a Linux server. In this section, you learn about the different options there are to connect from Linux to SMB shares.

Discovering Samba Shares

Before connecting to a Samba share, it is a good idea to just list the Samba shares that are available on the Samba server. To do this, you can use the **smbclient -L** command, followed by the name of the host that is offering Samba services. An example of this command is in Listing 37.4, where a list of shares is requested from localhost. Notice that the **smbclient -L** command will prompt for the root password; you can ignore it by just pressing Enter. To see which shares are available, no credentials are needed.

Listing 37.4 Listing Available Shares

```
[root@localhost ~]# smbclient -L //localhost
Enter root's password:
Anonymous login successful
Domain=[MYGROUP] OS=[Unix] Server=[Samba 4.1.1]

        Sharename       Type      Comment
        ---------       ----      -------
        sambagroup      Disk      My Samba Share
        IPC$            IPC       IPC Service (Samba Server Version 4.1.1)
Anonymous login successful
```

```
Domain=[MYGROUP] OS=[Unix] Server=[Samba 4.1.1]

                    Server                        Comment
                    ---------                     -------

                    Workgroup                     Master
```

Mounting Samba Shares

The most common way to access Samba shares is by mounting the share into the local Linux file system. To do this, on the Linux server which is going to be used as the Samba client, the cifs-utils package needs to be installed. While mounting the share, you need to specify a username and password. This username and password are going to be used as the mount credentials and apply to everyone who is using the mount.

> **TIP** Make sure the cifs-utils package is installed on the SMB client. Without it, you cannot mount Samba shares.

To mount an SMB file system, use the **mount** command followed by the name of the Samba user whose credentials you want to use. For instance, to mount a share as user lara, use **mount -o username=lara //server1/sambashare /mnt**. You then need to enter the password for the user specified and you'll be authenticated.

If you want to mount an SMB share automatically by using /etc/fstab, make sure that a username and a password are provided while performing the mount. Because it is not a good idea to put these in /etc/fstab directly, you can use a credentials file. If a credentials file is used, you create a credentials file containing user name and password in a location that is not accessible by ordinary users (such as the user root home directory). Then, you use the **credentials=** option to refer to the credentials file while mounting the Samba file system. In Exercise 37.3, you learn how to perform a mount this way. Also make sure that the credentials file is owned by root and the permission mode is set to 400.

Exercise 37.3 Mounting an SMB File System

Before performing the steps in this exercise, make sure that all steps as described in Exercises 37.1 and 37.2 have been performed and that the SMB share is available on server1. Perform all steps in this exercise on server2.

1. On server2, open a root shell. Install the cifs-utils package using **yum install cifs-utils**.
2. Create a mount point using **mkdir /mnt/lara**.
3. Type **smbclient -L //server1** to show that the Samba share you have created in the previous exercises is available. If you do not see it, fix it before continuing.
4. Type **mount -u username=lara //server1/sambashare /mnt/lara**. When prompted, enter the password **password**.
5. Verify that lara can write files in the share using **touch lara1**.
6. Disconnect the mount using **umount /mnt/sambashare**.
7. Now that you have verified that the Samba share is accessible through a local mount, let's verify that it can be accessed using a credentials file as well. As root, create the file /root/smbusers and give it the following contents:

```
username=lara
password=password
```

8. In /etc/fstab, add the following line:

```
//server1/sambashare           /mnt/lara cifs credentials=/root
/smbusers,_netdev   0 0
```

9. Type **mount -a**. The Samba share should now be mounted automatically. After verifying that it mounts using **mount -a**, you can reboot server2 to verify the mount comes up after a reboot as well.

Performing a Multiuser Samba Mount

In the previous section, you learned how to mount a Samba share with specific mount credentials. Although it works, it is not ideal to mount the share this way, as all users will be accessing the share with the same mount credentials. In RHEL 7, you can use the **multiuser** mount option to create a multiuser Samba mount.

When creating a multiuser Samba mount, the administrator mounts the Samba share as a user who has minimal permissions on the share. Regular users can then add their own SMB username and password in their current session to elevate their permissions to their own permission level. To do this, the **cifscreds** command is used.

To mount a multiuser mount, you need an SMB user with minimal permissions. Mount the Samba share as that user using the multiuser **mount** option and the **sec=ntlmssp mount** option, as in **mount -o multiuser,sec=ntlmssp,username =minimal //server/sambashare /mnt/multiuser**. Then, as the user that wants to access the share, use the **cifscreds** command to connect to the share.

The **cifscreds** command has four important options, as listed in Table 37.5.

Key Topic

Table 37.5 cifscreds Options

Option	Explanation
add	Adds the SMB credentials to the current user session. This option is followed by the name of the SMB server.
update	Updates the existing credentials. This option needs the name of the SMB server.
clear	Removes an entry from the current session. This option needs the name of the SMB server.
clearall	Clears all existing credentials from the session.

If the root user has mounted an SMB share using a user account that has minimal credentials, a user can use **cifscreds** to add her username to the current session. By default, the current username is used. If so desired, the **-u username** option can be used to use another username. So if currently user lara has logged in, use **cifscreds add server1**. Then, enter the password of user lara. Now the multiuser mounted Samba share can be accessed by lara, who will have all permissions assigned to her account to the share. In Exercise 37.5, you learn how to perform a multiuser Samba mount.

Exercise 37.5 Configuring Multiuser SMB Mounts

In this exercise, you continue working on the setup that has been created in previous labs.

1. Open a root shell on server2. Type **mkdir /mnt/multiuser** to create the mount point for the multiuser mount.
2. Create a credentials file to mount the multi user mount automatically. Use the filename /root/smb-multiuser and make sure it has the following contents:

```
username=lisa
password=password
```

3. In /etc/fstab, add the following line to perform the basic multiuser mount when the server boots:

```
//server1/sambashare            /mnt/multiuser       cifs
credentials=root/smb-multiuser,multiuser,sec=ntlmssp           0 0
```

4. Remove all other Samba mounts from /etc/fstab.
5. Type **mount /mnt/multiuser** to verify that the multiuser mount mounts correctly.
6. Try to write a file to /mnt/multiuser using **touch file1**. As user lisa has no write permissions to the share, this command will fail.
7. Still on server2, open a terminal session as user lara.
8. Type **cifscreds add server1** and enter the password for Samba user lara.
9. Write a file to the Samba share. Notice that the share is now read/write accessible.

Mounting Samba Shares Through automount

In some cases, it is useful if you can mount Samba shares through autofs. As discussed previously, there are different methods that allow you to use automount. You can use it through the autofs service or through systemd automount units. In this section, we focus on autofs automounts.

As is the case for any automount configuration, to start you need to create an /etc/auto.master file. In the auto.master file, you refer to the directory that needs to be monitored and the file through which it is going to be monitored. If you want to enable Samba home directories for automount, for example, give it the following contents:

```
/home/guests          /etc/auto.guests
```

Then, you need to create the file /etc/auto.guests. To mount home directories through this file, you start with a *, meaning "any directory that is accessed in /home/guests." Then you need to specify the mount options. For a CIFS mount, that is something like this:

```
-fstype=cifs,username=ldapusers,password=password\
   ://server1.example.com/homes/&
```

(Notice that this is all on one line.) Also make sure that the permission mode is set to 400 to make sure that nonroot users cannot see the Samba username and password. Notice that you can also configure it as a multiuser mount as described before. After creating this configuration, restart the autofs service, and you should be able to mount Samba home directories through automount. In Exercise 37.6, you learn how to automount the //server1/sambashare through automount.

Exercise 37.6 Mounting Samba Shares Through automount

In this exercise, you learn how to mount a simple Samba share through automount. To keep it simple, a fixed username and password are used. You use the //server1/sambashare that you have created in a previous exercise.

1. On server2, open a root shell.
2. Open the file /etc/auto.master and add the following line:
```
/srv/samba          /etc/auto.samba
```
3. Create a file with the name /etc/auto.samba and give it the following contents:
```
sambashare -fstype=cifs,username=lara,password=password\
  ://server1/sambashare
```
4. Use **chmod 400 /etc/auto.samba** to ensure that nobody but root can read the username and password in the credentials file.
5. Restart the autofs service using **systemctl autofs restart**.
6. Still on server2, access the Samba share by using **cd /srv/sambashare**. Type **mount** to verify that the share has indeed been mounted.

Summary

In this chapter, you learned how to set up an SMB file server and how to access SMB shares from Linux. Using these skills allows you to provide file services for Windows, OS X, and Linux clients. Mounting SMB shares allows you to access files that are stored on Windows servers from a Linux environment.

Exam Preparation Tasks

Review All Key Topics

Review the most important topics in the chapter, noted with the Key Topic icon in the outer margin of the page. Table 37.6 lists a reference of these key topics and the page numbers on which each is found.

Table 37.6 Key Topics for Chapter 37

Key Topic Element	Description	Page
List	Steps to configure a Samba share	804
List	Required packages	804
Table 37.2	Samba global parameters	806
Table 37.3	Common directory share options	807
List	How to create Samba users	808
Table 37.4	Samba-related SELinux settings	811
Table 37.5	cifscreds options	818

Complete Tables and Lists from Memory

Print a copy of Appendix B, "Memory Tables" (found on the disc), or at least the section for this chapter, and complete the tables and lists from memory. Appendix C, "Memory Tables Answer Key," also on the disc, includes completed tables and lists to check your work.

Define Key Terms

Define the following key terms from this chapter and check your answers in the glossary:

SMB, CIFS, Samba, share

Review Questions

1. What is the minimal configuration to put in smb.conf to create a share that grants access to the /data directory?
2. How do you configure a share that allows write access to all users that have write permissions on the Linux file system?
3. How do you limit write access to a share to members of a specific group only?
4. Which SELinux Boolean do you use to enable users to access home directories on this server through the SMB server?
5. How do you limit access to a specific share to hosts on the 192.168.10.0/24 network only?
6. Which command can you use as root to show a list of all Samba users currently defined on your server?

7. What does a user need to do to access a share that is configured as a multiuser share, after connecting to that server?
8. How do you mount a Samba share as a multiuser share where user lisa is used as the minimal user account?
9. How can you prevent users from seeing Samba mount credentials in the /etc/fstab file?
10. Which command enables you to list all Samba shares available on a specific server?

End-of-Chapter Labs

Configuring Samba is an important part of the skills that you should have as an RHCE. For that reason, the end-of-chapter labs here are relatively complex.

Lab 37.1

1. On server1, create two Samba shares. Configure this share with group access permissions. Use the users and groups that you have created in Chapter 6, "User and Group Management," for this purpose. If you do not have these users and groups, you can create the groups and assign some random users as member:
   - The share sales should be write-accessible by all members of the sales group, and have read-only access for members of the account group. No other users should have access to this share.
   - The share account should be write-accessible by all members of the account group and have read-only access for members of the account group. No other users should have access to this share.
2. Configure the firewall and SELinux for full access to the Samba shares.
3. On server2, configure a multiuser share for both shares. Create a Samba user account with minimal access to both shares. Configure /etc/fstab for automatic mounting of these shares.
4. Test the working of the multiuser mounts by accessing the shares as a member of each group. Verify read and write access to the shares.

The following topics are covered in this chapter:

- Understanding Email Basics
- Configuring Postfix Parameters
- Verifying a Working Mail Configuration

The following RHCE exam objectives are covered in this chapter:

- Configure a system to forward all email to a central mail server

CHAPTER 38

Setting Up an SMTP Server

Mail handling is an essential task that needs to happen on many Linux servers, no matter which specific service they are offering. In many cases, these services often need to send mail. That is why as an RHCE you need to be able to configure a server to forward mail to a central mail server. In this chapter, you learn how to do this.

Do I Know This Already Quiz

The "Do I Know This Already?" quiz allows you to assess whether you should read this entire chapter thoroughly or jump to the "Exam Preparation Tasks" section. If you are in doubt about your answers to these questions or your own assessment of your knowledge of the topics, read the entire chapter. Table 38.1 lists the major headings in this chapter and their corresponding "Do I Know This Already?" quiz questions. You can find the answers in Appendix A, "Answers to the 'Do I Know This Already?' Quizzes and 'Review Questions.'"

Table 38.1 "Do I Know This Already?" Section-to-Question Mapping

Foundation Topics Section	Questions
Understanding Email Basics	3, 5
Configuring Postfix Parameters	1, 2, 4, 8
Verifying a Working Mail Configuration	6, 7, 9, 10

1. Which of the following parameters enables you to specify on which network card the Postfix mail server should be listening for incoming connections?

   a. **inet_interfaces**

   b. **myorigin**

   c. **relayhost**

   d. **mynetworks**

2. Which of the following Postfix parameters enables you to specify where messages should be forwarded to?
   a. **inet_protocols**
   b. **relayhost**
   c. **mydestination**
   d. **mynetworks**

3. Which of the following mail handling roles describes the part of the configuration that is responsible for communicating with the mail server of the recipient?
   a. MUA
   b. MSA
   c. MTA
   d. MDA

4. Which is the name of the most important Postfix configuration file?
   a. /etc/postfix/postfix.conf
   b. /etc/postfix/master.cf
   c. /etc/postfix.conf
   d. /etc/postfix/main.cf

5. Which of the following is *not* a Postfix process?
   a. qmgr
   b. pickup
   c. postfix
   d. sendmail

6. After fixing a problem that prevented your mail server from reaching the destination mail server, you notice that messages are not sent immediately again. Which command can you use to mark all messages in the mail queue so that they will be delivered immediately?
   a. **postmaster**
   b. **postqueue -p**
   c. **postqueue -f**
   d. **sendmail**

7. Which log file contains detailed information about success and failure of message delivery?

   a. /var/log/postfix/maillog

   b. /var/log/maillog

   c. /var/log/mail

   d. /var/log/messages

8. Which command enables you to modify Postfix parameters?

   a. **postfix -e**

   b. **postconf -e**

   c. **postman -e**

   d. **postqueue -e**

9. While sending a message, you notice that it is not accepted on the recipient Postfix mail server. Which of the following parameters should you change to enable proper email reception?

   a. **inet_interfaces = all**

   b. **myorigin =**

   c. **mydestination =**

   d. **inet_protocols = ipv4**

10. You want to test your null mail client to verify that it can send email messages successfully. Which of the following reflects correct syntax to send a message from the command line to user root at server2, where no further action is required?

    a. **mail -s hello root@server2 <.**

    b. **mail -s hello root@server2.**

    c. **mail -s hello root@server2 >.**

    d. **mail hello root@server2**

Foundation Topics

Understanding Email Basics

When setting up an environment for handling email, it helps to understand what is happening. In this section, you learn about the different roles the participants in the email process can have. You also learn more about the email transmission process itself.

Understanding Roles in Mail Handling

Key Topic

In mail handling, the participants can have different roles:

- **MTA:** The MTA is the message transfer agent. This is the part of the mail solution that delivers messages from mail server to mail server. The MTA uses the Simple Mail Transfer Protocol (SMTP) to send messages to other servers on the Internet. To find the server that should be used for this purpose, the DNS Mail eXchange (MX) record is used. The core email communication on the Internet is between MTA servers only.
- **MDA:** When an MTA receives a message that is destined for one of the local users, the message is passed to the message delivery agent (MDA). The ultimate purpose of the MDA is to deliver the message into a user's mailbox; different programs can be used for this purpose. If nothing is configured, the message is delivered in the mailbox of the Linux user that exists locally on the server where the mail is coming in. On RHEL 7, the default location for this MDA is /var/spool/mail/$USER, such as /var/spool/mail/linda.
- **MUA:** When a user wants to send or read mail, a mail user agent (MUA) is used. This typically is the program that the user is using, such as the command-line mail client; the text user interface that is offered with Mutt, Pine, or Elm; or a graphical client such as Evolution or Thunderbird.

Another role that is important to understand is a machine running a null client. Such a machine is not capable of receiving any messages, but it has all the configuration that is needed to send mail messages to other hosts. A typical end-user workstation would be configured as a null client. On null clients, this usually happens by using a relay host. The RHCE objective wants you to be able to configure a null client.

The Email Transmission Process

Every RHEL server has a mail server process that is running by default. This process is started by the Postfix mail server. In its default configuration, this mail server process can send messages to other mail servers on the Internet, provided that the Domain Name System (DNS) configuration for the mail server domain is correct. Normally, if the IP address of the mail server can be resolved back to the domain name that the mail server is in, the mail server can send messages to other MTAs on the Internet. The default mail server process cannot receive messages, though.

To send an email, the client application (such as Mutt or Evolution) communicates with the outgoing mail server. This mail server relays the host to its final destination. To do this, the mail server looks at the /etc/nsswitch.conf file to see where it should look first for the name lookup. Then it either uses the /etc/hosts file, or DNS, to look up the MX record for the domain the message is sent to. If you send me an email at mail@sandervanvugt.com, for example, your MTA looks up the MX record of sandervanvugt.com. This MX record identifies the correct mail server, and if the destination mail server is configured to receive incoming messages, it delivers the message in the end-user mailbox.

The outgoing mail server may be configured to require authentication of the internal client. For the RHCE exam, you do not have to set up client authentication, apart from the my_network parameter, which allows you to specify which networks the outgoing mail server accepts clients from.

The recipient mail server, by default, delivers the message to the mailbox of the recipient user, which is in /var/spool/mail/$USER. If the recipient is a user, the message can be accessed using a command-line client such as Mutt, or you can even view the contents of the file with a text file viewer. Use, for instance, **cat /var/spool/mail/linda** to see whether there is mail for user linda in the spool. In many modern email solutions, the client does not access a shell on the server that handles incoming mail, but an additional service is used for this purpose. Typically, the Dovecot or Cyrus services provide user access to mail boxes and add functionality such as downloading messages using the Post Office Protocol (POP) or online mailbox access through Internet Message Access Protocol (IMAP).

Figure 38.1 illustrates what happens during the email process.

In Figure 38.1, a console user on server1.example.com wants to send a message to user2@example.org. To deliver this message, the following steps are performed:

1. user1@server1.example.com uses a mail client to write the message.
2. The user sends the message, which is further handled by the local Postfix process.

3. The local Postfix process is configured as a null client and relays the message to smtp.example.com, which acts as a relay host.
4. smtp.example.com performs a DNS MX record lookup to find that server2.example.org is configured to handle incoming mail for example.org.
5. The message is forwarded to server2.example.org.
6. server2.example.org delivers the message in the local mailbox of the user, which is in /var/spool/mail/$USER.
7. The user uses an MUA, which is configured to use IMAP to fetch the message from the local mailbox.

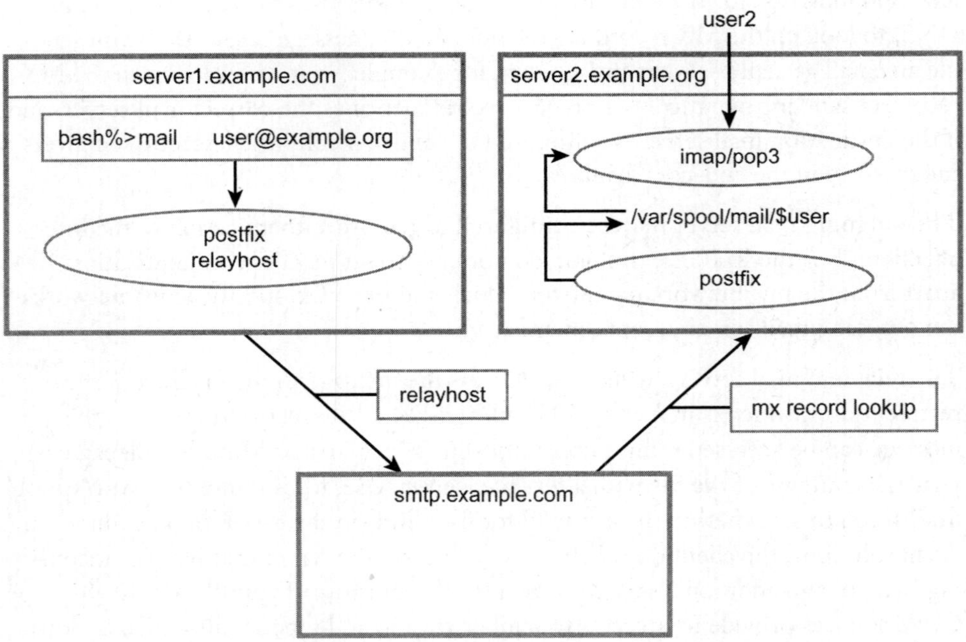

Figure 38.1 Mail transmission process overview.

Mail Server Solutions on RHEL 7

On Linux, different mail server solutions are available. In the past, the Sendmail mail service was the most common Linux mail server. It was complicated, though, and used a syntax that was hard to understand. Even though it was complicated, Sendmail became the standard for mail handling on Linux. Postfix was developed to be compatible with Sendmail but easier to configure.

On RHEL 7, Postfix is used as the mail service. Postfix consists of different processes that take care of specific tasks each. The processes are directed by the Postfix master service, which reads the /etc/postfix/master.cf configuration file to find out which services are used for specific tasks. This approach makes Postfix modular and pluggable; it is easy to replace one specific service with another service if needed. Some examples of Postfix processes are listed in Table 38.2, and Listing 38.1 shows partial contents of the /etc/postfix/master.cf configuration file.

Table 38.2 Postfix Server Processes Overview

Key Topic

Process	Purpose
master	The process that controls all other Postfix processes.
smtp	Responsible for SMTP communication between Postfix hosts.
pickup	Picks up messages after they have been placed in the message queue.
cleanup	Cleans up the message queue after the message has been delivered.
rewrite	If postfix maps are used to rewrite parts of the message header, the rewrite process takes care of that.
sendmail	The standard program that is used to send messages and which is implemented by Postfix.
qmgr	Generic process that manages the contents of the message queue.

TIP You do not have to know the names of all Postfix processes by heart. It does help, though, if you can recognize the Postfix processes while reading through the logs to understand why a message cannot be sent.

Listing 38.1 Partial Listing of the /etc/postfix/master.cf Configuration File

```
[root@server1 postfix]# head -n 20 master.cf
#
# Postfix master process configuration file.  For details on the format
# of the file, see the master(5) manual page (command: "man 5 master").
#
# Do not forget to execute "postfix reload" after editing this file.
#
```

```
# ==========================================================================
#  service type  private unpriv  chroot  wakeup  maxproc command + args
#                (yes)   (yes)   (yes)   (never) (100)
# ==========================================================================
smtp      inet  n       -       n       -       -       smtpd
#smtp     inet  n       -       n       -       1       postscreen
#smtpd    pass  -       -       n       -       -       smtpd
#dnsblog  unix  -       -       n       -       0       dnsblog
#tlsproxy unix  -       -       n       -       0       tlsproxy
#submission inet n      -       n       -       -       smtpd
#  -o syslog_name=postfix/submission
#  -o smtpd_tls_security_level=encrypt
#  -o smtpd_sasl_auth_enable=yes
#  -o smtpd_reject_unlisted_recipient=no
```

Configuring Postfix Parameters

To configure a Postfix mail server, you need to change the appropriate parameters. All the Postfix parameters are in the configuration file /etc/postfix/main.cf. The challenge is that this file contains many parameters that allow you to configure Postfix for many different use cases.

Postfix parameters can be configured through the **postconf** command, and alternatively they can be changed directly in the /etc/postfix/main.cf configuration file. In the following subsections, you'll learn which parameters are important and how to use them to configure Postfix to relay mail.

When working with Postfix parameters, it is a good idea to use the **postconf** command. The /etc/postfix/main.cf file may contain many lines with the result that it is easy to overlook parameters. Using the **postconf** command avoids making errors. To start with, you can use the **postconf** command without any options, which shows a list of all currently effective settings (including the default settings not visible in main.cf). **grep** enables you to easily find the argument that you need to change.

If the **postconf** command is followed by the name of a specific parameter, that specific parameter will be shown. To change **postconf** parameters, you can use the option **-e** followed by the parameter and its intended value. Use, for instance, **postconf -e 'inet_protocols = ipv4'** to set the value of the **inet_protocols** parameter to **ipv4**. Listing 38.2 shows partial output of the **postconf** command.

Listing 38.2 Partial **postconf** Output

```
[root@server1 postfix]# postconf | head -n 20
2bounce_notice_recipient = postmaster
access_map_defer_code = 450
access_map_reject_code = 554
address_verify_cache_cleanup_interval = 12h
address_verify_default_transport = $default_transport
address_verify_local_transport = $local_transport
address_verify_map = btree:$data_directory/verify_cache
address_verify_negative_cache = yes
address_verify_negative_expire_time = 3d
address_verify_negative_refresh_time = 3h
address_verify_poll_count = ${stress?1}${stress:3}
address_verify_poll_delay = 3s
address_verify_positive_expire_time = 31d
address_verify_positive_refresh_time = 7d
address_verify_relay_transport = $relay_transport
address_verify_relayhost = $relayhost
address_verify_sender = $double_bounce_sender
address_verify_sender_dependent_default_transport_maps = $sender_
dependent_default_transport_maps
address_verify_sender_dependent_relayhost_maps = $sender_dependent_
relayhost_maps
address_verify_sender_ttl = 0s
```

Understanding Essential Parameters

There are many parameters in the Postfix configuration. Only a few really matter for setting up an environment where mail can be forwarded to a central mail server. Make sure that you know all of them when taking the exam. Table 38.3 provides an overview of these.

Table 38.3 Essential Postfix Parameters

Key Topic

Parameter	Use
inet_interfaces	Interface(s) on which the Postfix service will offer services. By default, set to **loopback only**! Set to **all** to have Postfix listen on all network interfaces.
myorigin	Allows you to rewrite posted email to come from a specific domain instead of $myhostname. Most often used to strip off the hostname from the senders email address.

Parameter	Use
relayhost	Specifies which central mail server to forward messages to.
mydestination	Domains handled by this server. Mail addressed to a domain not listed in mydestination is rejected.
local_transport	Specifies what to use for local mail delivery. On servers that do not handle mail reception, set to "error: local delivery disabled."
inet_protocols	Specifies which protocol to use to offer services. Defaults to IPv6 if this is available. Set to **ipv4** to keep configuration easy.
mynetworks	Space-separated list of networks that are allowed to relay.

The first parameter to consider is **inet_interfaces**. By default, this is set to **loopback only**. There is nothing wrong with that if your mail server has to send outgoing mail only (which typically is the case if Postfix is running on a machine with the null client role), but if you want to configure your server for email reception, you must specify the IP address or addresses that your Postfix process will be listening on, as in **inet_interfaces = 10.0.0.1, localhost**.

The **myorigin** parameter is used to rewrite the origin of the message. If user linda on server1.example.com sends a message, the default setting makes the message appear to be coming from linda@server1.example.com. It is common to skip the host part in the recipient address, so that the message comes from linda@example.com. (Email recipients generally do not care which server the message was originally sent from.) To do this, variables are used. The **myorigin** parameter is set by default to **$myhostname**. Change it to **$mydomain** so that the domain part is shown only in the message header.

Key Topic

A very important part of the configuration is the **relayhost** setting. The relay host is usually a central mail server that has been configured with more advanced security settings and that takes care of sending email messages to other SMTP hosts on the Internet. Using a relay host has become more common as an attempt to tighten email-related security.

To forward all messages to a central relayhost, specify the name of that host here. The default behavior is that Postfix will do a DNS MX record lookup for what you specify. If you just specify the hostname, put it between square brackets so that no DNS lookup is done.

The **mydestination** parameter is important for receiving messages, not for sending messages. Email addresses for domains listed here are delivered into local mailboxes.

You need to configure your Postfix server with the **mydestination** parameter so that it knows the names of all domains that it is responsible for. In particular, you need to do this if your mail server is hosting several different mail domains. Make sure to include the domain names for all domains your mail server is receiving messages for.

The **local_transport** parameter is also for receiving email servers. It can be used to specify the name of a local destination to further process messages. You could use it, for instance, to have messages processed by a spam filter before they are delivered to the user mail box. According to the current RHCE specifications, you do not have to configure this parameter.

The **inet_protocols** parameter is important if you are setting up your own test environment. By default, Postfix uses IPv6. That means that DNS lookup for hostnames that are used (such as the relayhost) are done over IPv6 also. If you have a DNS server that has not been configured for IPv6, email delivery will fail. A simple fix for this problem is to use IPv4 only. To do this, make sure to set **inet_protocols = ipv4**. If your mail server is used in an environment where DNS is available and set up to handle IPv4 as well as IPv6 traffic, you do not have to change this parameter.

Finally, the **mynetworks** parameter is used to specify a comma-separated list of IP addresses and networks that are allowed to relay messages to your server. This is a basic protection against abuse, where on a fixed network only hosts on their own network will be accepted and messages from all others will be handled no further. Although using this parameter does increase the security of your server, it does not make it easier for mobile users. Users who will connect to unknown WiFi networks will have to use the mail server that is provided on that specific WiFi network because your mail server will reject them. If you want to use this setting to tighten security, you can consider adding virtual private network (VPN) security which ensures that users will always come from familiar networks.

Configuring Postfix to Relay Mail

To configure the mail server parameters you want to use, you can either edit the contents of /etc/postfix/main.cf directly or use the **postconf** command. If used without any arguments, the **postconf** command lists all the current 816 (and counting) configuration parameters that Postfix is using. If you use **grep** on the output of this command, you'll easily find the setting that you need to modify. You can also use **postconf** to modify settings by using the **-e** parameter followed by the setting you want to change. Exercise 38.1 shows how to do this.

TIP The RHCE objective states that you need to be able to configure Postfix to relay messages to another server. So, make sure that you can handle the tasks described in Exercise 38.1.

Exercise 38.1 Changing Postfix Parameters with postconf

1. On server1, open a root shell and type **postconf**. You'll see a long list of all current Postfix settings.
2. Type **postconf myorigin**. This shows the current value of the **myorigin** setting.
3. Type **postconf mydomain** to verify the current value of the **mydomain** parameter.
4. Enter **postconf -e 'myorigin = $mydomain'** to change the value of the **myorigin** parameter.
5. Repeat the command **postconf myorigin**. Notice that nothing has changed so far.
6. Type **postfix check**. This checks the contents of the /etc/postfix/main.cf file and alerts if anything is wrong with it (always a good choice before starting to use new configuration).
7. Reload Postfix, using **systemctl reload postfix**, and repeat Step 5. You'll see that the setting has now been changed.
8. Type **postconf -n**. This shows all parameters with a parameter that is different from the default.

TIP Read man 5 postconf for a complete overview and explanation of all of the 816 Postfix parameters. And make sure that you remember this man page while working on the RHCE Postfix-related assignments.

Now that you know how to change settings in Postfix, let's take a look on how to configure Postfix in a so-called null client configuration. As explained earlier, this is the configuration where users may run mail clients on the null client and the null client is configured for forwarding email messages to a relay host, but the local Postfix service does not accept any incoming mail. Notice that this configuration seems to be an exact match on the RHCE objective for Postfix configuration. In Exercise 38.2, you'll set up server1 as a null client and server2 as a server that accepts incoming messages.

Exercise 38.2 Configuring a Postfix Null Client Setup

Notice that in this exercise you configure two servers. The tasks that you perform on server1 show how to set up a null client. On server2, you configure a mail server that does accept incoming messages. This goes beyond the RHCE objective, but it is useful to know how to do it so that you can set up a working email configuration. To perform this exercise, you need to use DNS services. You can use the IPA server virtual machine (VM) that is provided at http://www.rhatcert.com for this purpose, or you can build your own IPA server according to the instructions in Appendix D, "Setting Up Identity Management."

1. Open a root shell on server1.
2. Verify that you can resolve server2 using **host server2**. The host command should get back with the IP address that server2 is currently using.
3. Type **postconf -e 'relayhost=[server2.example.com]'** to relay messages to server2.
4. Make sure your server can only relay messages that are sent from this server using **postconf -e 'inet_interfaces=loopback-only'**.
5. Type **postconf mynetworks** to verify that only messages originating from the loopback IP address will be accepted.
6. Type **postconf -e 'mydestination='**. This ensures that Postfix on server1 has no destinations.
7. Disable IPv6, using **postconf -e 'inet_protocols=ipv4'**.
8. Type **postconf -e 'mydomain=example.com'** to change the origin of each message that is sent.
9. Type **systemctl reload postfix** to restart the Postfix server on server1.
10. On server2, use the following commands to enable the server to receive messages that are relayed by server1:

```
postconf -e 'inet_interfaces=all'
postconf -e 'mydestination = example.com,server2.example.com'
postconf -e 'inet_protocols = ipv4'
```

11. On server2, type **firewall-cmd --add-service smtp --permanent** followed by **firewall-cmd --reload** to add the SMTP service to the firewall.

12. On server1, type **mail -s test1 root@server2.example.com <.**
13. On server2, as root, type **mail**. You should see the test message that has just been sent from the other server.

TIP Once more, on the exam, you do not have to know how to configure a mail server to receive incoming mail.

Verifying a Working Mail Configuration

Setting up a null mail client as previously described is not difficult. If you forget to change an essential setting, however, you might find yourself with a configuration that is not working. If that happens, it is good to know where to look to fix the problems. The following tips will help you find the problem:

- On the sending mail server, type **tail -f /var/log/maillog** to see what has happened to your message. Listing 38.3 shows relevant lines from the /var/log/maillog file, clearly indicating that the message was successfully sent after trying to connect to a server that could not be reached.

Listing 38.3 Using /var/log/maillog to Analyze the Mail Sending Process

```
[root@server1 postfix]# tail /var/log/maillog
Apr 21 03:41:21 server1 postfix/postfix-script[1879]: starting the
Postfix mail system
Apr 21 03:41:21 server1 postfix/master[1884]: daemon started -- version
2.10.1, configuration /etc/postfix
Apr 23 03:30:26 server1 postfix/postfix-script[1662]: starting the
Postfix mail system
Apr 23 03:30:26 server1 postfix/master[1664]: daemon started -- version
2.10.1, configuration /etc/postfix
Apr 23 07:35:47 server1 postfix/pickup[6298]: 968D09B46BB: uid=0
from=<root>
Apr 23 07:35:47 server1 postfix/cleanup[6831]: 968D09B46BB: message-
id=<20150423113547.968D09B46BB@server1.example.com>
Apr 23 07:35:47 server1 postfix/qmgr[1666]: 968D09B46BB: from=<root@
server1.example.com>, size=451, nrcpt=1 (queue active)
Apr 23 07:35:48 server1 postfix/smtp[6833]: connect to ASPMX.L.GOOGLE.
COM[2a00:1450:400c:c00::1a]:25: Network is unreachable
Apr 23 07:35:48 server1 postfix/smtp[6833]: 968D09B46BB: to=<mail@
sandervanvugt.nl>, relay=ASPMX.L.GOOGLE.COM[64.233.166.27]:25,
```

```
delay=1.1, delays=0.04/0.02/0.7/0.36, dsn=2.0.0, status=sent (250 2.0.0
OK 1429788948 fq4si13265111wjc.189 - gsmtp)
Apr 23 07:35:48 server1 postfix/qmgr[1666]: 968D09B46BB: removed
```

- On the sending mail server, type **postqueue -p** to display messages still waiting for delivery. This command will typically show results if the Postfix process on this server had a problem sending out the messages.
- If you think you have fixed the problems, on the sending mail server type **postqueue -f** to flush the mail queue. This triggers Postfix to immediately send all messages still waiting in the queue. Messages that get stuck in the mail queue are sent eventually, but according to the settings of the mail server, this might take a long time. So, when analyzing the mail flow on your server, it makes sense to help this process a bit.
- On the receiving mail server, read /var/log/maillog. If the message could not be delivered to the destination mailbox, in this log you'll often find an explanation as to why it could not be sent.

In Exercise 38.3, you create a small problem in the email delivery, which allows you to apply some troubleshooting solutions.

TIP It is easy to find configuration examples for all Postfix configurations you have to know on the exam. Many examples are stored in the /usr/share/doc/postfix-<version>/README files. If you use the command **grep null** on these files, for example, you'll find all the configuration necessary for setting up a null client configuration.

Exercise 38.3 Troubleshooting Mail Servers

1. On server2, type **firewall-cmd --remove-service smtp --permanent** followed by **firewall-cmd --reload**.
2. On server1, type **mail -s test1 root@server2.example.com <**.
3. On server2, verify whether the message has arrived by typing the **mail** command from a root shell. You will not see it.
4. On server1, type **postqueue -p**. Notice that the message is still waiting in the outgoing mail queue. Alternatively, you can use the **mailq** command.

5. On server1, type **tail /var/log/maillog**. You'll see a "no route to host" message, indicating that the destination mail server process could not be contacted.
6. On server2, type **tail /var/log/maillog**. You'll see no messages on server2 because the mail server cannot be contacted.
7. On server2, open the firewall by using **firewall-cmd --add-service smtp --permanent** and reload the firewall configuration by using **firewall-cmd --reload**.
8. On server1, type **postqueue -p**. You'll see the message still waiting in the mail queue.
9. On server1, type **postqueue -f** to flush messages currently in the queue. This triggers the mail server to send all pending messages.
10. On server1, type **postqueue -p**. You should see no more messages waiting in the queue.
11. On server2, open a root shell and type **mail**. You'll see the message has now been delivered.
12. On server1 and on server2 type **tail /var/log/maillog** again. This allows you to see what it looks like when a message has successfully been delivered.

TIP If a message gets stuck in the mail queue and you want to remove it, you can use the **postsuper -d** command.

Summary

In this chapter, you learned how to set up a basic Postfix configuration where a Postfix null client is configured to forward messages to a relay host, which takes care of further message handling. This does not teach you how to configure a completely working message solution, but it covers the RHCE objectives.

Exam Preparation Tasks

Review All Key Topics

Review the most important topics in the chapter, noted with the Key Topic icon in the outer margin of the page. Table 38.4 lists a reference of these key topics and the page numbers on which each is found.

Table 38.4 Key Topics for Chapter 38

Key Topic Element	Description	Page Number
List	Roles in mail handling	828
Table 38.2	Postfix server processes overview	831
Table 38.3	Essential Postfix parameters	833
Paragraph	The **relayhost** parameter	834

Complete Tables and Lists from Memory

Print a copy of Appendix B, "Memory Tables" (found on the disc), or at least the section for this chapter, and complete the tables and lists from memory. Appendix C, "Memory Tables Answer Key," also on the disc, includes completed tables and lists to check your work.

Define Key Terms

Define the following key terms from this chapter and check your answers in the glossary:

MUA, MTA, MDA, null client, relay host, mail queue, flush

Review Questions

1. Which parameter do you need to change to make sure that Postfix listens on other IP addresses than just the loopback address?
2. After sending messages from the null client that you have configured, you notice that all messages contain the server name in the sender mail address. Which parameter do you need to change in the Postfix configuration to make sure that it contains the domain name only?
3. You want your Postfix mail server to accept email messages for three different domains. Which parameter do you need to change to tell your mail server which domains it is responsible for?
4. You want to make sure that your Postfix server defaults to IPv4 and does not use IPv6 at all. Which parameter do you need to change to accomplish this?

5. You want to set up your null client to use smtp.example.com as the relay host. You also want to make sure that no DNS MX record lookup is done, but the message is sent directly to the relay host. Which line should be included in the postfix configuration file?
6. Which command enables you to get an overview of all Postfix parameters that are currently defined with the value they are using?
7. You have just tried to send a message which did not succeed. You have identified why the message could not be sent but notice that the message still has not been delivered. How can you schedule immediate message delivery?
8. Which file contains information about the message sending process?
9. Which SELinux contexts/Booleans must be changed to guarantee successful Postfix operations?
10. Which service must be added to the firewall configuration to guarantee successful email delivery?

End-of-Chapter Labs

In this chapter, you learned how to set up Postfix to relay messages to other mail servers. You also read how to analyze the mail flow. To prepare for the exam, you can now work on Lab 38.1, which you should be able to handle without too many problems.

Lab 38.1

1. Set up a configuration for email delivery. In this configuration, server1 is configured as the mail server that accepts the incoming message. Server1 is also the relay host that server2 will be using. Server2 is set up as a null client. Notice that in Exercise 38.1 you have done the opposite, so you need to change the parameters that have been configured in Exercise 38.1.

The following topics are covered in this chapter:

- Hardening the SSH Server
- Other Useful sshd Options
- Using Key-based Authentication with Passphrases
- Configuring SSH Tunnels

The following RHCE exam objectives are covered in this chapter:

- Configure key-based authentication
- Configure additional options described in documentation

CHAPTER 39

Configuring SSH

Secure Shell (SSH) is among the most important utilities that system administrators use. In Chapter 5, "Connecting to an RHEL Server," you learned how to use SSH to connect to a server using a password or key-based authentication. In this chapter, you learn about some of the more advanced configuration settings.

"Do I Know This Already?" Quiz

The "Do I Know This Already?" quiz allows you to assess whether you should read this entire chapter thoroughly or jump to the "Exam Preparation Tasks" section. If you are in doubt about your answers to these questions or your own assessment of your knowledge of the topics, read the entire chapter. Table 39.1 lists the major headings in this chapter and their corresponding "Do I Know This Already?" quiz questions. You can find the answers in Appendix A, "Answers to the 'Do I Know This Already?' Quizzes and 'Review Questions.'"

Table 39.1 "Do I Know This Already?" Section-to-Question Mapping

Foundation Topics Section	Questions
Hardening the SSH Server	1–5
Other Useful sshd Options	6–8
Using Key-based Authentication with Passphrases	9
Configuring SSH Tunnels	10

1. Which of the following is *not* a common approach to prevent against brute-force attacks against SSH servers?

   a. Disable X11forwarding

   b. Have SSH listening on a nondefault port

   c. Disable password login

   d. Allow specific users only to log in

2. Which of the following successfully limits SSH server access to users bob and lisa only?
   a. **LimitUsers bob,lisa**
   b. **AllowedUsers bob lisa**
   c. **AllowUsers bob lisa**
   d. **AllowedUsers bob,lisa**

3. Which of the following commands must be used to provide nondefault port 2022 with the correct SELinux label?
   a. **semanage ports -m -t ssh_port_t -p 2022**
   b. **semanage port -m -t ssh_port_t -p tcp 2022**
   c. **semanage ports -a -t sshd_port_t -p tcp 2022**
   d. **semanage port -a -t ssh_port_t -p tcp 2022**

4. Which of the following descriptions is correct for the MaxAuthTries option?
   a. After reaching the number of attempts specified here, the account will be locked.
   b. This option specifies the maximum number of login attempts. After reaching half the number specified here, additional failures are logged.
   c. After reaching the number of attempts specified here, the IP address where the login attempts come from is blocked.
   d. The number specified here indicates the maximum amount of login attempts per minute.

5. Which log file do you analyze to get information about failed SSH login attempts?
   a. /var/log/auth
   b. /var/log/authentication
   c. /var/log/messages
   d. /var/log/secure

6. SSH login in your test environment takes a long time. Which of the following options could be most likely responsible for the connection time problems?
   a. UseLogin
   b. GSSAPIAuthentication
   c. UseDNS
   d. TCPKeepAlive

7. Which of the following options is *not* used to keep SSH connections alive?
   a. TCPKeepAlive
   b. ClientAliveInterval
   c. ClientAliveCountMax
   d. UseDNS

8. Which file on an SSH client computer needs to be added to set the Server-KeepAliveInterval for an individual client?
   a. ~/.ssh/ssh_config
   b. ~/.ssh/config
   c. /etc/ssh/config
   d. /etc/ssh/ssh_config

9. Assuming that a passphrase protected public/private key pair has already been created, how do you configure your session so that you have to enter the passphrase once only?
   a. Copy the passphrase to the ~/.ssh/passphrase file.
   b. Run **ssh-add /bin/bash**, followed by **ssh-agent**.
   c. Run **ssh-agent /bin/bash** followed by **ssh-add**.
   d. This is not possible; you must enter the passphrase each time a connection is created.

10. Which of the following commands uses the source port 5555 on the local host to connect to a remote server called server2.example.com on port 80?
    a. **ssh -fNL 5555:localhost:80 root@server2.example.com**
    b. **ssh -fNL 5555:server2.example.com:80 root@server2.example.com**
    c. **ssh -fNL 5555:server2.example.com:80 root@localhost**
    d. **ssh -fNR 5555:localhost:80 root@server2.example.com**

Foundation Topics

Hardening the SSH Server

SSH is an important and also a convenient solution that helps you establish remote connections to servers. It is also a dangerous solution. If your server is visible directly from the Internet, you can be sure that sooner or later an intruder will try to connect to your server, intending to do harm.

Dictionary attacks are common against an SSH server. The attacker uses the fact that SSH servers usually offer their services on port 22 and that every Linux server has a root account. Based on that information, it is easy for an attacker to try to log in as root just by guessing the password. If the password uses limited complexity, and no additional security measures have been taken, sooner or later the intruder will be able to connect. Fortunately, you can take some measures to protect SSH servers against these kinds of attacks:

- Disable root login
- Disable password login
- Configure a non-default port for SSH to listen on
- Allow specific users only to log in on SSH

In the following subsections, you learn what is involved in changing these options.

Limiting Root Access

The fact that SSH servers by default have root login enabled is the biggest security problem. Disabling root login is easy; you just have to modify the PermitRootLogin parameter in /etc/ssh/sshd_config and reload or restart the service. After restarting, verify that you really cannot log in as root anymore.

TIP Some services automatically pick up changes in their configuration files. Most services pick up changes after the **systemctl reload servicename** command, whereas other services pick up changes only after a **systemctl restart servicename** command. To avoid wasting time on the exam, you should use **systemctl restart servicename** in all cases. At least you'll be sure that the service will pick up its new configuration.

After disabling root login, you must specify the username you want to use for login, by using **ssh user@servername** or **ssh -l user servername**. If you do not specify the username, it takes the name of the current user on the client who is trying to open an SSH session.

Configuring Alternative Ports

Many security problems on Linux servers start with a port scan issued by the attacker. Scanning all of the 65,535 ports that can potentially be listening takes a lot of time, but most port scans focus on known ports only, and SSH port 22 is always among these ports. Do not underestimate the risk of port scans. On several occasions, I found that an SSH port listening at port 22 was discovered within an hour after installation.

To protect against port scans, you can configure your SSH server to listen on another port. By default, sshd_config contains the line **Port 22** that tells SSH to listen on privileged port 22. To have SSH listen on another port, you must change port 22 into something else. Different ports can be used. You can choose to use a completely random port like 2022, but it can also be handy to configure SSH to listen on port 443.

Port 443 by default is assigned to web servers using Transport Layer Security (TLS) to offer encryption. If the users who want to access the SSH server are normally behind a proxy that allows traffic to ports 80 and 443 only, it may make sense to configure SSH to listen on port 443. You should realize, though, that by doing so port 443 cannot be used by your web server anymore; a port can be assigned to one service at a time only! So, do this only on a machine where you are not planning to run a TLS-enabled web server!

> **TIP** To avoid being locked out of your server after making a change to the SSH listening port while being connected remotely, it is a good idea to open two sessions to your SSH server. Use one session to apply changes and test, and use the other session to keep your current connection option. Active sessions will not be disconnected after restarting the SSH server (unless you fail to restart the SSH server successfully).

Modifying SELinux to Allow for Port Changes

After changing the SSH port, you also need to configure SELinux to allow for this change. Network ports are labeled with SELinux security labels to prevent services from accessing ports where they should not go. To allow a service to connect to a nondefault port, you need **semanage port** to change the label on the target port. Before doing so, it is a good idea to check whether the port already has a label. You can do this by using the **semanage port -l** command.

If the port does not have a security label set yet, use **-a** to add a label to the port. If a security label has been set already, use **-m** to modify the current security label. Use, for instance, the command **semanage port -a -t ssh_port_t -p tcp 2022** to label port 2022 for access by sshd.

Limiting User Access

Many options for sshd can be found by just browsing through the sshd_config file. One of the most interesting options to use is **AllowUsers**. This option takes a space separated list of all users that will be allowed login through SSH. Notice that this is a powerful option, limiting login to only these users. If the user root still needs to be able to directly log in, you have to include root as well in the list of allowed users.

When using this parameter, it makes sense thinking about which username you want to allow or deny access. In a scripted brute-force attack, intruders normally also try common user names such as admin, Administrator, and jsmith. It is easy to add a layer of security by selecting an uncommon username. Notice the following about the AllowUsers parameter:

- The AllowUsers option does not appear anywhere in the default /etc/ssh/sshd_config file.
- The AllowUsers option is a better option than PermitRootLogin because it is more restrictive than just denying root to log in.
- If the AllowUsers option does not specify root, you can still become root by using **su -** after making a connection as a normal user.

A parameter that looks promising, but is misleading, is MaxAuthTries. You might think that this option locks access to the SSH login prompt after a maximum number of failed login attempts. Such functionality proves useful when connecting to a local server (of which configuration can easily be changed if so required), but on an SSH server, it is a rather dangerous option, making it easy to perform a denial-of-service attack on the server. An intruder would only have to run a script that tries to log in as a specific user to block access for that user for an amount of time. That is why MaxAuthTries does not do what you might think it would do. It just starts logging failed login attempts after half the number of successful login attempts specified here.

Still, the MaxAuthTries option is useful. For analyzing security events related to your SSH server, it is not that interesting to know when a user by accident has typed a wrong password one or two times. It becomes interesting only after multiple attempts. The higher the number of attempts, the more likely it is that an intruder is trying to get in. SSH writes logs information about failed login attempts to the AUTHPRIV syslog facility. By default, this facility is configured to write information about login failures to /var/log/secure.

In Exercise 39.1, you apply the options that have been discussed so far.

Exercise 39.1 Configuring SSH Security Options

In this exercise, you learn how to apply common SSH security options. The sshd process should be configured on server1. Use server2 to test access to server1.

1. Open a root shell on server1, and from there, open the sshd configuration file /etc/ssh/sshd_config in an editor.
2. Find the **Port** line, and below that line add the line **Port 2022**. This tells the sshd process that it should bind to two different ports, which ensures that you can still open SSH sessions even if you have made an error.
3. Add the line **AllowUsers user** to the SSH configuration file as well.
4. Save changes to the configuration file and restart sshd, using **systemctl restart sshd**.
5. Type **systemctl status -l sshd**. You'll see a permission denied error for SSH trying to connect to port 2022.
6. Type **semanage port -a -t ssh_port_t -p tcp 2022** to apply the correct SELinux label to port 2022.
7. Open the firewall for port 2022 also, using **firewall-cmd --add-port=2022/tcp**, followed by **firewall-cmd --add-port=2022/tcp --permanent**.
8. Type **systemctl status -l sshd** again. You'll see that the sshd process is now listening on two ports.
9. Try to log in to your SSH server from your other server, using **ssh user@server1**. After the user shell has opened, type **su -** to get root access.

Using Other Useful sshd Options

Apart from the security related, there are some useful miscellaneous options that you can use to streamline SSH performance. In the next two subsections, you read about some of the most significant of these options.

Session Options

To start with, there is the **GSSAPIAuthentication** option, which on RHEL 7 is set to "yes" by default (which is in contradiction to what the man page states about it). This option is useful in an environment where Kerberos authentication is used. If you do not have Kerberos in your environment, you might as well switch it off, because having this feature on slows down the authentication procedure.

The next interesting option is **UseDNS**. This option is on by default and is used to have the SSH server look up the remote hostname and check with DNS that the resolved hostname for the remote host maps back to the same IP address. Although this option has some security benefits, it also involves a significant performance penalty. If client connections are slow, make sure to set it to no, to switch off client hostname verification completely.

The third session-related option is **MaxSessions**. This specifies the maximum number of sessions that can be opened from one IP address simultaneously. If you are expecting multiple users to use the same IP address to log in to your SSH server, you might need to increase it beyond its default value of 10.

Connection Keepalive Options

TCP connections in general are a relatively scarce resource, which is why connections that are not used for some time normally time out. You can use a few options to keep inactive connections alive for a longer period of time.

The **TCPKeepAlive** option is used to monitor whether the client is still available. Using this option (which is on by default) ensures that the connection for machines that are disappearing will be released. If used by itself, however, it might lead to a situation where unused connections are released as well, which is why it makes sense to use the **ClientAliveInterval** option. This option sets an interval in seconds, after which the server sends a packet to the client if no activity has been detected. The **ClientAliveCountMax** parameter specifies how many of these packets should be sent. If the **ClientAliveInterval** is set to 30, and the **ClientAliveCountMax** is set to 10, for instance, inactive connections are kept alive for about 5 minutes. It is a good idea to set this to match the amount of time you want to keep inactive connections open.

The **ClientAliveInterval** and **ClientAliveCountMax** options can be specified on a server only. There is a client-side equivalent to these options also. If you cannot change the configuration of the SSH server, use the **ServerAliveInterval** and **ServerAliveCountMax** to initiate connection keepalive traffic from the client machine. These options are set in the /etc/ssh/ssh_config file if they need to be applied for all users on that machine, or in ~/.ssh/config if applied for individual users.

Table 39.2 provides an overview of the most useful SSH options.

Table 39.2 Most Useful sshd Configuration Options

Key Topic

Option	Use
Port	Defines the TCP listening port.
PermitRootLogin	Allow/disallow root login.
MaxAuthTries	Used to specify the maximum number of authentication tries. After reaching half of this number, failures are logged to syslog.
MaxSessions	The maximum number of sessions that can be open from one IP address.
AllowUsers	Used to specify a space-separated list of users that are allowed to connect to the server.
PasswordAuthentication	Specifies whether to allow password authentication. This option is on by default.
GSSAPIAuthentication	Indicates whether authentication through the GSSAPI needs to be enabled. Used for Kerberos based authentication.
TCPKeepAlive	Set to yes if you do not want to clean up inactive TCP connections.
ClientAliveInterval	The interval in seconds that packets are sent to the client to figure out if the client is still alive.
ClientAliveCountMax	The number of client alive packets that needs to be sent.
UseDNS	If on, uses DNS name lookup to match incoming IP addresses to names.
ServerAliveInterval	The interval in seconds that a client sends a packet to a server to keep connections alive.
ServerAliveCountMax	The maximum number of packets a client sends to a server to keep connections alive.

Configuring Key-Based Authentication with Passphrases

By default, password authentication is allowed on RHEL 7 SSH servers. If a public/private key pair is used as explained in Chapter 5, this key pair is used first. If you want to allow public/private key based authentication only and disable password-based authentication completely, set the **PasswordAuthentication** option to no.

When you use public/private keys, a passphrase can be used. Using a passphrase makes the key pair stronger. Not only does an intruder have to get access to the private key, but when he does, he must also know the passphrase to use the key. This is why for establishing client/server connections with public/private keys, it is recommended to use passphrases. Without further configuration, the use of passphrases would mean that users have to enter the passphrase every time before a connection can be created, and that is inconvenient.

To make working with passphrases a bit less complicated, the passphrase can be cached for a session. To do this, you need the **ssh-agent** and **ssh-add** commands. Assuming that the public/private key pair has already been created, this is an easy two-step procedure:

1. Type **ssh-agent /bin/bash** to start the agent for the current (bash) shell.
2. Type **ssh-add** to add the passphrase for the current users private key. The key is now cached.
3. Connect to the remote server. Notice that there is no longer a need to enter the passphrase.

Notice that this procedure needs to be repeated for all new sessions that are created.

Configuring SSH Tunnels

The sshd service can be used for tunneling connections. Tunneling, in fact, is like port forwarding, where a UDP or TCP port is created that forwards traffic to another machine. The advantage of using SSH to create tunnels is that traffic that is sent through the tunnel is encrypted and for that reason invisible to potential intruders. When creating SSH tunnels, you can take two approaches:

- Use local port forwarding to create a local port that is connected to a remote service.
- Create remote port forwarding to forward a port on a remote server on the Internet to a local port.

Let's take a look at a few examples. In the command **ssh -fNL 4444:server.rhatcertification.com:80 root@server2.example.com**, a local port 4444 is defined. This port is forwarded to port 80 on server.rhatcertification.com, and this tunnel goes through an SSH session that is established as user root on server2.example.com (see Figure 39.1). Notice the use of options **-fN**. The option **-f** tells the **ssh** command to run in the background, and **-N** tells SSH that it does not have to start a command, which is typically what is needed for port forwarding.

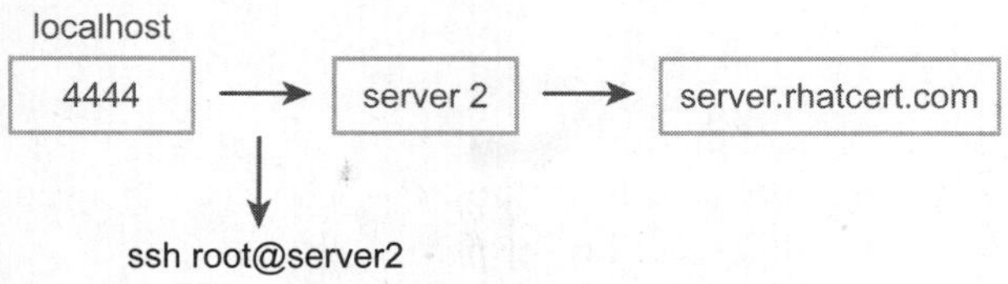

Figure 39.1 Local port forwarding overview.

The previous example works well if on localhost no SSH server is available that has open and unfiltered access to the Internet. If you do have an SSH server on localhost that is not limited by any firewall rules, the situation becomes a bit easier, and you can just type **ssh -fNL 5555:localhost:80 root@server2.example.com**. Using this command, you forward port 80 on server2.example.com to local port 5555. This might look a bit counterintuitive, but it does make sense. Just read the command as follows: log in as root to server2.example.com. Once on that host, forward port 80 on localhost (which at that time is server2.example.com) to port 5555 on the host from which the connection originated.

In remote port forwarding, you make a port on your local computer available to users on the Internet. To allow this to work, in the sshd_config file on the local machine, you must set **GatewayPorts** to **yes**. After doing so, you can use a command like **ssh -fNR 80:localhost:8088 root@lab.sandervanvugt.nl**. This command logs in as root on lab.sandervanvugt.nl, and as that user, forwards port 8088 on the remote server to local port 80. So, when a user addresses port 8088 on the remote host, that request is forwarded to port 80 on localhost. In Table 39.3, the three examples of port forwarding discussed in this section are summarized.

Table 39.3 Port Forwarding Examples

Key Topic

Command	Use
ssh -fNL 4444:server.rhatcertification.com:80 root@server2.example.com	Connect as root to server2.example.com to forward port 80 on server.rhatcertification.com to local port 4444.
ssh -fNL 5555:localhost:80 root@server2.example.com	Connect as root to server2.example.com to forward port 80 on that host to port 5555 on localhost.
ssh -fNR 80:localhost:8088 user@lab.sandervanvugt.nl	Connect as user to lab.sandervanvugt.nl to forward port 8088 to port 80 on localhost.

Summary

In this chapter, you learned how to configure the SSH server with advanced options. You also learned how to set security options for sshd and how to set specific clients options that help in keeping connections alive for a longer period. You have also learned how to set up local and remote port forwarding.

Exam Preparation Tasks

Review All Key Topics

Review the most important topics in the chapter, noted with the Key Topic icon in the outer margin of the page. Table 39.4 lists a reference of these key topics and the page numbers on which each is found.

Table 39.4 Key Topics for Chapter 39

Key Topic Element	Description	Page
Table 39.2	Most useful sshd configuration options	853
Table 39.3	Port forwarding exampless	855

Complete Tables and Lists from Memory

Print a copy of Appendix B, "Memory Tables," (found on the disc), or at least the section for this chapter, and complete the tables and lists from memory. Appendix C, "Memory Tables Answer Key," also on the disc, includes completed tables and lists to check your work.

Define Key Terms

Define the following key terms from this chapter and check your answers in the glossary:

port forwarding, SSH tunneling, passphrase, connection

Review Questions

1. Which two commands do you need to cache the passphrase that is set on your private key?
2. You want to disallow root login and only allow user lisa to log in to your server. How would you do that?
3. How do you configure your SSH server to listen on two different ports?
4. What options do you use to create an SSH tunnel where the **ssh** command will establish a background connection and will not expect any specific command?
5. When configuring a cache to store the passphrase for your key, where will this passphrase be stored?
6. You want to configure local port forwarding on your SSH server, where local port 5555 is forwarded to port 80 on server2.example.com. How do you do that?
7. Which command enables you to forward a port 8088 on server.somewhere.com to the web server listening on your local host?
8. How do you configure SELinux to allow SSH to bind to port 2022?
9. How do you configure the firewall on the SSH server to allow incoming connections to port 2022?
10. To allow for remote port forwarding, which additional setting must be configured in sshd_config?

End-of-Chapter Labs

In the end of chapter labs, you configure SSH for enhanced security and optimized connection settings. You also set up port forwarding. Use server1 to set up the SSH server, and use server2 as the SSH client.

Lab 39.1

1. Configure your SSH server in such a way that inactive sessions will be kept open for at least one hour. Also secure your SSH server so that it listens on port 2022 only and that only user lisa is allowed to log in. Test the settings from server2. Make sure that the firewall as well as SELinux are configured to support your settings.
2. Configure port forwarding in such a way that connections addressed to port 3333 on server1 are forwarded to the webserver on server2.

The following topics are covered in this chapter:

- Understanding the Need for Synchronized Time
- Setting up Time Synchronization
- Managing and Monitoring Time Synchronization with chronyc

The following RHCE exam objectives are covered in this chapter:

- Synchronizing time using other NTP peers

CHAPTER 40

Managing Time Synchronization

In Chapter 24, "Configuring Time Services," you learned how time on Linux is managed by using hardware time, system time, and network time. In this chapter, you learn more about network time and how the Network Time Protocol (NTP) is used to synchronize time between servers on a network.

"Do I Know This Already?" Quiz

The "Do I Know This Already?" quiz allows you to assess whether you should read this entire chapter thoroughly or jump to the "Exam Preparation Tasks" section. If you are in doubt about your answers to these questions or your own assessment of your knowledge of the topics, read the entire chapter. Table 40.1 lists the major headings in this chapter and their corresponding "Do I Know This Already?" quiz questions. You can find the answers in Appendix A, "Answers to the 'Do I Know This Already?' Quizzes and 'Review Questions.'"

Table 40.1 "Do I Know This Already?" Section-to-Question Mapping

Foundation Topics Section	Questions
Understanding the Need for Synchronized Time	1
Setting Up Time Synchronization	2–6
Managing and Monitoring Time Synchronization with chronyc	7–10

1. Many server applications depend on time synchronization. For some services, synchronized time is not that essential. Which of the following services will experience problems when time synchronization has been lost?
   a. DNS
   b. Kerberos
   c. LDAP authentication
   d. Database synchronization

2. If your RHEL 7 service is running IPA, which service takes care of time synchronization?
   a. timedatectl
   b. ntpd
   c. hwclock
   d. chronyd

3. Which service is used as the default service to synchronize time on RHEL 7?
   a. timedatectl
   b. ntpd
   c. hwclock
   d. chronyd

4. Which stratum is typical for a server that has established successful synchronization with an Internet time server?
   a. 1
   b. 3
   c. 7
   d. 10

5. What is the name of the chronyd configuration file?
   a. /etc/chrony/chrony.conf
   b. /etc/chrony.d/chronyd.conf
   c. /etc/chronyd.d/chronyd.conf
   d. /etc/chrony.conf

6. Which line would you include in the /etc/chrony.conf file to enable a server to fall back on its local clock if external synchronization is lost?
   a. **server local stratum 10**
   b. **server localhost stratum 10**
   c. **localhost stratum 10**
   d. **local stratum 10**

7. The **chronyc sources** command uses the column with the title S to indicate the status of the source as observed by the chrony process. What would you see for the source that chrony currently is synchronized with?

   a. #

   b. ?

   c. +

   d. x

8. Which command enables you to find out which servers the chrony process currently is synchronizing with?

   a. **chronyc servers**

   b. **chronyc status**

   c. **chronyc sync**

   d. **chronyc sources**

9. Which command enables you to display detailed synchronization information about current synchronization of the chrony process with its assigned time servers?

   a. **chronyc servers**

   b. **chronyc status**

   c. **chronyc tracking**

   d. **chronyc sources**

10. Which command enables you to see information about the drift rate and offset for each of the sources chrony is currently using?

    a. **chronyc sources**

    b. **chronyc sourcestats**

    c. **chronyc tracking**

    d. **chronyc status**

Foundation Topics

Understanding the Need for Synchronized Time

In some cases, it is not really a problem if time is not properly synchronized. In some cases, it is. When services are synchronizing information between the instances of the service that is offered by different machines, time stamps often play an important role. The number of services for which time synchronization is important is increasing, which is why any Linux server should have its time synchronized with an external authoritative server.

Services for which properly synchronized time is particularly important are databases and Kerberos. If several instances of databases are offered by different servers, these instances need to synchronize their tables. To do this efficiently, modifications in the database often are time stamped. Based on the time stamp that one server has set on the modification, another server can see whether data have been modified or not. This process requires time to be accurately synchronized. This principle applies not only to databases but also to other services that are using different data stores between which data has to be synchronized.

Another example where time synchronization is important is Kerberos-based authentication. In Kerberos-based authentication, authentication tickets are used. These authentication tickets are valid for a limited period of time only. To verify the validity of an authentication ticket, Kerberos servers need to synchronize time rather accurately.

To synchronize time in modern networks, the Network Time Protocol (NTP) is used. On Red Hat Enterprise Linux 7, the chronyd service provides NTP time synchronization.

Setting Up Time Synchronization

To set up time synchronization, you need to install and configure a service that takes care of it. On Red Hat Enterprise Linux 7, two different services may be used. The default service is chronyd, a newly designed service that takes care of time synchronization. You may also still encounter the old ntpd service.

TIP chronyd is the default service to synchronize time on RHEL. If you are using the IPA service, you'll notice that an integrated ntpd service is configured automatically. Because this integrated service is not compatible with chronyd, in that case chronyd needs to be disabled. An easy check to find out which service is taking care of time on your server, use the command **netstat -tulpen | grep 123**, which shows which service is offering time services on UDP port 123:

```
[root@server1 ~]# netstat -tulpen | grep 123
udp        0      0 0.0.0.0:123       0.0.0.0:*    0  169026    21804/chronyd
udp6              0 :::123               :::*      0  169027    21804/chronyd
```

In this chapter, we cover chronyd only, because it is the preferred service on RHEL 7.

Understanding NTP

To synchronize time, the Network Time Protocol is used. Before getting into detail about how to set up time synchronization, it makes sense knowing a bit about how NTP works.

To synchronize time in large network environments, you need a reliable clock. On networks that are connected to the Internet, reliable time is fetched from Internet servers that are connected to an external clock. This external clock is also referred to as the reference clock. Different models of hardware clocks are available, of which atomic clocks are the most reliable time sources.

In a network where many services are providing time, it is important to differentiate between reliable servers and less-reliable servers. To express the reliability of an NTP server, the concept of stratum is used. A low stratum is more reliable than a high stratum because a server with a low stratum number is closer to the reliable hardware clock than a server with a higher stratum number.

The stratum can be assigned by the administrator of the server when he configures the external clock, and a stratum can also be inherited from servers on the Internet (which is the more common scenario). At the top of the hierarchy are stratum 1 servers. These are directly connected to a hardware clock. A server that synchronizes directly with a stratum 1 server will itself be able to announce a stratum of 2 to others. By using the different stratums, NTP can select the most reliable server.

On the Internet, many stratum 1 servers that are publicly accessible are available. Often, the servers in pool.ntp.org are used for this purpose. You'll find out later in this chapter that servers from this pool are used as a default also by the chronyd service, which takes care of time synchronization on RHEL 7.

On normal operational NTP servers, you'll typically see low stratum only. Stratum 10 is commonly assigned to the internal clock. An NTP server as a backup can synchronize with its own internal clock, and to make clear to every server involved that that is not the most desirable solution, a stratum of 10 is assigned to the internal clock. If all servers in a network are synchronizing with their internal clock as external synchronization has dropped, then in fact NTP time synchronization is lost, because these servers will all announce a stratum of 11 (which is less reliable than the internal clock that offers stratum 10 synchronization).

If NTP synchronization could not be established on a server, this server typically will show a stratum 16.

Configuring chrony to Synchronize Time

The chronyd service uses the /etc/chrony.conf configuration file to set synchronization parameters. The default contents of this file contains everything that is needed to set up successful synchronization. Listing 40.1 shows a sample listing, containing a slightly modified configuration file.

Listing 40.1 /etc/chrony.conf sample contents

```
[root@server1 ~]# cat /etc/chrony.conf
# Use public servers from the pool.ntp.org project.
# Please consider joining the pool (http://www.pool.ntp.org/join.html).
#server 0.centos.pool.ntp.org iburst
##server 1.centos.pool.ntp.org iburst
#server 2.centos.pool.ntp.org iburst
#server 3.centos.pool.ntp.org iburst
server ipa.example.com iburst
peer server2.example.com

# Ignore stratum in source selection.
stratumweight 0

# Record the rate at which the system clock gains/losses time.
driftfile /var/lib/chrony/drift

# Enable kernel RTC synchronization.
rtcsync

# In first three updates step the system clock instead of slew
```

```
# if the adjustment is larger than 10 seconds.
makestep 10 3

# Allow NTP client access from local network.
#allow 192.168/16

# Listen for commands only on localhost.
bindcmdaddress 127.0.0.1
bindcmdaddress ::1

# Serve time even if not synchronized to any NTP server.
#local stratum 10

keyfile /etc/chrony.keys

# Specify the key used as password for chronyc.
commandkey 1

# Generate command key if missing.
generatecommandkey

# Disable logging of client accesses.
noclientlog

# Send a message to syslog if a clock adjustment is larger than 0.5
seconds.
logchange 0.5

logdir /var/log/chrony
#log measurements statistics tracking
```

Configuring the settings of the chronyd process is relatively easy because most settings are good as they are by default. If you do nothing and just start and enable the service, it automatically establishes time synchronization with time servers in pool.ntp.org, a pool of publicly available stratum 1 NTP servers.

If your server is not connected directly to the Internet, you might want to set up some staging in the configuration of time synchronization. It is relatively common to set up one or two central time servers in an organization that synchronize directly to NTP time sources on the Internet; the default chrony configuration would accomplish that.

At a second-tier level, servers can be configured to synchronize with these central servers. To configure this, you just need to enter a server line to enable synchronization with a specific server.

For complete redundancy, a third tier can be installed as well where servers are configured as peers to one another. In a peer configuration, no hierarchy exists between the servers, but the servers are communicating at the same level. If connection to the external server fails, the result is that NTP can still maintain a common time that all peers agree upon. Figure 40.1 shows what such a configuration could look like.

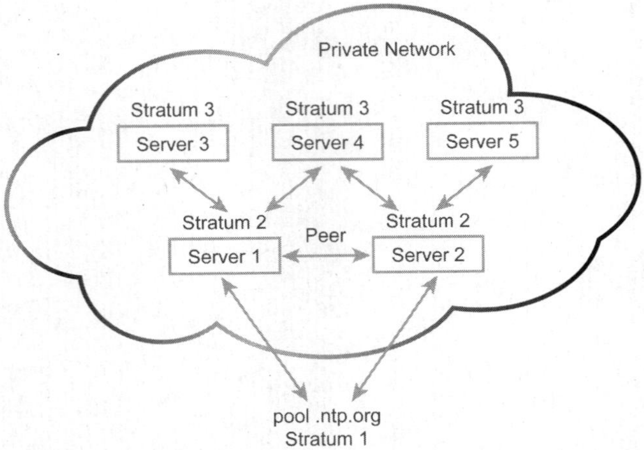

Figure 40.1 Setting Up Time Synchronization for Redundancy

To make the configuration completely foolproof, you can enable the line **local stratum 10**. This enables the server to fall back on the internal local hardware clock if external servers can be reached no longer. If that happens, every server will be on its own, but at least it will still have NTP time synchronization (even if it is unreliable time synchronization). This is not extremely useful, but is a bit. Some services check whether NTP time synchronization is established without checking how it is established. These services will work even if your server has stratum 10 NTP synchronization with itself only.

Managing and Monitoring Time Synchronization with chronyc

To check the current status of your chrony-based time synchronization, you can use the **chronyc** command. This command offers a rich utility that enables you to see what is going on. Table 40.2 provides an overview of the most important use cases of this command.

Table 40.2 chronyc Summary

Key Topic

Command	Use
chronyc sources	Shows current servers that chrony is synchronizing with
chronyc tracking	Gives detailed information about the current local time configuration
chronyc sourcestatus	Provides detailed information about the state of the remote servers

The command that you probably want to start with is **chronyc sources**. As you can see in Listing 40.2, this command provides information about the servers that your server currently is synchronizing with.

Listing 40.2 Showing Current Synchronization Sources with **chronyc sources**

```
[root@server1 ~]# chronyc sources
210 Number of sources = 2
MS Name/IP address          Stratum Poll Reach LastRx Last sample
===============================================================================
^* ipa.example.com           3   6    377    35   +1198us[+2533us] +/-   72ms
=? server2.example.com       0  10      0    10y  +0ns[   +0ns]    +/-    0ns
```

In the output of **chronyc sources**, different columns of output display. To start, the column M indicates what type of source is used. ^ is used for a server, = means a peer, and # is a locally connected reference clock.

The S column shows the current state of the source. A * in this column indicates the server that this server is currently synchronized with. If you see a +, chrony thinks that this is also an acceptable time source. A ? is used for a source to which connectivity has been lost. An x is a so-called false ticker, which means that its time is inconsistent with the majority of other sources. A ~ indicates that the source has shown too much variability, or that initial synchronization has not yet been established with that clock.

In the next columns, you can see the name or IP address of the remote server, followed by the stratum that was offered by that server. Poll indicates the poling interval, expressed in a power of 2. So, a value of 6 in this column would be 64 seconds total. The reach column contains the octal number 377 if the last eight polls have received a successful answer. LastRx indicates the last contact that has been established, and Last sample shows the offset between the local clock and the source at the last measurement.

The **chronyc sources** command gives nearly all the information that you would need to determine whether synchronization has been established successfully, but there are two other useful commands that you can use to get more details about the time synchronization status. The **chronyc sourcestats** command shows statistics about the state of the remote server (see Listing 40.3).

Listing 40.3 chronyc sourcestats Output

```
[root@server1 ~]# chronyc sourcestats
210 Number of sources = 2
Name/IP Address       NP  NR  Span  Frequency  Freq Skew  Offset  Std Dev
========================================================================
ipa.example.com        6   4   323    0.016       1.122   +485ns    26us
server2.example.com    0   0     0    0.000    2000.000     +0ns 4000ms
```

The **chronyc tracking** command gives detailed information about the clock and synchronization. Table 40.3 summarizes the meaning of the most significant parameters that are shown by this command, and Listing 40.4 shows its output.

Listing 40.4 Listing Displaying Synchronization Details with **chronyc tracking**

```
[root@server1 ~]# chronyc tracking
Reference ID    : 192.168.4.200 (ipa.example.com)
Stratum         : 4
Ref time (UTC)  : Thu Apr  9 16:22:37 2015
System time     : 0.000002353 seconds slow of NTP time
Last offset     : -0.000556652 seconds
RMS offset      : 0.006729999 seconds
Frequency       : 28.694 ppm fast
Residual freq   : -3.423 ppm
Skew            : 1.524 ppm
Root delay      : 0.047688 seconds
Root dispersion : 0.029117 seconds
Update interval : 64.1 seconds
Leap status     : Normal
```

Table 40.3 chronyc Tracking Columns

Parameter	Use
Reference ID	IP address or name of the remote source.
Stratum	Distance to the reference clock.
Ref time	The time in UTC when the last measurement from the reference source was processed.
System time	The difference between the NTP time and the local clock.
Last offset	The estimated local time difference on the last update.
RMS offset	The long-term average of the offset. Higher values indicate a more unreliable clock.
Frequency	The rate by which the clock would be wrong without chronyd correcting it.

> **TIP** Instead of using the **chronyc** command, you can also get much information about the current status of the chronyd service using the command **systemctl status chronyd**. Listing 40.5 shows example output of this command.

Listing 40.5 Showing Current chronyd Status Information with systemctl

```
[root@server1 ~]# systemctl status chronyd -l
chronyd.service - NTP client/server
   Loaded: loaded (/usr/lib/systemd/system/chronyd.service; enabled)
   Active: active (running) since Thu 2015-04-09 06:46:20 PDT; 4h 23min
ago
  Process: 21805 ExecStartPost=/usr/libexec/chrony-helper add-dhclient-
servers (code=exited, status=0/SUCCESS)
  Process: 21802 ExecStart=/usr/sbin/chronyd -u chrony $OPTIONS
(code=exited, status=0/SUCCESS)
 Main PID: 21804 (chronyd)
   CGroup: /system.slice/chronyd.service
           └─21804 /usr/sbin/chronyd -u chrony

Apr 09 06:46:20 server1.example.com systemd[1]: Starting NTP client/
server...
Apr 09 06:46:20 server1.example.com chronyd[21804]: chronyd version
1.29.1 starting
Apr 09 06:46:20 server1.example.com chronyd[21804]: Linux kernel
major=3 minor=10 patch=0
```

```
Apr 09 06:46:20 server1.example.com chronyd[21804]: hz=100 shift_hz=7
freq_scale=1.00000000 nominal_tick=10000 slew_delta_tick=833 max_tick_
bias=1000 shift_pll=2
Apr 09 06:46:20 server1.example.com chronyd[21804]: Frequency
-27791.393 +/- 450.547 ppm read from /var/lib/chrony/drift
Apr 09 06:46:20 server1.example.com systemd[1]: Started NTP client/
server.
Apr 09 06:46:24 server1.example.com chronyd[21804]: Selected source
192.168.4.200
Apr 09 09:30:53 server1.example.com chronyd[21804]: Source
192.168.4.220 offline
Apr 09 09:30:53 server1.example.com chronyd[21804]: Source
192.168.4.200 offline
```

You have now learned how NTP time synchronization works and how the chronyd service can be used to synchronize time. In Exercise 40.1, you apply these skills by setting up server and peer synchronization.

Exercise 40.1 Managing Time Synchronization with chrony

To perform this exercise, you need access to all three servers in the demo environment.

1. On all three hosts, ensure that hostname resolving is working, either through Domain Name System (DNS) or through the /etc/hosts file. Use ping to verify connectivity.
2. On labipa.example.com, make sure that the ntpd service is active by using **systemctl status ntpd**. This server needs to fetch time from the Internet, so no additional configuration is needed. If the service is not currently started, use **systemctl start ntpd** to start it. Notice that labipa does not use chrony because currently the IPA service has an integrated ntpd process that cannot run on a server that is also running chrony!
3. On labipa.example.com, make sure that NTP time is allowed through the firewall. Use **firewall-cmd --list-services** and verify that the ntp service is listed. If this is not the case, type **firewall-cmd --add-service ntp --permanent; firewall-cmd --reload** to add the service and activate it in the firewall configuration.
4. On labipa. type **ntpq -p** to verify that your server actually has established contact with time servers on the Internet.

5. On server1.example.com, open the /etc/chrony.conf file with an editor and make sure that it contains the following two lines:

```
server     labipa.example.com iburst
peer       server2.example.com
```

   Take out all other server lines because this server should synchronize with labipa only, and use peer synchronization with server2 as a backup.

6. Repeat step 5 on server2, but make sure that the peer line reads as follows:

```
peer       server1.example.com
```

7. On both servers, type **systemctl restart chronyd** and verify chrony operation using **systemctl status chronyd**.
8. On both servers type **chronyc sources**. This should show that both servers currently are synchronizing with labipa.example.com, as well as with one another.

Summary

For modern servers, it is important that time is synchronized because many services depend on having the right time. In this chapter, you learned how to configure the chronyd service for time synchronization. You learned how to configure NTP peers and servers, and you learned how to use the chronyc command-line utility to query NTP time status.

Exam Preparation Tasks

Review All Key Topics

Review the most important topics in the chapter, noted with the Key Topic icon in the outer margin of the page. Table 40.4 lists a reference of these key topics and the page numbers on which each is found.

Table 40.4 Key Topics for Chapter 40

Key Topic Element	Description	Page
Table 40.2	chronyc Summary	867

Complete Tables and Lists from Memory

Print a copy of Appendix B, "Memory Tables" (found on the disc), or at least the section for this chapter, and complete the tables and lists from memory. Appendix C, "Memory Tables Answer Key," also on the disc, includes completed tables and lists to check your work.

Define Key Terms

Define the following key terms from this chapter and check your answers in the glossary:

time stamp, NTP, stratum, chrony, reference clock

Review Questions

1. Why is accurate time synchronization important for database services?
2. Why does the Kerberos authentication service heavily depend on correct time synchronization?
3. Which service is used by default to synchronize time on RHEL 7?
4. What is the default stratum that is issues by a local reference clock?
5. Which firewall port must be open if you are configuring your server as an NTP peer?
6. Which line do you need to include in the chrony configuration file if you want to serve time, even if no external NTP servers can be reached?
7. Which stratum can you expect if there is no current NTP time synchronization?
8. Which command would you use on a chrony-enabled server to find out which servers it is synchronizing with?
9. How can you get detailed statistics about the current time settings for your server's chrony process?
10. Which command enables you to find information about the drift rate of the sources that chrony currently is using?

End-of-Chapter Labs

In this chapter, you learned how to organize NTP time synchronization using the chronyd service. At this point, you can work on the end-of-chapter lab to verify that you mastered the skills that are required to manage time synchronization on an RHCE level. To perform this lab, you need three different servers. Assuming that you are using the test environment that has been described in this book, in the labs the names labipa, server1, and server2 are used.

Lab 40.1

1. Configure the labipa.example.com for time synchronization with server in pool.ntp.org. As a backup, on this server specify that the local hardware clock should be used as a reference clock. If this happens, it should offer stratum 7.
2. Configure server1 and server2 to fetch their time from labipa.example.com and from nowhere else.
3. Also configure server1 and server2 as peers to one another.
4. Verify the working of the configuration using the appropriate commands.

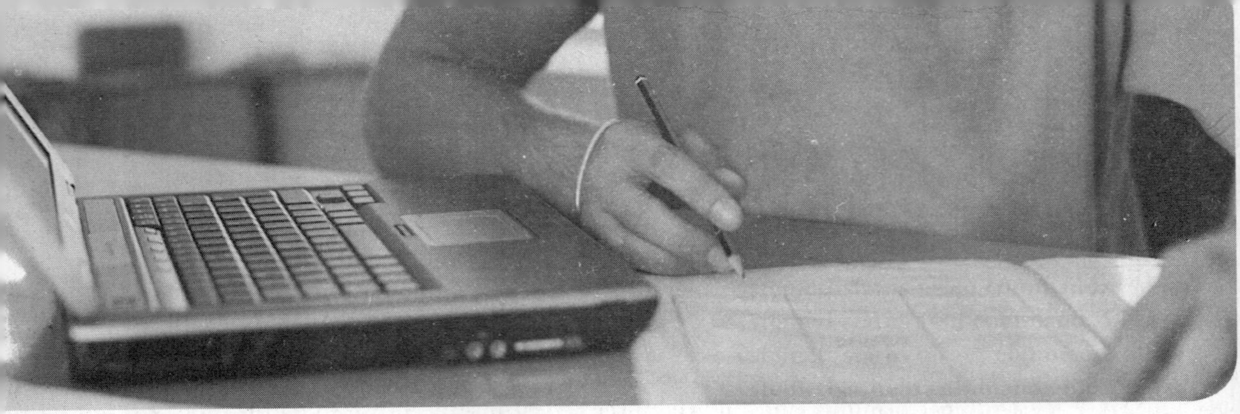

CHAPTER 41

Final Preparation

Congratulations! You made it through the book, and now it's time to finish getting ready for the exams. This chapter helps you get ready to take and pass the exam. In this chapter, you learn more about the exam process and how to register for the exam. You also get some useful tips that help you avoiding some common pitfalls while taking the exam.

Generic Tips

In this section, you get some generic tips about the exam. You learn how to verify your exam readiness, how to register for the exam, and what to do on the exam.

Verifying Your Readiness

Only register for the exam when you think that you are ready for it. This book contains a lot of material to help you verify your exam readiness. To start with, you should be able to answer all the "Do I Know This Already?" questions, which you find at the beginning of each chapter. You should also have completed all the exercises in the chapters successfully. At the end of each chapter, you'll find the end-of-chapter labs. These are the first real way of testing your readiness. The end-of-chapter lab questions are formulated in the same way as you might expect the real exam questions to be, so they are a good way of finding out whether you are ready for the exam.

Now that you have worked through all the material in this book, you are ready for the test exams in this chapter. Make sure that you can perform all the tests in the test exams before you register for the exam.

No sample answers are provided for the test exams, and that is on purpose. On the real exams, nobody tells you what you've done wrong if you fail on specific tasks. You should be able to find out yourself whether you have performed specific tasks successfully. If you are in doubt about specific tasks, chances are that you are just not ready for these tasks. The idea is that you should make sure that you feel comfortable with the exam topics.

Registering for the Exam

There are two ways of taking the RHCSA and RHCE exams. You can either take them as a classroom exam or as a kiosk exam. The classroom exam is typically on Friday only, and it is offered primarily by Red Hat to provide an exam at the end of a course. Therefore, most of the people who are with you in the exam classroom have taken 4 days of course training before taking the exam, and for that reason, classroom exam availability is limited.

For a long time, the classroom exam has been the only way to take the exam. For some time now, Red Hat has provided kiosk exams, too. A kiosk exam is an individual exam, where you work through the exam tasks on a kiosk computer. This is a monitored computer that is in a booth in an exam center, where you are monitored through multiple cameras while working on the exam tasks. The good thing about a kiosk exam is that it is individual and you schedule the exam time and place yourself at your convenience.

The exam can be registered through redhat.com or through a training company. It does not really matter where you buy it, because you end up at the same exam anyway. It might be easier, though, to get a discount while booking through a local training company. Booking through Red Hat will be faster normally, as you have direct access to Red Hat.

If you book a classroom exam, you get an invitation for the time and date the exam is scheduled. If you have booked a kiosk exam, you get a voucher code that you can use to book the exam venue, time, and date yourself.

On Exam Day

Make sure to bring appropriate identification to the exam. To be allowed to take the exam, you need an approved government ID. Normally, a passport or driver's license will do; other types of proof may be accepted in your country as well. Do not forget it; without ID, you will not be allowed to take the exam.

Second, make sure you are on time. It is a good idea to arrive to half an hour before the exam's scheduled starting time. If you are late, you will normally be allowed access to the exam, but you will not get extra time. So, just make sure that you are on time.

After proving your identity, you are introduced to the exam environment. Because of the nondisclosure agreement that every test-taker signs with Red Hat, I cannot tell you in detail what the exam environment looks like. I can tell you, though, that there will be an environment in which you have to work. Depending on the exam you are taking, this consists of one or more servers. There is also a list of tasks that have to be performed. Work your way through the tasks, read all well, and you will pass the exam.

During the Exam

The tasks that you have to work on during the exam are not necessarily presented in the most logical order. Therefore, it is a good idea to start reading through all the tasks before you start working on the first assignment. While reading through all the tasks, you can decide which is the best order to create the configurations needed. Determine the best possible order for yourself, because it may not be obvious.

Another very important tip is to read carefully. Not many people know how to read anymore, and you are probably among those people. IT administrators are very skilled in scanning web pages to retrieve the information that they need. That skill will not help you on the exam. Reading skills do. I cannot stress that enough. According to my estimate, 40% of all people who fail the exam fail because they do not read (they scan instead). So, let me give you some tips on how to read the exam questions:

- If English is not your native language, or if you master one or more additional languages, you can switch the language that questions are presented in. Maybe the English language question is not clear to you, but the question that was translated in another language is. So, if in doubt, read the translation as well.
- The English language questions are the most used and best scanned questions. Exam questions are perfect because Red Hat has made a tremendous effort to make them perfect. Given the fact that most of the exam candidates are working on English language questions, the quality of English language questions is the best. You are free to use translated questions, but you should use the English language questions as your primary source.
- To make sure that you do not miss anything, make a task list for each question. You have scratch paper with you during the exam. Use it to make a short list of tasks that you have to accomplish and work on them one by one. This approach helps you to concentrate on what the exam question is actually asking.
- After you have worked on all assignments, go have a cup of coffee (you are allowed to take a break during the exam). When you return, read all questions again to make sure that you did not miss anything. Taking a small break is important; it allows you to take distance from the exam, after which you read the questions as if it is the first time that you have seen them.

Another important part of the exam is the order in which you work on the assignments. Even without talking about specific exam content, some topics need to be fixed before other topics. Make sure that you deal with those topics first. If you do not, it will make it more difficult or impossible to fix the other assignments. Roughly speaking, here is the order in which you should work on the exam topics:

1. Make sure that your server boots and you have root access to it.
2. Configure networking in the way it is supposed to work.
3. Configure any repositories that you need.
4. Install and enable all services that need to be up and running at the end of the exam.
5. Work on all storage related tasks.
6. Create all required user and group accounts.
7. Set permissions.
8. Work on everything else.

The third thing that you need to know about the exam is that you should reboot at least a couple of times. A successful reboot allows you to verify that everything is working up to the moment you have rebooted. Before rebooting, it is a good idea to take out the rhgb and quiet options from the GRUB boot loader. Removing them allows you to see what actually happens and makes troubleshooting a lot easier.

Do not reboot just at the end of the exam because if at that moment you encounter an issue, you might not have enough time to fix it. You should at least make sure to reboot after working on all storage-related assignments.

The Nondisclosure Agreement

The RHCSA and RHCE certifications are the most sought-after certifications that currently exist in IT. They represent a real value because the person who took the RHCSA or RHCE exam has worked his way through a list of realistic assignments and knows how to do the job. It is in everybody's interest to help maintain this high value. The nondisclosure agreement is an important part of that.

The RHCSA and RHCE exams still represent real skills because the content of these exams is not publicly available. Please help keep these exams valuable by not talking about questions that you have seen on the exam. The person who knows which questions are asked will have an easier exam than you do, which means that the certificate value will diminish, which will also make your effort less valuable. So, please help protect what you have worked so hard for and do not talk about exam content to anyone.

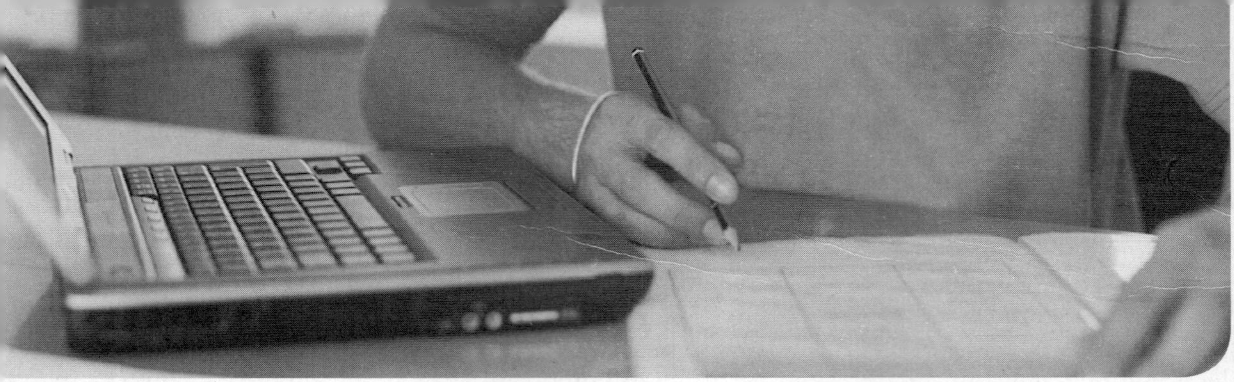

CHAPTER 42

Theoretical Pre-Assessment Exams

In this chapter, you find an RHCSA theoretical test and an RHCE theoretical test. Pre-assessment exams are the best way to determine what you know and what you do not. These theoretical exams are provided so that you can assess your skills and determine the best route forward for studying for the exams.

On the DVD, you will find video lessons that accompany these theoretical exams. These are unique videos that walk you through the configurations and help you determine what you know and what you still need to learn.

RHCSA Theoretical Pre-Assessment Exam

Let it be clear, the RHCSA and the RHCE exams are 100% practical exams. Therefore, you need to work on actual configuration tasks, and all that matters is that you deliver a working configuration at the end of the exam. Passing this practical exam does mean that you need to have some minimal knowledge, however. This chapter helps you checking whether this is the case.

In the pre-exam theoretical test, you are asked how you would approach some essential tasks. The purpose is to check for yourself whether you are on the right track. You do not have to provide a detailed step-by-step procedure. You just need to know what needs to be done. For instance, if the question asks how to set the appropriate SELinux context type on a nondefault web server document root, you know what you need to know if you say "check the semanage-fcontext man page.: If you do not have answers to any of these questions, you need to know that you need to do some additional studying.

In these pre-exam theoretical tests, some key elements are covered. This test is *not* 100% comprehensive; it just focuses on some of the most essential skills.

RHCSA Pre-Exam Theoretical Test

1. You need to create a shared group environment where members of the group sales can easily share permissions with one another. Which approach would you suggest?

2. You need to change the hostname of the computer to something else and do it persistently. How would you do that?
3. On your disk, you have to create a logical volume with a size of 500MB and the name my_lv. You do not have any LVM volumes yet. List the steps to be taken to create the logical volume and mount it as an Ext4 file system on the /data directory.
4. On the logical volume created in step 3, you need to set an ACL that gives members of the account group read and execute permissions. All other permission settings can be left as they are. How would you do this?
5. While booting, your server gives an error and shows "Enter root password for maintenance mode." What is the most likely explanation for this problem?
6. You need to access a repository that is available on ftp://server.example.com/pub/repofiles. How would you do this?
7. You want to manually edit the network configuration by modifying the relevant configuration file for the eth0 interface. What is the name of this file? Do you also need to do something else to make sure that the configuration is not changed back again automatically? Which service needs to be restarted to make the changes effective?
8. What configuration line would you add to which configuration file to schedule a cron job that executes the command "logger it is 2 AM" at 2 a.m. on every weekday? (You need to exclude Saturday and Sunday.)
9. You have changed the document root for your web server on a server that has SELinux enabled. What do you need to do to make sure that the web server is still operational after the change?
10. You do have access to the server console, but you do not have the root password to log in to that server. Describe step by step what you would do to get access to the server by changing the password of user root.
11. Describe exactly what you need to do to automatically mount home directories for LDAP users. The home directories are on nfs://server.example.com/home/ldapusers, and they should be automounted at /home/ldapusers on your local machine.
12. You need to install the RPM package that contains the file sealert, but you have no clue what the name of this package is. What is the best way to find the package name?

13. You have just downloaded a new kernel file from an FTP server; the update is not available in a repository. How do you use it to update your kernel in a way that allows you to install the new kernel but still keep the old kernel available for booting as a backup in case things go wrong?
14. You are trying to find relevant man pages that match the keyword user. You type **man -k user** but get the "nothing appropriate" message. How can you fix this?
15. How do you add a user to a new secondary group with the name sales without modifying the existing (secondary) group assignments?

RHCE Theoretical Pre-Assessment Exam

For all the following questions, make sure that SELinux and the firewall are fully operational and allowing access to the services, unless specified otherwise.

1. You have two servers, both with two network interface cards. How do you set these up for bonding or teaming?
2. Describe what you need to do to forward IP traffic on your server.
3. Describe what you need to do to export an NFS share thus that it is protected with the highest level of Kerberos security.
4. How would you configure automount to automatically mount Samba shares on //server/share.
5. Describe how you would set up two virtual web servers on your host for sales.example.com and account.example.com. Also make sure these virtual servers have their documentroot in /web/sales and /web/account.
6. What do you need to do to configure your firewall in a way that all traffic from the 10.0.0.0/8 network is blocked, while all services that are configured on your server are accessible?
7. How do you set up an iSCSI target that provides access to the /dev/vgroup/lv1 logical volume?
8. How do you connect to the iSCSI target that was created in step 7?
9. How do you set up an SSH server to listen on ports 2022 and 443 while allowing access only to user linda?
10. How do you set up a caching-only DNS name server that forwards all queries to someserver.example.com?

11. How would you create a simple MariaDB database, allowing you to store name, city, and phone numbers?
12. How would you make a physical backup of the database created in step 11?
13. How would you set up an SMTP mail server to forward mail to a central server?
14. Describe what needs to be done to create a Samba share /data that is accessible only for users that are a member of the sales group?
15. How would you configure your web server so that the entire sales website that was discussed in step 5 is accessible for members of the sales group only?

RHCSA Practice Exam A

Note: This exam is also available as a PDF on the book's DVD.

Note: The Premium Edition of this book contains four additional practice exams: two RHCSA and two RHCE. You can find information about upgrading to the Premium Edition in the front of this book.

RHCSA Practice Exam A

This test exam needs the following setup:

- An IPA server that is offering central services such as LDAP and NFS. The setup of such a server is described in Appendix D, "Setting Up Identity Management." Alternatively, you can use the test VMs provided on rhatcert.com.
- A cleanly installed virtual machine. Step 1 of this exam describes how to set up such a virtual machine based on a KVM setup. Notice that the IP addresses that are used in the virtual machines are based on the internal IP addresses in a KVM setup. If you are using another virtualization platform, make sure to change the IP addresses accordingly.

1. Install an RHEL 7 virtual machine. Use a 20GB LVM volume or disk backend file on the host as the storage backend for the virtual machine. Use the bridged network interface on the host for networking in the virtual machine. (This should normally be done automatically.) Make sure that the virtual machine meets the following requirements. All the tasks here will be performed on the server unless stated otherwise:
   - 20GB total disk space
   - IP address is 192.168.122.200
   - Set hostname to myserver1.example.com
   - A 10GB root partition and a 1GB swap partition, both created as primary partitions and nothing else
   - Install the Server with GUI installation pattern.

2. Make sure that the networking configuration on the VM is set up correctly. This includes DNS and routing settings. Use the same DNS and routing settings that are used on the host, and set the name of your server to server1.example.com.
3. Loop mount the installation ISO that you have used to install the virtual machine. After loop mounting it, use scp to copy three random RPM files to the /repo directory on your virtual machine.
4. Configure the /repo directory on the virtual machine as a repository. Also configure your virtual machine to use this repository.
5. Ensure that SELinux is in Enforcing mode. Where necessary, change settings to make SELinux fully functional.
6. Create a 200MB primary partition on your virtual machine hard drive. Mount this partition automatically on the directory /groups.
7. Make another 200MB partition. Make sure to do this in a way that allows you to add more partitions at a later stage. Create an LVM volume with the name lvdata in the volume group vgdata using this partition as the underlying physical volume. Mount the logical volume automatically on the directory /data.
8. Create four users: laura, lucy, lori, and linda. Create a group management of which laura and lucy are members. Create a group production of which lori and linda are members.
9. Create shared group directories for the groups you just created: /data/production and /data/management. Make sure the corresponding groups have all permissions they need to read and write files in their group directories. Also make sure that the groups have read and write permissions on all items that will be created in these directories. Ensure that only the user who has created a file is allowed to remove that specific file.
10. Install a kernel upgrade. After installing it, you should be able to select the old kernel as well as the new kernel while booting.
11. Create a cron job that shuts down your computer at 5 p.m. this afternoon.

RHCSA Practice Exam B

Note: This exam is also available as a PDF on the book's DVD.

Note: The Premium Edition of this book contains four additional practice exams: two RHCSA and two RHCE. You can find information about upgrading to the Premium Edition in the front of this book.

RHCSA Practice Exam B

This test exam needs the following setup:

- An IPA server that is offering central services such as LDAP and NFS. The setup of such a server is described in Appendix D, "Setting Up Identity Management." Alternatively, the test VMs that are provided on rhatcert.com can be used.
- A cleanly installed virtual machine. Step 1 of this test exam describes how to set up such a virtual machine based on a KVM setup. Notice that the IP addresses that are used in the virtual machines are based on the internal IP addresses in a KVM setup. If you are using another virtualization platform, make sure to change the IP addresses accordingly.
- Unless specifically mentioned, all tasks described below should be performed on the virtual machine.

1. Install an RHEL 7 virtual machine. Use a 12GB LVM volume or disk backend file on the host as the storage backend for the virtual machine. Use the bridged network interface on the host for networking in the virtual machine. (This should normally be done automatically.) Make sure the virtual machine meets the following requirements. All the following tasks are performed on the server unless stated otherwise:
    - 20GB total disk space
    - IP address is 192.168.122.200
    - Set hostname to server1.example.com
    - A 500MB boot partition

- A logical volume for the / file system with a size of 6GB
- A logical volume for swap with a size of 512MB
- Install the Server with GUI installation pattern.

2. Create a partition with a size of 500 MiB. Format this partition with the Ext4 file system and provide it with the label data. Mount this partition persistently through the /etc/fstab file on the /data directory.
3. Use the appropriate command to locate all files on your server that have a size greater than 100MB and store a list of their names in the file /root/bigfile.
4. Create the users lisa and lori. Set their passwords to expire after 90 days.
5. Generate an SSH key pair for the user root. Copy the appropriate key over to your host computer so that you can log in to the host computer without having to enter a password or passphrase.
6. Resize the logical volume that is used by the root file system and add 1 GiB to it. Ensure that the root file system is resized as well.
7. Create the groups profs and students. Make lisa a member of the group profs, and make lori a member of the group students without changing their primary group assignments.
8. Create a directory structure /data/profs and /data/students. Make the appropriate directories fully accessible to the members of their respective groups. In these directories, users should only be able to remove files of which they are the owner, and newly created files should be group owned automatically by the group that is owner of the directory. So if, for example, in /data/profs, user lisa creates a file, it should be group owned by the group profs automatically.
9. Set up file access permissions such that members of the group profs can read all files in the directory /data/students, existing files as well as new files. Also and without changing the umask, in this particular directory the others entity should get no access permissions at all.
10. Configure logging in such a way that all log messages with a priority of warn and higher are written to the /var/log/warnings file.
11. Set up logrotate on the /var/log/warning file such that it will be rotated on a monthly basis. Keep 11 old versions of the file.
12. Set up a firewall such that only the SSH process can be reached on your server.

RHCE Practice Exam A

Note: This exam is also available as a PDF on the book's DVD.

Note: The Premium Edition of this book contains four additional practice exams: two RHCSA and two RHCE. You can find information about upgrading to the Premium Edition in the front of this book.

RHCE Practice Exam A

This test exam needs the following setup:

- An IPA server that is offering central services such as LDAP and NFS. The setup of such a server is described in Appendix D, "Setting Up Identity Management." The IP address of the IPA server must be set to 192.168.122.200. Alternatively, the test VMs that are provided on rhatcert.com can be used.
- Two cleanly installed virtual machines with the names server1 and server2. Make sure they meet the following requirements. These tasks are not included in the actual exam time:
    - Both servers need to have two network interfaces. The IP addresses mentioned below can be set on any of these interfaces.
    - server1 has 1GB of unallocated disk space and the IP address set to 192.168.122.210.
    - server2 has its IP address set to 192.168.122.220.
    - Both servers are using the labipa.example.com servers as the DNS server.
    - The IP address of the host machine should be used as the default gateway.
    - A repository is available on server1. Create this repository by copying all RPM files from the installation DVD to the directory /repo and use **createrepo** on this directory to generate the repository index files.

As a general requirement, you must make sure that SELinux is in enforcing mode, allowing access to everything that you configure in this test exam. Also make sure that both servers have an operational firewall that is allowing access to all services mentioned in this test exam.

1. Configure server1 to offer the contents of the /repo directory as a repository, using an FTP server. Configure server1 and server2 to use the repository that is offered on server1.
2. Set up both servers to authenticate using Kerberos against the labipa.example.com server. A CA certificate is available in the home directory of the root user on the labipa server. To test successful setup, you can use the LDAP user lisa on the labipa server.
3. Set up a Kerberized NFS share on server1. The directory /srv/secure should be shared and secured with the best possible Kerberos security settings. A keytab file is available on the labipa.example.com server in the /var/ftp/pub directory.
4. On server2, configure a mount to the Kerberized NFS share on server1. The mount should be made automatically on the /mnt/secure directory when the server boots.
5. Configure an Apache web server. Two virtual hosts should be configured: sales.example.com and account.example.com. Create a documentroot for these servers in /web/account and /web/sales. In the document root, create an index.html file containing the text "this is the sales webserver" or "this is the account webserver."
6. Secure the Apache web server sales.example.com virtual host. It should only be accessible to user florence, using the password password. This user account has to be used for Apache authentication only and does not have to be created in any other way.
7. Write a script and give it the name /root/foobar. The script should offer support for two different parameters when launched. When using the parameter foo, it should create the file /tmp/foo; when using the parameter bar, it should create the file /tmp/bar. When using any other parameter, it should show an error message explaining to the user who launched it that an unsupported parameter was used.
8. Enable packet forwarding on server1.
9. Set up both servers with an aggregated network interface and make sure the IP addresses of the servers bind to these interfaces. You may use bonding or teaming at your convenience.
10. On server2, set up a caching only DNS name server. This name server should forward all DNS requests to labipa.example.com.

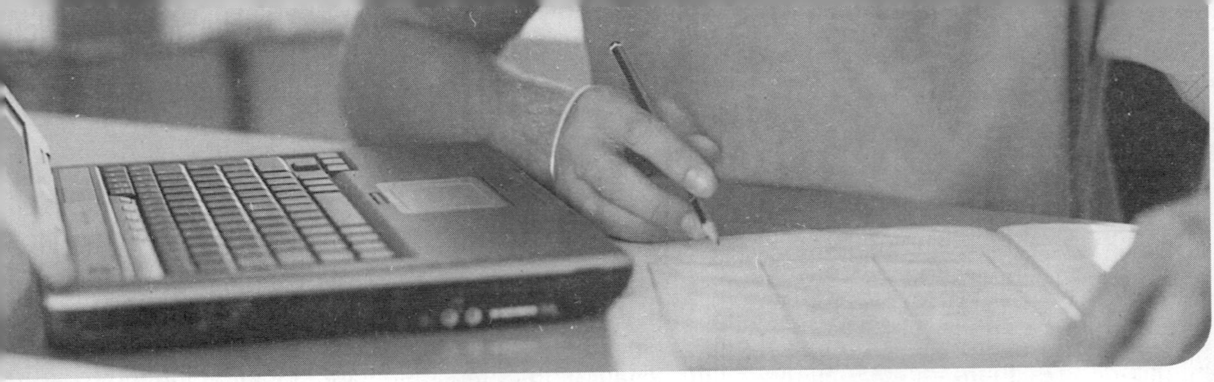

RHCE Practice Exam B

Note: This exam is also available as a PDF on the book's DVD.

Note: The Premium Edition of this book contains four additional practice exams: two RHCSA and two RHCE. You can find information about upgrading to the Premium Edition in the front of this book.

RHCE Practice Exam B

This test exam needs the following setup:

- An IPA server that is offering central services such as LDAP and NFS. The setup of such a server is described in Appendix D, "Setting Up Identity Management." The IP address of the IPA server must be set to 192.168.122.200. Alternatively, the test VMs that are provided on rhatcert.com can be used.
- Two cleanly installed virtual machines with the names server1 and server2. Make sure they meet the following requirements. These tasks are not included in the actual exam time:
  - Both servers need to have two network interfaces. The IP addresses mentioned here can be set on any of these interfaces.
  - server1 has 1GB of unallocated disk space and the IP address set to 192.168.122.210.
  - server2 has its IP address set to 192.168.122.220.
  - Both servers are using the labipa.example.com servers as the DNS server.
  - The IP address of the host machine should be used as the default gateway.
  - A repository is available on server1. Create this repository by copying all RPM files from the installation DVD to the directory /repo and use **createrepo** on this directory to generate the repository index files.

  As a general requirement, you must make sure that SELinux is in enforcing mode, allowing access to everything that you configure in this test exam. Also make sure that both servers have an operational firewall that is allowing access to all services mentioned in this test exam.

1. Configure server1 to offer the contents of the /repo directory as a repository using an FTP server. Configure server1 and server2 to use the repository that is offered on server1.
2. Set up SSH on both servers to listen on port 2022 as well as the default port 22. Allow login to the SSH server to user florence only. Create a local user account florence where needed to test the working of the modified SSH server.
3. Set up an SMTP server. All messages that are sent on server1 should be relayed to server2. Also set up server2 as a relay server.
4. On server2, create the groups sales and account. Create two users marcha and marion, who are members of the sales group, and suzan and cindy, who are members of the account group. Set the password for all users to password.
5. Configure a Samba server on server1. This server should share the directories /srv/samba/sales and /srv/samba/account. The sales share should be accessible by members of the sales group only; the account share should be accessible by members of the account group only. Copy all files that have a name starting with the letter *s* from the /etc directory to /srv/samba/sales, and copy all files that have a name starting with the letter *A* from the /etc directory to /srv/samba/account.
6. On server2, configure automount to mount the Samba shares you have configured in the previous step. The shares should be mounted on /mnt/sales and /mnt/account but only when a user accesses these mounts.
7. Write a script with the name testscript. While started, the script should test if the argument "test" was provided on script startup. If it was not, the script should become interactive and request the user to enter some random text.
8. Create a small MariaDB database. The name of the database should be addresses, and it should have two fields per record: name and city. Enter some records:

```
name          city
florence      lyon
julia         san francisco
```

9. Create a logical backup of the database and write it to a file with the name /root/addresses.bck.
10. Set up remote logging. All log messages that are generated on server1 should be stored locally on server1 but also forwarded to server2 using TCP only.

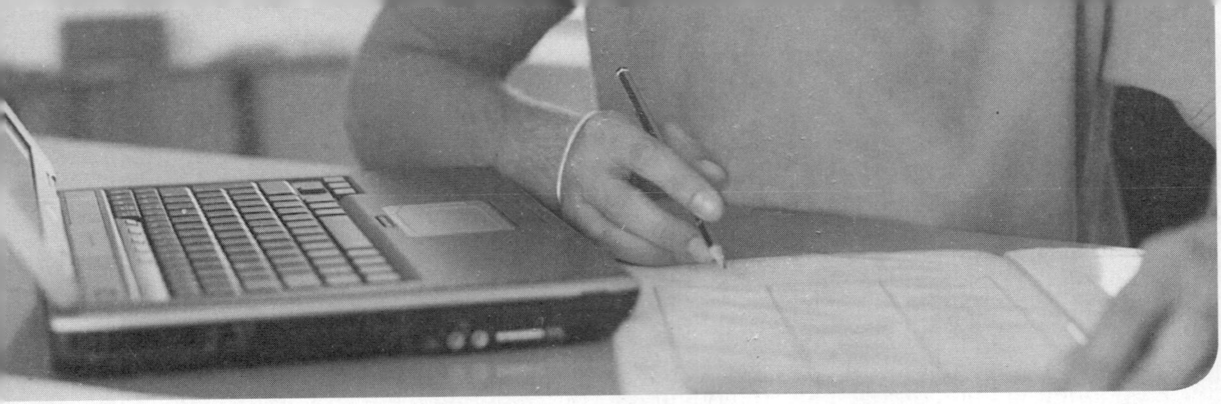

Index

Symbols

A

C

D

F

G

H

J

K

L

M

O

P

Q

R

S

T

U

V

W

X

Y

Z